Why You Need This New Edition

The most current cross-cultural research on a wide range of topics including ethnic and religious identity, psychological effects of globalization, spirituality, cross-cultural communication, evolutionary anthropology, cultural stereotypes, psychotherapy and counseling, mistakes of social perception, intelligence, collectivism and individualism, cultural adjustment, suicide, stigma of mental illness, national character, values, and methodology of research.

1. **A broader selection of applied problems** such as avoiding stereotypes and psycho-diagnostic biases, reducing mistakes in facial recognition, improving effectiveness of class-room learning, understanding spirituality, conducting survey research, and many others.

2. **A greater interdisciplinary perspective,** using research from contemporary psychol-ogy, as well as neurophysiology, genetics, anthropology, sociology, and microeconomics.

3. **More than 100 new reference sources** and new research data related to a diverse array of ethnic and religious groups.

4. **A new, revised, and expanded test bank** for instructors, which includes a comprehen-sive selection of questions for every chapter and ready-to-use-quizzes.

Fifth Edition

CROSS-CULTURAL PSYCHOLOGY

CRITICAL THINKING AND CONTEMPORARY APPLICATIONS

Eric B. Shiraev
George Mason University

David A. Levy
Pepperdine University

Ψ Psychology Press
Taylor & Francis Group

NEW YORK AND LONDON

First published 2013, 2010, 2007 by Pearson Education, Inc.

Published 2016 by Routledge
Routledge
Taylor & Francis Group
711 Third Avenue
New York, NY 10017

Routledge
Taylor & Francis Group
27 Church Road
Hove
East Sussex BN3 2FA

Routledge is an imprint of the Taylor & Francis Group, an informa business

Cover Image: © Brian Finestone/Fotolia
Cover Designer: Suzanne Behnke

Credits and acknowledgments borrowed from other sources and reproduced, with permission, in this textbook appear on the appropriate page within text and on pages 395–396.

ISBN: 9780205253234 (pbk)

Library of Congress Cataloging-in-Publication Data
Shiraev, Eric,
    Cross-cultural psychology : critical thinking and contemporary applications/
    Eric B. Shiraev, David A. Levy.—5th ed.
        p. cm.
    ISBN-13: 978-0-205-25323-4 (alk. paper)
    ISBN-10: 0-205-25323-7 (alk. paper)
    1. Ethnopsychology—Methodology.   I. Levy, David A., 1954–   II. Title.
    GN502.S475 2013
    155.8'2—dc23
                                                2012008752

CONTENTS

PREFACE

We cordially invite you to explore cross-cultural psychology of the twenty-first century. Just over 10 years ago, when we were preparing the first edition of this book, it was our initial hope that a number of students in North America would find it useful. We certainly did not anticipate that the text would soon find a receptive audience not only in the United States and Canada but also in the Netherlands, Russia, Indonesia, China, Turkey, Germany, and many other countries. Subsequently, a special edition of the book was published in India. Our book was then translated in China and is being translated in Indonesia. The rapidly growing interest in cross-cultural psychology is understandable. This field is new and exciting, fascinating in its content, important in its applications, and challenging in its goals and aspirations. Yet it is sometimes scarcely able to keep pace with the rapidly changing conditions of modern times.

Look at the world around us. Previously invincible barriers—both literal and metaphoric—that have separated people for hundreds, even thousands of years are increasingly cracking, crumbling, and finally collapsing before our eyes. Within a relatively brief period of history, the telephone, radio, television, motion pictures, and, more recently, computers, e-mail, cell phones, the Internet, and social networks are drastically altering our perceptions of time, space, culture, and each other. One key click and, in an instant, you are virtually on the opposite side of the planet, or even on a different planet.

We travel and migrate from one place to another on a scale previously unknown—even unimaginable—in human history. The United States alone naturalizes almost 700,000 new citizens and hosts nearly 725,000 international students every year. More countries are moving toward their economic and political unification. Hong Kong has been reunited with China. From Northern Ireland to Mauritania, from Bosnia to El Salvador, dozens of deadly ethnic, social, and religious conflicts have been stopped, and former enemies have begun to negotiate with one another. Millions of people learn about human rights and practice mutual tolerance. People understand that they share many common customs, ideas, and hopes. The world is indeed becoming a smaller place.

Or is it? Are such optimistic beliefs devoid of factual foundation, resting more on wishful thinking and hope than on empirical evidence? Are we guilty of committing a cognitive error, confusing what "is" with what "ought" to be? A pessimist can contend that the basic differences between cultural groups are, and always will be, irreconcilable. What appears to be "global civilization," "cultural enlightenment," or "social evolution" is largely illusory. Beneath this perilously thin veneer lurks raw human nature: selfish, greedy, and violent. To be sure, some progress has occurred. But many countries continue to be split along ethnic and religious lines. International terrorism remains a serious problem. Minority groups around the world continue to be ostracized, threatened, and assaulted. Millions of people belonging to various ethnic and religious groups continue to be the target of systematic violence. Local politicians reject pleas about human rights in their countries and label these appeals cultural "expansionism." Ethnic groups do not necessarily "blend" together, and the number of intercultural marriages is not on the rise. Tensions persist. Consider the Middle East, Sierra Leone, Timor, Sudan, Iraq, Kashmir, Afghanistan, Cyprus . . . is there any valid reason to believe that the list won't continue to grow? Can psychologists as professionals make a difference in this global but disunited world? Even if the world is becoming smaller, what does this mean? To some individuals, "smaller" implies a sense of community, connectedness, and camaraderie.

But to others, it is tantamount to cramped, crowded, and confining. Can we find a middle ground between these two views? Can we use the psychological knowledge gained in one country to understand the people in others? In searching for answers to questions such as these, we discovered an enormous body of theories, research, books, journal articles, and websites. Upon closer examination, however, what emerged was not particularly encouraging or even useful: lots of unsupported theories, lots of contradictory findings, lots of defensiveness and emotionally charged posturing, and lots of thinking that was a great deal less than clear. How does one even begin to sort through all of it? Is there a way to separate the proverbial wheat from the chaff? By what means can we thereby make informed decisions? These are some of the questions that we, the authors, have been struggling with for some time, and, in a nutshell, largely what prompted us to write this book. The background leading to our collaboration is briefly worth noting several respects. Although we both are of a similar age and share a number of common characteristics (from career choice to taste in music), we grew up in very different worlds. The first author (Eric) was born and raised in the city of Leningrad in the former Soviet Union, where he obtained his first academic degrees before moving to Virginia. He is a professor, author, and coauthor of 14 books. The second author (David) is from southern California, where he received his formal education and training and where he currently works as a psychology professor, psychotherapist, author, and researcher.

Thus, each of us brings a distinctly unique set of experiences and perceptions to this project. We were struck by both the similarities and differences in our respective backgrounds, and we sought to utilize these complementary contributions to maximum effect.

In discussing our past, we discovered that as we were entering college, neither of us knew very much about cross-cultural psychology. By the time we started graduate school (Eric at Leningrad State University and David at UCLA), our interest had begun to grow. But the real fascination with cross-cultural psychology emerged much later, specifically when each of us spent an extended period of time teaching in the other's home country. The appeal has never waned and continues to this day.

GOALS OF THIS BOOK   We have endeavored to distill and synthesize the knowledge gained from our own respective educational, research, training, and life experiences into a manageable set of four primary goals.

- To introduce the field of cross-cultural psychology to college students.
- To understand contemporary theories and research in cross-cultural psychology.
- To provide the reader—both instructors and students—with a useful set of critical thinking tools with which to examine, analyze, and evaluate the field of cross-cultural psychology in particular, and education in general.
- To assist current and future practitioners from a wide variety of fields and services.

INTENDED AUDIENCES   This book was designed with the following readers in mind:

1. As a primary or supplementary text for undergraduate college students from a diverse array of majors (including but not limited to psychology, sociology, anthropology, education, philosophy, journalism, political science, etc.).
2. As a supplementary text for graduate students in areas such as psychology, social work, education, law, journalism, nursing, business, and public administration.
3. Clinical psychologists, counselors, and social workers.
4. Educators and other practitioners who work in contemporary multicultural environments.

BRIEF OVERVIEW   The book consists of 12 chapters. Chapters 1 and 2 review the key theories, approaches, and research methods of cross-cultural psychology. Chapter 3 introduces principles of critical thinking and applies these tools directly to topics in cross-cultural psychology by identifying common errors and providing useful antidotes. Chapter 4 focuses on cross-cultural aspects of sensation, perception, and states of consciousness. Chapter 5 is devoted to the interface of cross-cultural psychology and intelligence. Chapters 6 and 7 comprise cross-cultural analyses of emotion and motivation, respectively. Issues related to human development and socialization are examined in Chapter 8. Chapter 9 focuses on the diagnosis, treatment, and explanation of psychological disorders from cross-cultural perspectives. The topics in Chapters 10 and 11 concern cross-cultural accounts of social perception and interaction. Last, Chapter 12 identifies several applied problems of cross-cultural psychology.

WHAT MAKES THIS BOOK DIFFERENT?

Emphasis on Critical Thinking

We firmly believe that critical thinking is perhaps the most vital and indispensable component of higher education and learning. Despite widespread consensus on this assertion throughout the educational community, however, it has been our experience that specific tools for critical thinking are rarely, if ever, provided to students during the course of their schooling. In other words, people may be convinced of the value of critical thinking, but they are left not knowing quite what to do about it. This book seeks to remedy that dilemma.

We view critical thinking as a series of skills that can be successfully taught and learned. As such, we provide the reader with specific strategies, methods, and techniques (along with lots of practice) to achieve this goal. For purposes of this book, each critical thinking principle ("Metathought") is illustrated primarily from the theory and application of contemporary cross-cultural psychology. Keep in mind, however, that these principles transcend the confines of any particular topic and can be utilized in a diverse array of fields.

In one sense, we use critical thinking to teach cross-cultural psychology; in another, we use cross-cultural psychology to teach critical thinking. This bidirectional relationship underscores the interdependence between the "content" and the "process" of thinking and learning.

Pedagogical Features to Enhance Learning

We have included a wide variety of pedagogical devices throughout the text.

- **Exercises and Activities.** There are more than 30 exercises strategically placed throughout the book. These can be utilized in any number of ways, including classroom discussions, demonstrations, debates, individual or group take-home assignments, term papers, and oral presentations. Boxes titled "Critical Thinking" were designed explicitly to provide practice in developing critical thinking skills as they relate to cross-cultural psychology.
- **Chapter Summaries** appear at the end of every chapter.
- **"A Case in Point" boxes:** In some instances, vivid examples or stories are best able to speak for themselves. A special feature in each chapter reviews and illustrates a number of controversial issues in cross-cultural psychology, displays cases and research findings, and introduces various opinions about human behavior in different cultural contexts.
- **"Cross-Cultural Sensitivity" boxes:** This section—featured in every chapter—presents some controversial remarks, statements, and actions that underscore the importance of empathy in interpersonal communications.

- **Quotations:** Scores of quotations appear throughout the text. These are intended to serve a number of functions, including the following: to provide divergent points of view, to pique the reader's interest and curiosity, to utilize humor as a means of facilitating learning, and to induce critical thinking. A sampling of sources includes Dr. Martin Luther King, Jr., Omar Khayyám, Confucius, Mahatma Gandhi, Lao-tse, Albert Einstein, P. T. Barnum, R. D. Laing, Jackie Mason, Miguel de Cervantes, the Bible, and common folk proverbs from a variety of cultures (Chinese, Russian, Yiddish, etc.).
- **Vignettes:** Each chapter begins with a vignette, a description of a real-life case, situation, or problem related to the chapter's subject.

Focus on Applied Contemporary Problems

We have dedicated ourselves to making this text as useful, practical, and relevant as possible. As a result, we made it a point to address a variety of applied contemporary themes and to present cross-cultural analyses for a series of complex problems that society faces today, or is likely to face in both the near and distant future. Throughout, we attempted to strike a balance between not making the book too theoretical (and, therefore, not particularly useful in the real world) or too concrete (which would not cultivate independent thinking).

Updates and Changes in the Fifth Edition

This edition of the book is updated with references to 129 new studies. In particular, there are new research and theoretical data on traditional and nontraditional cultures, ethnic identity, immigration, social perception, trance, intelligence, thinking, understanding emotions, violence, stigma of mental illness, physical abuse, sexuality, children's development, attitudes, verbal communications, mood disorders, culture-bound syndromes, schizophrenia, spirituality, customs, evolutionary psychology, treatment of psychological disorders, and acculturation.

The book includes new research data obtained on samples from the Netherlands, the United States, Belgium, Russia, Arab countries, India, China, Germany, Canada, Malaysia, Japan, Kenya, Romania, England, Cambodia, Botswana, Brazil, Zimbabwe, Finland, Iceland, Turkey, Austria, Mexico, and Taiwan. There are new data about various immigrant groups, Muslims, Christians, Asian Americans, Native Americans, Arab Americans, Hispanic Americans, and African Americans.

Chapters 1, 2, 5, 7, 10, 11, and 12 underwent the most significant rewriting and improvement. There are several new subtopics related to identity, values, self-perception, social and ethnic stereotypes, therapy, and applied problems.

To summarize, we wish to make our own values clear and not to present our opinions as if they were "facts" or "truths." We encourage debate and even disagreement. But we also believe that despite all the ethnic, cultural, religious, racial, and national differences, people can (and in fact should) learn to become more understanding, respectful, and tolerant of each other. Without appearing unduly optimistic, we do have faith in the enormous potential power of knowledge, reason, and compassion to help realize these goals.

It is true that cross-cultural psychology alone cannot solve the profound problems facing the human race. However, knowledge coupled with goodwill certainly can create a positive psychological climate that might eventually generate useful solutions. We hope that our enthusiasm about cross-cultural psychology and critical thinking is contagious and will serve to enhance your own academic, professional, and personal growth.

SUPPLEMENTS

Please find the companion website at www.routledge.com/9780205253234

ACKNOWLEDGMENTS

No project of this magnitude could have been realized without the invaluable contributions, assistance, and support of scores of individuals. We have benefited from the insightful feedback and advice of colleagues and reviewers, from the diligent efforts of research assistants, and from the patience and understanding of family members and friends. In particular, we wish to acknowledge Tamara Levy, Elizabeth Laugeson, Maykami L. McClure, Jacob Levy, Briana Levy, Zorro Levy, Emma Levy, Dmitry Shiraev, Dennis Shiraev, Nichole Shiraev, Oh Em Tee, Thomas Szasz, Fuji Collis, Don Kilburg Evangeline Wheeler, Alex Main, Susan Siaw, Gerald Boyd, Vladislav Zubok, Elena Vitenberg, Anthony Galitsky, Diana Smith, Mary Jo Carnot, Beverly A. Farrow, Bruno Bornet, Urszula Jakubowska, Yola Ghammashi, Buraq Amin, Alexandra Tyson, Alicia Hooper, Janett Chavez, Jason Smith, Sondra Saterfield, Joseph Morris, Judith Farell, William Lamers, Rita Chung, Michele Lewis, Fred Bemak, Vladimir Shlapentokh, Jane McHan, and Vinnie DeStefano.

We would also like to thank reviewers and commentators Denis Sukhodolsky, Yale University; Sergei Tsytsarev, Hofstra University; Cheryl Koopman, Stanford University; James Sidanius, Harvard University; William W. Lambert, Cornell University; Elaine P. Adams, Houston Community College; Karen L. Butler, Johnson C. Smith University; L. Kevin Chapman, University of Louisville; Kevin Chun, University of San Francisco; Fuji Collins, Central Washington University; McLin Dawn, Jackson State University; Chandler Gilbert Community College; G. William Hill, Kennesaw State University; Thomas Hodgson, SUNY-Empire State College; Corrine Lim-Kessler, Monmouth College; Na'im Madyun, University of Minnesota Twin Cities; Alex Main, Murdoch University; Pamela Mulder, Marshall University; Jill Norvilitis, SUNY College at Buffalo; Belinda Ramos, B. James Starr, Howard University; Yvonne Wells, Suffolk University; Evangeline Wheeler, Towson State University; and Leonard Wilhelm, Lakeland College for their insightful comments.

A special word of appreciation is due to the administrations, faculty, staff, and students at our respective academic institutions, where we have consistently been provided with an abundance of encouragement, assistance, and validation. We also would like to take this opportunity to acknowledge the tremendous support we received at virtually every stage of this project's development from the team at Pearson, in particular, Susan Hartman and Shivangi Ramachandran. We also thank Moganambigai Sundaramurthy from Integra Software Services for her invaluable help. On a more personal note, we wish to express our mutual feelings of thankfulness for our relationship to each other as collaborators, colleagues, comrades, and friends.

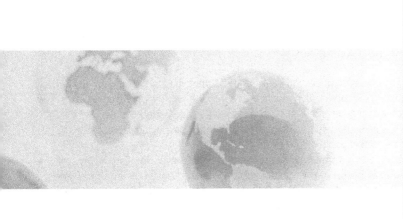

Understanding Cross-Cultural Psychology

Remember that all things are only opinions and that
it is in your power to think as you please.

MARCUS AURELIUS (112–180 C.E.)—
Roman Emperor and Stoic Philosopher

The West can teach the East how to get a living, but the East
must eventually be asked to show the West how to live.

TEHYI HSIEH (TWENTIETH CENTURY)—
Chinese Educator and Diplomat

I magine you develop a new method to overcome shyness and base your research on a sample of college students in the United States. Can you be sure that your method could decrease shyness in individuals living in China, Mexico, or South Africa? We know that social and cultural factors may impact the way people act, think, and feel and the same scientific study may yield different results in different groups. But how substantial are these impacts and differences? At least two answers are feasible here. If the influence of these factors is insignificant, then human behavior and psychological experience, regardless of where we were born and live, should be based on similar, almost universal mechanisms. On the other hand, if the impact is significant, then we, as humans, are very different because of our dissimilar backgrounds. Which side does psychology take? The problem is that for many years, psychology's answers to these questions were incomplete.

First of all, psychological research published in the United States in recent decades focused too narrowly on Americans, who comprise less than 5 percent of the world's population. Almost 70 percent of the research samples in these publications were in the United States, and only 5 percent were from Asia, Africa, and Latin America. To put simply, psychological research did not adequately represent the global population (Arnett, 2008).

Second, the most accepted international language of psychology is English. Scores of prominent journals appear in English. International conferences use English as an official language. Researchers who have limited knowledge of English, unfortunately, have a diminished opportunity to promote their research that would have otherwise enriched our knowledge of global psychological diversity.

Third, historically, most advanced psychological research was developed in a relatively small selection of countries. These are, mainly, the United States, Canada, France, Germany, and a very short list of other European nations. Without a doubt, scientists from these countries have made the most remarkable contributions to psychology. However, there are no less noteworthy and outstanding contributions coming from many other parts of the world, including China, Indonesia, India, Japan, Russia, South Africa, Turkey, Iran, and Mexico, to name a few. They often remain unknown to a majority of professional psychologists (Shiraev, 2011).

Cross-cultural psychology attempts to address these trends. Cross-cultural psychology seeks to identify and comprehend both the similarities and differences of people's behaviors and experiences. Most important, this discipline offers us the opportunity to connect with others through a deeper sense of appreciation and understanding.

WHAT IS CROSS-CULTURAL PSYCHOLOGY?

Before reaching adulthood, most of us do not choose a place to live or a language to speak. Growing up in cities, towns, and villages, no matter where—near a snowy Boston or in a humid Kinshasa—people learn how to take action, feel, and understand events around them according to the wishes of their parents, societal requirements, and traditions of their ancestors. The way people learn to relate to the world through feelings and ideas affects what these individuals do. Their actions, in turn, have a bearing on their thoughts, needs, and emotions.

Conditions in which people live vary from place to place. Human actions and mental sets—formed and developed in various environments—may also fluctuate from group to group. These kinds of differences—and of course, similarities—are studied by cross-cultural psychology (Gudykunst & Bond, 1997). **Cross-cultural psychology** is the critical and comparative study of cultural effects on human psychology. Please notice two important elements of the definition. This is a comparative field. Any study in cross-cultural psychology draws its conclusions from at least two samples that represent at least two cultural groups. Because cross-cultural psychology is all about comparisons, and the act of comparison requires a particular set of critical skills, this study is inseparable from critical thinking.

Cross-cultural psychology examines psychological diversity and the underlying reasons for such diversity. In particular, cross-cultural psychology studies—again, from a comparative perspective—the links between cultural norms and behavior and the ways in which particular human activities are influenced by different, sometimes dissimilar social and cultural forces (Segall et al., 1990). For example, do disaster survivors experience similar painful symptoms across cultures? If they do (Bemak & Chung, 2008), can a psychologist select a therapy aimed to treat posttraumatic symptoms in the United States and use it in other cultural environments, as in Sudan or Iran?

Cross-cultural psychology cares not only about differences among groups but also establishes psychological universals, that is, phenomena common for people in several, many, or perhaps all groups (Berry et al., 1992; Lonner, 1980). The structure of human personality—relatively enduring patterns of thinking, feeling, and acting—is, perhaps, one of such universals. For example, it was found that the same composition of personality is common in people in various countries (e.g., Germany, Portugal, Israel, China, Korea, and Japan). These universal traits include neuroticism, extraversion, openness to experience, agreeableness, and conscientiousness (Costa & McCrae, 1997). These findings have been supported in several global studies (Schmitt et al., 2007).

How is cross-cultural psychology different from **cultural psychology**? First and above all, cultural psychology seeks to discover meaningful links between a culture and the psychology of individuals living in this culture (which is defined below). The main message of cultural psychology is that human behavior is meaningful only when viewed in the sociocultural context in which it occurs (Segall et al., 1999). For instance, a cultural psychologist may be interested in describing how Buddhism affects both behavior and attitudes of young couples in Thailand. Or, a scientist may be interested in investigating how fundamental principles of Islam are incorporated into an individual's consciousness and personality traits (Monroe & Kreidie, 1997). Cultural psychology advocates the idea that behavior and mental processes are essentially the products of an interaction between culture and the individual.

Culture is simply how one lives and is connected to history by habit.

LE ROI JONES—Contemporary American Writer And Civil Rights Advocate

---

BASIC DEFINITIONS

Culture

For the purposes of this book, we define **culture** as a set of attitudes, behaviors, and symbols shared by a large group of people and usually communicated from one generation to the next. Attitudes include beliefs (political, ideological, religious, moral, etc.), values, general knowledge (empirical and theoretical), opinions, superstitions, and stereotypes. Behaviors include a wide variety of norms, roles, customs, traditions, habits, practices, and fashions. Symbols represent things or ideas, the meaning of which is bestowed on them by people. A symbol may have the form of a material object, a color, a sound, a slogan, a building, or anything else. People attach specific meaning to specific symbols and pass them to the next generation, thus producing cultural symbols. For example, a piece of land may mean little for a group of people living a few miles away. The same land, nevertheless, may be a symbol of unity and glory for the people living on this land (Brislin, 2000).

Cultures can be described as having both explicit and implicit characteristics. Explicit characteristics are the set of observable acts regularly found in this culture. These are overt customs, observable practices, and typical behavioral responses, such as wearing particular clothes. Implicit characteristics refer to the organizing principles that are inferred to lie behind these regularities on the basis of consistent patterns of explicit culture. For example, grammar that controls speech, rules of address, hidden norms of bargaining, or particular behavioral expectations in a standard situation may be viewed as examples of implicit culture.

Please remember that no society is culturally homogeneous. There are no two cultures that are either entirely similar or entirely different.

Society, Race, and Ethnicity

Some people use terms such as "society," "culture," "nationality," "race," and "ethnicity" interchangeably. However, these terms are different. A society is composed of people, whereas a culture is a shared way of interaction that these people practice. How does the term "culture" differ from "race," "ethnicity," and "nationality"?

Race is defined by most specialists as a group of people distinguished by certain similar and genetically transmitted physical characteristics. For example, Rushton (1995) looks at each race as a more or less distinct combination of heritable traits, morphological, behavioral, and physiological characteristics. As an illustration, narrow nasal passages and a short distance between eye sockets mark the Caucasian. Distinct cheekbones identify a Mongoloid. Nasal openings shaped like an upside-down heart typify a Negroid. Levin (1995) suggests that the differences among the races are also evolutionary. The Negroid race, according to this view, occurred first in sub-Saharan Africa approximately 110,000 years ago and later evolved in Mongoloid and Caucasian races. In general terms, blacks (Africans, Negroid) are those who have most of their ancestors from sub-Saharan Africa; whites (Europeans, Caucasoid) have most of their ancestors from Europe; and East Asians (Orientals, Mongoloid) have most of their ancestors from Pacific Rim countries. Of course, in referring to population or racial group differences, we are discussing *averages*. These three groups overlap substantially on almost all physical and psychological measures (Rushton & Jensen, 2005). It is essential to mention, however, the high or low frequency of occurrence of such physical— related to body—characteristics because most physical traits appear in all populations. For example, some Germans have frizzy hair and some Africans have red hair. There are many dark-skinned European Americans and light-skinned African Americans. To a contemporary biologist, "race" is a term used to describe a population that differs in distinguishable physical qualities. Members of this population are capable of breeding with members of other populations, but they generally do not. As a result, during a period of relative isolation, some specific physical characteristics emerge and are transmitted genetically. Geographical isolation was a race-creating factor in the past. Today, however, political, cultural, or religious factors are far more important in the explanations about the differences among races than are geographic factors.

Race can also be viewed as a social category. Because it indicates—first and foremost—particular experiences shared by many people who happen to belong to a category, it is called "race" (Gould, 1994, 1997; Langaney, 1988). Arthur Dole (1995), for example, recommended abandoning the term "race" altogether and instead using terms such as "continental origin" (African), "anthropological designation" (Caucasian), and "colonial history" (Latino) to describe large categories of people. Because race is a social construct, all racial differences may really reflect only the difference between arbitrarily established categories (Brace, 2005).

Race remains an important element of people's identification. For instance, in contemporary United States, the government, as well as many private organizations and agencies, may ask anybody applying for a job in those organizations to identify his or her race or origin, and there

TABLE 1.1 Major Racial Categories in the United States

White (includes people of European, Arab, and Central Asian origin)
Black (includes people of African origin)
Native American (includes people of American Indian, Eskimo, and Aleut origin)
Asian (includes people of East Asian and Pacific Islander origin)
Hispanic (includes people of South and Central American origin)

are formal guidelines for race identification (Table 1.1). The government also asks people their race when taking a census (Table 1.2).

Although the term "Hispanic" has been officially used by the U.S. government since 1980, it is generally not used in Latin America. Some believe the term "Latino" is more appropriate. The argument is that the term "Hispanic" emphasizes the Spanish heritage but not other origins (Comas-Diaz, 2001). To reach a compromise, some use the term "Latino-Hispanic."

In the United States, the term **ethnicity** usually indicates cultural heritage, the experience shared by people who have a common ancestral origin, language, traditions, and often religion and geographic territory. As you can see from the table, racial and ethnic minorities are expected to become 50 percent of the U.S. population by 2050. A **nation** is defined as group of a people who share common geographical origin, history, and language and are unified as a political entity—an independent state recognized by other countries. For example, those who acquire the status of a national of the United States, that is, become citizens, are either born in the United States or obtain their national status through a naturalization process. **Religious affiliation** indicates an individual's acceptance of knowledge, beliefs, and practices related to a particular faith. Europe, North America, and South America are predominantly Christian. Almost two-thirds of Muslims live in Asia. Since the beginning of polling almost 70 years ago, about 95 percent of Americans report consistently that they believe in God. However, the strength of their beliefs varies. Furthermore, about one-quarter of American adults have changed their religious affiliation since childhood and 25 percent of young adults under age 30 claim no affiliation with any religious institution (Pew, 2008). Overall, there are 78 percent Christians in the United States. More people, every year, identify themselves as Buddhist or Muslim, though these groups are relatively small: Each is less than 1 percent of the total population. Less than 2 percent identify themselves as Jews. Atheists or agnostics account for 4 percent of the total population. For global estimations of major religious affiliations, check the textbook's website, *www.ablongman.com/shiraev5e.*

There is a lot of confusion in the way people across countries use the terms "race," "ethnicity," "religious identity," and "nationality." Christian Arabs residing in Israel, for example, don't call themselves Israeli Christian Arabs. Although they are Israeli citizens, Arabs

TABLE 1.2 U.S. Population in 2010 and 2050 (The U.S. Bureau of the Census, Estimates)

Race/Origin	2010	2050
All people	308,936,000	420,000,000
White, non-Hispanic	201,112,000	210,283,000
Black	40,454,000	61,361,000
Hispanic-Latino	47,760,000	102,560,000
Asian	14,941,000	33,430,000

Source: U.S. Bureau of the Census

commonly see their Israeli identity as a civic or legal one, and not as cultural. On the other hand, for most of the Jewish population, Israeli citizenship serves as both legal and cultural identity (Horenczyk & Munayer, 2007). What is often labeled as "race" or "ethnicity" in the United States is often termed "nationality" in other countries.

A CASE IN POINT

Ethnicity and Nationality: How They Are Understood in the United States (an excerpt from Shiraev & Boyd, 2008)

There are different ethnic groups within most nations, and the United States is not an exception. Similarly, there could be different national groups within an ethnic group.

Same nationality, different ethnic groups:

Martha and Martin are both U.S. citizens. Nationally, they are both Americans. However, ethnically, Martha is Brazilian, because her parents emigrated from Brazil when she was a little girl and she received her U.S. citizenship a few years ago. Martin is a seventh-generation New Yorker. His ethnic roots are mixed: Irish, French, German, and Russian.

Same ethnic groups, different nationality:

Hamed and Aziza are both Palestinian exchange students living in New Jersey. Hamed's parents live in Tel-Aviv, and both he and his parents are Israeli citizens. Aziza is a Jordanian national and holds a Jordanian passport.

Source: Shiraev, E., & Boyd, G. The accent of success. © 2008 Ann Arbor: Reprinted by permission of University of Michigan Press.

CROSS-CULTURAL SENSITIVITY

Fairfax hospital emergency room was busy as usual on a typical Saturday afternoon. Perhaps in every emergency room the patient has little privacy, and whatever one says is heard by anyone who happens to be around. A young doctor was examining newly arrived patients—a usual routine to determine the seriousness of their symptoms. He just finished questioning a woman—she was apparently fine—and was about to leave to take care of another patient waiting nearby.

"Doctor, where did you go to school?" the woman asked.

"Wake Forest," the doctor replied.

"And what's your nationality?" the curious woman continued.

"I am American," replied the doctor with a smile.

"No, no, what is your nationality?" insisted the lady, putting an emphasis on the last word. "You look Chinese or Vietnamese to me."

"Ma'am, I am American, I was born here. My parents came from China, but they are U.S. nationals too. You can call me Chinese American."

"Oh, I see," concluded the lady loudly. "I knew I was right: You are Chinese."

Some people still associate the word "American" with a particular "European" look and "TV-anchor" accent. For some it is hard to comprehend that the United States has always been and will continue to be a multiethnic community. Skin color, name, and hair texture do not automatically determine a person's nationality or religion. "It is not big deal," said the doctor to one of the authors who witnessed this conversation and asked the doctor if he was offended by the woman's comments. "So long as I live I correct people's remarks about my ethnicity. Some people do not get it. It will never change." Doctors are not supposed to make wrong predictions. However, our hope is that this prediction was incorrect.

We should not forget that human groups are constantly moving and mixing with others. In the United States cultural diversity is encouraged and people have freedom to choose the group with which they want to be identified. Such phenomena as ethnic, religious, or national identity are becoming increasingly dynamic and based on choices of the individual. In some other countries, however, a person is prohibited from changing his or her religious affiliation.

Knowledge in Cross-Cultural Psychology

Knowledge is information that has a purpose or use. A fortune-teller is likely to explain to you that a dream is a mirror image of your future. A scientist, however, would likely explain the biological mechanisms of dreams, suggesting that they cannot predict anything. Pursuing various goals, people have developed different kinds of psychological knowledge. At least four types of knowledge about psychology can be recognized (Table 1.3).

The first type is **scientific knowledge**. This type of knowledge is derived from the systematic observation, measurement, and evaluation of a wide range of psychological phenomena. Observations are generalized in the form of scientific concepts and theories, which are typically tested by further empirical observations, verifications, and experimentation. Scientists propose new knowledge in the form of theories. Such theories arise from observation, hypotheses, and deductions. Predictions deriving from these theories are tested by experiments. Scientific views in psychology change. What was considered "scientific" has varied through history and from country to country. Some scientific theories have garnered academic respect during certain periods, only to be replaced later by other theories. Phrenology is an illustration. At a certain point in history, the link between bumps on the human skull and emotional and intellectual abilities of a person was considered scientific. Today such ideas are generally rejected.

The second type is that psychological knowledge represents a collection of popular beliefs and assumptions, often called folk theories. This knowledge is a type of "everyday psychology" that is formulated by the people and for the people. These assumptions vary from being general, such as the belief in the ability of dreams to predict the future, to quite specific, that a particular item of clothing will bring good luck. Popular beliefs may or may not be in line with major scientific theories. We may advice an angry person to take a deep breath and "cool down". Although the person's body temperature is unlikely to go down that quick, an angry reaction may be avoided.

TABLE 1.3 Four Types of Knowledge in Cross-Cultural Psychology

Type of Knowledge	Sources of Knowledge
Scientific	Knowledge accumulated as a result of scientific research of a wide range of psychological phenomena.
Popular (or folk)	Everyday assumptions ranging from commonly held beliefs to individual opinions about psychological phenomena.
Ideological (value-based)	A stable set of beliefs about the world, the nature of good and evil, right and wrong, and the purpose of human life—all based on a particular organizing principal or central idea.
Legal	Knowledge encapsulated in the law and detailed in official rules and principles related to psychological functioning of individuals.

On the other hand, millions of educated people today continue to be apprehensive about particular numbers: Many Christians avoid numbers 666 and 13, and number 4 is repulsed by many people in South East Asia. In many countries, people believe that when a black cat crosses your path, something bad could happen. Scores of people have faith in horoscopes.

As was the case many years ago, popular beliefs today have a tremendous influence on the lives of billions of people. Scientific knowledge remains in constant competition with popular beliefs, sometimes supporting them but often challenging many popular assumptions. For example, it is a common belief in many countries that immoral acts may cause mental illness (Haslam, 2005). Science, however, does not provide evidence to support these claims. Historically, many people routinely, but mistakenly, associate certain national or ethnic groups with salient personality traits or other salient features: Americans are ambitious and rude, British are courteous and grumpy, Chinese are obedient and polite, Russians are strong and unemotional, and so on. However, scientific research shows that such simplistic generalizations are inaccurate (Terracciano & McCrae, 2007).

The third type of knowledge is found in human values. In contrast to folk beliefs, this type of knowledge stems from cohesive and stable perceptions about the world, the nature of good and evil, right and wrong behavior, and the purpose of human life. Value-based knowledge is different from popular beliefs because it is grounded on a set of unwavering and articulated principles, which do not necessarily require empirical scrutiny. In a way, value-based knowledge tends to be dogmatic, in that its principles are not supposed to be challenged or questioned. For example, the deep-seated belief in the existence of the soul as a nonmaterial and immortal substance is an unquestionable value to many people. Religion as a social institution offers one of the most prominent kinds of value-based knowledge. In contemporary South Korea, for example, Blackberries and iPads coexist with traditions of direct communication with multitudes of gods and spirits. Such communication is enabled by several hundred thousands of professional mediators, called *manshin* (Sarfati, 2010).

Finally, the fourth type of knowledge is represented by **legal knowledge**. This knowledge exists in the form of laws and other prescriptions established by authorities (from tribal or community leaders to a central government). This knowledge includes the rules and principles that can be used by authorities and people themselves to pass judgments about psychological aspects of human behavior. Legal knowledge provides grounds for important decisions about life and death, marriage, people's sanity, ability to raise children, and so forth. What is considered death in most Western societies from the legal standpoint has little to do with people's religious beliefs in existence of the soul. The legal indicator of physical death is the secession of brain activities. The issues of whether the person is mature enough to get married and competent to stand trial are not decided by custom but by some legal rules. Spanking and smacking as forms of punishment of children are widely practiced all over the world. Many parents consider some physical violence against children normal. In the United States, however, most parents recognize that an act of physical violence against their own child would be viewed simply illegal.

It is critical for psychologists to treat all types of knowledge with sensitivity, understanding, and respect. The four types of knowledge are deeply interconnected. Commonsense assumptions, such as how to deal with deep sadness or how to interpret dreams, have always been part of people's knowledge about mental phenomena. At certain times in history, value-based doctrines, often embedded in organized religion, have had a tremendous impact on popular, scientific, and legal knowledge. Value-based, deep-seated cultural knowledge tends to resist rapid changes, but it transforms too. Legal psychological knowledge changes together with continuous transitions taking place in society (Shiraev, 2011).

CULTURAL TRADITIONALISM

Two types of cultural roots can be recognized. One is so-called **traditional culture.** It is a cultural construct based on traditions, rules, symbols, and principles established predominantly in the past. The other type is **nontraditional culture** (often called modern), which is based on new principles, ideas, and practices. The prevalence of science-based knowledge and technology-driven developments is typically associated with nontraditional cultures. The traditional culture tends to be confined in local and regional boundaries. It tends to be conservative and intolerant to innovations. The nontraditional culture tends to be absorbing and dynamic. The image of reality in contemporary nontraditional cultures is expanding. Traditional cultures tend to be restricting: The image of reality embraces only a certain set of ideas associated with a particular religious doctrine, tribe, ethnic group, or territory. The differences between traditional and nontraditional cultures have been listed in Table 1.4.

Traditional society structures people's lives and gives them little choice in their actions: Most things in their lives are ascribed by authorities and prescribed to people with little room for change. Traditional societies via religious and other cultural imperatives prescribe to the individual understandings of good and evil, desirable and unpleasant things, valuable and worthless actions, and sanity and insanity. In traditional Chinese culture, women's roles were outlined primarily by their family roles: daughter, wife, and mother, who should obey, respectively, their father, husband, and son (Cheung & Halpern, 2010). Modern cultures of the United States and other Western countries stand for new gender roles emphasizing equality between men and women. In contrast, gender roles in traditional cultures remain discriminatory allowing women fewer educational and social opportunities compared to men. It should be understood, however, that traditional values and norms are not always protected by coercion and safeguarded by obedience. Many people representing traditional cultures accept their norms willingly. Some of them do not want to face uncertainty caused by knowledge and practices that are new to them. Others do not want to lose their cultural identity. Nontraditional cultures, in general, embrace the freedom to choose. This may lead to the development of psychological problems. Psychologist Barry Schwartz (2004) showed that people in contemporary consumption-oriented communities spend too much time choosing

TABLE 1.4 A Comparison Between Traditional and Nontraditional Cultures

Traditional Cultures	Nontraditional Cultures
Most social roles are prescribed to individuals.	Most social roles are achieved by individuals.
In evaluations of individual behavior, the emphasis is placed on custom and routine.	In evaluations of individual behavior, the emphasis is placed on individual choice.
There is a clear distinction between good and evil in human behavior.	The distinction between good and evil in human behavior is relative.
Truth is not debatable; it is established and does not change.	Truth is revealed through the competition of ideas.
Individuals' choices are restricted to the boundaries of social prescriptions. Example: premarital, extramarital, and homosexual behavior are restricted.	Individuals' choices are not strongly restricted to the boundaries of social prescriptions. Example: premarital, extramarital, and homosexual behavior are generally tolerated.

among different foods, furniture, cars, clothes, and vacation destinations. This array of options can lead to so-called choice congestion and frustration concerning mistakes people make when exercising their options.

EMPIRICAL EXAMINATION OF CULTURE

We often refer to people by saying, "She is from a different culture," or "Let us consider his unique cultural background." Are there different types of cultures? Many academic psychologists have been working and continue to work on the premise that cultural differences can be conceptualized in terms of cultural dichotomies. Among such dichotomies are high- versus low-power distance, high- versus low-uncertainty avoidance, and collectivism versus individualism.

Power distance is the extent to which the members of a society accept that power in institutions and organizations is distributed unequally (Hofstede, 1980). It is assumed that there are cultures high and low on power distance. Most people in "high-power distance" cultures generally accept inequality between the leaders and the led, the elite and the common, the managers and the subordinates, and breadwinners and other family members.

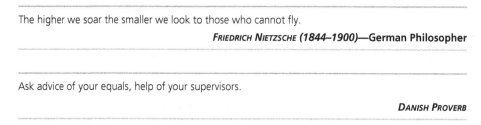

The higher we soar the smaller we look to those who cannot fly.

FRIEDRICH NIETZSCHE (1844–1900)—**German Philosopher**

Ask advice of your equals, help of your supervisors.

DANISH PROVERB

An old caste-based Indian society is one of high-power distance. Expectedly, there are also cultures low on power distance, in which equality is a preferred value in relationships. Studies reveal that people in hierarchical, high power-distance cultures tend to assign stricter behavior rules associated with social status (e.g., "when you become a father you should always act like a respectable head of the family"). On the other hand, people in egalitarian, low power-distance cultures are less preoccupied with the behavioral rules attached to the status ("a father is just a man, after all"). In many studies, it has been shown, for instance, that the United States is viewed as a relatively egalitarian, low power-distance culture. Alternatively, Japan and South Korea are commonly viewed as more hierarchical and higher in power distance (Matsumoto, 2007). Studies also show that on the individual level, high measures of power distance may be rooted in an individual's social dominance orientation, a measure of a person's preference for hierarchy within any given social system (Sidanius & Pratto, 2001). People accepting social hierarchy tend to see social, gender, ethnic, and other groups as unequal. These attitudes are most likely formed early in life (Lee et al., 2007).

If life were eternal all interest and anticipation would vanish. It is uncertainty, which lends its fascination.

YOSHIDA KENKO (1283–1350)—**Japanese Official and Buddhist Monk**

If you forsake a certainty and depend on an uncertainty, you will lose both the certainty and the uncertainty.

Sanskrit Proverb

Uncertainty orientation refers to common ways used by people to handle uncertainty in their daily situations and lives in general. This phenomenon is measured on a continuum between uncertainty acceptance and uncertainty avoidance.

Uncertainty avoidance is the degree to which the members of a society feel uncomfortable with uncertainty and ambiguity. People in cultures high on uncertainty avoidance tend to support beliefs promising certainty and to maintain institutions protecting conformity. Likewise, people in cultures low on uncertainty avoidance are apt to maintain nonconformist attitudes, unpredictability, creativity, and new forms of thinking and behavior. People who accept uncertainty tend to respond to uncertain situations by seeking information and engaging in activities that directly resolve the uncertainty. People who are certainty oriented tend to refer to rules, customs, or opinions of other people, including authority figures, to resolve uncertainty (Sorrentino et al., 2008). Research shows that people in Eastern and Western cultures tend to differ in how they handle uncertainty. In particular, Eastern cultures such as Japan or China tend to be more "uncertainty avoidant" than Western cultures such as France or Canada (Hofstede, 1980).

Collectivism and **individualism** are perhaps the most frequently mentioned and examined cultural characteristics (Triandis, 1989). Individualism is typically interpreted as complex behavior based on concern for oneself and one's immediate family or primary group as opposed to concern for other groups or society to which one belongs. Collectivism, however, is typically interpreted as behavior based on concerns for others and care for traditions and values. Collectivism and individualism can be studied on the level of so-called "strong ties" (among family members and close friends) and also on the level of "weak ties" appearing among casual acquaintances (Granovetter, 1973). Group norms in collectivist cultures—above anything else—are likely to direct individual behavior. People in collectivist cultures, in general, tend to prefer harmony-enhancing strategies of conflict resolution. People in individualistic cultures prefer more competitive strategies. Collectivism is expected to be high in the Asian countries, the traditional societies, and the former communist countries. Individualism is high in Western countries (Triandis, 1996). North Americans, according to studies, in comparison to Western Europeans and Asians, show the predominance of independence and individualism, as opposed to interdependence and collectivism of other groups (Kitayama et al., 2010).

What man wants is simply independent choice, whatever that independence may cost and wherever it may lead.

FYODOR DOSTOEVSKY (1821–1881)—**Russian Novelist**

COLLECTIVISM AND INDIVIDUALISM: FURTHER RESEARCH

Harry Triandis (1996) offered a more detailed and sophisticated understanding of the individualism–collectivism phenomenon. He suggested examining vertical and horizontal dimensions of collectivism and individualism. In the vertical cultural syndrome, people refer to each other from power and achievement standpoints. They communicate with each other as employees and employers and as leaders and the led. People are also engaged in various activities as friends, family members, and coworkers. Thus, benevolence and equality may represent the horizontal cultural syndrome. Totalitarian regimes, for example, are likely to emphasize equality (horizontal level) but not freedom. Western democracies tend to emphasize freedom (vertical level) but not necessarily equality (Kurman & Sriram, 2002).

People in more traditional societies such as India tend to be vertical collectivists. People in the United States may be viewed as vertical individualists. People in Sweden are seen as horizontal collectivists. Why? Americans tolerate inequality to a greater extent than people in Sweden do; Swedes for many years have been willing—at least many of them—to be taxed at higher rates so that the income inequality is reduced. Indeed, economic inequality between the top and bottom 10 percent of the population is three times lower in Sweden than it is in the United States (Triandis, 1996). These numbers haven't changed significantly in recent years.

National examples of collectivism and individualism vary. For instance, collectivism in the United States is expected to be different from collectivism in Asia. The Asian form of collectivism puts pressures on individuals to avoid disagreements with others, because in Asian cultures a concern about harmony with and happiness of others may be seen as more important than one's own personal comfort (Barnlund, 1975, 1989).

Fijeman and colleagues (1996) conducted a classic study in Hong Kong, Turkey, Greece, the Netherlands, and the United States. The subjects were college students who were asked to express their opinions regarding eight hypothetical situations of psychological and economic need. In particular, the participants were asked to indicate their readiness to help others with money, goods, or personal hospitality. This study challenges some simplifications in the traditional understanding of collectivism and individualism. The main point is that people in collectivist cultures not only expect to contribute to others but also expect others to support them back. People in individualist cultures not only expect to contribute less to others but also tend not to expect others to help or support them, thus reducing their own expectations of entitlement.

"Independence" and "interdependence" also became frequently used terms in cross-cultural psychology. In some cultures, most people seek to maintain their independence from others by attending to their individual selves and by expressing their unique inner attributes. In other cultures, people are interdependent and accentuate attention to others, fitting in and maintaining harmonious relationship with people of higher-, lower-, or equal-status levels (Markus & Kitayama, 1991). Studies show that compared with Asians, Western Europeans such as the British and the Germans tend to be more independent in their relationships and decisions. Compared with Western Europeans, European Americans are even more independent (Kitayama et al., 2009).

CULTURAL SYNDROMES

Every category displayed earlier is a label, which tends to describe one or several characteristics of a culture. Harry Triandis (1996) introduced the concept "cultural syndrome" as the pattern, or combination, of shared attitudes, beliefs, categorizations, definitions, norms, and values that is organized around a theme that can be identified among those who speak a particular language, during a specific historic period, in a definable geographic region. Examples of such syndromes include tightness—particular rules and norms applied to social situations and sanctions applied to those who violate these norms; cultural complexity—a number of different cultural elements; and activity and passivity (e.g., action vs. thought). Another example is honor—attitudes and practices that support aggressive actions in the name of self-protection. Psychologists also refer to syndromes similar to collectivism and called *communalism* in African contexts (Boykin et al., 1997), *familism* (as family orientation) in many Hispanic contexts (Galanti, 2003), and a combination of filial piety, conformity, family recognition, emotional self-control, and humility in many Asian contexts (Park & Kim, 2008).

Another cultural syndrome is embeddedness. Cultures measured high on embeddedness regard the family or extended in-group rather than the autonomous individual as the key social unit. Embedded cultures focus on the welfare of the in-group and limit concern for outsiders' well-being. This means that the more embedded the culture in a country, the less people should help or care about strangers. Embedded cultures emphasize restraint of actions that might disrupt in-group solidarity or the traditional order. Researchers have identified several countries that scored high on embeddedness: Singapore, Malaysia, Bulgaria, and Thailand. Countries in between are the United States, China, and Brazil. Low embeddedness is found in Austria, Spain, Denmark, Sweden, and the Netherlands (Knafo et al., 2009).

Cross-cultural psychologists use several approaches to examine human activities in various cultural settings. Consider several of them.

EVOLUTIONARY APPROACH

Evolutionary Approach is a theoretical model that explores the ways in which evolutionary end factors affect human behavior and experience and thus lay a natural foundation for human culture. Culture is just a form of existence that provides for fundamental human needs and subsequent goals. According to this approach, the prime goal of human beings is survival.

According to the natural selection principle, described by Charles Darwin, some organisms—due to various, primarily biological, reasons—are more likely to survive than others. Typically, healthy, strong, and adaptive individuals have better chances of survival than weak, unhealthy, and slow-adapting human beings. If members of a particular group are better fit to live in an environment than members of other groups, the first group has more of a chance to survive and, consequently, develops a social infrastructure. Therefore, its members have a chance to live in improved social conditions that will make people more competitive. Natural selection also removes cultural practices, norms, and beliefs that have outlived their usefulness.

Competition steadily develops society by favoring its best-fit members. Survivors pass on their advantageous genes to their offspring. Over generations, genetic patterns that promote survival—such as aggressiveness, initiative, curiosity, or obedience—become dominant and then form foundations for a culture. Biological differences between men and women—such as size, strength, bodily hormones, and reproductive behavior—laid foundation for cultural customs that reinforce inequality between the sexes.

Proponents of this approach offer natural and evolutionary explanations for a diverse array of human behaviors. Psychologists Beatrice and John Whiting, for example, believed that all people share a common evolutionary past that provides them with uniquely human tools for adapting to their diverse environments, raise children, and pass on to the next generation habits of survival and well-being (Edwards & Bloch, 2010). According to Satoshi Kanazawa (2010), people tend to act in accordance with the situations that existed in their ancestral environment. Thus, humans are evolutionarily designed to be altruistic toward their family members or ethnic groups. They tend not to be altruistic toward strangers. This is mainly because our ancestors for centuries lived in small groups; today, large cities and nations are evolutionarily novel and thus require caution and even mistrust as adoptive behaviors (Kanazawa, 2010).

According to evolutionary theorist Geoffrey Miller, the brain, like the peacock's tail, is designed through evolution to attract the opposite sex. Both sexes have a reason to "show off" in an attempt to attract a mate, but men and women have different criteria for making their choices. Compare, for instance, altruism and greed. These two phenomena appear different, but they also have something in common: Both involve wasteful deployment of resources, and both are signals demonstrating that an individual has these resources. The difference between men and women, according to Miller, is that women naturally tend to act altruistically, while men tend to be the conspicuous and greedy consumers. From the evolutionary viewpoint, women tend to seek material support in a partner, while men require self-sacrifice from women (Miller, 2000).

SOCIOLOGICAL APPROACH

This is a general view of human behavior that focuses on broad social structures that influence society as a whole, and subsequently its individuals. Several prominent sociological theories have had a profound impact on scientific and comparative understanding of human behavior in cultural contexts. On the whole, these theories suggest that social forces shape the behavior of large social groups, and human beings develop and adjust their individual responses in accordance to the demands and pressures of larger social groups and institutions. Thus, culture is both a product of human activity and its major forming factor.

Several views were confined within this approach. One of them was developed in the works of Emile Durkheim (1924), Talcott Parsons (1951), and other prominent social scientists. According to this view, society, as a complex system, functions to guarantee stability and solidarity among its members. Once created by people, society turns and confronts its creators, demanding subordination and obedience. Cultural norms and values become extremely important regulators of human behavior. Society provides a moral education for restraining the needs of its members.

This system worked perfectly, according to Durkheim, in traditional societies prior to the industrial revolution in the 1800s. However, with the improved living conditions and progression of personal freedom, many individuals in industrialized societies avoid moral obligations. As a result, people receive little moral guidance in their lives. Lack of moral mutual support results in violence, crime, suicide, and other anomalies.

According to the views of another prominent social scientist, Max Weber (1922), preindustrial societies develop traditions. Passing traditions on from generation to generation, these societies evaluate particular actions of individuals as either appropriate or inappropriate. Capitalist societies, on the contrary, endorse rationality. Rationality is a deliberate assessment of the most efficient ways to accomplish a particular goal. Reason defeats emotions, calculation replaces intuition, and scientific analysis eliminates speculation. Modern success-oriented societies promote values of efficiency and achievement. Members of such societies see each other on the basis of what they are, not who they are, as happens in traditional societies.

According to the conflict theory developed by Karl Marx more than a century ago, economic factors are the prime causes of human behavior and beliefs. Each society is divided roughly into two large and antagonistic social classes. The owners of the resources are members of the most powerful social class. Those who own neither resources nor technologies (the majority) become a social class without access to power. In an attempt to preserve power, the ruling class creates government, ideology, education, law, values, religion, and arts. Thus, each society contains at least two subsystems or cultures: the culture of the ruling class and the culture of the oppressed. The oppressed classes create their own beliefs, values, norms, and traditions. These norms and traditions reflect the class's need for social and political equality.

In class society everyone lives as a member of the particular class, and every kind of thinking, without exception, stamped the brand of a class.

MAO TSE TUNG (1883–1975)—**Chinese Communist Leader**

According to Marx, people of the same social class, but of different ethnic groups, have much more in common than people of the same ethnic or national group, but of antagonistic social classes. When people are equal, when there are no differences among social classes regarding their access to resources and technologies—all national, ethnic, and racial differences will eventually disappear.

ECOCULTURAL APPROACH

People constantly interact with the environment, thus transforming it and themselves (Goodnow, 1990). The individual is not a passive and static entity influenced by the environment, but as a dynamic human being who interacts with and changes the environment (Bronfenbrenner, 1979; Harkness, 1992). For example, parents educate their children and at the same time learn themselves. At the turn of the twentieth century, the American sociologist Fredrick Turner (1920) argued that while facing the challenges of the frontier, Americans developed both individualistic and egalitarian culture as conquerors and builders. Today's America's culture is a mixture of the unique American and global features (Schwartz et al., 2010).

John Berry suggests that among the major environmental factors influencing individual psychology are (1) ecological and (2) sociopolitical settings (Berry, 1971; Berry et al., 1992). The natural setting in which human organisms and the environment interact is called the **ecological context**, which includes the economic activity of the population. Factors such as presence or absence of food, quality of nutrition, heat or cold, and population density have a tremendous impact on the individual. **Sociopolitical context** is the extent to which people participate in both global and local decisions. This context includes various ideological values, organization of the government, and presence or lack of political freedoms. Through (1) genetic transmission, (2) cultural transmission, and (3) acculturation, people adjust to the existing realities and acquire roles as members of a specific culture. When ecological, biological, cultural, and acculturation factors are identified and taken into consideration, the psychologist ought to be able to explain how, why, and to what extent cultural syndromes differ from one another.

Even small cross-cultural differences can be associated with both environmental and social conditions. In Brazil, for example, one study found that pretend play is more developed in urban children of higher socioeconomic status than in other youth groups growing up in more difficult conditions. It is quite possible that the lives of poor children are preoccupied with material survival issues that require immediate and concrete solutions. Children in wealthier areas can be frequently engaged in symbolic and abstract thought associated with pretend play (Gosso et al., 2007).

Or, take climate, for example. Harsher climates involve a wide variety of risks and challenges, including food shortages, stricter diets, and health problems. People living in harsh climates persistently face greater risks and require tough adjustments, compared to people living in mild climates. People have to provide for themselves special clothing, housing, and working arrangements, special organizations for the production, transportation, trade, and storage of food, and special care and cure facilities. People in colder areas, by far, are wealthier than those in hotter areas. This unequal access to resources might affect several cultural syndromes (Van de Vliert, 2006). Could you guess which ones?

Economic and political stability is an important factor affecting long-term customs and beliefs. Persistently, over many years, some countries remain stable, while others stay very unstable. Among the most stable countries are Sweden, the United States, the United Kingdom, Canada, the Netherlands, and the Irish Republic. The most unstable ones are Sudan, Afghanistan, Iraq, Haiti, Zimbabwe, Chad, Ivory Coast, and Central African Republic. The vast majority of

A CASE IN POINT

An Ecocultural Approach: Culture and Availability of Space

Crowding has become one of the most significant elements of Japanese society. People are squeezed and squashed on the train, elbowed on the crowded street, and kicked in the swimming pool with 10 other people in the same lap lane. Almost all of Japan's 130 million people live in huge urban conglomerates, where space is extremely tight and expensive. The average Tokyo dwelling is about 620 square feet. Most Japanese houses do not have basements, the number of bathrooms is usually one, and front doors in many dwellings open directly into the road because many streets have no sidewalks. Many large companies own guesthouses for entertaining by their top executives, who often don't have a home large enough to accommodate dinner guests.

stable countries are democratic and free (Jane's Information Group, 2008). Do you think that long-term social stability and freedom would affect people's behavior and the cultural syndromes? If yes, in which way?

THE CULTURAL MIXTURES APPROACH

Dutch psychologists Hubert Hermans and Harry Kempen (1998) directed their attention to cross-cultural interaction, interconnected systems, and multiple cultural identities called "cultural mixtures." The "old" cross-cultural psychology, as the authors argue, assumed that cultures are generally static and confined within particular geographic locations. However, the ongoing social, economic, technological, and political realities have already transformed contemporary cultures, which have become heterogeneous and extremely complex (Faiola, 2003). Cultures are moving and mixing. People have more freedom to choose what cultural messages they want to receive. Phenomena such as culture identity are becoming increasingly dynamic, absorbing the commingling of different backgrounds, interests, ideas, and choices in one individual self. Immigration creates a distinctive new culture, one that is different from both the old and the new context (Raghavan et al., 2010). For example, many immigrants from Latin America in the United States might be fluent in two languages, support individualistic values in some situations such as business and collectivistic values in other contexts such as community, and identify both with the United States and with their country of origin (Chen et al., 2008).

Because the process of globalization involves so many areas of human activities and crosses so many cultural and national boundaries, the psychological values of tolerance and openness become essential in people's lives (Friedman, 2000; Giddens, 2000).

Psychologists have developed at least three views on how local cultures will respond to globalization. The first view predicts that globalization will inevitably lead to the weakening of local cultures and the development of a new international culture. Individualism, competition, and pursuit of efficiency will become global trends. Improving living standards and the proliferation of the Internet will eventually create similar lifestyles (Ho-Ying Fu & Chi-Yue, 2007).

The second view is based on the assumption that today's globalization patterns will eventually pull cultures further apart. The importance of local traditions and ethnic customs will be maintained by most people's fear of globalization. This tendency will result in strengthening of traditional views and religious affiliations, which will inevitably spark many ethnic and religious conflicts. As a result, globalization will affect the lives of a small proportion of the world population, living mostly in wealthy areas.

According to the third view, globalization will probably make a difference for only half of the world's population. These people will have access to modern technologies, education, and travel. The other half of the planet population will remain in relative isolation due to either rampant poverty or restrictive government policies, or both. At the same time, large groups of people will remain in the state of cultural transition marked by psychological uncertainty and elevated anxiety trying to adjust to global transitions (Arnett, 2002).

THE INTEGRATIVE APPROACH: A SUMMARY

To combine and critically apply these and possibly other approaches to cross-cultural psychology, let us introduce two general concepts that will be used throughout this book: **activity** and **availability of resources.**

For the cross-cultural psychologist, human behavior is not only a "result" or "product" of cultural influences, but people are also free, active, and rational individuals who are capable of exercising their own will. Activity is a process of the individual's goal-directed interaction with the environment. Human motivation, emotion, thought, and reactions cannot be separated from human activity, which is (1) determined by individual, socioeconomic, environmental, political, and cultural conditions and also (2) changes these conditions. In fact, human psychology develops within human activity and manifests through it (Vygotsky, 1932). Imagine, for example, a child who grows up in a zone of an ethnic conflict and for whom survival becomes a primary activity. Such a child develops emotions, motivation, and cognitive processes quite different from those children who grew up in safe conditions. At the same time, because this child can also engage in activities similar for children in most environments—such as playing, learning arithmetic, thinking about the future, helping parents, to name a few—he or he will be likely to share many common psychological characteristics with his or her counterparts around the world. Cultures may be similar and different in terms of the most common activities of their members.

Presence of resources essential for the individual's well-being largely determines type, scope, and direction of human activities. There are societies with plenty of resources available, and there are regions in which resources are extremely scarce. Geographic location, climate, natural disasters, or absence of such may determine how much resources are available to individuals.

Poverty, for instance, is clearly linked to a shorter life span and poorer health. The poor tend to live in more harmful environments and are more likely to be exposed to diseases and other risks than those who are not poor. Malnutrition in childhood, particularly during the first year of life, childhood infections, and exposure to accidents and injuries all make chronic and sometimes disabling diseases more likely in adult life, causing substantial changes in individual activities. Overall, would poverty affect the way people make decisions and see themselves, others, and their environment? This question will be addressed throughout the text.

Presence of resources does not mean equal availability to all members of that society. **Access to resources** is another important factor that unifies and separates people and cultures from one another. People's access to resources—and this will be a focus of our attention as well—affects many aspects of culture and individual behavior. Most psychological studies that examine ethnic and cultural minorities point at inequality and oppression as major causes of psychological differences between minorities and mainstream cultural groups (see, for example, Jenkins, 1995). As an example, oppression is often defined as an unequal distribution of resources that causes a sense of psychological inferiority among the oppressed (Fowers & Richardson, 1996). Every year researchers from the United Nations measure standards of living in most countries in the world. Average levels of people's education and income, combined with expected length of lifetime, are used as the criteria determining standards of living. For many years, countries such as Norway, Sweden, Australia, Canada, France, Japan, and the United States have occupied positions in the top ten. Unfortunately, other countries chronically finish last on the list. For 20 years, the bottom 20 countries on the list have been African.

However, more than material resources and access to them determine major characteristics of culture and culture-linked behavior. Ideas and practices that implement these ideas are insepa-rable from individual psychology. As mentioned earlier, Weber revolutionized scientific views on the role of ideas in human life. Take, for example, the role that people assign to their families and ancestors. Since ancient times in Chinese society the family—not the individual—has been regarded as the basic social unit. The human being, therefore, was valued primarily as part of a larger community and not necessarily as an independent individual. However, China is changing today: The large family is disappearing (most families have only one child), and capitalism is gradually replacing communism in people's daily lives. These changes may cause a profound impact on China's culture and its people.

To forget one's ancestors is to be a brook without a source, a tree without a root.

CHINESE PROVERB

INDIGENOUS PSYCHOLOGY

Kim and Berry (1993) define indigenous psychologies (plural is a suitable form because apparently any group of people can develop its own psychology) as the scientific study of human behavior, or the mind, that is designed for a people and native not transported from other regions.

A CASE IN POINT
Wealth and Individualism

There is a positive correlation between wealth and individualism (McClelland, 1961); how-ever, a society can accumulate wealth but remain collectivist, such as Kuwait or Singapore. One might argue that capitalism should promote indi-vidualism. Capitalism is based on the principle of competition that is protected by democratic political freedoms, which guarantee power for the majority—if the majority establishes its power through elections. Such free competi-tion requires a surplus of available resources. Others, however, may also successfully argue that collectivism is based on cooperation and does not exclude competition: people may com-pete among themselves while still basing their relationship on principles of cooperation.

One of the assumptions in contemporary cross-cultural psychology is that it is not possible to fully understand the psychology of the people in a particular ethnic or any other social group without an advanced understanding of the social, historic, political, ideological, and religious premises that have shaped this group's behavior and experience. Therefore, indigenous theories, including indigenous psychology, are characterized by the use of conceptions and methodologies associated exclusively with the cultural group under investigation (Ho, 1998).

ETHNOCENTRISM

College students in several countries were asked to draw a map of the world in 10 minutes, putting in as much detail as possible. In almost all cases, the students' own country was drawn disproportionately large (Whittaker & Whittaker, 1972). Perhaps what is most familiar to us tends to be exaggerated.

Ethnocentrism, in a way, is an exaggeration. This is the view that supports judgment about other ethnic, national, and cultural groups and events from the observer's own ethnic, national, or cultural group's outlook. In psychology, for example, various theories that rely on concepts alien in the studied culture are subject to the pitfalls of ethnocentrism. For those who grew up in one place and have never been exposed to other countries, the differences between Chile and Argentina, France and England, and blacks and Hispanics in the United States would appear insignificant. Ethnocentrism narrows our perception of other countries and social groups. Ethnocentrism is also a distortion of reality.

In most cases, being ethnocentric is also judging from the position of a cultural majority. Values and norms accepted by any majority have great power because of the sheer size of the majority and because of the fact that its members hold most positions of power.

MULTICULTURALISM

Seeking equality in treatment for all social and cultural groups has become a standard in contemporary psychology (Fowers & Richardson, 1996; Sears, 1996). **Multiculturalism** not only encourages recognition of equality for several ethnic or religious groups in one country but also promotes the idea that various cultural groups have the right to follow their own values and practices. Biculturalism as a kind of multiculturalism involves combining features of two cultures into one unique blend. Immigrants may easily embrace dual ethnic identities, speak two languages fluently, and raise their children bilingual as well (Ng & Lai, 2011). Biculturalism may appear in simple customs. For example, many Cuban Americans celebrate the Thanksgiving holiday with a combination of traditional Thanksgiving food and Cuban cuisine (Chen et al., 2008).

A BRIEF HISTORY OF THE FIELD

Cross-cultural psychology, a relatively new field, descended from scientific general psychology. It is also part of an intellectual tradition, rooted mainly in Europe but developed primarily in the United States. However, the old roots of cross-cultural psychology spread back in the history of contemporary science. Beyond its historical links with general psychology, cross-cultural psychology has diverse influences, including some that originate in disciplines such as anthropology, physiology, sociology, history, and political science. Please note that many specific views that contributed to modern cross-cultural psychology will be described in every chapter. Therefore, only a few important trends will be mentioned here.

Despite our scarce and incomplete knowledge about ancient philosophers and their scientific creations, it is possible to suggest that the scientists were aware of human diversity and emphasized the existence of some group and social differences in human behavior. After a relatively stagnant period in the Middle Ages, some essential changes in human scientific interest of diversity started to emerge, especially after the fifteenth century (Jahoda & Krewer, 1997). Among some of the contributing factors to such a trend were advances in science, growing number of contacts with other people, geographic expeditions, and trade. Perhaps the most radical changes in human thought on diversity occurred during the Enlightenment era, between the seventeenth and nineteenth centuries. By means of books and systematic education, many argumentative debates on the nature of human beings began to reach the minds of thousands of educated people. Works and publications of René Descartes in the Netherlands, Francis Bacon and David Hume in England, Immanuel Kant in Prussia, Denis Diderot and Jean Jacques Rousseau in France, and other prominent thinkers have shaped many contemporary views on reason, emotion, values, and behavior.

By the end of the nineteenth and the beginning of the twentieth century, the interest in the comparative subject in social sciences continued to grow. Anthropologists, psychologists, and social scientists, such as Emile Durkheim and Gabriel Tarde in France, Vladimir Bekhterev in Russia, and others, tried to offer an attractive theory or simple analogy (i.e., "social instinct" or "imitation") as explanations for cross-cultural human behavior. Gradually, the focus of research was changing from speculative to empirical. Francis Galton conducted his comparative research on intelligence. William Rivers undertook data-gathering expeditions to New Guinea, and Richard Thurnwald went to Melanesia to study people's cognitive functions. Psychological studies and anthropological observations in the middle of the twentieth century led many scientists to believe the key to the understanding of human behavior was the interaction between individuals and their cultural environment. By the 1960s, cross-cultural psychology began to establish itself as an independent discipline.

Among many notable developments, the 1960s were marked by the publication of an international study of cultural influences on visual perception (Segall et al., 1966) and the launch of the *International Journal of Psychology* (1966). At this time, cross-cultural psychology was informally established by the publication of the *Journal of Cross-Cultural Psychology* in 1970. Today, the editors of the journal focus on studies that describe the relationships between culture and psychological processes. They believe that all psychology is cultural and all cultures are psychological. They seek to publish papers that present culture as a mediating and moderating variable or antecedent to all behaviors. The journal encourages comparisons between two or among more cultures. It also includes studies of some cultural comparisons between minority or ethnic groups in one country (*http://www.iaccp. org/drupal/*).

In 1972, the International Association for Cross-Cultural Psychology and the Society for Cross-Cultural Research were established. By the 1980s, two important books were published: one the first edition of the *Handbook of Cross-Cultural Psychology* (Triandis et al., 1980) and the other the *Handbook of Cross-Cultural Human Development* (Munroe et al., 1981). In 1997, the second edition of the *Handbook of Cross-Cultural Psychology* was published. An encyclopedia of cross-cultural psychology is underway. Today, cross-cultural psychology is an international discipline. Many specialists represent this field from virtually every country in the world.

Exercise 1.1

Your Name and Your Culture

We seldom choose our names. Somebody else—usually our parents—decides how to name us. But do you think that our names may reflect to some degree our culture and individual personality? Let's analyze in several steps. Answer these questions.

Step 1. What is your name? Do you have a first and a second name? Explain how your names were given to you and why. What do your names—the first and middle—mean? How do people who know you call you? How do you like to be called?

Step 2. Describe how the names are given in your culture. For example, in the U.S. south it is somewhat common to give two (or even more) first names. In Russia, Ethiopia, or many other countries, your middle name is commonly the first name of your father. Do you think your name represents the culture with which you identify yourself? If you have to live in a different country, would you consider changing your name so that it sounds culturally more appropriate?

Step 3. Do you like your name and how do you feel about it? How do strangers treat you when they hear your first and last name? Do you think your name reflects your individual personality? If yes, in which way?

Chapter Summary

- Cross-cultural psychology is the critical and comparative study of cultural effects on human psychology. As a comparative field, cross-cultural psychology draws its conclusions from at least two samples that represent at least two cultural groups. The act of comparison requires a particular set of critical thinking skills.

- Cross-cultural psychology examines psychological diversity and the underlying reasons for such diversity. Using a comparative approach, cross-cultural psychology examines the links between cultural norms and behavior and the ways in which particular human activities are influenced by various cultural forces. Cross-cultural psychology establishes psychological universals, that is, phenomena common for people in several, many, or perhaps all cultures.

- Cultural psychology seeks to discover meaningful links between culture and psychology of individuals living in this culture.

- At least four types of knowledge about psychology can be recognized: scientific, popular (folk), ideological (value-based), and legal. It is critical for cross-cultural psychologists to treat all types of knowledge with sensitivity, understanding, and respect.

- No society is culturally homogeneous. There are no cultures that are either entirely similar or completely different. Within the same cultural cluster there can be significant variations, inconsistencies, and dissimilarities.

- Cross-cultural psychologists establish and conceptualize the main culture's features in terms of cultural dichotomies. Among such dichotomies are high- versus low-power distance, high- versus low-uncertainty avoidance, masculinity versus femininity, and collectivism versus individualism.

- Evolutionary approach is a theoretical model that explores the ways in which biological factors affect human behavior and thus lay a natural foundation for human culture. The sociological approach focuses on broad social structures that influence society as a whole and, subsequently, its individuals. There are particular social forces that shape the behavior of large social groups, and human beings develop and adjust their individual responses in accordance to the demands and pressures of larger social groups and institutions.

- According to an ecocultural approach to cross-cultural psychology, the individual cannot be separated from his or her environmental context. People constantly exchange messages with the environment, thus transforming it and themselves.

- According to a "culture mixtures" approach, researchers should switch their attention from traditional views on culture to new cultural mixtures, contact zones, interconnected systems, and multiple cultural identities.

- An "integrative" approach to cross-cultural psychology emphasizes human activity, a process of the individual's goal-directed interaction with the environment. Human motivation, emotion, thought, and reactions cannot be separated from human activity, which is (1) determined by individual, socio-economic, environmental, political, and cultural conditions and also (2) changes these conditions. Two factors—presence of and access to resources—largely determine type, scope, and direction of human activities.

- Indigenous theories are characterized by the use of conceptions and methodologies associated exclusively with the cultural group under investigation. Indigenous psychology is the scientific study of human behavior or the mind and is designed for a people and native, not transported from other regions.

- Ethnocentrism is the view that supports judgment about other ethnic, national, and cultural groups and events from the observer's own ethnic, national, or cultural group's outlook. Multiculturalism is a view that encourages recognition of equality for all cultural and national groups and promotes the idea that various cultural groups have the right to follow their own unique paths of development and have their own unique activities, values, and norms.

Key Terms

Access to Resources The indicator of availability of material resources to a population.

Activity A process of the individual's goal-directed interaction with the environment.

Availability of Resources A measure indicating the presence of and access to resources essential for the individual's well-being.

Collectivism Behavior based on concerns for other people, traditions, and values they share together.

Cross-Cultural Psychology The critical and comparative study of cultural effects on human psychology.

Cultural Psychology The study that seeks to discover systematic relationships between culture and psychological variables.

Culture A set of attitudes, behaviors, and symbols shared by a group of people and usually communicated from one generation to the next.

Ecological Context The natural setting in which human organisms and the environment interact.

Ethnicity A cultural heritage shared by a category of people who also share a common ancestral origin, language, and religion.

Ethnocentrism The view that supports judgment about other ethnic, national, and cultural groups and events from the observer's own ethnic, national, or cultural group's outlook.

Ideological (Value-Based) Knowledge A stable set of beliefs about the world, the nature of good and evil, right and wrong, and the purpose of human life—all based on a certain organizing principal or central idea.

Individualism Complex behavior based on concern for oneself and one's immediate family or primary group as opposed to concern for other groups to which one belongs.

Legal Knowledge A type of knowledge encapsulated in the law and detailed in official rules and principles related to psychological functioning of individuals.

Multiculturalism The view that encourages recognition of equality for all cultural and national groups and promotes the idea that various cultural groups have the right to follow their own paths of development.

Nation A large group of people who constitute a legitimate, independent state and share a common geographic origin, history, and, frequently, language.

Nontraditional Culture The term used to describe cultures based largely on modern beliefs, rules, symbols, and principles, relatively open to other cultures, absorbing and dynamic, science-based and technology-driven, and relatively tolerant to social innovations.

Popular (or Folk) Knowledge Everyday assumptions ranging from commonly held beliefs to individual opinions about psychological phenomena.

Power Distance The extent to which the members of a society accept that power in institutions and organizations is distributed unequally.

Race A large group of people distinguished by certain similar and genetically transmitted physical characteristics.

Religious Affiliation A term indicating an individual's acceptance of knowledge, beliefs, and practices related to a particular faith.

Scientific Knowledge A type of knowledge accumulated as a result of scientific research on a wide range of psychological phenomena.

Sociopolitical Context The setting in which people participate in both global and local decisions; it includes various ideological issues, political structures, and presence or absence of political and social freedoms.

Traditional Culture The term used to describe cultures based largely on beliefs, rules, symbols, and principles established predominantly in the past, confined in local or regional boundaries, restricting and mostly intolerant to social innovations.

Uncertainty Avoidance The degree to which the members of a society feel uncomfortable with uncertainty and ambiguity.

Uncertainty Orientation Common ways in which people handle uncertainty in their daily situations and lives in general.

2

Methodology of Cross-Cultural Research

A blind man who sees is better than a seeing man who is blind.

PERSIAN PROVERB

N ot long ago we were conducting a comparative Russian–American study on the perception of obedience. After we translated the survey questions from English to Russian, made a thousand copies of the questionnaire, and videotaped testing materials, we flew to Russia to gather our research data. We studied a wide variety of samples, from schoolchildren to construction workers, from engineers to psychology majors. There was only one problem. We needed to get access to Russian police officers but couldn't get permission from a county police chief. To our elation, however, after a few days of delays we finally were allowed to interview 100 police officers. We rushed to the police station, met with a local police chief, and handed him cash for "using" his officers as research subjects.

   The procedure went well and when the last policeman had filled out the questionnaire, we went back to the chief's office to thank him for his assistance. "Oh, you are very welcome," he replied with a smile. "I really wanted to help you to get the best results. I told my lads"—he referred to the policemen—"to be serious and give you their best answers. I told them that it is a comparative study and that they should have given you the most decent answers."

We couldn't believe what he was saying to us! Did he really instruct his policemen to give us only "decent," that is, socially desirable answers? If that was the case, we could not have used the results of the study because all other U.S. and Russian subjects did not receive any instructions from their bosses about how to answer the questionnaire. And now, an officer tries to create a better image of Russian police officers and instructs his subordinates about how to answer questions!

This is perhaps one of the most common methodological problems of any comparative research: the subjects' attempts to present themselves as better than they usually are, assuming that their answers will be compared with their counterparts' surveys overseas. How could we have prevented such a situation? Perhaps we should have better hidden the fact that we were conducting a comparative research study. However, the next day one of our colleagues clarified the situation for us. He asked whether we knew why it took the police chief several days to give us the "green light" to conduct this research. When we said we didn't, he enlightened us. "The chief was making phone calls and gathering information about you and your research project. You did not have a chance to hide that this was a comparative study. Please don't blame yourself. That's the Russian environment: you have to second-guess and verify everything. The police chief did everything that he was supposed to do and any other cop in his place would have done the same. In a way, you had a representative sample."

To better understand the diversity of human behavior and experience, psychologists have to gather reliable evidence—verifiable facts and consistent data interpreted in the most unbiased way. This chapter deals with research methodology in cross-cultural psychological studies. It gives an overview of the most popular methods used by cross-cultural psychologists and offers critical suggestions about the process of gathering facts and interpreting data in comparative studies.

GOALS OF CROSS-CULTURAL RESEARCH

Imagine, a researcher wants to find similarities and differences between arranged marriage practiced in India and nonarranged marriages in the United States and how they affect marital stability. What does the psychologist aim to pursue in this particular project?

First, the researcher wants to *describe* some major findings of this research. Suppose one of the most important differences is so-called conflict-avoiding behavior of both spouses in the arranged-marriage family: They tend not to escalate tensions and try to resolve every minor problem in their relationship before the problem grows unsolvable.

Then, when some differences between ethnic groups are found, the researcher tries to *explain* whether these factors affect stability. If they do, then why and how does this influence take place? After an explanation is offered, the psychologist tries to disseminate the received data and their interpretations. The psychologist may attend a conference, share the data with colleagues and students, or publish an article in a scholarly journal.

The practical value of the study may be significant if it not only explains but also *predicts* the factors that determine successful marital relationships. For example, the psychologist could suggest that conflict-avoiding behavior is effective primarily in arranged-marital relationships, but not in other types of marriages in which conflict resolution behavior is more efficient than conflict-avoiding activities. If this is the case, practitioners could use these research data to help other people to better understand and manage—that is, effectively *control*—their family relationships.

By and large, research methodology in cross-cultural psychology can be divided into two categories: quantitative and qualitative.

QUANTITATIVE RESEARCH IN CROSS-CULTURAL PSYCHOLOGY

Because cross-cultural psychologists are interested in establishing similarities, differences, and other statistical relationships that occur between two or among several variables, the most common data are **measures of central tendency**. The measure of central tendency indicates the location of a score distribution on a variable; that is, it describes where most of the distribution is located. There are three measures of central tendency: the mode, the median, and the mean.

The most frequently occurring score is called the **mode**. For example, you compare the test performances of two groups of people: A and B. Then you find out that most people in group A received 10 points for the test and most people in group B received 7 points; you can compare 10 and 7 as the groups' modes. Mode in most cases does not provide accurate accounts of the scores in the studied groups. Therefore, a better measure of central tendency can be used— the **median**. When 50 percent of all scores are the score X or a score less than X, the median will be X. For example, if you have the scores 1, 2, 2, 2, 3, 4, 5, 5, 5, the median would be 3 because half of the distribution—scores 1, 2, 2, 2—is before the 3 and half of the distribution—scores 4, 5, 5, 5—is after the 3. The numerical value of the scores is not what determines the median. In brief, the median is the score at the 50th percentile. For example, you want to know the socioeconomic status of the population in the country in which you conduct research. You will have to find a point on the country's income distribution scale that indicates a 50 percent level. Suppose this point is $12,000. This measure will indicate that $12,000 is the median income in this country. The median, however, does not adequately describe some data. Imagine a child is taking a test on cognitive development and receives the following scores: 2, 3, 3, 4, 9, 9, 9. The median in this case will be 4; however, this description virtually ignores the high scores received on the last three tests. The student could have gotten scores 6, 6, and 6 instead of 9, 9, and 9; however, the median will still be 4.

The most convenient and frequently used measure of central tendency in cross-cultural psychology is the **mean**. The mean indicates the mathematical central point of a distribution of scores. It is determined by adding up all the scores and dividing by the number of scores you just added. For example, by adding the scores 2, 3, 7, 8, 15, and dividing the sum (35) by 5, which is the number of scores, you would have a mean of 7. However, this measure does not always accurately describe highly skewed distributions. Imagine, for example, that you examine aggressive reactions in people's behavior during an experiment. In four experimental conditions the score of angry reactions is 10. The mean will be 10. Then on the fifth condition the score is 0. That will bring the mean down to 8, which could be somewhat misleading because any observer unfamiliar with this research would assume that all the scores were distributed around 8. Therefore, when you collect statistical data you always have to be aware of the distance between the two most extreme scores in your set of data (the range) and deviations of the scores around the mean (the variance).

QUANTITATIVE APPROACH: MEASUREMENT SCALES

When you measure distance, weight, volume, motion, or temperature, the results represent quantity, magnitude, or degree. Human activities can be measured along these dimensions too. Choosing a correct measurement scale becomes a crucial factor for the overall success of any psychological research. There are four types of measurement scales: nominal, ordinal, interval, and ratio. With a nominal scale, each score does not indicate an amount. This scale does not measure any rank or order and is used mostly for identification purposes. For example, in the question, "What languages do you speak?" the scale *English–Spanish–Mandarin–Arabic–Other* is a nominal scale. Remember the description of the mode? In fact, the mode is usually used to describe central tendency when the scores reflect a nominal scale of measurement (Heiman, 1996).

In an ordinal scale, the scores designate rank order. A rank order may indicate the subject's preference, attitude, or opinion. For example, you may ask your subjects from two countries to pick and rank the most valuable traits in a personal friend: assertiveness, honesty, intelligence, creativity, confidence, sense of humor, and so on. This procedure will require use of an ordinal scale. This scale, however, as you see, does not measure the distance between the ranks.

In an interval scale, each score indicates some amount. There is presumably an equal unit of measurement separating each score. In the question, "Do you support or oppose sexual relations between any two unmarried individuals?" the scale *Definitely support* (+2), *Conditionally support* (+1), *Do not know* (0), *Conditionally oppose* (–1), *Definitely oppose* (–2) is a rank scale. The scores here could be either positive or negative (e.g., the Fahrenheit scale), and zero does not indicate a zero amount. In other words, there is no true zero point.

With a ratio scale the scores reflect the true amount of the present variable, and zero truly means that zero amount of the variable is present. Ratio scales cannot include negative numbers and are used to measure quantitative variables, such as the amount of time spent watching television, the number of errors made on the test, or number of hits on a website.

QUANTITATIVE APPROACH: LOOKING FOR LINKS AND DIFFERENCES

A specialist or student conducting research in cross-cultural psychology often needs to establish *correlations*, or the relationships between two or among several variables. If in one set of data, when variable X is low, variable Y is also low, and when variable X is high, variable Y is also high, we have a positive correlation between the variables. If, according to another data set, when variable A is low, variable B is high, and when variable A is high, variable B is low, we have a negative correlation. For example, the relationship between frequency of picture exposure and picture liking is positively correlated. In a study conducted by Zajonc (1968), different people were shown photographs of different faces, and the number of times each face was shown was varied. The more often the subjects saw a particular photograph, the more they reported liking the face pictured on it. As an illustration of negative correlation, we can look at marital stability: Divorce rates around the world are negatively correlated with fertility rates. This means that the more the number of children a family has, the lesser the chance of divorce (Lucas et al., 2008).

A measure of correlation—**correlation coefficient**—contains two components. The first is the sign that indicates either positive or negative linear relationship. The second is the value. The larger the absolute value, the stronger the relationship. For example, the intelligence scores of identical twins raised either together or apart are highly correlated: +0.88. The intelligence scores of nonrelatives raised together are relatively low: +0.20 (Bouchard et al., 1990). Correlational studies can describe the relations between global, general variables that are established in large samples. As an illustration, in a study of 59,169 persons in 42 nations, a strong positive correlation was established between marital status and subjective well-being: In other words, people who are married tend to feel better than those who are not married. This correlation appears similar across the world (Diener et al., 2000). Correlational studies can also deal with "smaller" issues and samples. Based on a survey with face-to-face interviews of 335 adults without tattoos (mean age was 49) randomly selected from relatively large city, one researcher found that age and attitude toward religion were associated with individuals' perception of tattoos (Lin, 2002). This means that people who are older and more religious were less likely to have tattoos on their bodies.

Does correlation establish a cause-and-effect relationship between the variables? A psychologist who, for example, finds a positive cross-cultural correlation between (1) violent crime and (2) level of poverty in a particular country, in most cases, would not be able to make a conclusion about which, if either, factor was the cause, and which, if either, was the effect or result. In other words, poverty may cause crime, crime can contribute to poverty, or a third variable—unknown to the psychologist—may contribute to both. For a more detailed critical analysis of correlation see Chapter 3.

QUALITATIVE APPROACH IN CROSS-CULTURAL PSYCHOLOGY

Qualitative research is conducted primarily in the natural setting, where the research participants carry out their daily activities in a nonresearch atmosphere. Psychologists try to detect and describe some illicit or unspoken aspects of culture, hidden rules, innuendo—the so-called contexts that are often difficult to measure by standard quantitative procedures (Marsella, 1998). It is obvious that the use of these methods can bring the element of subjectivity to cross-cultural research, which can produce both positive and negative outcomes. In what other instances might you use qualitative over quantitative research? You may try qualitative procedures when dealing with phenomena that are difficult to measure (such as dreams, pictures, drawings, songs); subjects or topics for which standardized measures are not suited or not available (subjects who are illiterate or unable to use answer scales; see Tutty et al., 1996); and variables that are not

A CASE IN POINT
Looking for Causes

A study, conducted in Finland, found that Finnish women who had cosmetic breast implants were three times more likely to commit suicide than the general population (Kaufman, 2003). These results were similar to the findings from a comparable study of Swedish and U.S. women conducted by the National Cancer Institute. In the United States, six recent studies show the following result: The suicide rate for women who have undergone breast augmentation is approximately twice the expected rate based on estimates of the general population (Sarver et al., 2007). The question is why? A common response of the media after the publication of the Finnish study was that breast implants caused a high risk of suicidal behavior. This is indeed a possibility: the high suicide rate might be a function of the problems, discomfort, pain, or serious regrets that occur in some women months and years after their surgery. It is also possible that the high suicide rate reflects the psychological makeup of women who seek implants. In other words, women who want to have breast implants, as a group, might be more likely than all other women to have specific psychological problems than the general population.

completely conceptualized or operationally defined (in many cultures, sexual harassment, or mental illness; see Chapter 9).

Researchers often have to combine both qualitative and quantitative methods. Let us go back to the opening vignette. In this example, the sample participants and their answers were influenced by the police chief. We might choose a qualitative design for this study—in addition to quantitative procedures—because it is difficult to measure the extent to which the survey answers were influenced by the police chief's actions.

One form of qualitative research is **psychobiographical research**, or an in-depth analysis of particular individuals—usually outstanding persons, celebrities, and leaders—representing different countries or cultures. Most of the time, specialists try to collect empirical evidence in order to compose a personal profile of the individuals under study. To collect such evidence, diaries, speeches, letters, memoirs, interviews, and witnesses' accounts are examined.

Qualitative and quantitative methods are not mutually exclusive, and in many cases, psychologists choose both in their research. For example, in one study of immigrant groups, the researchers first used a qualitative method to understand the studying samples better and only then designed and applied quantitative procedures (Roer-Strier & Kurman, 2009).

A CASE IN POINT

A Sample of a Multistep Approach to Cross-Cultural Research Design

Step 1. Describe a problem (an issue) you have to investigate. Review the scholarly literature on the topic. You may use popular journals, magazines, and newspapers for additional references. Check available sources in the language of the country or countries you examine, if necessary.

Step 2. Identify your research goal, that is, explain what you want to achieve as a result. Then, introduce one or several hypotheses for your study. You can use at least two strategies: (1) inductive: you collect data first and then make a conclusion about the studied samples; (2) deductive: you select a theoretical concept first; then you collect data to demonstrate or reject the selected hypothesis.

Step 3. Identify and describe the research sample of your study: groups of people, newspaper reports, children's drawings, texts, and so on.

Step 4. Choose or design a methodology for your project. Make sure that your method does not violate research ethics. Refer to your local Human Subjects Review Board for approval. Put together a schedule (timetable) for your project.

Step 5. Conduct a pilot study, a preliminary exploration of the method to see how your methodology works and whether there are any obstacles to data collection.

Step 6. Collect research data.

Step 7. Interpret your data using statistical procedures.

Step 8. Present the results and analyze them critically in a report.

Step 9. In your report, suggest where and how your data should be or could be used (i.e., in education, therapy, conflict-resolution, etc.).

MAJOR STEPS FOR PREPARATION OF A CROSS-CULTURAL STUDY

A solid cross-cultural study should address all basic requirements applied to an empirical study in general psychology (see A Case in Point, p. 29).

Ultimately, the researcher attempts to explore both the significance and meaning of cross-cultural differences or similarities. Because research in cross-cultural psychology is comparative, investigative strategies may pursue at least two goals.

Choosing an **application-oriented strategy**, researchers attempt to establish the applicability of research findings obtained in one country or culture to other countries or cultures. In this type of research, a methodology or procedure tested in a particular cultural context (e.g., in Japanese collectivist society) is tested in a different cultural setting (e.g., in Finnish individualist society). To illustrate, an Argentinean psychologist who created a unique form of behavioral therapy may conduct an examination of the therapy's effectiveness in neighboring Chile.

Comparativist strategy focuses primarily on similarities and differences in certain statistical measures in a sample of cultures. For example, a Canadian researcher establishes that educational level of family members and size of the family are negatively correlated on the national level. Then she would use a comparativist strategy to identify similarities or differences in the relationships between education and family size in a sample of other countries.

A crucial element for a successful comparative study is the selection of methodology. Often, the same method can be used in different countries without any modifications other than translation. One example of such direct application of the same method is a study conducted by Hofstede (1980), when the original questionnaire was translated into 10 languages in 53 countries. In other cases, an adaptation of the original method is necessary, which usually includes the rephrasing of questions or statements, adding or deleting some words to clarify meaning, breaking up sentences, and so on. Some authors believe that many psychological tests from one culture can be effectively applied—after adaptation, of course—in other countries (Butcher et al., 1998). Others suggest that, on some occasions, an entirely new method should be designed for a comparative study. As an example, Cheung and colleagues (1996), arguing that Western personality inventories were inadequate to measure the main elements of Chinese personality, put together a new personality questionnaire specifically for Chinese people.

One of the major concerns of any cross-cultural study is **equivalence**. This term stands for the evidence that the methods selected for the study measure the same phenomenon across other countries or cultures chosen for the study. For example, if an investigator tries to make cross-cultural comparisons of leadership behavior of men and women, he or she should be aware that the empirical results of this study should be discussed together with the specific political and cultural contexts within which the leaders were studied (Ayman & Korabik, 2010). For instance, a leader's decisiveness and indecisiveness may depend not only on cultural and gender factors but also on a wide range of specific political circumstances.

SAMPLE SELECTION

There are at least three strategies for sample selection (van de Vijver & Leung, 1997). One strategy is availability or convenience sampling, in which the researcher chooses a culture by chance or, most likely, because of the researcher's professional or personal contacts in the country in which the samples are selected. For instance, if you have a former classmate and good friend working as a professional psychologist in India, will you hesitate to collaborate with her in a comparative study? Convenience sampling is very popular but has certain limitations because some cultural or ethnic groups are likely to receive more attention than others. Which groups, in your view, will have an advantage here?

A second type of sampling is called systematic. The psychologist selects national or ethnic samples according to a theory or some theoretical assumption. The samples may be selected because they represent people who practice different customs. For example, a psychologist who studies marital satisfaction in arranged families may choose countries with and without the arranged-marriage tradition. In one category will be included Germany, Spain, Chile, and Australia. In the other category, countries such as India, Pakistan, and Somalia will be selected.

A third sampling strategy, random sampling, is when a large sample of countries or groups is randomly chosen; that is, any country or group has an equal chance of being selected in the research sample. As an illustration, this method was used by Schwartz (1994), who, in one of the most fascinating comparative projects in psychology, examined human values in 36 randomly selected countries. This method was also used by David Schmitt and his colleagues to measure the personality traits of 17,837 individuals from 56 nations (Schmitt et al., 2007).

In a **representative sample**, the characteristics of a sample accurately reflect the characteristics of the population. The determination of the size of a representative is the chief problem of practically all studies in cross-cultural psychology. There are some statistical methods that determine more or less accurately the size and type of the sample (Heiman, 1996). In general, the smaller the sample, the greater the sampling error, and the greater the result of chance factors. (The sampling error indicates the extent to which the sample is different from the population it represents.) Conversely, the larger the sample, the lower the sampling error. For example, a study that establishes a cross-cultural negative correlation between power distance on one hand and leader communication and psychological approachability on the other is likely to contain very small sampling error because it was conducted on a sample of 39 countries of different cultures (Offermann & Hellmann, 1997).

One of the most reliable methods of designing a representative sample is random sampling. A random sample is expected to be representative. The mean score received for a representative sample is likely to be a good estimation of the entire population. However, this is just a general assumption. Even random sampling may produce an unrepresentative sample, the one that was perhaps described in the opening vignette.

Research has shown, time and again, that estimates derived from large samples are more *reliable* than those derived from small samples. Nevertheless, when forming judgments, we typically do not take this principle into account. As a consequence, despite the fact that data collected from small samples cannot be counted on as trustworthy predictors of a population's characteristics, we are prone to commit the error of overgeneralizing from too small a sample. Let us illustrate this concept mathematically. What do you think: Does "7 out of 10" look like better odds than "60 out of 100"? Yes, it looks like the first one is better. However, which of these indicators is more reliable? The more reliable indicator is the "60 out of 100" because it is drawn from a larger, that is, more reliable sample.

The sample should be representative of a larger ethnic, national, or other social group. Two national samples cannot be claimed if they comprise, for example, French suburban middle-class professionals and Uruguayan college students from Montevideo. In this case it will be unclear what differences are measured: either between two national groups or between students and suburban residents. Even the results of the famous Hofstede study (1980) that were based on a large sample of 88,000 IBM employees in more than 60 countries should be accepted with caution. Because all the studied individuals were employees of a large international corporation, the sample could only conditionally represent the diverse populations of respective countries.

CRITICAL THINKING

Sampling and the Interpretation of Results

Buda and Elsayed-Elkhouly (1998) paired samples from the United States, Egypt, and Persian Gulf states (namely, Kuwait, Saudi Arabia, and United Arab Emirates). The U.S. sample displayed significantly higher scores on individualism than the Arab sample did. In addition, a difference was detected between the Egyptian and Gulf samples; Egyptians scored lower on collectivism than their counterparts. The authors attribute these differences to Egyptian exposure to Western influence. Many Egyptian citizens travel to other countries and are influenced by Western culture, especially in the capital city of Cairo.

However, looking critically at the samples selected, a point of concern may be raised. The overall sample of this study was 400 subjects, which included approximately 130 women. The Egyptian sample included 224 men and 75 women; of the 102 American subjects, 55 were women; the Gulf sample contained exclusively men. Overall, did this study measure differences among three national groups or did it actually display the differences between male subjects from the Gulf countries, mostly men from Egypt, and a mixed sample from the United States?

One of the substantial weaknesses of cross-cultural research is its overwhelming reliance on research samples comprising students. In various ways, students are not necessarily a representative sample of their nations. Students are better educated, tend to be younger, and frequently more affluent than the general population (Oyserman et al., 2002).

All in all, when selecting and analyzing samples for cross-cultural research, one should beware of substantial differences in the demographic and social characteristics of the chosen subjects.

OBSERVATION IN CROSS-CULTURAL PSYCHOLOGY

If you are recording people's behavior in their natural environments (e.g., on the streets of Madrid and Mumbai) with little or no personal intervention, this procedure is called **naturalistic observation**. A scientific, cross-cultural observation is difficult to design because it should use identifiable and measurable variables (LeVine, 2010). An example of cross-cultural observation could be a study of different walking patterns in several countries (see Chapter 10) in which the researcher had no impact on how fast the individuals walked on the street. Most of the time, spontaneous observation is biased, and the observer's attitudes can have an impact on the results of observation. For a Chinese observer, for example, most U.S. elementary schoolchildren may seem "unrestrained" and "hyperactive." By contrast, to a psychologist from the United States, Chinese pupils in the classroom may appear "restrained" and "hesitant."

In the **laboratory observation**, the subjects are brought in, and you—as a psychologist—design specific situations or prepare a set of stimuli and then ask the participants to respond.

The use of this method requires the researcher to display patience and skepticism. One question should be persistently asked: "Did I observe everything about the studied issue, or is there anything else hidden from me?" An interesting illustration of observation is a study of the

Utku Inuit culture (Briggs, 1970). The researcher initially found—as a result of observation—a virtual absence of anger reactions among members of this ethnic group. Does this observation mean that these individuals do not experience anger? Not at all. A more patient observation provided a new set of data. Even though there were no displays of anger in interpersonal relationships of the Utku Inuit, anger could still be vented in at least two ways: against dogs and against those persons who were expelled from the community.

SURVEY METHODS

Surveys are, perhaps, the most common technique of data collection in cross-cultural psychology. In a typical survey, the researcher asks the subject to express an opinion regarding a particular topic, issue, or issues. There could be open-ended and, more commonly, multiple-choice questions. Open-ended questions give subjects some freedom to express themselves, to explain many nuances of their thoughts and feelings. However, such answers are difficult to interpret quantitatively. Moreover, some subjects—small children or people with little language proficiency or those who are afraid to give away information about themselves—have difficulty articulating their ideas. Multiple-choice questions, although easier to analyze, also limit the choice of an answer for the respondent. Moreover, in Chapter 5 we will argue that, in some instances, lack of familiarity with formal response scales may affect individual test scores. In many communities, for example, the use of imported questionnaire techniques is constrained by higher rates of illiteracy and people's reluctance to deal with the unfamiliar.

There are direct and indirect surveys. In **direct surveys**, the interviewer maintains or can maintain a direct communication with the respondent and is able to provide feedback, repeat a question, or ask for additional information. In **indirect surveys**, the researcher's personal impact is very small because there is no direct communication between the respondent and the interviewer. The questions are typically written and handed in, mailed, or sent electronically to the respondents in their homes, classrooms, or work places.

Direct surveys are conducted in several ways, the most common of which are face-to-face and telephone. In face-to face surveys, the interviewer can see the respondents who are usually at their residences or work places, but not exclusively there. Telephone surveys—although there is no visual contact between the respondent and the researcher—are also based on direct interaction. This type of survey is usually the least expensive one and can be successfully used in places where there is unlimited access of the population to telephones.

One of the most common difficulties of surveys is a researcher's inability to identify those respondents who are not sincere in their responses. In some cases, the subjects want to present themselves in a socially appropriate way. For example, parents tend to be reluctant to admit that they use socially inappropriate child-rearing practices such as spanking or other forms of violence (Iusitini et al., 2011). In surveys about sexual practices, men tend to report about engaging in sex at earlier ages, more often, and with more sexual partners than do women. In reality, these reported gender differences may be caused by many women being unwilling to give truthful responses about their sexual behavior, as they are more likely to consider such topics inappropriate and shameful. In one study, the psychologists asked male and female students questions about their sexual attitudes and behaviors. The participants believed they were connected to a lie detector machine (a polygraph device). The students, who filled out written questionnaires, were told the machine was responsive enough to detect untruthfulness even in written responses. However, the polygraph was not turned on. Interestingly, under these conditions the women's answers were very close to the men's responses in some areas of sexual behavior when they

CROSS-CULTURAL SENSITIVITY

What kind of obstacles should a Western researcher anticipate when deciding to conduct a survey in a country located thousands of miles away from home? Can people be asked at random and in person? This might create a problem. Imagine a foreign researcher in a small town asking people questions and writing their answers down on a piece of paper. Do we expect people to be open with the researcher? Perhaps some alternative survey methods should be used in such situations. For example, Ho (1998) describes a procedure that is used in psychological research in the Philippines. This is a special unobtrusive survey procedure called *pagtatanung-tanong* that can be used in relatively small, stable, and homogeneous communities. One of the advantages of this method is that the researcher avoids making the interviewees feel that they serve as "subjects" and their answers are used as research information. Using this method the researcher may ask questions in natural, nondisruptive contexts. The researcher is conversing with people, "asking around." The questions may be asked in sequence, and they may lead to the formulation of new questions and further clarifications if needed. Inconsistency in the answers would indicate that there is a diversity of opinions among interviewees. If the answers are consistent, this might indicate a particular trend in people's opinions. Conducting this type of research does not disturb people and allows some sensitive issues to be addressed that—in the case of a "standard" opinion poll—would have been unanswered.

thought the lie detector was on. Men's answers didn't change as much as did women's under these different testing conditions (Alexander & Fisher, 2003). The researchers believed that in this study, many women preferred to give "socially acceptable" answers.

Another drawback of surveys is cultural differences in the way people see themselves. For example, Americans typically see themselves as highly conscientious and hardworking: They work longer hours than people in many other countries, and the American economy remains the most productive in the world. However, surveys show that people from Ethiopia, Tanzania, and Zimbabwe—all with lower economic scores—evaluate self even higher as the most conscientious and hardworking nations. Furthermore, respondents from Chinese, Korean, and Japanese samples evaluate themselves among the least hardworking in the world! These results suggest that people's self-perceptions must always be considered with caution (Schmitt et al., 2007).

To receive reliable survey information in countries under authoritarian regimes can often be extremely difficult. Several reasons exist (Mills & Singh, 2007). First, these governments discourage individuals from providing any information (e.g., reports about corruption or violence) that could damage the government's "reputation." Second, people tend to be unsure about the privacy of information they share, especially if the information concerns their private lives. A written statement provided by a psychologist guaranteeing privacy means little to them. Third, some individuals are willing to provide socially desirable information to avoid potential problems with authorities, as described in the case early in this chapter.

EXPERIMENTAL STUDIES

To conduct an **experiment**, you put randomly assigned subjects in particular experimental conditions. By varying these conditions, you try to detect specific changes in the subjects' behavior, attitudes, emotions, and so on. In an experiment, the condition(s) that are controlled, that is, can be changed by you, are called the **independent variable(s)**. The aspect of human activity that is studied and expected to change under influence of the independent variable is called the **dependent variable**. As an experimenter, you control the independent variable: You change the conditions of the experiment.

In a typical cross-cultural experiment, two or more groups are put in preferably identical experimental conditions. Ethnicity, nationality, or other cultural identification of the members of studied groups will typically represent the independent variable. If the experiment is designed properly, any differences in subjects' activity measured by the experiment could be explained, hopefully, as caused by the subjects' cultural background.

A simple illustration of an experimental procedure can be drawn from a classical study of flag preference in schoolchildren of two groups: Arabs and Jews. The researcher measured how often children of the two groups, both living in Israel, would choose symbols representing their national identity: either Israeli or Palestinian flags. In this study, the decision to choose a picture with a particular flag on it was the dependent variable. Pictures containing depictions of various flags were the independent variable—and that variable was manipulated by the experimenter. In this experiment, after responses of the participating children were recorded, it was found that the Arab and Jewish schoolchildren in Israel were significantly different in their flag preference, clearly divided along their Arab–Jewish origins (Lawson, 1975). In another experiment, two groups of people selected randomly—one in Westchester County, New York, the other in Bern, Switzerland—were approached via telephone by a caller (researcher) who would tell these people (subjects) that her car had broken down and she was out of change at a pay phone. She asked the subjects to call her friend. The response rates showed that the Swiss subjects from Bern were significantly more helpful than people from the U.S. sample (Gabriel et al., 2001).

CONTENT ANALYSIS

Content analysis is a research method that systematically organizes and summarizes both the manifest (what was actually said or written) and latent (the meaning of what was said and written) content of communication. The researcher usually examines transcripts of conversations or interviews, television or radio programs, letters, newspaper articles, and other forms of communication. The main investigative procedure in content analysis consists of two steps. Initially, the researcher identifies coding categories. These can be particular nouns, concepts, names, or topics. First-level coding is predominantly concrete and involves identifying properties of data that are clearly evident in the text. Second-level coding is more abstract and involves interpreting what the first-level categories mean.

Content analysis of responses is especially valuable when researchers—for various reasons—cannot use standard questionnaires. For example, a study of undocumented aliens in the United States (Shiraev & Sobel, 2006) revealed that the vast majority of the subjects selected for this research did not want to give written answers because of their fear of being detained by immigration authorities. The subjects preferred verbal communication with the interviewer who could use a digital recorder. For this reason, a quantitative version of the basic interview that contained numerical scales could not have been used in many occasions. Instead, a special qualitative version of the interview was prepared to fit the new requirements of a "verbal" interview (see A Case in Point box, p. 36).

The researcher must make sure to verify the sources of the received information, especially when analyzing stories or autobiographies. Sure, we should trust people and believe that their accounts are accurate. However, people can make honest mistakes in recollecting or remember only those events or facts that support their point of view. There are quite a few so-called impersonator autobiographies written by Western authors on behalf of some ethnic, economic, or other minority groups. Historians, for example, are well aware of such spurious sources of information (Browder, 2000).

A CASE IN POINT
A Modification of an Interview Question

Question 14 from the "Standard" Interview:

"In the past, have you ever had bad dreams (nightmares) about being forced to leave (or be deported from) the United States?"

Measurement Scale:

Constantly Frequently Occasionally Seldom Never Cannot tell

Modified Question 14 for a New Version of the Interview:

"Now tell me please, in the past, have you ever had bad dreams (nightmares) about being forced to leave (or be deported from) the United States?"

Additional Questions to Be Asked in the New Version of the Interview:

"If yes, do you remember them?" "Could you please describe (one) some of them?" "Do you have such dreams often?" "How often?"

FOCUS GROUP METHODOLOGY

Focus group methodology is used frequently both in academic and marketing research. The principal advantage of this method is the opportunity to analyze social, gender, and ethnic discourse on some issues in depth: for example, whether a particular fashion product would have any success among a certain ethnic group or whether a psychotherapeutic procedure would be appropriate for particular national groups.

The most common use of this method is a procedure in which a group responds to specific social, cultural, or marketing messages. The typical focus group contains 7–10 participants. Based on the goal of specific research, the group could be either homogeneous or heterogeneous (ethnically, nationally, professionally, etc.). However, the use of focus group methodology presents a number of problems for cross-cultural psychologists because these groups do not usually represent randomly selected samples. Also, due to the lack of external validity of any particular focus group outcome, specialists agree that the validity of the focus group method in general—and in cross-cultural psychology in particular—rests on the repetition of findings across different groups (Kern & Just, 1995).

META-ANALYSIS: RESEARCH OF RESEARCH

Imagine that you study the relationship between family climate and mood disorders in various countries and find that there are more than 30 studies available on this subject and they were all published between 1982 and 2012. How can a scientific generalization be made from all these studies? Is it possible to analyze these data and make a conclusion about the links—or absence of—between the individual's job satisfaction and job performance? You might realize that a standard comparative review is not a solution. These studies are difficult to compare because they appear to be extremely diverse. Some of them are based on interviews with a few dozen people, whereas others included hundreds of participants from different countries at different times (Ng et al., 2009).

A special statistical method allows cross-cultural psychologists to do quantitative analysis of a large collection of scientific results and integrate the findings. It is called **meta-analysis**. In brief, meta-analysis refers to the analysis of analyses—usually called "combined tests"—of a large collection of individual results in an attempt to make sense of a diverse selection of data. One of the attractive features of this method is the reliance on statistical formulas, and an imperative to include a large selection of studies, not only those that appear to be "good" and "interesting." This method often shows results that are difficult to see in individual studies. For instance, meta-analysis of rewarding behavior such as praise, encouragement, and so on across cultures (25 studies altogether) has shown that results yielded by student samples differed from those collected from samples of employees (Fischer & Smith, 2003).

Meta-analysis has some disadvantages, however. The method attempts to compare studies that deal with variables that are defined differently. For example, if two researchers identify collectivism in their own dissimilar ways, any comparisons of the two would produce invalid and unreliable results. Moreover, many studies use unlike measuring techniques and are often based on results obtained from dissimilar subject pools. And finally, meta-analysis pays attention to largely published studies that represent significant findings. Therefore, nonsignificant findings are either overlooked or ignored, and this may add to some bias in the process of sample selection.

A HIDDEN OBSTACLE OF CROSS-CULTURAL STUDIES: TEST TRANSLATION

The majority of cross-cultural projects—especially of the survey type—require translation from the researcher's language to another language or languages. In such cases, one of the most difficult tasks appears before the investigator: to make sure that the translated version of the method is as close to the original version as possible. However, even a well-translated version of a test is always different from the original one. Languages have dissimilar grammar rules and sentence structures. At first glance some identical words may have different meanings, such as the words "friend" in English and *amigo* in Spanish. Some words require additional clarifications. Take, for example, the word "cousin." In Arabic and Russian languages this word is translated in a particular way so that it always indicates the cousin's sex. An English version, however, does not typically specify who this person is: "he" or "she." Metaphors (such as "pie in the sky") and vague words (such as "probably" or "frequently") should also be routinely avoided because they are difficult to translate (Brislin, 1970).

Some words and phrases, common in the vocabulary of the average person in the United States, may have no equivalents in other languages. As an example, the phrase "privacy" requires additional detailed explanations when it is translated in some other languages. If you have trouble believing that this is possible, ask anyone—a Spanish, Arabic, Urdu, Vietnamese, or Hebrew-speaking person—to translate the phrase "privacy" into their language. They will perhaps come up with a phrase in their native tongue. Then ask another person from the same country to translate this phrase back to English. You will likely receive anything but "privacy" as a result of this translation.

A CASE IN POINT

Test Translation

For illustration, we will use a brief description of the procedure conducted by Kassinove et al. (1997) for a translated version of a State-Trait Anger Expression Inventory. To examine the possible universality of a theoretical model of anger created by Spielberger (1980), a special Russian State-Trait Anger Expression Inventory was created. In this questionnaire, a subject had to indicate agreement with several statements that stand for different manifestations and experiences of anger. The statements—taken from the original U.S. version of the inventory—were translated from the English language to Russian by a native Russian-speaking psychologist with assistance from a Russian psychiatrist. The new translated items were then back-translated by an advanced clinical psychology doctoral candidate at Hofstra University, New York. This person and an assistant were born and educated in the former Soviet Union. Because of the presence of some unique idioms used in English to describe anger—for example, "harboring grudges," "keeping cool," or "feeling burned up"—several items did not receive an exact Russian translation. To overcome this obstacle, adjustments were made to re-create several items in the Russian version. Another Russian-speaking U.S. assistant back-translated these items from Russian to English. The complete research team then held special discussion sessions to reach a consensus about the most disputed translations. Such careful translation and back-translation procedures with the help of several researchers create an internally consistent and theoretically sound assessment device for the psychometric measurement of anger in Russian-speaking individuals. A similar technique was used by Denis Sukhodolsky and his colleagues to validate their internationally acclaimed Anger Rumination Scale used today to study anger management in several countries and in various cultural groups (Sukhodolsky et al., 2001).

All in all, there are some generic rules that can be used for successful translation in cross-cultural studies.

- First, the translation process from the beginning ought to be conducted by bilinguals, that is, by people proficient in both languages. They should conduct the so-called back-translation: Initially, they translate the original version of the method and then transfer this version back into the original language. Then both versions are compared and corrected if necessary (Mayer & Trommsdorff, 2010).
- Second, it is quite beneficial to have several people do the translation so that there will be several versions of it. These versions can then be compared and converted into one (Heine et al., 2002).
- Third, both versions of a questionnaire can be administered on the same bilingual individuals. If the investigator gets similar results on both versions, this is a good indicator that the translation was conducted successfully.

COMPARING TWO PHENOMENA: SOME IMPORTANT PRINCIPLES

How similar are people in Tokyo and New York in terms of thoughts, emotions, and reasoning? Theoretically, there are two answers to this question, each one reflecting a distinct approach to cross-cultural psychology (Berry et al., 1992). Psychologists supporting the

absolutist approach (often called the universalist approach) will argue that psychological phenomena are basically the same in all cultures: Honesty is honesty, sexual abuse is abuse, and depression is depression, no matter where, when, or how the researcher studies these and other psychological phenomena. Within this approach, there is a tendency to use the standards of one group as the norms for viewing other groups. From the absolutist perspective, psychological processes are expected to be consistent across different cultures. However, the occurrences of certain processes and behaviors may vary from culture to culture. A scientist, therefore, can study human activity from a position "outside," comparing different cultures and using similar criteria for such comparisons. Assessments of such characteristics are likely to be made using standard—for one country—psychological instruments and their translated versions. Evaluative comparisons can be frequently made from these assessments (Segall et al., 1999).

The second, the **relativist approach**, suggests that human behavior in its full complexity can be understood only within the context of the culture in which it occurs. Anthropologists were among the first to encourage psychologists not to use moral standards of one culture to judge others (Benedict, 1934). Therefore, the scientist should study an individual's psychology from within his culture. Since there are no context-free psychological processes or behaviors, valid comparisons cannot be made among cultures. In other words, from the relativist view practically any cross-cultural comparison is biased.

Quite often in cross-cultural literature, the reader will find the expressions "etic" and "emic." The term *etic* refers to the absolutist position, whereas *emic* stands for the relativist approach. As expected, it is difficult to find a psychologist who is a die-hard absolutist or relativist. Most cross-cultural psychologists today accept a view that combines these two approaches. Some phenomena in psychology are universal for all social groups, both large and small, including cultures and subcultures. However, there are psychological phenomena that are unique for only particular social and cultural conditions. Therefore, psychological comparative measures should be developed in culturally meaningful terms, and comparisons and interpretations of findings have to be made cautiously. This approach does not separate the etic and emic concepts. Instead, it somewhat interconnects them. One of the tasks of cross-cultural psychology then is to determine the balance between both universal and culturally specific characteristics of human behavior, emotion, motivation, and thought.

Even though the absolutist and relativist approaches seem to be dissimilar, they both make sense. Take, for example, the relativist standpoint on phenomenon such as greeting procedures. For anyone examining human communication across countries, it will soon become obvious that the rules of contact are quite different. In some cultures, such as the United States and Canada, a handshake is appropriate for both men and women. In Slavic countries, most women do not normally shake hands when they meet another person. In Northern Europe, men rarely kiss each other when they meet, whereas in the Middle East this type of greeting is appropriate. Direct eye contact is considered appropriate in many countries, with the exception of some East Asian cultures, where people, in most cases, greet each other with a bow, without eye contact. Even the distance of conversation varies substantially across countries and regions (see Chapter 11 for more detail on this issue). Therefore, it is very difficult to study greeting styles in different cultures because in these cases, according to a U.S. expression, we would be comparing "apples to oranges."

The absolutist (universalist) approach is defendable too. Imagine yourself for a minute as a professional psychologist who studies physical and sexual abuse against women in a particular country. By studying cases, and conducting individual interviews, you uncover evidence that women in this country are abused to a significantly greater extent than U.S. women are. Some critics, that is, supporters of the relativist view, might suggest that your data are invalid because "American" views on abuse cannot be applied to other national samples. You, however, could argue that there is no such thing as "cultural" justification for abuse, as there should not be a "cultural" justification for violence and murder.

ON SIMILARITIES AND DIFFERENCES: SOME CRITICAL THINKING APPLICATIONS

Without comparisons, there is no cross-cultural psychology. When we compare—take, for example, emotional expressions in two countries or test scores in two national or ethnic groups—we look for either similarities or differences between two variables. When comparing any two phenomena, initially they may "match" with respect to their mutual similarities. But no matter how many features they might share in common, there is no escaping the inevitable fact that at some point there will be a "conceptual fork" in the road, where the phenomena will differ. We may refer to this juncture as the point of critical distinction (PCD), before which the phenomena are similar and after which they are different. When we are attempting to define, compare, and contrast any two phenomena, it is imperative that we identify and examine the PCDs that are relevant to the particular events under examination. If, for instance, we are interested in exploring the similarities between the events, we should examine the variables that appear before the PCD; if, by contrast, we wish to analyze the differences between the same two events, we should focus on the variables that appear at and after the PCD. Of course, to gain a full and comprehensive understanding of their relationship, we should examine the variables that appear both before and after the PCD, with particular attention to the PCD itself.

When a difference is found, we often contrast the samples and the larger populations they represent. However, when we contrast individualism and collectivism, for example, we should realize that these two opposites depend on each other for their very conceptual existence. Without one, its opposite ceases to exist. How can we possibly define the concept of "collectivism," for example, without also addressing what we mean by "individualism"? How can we define "biased" in the absence of defining "unbiased"? Can we ever truly understand "conformity" without also understanding "dissent"? This same principle holds true for scores of other opposites: feminine and masculine, subjective and objective, low-power distance and high-power distance, altruism and selfishness, high context and low context, coercion and consent, ability and disability, hunting culture and gathering culture, adaptive and maladaptive, and functional and dysfunctional. Remember, to define or understand any phenomenon or issue, its theoretical opposite should also, whenever possible, be addressed and explored. As these examples illustrate, to contrast a phenomenon with its polar opposite is to give definition to both terms.

We have talked about some studies that involve self-evaluation. Peng et al. (1997) and other psychologists noted that people from different cultural groups pay attention first to their own culture when they describe their own beliefs and values. Therefore, in a culture with predominantly collectivist values, collectivism may not be rated high because it is part of everyday life. The same can be suggested about other points of psychological self-evaluation. A 5-foot, 10-inch man is likely to be seen as tall in some contexts (e.g., for children or most Vietnamese women) and short to other people (e.g., for professional basketball players or men in Iceland who are among the tallest in the world). Chinese tend to evaluate themselves in comparison with other people in China, whereas people in the United States most likely evaluate themselves with reference to other U.S. citizens (Heine et al., 2002). As you remember, people in countries such as Japan and Korea tend to evaluate themselves critically, considering self as not necessarily hardworking. Yet the facts and observations suggest otherwise. Both Japan and Korea are highly productive and economically successful nations. In the Japanese language, there is a special word referring to death from overwork—*karoshi*. Similarly, in Korea, unexpected natural death has been the leading work-related cause of death (Park et al., 1999). To understand why people in these countries give themselves such low evaluations, we should realize that hard work and conscientiousness are usually estimated with respect to larger cultural norms. If everyone is expected to be hardworking, punctual, and reliable, many people may see themselves as not meeting the standards of "perfection" set by cultural norms. As a result, most people report in surveys that they are less organized and less determined than they ought to be. These are examples of cultural response bias (Schmitt et al., 2007).

CULTURAL DICHOTOMIES

There Are Fewer Differences than One Might Think

As was mentioned earlier, mainstream cross-cultural psychology operates in a tradition of cultural dichotomies reflecting a classificatory approach to culture. Typically, these dichotomies have been formulated as contrasts between Western and non-Western cultures. The Westerners (mostly citizens of the richest European and American nations, including some other countries who share major Judeo-Christian values) are commonly associated with individualism, independence, and "egocentrism" (i.e., the individual is of paramount value). The non-Westerners are associated with collectivism, interdependence, and "sociocentrism" (i.e., community and society are supreme values). However, such generalizations are often simplistic and inaccurate (Hermans & Kempen, 1998). Cultural dichotomies do not and cannot meet challenges raised by the process of global, technological, and demographic changes. But most important, such stereotypical distinction between the "West" and "non-West" often turns labels and symbols into "things," a typical reasoning error (see Chapter 3 for a more detailed discussion). As a result, entire nations that are diverse and heterogeneous may be endowed and labeled with the qualities of homogeneous and distinctive objects. Using such assumptions, people may not only *think* that U.S. citizens are individualists but also *communicate* with them as if all people in the United States were selfish. Likewise, they may not only think that Japanese are collectivists, but also interact with them as if they all were unselfish. Several studies (like one, for example, based on responses from six Asian and six Western samples) show that despite popular assumptions about the existence of profound differences in the way people of different cultures perceive history and major world events, the similarities are overwhelming (Liu et al., 2005).

Any given group (or individual), in reality, falls somewhere between the two hypothetical extremes. Moreover, these orientations are relative to different social contexts. For instance, a person may be individualistic within her own culture, yet much more collectivistic compared with other cultural groups. Similarly, a person might strongly favor collectivism, but the culture in which he or she lives may be somewhat more individualistic than other cultures.

There Are More Differences than One Might Expect

When the researcher works with samples in Western, technologically developed nations, he should understand that most of these countries enjoy considerable cultural and social diversity. For example, imagine a psychologist conducting a three-country study of first-year students' attitudes toward verbal abuse. The research samples are carefully selected. They contain students of the same age, with an equal proportion of men and women. However, what can remain undetected in the study are (1) national differences in higher education and (2) the ways in which people in the studied countries become students. In this hypothetical case, researchers should be aware of a highly competitive system of higher education in Germany and Japan: to become a student, it is necessary to take and pass difficult qualifying exams on different subjects. Many young men and women fail in the process. Critical evaluation of the subject pool of this hypothetical study, therefore, could reveal the fact that this project does not measure the difference among three compatible representative samples. Instead, it attempts to uncover differences between (1) highly educated, motivated, and relatively successful Japanese and German men and women and (2) a randomly selected "average" group of U.S. college students who did not go through as difficult a process of precollege selection as did their counterparts overseas.

If rain were coming, we would see clouds.

ARABIC SAYING

AVOIDING BIAS OF GENERALIZATIONS

People tend to form inaccurate assumptions about others. We may base our impressions on certain cross-cultural comparisons. But what kinds of comparisons are we looking for? By and large, our attention is drawn to the studies that demonstrate the most conspicuous, prominent, or salient differences. We then are prone to overgeneralize from these few outstanding examples to the group as a whole, the result of which is an inaccurate generalization.

Consider an interesting research finding. It was established that in Chinese romantic love songs, topics of negative or pessimistic expectations are more prevalent than they are in U.S. love songs. This conclusion was made after an analysis of 80 Chinese and U.S. songs was conducted (Rothbaum & Tsang, 1998). Do these findings indicate that people in China are more pessimistic than those in the United States? Maybe they are. Maybe they are not. Pessimism in songs does not necessarily and accurately reflect people's pessimistic attitudes in real life.

To avoid making quick generalizations from research findings, we offer the following recommendations for critical evaluation of cross-cultural research data.

- What were the size and representation of the chosen samples in this project? If the study included only 50 subjects from two countries who answered several-question surveys regarding attitudes toward religion, it is not possible to make reliable conclusions about religious differences between the studied nations.
- Was the method chosen for the study adequate in different cultural settings? Was it translated properly? When it could be demonstrated that the instrument, produced in one setting, was nonetheless applicable in many other settings, differences obtained with that instrument could be taken as reflections of some cultural variables.

- Are the data convincing? To make sure that the results of the study reflect a particular trend and are not due to chance alone, the researcher should repeat the same study to accept the data with confidence or find out about other similar studies.
- Are there any factors that could have affected the outcome that were not taken into consideration during the study? For instance, psychophysiological events are believed to be the same across cultures. In fact, they largely do not belong to the sphere of interest of cross-cultural researchers. However, such physiological factors can produce unexpected effects (Berry et al., 1992). As an example, studies on alcohol consumption and smoking (see Chapter 9) show the significance of physiological factors in cross-cultural studies.

When comparing large groups such as U.S. whites, blacks, Latinos, Asians, or any other ethnic or religious groups, do not forget that these groups are far from being homogeneous. Among them are individuals who are educated and those who are not, who are wealthy and poor, and who live in cities and small towns. In cross-cultural research, it is always useful to request additional information about the countries in which you do research. For example, the diversity or homogeneity of the population and people's experience of such diversity may affect observation procedures. According to Matsumoto (1992), individuals from homogeneous societies (Japan, for example) may detect and identify other people's emotions less accurately than people from heterogeneous societies do (the United States, for example).

Furthermore, people may have either strong or weak psychological attachment to their cultural heritage, norms, customs, and values compared to other people who belong to the same group. Every social group has individuals with very high intellectual skills as well as individuals with very low scores. Among immigrants, there are scientists and engineers who emigrated from their home countries for economic reasons and political refugees who escaped political persecution. Taiwan and China may represent one culture in someone's view; however, these nations are different ideologically, politically, and even philosophically. The citizens of these political entities may have quite different lifestyles and opinions on various issues.

Herein lies the tragedy of the age: not that men are poor—all men know something of poverty; not that men are wicked—who is good? Not that men are ignorant—what is truth? Nay, but that men know so little of men.

W.E.B. Du Bois—**American Sociologist, Writer, and Teacher**

KNOW MORE ABOUT CULTURES YOU EXAMINE

If an experimental study shows that the Chinese subjects, compared to Western and Japanese subjects, are more likely to disregard or ignore a "stranger" who appears to be irrelevant to their affiliations and involvements, does this mean that people in China are selfish? Not at all. We must understand that any experiment results should be interpreted carefully and individual scores should not refer to the entire society (Tafarodi et al., 2009). To be proficient in cross-cultural research, you should know methodology and also be familiar with the cultural groups you study.

Therefore, you should also make yourself familiar with geography, sociology, anthropology, and global studies. People of one nationality are very diverse. If you conduct research in Brazil, you will find that remarkable differences between the Northeast with its Afro-Brazilian roots and the North with its native Indian roots (Hofstede et al., 2010). If you find that American women relative to the Russians look for some positive psychology traits in their partners and the Russian women seek earning potential and maturity you should certainly refer your findings to the different social and political contexts in these two countries (Pearce et al., 2010). If you study immigrant populations in the United States or United Kingdom, you will certainly be aware of the different "waves" or generations of immigrants who are likely to be different in many ways from their linguistic proficiency to the reasons for immigration (Schwartz et al., 2010).

Grieve not that men do not know you; grieve that you do not know men.

Confucius (551–479 b.c.e)—**Chinese Philosopher**

In the process of designing interviews, psychologists should also be mindful of the traditional practices, values, and beliefs of the cultures they are attempting to study. For example, creating an assessment about suicidal ideation is expected to be difficult with Muslim clients, especially with those who have not been exposed to Western culture. Islam strictly forbids suicide and considers it a criminal act. Therefore, direct questions such as "Have you ever thought about taking your own life?" are likely to yield little information as the vast majority of respondents would deny such thoughts. However, a therapist could instead ask, "Do you think that God would let you die?" in an effort to circumvent the stigma of suicide and thus engender more detailed responses (Ali et al., 2004; Hedayat-Diba, 2000).

Overall, watch, analyze, doubt, and observe again! It is quite possible that the differences among examined samples in a comparative study may be explained in several ways. One study compared the dreams of 562 Hispanic individuals from Mexico, Spain, and Venezuela who were asked to make assessments of their dreams. These data then were contrasted with the data obtained from a non-Hispanic American sample. The results revealed some cultural differences. For example, the number of recalled dreams reported by non-Hispanic respondents was significantly higher than in all three Hispanic groups. Moreover, both Mexican and Venezuelan participants had greater negative emotions associated with their dreams than Spanish and U.S. participants. The author explained the difference in the number of reported dreams by suggesting that Hispanic groups are more passive in their coping styles. Moreover, they consider unpleasant dreams a bad omen and, therefore, simply do not want to reveal them as often as non-Hispanics do (Domino, 1986).

However, these differences may be attributed to other features—if one looks carefully at some subtle factors. Even though the subjects of this study were people of the same occupational status, they could be significantly different in terms of their living conditions and sleeping arrangements. Non-Hispanic American and European families typically have fewer children and more individual privacy in their homes and apartments than do families in many other countries. Sleep patterns may affect how well dreams are retrieved from memory.

You should also anticipate that research participants from collectivist countries might present themselves as more collectivist than they usually are because of the social desirability of collected behavior in the society under examination. In other words, people can reply and act in a certain way, not necessarily because this is their typical behavior, but because they want to impress the researcher and give her a socially desirable answer. Some studies of the mental health in East Asian countries (China, Japan, and Korea, for instance) revealed that people were giving different information when they wrote about their feelings on a piece of paper and when they told about their experiences in the presence of a professional psychologist (Park, 1988).

A CASE IN POINT

A Sample Study of Collectivism–Individualism

Marshall (1997) examined two samples in New Zealand and Indonesia; both samples included garbage collectors, bus drivers, and senior college professors. Each social category contained 25 respondents, for a total sample of 150 people. Each group was given a questionnaire that contained 14 statements: seven characteristics of an individualistic orientation and seven representing a collectivist orientation. The respondents had to suggest their agreement with the statements on a 5-point scale.

Collectivist statements:

I cannot be happy if any of my friends are unhappy. I feel good to work as a part of a large organization. I like to share my problems with my friends. It is wiser to choose your friends from people with similar social and family backgrounds as yourself. The people at work depend on me, so I should not let them down no matter how badly the organization cheats me. Most of my decisions are made together with relatives and friends. My first duty is to ensure the well-being of my relatives.

Individualistic statements:

If the organization I work for suffered financial difficulties and asked me to accept a substantial drop in pay, then I would look for another job. I usually do what I feel is best for me, no matter what others say. Happiness lies in maximizing my personal pleasure. Ideally, I would like to work for myself or own my own company. I deeply resent any invasion of my personal privacy. My happiness depends on my state of mind, regardless of how those around me feel.

The results revealed a trend: Indonesian participants were more collectivistic and less individualistic than their counterparts from New Zealand. Because this study examined the same professional groups, the differences between samples may be explained, from the author's point of view, by cultural differences, that is, collectivism and individualism.

Question

What other explanations can you offer for the differences found in this project? Please consider that New Zealand is more advanced economically than Indonesia and there is—contrary to Indonesia—a large middle class in New Zealand.

Exercise 2.1

1. Please identify several potential sampling errors in the cases given below:

   Case 1. A professor studies students' ethnic stereotypes. There are 55 people in his class. On Monday morning, 25 showed up for class. The professor asks these students to fill out questionnaires, assuming that a group of 25 is a representative sample for this particular class.

   Case 2. A student union conducts a poll among students by collecting 300 responses from 150 men and 150 women. The interviews take place in the college library where patrons are approached at random and asked to answer a few questions.

Case 3. A radio talk show host decides to study people's opinions about affirmative action and asks listeners to send their e-mails to the station.

2. It is crucial to know that your question is understood correctly by participants. People typically do not answer what you ask but what they think you mean by asking (Zaller, 1992). Following are some rules that might be useful in any survey research:

- Don't ask persuasive questions ("People condemn this initiative. Do you?").
- Don't put two questions in one ("How often do you feel anxiety and frustration?").
- Don't ask questions that are difficult to comprehend ("Which paradigm can become the explanatory model for these phenomena?").
- Don't ask rhetorical questions ("When will the world start living without violence?").
- Don't ask questions that already have "ready" answers ("Do you think that people can discriminate against each other?").

Using these tips, could you detect what is wrong with the questions below? Please correct and rewrite them.

1. Do you think people emigrate to another country because they look for better lives?
2. How often do you discuss ethnic or social problems with your parents?
3. What is your favorite TV or radio talk show?
4. How often do you feel depressed, frustrated, or angry watching the evening news?
5. If prejudice is caused by unconscious factors, to what extent do these variables overlap with the previously established contextual conditions?
6. What is your parents' ethnic background?

Chapter Summary

- There are four basic goals of research in cross-cultural psychology: description, interpretation, prediction, and management. After identifying the goals, the researcher has to choose a methodological approach that is most appropriate for the implementation of these goals. In general, research methodology in cross-cultural psychology may be divided into two categories: quantitative and qualitative.

- Quantitative research in cross-cultural psychology involves the measurement of certain aspects of human activity from a comparative perspective. The variables chosen for examination have to be studied empirically, primarily through observation, as opposed to other forms of reflection, such as intuition, beliefs, or superstitions. The most common data are measures of central tendency: the mode, the median, and the

mean. There are four types of measurement scales: nominal, ordinal, interval, and ratio.

- Among the most important statistical methods used in cross-cultural psychology are correlational methods that establish relationships between two variables and the *t*-test for independent samples, which aims to estimate whether the difference between two samples occurred by chance.

- Qualitative research is conducted primarily in the natural setting, where the research participants carry out their daily activities in a nonresearch atmosphere. Qualitative studies are also conducted when there are difficulties in measuring variables, in situations when the subjects cannot read or use answer scales or when there are no standardized measurement instruments available. Qualitative research is also useful in situations in which variables are not completely conceptualized or operationally defined. The qualitative method can be useful when the experiences and priorities of the research participants heavily influence the research.

- Choosing an application-oriented strategy, researchers attempt to establish the applicability of research findings obtained in one country or culture to other countries or cultures. The comparativist strategy, on the contrary, focuses primarily on similarities and differences in certain statistical measures in a sample of cultures.

- There are several strategies for sample selection. One strategy is availability or convenience sampling. Another type of sampling, called systematic, involves the psychologist selecting national or ethnic samples according to a theory or some theoretical assumption. A third sampling strategy is random sampling. In this case, a large sample of countries or groups is randomly chosen; that is, any country or group has an equal chance of being selected in the research sample.

- Cross-cultural psychologists use all the typical psychological methods of investigation: observation, survey, experiment, content analysis, psychobiography, meta-analysis, focus group, and other procedures.

- The majority of cross-cultural projects—especially of the survey type—require translation from the researcher's language to other language or languages. In such cases, one of the most difficult tasks that appears before the investigator is to make sure that the translated version of the method is as close to the original version as possible.

- There are at least two approaches to the analysis of cross-cultural data. Psychologists supporting the absolutist approach argue that psychological phenomena are basically the same across cultures. However, the occurrences of certain processes and behaviors may vary from culture to culture. The relativist approach implies that human behavior in its full complexity can be understood only within the context of the culture in which it occurs.

- Cross-cultural psychologists should see similarities in different phenomena; likewise, similarities should not overshadow potential differences between samples. The specialist should be aware that to contrast a phenomenon with its polar opposite is to give definition to both terms. All polar opposites are dependent on each other for their very conceptual existence.

- Cross-cultural psychologists should avoid biases of generalization. At the same time, it should be understood that cross-cultural psychology requires a great deal of imagination and abstraction. Concrete human activities take place in diverse and unique contexts with a huge variety of underlying factors. To understand and compare psychological phenomena the researcher should assume that the number of such factors is relatively limited.

Key Terms

Absolutist Approach A view in cross-cultural psychology that psychological phenomena are basically the same in all cultures.

Application-Oriented Strategy An attempt to establish the applicability of research findings obtained in one country or culture to other countries or cultures.

Comparativist Strategy An attempt to find similarities and differences in certain statistical measures in a sample of cultures.

Content Analysis A research method that systematically organizes and summarizes both the manifest and latent content of communication.

Correlation Coefficient A number that summarizes and describes the type of relationship present and the strength of the relationship between variables X and Y.

Dependent Variable The aspect of human activity that is studied and expected to change under the influence of an independent variable(s).

Direct Surveys The type of surveys in which the interviewer maintains or can maintain a direct communication with the respondent and is able to provide feedback, repeat a question, or ask for additional information.

Equivalence Evidence that the methods selected for the study measure the same phenomenon across other countries chosen for the study.

Experiment The investigative method in which researchers alter some variables to detect specific changes in the subjects' behaviors, attitudes, or emotions.

Focus Group Methodology A survey method used intensively in both academic and marketing research. The most common use of this method is a procedure in which a group responds to specific social, political, or marketing messages. The typical focus group contains 7–10 participants, who are either experts or represent potential buyers, viewers, or other types of customers.

Independent Variable The condition(s) that are controlled by the researcher.

Indirect Surveys The type of surveys in which the researcher's personal impact is very small because there is no direct communication between the respondent and the interviewer. The questions are typically written and handed in, mailed, or e-mailed to the respondents in their homes, classrooms, or work places.

Laboratory Observation Recording people's behavior in an environment created by the researcher.

Mean The mathematical central point of a distribution of scores.

Measure of Central Tendency The measure that indicates the location of a score distribution on a variable, that is, describes where most of the distribution is located.

Median The score in a distribution located at the 50th percentile.

Meta-Analysis The quantitative analysis of a large collection of scientific results in an attempt to make sense of a diverse selection of data.

Mode The most frequently occurring score in a distribution.

Naturalistic Observation Recording people's behavior in their natural environments with little or no personal intervention.

Psychobiographical Research A longitudinal analysis of particular individuals, usually outstanding persons, celebrities, and leaders, representing different countries or cultures.

Relativist Approach A view in cross-cultural psychology that psychological phenomena should be studied only from "within" a culture where these phenomena occur.

Representative Sample A sample having characteristics that accurately reflect the characteristics of the population.

Survey The investigative method in which groups of people answer questions about their opinions or their behavior.

Critical Thinking in Cross-Cultural Psychology

What luck for rulers that men do not think.

ADOLF HITLER (1889–1945)—
German Nazi Leader

*It's good to be open-minded, but not so open that your
brains fall out.*

JACOB NEEDLEMAN—
Contemporary American Writer

*Only two things are infinite, the universe and human
stupidity, and I'm not sure about the former.*

ALBERT EINSTEIN (1879–1955)—
German-Swiss-American Physicist

This story could have been told in New Orleans. Or maybe in New York. Or perhaps in Tokyo, Cape Town, or Buenos Aires. A woman walks into a doctor's office complaining that she's a zombie. The doctor, trying his best to convince her otherwise, says, "You're walking and talking, aren't you?"

"Zombies walk and talk," replies the patient.

"Well, you're breathing, too."

"Yes, but zombies breathe."

"Okay, what *don't* zombies do? Do they bleed?"

"No, *of course not,*" says the patient.

The doctor replies, "Good. Then I'm going to stick this needle into your arm and we'll see if your idea is right or wrong."

So he plunges the needle deep into the woman's arm, and, sure enough, blood starts to pour out of the wound. The woman is aghast. In utter dismay, she turns to the doctor and says, "My God, I was wrong....Zombies *do* bleed."

What is the moral of this story? Compelling facts are quite often not compelling enough. What matters more is our interpretation of these facts. One of the most significant characteristics of our thinking is the way in which we become personally invested in—and then tightly cling to—our beliefs and interpretations. This tendency, called the belief perseverance effect, can frequently lead us to freely distort, minimize, or even ignore any facts that run contrary to our reality.

Thinking is one of the most essential of all human characteristics. It is intrinsic to almost everything we do. But do we ever think about thinking? How often do we subject our thinking process to critical analysis?

Educators rightfully profess that learning how to think critically is one of the most vital and indispensable components of learning; yet, specific tools for **critical thinking** are rarely, if ever, provided to us. Thus, although we may be convinced of the value of critical thinking, we are left not knowing quite what to do about it.

Herein lies the theme of this chapter, the express purpose of which is to improve your thinking skills, to teach you to think critically, to help you think about thinking—in a word, to promote **metathinking** in cross-cultural psychology. Metathinking is not a magical, mystical, or mysterious abstraction. It is not an unattainable gift that is miraculously bestowed on the intellectual elite. Rather, it is a skill (or, more accurately, a series of skills) that can be successfully taught and learned (Levy, 2010). The thought principles or **metathoughts** (literally, "thoughts about thought") contained in this chapter are cognitive tools that provide the user with specific strategies for inquiry and problem solving in cross-cultural psychology. In this way, they serve as potent **antidotes** to thinking, which is often prone to be biased, simplistic, rigid, lazy, or just plain sloppy.

For the purposes of this book (portions of which were adapted from Levy, 2010), each metathought is illustrated primarily from the theory and application of contemporary cross-cultural psychology. Keep in mind, however, that these principles transcend the confines of any specific topic and can be utilized in a diverse array of fields, ranging from philosophy and theology to law, political science, history, sociology, anthropology, journalism, business, medicine, sports, and the arts—in fact, in all areas of education and learning.

Description is always from someone's point of view.

RHODA KESLER UNGER (1939–)—American Psychologist

It's a recession when your neighbor loses his job; it's a depression when you lose your own.

HARRY S. TRUMAN (1884–1972)—Thirty-Third U.S. President

THE EVALUATIVE BIAS OF LANGUAGE: TO DESCRIBE IS TO PRESCRIBE

Language serves many functions. Certainly one of its most common and most important purposes is to help us describe various phenomena, such as events, situations, and people: "What is it?" Another purpose is to evaluate these same phenomena: "Is it good or bad?" Typically, we consider descriptions to be objective, whereas we consider evaluations to be subjective.

However, is the distinction between objective description and subjective evaluation a clear one? The answer, in the vast majority of cases, is no. Why? Because words both describe *and* evaluate. Whenever we attempt to describe something or someone, the words we use are almost invariably value laden, in that they reflect our own personal likes and dislikes. Thus, our use of any particular term serves not only to describe but also to *prescribe* what is desirable or undesirable to us.

This problem is not so prevalent in describing objects as compared with people. Let us take, as an illustration, the terms *cold* and *hot*. For material substances, both terms refer literally to temperature: "That liquid is very cold," or "That liquid is very hot." When we use these same terms to describe an individual, however, they take on a distinctly evaluative connotation: "That person is very cold," or "That person is very hot."

Our best attempts to remain neutral are constrained by the limits of language. When it comes to describing people (e.g., in conducting research), it is nearly impossible to find words that are devoid of evaluative connotation. Incredible as it may seem, we simply do not have neutral adjectives to describe personality characteristics, whether of an individual or an entire group. And even if such words did exist, we still would be very likely to utilize the ones that reflect our own personal preferences.

The evaluative bias of language is illustrated in Table 3.1 and the accompanying exercise. Let us say that two different observers (Jenny and Lee), each with a different set of values, are asked to describe the same person, event, or group.

Notice how the words they use reveal their own subjective points of view.

TABLE 3.1 The Same Person as Described from Two Perspectives

From Jenny's Value System	From Lee's Value System
old	mature
naive	idealistic
reckless	brave
manipulative	persuasive
spineless	cooperative
childish	childlike
weird	interesting
obsessed	committed
anal retentive	tidy
dependent	loyal
codependent	empathic
narcissistic	high self-esteem
lunatic	visionary
psychotic	creative
bum	vocationally disadvantaged
sociopath	morally challenged
dead	ontologically impaired

Exercise 3.1

The Interdependence of Values, Perceptions, and Language

Ready to try some on your own? Remember that you are to select words that reveal Lee's personal attitudes and values, which are consistently more "positive" than Jenny's. (Some suggestions appear on our website at www.ablongman.com/shiraev3e.)

Jenny	Lee	Jenny	Lee
problem	_____	abnormal	_____
failure	_____	ethnocentrism	_____
terrorist	_____	chauvinism	_____
hostage	_____	cultural impurity	_____
murder	_____	discrimination	_____
genocide	_____	reverse discrimination	_____
brainwashed	_____	child abuse	_____
handicapped	_____	child neglect	_____
disabled	_____	handout	_____
primitive	_____	kleptomaniac	_____

This metathought also underscores the reciprocal influence of attitudes and language. That is, not only do our beliefs, values, and perceptions affect our use of language, but our use of language in turn influences our beliefs, values, and perceptions (see bidirectional causation, p. 75). For example, by referring to a person or group as *sick*, we are more inclined to perceive them as sick, which in turn leads us to label them sick, which prompts us to assume that they are sick, and so forth.

The bidirectional relationship between attitudes and language has direct relevance to the use (and misuse) of "politically correct" terminology. Consider the ways in which names applied to various ethnic groups have changed as a function of different social and historical contexts. What values might be related to, for example, the use of *Indian* versus *Native American*? *Iranian* versus *Persian*? *Oriental* versus *Asian*? *Colored* versus *black* versus *Negro* versus *Afro-American* versus *African American*? Why is *person of color* "in," while *colored person* is "out"? Similarly, what do the terms *pro-choice* and *pro-life* not so subtly imply about the moral stance of anybody who happens to have a different point of view? In these cases and countless more, we see how values both shape and are shaped by our use of language.

Antidotes

1. Remember that descriptions, especially concerning personality characteristics, can never be entirely objective, impartial, or neutral.
2. Become aware of your own personal values and biases and how these influence the language that you use.
3. Avoid presenting your value judgments as objective reflections of truth.
4. Recognize how other people's use of language reveals their own values and biases.

He that is not with me is against me: and he that gathereth not with me scattereth.

MATTHEW 12:30

DIFFERENTIATING DICHOTOMOUS VARIABLES AND CONTINUOUS VARIABLES: BLACK AND WHITE, OR SHADES OF GRAY?

Some phenomena in the world may be divided (or *bifurcated*) into two mutually exclusive or contradictory categories. These types of phenomena are **dichotomous variables**. For example, when you flip a coin, it must turn up either heads or tails—there is no middle ground. Similarly, a woman cannot be "a little bit," "somewhat," or "moderately" pregnant—she is either pregnant or not pregnant. Here are some other examples:

- A light switch is either on or off.
- An individual was either born in Rwanda or he wasn't.
- A person is either male or female (with some rare exceptions).

Other phenomena, by contrast, consist of a theoretically infinite number of points lying between two polar opposites. These types of phenomena are **continuous variables**. For example, between the extremes of black and white there exists a middle ground that comprises innumerable shades of gray.

The problem is that we often confuse these two types of variables. Specifically, people have a natural tendency to dichotomize variables that, more accurately, should be conceptualized as continuous. In particular, most person-related phenomena are frequently presumed to fit into one of two discrete types (either category A or category B), rather than as lying along a continuum (somewhere between end point A and end point B). In the vast majority of cases, however, continuous variables are more accurate and therefore more meaningful representations of the phenomena we are attempting to describe and explain.

With particular respect to cross-cultural psychology, the potential pitfall of false dichotomization is illustrated by the concepts of *individualism* and *collectivism* (see Chapter 1). What are some examples of continuous variables that frequently are assumed to be, or treated as if they were, dichotomous?

normal–abnormal

mental health–mental illness

introverted–extroverted

biased–unbiased

competitive–cooperative

autonomous–dependent

functional–dysfunctional

adaptive–maladaptive

Exercise 3.2

Identifying Dichotomous versus Continuous Variables

The following exercise will give you some practice at differentiating dichotomous and continuous phenomena. For each of the terms below, indicate those that refer to dichotomous phenomena (D) and those that refer to continuous phenomena (C). (Answers appear on our website at www.ablongman.com/shiraev3e.)

feminine–masculine: _____

married–single: _____

conscious–unconscious: _____

prejudiced–unprejudiced: _____

slavery–freedom: _____

racist–nonracist: _____

homosexual–heterosexual: _____

licensed–unlicensed: _____

integration–segregation: _____

alcoholic beverage–nonalcoholic beverage: _____

sexist–nonsexist: _____

perfect–imperfect: _____

young–old: _____

present–absent: _____

rich–poor: _____

liberal–conservative: _____

airborne–grounded: _____

responsible–not responsible: _____

acculturated–unacculturated: _____

mailed–unmailed: _____

democracy–dictatorship: _____

guilty verdict–not guilty verdict: _____

heterogeneous–homogeneous: _____

materialistic–spiritualistic: _____

traditionalist–reformist: _____

addicted–not addicted: _____

similar–different: _____

dead–alive: _____

tolerance–intolerance: _____

successful basketball shot–unsuccessful shot: _____

power on–power off: _____

subjective–objective: _____

politically correct–politically incorrect: _____

Antidotes

1. Learn to differentiate between variables that are dichotomous and those that are continuous.
2. Remember that most person-related phenomena—such as traits, attitudes, and beliefs—lie along a continuum.
3. When making cross-cultural comparisons, try to avoid artificial or false dichotomies (Hermans & Kempen, 1998).

In order to generalize about fruit, it is perfectly appropriate to combine apples and oranges.

Robyn M. Dawes—Contemporary American Psychologist

Everyone and anyone is much more simply human than otherwise, more like everyone else than different.

HARRY STACK SULLIVAN **(1892–1949)—American Psychiatrist**

THE SIMILARITY–UNIQUENESS PARADOX: ALL PHENOMENA ARE BOTH SIMILAR AND DIFFERENT

By way of introducing this metathought, let us examine the following problem: Which of the following four words does not belong with the other three?

    A. Canadian   *B.* Italian   *C.* Cuban   *D.* Hindu

The correct answer to this question is *D*, because *Hindu* is the only term that represents a religion rather than a nationality. But wait, the correct answer is *B*, because none of the others is European. Then again, the correct answer is *C*, because this is the only group with a communist government. Is that it? Not quite. The correct answer is *A*, because Canadian is the only word on the list that contains an even number of letters.

So which is it? Can it be that all four answers are correct? If so, how can every term be both similar to and different from the others? The solution to this apparent paradox lies in the cognitive schema or perceptual set with which one initially approaches the problem. More specifically, it is a function of the particular dimensions or variables on which one has evaluated the response options.

As you can see, determining the similarities and differences between any set of events— two cultures, for example—is dependent on the perspectives from which you choose to view them. In this way, phenomena can be seen at the same time as both unique from and similar to other phenomena.

Let us examine briefly the interlocking processes of comparing and contrasting phenomena. First, how do we determine the degree to which phenomena are similar? To begin with, any two phenomena in the cosmos share at least one fundamental commonality: They are both phenomena. With this as a starting point, they may subsequently be compared along a virtually infinite array of dimensions, ranging from the broadest of universal properties to the minutest of mundane details.

For instance, when you compare two groups of people, you can focus on physical features (height, weight, hair and eye color, health, strength, attractiveness), demographic characteristics (age, ethnicity, nationality, culture, religion, income, occupation), social context (competitive, cooperative, structured, ambiguous, restrictive, permissive), personality attributes (intelligence, motivation, maturity, creativity, psychological problems, attitudes, values, beliefs, goals), personal tastes (in art, music, food, clothing, wallpaper), and so on.

Exercise 3.3

Exploring Similarities and Differences

The following exercise will give you some practice at comparing, contrasting, and identifying points of distinction from a diverse array of sociocultural phenomena. First, browse through the list below and select three word pairs that, for whatever reason,

capture your interest. Then, utilizing any dimensions or sorting variables that might be helpful, for each pair, answer the following questions: (1) "How are they similar?" and (2) "How are they different?"

God and Satan

heaven and hell

religion and art

religion and science

religion and mythology

religion and psychotherapy

religion and slavery

religion and freedom

Judaism and Christianity

Catholicism and Protestantism

Buddhism and Hinduism

the Bible and the Koran

the Bible and the Constitution

religious leaders and political leaders

religious conversion and cult indoctrination

television evangelists and infomercial salesmen

men and women

homosexuality and heterosexuality

Western philosophy and Eastern philosophy

Jewish Americans and African Americans

Native American tribes and African tribes

Spanish culture and Mexican culture

Japanese art and Chinese art

Israeli music and Arabic music

Italian food and French food

racism and sexism

ignorance-based racism and hostility-based racism

racial inequality in 1950 and racial inequality in 2013

white supremacists and black nationalists

prejudice against women and prejudice against teenagers

affirmative action and discrimination

discrimination and reverse discrimination

government and parents

nations and families

patriotism and nationalism

customs and laws

Democrats and Republicans

Capitalism and Socialism

Communism and Nazism

infancy and old age

the Olympics and war

your cultural background and the president's cultural background

your cultural background and your best friend's cultural background

your cultural background and your adversary's cultural background

What is the purpose of this exercise? First, it illustrates that any two phenomena, no matter how seemingly disparate at first glance, always share at least some similarities. Second, phenomena invariably are differentiated by various points of critical distinction, which, in essence, define the boundaries delineating one phenomenon from another. Third, by utilizing this method of comparing and contrasting phenomena, you probably gained new insights and discovered some fresh perspectives into these relationships that you heretofore might not have considered. Fourth, given the fact that any two events are similar *and* different, it is crucial to take them *both* into account in your assessment of the phenomena.

Keep these principles in mind whenever you are faced with the task of comparing and contrasting sociocultural phenomena. You are likely to be more than just a little surprised each time you realize that the dimensions or variables you select for purposes of evaluation ultimately will determine just how "similar" or "unique" the phenomena turn out to be.

Antidotes

1. When comparing and contrasting any two phenomena ask yourself, "In what ways are they similar?" *and* "In what ways are they different?"
2. Before beginning your evaluation, ask yourself, "What is the purpose of this analysis?" Asking this question will help you to choose the most appropriate and relevant dimensions and sorting variables.
3. Carefully and judiciously select the dimensions on which you will evaluate various phenomena. Recognize that the dimensions you select will ultimately determine the degree of "similarity" or "uniqueness" displayed between the two phenomena.
4. Despite what may appear to be an overwhelming number of similarities between two events, always search for and take into account their differences; conversely, regardless of what may seem to be a total absence of commonalities between two events, search for and take into account their similarities.
5. Do not allow yourself to be swayed by individuals who maintain that "These events are exactly the same," or "You can't compare these events because they have absolutely nothing in common."

A good circus should have a little something for everybody.

ATTRIBUTED TO P.T. BARNUM

There's a sucker born every minute.

P.T. BARNUM (1810–1891)—**American Showman**

THE BARNUM EFFECT: "ONE-SIZE-FITS-ALL" DESCRIPTIONS

A **Barnum statement** is a personality description about a particular individual or group that is true of practically all human beings; in other words, it is a general statement that has "a little something for everybody." The **Barnum effect** refers to people's willingness to accept the validity of such overly inclusive and generic appraisals.

Barnum statements pervade the popular media, from broadcast to print, in the form of self-help primers, astrological forecasts, psychic hotlines, biorhythm and numerology readings, and interpretations of dreams, palms, or favorite colors. A few studies of the Barnum effect showed its presence in several national groups including Chinese and Western respondents (Rogers & Soule, 2009). To find them, you need look no further than the contents of your most recent fortune cookie. (See Levy, 1993, for a satirical essay on this topic, "The One-Size-Fits-All Psychological Profile.")

These statements are frequently used in our everyday descriptions of both individuals and specific sociocultural groups with whom we interact. For instance, we may confidently announce, "Immigrants have self-esteem issues." (Who *doesn't*?) Or "Chinese are sensitive to criticism." (Who *isn't*?) Or "Women do not want to be rejected." (Who *does*?)

The variations on this theme are virtually infinite. To list but a few: "He has a streak of prejudice in him." "She has some sensitive spots about her cultural background." "Hindus search for meaning of life." "Caucasians favor members of their own group." "Italians enjoy food." "Minorities just want their rights." "Republicans care about family values." "Homosexuals

A CASE IN POINT
"Your Personality"

A number of researchers have presented subjects with Barnum-like personality descriptions, such as those below (Forer, 1949).

"You have a strong need for other people to like and admire you. You have a tendency to be critical of yourself. ... At times you have serious doubts as to whether you have made the right decision or done the right thing. You prefer a certain amount of change and variety and become dissatisfied when hemmed in by restrictions and limitations. You pride yourself on being an independent thinker and do not accept other opinions without satisfactory proof. You have found it unwise to be too frank in revealing yourself to others. At times you are extraverted, affable, sociable; at other times you are introverted, wary, and reserved. Some of your aspirations tend to be pretty unrealistic."

Source: Forer, B. R. (1949). The fallacy of personal validation: A classroom demonstration of gullibility. Journal of Abnormal and Social Psychology, 44, 118–123. Reprinted by permission of the American Psychological Association.

are concerned with sex." (See our website for an extended list of Barnum statements related to sociocultural groups: www.ablongman.com/shiraev5e.)

When subjects in the experiments were led to believe that the bogus personality description was prepared especially for them, and when it was generally favorable, they nearly always rated the description as either "good" or "excellent" (Dickson & Kelly, 1985). In fact, when given a choice between a fake Barnum description and an authentic personality description based on an established test, people tended to choose the phony description as being more accurate (see Snyder et al., 1977, for a review of research in this area).

Exercise 3.4

"De-Barnumizing" Barnum Statements

Begin this exercise by selecting a few Barnum descriptions. Then, "de-Barnumize" each statement by incorporating any potentially useful qualifiers, modifiers, or adverbs. To get you started, here are two examples:

Barnum statement: *Roberto is sensitive to criticism.*

De-Barnumized statement: *Roberto is particularly sensitive to criticism.*

Barnum statement: *Native Americans have an appreciation for nature.*

De-Barnumized statement: *Compared to modern, industrialized societies, Native Americans display a greater appreciation for nature.*

Now try one of your own:

Barnum statement:_____

De-Barnumized statement: _____

_____

Antidotes

1. Learn to differentiate Barnum statements from person- and group-specific descriptions and interpretations.
2. Be aware of the limited utility inherent in Barnum statements. Specifically, remember that although Barnum statements have validity about people in general, they fail to reveal anything distinctive about any given individual or sociocultural group.
3. Whenever feasible and appropriate, make it a point to reduce the Barnum effect by qualifying personality descriptions and interpretations in terms of their magnitude or degree.

No two people look at one individual from the same point of view. For instance, I have a girlfriend. To me, she's the most remarkable, the most wonderful person in the world. That's to me. But to my wife . . .

JACKIE MASON (1936–)—**American Comedian**

A monkey, in his mother's eye, is a gazelle.

ARABIC SAYING

Two-thirds of what we see is behind our eyes.

CHINESE PROVERB

THE ASSIMILATION BIAS: VIEWING THE WORLD THROUGH SCHEMA-COLORED GLASSES

One of the most fundamental and pervasive of all human psychological activities is the propensity to categorize. People appear to possess an innate drive to classify, organize, systematize, group, subgroup, and otherwise structure the world around them.

We categorize everything from persons, objects, places, and events to concepts, experiences, feelings, and memories. The phenomenon is omnipresent, the breadth is enormous, and almost nothing is immune: gender and race, religions and occupations, cultures and nations, subatomic particles and celestial constellations, and time and space.

We can conceptualize all such categories as mental representations, or **schemas**. A schema is a cognitive structure that organizes our knowledge, beliefs, and past experiences, thereby providing a framework for understanding new events and future experiences (see Cantor & Mischel, 1979; Fiske & Taylor, 1991; Levy et al., 1988; Piaget, 1952; Taylor et al., 1994). Put another way, schemas (or *schemata*) are general expectations or preconceptions about a wide range of phenomena. In the cross-cultural domain, these include perceptual sets about people based on their age, gender, race, religion, vocation, socioeconomic status, political affiliation, social role, or any other characteristic. In fact, we may view stereotypes as equivalent to group schemas (Hamilton, 1979, 1981). (See Chapter 10.)

What function do schemas serve? First and foremost, they enable us to process the plethora of stimuli we continually encounter in a relatively rapid, efficient, and effortless manner. In other words, schemas reduce our cognitive processing load. Whenever we are faced with new information, we quickly and automatically compare it to our preexisting schemas, which greatly simplifies the task of organizing and understanding our experiences.

What happens when we come across information that is discrepant from our preconceptions? Put another way, what do we do when there is a clash between the data and our schemas? The Swiss psychologist Jean Piaget (1954, 1970) identified two complementary processes that we utilize in such situations: *accommodation* and *assimilation.* According to Piaget, both of these responses are integral components of cognitive development and constitute the means by which we adapt to our environment and construct our reality (see Chapter 8).

Accommodation refers to the process wherein we modify our schema to fit the data. In other words, we change our preexisting beliefs so that they make room for (i.e., "accommodate") new information. Assimilation, by contrast, means to modify the data to fit our schema. Here, we incorporate new information into our preexisting beliefs—even if it means distorting the information itself.

The conduct of scientific investigation involves the processes of both assimilation and accommodation. Specifically, psychologists use theories to help them make sense out of an overwhelming array of seemingly disjointed, frequently bewildering, sometimes incoherent, and all-too-often ambiguous events. In other words, they assimilate observed phenomena into their conceptual schemas. And so long as the data and the theory "fit" each other, assimilation effectively and successfully serves its purpose. Suppose, however, that a particular observation disconfirms or contradicts the scientist's expectations; that is to say, the new datum does not fit the old theory. Now what? In the pursuit of knowledge, good scientists put aside their pride, their stubbornness, and their egos, and they alter their theory to accommodate the facts.

Do people, in general, make appropriate use of assimilation and accommodation? The answer, by and large, is no. Time and again the discrepancies between data and schemas typically are resolved more in the direction of assimilation than accommodation. In other words, we are inclined to make the data fit the schema, rather than the other way around.

Because schematic processing occurs automatically and relatively unconsciously, it is very resistant to change—even when it is fraught with errors. We tend to overlook, misconstrue, or outright reject valid information when it is not consistent with our schemas. In a word, a fundamental and pervasive liability of schematic processing can be seen as a problem of assimilation.

This **bias** manifests itself in a wide variety of forms and contexts. Specifically, it leads us to rely excessively on vivid, but not necessarily appropriate, information to fill in gaps in our knowledge with schema-consistent, but erroneous, information, to conduct biased searches for evidence, to recall or misinterpret information about past events so that it validates our schemas, to unwittingly elicit the very events that we expect to find, and to engage in and perpetuate sociocultural stereotyping.

In sum, schemas bias our perceptions of reality to make them consistent with what we already believe. As such, the **assimilation bias** represents a significant obstacle to clear thinking and effective problem solving. In viewing the world through "schema-colored glasses," we subject virtually all the incoming information to varying degrees of distortion, misinterpretation, and invalidation.

A vivid case in point is provided by Dawes (1994), who tells of an incident involving flagrant gender bias in decision making. The dean of a major medical school, perplexed as to why his institution was unsuccessful in its attempts to recruit female students, asked a colleague of Dawes to investigate the problem. What emerged was striking. One of the interviewers had been rating applicants with respect to their "emotional maturity," "seriousness of interest in medicine," and "neuroticism." As it turned out, the vast majority of females did not receive positive evaluations on any of his criteria. Specifically, whenever the woman was not married, he judged her to be "immature." When she was married, he concluded that she was "not sufficiently interested in medicine." And when she was divorced? "Neurotic," of course. No win. No escape. No admittance.

Exercise 3.5

Changing the View with Different Lenses

The following exercise will give you some practice at viewing the same phenomenon through different sociocultural lenses. Select one of the perspectives from the list below (or of your own choosing) and write a few statements as to how that individual might perceive, explain, or react to a teenager from Oregon who engages in body piercing. Then, "switch lenses" by viewing the same teenager from a different perspective.

parental figure(s) • Zulu tribal chief • Midwestern farmer • Hollywood casting agent • Marine drill sergeant • Holocaust survivor • New Age philosopher • inner-city gang member • psychiatrist • cultural anthropologist • vocational counselor • fashion designer • rap artist • priest • shaman • underground photographer • pimp • yuppie • sexual sadomasochist

Antidotes

1. Do not underestimate the extent to which your prior beliefs, knowledge, and expectancies (schemata) can affect your current experience, impressions, and perceptions.
2. Try to become as aware as possible of schemata that are important to you; awareness of schemata increases your ability to modify them.
3. Experiment with temporarily lowering or altering your "perceptual filters" or "schema-colored glasses" by attempting to understand someone else's subjective (phenomenological) perceptions and experience.
4. Learn to differentiate your use of assimilation versus accommodation, particularly when you are faced with a discrepancy between your beliefs (schemas) and the information (data). Beware of the general tendency to assimilate rather than to accommodate.
5. Prod yourself to accommodate when, out of habit, reflex, or just sheer laziness, you would typically be inclined to automatically assimilate.

All that glitters is not gold.

ANONYMOUS

If my theory of relativity is proven successful, Germany will claim me as a German and France will declare that I am a citizen of the world. Should my theory prove untrue, France will say that I am a German and Germany will declare that I am a Jew.

ALBERT EINSTEIN (1879–1955)—German-Swiss-American Physicist

THE REPRESENTATIVENESS BIAS: FITS AND MISFITS OF CATEGORIZATION

In everyday life, we are frequently called on to make rapid judgments in circumstances that do not lend themselves to thoroughness or accuracy. Consider the following scenarios:

- At a job interview, you have a limited amount of time to figure out how to create the right impression.
- In a counseling setting, you might be assigned the task of expeditiously evaluating an individual from a cultural group about which you know very little.
- While traveling in a foreign country, you are approached by a group of strangers, and you need to quickly determine their intentions.

An ideal strategy for making decisions in these situations (and countless others like them) would involve the opportunity to conduct a comprehensive and systematic analysis of the problem, collect relevant data, test various hypotheses, draw appropriate inferences, thoroughly evaluate the pluses and minuses of all possible outcomes, and arrive at the optimum conclusions before having to take final action.

Well, so much for the ideal. For obvious reasons, such a strategy is impractical in most real-life circumstances. We simply do not have the time, information, or resources (not to mention incentive) that would enable us to solve most problems in this manner. Nevertheless, we proceed to make decisions and give answers in the face of varying degrees of uncertainty.

Cognitive psychologists Tversky and Kahneman (1974) theorized that people use a variety of mental shortcuts, or **heuristics**, that reduce complex and time-consuming tasks to more simple, manageable, practical, and efficient problem-solving strategies. We all have a repertoire of such shortcuts that we tend to use automatically, without necessarily considering their accuracy or validity in each situation.

Unfortunately, these shortcuts are double-edged swords. On one hand, they permit highly efficient information processing and rapid solutions to the problem. In other words, they help us to make quick "seat-of-the-pants" decisions. On the other hand, they do so at the expense of thoroughness and precision. In essence, we trade accuracy for speed. Thus, the price we pay for their efficiency can be bad judgments.

Tversky and Kahneman (1973, 1982) identified a number of such shortcuts, the most basic of which they termed the **representativeness heuristic**. Essentially, this involves judging the likelihood that something belongs to (i.e., "represents") a particular category. Stated slightly more formally, representativeness is a method of estimating the probability that Instance A is a member of Category B. In 2002, Kahneman won the Nobel Prize in economics. His works have explained how people make right and wrong economic and business decisions.

We use the representativeness heuristic to identify phenomena in our environment by intuitively comparing the phenomenon (be it people, objects, events, research data, or ideologies) to our mental representation, prototype, or schema of the relevant category. In so doing, we are attempting to ascertain if there is a "match" on the basis of whether the phenomenon's features are similar to the essential features of the category. If there is a match, we conclude that we have successfully identified the phenomenon; if not, we continue our cognitive search.

One of the most common uses of the representativeness heuristic involves judging whether a person belongs to a specific group based on how similar he or she is to the "typical" member of that group. In this way, we may conclude, for example, that Ted (A) is Jewish because he looks like your prototype of a Jewish person (B). Or that Jane (A) is a lesbian because she behaves like your stereotype of a lesbian (B). In like manner, we use the representativeness heuristic for identifying everything from ideological categories (religious, philosophical, political) to causal explanations (random, unintentional, malevolent). As you can readily see, this simple act is fundamental to all subsequent inferences and behaviors: Before any other cognitive task can be addressed, we first must answer the question, "What is it?"

Although in most instances the representativeness heuristic yields quick and relatively accurate results, it sometimes produces systematic errors in information processing. This effect, which we refer to as the **representativeness bias**, can occur as a result of numerous factors. Some of these factors include our reliance on inaccurate or faulty prototypes, our failure to take into account pertinent statistical data (such as base rates, sample size, and chance probability), and our inclination to allow our motivational needs to bias our cognitive search and subsequent evaluations.

Exercise 3.6

Examining Sociocultural Schemas and Stereotypes

As an exercise in identifying and exploring the nature and content of your own cognitive schemata, select three specific instances drawn from various sociocultural categories (such as ethnic background, occupation, religion, socioeconomic status, or political affiliation). You can choose from the following list or come up with any other examples that might be more relevant to your own life experience.

Russian • Italian • German • French • Mexican • Arab • Chinese • Native American • South African • Iranian • New Yorker • lawyer • soldier • actor • therapist • rock musician • police officer • taxicab driver • corporate executive • professional athlete • politician • nurse • nun • insurance salesperson • truck driver • convenience store clerk • mortician • Buddhist • Jehovah's Witness • Jews for Jesus • Scientologist • Republican • environmentalist • welfare recipient • yuppie • gay activist • vegetarian • heroin addict • alcoholic • single parent • senior citizen • a person with AIDS

First, note the initial thoughts, impressions, or images that come to mind regarding the category. Next, rate (on a scale from 1 to 5) the degree to which your schema for that category is *specific* (well defined, vivid, clear) versus *broad* (diverse, loose, vague). Then describe in detail the particular content (i.e., your personal perceptions) of each schema. Now try to determine and describe the schema's etiology (origin) and development. Last, try to recall (or imagine) an occasion where you came across an instance that clearly was inconsistent with (i.e., did not "fit") your schema. How did (might) you respond? What happened (might happen) to the schema itself?

Social Schema #1: _____

Distinctness of Schema: *Specific*   1   2   3   4   5   *Broad*

Content: _____

_____

Etiology and development: _____

_____

Your response to schema-inconsistent event: _____

_____

Before concluding this metathought, two final points deserve mention. Despite the problems, pitfalls, and liabilities associated with the use of cognitive heuristics, we persist in relying on them as an integral component of our decision-making processes. Why? One of the main reasons is that, on the whole, they provide us with more right answers than wrong ones. Moreover, even in those circumstances in which they are incorrect, the results typically are inconsequential.

One significant exception, however, can occur in relation to our use of prototype categories about particular groups of people, based on, for example, their race, gender, culture, nationality, religion, sexual orientation, and even psychological diagnosis. When viewed in this context, such group-related schemata are equivalent to stereotypes. Thus, when heuristics such as representativeness are utilized with respect to these categories, extreme caution is advised. As history has repeatedly demonstrated, stereotyping can have far-reaching and potentially harmful social consequences, not the least of which include prejudice, bigotry, and discrimination— outcomes that are far from inconsequential.

Antidotes

1. In situations in which you are likely to utilize the representativeness heuristic, make a conscious effort to consider the possibility that the prototype in question might be inaccurate, biased, or incomplete.
2. Take into account relevant statistical information, such as base rates, sample sizes, and chance probability.
3. Beware of the natural tendency to overestimate the degree of similarity between phenomena and categories.
4. Recognize that your personal attitudes about people and group prototypes can bias your comparisons and subsequent judgments.

When a dog bites a man, that is not news. But when a man bites a dog, that is news.

JOHN B. BOGART (1836–1920)—American Journalist

One picture is worth a thousand words.

ANONYMOUS

THE AVAILABILITY BIAS: THE PERSUASIVE POWER OF VIVID EVENTS

As a means of introducing this metathought, let us begin with a brief quiz. Give your best estimates for the following questions:

1. What are the odds of sustaining a fatal accident traveling by car as compared with traveling by commercial airplane?
2. Which racial group comprises the largest proportion of U.S. citizens living in poverty: blacks, whites, or Hispanics?
3. Which age group is at highest risk for committing suicide: teens, middle age, or elderly?
4. Which country has a higher suicide rate: South Korea or the United States?

Setting aside for the moment the actual answers to these questions, spend a few moments considering the cognitive processes you utilized in reaching your conclusions. How, specifically, did you go about arriving at your estimates for each question? Did you notice any similarities in the mental strategies you employed?

If you are like most people in this way, your estimates probably would have been determined primarily on the basis of how easily or quickly specific instances of each question came to mind. And what types of instances are likely to stand out in memory? In general, the most powerful impressions are created by events that are particularly vivid, dramatic, important, personally relevant, or otherwise salient to us. We are also prone to more quickly think of instances that are simply easy to imagine.

Unfortunately, however, the problem in relying on the ease with which events can be retrieved from memory for determining their likelihood is that our perceptions cannot necessarily be counted on as an accurate reflection of reality. Specifically, this strategy leads us to over-estimate their actual occurrence, frequency, or distribution in the world.

Did you inadvertently succumb to this bias in answering any of the questions posed above? Let us examine each one in turn.

1. Few events are more disturbing than the graphic sights and sounds of a catastrophic airplane crash. Even a mere glimpse of these horrific images on the 11 o'clock news is likely to stamp in our minds a potent and indelible impression. Such tragic accidents, therefore, become easily accessible and readily available in our memory. As a consequence, many people erroneously jump to the conclusion that they are at greater risk when traveling by commercial airplane than by car. Yet, mile for mile, people are nearly 100 times more likely to die in an automobile accident than in a commercial plane accident (Greenwald, 1986; Rich, 1999).

2. Nearly *half* of all poor individuals in the United States are white, approximately one-quarter are black, and just under one-quarter are Hispanic. Why might people be inclined to overestimate the proportions of racial minorities? In addition to the salience of their skin color, these groups do, in fact, display disproportionately higher rates of economic hardship. Specifically, almost 30 percent of Hispanics and blacks in the United States are living below the poverty level, whereas less than 10 percent of whites are poor (U.S. Bureau of the Census, 2008).

3. Although the overall national suicide rate among the elderly (65 and over) has dropped significantly during the past 60 years, this group still displays the highest proportion of self-inflicted deaths in the United States. This fact is likely to come as a surprise to many people who would identify teens as the age group at greatest risk. What might account for this misperception? There are at least three possible factors. First, whenever a teenager takes his or her own life, the event is particularly salient to us. We find it shocking, disturbing, and especially tragic that a young person, full of future potential, would choose irrevocably to end it all. Second, when it comes to suicide *attempts*, at least two-thirds of individuals who try (but fail) to kill themselves are under the age of 35 (Bernman et al., 2005). Here again, the salience even of "unsuccessful" suicide attempts by younger people can exert a disproportionate impact on our impressions and distort our perceptions. Third, the actual rate of "successful" suicides among teenagers (and even children) has, in fact, risen dramatically over the past several decades (Berman & Jobes, 1992; Brenton, 2004). Looking across cultures, the increase in adolescent suicide is not unique to the United States but appears in 23 out of 29 countries that have been studied. This trend may also lead us to overestimate the occurrence of suicide in younger age groups. Now consider suicides committed by the elderly. In general, they do not draw as much attention. They do not capture our focus. They do not startle us as particularly newsworthy. The net effect? "Out of sight, out of mind."

4. The suicide rate in the United States is 11 cases per 100,000 people. The suicide rate in Russia or South Korea is approximately 30 per 100,000—three times the U.S. rate. Still, many people believe that suicide rates are substantially higher in the United States than in other countries. What is the reason for this misperception? Among several reasons is the attention paid by the U.S. media to various stories involving suicide, especially among celebrities. It is also assumed by some people that Western industrial countries "should" have higher suicide rates than the rest of the world because of factors such as high stress and lack of emotional support systems. Although these assumptions may be correct, they are only assumptions. They cannot explain the complicated picture of suicide and its causes across the world.

The specific cognitive strategy demonstrated in the above examples has been termed the **availability heuristic** (Tversky & Kahneman, 1973) because it refers to the process of drawing on instances that are easily accessible or "available" from our memory. This heuristic helps us to answer questions concerning the frequency ("How many are there?"), incidence ("How often does something happen?"), or likelihood ("What are the odds that something will occur?") of particular events.

If examples are readily available in memory, we tend to assume that such events occur rather frequently. For instance, if you have no trouble bringing to mind examples of X (Southern hospitality, for instance), you are likely to judge that it is common. By contrast, if it takes you awhile to think of illustrations of Y (Germans' sense of humor, for example), you are prone to conclude that it is uncommon. In sum, when an event has easily retrieved instances, it will seem more prevalent than an equally frequent category that has less easily retrieved instances.

As is the case with the representativeness heuristic, very little cognitive work is needed to utilize the availability heuristic. Further, under many circumstances, the availability heuristic provides us with accurate and dependable estimates. After all, if examples easily come to mind, it is usually because there are many of them.

Unfortunately, however, there are many biasing factors that can affect the availability of events in our memory without reflecting their actual occurrence. Problems arise when this strategy is used, for instance, to estimate the frequency or likelihood of rare, though highly vivid, events as compared with those that are more typical, commonplace, or mundane in nature. When our use of the availability heuristic results in systematic errors in making such judgments, we may refer to this as the **availability bias**.

Perhaps the single most important factor underlying the availability bias is our propensity to underuse, discount, or even ignore relevant base-rate information (i.e., data about the actual frequency of events in a particular group) and other abstract statistical facts in favor of more salient and concrete, but usually less reliable, anecdotal evidence. As a consequence, personal testimonials, graphic case studies, dramatic stories, extraordinary occurrences, and bizarre events all are liable to slant, skew, or otherwise distort our judgments.

With respect to sociocultural issues, a significant problem resulting from the availability bias concerns our proclivity to overgeneralize from a few vivid examples, or sometimes even just a single vivid instance. This error is responsible, at least in part, for the phenomenon of stereotyping (see Chapter 10).

In general, how do we formulate our beliefs about particular groups of people, whether racial, cultural, national, religious, political, occupational, or any other category? We typically base our impressions on observations of specific members of the group. But which members? By and large, our attention is drawn to the most conspicuous, prominent, or salient individuals. We then are prone to overgeneralize from these few extreme examples to the group as a whole, the result of which is a role schema or stereotype. In this way, the availability bias leads us to perpetuate vivid but false beliefs about the characteristics of a wide variety of groups in our society.

The moral? We tend to be more persuaded by an ounce of anecdotal evidence than by a pound of reliable statistics. Although vivid and dramatic events can make for appetizing fiction, they are ultimately unsatisfying to those with a taste for reality.

Antidotes

1. When estimating the frequency or probability of an event, remind yourself not to reach a conclusion based solely on the ease or speed with which relevant instances can be retrieved from your memory.
2. Take anecdotal evidence not with a grain but with several large shakers of salt. Although personal testimonies and vivid cases may be very persuasive, they are not inherently trustworthy indicators of fact.
3. Make a conscious effort, whenever feasible, to seek out and utilize base-rate information and other pertinent statistical data.
4. Remember that the best basis for drawing valid generalizations is from a representative sample of relevant cases.

Don't call a man honest just because he never had the chance to steal.

YIDDISH PROVERB

THE FUNDAMENTAL ATTRIBUTION ERROR: UNDERESTIMATING THE IMPACT OF EXTERNAL INFLUENCES

How do we explain the causes of people's behavior? We typically attribute their actions either to their personality or to their circumstances. Put another way, we make dispositional attributions or situational attributions. Dispositional attributions involve assigning the causes of behavior to people's personality traits, characteristics, or attitudes, that is, to "internal" influences. Situational attributions, in contrast, involve assigning the causes of behavior to people's circumstances, surroundings, or environment, that is, to "external" influences (see Chapter 10).

In reality, of course, behavior is due to combinations of many factors, both internal and external, that vary in the degree to which they are responsible for causing a person's actions. However, in arriving at causal attributions, we have a tendency to overestimate people's dispositions and to underestimate their situations. In other words, we are prone to weigh internal determinants too heavily and external determinants too lightly. We are thus likely to explain the behavior of others as resulting predominantly from their personality, whereas we often minimize (or even ignore) the importance of the particular context or situation. This mistake is so prevalent, in fact, that social psychologist Ross (1977) termed it the **fundamental attribution error**.

What are some illustrations of this attributional bias? If a person does not make eye contact when talking to you, you might presume that the individual is "untrustworthy," "shy," or "sneaky." If someone brings you a gift for no apparent reason, you might conclude that the person is "thoughtful," "generous," or perhaps even "manipulative." Notice how these attributions essentially disregard any external or situational factors that might be responsible for producing these behaviors.

To take another example, consider the dilemma of the homeless. Some people are prone to explain a homeless person's condition in terms of personality factors, such as laziness, moral weakness, drug abuse, or mental illness. These attributions, however, fail to take into account the situational factors that can (and do) perpetuate homelessness, such as a lack of affordable housing, job scarcity, discrimination, and an unstable economy.

This same principle applies to our attributions about a diverse array of other specific subgroups within our society. How do we explain differences between, for instance, men and women? We explain them, by and large, in terms of inherent dispositions. We may thus conclude that men are "innately" more competitive or that "it's in their nature" for women to be more cooperative, while overlooking societal expectations, constraints, and sanctions that shape gender-role behavior. Along these same lines, can you think of situational factors that might have led one particular group toward athletic achievement and another toward academic achievement? Small business ownership? Underground crime? Overrepresentation in positions of upper management? Underrepresentation in the military? Having many children? Poor test performance? Eating disorders? Violence? All told, we are liable to ignore such sources of external influence that could account for intergroup differences in behavior.

Exercise 3.7

Exploring the Effects of Social Context

This exercise serves to underscore the enormous, yet typically unnoticed, power of the social situation in influencing our feelings, attitudes, and behavior. Imagine yourself in the following scenarios and how you might respond to the simple question, "So, how are you doing?" For each situation, indicate not only what you might say, but also provide a brief description of your probable thoughts, demeanor, and the emotional tone of your response.

At a job interview: _____

At a class reunion: _____

At a funeral:_____

With your parents: _____

With your best friend: _____

With a total stranger: _____

With someone who is hearing impaired: _____

With someone who is wheelchair bound: _____

With someone who is physically very attractive: _____

With someone who is physically very unattractive: _____

In a foreign country where you do not speak the language: _____

When approached by a homeless child: _____

When approached by a homeless adult: _____

When approached by a police officer: _____

When approached by a prostitute: _____

When approached by a group of Hispanic youths: _____

When approached by a group of Hispanic tourists: _____

When approached by a group of Japanese tourists: _____

When approached by a group of people singing and dancing in orange robes and offering you free incense: _____

In looking over your answers, observe that *all* the variability in your responses is attributable to the situations themselves, since both you and the initial question were fixed and held constant. One final point deserves mention. Can you determine which of these responses reflects the "real" you? Notice that this question is, in itself, virtually unanswerable without also taking into account the context of the situation.

What is responsible for this attributional error? Social psychologists have identified two principal sources: **cognitive biases** and **motivational biases**.

Cognitive biases refer to systematic mistakes that derive from limits that are inherent in our capacity to process information. Because we are not capable of perceiving everything in our environment, our focus is automatically drawn to the most prominent or "eye-catching"—that is, perceptually salient—stimuli. This can lead us to formulate biased and inaccurate causal attributions (Taylor & Fiske, 1975). Specifically, we are prone to equate the most perceptually salient stimuli with the most causally influential stimuli.

In contrast, motivational biases refer to systematic mistakes that derive from our efforts to satisfy our own personal needs, such as the desire for self-esteem, power, or control. Simply put, motivational biases serve the function of making us feel better, even if they do so at the expense of distorting, obscuring, or falsifying reality.

Are we motivated to prefer one type of causal attribution over another? It would appear so. In the case of Western cultures in particular, we are told from early childhood to believe that people can control their destiny and are the masters of their fate. As such, society generally condones dispositional attributions, while it discourages situational attributions. In this way, we can fool ourselves into overestimating the degree of control that we actually do have, while underestimating the impact of external factors that lie beyond our control. We are prone, therefore, to exaggerate our perceptions of controllability.

One very unfortunate consequence of this motivational bias is that people who are harmed by forces that are truly out of their control may be held more responsible for their circumstances than they should be. In other words, our illusion of control may lead us to blame people for the bad things that happen to them.

Why does this occur? Lerner (1970) theorized that we have great difficulty accepting the unfairness and injustices of life. Further, we have a strong need to believe that we live in a "just world" in which good is rewarded and bad is punished. This belief leads us to conclude that people get what they deserve and deserve what they get: "What goes around, comes around."

Instances of such attributions abound:

- *Rape victims must have behaved seductively.*
- *Homosexuals must have brought AIDS on themselves.*
- *People with physical disabilities must have done something wrong.*
- *People in poor countries must be responsible for what is happening to them economically.*
- *Victims of persecution must be guilty of something, or they wouldn't be persecuted.*

What compels people to make such attributions? Once again, we do it, in all likelihood, to preserve our illusion of control. It is psychologically more comforting to blame others for the disasters that befall them, rather than face the cold reality that we live in an unjust world in which such events can happen at random. After all, if negative events are uncontrollable, they could just as easily happen to *us*. In other words, by assigning dispositional attributions, we hope to experience a greater sense of control over our destiny. Further, it provides a justification for our indifference to (or even oppression of) society's victims: If people themselves are responsible for their own plight, there is no need for the rest of us to help them. (In fact, they probably *deserve* it.)

Antidotes

1. Do not underestimate the power of external, situational determinants of behavior.
2. Remember that at any given time how people behave depends both on what they bring to the situation ("who" they are) as well as on the situation itself ("where" they are).
3. Keep in mind that this attributional error can become reversed, depending on the perceiver's point of view. Specifically, although people are prone to underestimate the impact of others' situations, they tend to overestimate the impact of their own situations.
4. Be sure to take into account both cognitive and motivational biases that are responsible for producing these attributional errors.

Respect a man, and he will do the more.

ANONYMOUS

To believe a thing impossible is to make it so.

FRENCH PROVERB

THE SELF-FULFILLING PROPHECY: WHEN EXPECTATIONS CREATE REALITY

The attitudes and beliefs that we hold toward other people can—with or without our intent— actually produce the very behaviors that we expect to find. In other words, a perceiver's assumptions about another person may lead that person to adopt those expected attributes. This phenomenon is known as the **self-fulfilling prophecy**.

In what is probably the most famous—and still controversial—study of the self-fulfilling prophecy, Rosenthal and Jacobson (1968) informed teachers at a San Francisco elementary school that on the basis of a reliable psychological test, some of the pupils in their classroom would show dramatic spurts in academic performance during the upcoming school year. In reality, there was no such test, and the children designated as "intellectual bloomers" were chosen at random. Nevertheless, when the children's performance was assessed several months later, those students who had been earmarked as "bloomers" did, indeed, show an improvement in their schoolwork; even more remarkably, their IQ scores had increased. The teachers thus unwittingly created the very behaviors that they expected.

The self-fulfilling prophecy has been demonstrated with a diverse array of both positive and negative perceiver expectancies, including hostility (Snyder & Swann, 1978), extraversion (Snyder, 1984), gender stereotypes (Skrypnek & Snyder, 1982), racial stereotypes (Word et al., 1974), and even stereotypes concerning physical attractiveness (Snyder et al., 1977). These studies underscore how prejudice of any kind can set in motion a self-perpetuating and ever-escalating vicious cycle of adverse repercussions (see bidirectional causation, p. 75), in which the self-fulfilling prophecy serves to influence not only how the prejudiced person behaves toward the victim but also how the victim may then behave in a way that confirms the person's initial prejudices.

Not only are we seldom aware of the extent to which our expectations can influence the behavior of others, but we probably are even less aware of how the expectations of others are capable of influencing *our* behavior. It is thus important to remember that our actions are shaped not only by our own attitudes but also by the expectations of those with whom we interact. Put another way, we are continually cultivating the constructions of each other's social realities.

Given the ubiquity of the self-fulfilling prophecy, we would do well to consider its potential impact in all of our social interactions. In an ethnic minority community, for instance, what do you suppose might occur if a police officer were to expect neighborhood residents to be hostile and dishonest? Resistant? Helpless? Paranoid?

In like manner, what if a resident expects police officers to be hostile and dishonest? Unfair? Callous? Abusive? The police and community can ultimately end up creating a reciprocally reinforcing projection system that supports their respective initial expectations, much of which may be occurring outside of their direct awareness.

Exercise 3.8

Exploring Manifestations of the Self-Fulfilling Prophecy

As an exercise, select two scenarios—either hypothetical or factual—involving the self-fulfilling prophecy. In making your selections, consider a variety of topics (e.g., stereotyping, prejudice, child rearing, testing, competition), settings (e.g., research, classroom, workplace, religious), and societal or governmental policies, programs, and laws (e.g., welfare, unemployment, affirmative action, desegregation, immigration, bilingual education, sexual harassment, mandatory retirement). Then for each scenario, present your thoughts as to how Person A's expectations might influence his behavior toward Person B. Last, discuss how Person A's actions could cause Person B to behave in accordance with Person A's prior expectations. In other words, identify some of the specific factors or events that you believe are capable of transforming Person A's initial expectations into the reality of Person B's subsequent attitudes and behavior.

Scenario: _____

Effects of Person A's expectations on behavior toward Person B:

_____

_____

Effects of Person A's behavior on Person B's subsequent actions:

_____

_____

Antidotes

1. In all of your social interactions, remember that expectations can, in themselves, create their own reality.
2. Make a conscious effort to become aware of your own expectancies and the ways in which they may lead you to induce those very behaviors in others.
3. Do not forget that your own behavior is not immune to the influence of the self-fulfilling prophecy. Specifically, keep in mind that your behavior can be shaped by the expectations other people have of you.
4. In conducting research, initiate safeguards to reduce the potential impact of expectancy effects. This may be accomplished by, for example, keeping the experimenters unaware of (i.e., "blind" to) the specific purpose, goals, or hypotheses of the study.

CORRELATION DOES NOT PROVE CAUSATION: CONFUSING "WHAT" WITH "WHY"

A correlation is a statement about the relationship or association between two (or more) variables. Correlations thus enable us to make predictions from one variable or event to another. That is, if two events are correlated (or "coappear"), then the presence of one event provides us with information about the other event. A correlation does not, however, necessarily establish a causal relationship between the variables. In other words, causation cannot be proven simply by virtue of a correlation or coappearance.

As an example, let us consider the correlation between creativity and psychological disorders (see, e.g., Andreason & Canter, 1974; Andreason & Powers, 1975; Jamison, 1993). Great painter Vincent van Gogh, Russian novelist Fyodor Dostoyevsky, and American writer Ernest Hemingway all suffered from emotional disorders that seriously disrupted their lives. More recently, popular U.S. comedians John Belushi and Chris Farley developed serious (and ultimately fatal) drug addictions. Based on these observations, what may we conclude? That psychological disorders cause creativity? Perhaps. But maybe creativity causes psychological disorders? Then again, isn't it possible that creativity and psychological disorders reciprocally affect each other? To complicate matters further, what about the possibility that some other variable, such as a genetic predisposition, causes both creativity and psychological disorders?

Put another way, given a correlation between A and B: Does A cause B? Does B cause A? Do A and B cause each other? Does C cause A and B? Could there be some combination of these causal relationships? Unfortunately, a correlation alone does not (in fact, cannot) provide us with the definitive answers to these questions. The following are some examples of correlated variables about which people frequently (but erroneously) may infer causality.

> **Example 1:** Research indicates that watching violent television programs appears to be mildly but positively correlated with aggressive behavior. This correlation does not, however, prove that TV violence causes aggressiveness. Perhaps aggressive people

prefer to watch violent TV programs. Maybe aggressiveness and TV violence, in a "vicious cycle," feed off each other (see bidirectional causation, p. 75). Or consider the possibility that family conflict causes both aggressive behavior and the watching of TV violence.

Example 2: Do you know that there is more aggression in hot meteorological conditions than in cold ones? For example, rates of homicide and rape are generally higher in warmer than in colder climates (Anderson, 1987). Why? It would be absurd, of course, to propose that the weather is affected by violent crimes. It certainly is much more likely that meteorological conditions somehow affect violent behavior. However, we do not know if other factors, such as poverty, density of population, or government policies affect incidents of homicide and rape.

Example 3: Suppose that certain ethnic minority groups display disproportionately higher rates of delinquency, academic failure, teenage pregnancy, drug abuse, criminality, or psychopathology. In other words, let us assume a relationship exists between group membership (e.g., Hispanic Americans) and the incidence and severity of these problems. What could account for this trend? One of the most commonly overlooked but critical factors is socioeconomic status. Specifically, poverty appears to be a much stronger predictor for such behaviors than is ethnicity itself. Now, what if (as happens to be the case) such groups are, on average, located at a lower rung on the socioeconomic ladder? We could be inclined erroneously to focus on skin color and ethnic identity, while underestimating the effect of economic circumstances (see the section "The Fundamental Attribution Error: Underestimating the Impact of External Influences").

Example 4: Similarly, let us examine the debate regarding racial (specifically black versus white) differences in IQ scores. In their controversial book, *The Bell Curve* (1994), Herrnstein and Murray propose that such correlations can be explained primarily in terms of differential genetic inheritance (see also Jensen, 1973; Rushton, 1994, 1995). Needless to say, this conclusion cannot be accepted without taking into account factors such as the roles of socioeconomic status, access to quality schooling, parental role modeling, family structure, peer influence, cultural norms, as well as both personal and societal expectations (see self-fulfilling prophecy).

Consider also correlations between incidents of homelessness and mental illness, teen pregnancy and welfare benefits, poor grades in school and legal troubles, ethnicity and alcohol consumption, and gender roles and mass media. In all these instances (and countless more), beware of concluding causation based solely on correlation or coappearance. Further, when a correlation is observed, be sure to examine all plausible pathways and directions of causation.

One particular type of faulty reasoning, the **post hoc error**, refers to the mistaken logic that because Event *B* follows Event *A*, then *B* must have been caused by *A*. This error, also known as **parataxic reasoning** (Sullivan, 1954), may be seen as a kind of "magical thinking," because events that occur close together in time are construed as causally linked. As it turns out, most superstitions are based on parataxic reasoning. For example, if a football coach does not shave before a game, and his team then wins, he might assume that not shaving somehow caused the success. As a result, he may adopt this superstitious behavior for future games.

Exercise 3.9

Exploring Correlation and Causation

To give you some practice at applying these principles, try to identify some of the possible causal relationships, pathways, and explanations that could account for each of the correlations presented below.

Example

"Eveningness" and optimism appear to be negatively correlated (Levy, 1985); that is, people who are "evening types" tend to be more pessimistic than "morning types." Why might this be true?

1. Optimism may cause "morningness."
2. Morningness may cause optimism.
3. Optimism and morningness may affect each other.
4. Satisfying job may cause both optimism and morningness.

Exercise A

Many societies believe that the most effective way to control or deter aggression is through the use of punishment, including the death penalty. The preponderance of research evidence, however, shows a positive correlation between murder rates and the number of executions, rather than the negative relationship predicted by deterrence theories (see Segall et al., 1997). Assuming this correlation is valid, how might it be explained?

1. _____
2. _____
3. _____
4. _____

Exercise B

Suppose you read an article reporting a negative correlation between religiosity and depression (i.e., the less religious, the more depressed). What factors could account for this relationship?

1. _____
2. _____
3. _____
4. _____

As these examples illustrate, although correlations may provide us with accurate—and frequently very useful—information regarding "what" relationships exist, they cannot be counted on to answer the question "why?" Even in those circumstances in which a correlation strongly *implies* causation, it does not *prove* causation.

Antidotes

1. Remember that a correlation or coappearance is not, in itself, proof of causation.
2. Keep in mind that correlations enable us to make predictions from one event to another; they do not, however, provide explanations as to why the events are related.

3. When a correlation is observed, consider all possible pathways and directions of causation. For example, if Event *A* and Event *B* are correlated, does *A* cause *B*? Does *B* cause *A*? Do *A* and *B* cause each other? Does *C* cause *A* and *B*?

The ancestor of every action is a thought.

RALPH WALDO EMERSON **(1803–1882)—American Poet and Philosopher**

Thought is the child of action.

BENJAMIN DISRAELI **(1804–1881)—English Statesman and Novelist**

BIDIRECTIONAL CAUSATION AND MULTIPLE CAUSATION: CAUSAL LOOPS AND COMPOUND PATHWAYS

Bidirectional Causation

Although we typically tend to think of causal relationships as being **unidirectional** (Event *A* causes Event *B*), frequently they are **bidirectional** (Event *A* causes Event *B* and Event *B* causes Event *A*). In other words, variables can, and frequently do, affect each other. This relationship may also be referred to as a causal loop or, depending on our subjective evaluation of the particular situation, either a "healthy spiral" (if we happen to like it) or a "vicious cycle" (if we do not). (In this regard, see the section "The Evaluative Bias of Language: To Describe Is to Prescribe.")

As an illustration of this principle, let us look at the widely debated psychological question, "Does thought cause emotion, or does emotion cause thought? Which comes first? Which is the cause and which is the effect?" (see Berscheid, 1982; Mandler, 1975; Weiner, 1980; Zajonc, 1980). When viewed as a bidirectional relationship, however, the argument may be moot: clearly, thoughts and feelings affect each other.

Consider also the bidirectional relationship between psychological disturbance and one's social environment. Specifically, it is probable that cold, rejecting, and hostile parents can cause emotional and behavioral problems in their children. At the same time, do not ignore the possibility (even the likelihood) that children with emotional and behavioral problems also might cause their parents to become cold, rejecting, and hostile.

Bidirectional relationships are as interesting as they are plentiful:

- self-esteem and popularity
- motivation and encouragement
- curiosity and knowledge
- respect and responsibility
- frustration and helplessness
- apathy and powerlessness
- criticism and defensiveness

- paranoia and secrecy
- education and opportunity
- opportunity and success
- money and power
- poverty and failure
- discrimination and defiance
- violence and prejudice

Exercise 3.10

Identifying and Disentangling Causal Loops

As an exercise, consider the bidirectional relationship between unemployment (Event *A*) and delinquency (Event *B*).

- First, describe some ways that unemployment (*A*) might result in delinquency (*B*).
- Next, describe some ways that delinquency (*B*) can lead to unemployment (*A*).
- Is it possible to determine which is (or was) the "initial" cause? If so, how?
- Under what circumstances might it be important to identify which was the initial cause?
- Under what circumstances might it be *unimportant* to identify which was the initial cause?

For some more practice, select another bidirectional relationship (either from the above-mentioned list or an original example from your own experience).

As you can see, "cause" and "effect" are relative terms: A cause in one instance becomes an effect in another. From this perspective, asking the question, "Which comes first?" although interesting, may be unnecessary, irrelevant, or even unanswerable. Thus, when faced with such chicken-and-egg questions, remember that your answer may depend entirely on where you happen to enter the causal loop.

Multiple Causation

Immigrants to the United States and Canada from the Indian subcontinent display higher rates of coronary heart disease than the population of the countries to which they moved (Bahl et al., 2001). What is the cause?

Actually, the form of this question is somewhat misleading in its implication that there is a *single* cause. In point of fact, any effect may be, and usually is, the result of not just one but several causes, which are operating concurrently. Virtually every significant behavior has many determinants, and any single explanation is inevitably an oversimplification. Thus, in this case, we would need to consider a wide range of possible factors (e.g., genetic, dietary, stress, family norms, and cultural traditions), all of which could, to varying degrees, be involved. Dutch professor Ruut Veenhoven (2008) has shown through his research that, despite common assumptions, happiness is not entirely based on economic factors alone, such as jobs or prices. In Great Britain, for instance, different indicators of happiness haven't changed much for 40 years despite economic ups and downs. Brits steadily score as one of the happiest nations. Scandinavian countries such as Iceland, Denmark, or Finland receive even higher scores. People in Iceland, for example, according to surveys, are happier than those in Sweden, but they spend only half as much on social welfare. Americans, despite recent economic slowdowns, report that they are getting happier. Studies also show that in individualistic cultures, people rely on their emotions when they assess their own happiness. In predominantly collectivist cultures, people tend to seek social cues or other people's responses to make a judgment (Suh et al., 2008).

To take another example, what causes depression? Is it caused by early childhood trauma? Or a perceived failure? Or unrealistic expectations? Or a faulty belief system? Or learned helplessness? Or a biochemical predisposition? Or lack of opportunity?

Now, try replacing each *or* with *and*. Depression thus may be seen as caused by a variety of factors, including early childhood trauma, *and* a vital loss, *and* a perceived failure, *and* unrealistic expectations, *and* a faulty belief system, *and* internalized anger, *and* learned helplessness, *and* a biochemical predisposition, *and* a lack of opportunity.

Exercise 3.11

Exploring Compound Pathways

Applying the same principle, consider the multiple determinants of *homophobia*. List as many possible factors as you can think of (suggested answers appear on our website at www.ablongman.com/shiraev5e). Do the same with some other topic related to cross-cultural psychology. (You might browse through the index of this book for some ideas.)

In sum, every time you are faced with a question, issue, or problem that is presented in terms of *either/or*, stop for a moment. Now, try replacing *either/or* with *both/and*. For example, the statement, "Prejudice is caused by either ignorance or hatred," becomes "Prejudice is caused by both ignorance and hatred" (and probably many other factors as well). Then ask yourself, "Is this new formulation *useful*?" In a great number of situations, you are very likely to find that it is.

Antidotes

1. Do not assume a priori that the causal link between two variables is a unidirectional "one-way street."
2. When investigating directions of causation, consider the possibility that the variables are linked in a causal loop, that is, each might be both a cause and an effect of the other.
3. Remember that in a case of bidirectional causation, which variable appears to be the "cause" and which variable appears to be the "effect" may depend entirely on the point at which you happen to enter the causal loop.
4. In attempting to explain why an event occurred, do not limit your search to one cause. Instead, explore multiple plausible causes, all of which may be responsible for producing the effect.
5. When faced with an *either/or* question, always consider the possibility that the answer might be *both/and*.

Empirical principles are wholly unsuited to serve as the foundation for moral laws.

IMMANUEL KANT **(1724–1804)—German Philosopher**

It is of fundamental importance not to make the positivist mistake of assuming that, because a group are "in formation," this means they are necessarily "on course."

R. D. LAING **(1927–1989)—Scottish Psychiatrist**

THE NATURALISTIC FALLACY: BLURRING THE LINE BETWEEN "IS" AND "SHOULD"

One very important way in which our personal values can bias our thinking is when we equate our description of what *is* with our prescription of what *ought* to be. This occurs, for instance, whenever we define what is good in terms of what is observable. This error in thinking is called the **naturalistic fallacy**.

Examine the following statements: "What's typical is normal; what's normal is good. What's not typical is abnormal; what's abnormal is bad." Notice how, in each case, a description of what exists becomes converted into a prescription of what we like or dislike.

As Scottish philosopher Hume pointed out more than 200 years ago, values, ethics, and morality are based not on logic or reason but on the sentiments and public opinions of a particular society. Thus, no description of human behavior, however accurate, can ever ordain what is "right" or "wrong" behavior. It makes no difference whether we are studying cultural customs, religious convictions, political beliefs, educational practices, recreational activities, sexual proclivities, or table manners. If most people do something, it does not make it right; if most people do not, it does not make it wrong.

Of course, the converse is also true: If most people do something, it does not make it wrong; if most people do not, it does not make it right. In other words, there is no need to idealize someone just because he or she is different from the crowd. Likewise, we need not condemn someone solely for doing what others do. The point is that, in any case, we must be careful not to confuse objective description with subjective value judgment.

Let us briefly elaborate on these four variants of the naturalistic fallacy.

1. *common = good* The error here is to equate what is average, conventional, or popular with what is right. What are some of the assumptions underlying this perspective? "Everybody does it, so it must be okay." "The majority knows best." "All those people just can't be wrong." To take a concrete example: "Because the vast majority of people in a particular country approve of physical punishment of children, this opinion must be the right one."

2. *uncommon = bad* On the flip side of the same coin, that which departs from the norm is presumed to be wrong. Whether judging deviant behavior, unpopular beliefs, unusual customs, or unconventional appearances, the verdict is inevitable—if it's different, it's condemned. Example: "Since only a small minority of the world's population is homosexual, homosexuality must be wrong."

3. *common = bad* In this scenario, an individual rejects something solely because the majority accepts it, separate and apart from its own merits or drawbacks. On what basis? "The masses are always wrong." "If most people do it, it can't be good." "Since society is a flock of mindless sheep, anything they stand for is bound to be immoral." Example: "The establishment believes in marriage, therefore I certainly do not."

4. *uncommon = good* Along the same lines, any deviation from what is normal is deemed, per se, to be desirable, irrespective of its inherent value. Why? "Anything that's different is better than what's average." "If it's unusual, it's good." "Anybody who has the courage to rebel against conventional thinking must have something important to contribute." Example: "I would rather have people look at me as strange than not notice me at all."

To view this phenomenon in a cross-cultural perspective, consider some of the practices that, in the past, have been widely accepted as correct: human sacrifice, slavery, child labor, public execution, denial of religious freedom, involuntary medical treatment, and the burning of books, heretics, and witches. By today's standards, it may seem painfully clear to most of us that these practices were morally wrong. Yet, what are the chances that future generations will dismiss—perhaps even mock—much of what we currently take for granted as right? (Can you foresee any in particular?)

Exercise 3.12

Exploring Manifestations of the Naturalistic Fallacy

As an exercise, try to think of specific examples that represent each of the categories below. (To help get you started, look through the following list of topics: gender roles, racial segregation, civil disobedience, affirmative action, birth control, child rearing, war, psychopathology, artistic expression, fashion, music, advertising, illegal immigration, personal hygiene.)

Common, therefore good: _____

Uncommon, therefore bad: _____

Common, therefore bad: _____

Uncommon, therefore good: _____

T. H. Huxley once noted that "the cosmic process has no sort of relation to moral ends" (cited in Miner & Rawson, 1994). His assertion notwithstanding, our view of nature itself is subject to the naturalistic fallacy. This happens when we equate what is "natural" with what is "right." Or when we proclaim that "things are as they should be." Or presume that whatever occurs in nature is good because nature is, in itself, good. How could it not be good? After all, just consider snowcapped mountains, golden sunsets, fragrant flowers, the miracle of birth, the instinct to survive, indeed life itself. From herbal remedies to organic pesticides, if it is from nature, then it is inherently good.

There is only one small wrinkle. Perhaps, not surprisingly, we are less inclined to cite examples from nature that we do not happen to like. What about birth defects and leprosy? Or drought and famine? Earthquakes and monsoons? Strychnine and oleander? Are these phenomena any less a part of nature? Are they somehow "unnatural"?

In essence, nature is held to a double standard: We embrace the "good" parts and ignore, dismiss, or rationalize away the "bad" parts. But we cannot have it both ways. Nature is, morally speaking, just nature. The values we impart to it are a different matter.

Even social scientists are not immune to committing this error. A case in point is the field of evolutionary psychology. Proponents of this approach, basing their theories on the Darwinian principles of natural selection and adaptation for reproductive success, offer evolutionary explanations for a diverse array of human behaviors, including aggression, intelligence, morality, prejudice, territoriality, xenophobia, mating, sexual preference, and infidelity (see Barkow et al., 1992; Futuyma, 1979; Symons, 1979; Wright, 1994).

For instance, according to these theorists, men are genetically predisposed to seek out a variety of nubile young females as sex partners. Women, in contrast, naturally prefer fewer, monogamous relationships with wealthy and powerful men. Further, evolution determines that men, compared with women, inherit a greater proclivity to kill their spouses over sexual infidelity.

For the sake of argument, let us set aside the numerous criticisms of evolutionary psychology (e.g., Holcomb, 1996; Schlinger, 1996) and assume that these theories are valid.

CROSS-CULTURAL SENSITIVITY

What does it mean to follow the principles of "multiculturalism"? Does it suggest that we should accept anything and everything that happens in other cultures, whether in different countries or even within our own country? Does it mean that cross-cultural psychologists should set aside their own values and tolerate, for instance, the sexism and discrimination against women that are widely practiced, particularly in many countries? Would a multiculturalist perspective dictate the acceptance of polygamy in other countries, even though it is a federal offense in the United States? Should we cease condemning certain groups for their religious intolerance? Are we obliged—on the grounds of multiculturalism—to approve sexual harassment in Russia, for example, as an acceptance of certain cultural norms? Do we remain silent about forceful female circumcision in Africa, a practice considered body mutilation in Europe and the United States? After all, who are we to judge? "This is what they do in her culture." Consider the fact that from their perspective, many of *our* practices may seem immoral.

The school of thought that attempts to reduce (or even eliminate) particular moral and cultural values from study and research and maintains that any value is good so long as it exists in a particular culture context is called *cultural relativism*.

What do you think about cultural relativism? Are there any limits to this perspective? Do you believe that everything truly is relative, and that there are not more universal standards by which to evaluate different cultural practices? Is it possible to reconcile the dilemma between respecting the beliefs of others without sacrificing one's own? Is there a point at which values such as tolerance and acceptance become potentially harmful? Can you draw a line between relativism and multiculturalism?

Where does that leave us? What are the implications? That sexual double standards are "natural" and therefore acceptable? Would this justify promiscuity, adultery, deceit, and betrayal? Are greed, materialism, racial segregation, and war to be sanctioned? Could we really criticize or condemn someone for infidelity? How can we hold people accountable for spousal abuse, statutory rape, or murder? After all, it's "in their nature."

Clearly, even if evolution does influence what we do, this does not inherently make it morally good, desirable, or correct. Put another way, what is "true" isn't necessarily "right." It would be erroneous, for example, to condone acts of violence solely on the grounds that aggression is an intrinsic product of our genetic inheritance. It is one thing to *explain* human conduct; it is quite another to *excuse* it. Maybe our behavior is, in part, attributable to the process of natural selection. Then again, perhaps, to borrow a line from the movie *The African Queen*, "nature is what we were put on earth to overcome."

Antidotes

1. Do not make the mistake of equating statistical frequency with moral value. Thus, if most people do something, that does not intrinsically make it right; if most people do not, that does not therefore make it wrong. In like manner, if most people do something, that does not make it wrong; if they do not, that does not make it right.
2. Learn to differentiate objective descriptions from subjective prescriptions. Specifically, do not confuse one's description of what "is" or "isn't" with one's prescription of what "should" or "shouldn't" be.

To be positive: To be mistaken at the top of one's voice.

AMBROSE BIERCE (1842–1914)—**American Journalist and Poet**

The great tragedy of Science—the slaying of a beautiful hypothesis by an ugly fact.

T. H. HUXLEY (1825–1895)—**English Biologist and Writer**

THE BELIEF PERSEVERANCE EFFECT: "DON'T CONFUSE ME WITH THE FACTS!"

In our attempts to understand the world around us and to navigate our way through life, we adopt a wide variety of beliefs, the content of which ranges from the mundane (the best brand of detergent, the most flattering hairstyle) to the profound (the meaning of life, the existence of God). One of the most significant characteristics of our beliefs is the degree to which we become personally invested in them. The attachment may be so strong that our beliefs feel as if they are a vital and indispensable component of our very identity.

What happens, then, when our beliefs are challenged by new facts (such as research data)? Particularly those beliefs that we happen to like? Or those that we regard as important? Or those that we have come to accept as truths?

If we were to respond to such challenges in a purely rational manner, we would simply detach our personal feelings from the dispute, evaluate the substance of the challenge as objectively and dispassionately as possible, and, then, if appropriate, modify our beliefs accordingly. We would, in other words, accommodate the new information by modifying our preexisting schemas (see assimilation bias, p. 59).

But we are not always so rational. In fact, sometimes we are not rational at all. Specifically, when our beliefs are being challenged, we are prone to feel that we are being personally challenged. When our beliefs are criticized, we feel criticized. When our beliefs are attacked, we feel attacked. Our first impulse, therefore, typically is to protect our beliefs, as if to protect ourselves. As such, we tend to cling to our beliefs, sometimes even in the face of contrary evidence. This bias in thinking is called the **belief perseverance effect** (see Lord et al., 1979).

When we engage in belief perseverance, we usually respond to such challenges by discounting, denying, or simply ignoring any information that runs counter to our beliefs. That is, we treat potentially disconfirming evidence or arguments as if they did not really exist. For example, suppose a friend of yours adamantly maintains that "rape is an act of violence, not of sex." In response, you point out that it isn't an "either/or" question; rape can be, and is, an act of both violence and sex. You explain further that the particular means of the assault differentiates rape from other types of violent acts (see similarity–uniqueness paradox). We would not call it "rape" if, for instance, a person were knifed in the back. Rape, in contrast, is a violent act specifically involving the sex organs. As such, it need not necessarily even entail the assailant's sexual pleasure or sexual gratification to be considered a sexual act. "In other words," you conclude, "rape is an act of sexual violence." Your friend pauses a moment, apparently mulling it over, and then replies, "Oh, I see what you mean. That makes a lot of sense. But I *still* think that rape is an act of violence, not of sex."

In fact, our beliefs can be so intractable that they stubbornly persevere even when we acknowledge that the evidence supporting them is erroneous. This was evidenced in a research study in which subjects were administered a personality test that purportedly showed them to be especially "socially sensitive" (Ross et al., 1975). Subjects were subsequently informed that the test actually was *fake* and therefore provided invalid results. Even with this knowledge, however, subjects still persisted in believing that they were socially sensitive. Other studies have corroborated the general conclusion that it requires much more compelling evidence to change our beliefs than it did to create them in the first place (Ross & Lepper, 1980).

Can we engage in belief perseverance without rejecting contradictory information? What if we are not able, or even choose not, to discount, deny, or ignore potentially disconfirming evidence? Is there any way that we can continue to cling to our cherished beliefs and still emerge victorious? The answer, as you probably have already anticipated, is yes. Like the martial arts expert who masterfully redirects and transforms his opponent's force to his own advantage, in a brilliant feat of logical contortionism, we simply find a way to bend, twist, or reframe the information so that it actually *supports* our original belief.

Let us now turn to a sampling of variations on this very robust theme (Table 3.2). Of particular interest, note how the participants in these brief scenarios are able to support their positions by employing a creative assortment of flaws in thinking, including tautologous logic, misattributions of intentionality based on consequences, confusing feelings with truth, and errors

TABLE 3.2 Illustrations of the Belief Perseverance Effect

Employer: New Yorkers always do a better job. I've known it since my youth.

Employee: But our new sales rep from Los Angeles outsold every New Yorker in the department.

Employer: Yeah, but if we had given the same region to a New Yorker, we would have made *twice* the profit.

Minority group leader: I am absolutely certain that there's a government plot against us.

Interviewer: Now, hold on. Do you have any *evidence* that there's a plot against you?

Minority group leader: No, but do you have any evidence that there *isn't*?

Religious person: All atheists, at their core, are profoundly depressed due to a lack of belief in God.

Atheist: I don't believe in God, and I am not depressed.

Religious person: Then you might not realize it, but you actually *do* believe in God. Or maybe you are depressed but just aren't aware of it.

Sociopolitical theorist: Jews control the media.

Reporter: But the vast majority of people who head the networks and newspapers aren't Jewish.

Sociopolitical theorist: Exactly my point. All that proves is how *clever* they are in creating the *appearance* that they do not have any power. They have *so much* control that they've been able to dupe you into believing that they do not have *any* control.

Female group therapy member: All men really want is sex and nothing else.

Male group therapy member: I'm a man, and that's not all I want.

Female group therapy member: Well, then either you're lying to me, or you're lying to yourself, or you're not really a man.

in deductive and inductive reasoning. (These examples were drawn directly from our own experiences in a variety of settings, including classrooms, workshops, therapy sessions, media broadcasts, and waiting in line at a movie theater.)

Exercise 3.13

The Perseverance of Sociocultural Beliefs

As an exercise in further examining the various manifestations of belief perseverance, try completing the following scenarios on your own:

PERSON A: Aryans are the master race

PERSON B: Then how come they *lost* World War II? Especially to "inferior" races?

PERSON A: _____

PERSON A: The terrorist is insane.

PERSON B: But he claims to be completely responsible for his actions.

PERSON A: _____

PERSON A: You're a racist.

PERSON B: No, I'm not.

PERSON A: _____

PERSON A: The only reason she got the job is because she's an ethnic minority.

PERSON B: _____

PERSON A: _____

PERSON A: The only reason she didn't get the job is because she's an ethnic minority.

PERSON B: _____

PERSON A: _____

PERSON A: Racial discrimination in America is worse now than it was 50 years ago.

PERSON B: _____

PERSON A: _____

PERSON A: Immigrants coming to this country are just looking for a "free ride."

PERSON B: _____

PERSON A: _____

PERSON A: Homosexuality is a mental illness, just like any other mental illness.

PERSON B: _____

PERSON A: _____

PERSON A: The Holocaust didn't really happen.

PERSON B: _____

PERSON A: _____

PERSON A: God is on our side.

PERSON B: _____

PERSON A: _____

Antidotes

1. Keep an open mind to different, and especially challenging, points of view.
2. Remind yourself (and others as well) to think carefully about how you evaluate evidence and to closely monitor your biases as you formulate your conclusions.
3. Make it a point to actively *counterargue* your preexisting beliefs. That is, ask yourself directly in what ways your beliefs might be wrong. One specific method of doing so is to *consider the opposite*.
4. When faced with a discrepancy between your beliefs and the facts, resist the natural tendency to assume that your beliefs are right and the facts must somehow be wrong.

CONCLUSIONS: "TO METATHINK OR NOT TO METATHINK?"

Last, let us turn to an evaluation of this chapter's principal content: the metathoughts themselves. In a sense, metathoughts may be seen as cognitive schemas. As such, they provide the same benefits—and, of course, are subject to the same liabilities—inherent in all schematic processing (see assimilation bias, p. 59). More specifically, in terms of advantages, they can

- significantly reduce or eliminate a wide variety of systematic biases, errors, and mistakes in thinking related to cultural and cross-cultural phenomena;
- improve the clarity of thinking and the accuracy of solutions;
- open pathways to new perspectives and alternative points of view;
- promote and facilitate innovative and creative approaches to problem solving;
- serve as a foundation for identifying other as-yet-unidentified cognitive errors (i.e., new metathoughts), as well as their antidotes.

As for disadvantages, their use

- requires more time and effort (particularly at first) to analyze theories and facts;
- involves greater complexity at the cost of simplicity;
- is likely to result in increased ambiguity;
- can sometimes leave you feeling frustrated or confused;
- may be impractical or inappropriate in some situations.

In sum, like all other choices, the acceptance or rejection of these ideas entails costs as well as benefits. Thus, once you have made the effort to study, understand, and apply these metathought principles in cross-cultural psychology and your own life, take stock of their pluses and minuses. By weighing them out in this manner, you will be able to make much more informed choices as to your particular course of action. Either way, the decisions ultimately are yours.

Thomas Szasz once remarked, "I do not have the answer to every one of life's problems. I only know a stupid answer when I see one" (quoted in J. Miller, 1983). In like manner, the metathoughts will not necessarily provide you with the best solutions to all of the questions that you will ask or that will be asked of you. Nevertheless, cultivating your skills of critical thinking in cross-cultural psychology certainly will, at the very least, enable you more easily and consistently to identify and discard "the stupid ones," thereby freeing your time, energy, and resources for more productive endeavors.

Chapter Summary

- Critical thinking is one of the most vital and indispensable components of learning. The thought principles or metathoughts (literally, "thoughts about thought") presented in this chapter are cognitive tools that provide the user with specific strategies for inquiry and problem solving. In this way, they serve as potent antidotes to thinking that is often prone to be biased, simplistic, rigid, lazy, or just plain sloppy.

- In describing phenomena, particularly social phenomena, the language that people use invariably reflects their own personal values, biases, likes, and dislikes. In this way, their words can reveal at least as much about themselves as the events, individuals, and groups they are attempting to describe.

- Dichotomous variables are a matter of classification (*quality*), whereas continuous variables are a matter of degree (*quantity*). The problem is that people have a tendency to dichotomize variables that, more accurately, should be conceptualized as continuous.

- All phenomena are both similar to and different from each other, depending on the dimensions or sorting variables that have been selected for purposes of evaluation, comparison, and contrast. No phenomenon is totally identical or totally unique in relation to other phenomena.

- Barnum statements are "one-size-fits-all" descriptions that are true of practically all human beings, but that do not provide distinctive information about a particular

group or person. Thus, the problem with Barnum statements is not that they are wrong; rather, because they are so generic, universal, and elastic, they are of little value.

- The *assimilation bias* represents a significant obstacle to clear thinking and effective problem solving. In viewing the world through "schema-colored glasses," we subject virtually all the incoming information to varying degrees of distortion, misinterpretation, and invalidation.

- To identify any given phenomenon, we automatically and intuitively compare it with our mental representation, prototype, or schema of the relevant category. Errors due to the *representativeness bias* can occur as a result of faulty prototypes, failure to consider relevant statistical data, or motivational biases.

- We utilize the availability heuristic whenever we attempt to assess the frequency or likelihood of an event on the basis of how quickly or easily instances come to mind. Thus, vivid examples, dramatic events, graphic case studies, and personal testimonies, in contrast to statistical information, are likely to exert a disproportionate impact on our judgments. In this way, anecdotes may be more persuasive than factual data.

- In arriving at causal attributions to explain people's behavior, we have a tendency to overestimate the impact of their internal personality traits (dispositions) and to underestimate the impact of their environmental circumstances (situations). This *fundamental attribution error* appears to be due to cognitive biases and motivational biases.

- The assumptions, attitudes, and beliefs that we hold toward other people can, with or without our intent, actually produce the very behaviors that we expect to find. Similarly, our own behavior may inadvertently be shaped by other people's expectancies of us. In sum, with the *self-fulfilling prophecy*, expectations can generate their own reality.
- Correlations may provide us with accurate and useful information regarding "what" relationships exist, but they cannot be counted on to answer the question, "why?" Even in those circumstances in which a correlation strongly implies causation, it does not prove causation.
- In contrast to unidirectional causation, when Event *A* causes Event *B,* in bidirectional causation Event *A* and Event *B* are linked in a circular or causal loop, in which each is both a cause and an effect of the other. In such instances, the pathway of causation is a "two-way street." Further, any given event can be, and typically is, the result of numerous causes.
- The frequency of an event does not inherently determine its moral value or worth. What is common, typical, or normal is not necessarily good; what is uncommon, atypical, or abnormal is not necessarily bad. Conversely, what is common is not necessarily bad, and what is uncommon is not necessarily good.
- We have a tendency to stubbornly cling to our beliefs, sometimes even in the face of disconfirming evidence. Thus, when these beliefs are challenged, we feel impelled to protect them, almost as if we were protecting ourselves. One consequence of this belief perseverance effect is that it generally requires much more compelling evidence to change our beliefs than it did to create them in the first place.

Key Terms

Antidote A remedy to prevent or counteract an adverse effect.

Assimilation Bias The propensity to resolve discrepancies between preexisting schemas and new information in the direction of assimilation rather than accommodation, even at the expense of distorting the information itself.

Availability Bias Any condition in which the availability heuristic produces systematic errors in thinking or information processing, typically due to highly vivid although rare events.

Availability Heuristic A cognitive strategy for quickly estimating the frequency, incidence, or probability of a given event based on the ease with which such instances are retrievable from memory.

Barnum Effect A phenomenon that refers to people's willingness to accept uncritically the validity of Barnum statements.

Barnum Statement Any generic "one-size-fits-all" description or interpretation about a particular individual that is true of practically all human beings.

Belief Perseverance Effect The tendency to cling stubbornly to one's beliefs, even in the face of contradictory or disconfirming evidence.

Bias A prejudicial inclination or predisposition that inhibits, deters, or prevents impartial judgment.

Bidirectional Causation A mutual, reciprocal relationship between two variables wherein each is both a cause and an effect of the other.

Cognitive Bias Any systematic error in attribution that derives from limits that are inherent in people's cognitive abilities to process information.

Continuous Variable Any variable that lies along a dimension, range, or spectrum, rather than in a discrete category, that can theoretically take on an infinite number of values and is expressed in terms of quantity, magnitude, or degree.

Critical Thinking An active and systematic cognitive strategy to examine, evaluate, and understand events, solve problems, and make decisions on the basis of sound reasoning and valid evidence. More specifically, critical thinking involves maintaining an attitude that is both open minded and skeptical; recognizing the distinction between facts and theories; striving for factual accuracy and logical consistency; objectively gathering, weighing, and synthesizing information; forming reasonable inferences, judgments, and conclusions; identifying and questioning underlying assumptions and beliefs; discerning hidden or implicit values; perceiving similarities and differences between phenomena; understanding causal relationships; reducing logical flaws and personal biases, such as avoiding oversimplifications and overgeneralizations; developing a tolerance for uncertainty and ambiguity; exploring alternative perspectives and explanations; and searching for creative solutions.

Dichotomous Variable Any variable that can be placed into either of two discrete and mutually exclusive categories.

Fundamental Attribution Error A bias in attempting to determine the causes of people's behavior that involves overestimating the influence of their personality traits, while underestimating the influence of their particular situations; that is, overutilizing internal attributions and underutilizing external attributions.

Heuristic A mental shortcut or rule-of-thumb strategy for problem solving that reduces complex information and time-consuming tasks to more simple, rapid, and efficient judgmental operations, particularly in reaching decisions under conditions of uncertainty.

Metathinking The act of thinking about thinking; engaging in a critical analysis and evaluation of the thinking process.

Metathoughts Literally, thoughts about thought, which involve principles of critical thinking.

Motivational Bias Any systematic error in attribution that derives from people's efforts to satisfy their own personal needs, such as the desire for self-esteem, power, or prestige.

Naturalistic Fallacy An error in thinking whereby the individual confuses or equates objective descriptions with subjective value judgments, in particular, by defining what is morally good or bad solely in terms of what is statistically frequent or infrequent.

Parataxic Reasoning A kind of "magical thinking," frequently responsible for superstitious behaviors, in which events that occur close together in time are erroneously construed to be causally linked.

Post Hoc Error A shortened form of *post hoc, ergo propter hoc* ("after this, therefore because of this"), referring to the logical error that because Event *B* follows Event *A*, then *B* must have been caused by *A*.

Representativeness Bias Any condition in which the representativeness heuristic produces systematic errors in thinking or information processing.

Representativeness Heuristic A cognitive strategy for quickly estimating the probability that a given instance is a member of a particular category.

Schema A cognitive structure or representation that organizes one's knowledge, beliefs, and past experiences, thereby providing a framework for understanding new events and future experiences; a general expectation or preconception about a wide range of phenomena.

Self-Fulfilling Prophecy A phenomenon wherein people's attitudes, beliefs, or assumptions about another person (or persons) can, with or without their intent, actually produce the very behaviors that they had initially expected to find.

Unidirectional Causation A relationship between two variables wherein one is the cause and the other is the effect.

CHAPTER

4

Cognition: Sensation, Perception, and States of Consciousness

We do not see things with our eyes; we see them through our eyes and with our minds.

ANONYMOUS

As a rule, what is out of sight disturbs men's minds more seriously than what they see.

JULIUS CAESAR (100–44 B.C.E.)— *Roman Statesman*

At the end of class Albert raised his hand and asked a question: "Do cross-cultural psychologists acknowledge important differences between Europeans and non-Europeans in America?" He then contended that for centuries, the ancestors of the former group relied mostly on visual perception. Europeans, he said, must see, verify, measure, and then rationalize their impressions. They do not feel or believe a priori; they must experience everything before their own eyes. Africans, he said, referring to his own ancestors, were different because of environmental conditions that caused them to rely mostly on hearing and touch. They felt objects and vibrations through their skin, could masterfully express themselves through their voices, and did not always need visual verifications. Albert concluded that due to such perceptual differences between European and African ancestors, European Americans are more likely to succeed in engineering, science, and writing, whereas African Americans tend to excel at playing music, singing, and other nonvisual arts. "Do you have any evidence to support your idea?" one of the students asked. "You see, you need verifications. I do not have them. I simply feel this way," responded Albert, laughing at his own answer.

Was Albert right when he daringly suggested the sensory differences between Africans and Europeans? Are there any significant sensory differences among people of various cultures? Or maybe people see, hear, and feel the physical world in the same way? If not, what particular characteristics of vision, hearing, smell, touch, or taste have the strongest cultural roots? How do cultures affect our consciousness? On a more "practical" side, should fashion designers pay attention to certain colors either liked or disliked by particular ethnic or national groups? Do pilots in all countries prefer to scan the control board in front of them from left to right? Do people see similar dreams? We will try to address these and other questions throughout this chapter. First, let us begin with a brief review of the most basic principles underlying human cognitive processes.

SENSATION AND PERCEPTION: BASIC PRINCIPLES

The process by which receptor cells are stimulated and transmit their information to higher brain centers is called **sensation**. You see a blue star in the evening sky or feel a dull pain in your arm—all sensations begin from an environmental stimulus, either external or internal, in the form of energy capable of exciting the nervous system. Sensation converts external energy into an internal neurophysiological process, which "results" in a particular psychological experience: We see the star and feel the pain. Do we feel all environmental stimuli? Obviously not, because certain stimuli are not experienced at all. The minimum amount of physical energy needed for an individual to notice a stimulus is called an **absolute threshold**. The **difference threshold** is the lowest level of stimulation required to sense that a change in the stimulation has occurred. **Sensory adaptation** is the tendency of the sensory system to respond less to stimuli that continue without change. We can adapt, for example, to particular conditions, such as heat or cold, the presence or absence of air pollution, and spicy food. Residents of a small resort town in Spain are less likely to attend to the air they breathe, whereas a tourist visiting this town from a polluted Mexico City or Los Angeles is likely to notice the incredible freshness of the air. Constancy of our sensory processes refers to the experience of an object or quality as unchanging under changing conditions. For example, the color of a banana appears constant to the human eye under several conditions despite the fact that the actual wavelengths of the light reflected by the surface of the banana under these varied conditions are different (Kanazawa, 2010).

For each of the five senses (vision, hearing, smell, touch, and taste), discrete neural pathways normally carry sensory information, a signal, to specific regions in the brain. The nature of sensation depends on the area of the brain that is activated by a signal. For example, electrical stimulation of the primary visual cortex, which is located in the occipital lobes of the brain, produces visual sensations, whereas stimulation of the auditory complex in the temporal lobes is experienced as sound. Color sensation is a process based on the functioning of three different types of cones in the eye's retina. Each cone responds to wavelights, but fires most persistently at a particular point on the spectrum. Thus, short-wavelight cones are responsible for the sensation of blue, middle-wavelight cones produce the sensation of green, and long-wavelight cones produce red sensations. Mixing these three primary colors together, most individuals detect as many as 1,000 color shades (Brown & Wald, 1964). When a person detects a smell, information from the receptors travels directly to the primary olfactory complex in the frontal lobes. Taste receptors consist of two paths. The first path is connected to the primary gustatory cortex in the brain, which allows people to detect tastes. The second path is connected to the brain's limbic system, which can generate immediate emotional and behavioral responses to tastes. Several receptors in the skin feed into a single sensory neuron that is connected to the spinal cord. This allows for immediate reflexive action, such as the quick movement after touching something hot.

The process that organizes various sensations into meaningful patterns is called **perception**. Physiologists assert that perception involves activation of association areas in the cortex, thus integrating prior knowledge with current sensation. Three colored vertical stripes—blue, white, and red—displayed in sequence on a piece of material will have little meaning for a boy from Bangladesh or Northern Ireland. However, for a French adult, this sequence of colors would be associated with the French national flag. When one of us takes a guitar and plays the first cords of the song *Stairway to Heaven*, many U.S. or British students identify it as a classic rock ballad written by Led Zeppelin. However, those who grew up outside the Western tradition of rock music interpret these notes as nothing more than a "melody."

Sensation and perception are two basic processes first studied in psychological laboratories more than 100 years ago in several countries, including Germany, France, Russia, Great Britain, and the United States. Comparative analysis of the data obtained by these laboratories shows remarkable quantitative and qualitative similarities in both sensory and perceptual processes in people of different countries (Yaroshevski, 1996). However, in most experiments, psychologists studied sensation using a "standard"—for psychological research in the 1800s—sample of subjects: the researchers themselves, their academic assistants, and, of course, the students. Therefore, the data in such studies were obtained mainly from highly educated, white male subjects. Cross-cultural investigation of sensation began with the research conducted by Rivers (1901) and associates, who selected their subjects in Europe and Torres Strait Islands, a territory near Australia. Rivers examined a popular assumption about the extraordinary visual sharpness of non-Europeans. The assumption was disproved: The vision of the Torres Strait Islanders was not found to be outstanding.

HOW CULTURE INFLUENCES WHAT WE PERCEIVE

Our experience with the environment shapes our perception by creating perceptual expectations. These expectations, known as a **perceptual set**, make particular interpretations likely to occur and increase both the speed and efficiency of the perceptual process. Perceptual sets common in people of a particular culture—and most relevant to their experience—are not necessarily developed in individuals from other cultures.

Personal experience influences one's sensation and perception. If many individuals from a particular group share such experiences, there should be some common group-related sensory or perceptual patterns. For example, we are usually aware of the aroma outside a restaurant when we are hungry, yet we are much less sensitive to it when our stomach is full. In general, if we need something, we pay attention to the stimuli that are linked to the gratification of the need. But what if a person is constantly deprived of food or water, like millions of people on earth are? In one study, researchers examined the effects of food and water deprivation on word identification (Wispe & Drambarean, 1953). The deprived participants perceived the need-related words (words standing for food and drinks) at shorter exposure times than the nondeprived subjects. In another study, researchers compared the perceptual experiences of children from poor and wealthy families (Bruner & Goodman, 1947). They asked children to adjust the size of a circle of light to match the sizes of various coins: a penny, a nickel, a dime, and a quarter. Children from wealthier families tended to see the coins as smaller than they actually were, whereas children from poor families overestimated the size of the coins. The investigators argued that the need for money among children from poor homes influenced their perception of the coins. This interesting finding has been reproduced in Hong Kong with similar results (Dawson, 1975).

Environmental conditions affect sensation and perception in many ways. Studies have shown that hunter and gatherer cultures have a lower rate of color blindness among their members than societies practicing agriculture. Indeed, from an evolutionary standpoint, not many color-blind hunters could have survived because of their inability to distinguish details, colors, and contours, a skill critical in hunting or gathering activities (Pollack, 1963). Another example refers to the level of noise in the surrounding environments. People who live in deserts do not suffer hearing loss to the extent that city dwellers do (Reuning & Wortley, 1973). In deserts, the level of noise is significantly lower than it is in urban areas, and this could explain, in part, the difference in hearing problems.

The absence of experience can become a significant factor that affects perception. For example, researchers raised kittens in complete darkness except for several hours each day. During these brief periods, the kittens were placed in a cylinder with either horizontal or vertical stripes (Blakemore & Cooper, 1970). The animals could not observe their own bodies, and the only object they saw were the stripes. Five months after the beginning of the experiment, the kittens reared in "horizontal" environments were unable to perceive vertical lines. Their brains lacked detectors responsive to vertical lines. Similarly, the kittens reared in "vertical" environments were unable to perceive horizontal lines. The animals' brains adapted to either "horizontal" or "vertical" worlds by developing specialized neuronal pathways. Similar results were obtained in studies of individuals who were born blind but obtained sight after a surgical procedure later in life (Gregory, 1978). Most of these people could tell figure from ground, detect colors, and observe moving objects. However, many of them could not recognize objects they previously knew by touch. The absence of a visual experience affected these people's cognition after sight was gained!

On the whole, environmental conditions, as well as activities and experiences, determine culture-related differences and similarities in sensation and perception. Children learn to pay attention to certain stimuli, ignore others, and develop particular cognitive preferences for some culture-related images, smells, tastes, and sounds (Shiraev & Boyd, 2001).

CRITICAL THINKING
Origin and Sensory Preferences

This chapter opened with an episode in which Albert raised a question about basic cultural and psychological differences between African Americans and European Americans. His hypothesis resembles the so-called compensation hypothesis: Africans are likely to excel in auditory (hearing) tasks, whereas Europeans deal more effectively with visual (seeing) stimuli. In other words, Africans may prefer to communicate through the auditory modality, whereas white Europeans might favor written communications. If Africans, compared to Europeans, appear to have difficulty with the study of mathematics, this can be "compensated" by a high facility for learning languages and a good sense for rhythm and music (McLuhan, 1971). According to Shade (1991), one of the important features in African American perceptual style is the preference of auditory, aural, and tactile perceptions, compared with predominantly visual perceptions common in European Americans. African Americans are trained to concentrate on people rather than abstract ideas and nonhuman objects. A similar suggestion was extended to the

(continued)

(continued)

field of art. Auditory and tactile sensations and perceptions were proposed as being specifically African and quite different from the visual culture of the Europeans. Some authors propose the existence of *verve*, a special element of African psychology. This is an energetic, intense mental set or preference to be simultaneously attuned to several sensory stimuli rather than singular events or a linear set of stimuli (Boykin, 1994).

These hypotheses are intriguing; however, there are very little empirical data to support assumptions about substantial sensory differences between Africans and Europeans. Empirical studies have also come up short in supporting the hypothesis of physiological differences between visual and auditory transmission of information among different cultures. No evidence was found to back a hypothesis about the superiority of black students in auditory judgments and white students in visual judgments. Empirical evidence on the prominence of auditory, tactile, or kinesthetic cues for Africans is also very limited.

HOW PEOPLE PERCEIVE PICTURES

Perception of pictures is linked to a person's educational and socialization experience or the lack thereof. In a study conducted among the Mekan—a remote group in Ethiopia with limited access to formal schooling and little exposure to pictures—scientists used detailed drawings of animals. With few exceptions, the subjects identified the animals, but only after some time and with obvious mental effort (Deregowski et al., 1972). Hudson (1960), who studied how South Africans perceived and interpreted safety posters and signs, provided another demonstration of the links between educational experience and perception. The number of misinterpretations of the posters was much lower for urban and more educated subjects than for rural and less educated individuals. Numerous experiments have demonstrated that people generally have more difficulty in judging pictures of faces of other ethnic groups compared to faces of their own group (Meissner & Brigham, 2001). In one such study, two samples of Turkish-born and Austrian children living in Europe were asked to look at the photographs of Turkish and German faces and match photographs of faces in frontal and angled views. Turkish children were faster in matching Turkish faces than were Austrian children. There was no difference in perception of German faces: Both groups matched them equally fast. Most likely, as this research suggests, the Turkish-born children have had more frequent interpersonal contact with Germans than the Austrian kids with Turkish groups (Sporer et al., 2007).

There is evidence that scanning patterns are subject to some cultural variations. The most significant finding is that the direction we examine pictures—from left to right, from right to left, or from top to bottom—is linked to our reading habits (Goodnow & Levine, 1973). For example, it is likely that people in England, Argentina, or Canada, who read from left to right, also have a left–right scanning pattern; Arab and Hebrew readers, who read from right to left, should demonstrate a right–left scanning pattern; and Japanese readers, who read from top to bottom, should have a top–bottom pattern of picture scanning. However, there are exceptions to this rule. For example, in a test on the copying of geometric figures, Hebrew subjects showed a left–right preference. How did the researchers explain this finding? Both Hebrew and English scripts require mainly left-to-right strokes for single letters. In comparison, in the Arab language, the right-to-left direction is required for the writing of individual letters. Therefore, from a practical standpoint, it is always useful to examine not only reading but also writing patterns of a particular culture. These findings can raise interesting assumptions about how some professionals (i.e., pilots, operators, etc.) of different cultural backgrounds scan signals from monitors and other visual indicators.

Visual scanning is related to writing and drawing. Take, for instance, the drawing of circles. The differences between cultural groups are perhaps based on the way people learn to

A CASE IN POINT

Picture Interpretation and Access to Media

Liddell (1997) reported that children in South Africa were less skilled interpreters of pictures than their European counterparts, and this tendency was first noticed as early as in the 1960s. The differences between the samples were larger for African children from rural areas. The mistakes in picture interpretation included making mistakes in depth perception, identification of face blemishes, and interpretation of motion markers. Also, South African children had more difficulties than children in the European sample in creating narrative—short descriptive—interpretations of the pictures. Do these results suggest that because pictures may be a relatively poor source of organizing the South African children's knowledge, the authors of school textbooks should limit the usage of pictures?

We want you to think about the results from a different perspective. The children in the examined samples, despite recent progress in communications, still face a tremendous lack of opportunities compared with their European, Asian, or North American peers. Limited access to television and movies, inability to use personal computers at home, limited access to computers at school, lack of pictorial materials at home, and many other poverty-related problems can contribute to the significant limitations in the child's use of pictures. Make your call now. Should you suggest cutting the number of pictures in South African textbooks or should you rather insist that the child have better access to pictorial materials outside the classroom?

write in their native language. If writing requires more clockwise movement, then the child is more likely to make his or her circles in the same manner. In a comparative Japanese–U.S. study the direction of circle drawing for U.S. students and Japanese students was compared. Results showed that with advancing grade, U.S. students increasingly drew circles in a counterclockwise direction whereas the Japanese increasingly drew them in a clockwise direction (Amenomouri et al., 1997). Another study showed that children who speak Hebrew tend to draw circles in a clockwise direction more often than the other two groups studied, whose language was French or English (Zendal et al., 1987).

Studies also show that people, including residents of big cities, are substantially faster and more accurate at visually detecting animals compared to nonliving objects such as moving cars (New et al., 2007). Ian Spence and his colleagues (Spence et al., 2006) found differences in men's and women's ability to distinguish objects that appear in their field of vision. Such differences were not overwhelming; yet, it was found that men were generally better at remembering and locating general landmarks in pictures, while women were better at remembering and locating food.

Some intriguing perceptual differences were found in comparative studies of Weston and East Asian subjects. East Asians tend to be more holistic, and Westerners tend to be more analytic. Numerous studies show that people from Asian cultures, including China, Japan, and Korea, pay more attention to contexts and backgrounds of pictures that they see than people from Western cultures who tend to focus in the center or the central figure of these pictures (Ko et al., 2011). East Asians are also slower than Americans at detecting changes in the center of the screen but allocate their attention more broadly than Americans (Boduroglu et al., 2009). What is the source of these differences? One possibility is that they reflect different cultural styles in what is considered as informative and worthy of report about observed scenes (Masuda & Nisbett, 2006). We will return to these differences again in Chapter 5.

PERCEPTION OF DEPTH

Depth perception refers to the organization of sensations in three dimensions, even though the image on the eye's retina is two dimensional. Look at the drawing of the famous Devil's tuning fork (below). Now we challenge you to draw the fork by memory, without looking at the picture. Why is it difficult? The picture is two dimensional with several confusing depth cues. However, the brain, because of our experience with depth cues, interprets this object as three dimensional. It is interesting that many people without formal schooling or previous exposure to three-dimensional pictures do not find this particular picture confusing (Deregowski, 1974; Hudson, 1960). Those who are not familiar with how to interpret depth cues—usually due to environmental conditions, extreme poverty, and lack of formal schooling—will perceive them as two dimensional. Some non-Western subjects experience difficulty with pictorially presented depth stimuli. However, according to several studies, education and training can significantly improve depth perception (Leach, 1975; Nicholson et al., 1977).

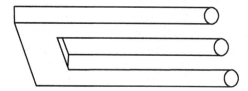

Altogether, picture perception is a combination of cognitive skills. Some national, regional, or culture-specific conditions determine which skills improve in individuals and which skills remain underdeveloped.

Beware in case you lose the substance by grasping at the shadow.

Aesop (Sixth Century b.c.e.)—Greek Fabulist

ARE PEOPLE EQUALLY MISLED BY VISUAL ILLUSIONS?

Look at the figures below. They represent famous visual illusions. In the Müller–Lyer illusion, the line on the left appears shorter than the line on the right. In the Ponzo illusion, the upper line appears larger than the one at the bottom. In the horizontal–vertical illusion, the vertical line appears to be larger than the horizontal one. The vast majority of us are susceptible to these illusions; even though we know that the lines are equal in length, they appear unequal to us. However, such susceptibility is not common in all individuals, and there are some cultural variations in how people perceive visual illusions.

For example, a study of receptiveness to the Ponzo illusion in the United States and Guam suggested that non-Western and rural subjects showed less susceptibility to the illusion than the individuals from either Western or urban areas (Brislin, 1993). Likewise, on both the Müller–Lyer and horizontal–vertical illusions, the Western samples, living primarily in industrial urban environments, were more illusion prone than any of the non-Western samples. Subjects from regions with open landscapes were more susceptible to the horizontal–vertical illusion than subjects from regions in which such views are rare (Segall et al., 1966).

How can we interpret such perceptual differences? As suggested earlier in the chapter, if certain groups differ in their visual perception, such differences may be influenced by the different experiences of the members of these groups. According to a popular "carpentered world" hypothesis (Segall et al., 1966), people who are raised in an environment shaped by carpenters—most of us live in rectangular houses with rectangular furniture and similar street patterns—tend to interpret nonrectangular figures as representations of rectangular figures seen in perspective. They also have a tendency to interpret the lines in the horizontal plane that look as if they are moving away from an observer as appearing to be shorter than the lines that cross the viewer's line of vision (the horizontal–vertical illusion).

Virtually, all people who had formal schooling got used to converting two-dimensional pictures into three-dimensional images even though pictures on computer screens and photographs in magazines are displayed on a flat surface. Certain perceptual sets (see the beginning of the chapter) allow people to see "flat" objects as if they actually exist in "volume" (Segall et al., 1990).

SOME CULTURAL PATTERNS OF DRAWING

Individuals with no formal schooling, young children, and early artists a few thousand years ago did not acquire the ability to convert three-dimensional perceptions into two-dimensional paintings or sketches. In some cultural groups, their paintings often display objects, details, and surroundings independently of one another. For instance, Australian Aborigines usually depict the trunk of a crocodile as seen from above, while the head and the tail are drawn as being seen from the side (Dziurawiec & Deregowski, 1992). Beveridge (1940) and Thouless (1932) found that African drawings available to them were less affected by visual cues than were European drawings. With the lack of perspective in African pictures, objects were depicted as they were in reality rather than how they actually appear to the observer.

Perceptual distortions are easily found in various forms of drawings. For instance, in many national art traditions a linear perspective does not occur. Numerous perceptual distortions are found in modern art, as well as in ancient Egyptian and medieval Spanish art (Parker & Deregowski, 1990). The polydimensional representation of space has been used at some period in most cultures. In much of ancient Egyptian and Cretan painting, for instance, the head and legs of a figure were shown in profile, but the eye and torso of a figure were drawn frontally. In Indian and early European paintings, created before the seventeenth century, figures and other vertical forms were represented as if seen from ground level, whereas the horizontal planes that figures and objects stood on were shown as if viewed from above. Paul Cezanne (1839–1906), a famous French artist, represented things on his paintings as if seen from different directions and at varying eye levels. Cubism, one of the prominent schools in modern art, aimed to give the viewer the time experience of moving around static forms in order to examine their volume and structure. In cubist pictures, the viewer is specifically encouraged to examine the surfaces of depicted objects from every possible angle.

PERCEPTION OF COLOR

Color has three universal psychological dimensions: hue, brightness, and saturation. Hue is what people mean by color, brightness refers to a color's intensity, and saturation indicates a color's purity. If there are similar underlying physiological mechanisms of color perception, does this mean that perception of color has very little cultural variation? Are culturally sanctioned activities able to influence color perception?

According to language-related theories of color perception—that emphasize the role of language in the identification and labeling of colors in each and every language—there are words that are linked to various units of the visible spectrum (Berry et al., 1992). The developing child learns these words and starts to use them in order to identify colors. It is interesting that even though the vast majority of healthy individuals are able to detect the same range of colors, there are languages that lack certain words for particular colors. For example, the color red is always represented by a separate word, whereas the colors green and blue are sometimes not distinguished linguistically. An explanation for this finding is based on an assumption that due to environmental conditions, the less vivid colors were less salient to non-Europeans and for that reason less likely to be identified and labeled with a separate word (Ray, 1952).

There were other attempts to explain such a perceptual confusion between the colors green and blue. Some studies stress physiological differences between racial groups in terms of their color perception. For instance, Pollack (1963) demonstrated that certain visual perceptual skills might be related to factors such as retinal pigmentation. He found that persons with denser retinal pigmentation had more difficulty detecting contours and showed relative difficulties in perceiving the color blue. Studies of color preferences showed that women across countries tend to choose and like reddish hues, such as pink. On the other hand, men had a preference for greenish-blue colors. The researchers suggest that the differences in color preferences may be connected to the evolutionary ability of the female brain to deal with gathering of food products such as fruits, while men's brains tend to be "wired" to be better hunters in green and lush environments (Hurlbert & Ling, 2007). However, physiological and evolutionary explanations of cultural differences in the detection of color did not gain as much popularity as the theories that emphasize the importance of learning experiences and linguistic norms of perception.

The subjective social and individual psychological meaning of color can be crucial to our understanding of color perception. There are strong universal trends in people's feelings about colors. In one prominent study, data from 23 countries revealed stable cross-cultural similarities. The concept "red" was perceived as being quite salient and active. "Black" and "gray" were considered bad, whereas "white," "blue," and "green" were considered good. "Yellow," "white," and "gray" were persistently seen as passive (Adams & Osgood, 1973).

The history of human civilization gives many examples about other trends in color interpretation. Take, for example, the color red. In many nations it became a political symbol of violence, revolution, and revolt. In communist China and the Soviet Union, government officials made red banners the official flags of their countries. The official flag of Nazi Germany was also red. Rebellious students in Europe waved red flags during antiestablishment demonstrations in the 1960s. Guerrilla fighters in South and Central America, Southeast Asia, and South Africa chose red as the color of their armed struggle. In the 1970s, one of the most notorious terrorist groups in Italy carried the name Red Brigades. Yet in Japan, the red color stood for philanthropy and vitality and the red circle on the national flag represents the sun.

In Druze culture, a religious community living primarily in Lebanon, Syria, and Israel, colors are associated with five cosmic principles. These principles are represented by the five-colored Druze star: reason (green), soul (red), word (yellow), precedent (blue), and immanence (white).

Another interesting set of facts is related to human perception of black and white. More than three decades ago, researchers found that preschool children in the United States from various racial groups tended to prefer light- to dark-skinned people on pictures and photographs and to favor the color white over black. European children also displayed a tendency toward the positive evaluation of light-skinned figures relative to dark-skinned ones (Best et al., 1975). Moreover, cross-cultural research has established that people associate the color white with more positive feelings than black and that this bias seems to emerge by the preschool years. Subsequent research has shown that native African children share the same color bias (Williams & Best, 1990). The association of the color white with something "good," "pure," and "familiar" and black as primarily "negative," "unclean," and "unknown" is common in many cultures. The investigators speculate that the pan-cultural preference for light over dark may reflect a generalization from light and dark cycles of the day. Light is generally associated with certainty and safety, whereas darkness is more likely to represent danger and uncertainty. Nature may have endowed humans with a tendency to dislike the dark, just as it has endowed them with a susceptibility to a fear of snakes and spiders. Sea pirates raised black banners over their ships as a symbol of intimidation. In Christianity, angels are white and demons are black. In the Islamic context, the color white is symbolic of purity and equality of all people. As in many places on the earth, a typical Bulgarian bride would be dressed in white on her wedding. However, the bride's bouquet would never consist of white roses, as the white rose is indicative of death, according to Bulgarian folk beliefs. In addition, people from various religious backgrounds wear black clothes when they are mourning. In the English language, definitions of the word "black" include "without any moral light or goodness," "evil," "wicked," "indicating disgrace," and "sinful." Definitions of "white" include "morally pure," "spotless," "innocent," and "free from evil intent." In 1993, during a period of economic recession, when a newspaper asked Russians what color they associated with their lives, 42 percent said gray and 21 percent said black. Most of them felt as though they entered into "darkness" when things were extremely difficult (Kelley, 1994).

A CASE IN POINT
A Few Color-Related Idioms in Several Languages

In English and Serbian people may say that they "feel blue," which stands for sadness. In Portuguese, "everything is blue" stands for "everything is well." However, if a German is "blue," this person is intoxicated. In contrast, in Arabic, having a "blue day" may stand for having a bad day. In Russian, if you called a man "blue," you must have implied that he is gay. However, "blue" in Russian can be also referred to a cherished dream. In German, to "see red" means the same that it does in English. The "white lie" denotes the same in Arabic and in English. In German, distant and indefinite future is gray. The expression "rose-colored glasses" has the same meaning in Russian, German, and English. The expressions "pink elephants" and "yellow press" have the same meaning for people in New York, London, and Belgrade. People can turn "green," which indicates "being extremely angry" in many languages. Similarly, "blue blood" stands for aristocracy in dozens of tongues. "Yellow eye" stands for envy in Arabic, and "yellow smile" stands for embarrassment in Brazil. "Brown" in Russian may indicate fascist beliefs, and "gray" stands for boredom.

Information for this case was provided by Mirjana Simic, Walid Abdul-Jawad, Manal Alafrangi, Pedro DeAraujo, Fahad Malik, Makoto Tanaka, and Denitza Mantcheva.

In summary, it appears that there is a significant degree of similarity in the way color terms are used in different cultures. Verbal labels, if they are not available in the lexicon of a language, can be readily learned. Systematic formal schooling and the availability of various informational sources—such as books, television, and computers—can play a significant role in such learning.

OTHER SENSES

So far in this chapter, our attention has been directed at vision, the most systematically studied modality in cross-cultural psychology. There is significantly less information concerning other types of sensation or perceptual cross-cultural processes. Let us consider some relevant data.

Hearing

Psychology textbooks emphasize the universal nature of human auditory sensation and perception processes. Most variations in hearing are based on individual physiological differences, which are related to age, education, professional training, environmental conditions, and general experience. The most important differences are related to the meanings attached to particular sounds in different cultures. During childhood and the following periods of socialization, individuals get used to particular voices, sounds, and even noises, and subsequently interpret them according to the norms established in their culture. For more information on speech perception, see Chapters 8 and 10.

Taste

People across the world respond to four basic tastes: sweet, sour, bitter, and salty. It has been shown that individuals of different ethnic groups vary only insignificantly in their ability to detect these four primary tastes. However, as might be expected, there are tremendous cross-cultural variations in taste preferences and beliefs about basic flavors (Laing et al., 1993). For example, people in the regions closer to the equator generally prefer spicier foods, compared with their counterparts living farther to the north or south. Therefore, Italians will likely consider Scandinavian cuisine as dull, whereas many people in Sweden or Denmark will refer to Lebanese food as spicy. Across the globe, human beings have learned to avoid rotten or spoiled foods. Tastes associated with such products are typically described as very unpleasant. However, because of certain customary food practices passed on from one generation to the next, people in various parts of the world eat and enjoy a wide range of decayed or fermented foods (Rozin & Fallon, 1987). The smell and taste of such products tend to be extremely unpleasant to individuals unfamiliar with them. However, for those people who have eaten these foods since childhood, because of the adaptation process, their taste and smell are enjoyable. As an example, cheese is liked in many parts of the world. However, people who primarily eat cheese produced out of cow milk are likely to find cheeses made out of goat milk objectionable. Yogurt as a fermented milk product is widely consumed in some parts of the world. Don't ask people who are not familiar with yogurt to try it: Only few would dare. Many people in China enjoy decayed eggs. Would you try one if you are not from China? Can you come up with other examples? We will get back to the topic of taste perception when we analyze hunger in Chapter 7.

Smell

Even though researchers today understand the physiology of the olfactory sense, our knowledge about how smell affects behavior is very limited. There are data suggesting that exposure to a substance (underarm secretion) may affect the menstrual cycle in women (Cutler et al., 1986). In another study, investigators examined the positive impact on safe driving of having a pleasant odor in the car (Baron & Kalsher, 1996). However, data on cross-cultural variations in olfactory perception are mostly anecdotal and focus mainly on cross-cultural differences in odor preferences and prevailing odors.

Touch

The sense of touch is a combination of at least three qualities: pressure, temperature, and pain. The last one has received the most attention from cross-cultural psychologists. Many individual and situational characteristics (e.g., skin texture, age, social status, presence or absence of other people, and level of individual motivation) can determine perception of pain. Passively experienced anxiety can increase pain. Fear, anger, or stress can inhibit it. Love and pride can cause some people to hide even the most excruciating pain.

    Some specific cultural norms and expectations influence people's experience of pain (Morse & Park, 1988). For example, subjective reports of labor pain are lower in societies where childbirth is not considered to be a defiling event and where little help or comfort is offered to women in labor. Differences in the ability to endure pain are often a function of the circumstances in which the perception of pain is occurring. People exposed to harsh living and working conditions may become more stoical and less susceptible to pain than those who live and work in comfortable conditions (Clark & Clark, 1980). People without adequate access to health care may use a higher threshold to define unbearable pain, compared with those with guaranteed medical care (Halonen & Santrock, 1995).

    Across cultures, people appear to place a high value on clothing previously worn by loved ones. Touching (and often wearing) a loved person's garments is commonly accompanied with positive emotional experiences. However, people in most circumstances tend not to touch objects worn by a stranger, especially if these clothes contain body residues such as hair or moisture (Rozin & Fallon, 1987). Proprioceptive sense helps people register body position and movement. Individual variations in our ability to detect and then coordinate body position can be

CROSS-CULTURAL SENSITIVITY

A Massachusetts training police officer in an interview with a local newspaper, the *Cambridge Chronicle*, suggested that members of ethnic groups accustomed to eating spicy foods are less susceptible to the use of pepper spray against them. Members of ethnic groups who have consumed cayenne peppers from the time they were small children, the officer explained, might have a greater resistance to the spray. Among these "high-resistance-to-pepper-spray" groups are Mexican Americans, Pakistanis, and members of Louisiana's Cajun population. Fortunately, the Cambridge police commissioner later corrected his subordinate and said that there is no scientific evidence to support any statements about the pepper spray susceptibility of certain ethnic groups (Police Apologize for Spice Remark. *Reuters*, August 16, 1999). Medical studies have shown that any person's single exposure to pepper spray causes immediate changes in mechanical and chemical sensitivity of the eye that persist for a week (Vesaluoma et al., 2000).

significant. The evidence of cultural differences and similarities is mostly anecdotal. Some well-known facts about a few Romanians who are good in gymnastics, some Russians who are superb in ballet, and certain East Asians who are excellent in martial arts should not encourage anyone to make any valid generalizations.

Nothing really belongs to us but time, which even he has who has nothing else.

BALTASAR GRACIAN (1601–1658)—Spanish Writer and Jesuit Priest

PERCEPTION OF TIME

Talk to several people who have traveled or lived abroad. They could tell you how people in different cultures perceive and treat time guidelines. One of our colleagues from the Caribbean recently said that on his island people are generally not in a hurry compared with people from the United States, who usually are. Indeed, it is believed that Westerners tend to define punctuality using precise measures of time: 1 minute, 15 minutes, an hour, and so forth. In other cultures, time can be measured by significantly longer intervals (Hall, 1959). These days, however, information technology is making our time perception more uniform.

In other studies published over an extended period (Abou-Hatab, 1997; Meleis, 1982), researchers paid attention to this interesting aspect of Arab culture: its less-structured time orientation than one developed in most individuals in Western cultures. For example, individuals of Arab descent in traditional settings may display a tendency to be more interested in and focused on events or circumstances that are present or occur "now" and may pay less attention to those expected or scheduled to happen sometime in the future. Some studies suggest that this tendency in perception of time may have an impact on how patients or clients of Arab descent perceive their tasks during therapy. Some of them may need extra effort from the therapist to accept a particular timetable for behavioral or cognitive changes (Erickson & Al-Timimi, 2001). It is also important, though, to be cautious and not overgeneralize: Being Arab or Arab American does not mean to have a certain predetermined perception of time that is different from other people's perception.

There are different ways of arranging time in a definite order known as calendars. Most people on earth use the Gregorian calendar, which has religious origin and, since its adoption in the sixteenth century, counts years since the incarnation of Jesus. Other major religions also have their own calendars. The first year of the Islamic calendar, for example, is the year when Mohammed moved from Mecca to Medina. In North Korea today, the official calendar starts on the birthday of the late communist leader Kim Il-sung in 1912. The official calendar of Taiwan also starts in 1912, the year of the founding of the Republic of China.

Akbar (1991), who compared perceptions of time in European American and African cultures, also acknowledged the Westerners' emphasis on precise measurement of time. He suggested that time in the European and North American cultures is treated as a commodity or product that can be bought and sold as any other item for consumption, whereas in the African system, time is not viewed as a commodity.

The African time concept is very elastic and includes events that have already taken place, those that are taking place right now, and even those that will happen. Time can be experienced through one's own individual life and through the life of the tribe to which each individual belongs (Nobles, 1991). In Swahili—the language widely used in Eastern and Central Africa—two words indicate time: *sasa* and *zamani*. The first word stands for the present and generates a sense of immediacy. The second one indicates the past, but not merely as a "warehouse" of time. It is also a connector of individual souls. Most African peoples perceived human history in the natural rhythm of moving from *sasa* to *zamani*. The life cycle is renewable. After physical death, as long as a person is remembered by relatives and friends who knew her, this person would continue to exist in the *sasa* dimension. When the last person who knew the deceased also dies, that means the end for that individual.

Hamermesh (2003) conducted a cross-cultural analysis of affluent people in the United States, Germany, Australia, Canada, and South Korea. Hamermesh discovered that across cultures, people express dissatisfaction about the lack of time they experience as their incomes rise. As people's wealth increases, so do the number of opportunities available to them. As this demand increases, however, the "supply" of time does not grow. Therefore, time becomes more valuable, and people become increasingly frustrated about the lack of it.

Did you know that age and aging might be related to an individual's perspective of time, at least in people of the industrial world? In turn, this changing individual time perspective may impact many other personal attitudes (Cutler, 1975). Perhaps for most people, in early childhood, the dominant perception is that time is limitless. Early adulthood brings the realization that time is a scarce resource. Middle age and later stages lead to the perception that time becomes seriously limited. As Gergen and Black (1965) pointed out, orientations toward problem solving in international politics are substantially related to one's psychological perception of personal future time: Older politicians may be in a "hurry" to resolve conflicts. Renshon (1989) also argued that in the arts, the phenomenon of late-age creativity and boldness occurs relatively often. The last works of Shakespeare, Rembrandt, Verdi, Beethoven, Tolstoy, and Picasso all suggest that the final stages of the life cycle often bring release from conventional concerns and free artists to make major creative statements that represent a culmination of their vision.

Various authors have reported about a seemingly cross-cultural tendency: People notice an apparent accelerating of self-reflected time flow experienced with age. In diaries, self-observations, personal recollections, and other sources, many older people notice that time runs faster now than it did when they were younger. These observations, however, are subjective and were not verified in experiments. Laboratory studies that measured the impact of age on perception of time intervals, however, were few and inconsistent in their results (Wearden et al., 1997).

Culture opens the sense of beauty.

RALPH WALDO EMERSON (1803–1882)—American Poet and Philosopher

---

Beauty is nothing other than the promise of happiness.

STENDAHL (1783–1842)—French Novelist

PERCEPTION OF THE BEAUTIFUL

The song "Let It Be" performed by the Beatles or a Mexican folk song, a dress designed by Versace or a Peruvian picturesque poncho, a Persian rug or a Nigerian ivory statuette, the Taj Mahal mausoleum or a Chinese porcelain vase—these creations can be enjoyed by anyone and everyone on the planet. The term **aesthetic experience**, or perception of the beautiful, is used to identify the feeling of pleasure evoked by stimuli that are perceived as nice, attractive, or rewarding. Researchers suggest that aesthetic responses are underpinned by the amount of corti-cal arousal produced by some stimuli in the brain (Berlyne, 1960, 1974). People seek certain stimuli because the activity of dealing with them is pleasant. Others consider aesthetic apprecia-tion as curiosity and stimulus-seeking activities (see Chapter 7 on intrinsic motivation). Berlyne (1971) found that the characteristics of a stimulus that generally evoke curiosity, joy, and appre-ciation are those such as novelty, ambiguity, incongruity, and complexity.

Several common perceptual mechanisms lead to similarities across cultures in aesthetic appreciation. For example, there are empirical studies in which subjects from different cultures displayed similarities in their evaluation of different works of art, primarily paintings (Child, 1969). Many similarities in perception and appreciation of beauty were found in different cul-tural groups despite socioeconomic differences among them (Berlyne, 1974; Ross, 1977). For instance, in a survey conducted by Nasar (1984), both Japanese and U.S. subjects were asked to evaluate videotapes and slides of urban street scenes in each country. An examination of pref-erence scores revealed that both groups preferred foreign scenes to native ones, as well as the scenes of orderly and clean streets with very few vehicles on them.

Beware though. There are tremendous inconsistencies in how people see and interpret both beautiful and ugly creations. For instance, in the history of Western painting, impressionism as a new artistic genre was publicly ridiculed and rejected. Many years later it became an internation-ally acclaimed style and collectors began to pay huge sums of money for impressionist paintings. When the Eiffel tower was first erected in Paris, many people condemned this grandiose land-mark and considered it ugly. Today, who can imagine Paris without the Eiffel tower?

What is considered tasteful and beautiful is not confined within geographic regions or among particular ethnic groups. Many national patterns become international, captivating the minds and influencing the behavior of millions of people. To illustrate, consider *kawaii*, a Japanese artistic style of design. Rooted in the celebration of youthfulness and cuteness, conveyed by neat stories and playful designs of bright colors, *kawaii* has become popular outside of Japan and can even be seen influencing street fashion in Europe, the United States, and many other countries. Another Japanese school of flower arrangement called *ikebana* has received wide international acclaim and found scores of followers around the world (Faiola, 2003).

Cultural aesthetic standards can be numerous and widely defined; they can also be lim-ited in appearance and narrowly defined. For example, in the countries in which governments

CRITICAL THINKING
As Beautiful as... Your Money Can Buy

Beautiful things sell. Art collectors and art dealers around the world know this well. Today many classical paintings change hands, not for thousands, but millions of dollars! However, does the price tag on a painting or sculpture determine how beautiful the creation is? Why are the smallest paintings by Cezanne or pencil sketches by Leonardo almost priceless, whereas a beautiful original colorful landscape could be purchased for €20 from a street artist in Rome? Do you agree that sometimes people first assign and attach value to particular pieces of art and only then do they begin to evaluate this object from the standpoint of aesthetic perception? If a sculpture is considered "famous" or a song "popular" by most members of our society, are we likely to consider the sculpture as "beautiful" and the song as "nice"? Do you think that our evaluation of a song, painting, fashion style, or dance changes according to how well or how poorly it is advertised or promoted?

or ideological institutions control the media, and therefore restrain the free flow of information, such standards of beauty and ugliness are typically precisely defined. Because of the lack of available information, scarcity of products, and ideological pressures, people's choices are limited and certain items—clothing, music, or even hairstyles, for example—quickly become dominant (Sears et al., 2003; Shiraev & Bastrykin, 1988).

PERCEPTION OF MUSIC

The traditional music of different cultures may fluctuate in notion and harmony. For instance, conventional Western harmony is different from Japanese and Indian styles (Sadie, 1980). In many non-Western traditions, the idea of the note as a stable, sustained pitch is foreign. Some Indian and Japanese musical intervals—or tonal dyads differing only slightly in frequency ratio—are perceived as extreme dissonance in the West and are usually avoided by composers and musicians. However, these intervals appear to be beautiful and are used freely in the classic music of these two countries (Maher, 1976).

Contemporary Western music notation reflects the underlying general perception of beauty developed in Western culture. Perceptual problems that can cause displeasure in the Western listener—born and raised in Sweden, Italy, or Ukraine—may occur because of the different scales, intervals, and rhythmic patterns used in Western and non-Western music. In non-Western cultures—for example, in Middle Eastern Islamic countries—classical music for the most part is not written down in advance, as is the practice in Europe and America. Notwithstanding the fact that written notations are found in many cultures around the world, in many non-Western countries, classical music is usually improvised on frameworklike patterns. In fact, in these societies many types of music exist mostly in performance. One should not exaggerate, nevertheless, cultural differences in musical perception. Contemporary mass media, global trade, and interpersonal contacts provide unique opportunity for many people to learn, understand, and appreciate different musical styles.

Let us make some preliminary conclusions. As we have learned, most psychologists share the contemporary belief that sensory differences among cultures are insignificant and their impact on human behavior is minimal. In general, the universal similarity in the anatomy and physiology of human sensory organs and the nervous system seems to suggest that sensory impressions and their transmission through the perceptual system are basically the same across cultures. Despite similarities, however, people may see beautiful and ugly things differently, and there is a substantial weight of cultural factors in our aesthetic perception.

Most of the time, healthy adults are aware of their sensations and perceptions. A street vendor in Spain or a teacher in Pakistan can describe what they see or hear and are able to separate the "objective" reality from thoughts about it. No matter what we do, either paying careful attention to some events or **daydreaming** about others, we are aware of our subjective experiences.

The ultimate gift of conscious life is a sense of mystery that encompasses it.
LEWIS MUMFORD—Twentieth-Century U.S. Historian and Critic

Suffering is the sole origin of consciousness.
FYODOR DOSTOYEVSKY (1821–1881)—Russian Novelist

CONSCIOUSNESS AND CULTURE

Culture is an inseparable attribute of human **consciousness**—the subjective awareness of one's own sensations, perceptions, and other mental events. It is a process that has several stages or states. The "normal" flow of consciousness may consist of periods of full attention and concentration or relative detachment from the outside events. Periods of wakefulness are altered by periods of sleep. Under various circumstances, the normal flow of consciousness can be altered by meditation, psychoactive substances, trance, or hypnotic suggestion. However, the very concept of consciousness is elusive, thus making its cross-cultural examination particularly difficult.

From the dawn of scientific exploration of mental life, ancient thinkers were aware of consciousness. Major ideas about human consciousness were developed within the Christian, Muslim, Jewish, Hindu, Buddhist, and other theological schools of thought (Smith, 1991). They developed fundamental ideas about the soul as immortal, divine, and separable from the body. With further development of philosophy and science, two types of fundamental views on consciousness were established. One view was held by the monists, who believed in the inseparability of the body and soul. The second view was held by the dualists, who recognized an independent existence of body and soul. Both philosophical platforms still affect many people's personal views on consciousness.

The idea of individual consciousness as dependent on socialization experiences and other cultural factors was developed throughout the twentieth century by a number of psychologists (Piaget, 1963; Vygotsky, 1932; Wundt, 1913). According to psychological anthropologist Hallowell (1955), people live within a **behavioral environment**, a mental representation of time, space, and the interpersonal world. Specific cultural beliefs and practices shape the individual's behavioral environment. For example, among the Ojibwa Indians studied by Hallowell, their behavioral environment included the self, other people, their gods, existing relatives, and deceased ancestors. Thus, when considering an action with moral consequences, the Ojibwa take into account possible impacts of the action on spirits and relatives.

Consciousness directs human behavior in ways that are adaptive in particular physical and social environments. People tend to focus on things that are important for survival or the accomplishment of a goal. A motorist in New York will definitely pay attention to traffic reports on the car radio, whereas his guest from South Africa may not attend to them at all. Consciousness devotes extra cognitive resources to information that may be particularly meaningful for individual adaptation. For instance, the contents of the consciousness of Ifaluk, a people of Micronesia in the Pacific Ocean, reflect the way their culture structures reality: People are aware of their immediate location at all times because life depends on successful navigation of the surrounding ocean (Lutz, 1982).

There are popular opinions about the main attributes of Western consciousness as being linear, pragmatic, and rational (Jackson, 1991). If this is the case, these elements of consciousness should be overwhelmingly present in various forms of Western art. If consciousness is rational, it should be reflected in "rational" forms of artistic expression. However, the history of Western art (literature and painting, for example) shows numerous examples of nonlinear, mystical, multidimensional, and irrational views reflected by the writer's pen or the artist's paintbrush. Existentialism and symbolism in literature, cubism and primitivism in painting, and modernism in music are all examples of irrational and nonlinear perception and reflection of reality by Western artists. Perhaps one of the best illustrations of a nonlinear perception of life is the literary world of Gabriel García Marquez, one of the most significant writers of the twentieth century. A Colombian native, he spent most of his life in Mexico and Europe as a journalist and writer. Take, for example, his most famous novel, *One Hundred Years of Solitude*. The main characters in the book live within several time dimensions. It seems that they are not concerned with time at all. Occasionally, the past is diminished into a single moment, and then the future becomes present and twisted in a mysterious way. The dead return home, and those who are alive disappear in the skies without a trace. Consciousness becomes circular and brings back memories and transfers individuals in time and space. Analyzing Marquez's work, one can find elements of Catholic religious doctrine, Spanish cultural tradition, and Native Indian beliefs. Perhaps such a mixture of different influences reflected in the author's mind and in his literary works reveals many fascinating aspects of human consciousness. Please read *One Hundred Years of Solitude* by Marquez. Will you find it difficult to confine human consciousness within the simplistic boundaries of Western or non-Western labels?

Sleeping is no mean art: For its sake one must stay awake all day.

FRIEDRICH NIETZSCHE **(1844–1900)—German Philosopher**

In the drowsy dark cave of the mind dreams build their nest with fragments dropped from day's caravan.

RABINDRANATH TAGORE **(1861–1941)—Bengali Poet and Novelist**

SLEEP AND CULTURAL SIGNIFICANCE OF DREAMS

At this moment, about a third of the world population is sleeping. **Sleep** is a nonwaking state of consciousness characterized by general unresponsiveness to the environment and general physical immobility.

During sleep, responsiveness to external, and particularly visual, stimulation is diminished, but it is not entirely absent (Antrobus, 1991). There are tremendous individual variations in how "wakeful" we are when sleeping. In addition, cultural practices, sleeping arrangements, and general environmental conditions can influence people's responsiveness to external stimulation during sleep. There are also significant individual variations in terms of duration of sleep. In every country around the world, some individuals sleep for five or six hours, whereas others need nine or ten hours. Duration of sleep may vary from culture to culture. As an illustration, in a study of the sleep–wakefulness cycle in Mexican adults, Taub (1971) found that the average duration of sleep in Mexican subjects was longer than in other Western countries.

Since the dawn of their existence, humans have wondered about both the nature and significance of **dreams**, storylike sequences of images occurring during sleep. McManus and coauthors (1993) make a distinction between two types of cultures in terms of their interpretation of dreams. *Monophasic* cultures value cognitive experiences that take place only during normal waking phases and do not incorporate dreams into the process of social perception and cognition. Dreams are regarded as indirect indications of the dreamer's concerns, fears, and desires (Bourguignon, 1954). *Polyphasic* cultures value dreams and treat them as part of reality. The first type of culture is typically associated with a materialistic worldview on psychological experience. The second type of culture is associated with the spiritual or traditional view.

For many years, people considered dreams as experiences accumulated by the dreamer's traveling soul or revelations conveyed to the dreaming individual from the spiritual world. This polyphasic view on dreams can be found in contemporary cultural groups. Moss (1996) describes several core elements in the traditional dream practice of Iroquois, a Native American tribe. Dreams are perceived as flights of the soul, which leaves the body and travels in space and time. Therefore, dreams are real events and should be taken literally. Dreams demand action because they indicate something that the person has failed to perform while awake. For Iroquois, dreams also yield information about future events. Similarly, Araucanos in Chile believe that dreams help to communicate with other people and are related to future events (Krippner, 1996). Among many native peoples in Australia, it is believed that one can travel in his or her dreams for particular purposes. Among some African tribes there is a conviction that both the living and deceased relatives can communicate with the dreamer. Dreams can be transmitted from one person to another, and some people can do so with malicious purposes. Some Zambian shamans imply they can diagnose a patient's illness through information contained in that person's dreams (Bynum, 1993).

Traditional psychological theories of dream interpretation—including psychoanalysis—pay most attention to the latent, hidden content of dreams. Usually therapists would try to interpret the meaning of the dream, something that is not obvious to the dream-teller, who is actually a person who receives psychological counseling. Less attention in most Western therapies is given to the manifest content, that is, to the sequence of events reported by the dream-teller. In polyphasic cultures, people typically consider dreams as a source of individual guidance; dreams are readily shared with others and their meanings discussed (Murray, 1999). Studies of dream interpretations in traditional societies show that the actual content of the dream—the story told by the person—is often interpreted literally by individuals and may serve as an important process that initiates adaptive behaviors (Pratt, 2000).

Contemporary science develops several views on the nature of human dreams. Some physiologists, for example, suggest that dreams have no hidden psychological meaning (Crick & Mitchison, 1983). Others theories suggest (Hobson, 2002) that during this altered state of consciousness, the brain stem is activating itself internally. This activation does not contain any ideas, emotions, wishes, or fears. The forebrain produces dream imagery from "noisy" signals sent to it from the brain stem. As this activation is transmitted through the thalamus to the visual and association zones of the cerebral cortex, the individual tries to make sense of it. Because the initial signals are essentially random in nature, the interpretations proposed by the cortex rarely make complete logical sense. However, the issues most relevant to the individual enter dreams in some way because the incoming signals are compared with the dreamer's existing knowledge and attitudes (Cartwright, 1992; Foulkes, 1985). In other words, experiences should influence our dreams (Kern & Roll, 2001).

A study of a sample of Zulu South Africans (aged 25–92 years) showed substantial differences between urban and rural subjects. Less educated and less affluent individuals from the country tended to consult with dream interpreters and act in response to dreams much more often than the urban participants. Moreover, subjects with less education were more likely than others to report the specific impact of dreams on their lives. More older, rather than younger, respondents experienced dreams as a direct communication with ancestors and were more likely than others to respond to dreams with prayer and rituals (Thwala et al., 2000).

Despite significant differences in the manifest content of dreams (i.e., the actual content of the recalled dream), the latent content (the dream's meaning) is believed to be cross-culturally comparable. The similarities in the way people describe the content of their dreams were demonstrated in an early Japanese–U.S. study (Griffith et al., 1958). Students in both groups reported having dreams about falling, eating, swimming, death, snakes, finding money, examinations, being unable to move, and various sexual experiences.

Dream scenarios are personal, but they are enacted within the stage set by the dreamer's sociocultural reality (Roll et al., 1976). Take, for example, a study in which the dreams of more than 200 Finnish and Palestinian children were compared (Punamaki & Joustie, 1998). Half the subjects were selected from working-class and middle-class Finnish suburbia and half were taken from two areas in the Middle East. One represented the Gaza Strip, an area with frequent military confrontations. The other area was not known for any violent outbursts. Children in both groups were asked to report their dreams daily during a seven-day period. The recorded dreams were content analyzed. It was found that life in a violent environment was linked to a greater extent to dream content than the culture and other personal factors. The Palestinian children who lived in the violent social environment reported having predominantly intensive and vivid dreams, which incorporated aggression and persecution as main themes, more often than the other children studied did. It was also found that in Arab children's dreams there were predominantly external scenes of anxiety that typically involved fear. In Finnish children, dreams contained anxiety scenes that involved mostly guilt and shame. The authors interpreted the results by referring to social and cultural conditions in the studied samples. The Finnish society is considered to be more individualistic than the Palestinian society and therefore more oriented toward the experiences directed into individuals themselves. The Finnish children are less interdependent than Arab children. Also, according to the established cultural traditions, the Finnish understanding of dreaming is based predominantly on Freudian influences that emphasize the importance of individual psychological reality. According to the Arab tradition, dreaming is mainly understood as an external message from forces to guide the dreamer.

Keep in mind one important difference between these two cultures. Finland is an economically advanced and democratic European country with one of the highest incomes per capita in the world. Palestinian people for many years have experienced poverty and injustice and have suffered from constant struggles between various political groups for power. It is plausible to propose that everyday stressful experiences can contribute to dream content.

Specialists in Turkish folklore identify a typical theme in dreams reported by males: the quest, both physical and spiritual, for the most gorgeous and beautiful woman in the world. According to one explanation (Walker, 1993), this preoccupation may be linked to the tradition of arranged marriage. According to this practice, many Turkish men cannot see their brides before the time of the wedding. This emotional deprivation creates a state of secret admiration and fascination of the future wife. Another explanation, however, can be offered: Because the relatives of the bride and groom commonly arrange many Turkish marriages, most men's relationships with women lack the important elements of romanticism and adventure. As a result, men "compensate" in their dreams for this missing romantic activity and experience.

Tedlock (1987) suggested that people's reports about their dreams include more than the dream report. She also wrote that what one tells about a dream is based on a particular cultural concept of the dream and culturally sanctioned ways of sharing dream content. Using particular rules of communication, we may report some elements of our dream and delete others. In short, our culture may change our experience of dreams, and therefore our dreams are loaded with cultural elements that include not only dream content but also the ways in which dreams are communicated (Ullman & Zimmerman, 1979).

Imagine now somebody from a different country is sharing with you a recent dream. Can you interpret its contents? Some people claim that they can interpret any dream right after hearing it. You have to doubt the validity of such propositions. Besides hidden psychological factors, there are numerous contextual influences that affect not only the dream but also the way it is recalled, shared, and interpreted. These are some questions that you perhaps have to ask when

CRITICAL THINKING
Can Dreams Predict Anything?

There are popular stories about famous discoveries taking place during sleep. The famous benzene ring and the periodic system of chemical elements were allegedly "discovered" by their authors when they were dreaming. In many famous fairy tales, literary works, and film creations, heroes and heroines read important life forecasts in their sleep. We all know that in every country, there are people who believe that dreams can predict the future or may be considered an omen of something to come. It is a belief in Turkey that if one discloses a dream about receiving a favor before the favor is offered, then the event foretold in the dream may end in disaster (Walker & Uysal, 1990). A popular Russian calendar of dreams predicted that a tooth lost in one's dream should mean a misfortune for this person in the future. Around the world, books are written and manuals published on how to interpret each particular

dream. Why do so many people maintain such an attitude toward dreams? We have to take into consideration how powerful people's superstitions are as regulators of behavior. We follow them often without a conscious attempt to think critically. Meanwhile, some dreams may be rationalized. Imagine a person has a dream about a car accident. When the dream content does not coincide with an actual car accident the day after the dream, the content of the dream can be easily forgotten. If an accident really happens, he or she is likely to refer to the dream: "I knew this was going to happen." Similarly, when dream content coincides with a conscious attitude, we tend to hold an opinion about the possible motivational power of dreams. In general, knowledge about dreams and critical thinking abilities can diminish an individual's dependency on dreams as predictors of the future.

you listen to someone's dream. What motivates the person to recall and tell a dream? (Is it a teacher's assignment, your request, or a spontaneous conversation?) Under what circumstances is the dream recalled? Who is present during the dream recollection? What is the relationship between the dream-teller and the listener? How is dreaming understood in the teller's culture? How is dreaming understood in the listener's culture? What meaning do certain dream symbols carry in the studied culture?

No matter how psychologists explain dreams, researchers can provide plenty of interesting facts about the interaction between culture and the psychological experiences of dreams (Roll, 1987). Dreams not only reflect our private world of hopes, fears, and concerns but also mirror the environment in which people live.

The supernatural is the natural not yet understood.

Elbert Hubbard (1856–1915)—American Author

BEYOND ALTERED STATES OF CONSCIOUSNESS

Altered states of consciousness (ASC) is the general name for phenomena that are different from normal waking consciousness and include mystic perceptual and sensory experiences, such as meditation, hypnosis, trance, and possession (Ward, 1994). Like Cinderella in the famous fairy tale—a neglected outcast daughter in her stepmother's family—ASC for many years were not highly regarded by Western academic psychologists. The rapid development of empirical research based on the pragmatism and positivism of European science coupled with the skepticism encouraged by the Enlightenment era contributed to the lack of scholarly attention to ASC. Under the influence of the Protestant tradition and in Western Europe, ASC is considered mostly as abnormal phenomena linked in some cases to mental illness (Warner, 1994).

Meanwhile, ASC is a widely reported phenomenon across the globe. The different forms of ASC are identified in the majority of societies and may be viewed as a special form of human experience (Laughlin et al., 1992; Ward, 1994). Let us consider several kinds of alternative states of consciousness.

Trance is a sleeplike state marked by reduced sensitivity to stimuli, loss or alteration of knowledge, and automatic motor activity. Trances are often induced by external sources, such as music, singing, and direct suggestion from another person. Trances may provide a sense of protection, wisdom, and greatness. For the group, it can provide a sense of togetherness and unity. Mass religious ceremonies, collective prayers, rock concerts, political gatherings, and other collective actions can induce a trance in the participants. There is a difference between a visionary trance, when a person is experiencing hallucinations, and a possession trance, when a person reports that his body is invaded or captured by a spirit or several spirits. The possession experience is usually, but not always, recalled with fear and hesitation because of its traumatic significance. Trancelike and possession experiences are described as parts of religious practices in many cultures (Bourguignon, 1976; Rosen, 1968). According to one survey, visionary or possession trance states were reported in 90 percent of the countries in a large world sample (Bourguignon, 1994).

Several religious groups consider trances as part of their regular religious experience (Taves, 1999). Incidences of visionary trances are more common among men than in women and in hunter–gatherer societies. Possession trance is more typical among women and those who are not from hunter–gatherer cultures (Bourguignon, 1976; Gussler, 1973; Lee & Ackerman, 1980). Some psychologists develop a view that many shamanic practices involving ritualistic trance affect the brain's serotonin and opioid neurotransmitter systems—all affecting an individual's emotional states, behavioral responses, and even the belief system (Winkelman, 2000). The same way as Prozac or Xanax (alprazolam) can change mood and anxiety manifestations, many shamanic practices affect other people's experiences. However, many of these individuals are not aware of this effect and continue to believe that shamans are capable of supernatural or magic healing. Many cultural groups today continue to practice self-induced trance as a form of "purification" from evil and emotional healing. For example, some Jewish groups in the Middle East practice Stambali—a trance-inducing ritual used for the promotion of personal well-being and as a form of crisis intervention (Somer & Saadon, 2000).

There have been attempts to evoke trance states and similar experiences in laboratory settings. Neurophysiologist Michael Persinger conducted one of the most significant studies on this topic. The subjects in this study reported trance experiences when the temporal lobes in their brains were stimulated artificially with a weak magnetic field. Specifically, they reported feelings of great and "eternal" presence, omnipotence, serenity, and wisdom. According to a theory, trance is associated with the release of opiates in the body, which induces a temporary state of elation, euphoria, and excitement (Persinger, 2003). Such experiences are interpreted in a variety of ways ranging from "divine" to "weird." These interpretations are contingent on the context in which the trance takes place, as well as the cultural background of those experiencing it: Religious subjects would talk about spiritual experiences, while skeptics would mention sensory disturbances.

Possession is explained better when it is evaluated simultaneously from the observer's standpoint, the victim's point of view, and the perspective of the community at large (Lee &

Ackerman, 1980). In this context, there are several scientific explanations related to the previous case and other similar episodes of "demonic possession." One explanation appeals to the stress accumulated by victims from job dissatisfaction, work conflicts, and economic hardship. Individuals who claim possession are provided with culturally acceptable outlets for their previously restrained frustration (Halperin, 1996).

Beliefs about possession are also documented in many Slavic, German, and Scandinavian folk tales. In Morocco, as in many other Islamic countries, folk beliefs about possession include the concept of demons or *jinni*. These demons like wetness and prefer to live near water, under old trees, in washrooms, in old ruins, as well as in cemeteries and waste dumps. If disturbed, these creatures get enraged, possess someone's body, and take revenge on this person's psyche. Many individuals who experienced symptoms of possession say they can identify the time and the place in which the possession took place. Some claim to have stepped on a demon while walking in the garden at night. Others believe they disturbed a demon who lived in the bathroom pipes or in nearby bushes.

Similar beliefs in demonic possession as the cause of particular mental disorders are found among people in many cultural and religious groups. The best-selling novel by William Peter Blatty (known to most people as *The Exorcist*, in a Hollywood movie version) is a literary case of a wealthy mother in the United States who, unable to find effective medical treatment for a child who suffers from severe and disturbing psychological symptoms including possession trance, turns to religious healers (see Exercise 4.2).

In 2005, a Romanian monk and four other people were charged in the death of a 23-year-old nun during an apparent exorcism. The woman was allegedly left without food for three days and died due to dehydration, exhaustion, and lack of oxygen. The monk, who belongs to the Orthodox branch of the church, reportedly explained that his actions were an attempt to rid the woman of the devil inside her.

Contemporary Korean shamanism called *musok* continues to flourish in a modern-day society of electronic devices and instant communication. In South Korea, such direct communication also extends to multitudes of gods and spirits. Several hundred thousands of

A CASE IN POINT

Mass Hysteria and Possession as Altered States of Consciousness

Lee and Ackerman (1980) documented and analyzed an interesting case of mass possession at a small college in West Malaysia. The incident involved several, mostly female, students who manifested various physical symptoms and bizarre behaviors, such as difficulty breathing, convulsive muscular contractions, and screaming. The victims were oblivious of their surroundings, went through dance frenzies, reported demonic possessions, and complained about seeing strange creatures. The possessed claimed that they became other beings, because of the spirits that had taken over the body. *Bomohs* or traditional Malai healers were called to help. They treated the possessed individuals by sprinkling them with holy water, sacrificing a small animal in an attempt to pacify the offended spirits, and giving victims talismans to protect them from evil spirits. Notably, when the healers confirmed the existence of spirits in the victims' bodies, it provoked further incidents of possession. Moreover, most people in the area believed that the symptoms of this altered state of consciousness were contagious.

professional mediators, mostly women called *manshin*, help with these contacts and perform possession–trance techniques (Sarfati, 2010).

Nowhere can man find a quieter or more untroubled retreat than his own soul.
                          MARCUS AURELIUS (112–180)—**Roman Emperor and Stoic Philosopher**

Meditation is a quiet and relaxed state of tranquility in which a person achieves an integration of thoughts, perceptions, and attitudes. Usually, this state is attained with the cooperation of a special principle or belief. People who meditate often describe their experience as leading to liberation from the self or an expansion of conscious awareness. In Buddhism, for example, it is believed that meditation leads to a deepened and clearer understanding of reality (Ornstein, 1977). During meditation, a special state of consciousness can be achieved in which obstacles of private desire are completely consumed.

Meditation can be highly therapeutic because it might reduce stress (Collings, 1989). Contrary to contemporary scientific principles of psychotherapy, which require control over the outcome of one's actions, in many types of meditation principles of detachment from others are valued. A meditating person withdraws the senses from objects of pleasure or hardship. If the complete state of detachment is reached, then the individual is able to feel tranquility, serenity, and love. Those trained in detachment are far less subject to the stresses and strains of life, compared with people who do not practice meditation.

The contemporary psychological evidence suggests that the most fundamental mechanisms of sensation, perception, and the main states of consciousness, including both the normal flow of consciousness and its altered states, are universal across cultures. In all, the important differences are primarily concerned with the specific content of these experiences and the ways people process information according to both overt rules and covert practices of their countries and communities. With the development of technologies and human interaction, different human experiences are rapidly learned by various cultural groups through television, movies, art, the Internet, interpersonal contacts, and many other forms of communication. People learn more about each other by revealing their dreams and religious experiences and through understanding different mental realities. Still, we know little about our diverse cognitive world and the cultural backgrounds underlying it. Studies continue.

Exercise 4.1

A Cross-Cultural Psychoanalytic Interpretation of Dream Content

Clarissa P. Estes (2003) in her book *Women Who Run with the Wolves* suggests that dreams may reflect complex feelings that the dreamer, in real life, is unable to discuss openly. In short, dreams release our suppressed concerns. Please read some of the author's interpretations of several common dreams. They, as Estes believes, are typical in women of all cultural and social backgrounds.

In this dream, a woman is helping an old person to cross the street. Suddenly, the old person smiles diabolically and "melts" on her arm, burning her deeply (or harms her in some other way). The dream sends a message that malevolent things are disguised as benevolent things. The woman tries to avoid threatening facts, but the dream shouts a warning to her: Stay away from somebody and be careful in your current relationships.

In the "scary dark man" dream, a frightful intruder appears in the woman's apartment or house. She can feel his presence, his breath. The woman experiences horror and helplessness. She cannot scream for help or dial an emergency number. This dark man may appear as a thief, Nazi, rapist, terrorist, and so forth. The meaning of the dream is that the woman should awaken and reconsider her life again: Something frightening is going on inside her. This is a dream of a woman who is "drying out," who is deprived of her creative function, and so far makes no effort to help herself (p. 66).

In the "injured animal" dream, a woman sees an injured or wounded animal. This dream could represent a serious violation of the woman's freedom and other basic rights. Being unable—due to cultural censorship—to understand why her rights are violated, the woman accepts this safe way of symbolic expression of her concerns. An injured animal dream appears especially often in women in cultures in which they are deprived of their rights, abused, and discriminated against (p. 276).

If a disembodied voice is heard in the dream (the voice that does not belong to a particular person or creature), this could mean that the woman's life is coming to an extreme. It could be a sign that she has "too much positive stimulation" or "too many responsibilities," and so forth. The woman is either "overloved" or "underloved" and either "overworked" or "underworked." Bottom line, she must reevaluate her current life (p. 278).

Assignment

Write your critical comments regarding each of these interpretations. Could you agree with some of these explanations? What interpretations do you disagree with? Explain why.

Exercise 4.2

Watch the classic movie **The Exorcist,** *which you can rent in any video store. Answer the following questions.*

What kind of altered states of consciousness can we recognize in the main character of the movie: visionary trance or possession trance? How did it develop?

There is a tradition found in many tribes around the world, such as in Mission Indians in California, to assign special duties of communicating with the spirit world to a medicine man (Caprio, 1943). In the movie, who was given the duty to negotiate and eventually expel the spirit from the girl's body? What did he specifically do?

Please summarize and generalize the diagnoses given to the girl by various doctors. What other cultures were mentioned in the conversations or can be seen in the movie? Try to give your opinion of why the theme of possession is still very popular among educated people.

Chapter Summary

- Our experience with the environment shapes our perception by creating perceptual expectations. These expectations, known as a perceptual set, make particular interpretations more likely to occur. They allow people to anticipate what they will encounter and, therefore, increase both the speed and efficiency of the perceptual process.

- Studies on cross-cultural differences in the perception of simple patterns showed only small variations. Cross-cultural similarities in the drawing of visual patterns suggest the presence of a common mechanism for perceptual processes. Shape constancy of perception is significantly influenced by learning experiences. Culturally specific conditions determine which skills will improve in individuals in a particular culture and which skills will remain underdeveloped.

- Psychologists offer several hypotheses that explain cultural differences in illusion susceptibility. The carpentered world hypothesis postulates a learned tendency among people raised in an environment shaped by carpenters to interpret nonrectangular figures as representations of rectangular figures seen in perspective.

- There is a strong degree of similarity in the way color terms are used in different cultures. Moreover, verbal labels, if they are not available in the lexicon of a language, can be readily learned. Education, travel, interpersonal contacts, and the media can play a significant role in the development of color recognition and labeling.

- There are perhaps common perceptual mechanisms that lead to similarities across cultures in the perception of time and in aesthetic appreciation. Many similarities in perception of the beautiful were found in different cultural groups despite apparent socioeconomic differences among them. Because the traditional music of different cultures may differ in notion and harmony, there are some cultural differences in the perception of musical harmony.

- The universal similarity in the anatomy and physiology of human sensory organs and the nervous system seems to make it likely that sensory impressions and their transmission through the perceptual system are comparable across cultures.

- Consciousness is a process that has several stages or states. The "normal" flow of consciousness may consist of periods of full attention and concentration or relative detachment from the outside events.

Periods of wakefulness are altered by periods of sleep. Under various circumstances, meditation, psychoactive substances, trances, or hypnotic suggestion can alter consciousness. The understanding of consciousness is based on general cultural views of mental life and the relationship between body and soul.

- From a cultural standpoint, the normal flow of consciousness directs our behavior in ways that are adaptive in particular physical and social environments. Individual consciousness is dependent on socialization experiences, which, in turn are based on cultural factors, collective forms of existence, or shared collective experiences. Human consciousness develops together with the development of both physical and social environments. Increasing knowledge of the world at the same time broadens consciousness.

- Both duration and patterns of sleep may vary individually and from culture to culture. Despite significant differences in the manifest content of dreams, the latent dream content is believed to be generally similar in people living in different cultures. Dreams not only reflect our private world but also mirror the environment in which we live. The dreaming individual's brain organizes and retrieves various images in a "culturally ascribed" manner.

- Phenomena such as meditation, trance, hypnosis, and near-death experiences during coma are very common in practically every culture. While analyzing them a specialist should take into consideration personal characteristics of the studied individuals, their educational level, and position within the society. Specialists should also notice that certain life circumstances can influence individual experiences. Another set of conditions is a predominant cultural attitude toward altered states of consciousness expressed in the media, people's everyday conversations, or public opinion (if data are available).

Key Terms

Absolute Threshold The minimum amount of physical energy needed for the observer to notice a stimulus.

Aesthetic Experience A term used to identify the feeling of pleasure evoked by stimuli that are perceived as beautiful, attractive, and rewarding. The term also refers to displeasure evoked by stimuli that are perceived as ugly, unattractive, and unrewarding.

Altered States of Consciousness (ASC) The general name for phenomena that are different than normal waking consciousness and include mystic experiences, meditation, hypnosis, trance, and possession.

Behavioral Environment A mental representation that orients people to dimensions such as time, space, and the interpersonal world.

Consciousness The subjective awareness of one's own sensations, perceptions, and other mental events.

Daydreaming Turning attention away from external stimuli to internal thoughts and imagined scenarios.

Depth Perception The organization of sensations in three dimensions, even though the image on the eye's retina is two dimensional.

Difference Threshold The lowest level of stimulation required to sense that a change in the stimulation has occurred.

Dreams Storylike sequences of images occurring during sleep.

Meditation A quiet and relaxed state of tranquility in which a person achieves an integration of emotions, attitudes, and thoughts.

Perception The process that organizes various sensations into meaningful patterns.

Perceptual Set Perceptual expectations based on experience.

Sensation The process by which receptor cells are stimulated and transmit their information to higher brain centers.

Sensory Adaptation The tendency of the sensory system to respond less to stimuli that continue without change.

Sleep A nonwaking state of consciousness characterized by general unresponsiveness to the environment and general physical immobility.

Trance A sleeplike state marked by reduced sensitivity to stimuli, loss or alteration of knowledge, rapturous experiences, and the substitution of automatic for voluntary motor activity.

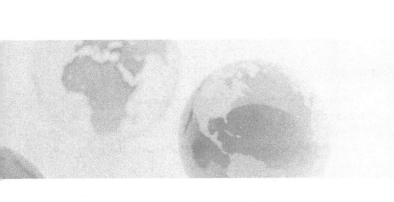

Intelligence

To learn about other people is science, to learn to know yourself is intelligence

CHINESE PROVERB

Our friend Charles Wiley—a journalist who has visited almost every country in the world—showed us a photo that he took in the People's Republic of China. We were at Charles's house, and his guests took turns staring at the photo. On the picture, there was an entrance to Jinan University in Guangzhou. The large sign at the entrance read (as Charles translated to us): "Be loyal to the country, be faithful to your friends, persevere with your mission, be respectful to your parents and teachers." "You see," said one of the guests. "This is why the Chinese have such great test scores. They learn about discipline and hard work from early childhood. Look at their IQ numbers. They are ahead of everybody and it's no wonder. I wish I could send my two teenagers to China. Maybe there they would learn something useful." Everybody laughed, and the conversation quickly switched to football. Two months later, one of us—who got a copy of the photo—showed it to a colleague who was born in Beijing. "You know," he replied, "you are asking me whether loyalty and respect are prime educational and cultural values in China. I do not want to disappoint you. It looks fine on the paper but in reality things are different. Do you think that *all* people there are just puppets who do whatever the government tells them to do? Do you think that *all* people there are loyal to their friends?" "No, but we're talking about the overall relationship between self-discipline and high test scores." "Oh, self-discipline....It's family pressure," the friend replied with a mysterious smile. "You have to understand the Chinese family. Intelligence is a result of family influence."

DEFINING INTELLIGENCE

First of all, what is **intelligence**? Ask psychology professors at your college or university. If you ask 10 of them, you will receive nine different definitions. Just nine? What about the tenth teacher? (If you are asking this question now you are already revealing curiosity, an important feature of your intelligence.) The tenth professor will simply refer you to the introductory psychology textbook currently in use.

A quick glance through several introductory psychology textbooks published in the 2000s would reveal that intelligence is defined in a variety of ways. For example, intelligence may be described as a set of mental abilities; the capacity to acquire and use knowledge; problem-solving skills and knowledge about the world; the ability to excel at a variety of tasks; or as a skill that allows us to understand, adapt, learn, reason, and overcome obstacles. Which point of view should we choose? First, most definitions include the word "knowledge." Intelligence is knowing and understanding the reality. Then, most definitions draw attention to problem solving, which leads to an assumption that intelligence is a set of mental skills that helps individuals to reach goals. Intelligence is also an ability to use knowledge and skills in order to overcome obstacles. And finally, intelligence helps in the adaptation to changing conditions.

Such an inclusive understanding of intelligence can be useful for cross-cultural psychologists because it allows them to incorporate the cultural factor in the discussion of intelligence. Indeed, people live in different environments and acquire knowledge and skills necessary to pursue goals and adapt to different cultural settings.

Intelligence is also inseparable from **cognition**, a diversified process by which the individual acquires and applies knowledge. It usually includes processes such as recognition, categorization, thinking, and memory.

There are several scientific approaches to intelligence. Let us consider them briefly, using the previous vignette as a starting point for discussion.

Some researchers, especially during the earlier stages of intelligence testing at the beginning of the twentieth century, suggested the existence of a general factor—or central cognitive function—that determines a certain level of performance on a variety of cognitive tasks (Spearman, 1927). The existence of this central cognitive function was evidenced by a set of positive correlations among performances on verbal, spatial, numerical, and other assessment problems. People with high academic ranking tended to score well on measures such as general knowledge, arithmetic ability, and vocabulary. On the contrary, people with low scores on verbal tasks were likely to have low scores on other tests. This approach inevitably encouraged the assumptions that some ethnic and racial groups are fundamentally different in their intellectual abilities.

Over the years, the idea of "one factor" that determines intellectual functioning has been frequently challenged. One such critic, Thurstone (1938), proposed the existence of not only one but rather three intellectual skills: verbal, mathematical, and spatial.

Sternberg (1985, 1997) also supported a hypothesis about a multidimensional structure of intelligence and suggested the existence of three fundamental aspects of intelligence: analytic, creative, and practical. According to his arguments, most intelligence tests measured only analytic skills. Analytic problems in the test are usually clearly defined, have a single correct answer, and come with all the information needed for a solution. On the contrary, practical problems are usually not clearly defined. The person has to seek additional information and offer various "correct" solutions to the problem under consideration.

To solve these problems successfully, the person would need to have accumulated everyday experiences and be motivated enough to find the solution.

Studying the diversity of human behavior and achievement, Gardner (2007) argued that along with logical, linguistic, or spatial intelligence measured by psychometric tests, there are other special kinds of musical, bodily kinesthetic, and personal intelligence (a person's ability to understand himself or herself, or other people). However, as you may see, the ability to plan, evaluate a particular situation, and make useful decisions about the situation is essential for human survival and well-being. Then again, skills such as musical and body kinesthetic—in most cases—are not necessarily essential for human endurance and adaptation.

From the beginning of the empirical studies of intelligence, culture was claimed to be its important "contributor." For example, Piaget (1972) argued that intelligence has similar cross-cultural developmental mechanisms. On one hand, children in all countries assimilate new information into existing cognitive structures. On the other hand, these cognitive structures accommodate themselves to the changing environment. Vygotsky, a Russian psychologist (1978), believed that intelligence could not be understood without taking into consideration the cultural environment in which the person lives.

In psychology, most attention has been given to the so-called **psychometric approach to intelligence**. This view is based on an assumption that our intelligence can "receive" a numerical value (Wechsler, 1958). This approach is also probably the most controversial one because of an ongoing debate about how accurately these values can be assigned and interpreted.

From an introductory psychology class you perhaps remember that, typically, most intelligence tests contain a series of tasks. Each test contains several subtests that measure various cognitive skills. When you take the test, you are asked to solve verbal and nonverbal problems, make perceptual judgments, solve puzzles, find word associations, explain pictures in your own words, memorize sequences of words or numbers, and so on. After your answers are checked, your score is converted into a special score. Then your score is compared with the average score of your peers—presumably, and in most cases, this includes people of the same nationality and age group as you are. In fact, the comparison will yield your actual intelligence quotient, or for short, IQ. Approximately 95 percent of the population have scores on IQ tests within two standard deviations of 15. That means IQs of most people—95 out of 100—will be somewhere between 70 and 130.

There has long been intense controversy about the validity of measures and interpretation of intelligence test scores, and there are at least two major points in debates about intelligence testing:

1. What do intelligence tests actually measure?
2. How can it be proven that the test score was not influenced by factors such as the attitudes, motivation, or emotional states of test takers?

Critically important for those who attempt to interpret cultural differences on intelligence scores are (1) the distinction between cognitive potential, (2) cognitive skills developed through interaction with cultural environment, and (3) scores on a particular test. The problem is that the standard tests may not provide for the direct assessment of cognitive skills shaped by a particular cultural environment. Unless intelligence tests accommodate the activities that people perform in their day-to-day life, the tests created in one culture will continue to be biased against other cultural groups. This means that the test performance may not represent the individual's cognitive potential (Vernon, 1969). Moreover, factors such as language, test content, and motivation reportedly contribute to an individual's performance on tests (Sternberg, 2007). For example, there are many aspects of human intelligence, such as wisdom and creativity, that many tests are simply not designed to measure.

By nature, men are nearly alike; by practice, they get to be wide apart.

CONFUCIUS **(441–479 B.C.E.)—Chinese Philosopher**

Another major point of most discussions is how to interpret the numerical value of intelligence. If 12-year-old boys and girls from a northern part of a city scored 90 on a test, whereas those from a southern part scored 105 on the same test, what does this mean? The most fired debates take place when intelligence value is assigned to ethnic or national groups. Apparently, some significant differences among people in body size, shape, and skin color do not evoke such heated discussions, and, as a result, emotions often overshadow a fair discussion of group differences between intelligence scores.

Before we continue our analysis, let us express one concern. As we just suggested, few issues in psychology have become as divisive as the concept of intelligence. Around the world the debates about intelligence are often motivated by a variety of political, ideological, and group interests (Helms, 2006). In some cases, a particular political agenda comes first and psychology serves as a provider of data. Scientific arguments are often put aside. We accept, of course, that people who want to advance their particular views could use psychology for this purpose. Therefore, the goals of cross-cultural psychology perhaps will be better served if these views are not rejected outright but are critically analyzed.

ETHNIC DIFFERENCES IN IQ SCORES

Most of the questions that cross-cultural psychology attempts to address are concerned with a set of measurable similarities and differences among different cultural, ethnic, and national groups. Are ethnic groups characterized by a particular pattern of intellectual ability? For example, can one prove that Italians, in general, are more creative than Germans, but that the German mode of thinking is more "precise" than the Brazilian mode? Do some cultural groups have a "better" memory than others? Do poverty and other devastating social problems influence intelligence? Is systematic formal schooling the key to human intellectual equality? Is such equality achievable in principle? In Chapter 4, we have mentioned about some cognitive differences between Western and East Asian subjects. We now turn to IQ scores.

In the United States, early attempts to measure IQs began more than 100 years ago. These studies examined schoolchildren, army recruits, and immigrants arriving in this country. For example, in 1921, the National Academy of Sciences published the results of one of the first massive national studies on intelligence. The results allowed the organizers of this study to rank newly arrived immigrants according to their IQ scores. This is how the "intellectual" order of the immigrants looked: England, Holland, Denmark, Scotland, Germany, Canada, Belgium, Norway, Austria, Ireland, Turkey, Greece, Russia, Italy, and Poland. In addition, the data showed the first evidence that blacks generally scored lower than whites on those tests. It was also reported that the Polish in this study did not score significantly higher than the blacks did (Kamin, 1976).

Today various tests show differences in intelligence scores among large cultural groups. For example, in the United States, Asian Americans (of East Asian origins) score the highest, followed by European Americans, Hispanics, and lastly African Americans. Thus, on the average, African American schoolchildren score 10–15 percent lower on a standardized intelligence test than white schoolchildren do. Similar results were reported for adults (Rushton & Jensen, 2005; Suzuki & Valencia, 1997). For better comprehension of the differences between some of the groups, just imagine that the average white person tests higher than about 80 percent of the population of blacks and an average black person tests higher than about 20 percent of the population of whites. According to studies, some racial-group differences in IQ appear in early childhood. For example, on the Differential Aptitude Battery, by age 6, the average IQ of East Asian children was 107, compared with 103 for white children and 89 for black children (Lynn, 1996). The size of the average black–white difference does not change significantly over the developmental period from three years of age and beyond.

The mean intelligence test scores for Latino groups are usually between those of blacks and whites. If we divide U.S. citizens along their religions, we will find that Jews, and specifically Jews of European origin, test higher than any other religious group in the United States. Studies of Korean and Vietnamese children adopted into white homes in the United States show that they tend to grow to have IQs 10 or more points higher than their adoptive national norms (Rushton & Jensen, 2005). Even though it is established that Americans of Japanese, Chinese, and Korean ancestry have higher scores than American whites, there is no consistency in research findings. The differences in scores that do occur are usually in the low single digits. The average difference between black and white IQ scores is established at every level of the socioeconomic ladder. In other words, upper-class blacks have lower test scores than upper-class whites, and lower-class whites have higher test scores than lower-class blacks. Cultural disparities in cognitive performance are found around the world. In India, members of the higher castes obtain higher mean scores and examination marks than do those of the lower castes. In Malaysia, members of the Chinese and East Indian minority communities have higher mean scores than those of the majority Malay population. In South Africa, members of the white, East Indian, and colored population groups obtain higher mean scores than members of the indigenous black African majority (Lynn & Vanhanen, 2002).

Some groups are found to have higher scores on certain scales and lower scores on others. For instance, the verbal intelligence scores of Native Americans were found to be lower than these same scores were for other ethnic groups. However, some studies showed the existence of high visual–spatial skills in Native American groups (McShane & Berry, 1988). East Asians score slightly higher than whites on nonverbal intelligence and equal or slightly lower on verbal intelligence. Moreover, studies suggest that the visual and spatial abilities of East Asians are superior to their verbal abilities, despite substantial political and socioeconomic differences among East Asian countries (Herrnstein & Murray, 1994).

It is not enough to have a good mind; the main thing is to use it well.

RENÉ DESCARTES (1596–1650)—**French Philosopher and Mathematician**

EXPLAINING GROUP DIFFERENCES IN TEST SCORES: INTELLIGENCE AND INTELLIGENT BEHAVIOR

In an attempt to explain some group differences on intelligence test scores, Sternberg (1997) suggested distinguishing between intelligence and intelligent behavior. Intelligence, from his standpoint, is a mental process that may or may not result in particular behavioral responses. These behaviors vary from culture to culture. Something considered intelligent among members of one culture may not be viewed as such in other cultures. If a Washingtonian knows how

CROSS-CULTURAL SENSITIVITY

Because of stereotyping (see Chapter 10 on social perception), some people may believe that all members of a group—or at least most of them—have either high or low IQ scores. This view is incorrect and may have an indirect impact on school performance and perhaps other activities. How? Imagine, for instance, a teacher knows there are five Hispanic and three black children in her class. Making a stereotypical judgment, the teacher would assume that these children should have lower intelligence test scores and, therefore, are less capable of learning than other children in class. This stereotype may create an expectation and attitude that result in the teacher, having only good intentions, giving "easier" assignments to these children, and not challenging them in their educational effort.

to negotiate the conditions of a three-year lease with a car dealer, this skill may not be—and likely will not be—very useful at a farm market in Istanbul or Helsinki. Dealing with different cultural contexts, people develop different cognitive skills and acquire dissimilar ways of thinking and learning that are useful in their particular cultural environment. Take, for example, the way people use categories to describe their experience. Traditionally, among navigators in Southeast Asia, the word "south" is often used to refer only to "seaward," which can be any side of the horizon (Frake, 1980). This centuries-old understanding of directions is inappropriate and confusing to visiting foreigners.

However, people may share some general understandings about what intelligence is because the underlying psychological mechanisms of intelligence are expected to be quite similar in all individuals. Among these processes are abilities to understand a problem, identify its type, prepare a solution, find resources to solve the problem, manage the process of solution, and, finally, evaluate the outcome of behavior. Nevertheless—and this is a key element in the understanding of intelligent behavior—the specific content of such behavior in each of these stages is determined by the specific environment in which the individual lives (Farhi, 2007). A chess master in India uses these strategies to make particular moves on a chessboard, whereas a farmer in Bosnia, using the same psychological mechanisms, secures a good deal buying a new tractor.

Reasoning that is causal, scientific, and based on empirical facts is not applicable in all cultures all the time (Shea, 1985). A ritualistic dance of a Brazilian tribesman may be considered "unintelligent" behavior by many people in London or Tokyo: "Look at him, he is dancing to stop the rain," some taunt sarcastically. These same taunting individuals, however, go every week to their temples and churches and, by doing this, commit themselves to similar ritualistic acts. Moral? People develop cognitive skills best adapted to the needs of their lifestyle (Dasen et al., 1979).

DO BIOLOGICAL FACTORS CONTRIBUTE TO INTELLIGENCE?

According to the **nativist view**, most cognitive phenomena are inborn. They unravel as a result of biological "programming," and environmental perception requires little active construction by the organism. Hypothetically, according to this view, a boy in Nepal and a girl in Venezuela are both expected to develop some elements of conceptual thinking by approximately the age of seven. No one can make these children think conceptually when they are four years old. This view argues that hereditary factors determine both the depth and scope of our intellectual skills.

These are not just the empty statements of a handful of researchers. In the 1980s, two scientists asked more than 1,000 scholars to give their opinion about IQ, in particular about the differences in IQ scores among ethnic groups. Even though only 1 percent suggested that the differences are always caused by genetic factors, almost 45 percent of the professionals reported that the differences are the product of both genetic and environmental variations (many could not or did not want to give a definitive answer). Remarkably, of all those interviewed only one in seven said that the difference is entirely due to environmental factors (Snyderman & Rothman, 1988). French neuroscientist Stanislas Dehaene (2002) maintains that the mathematical ability of humans may be imbedded in the brain and could be generally independent of memory and reasoning. Moreover, an individual's learning experience, school programs, and even spoken language (like French) may even suppress the development of certain inborn mathematical skills. Dehaene also argues that some languages, like Chinese, may be more helpful to develop a person's basic natural mathematical abilities.

Further support to the assumption that an individual's ability to be successful on cognitive tests is somehow biologically "programmed" and may be less dependent on this person's educational effort comes from a study conducted by Derek Briggs (2001). He found that young people who take preparation courses for college admission tests (such as the SAT in the United States) show only a small improvement in their scores. In other words, whether people study for this test or not, the results of these two groups are likely to be the same. Although some critics reasoned that the conclusions of this study simply pointed out the little effectiveness of the preparation courses, others suggested that certain cognitive skills cannot be improved over a short period of time, which indicates the existence of "deeper" roots of these skills.

There is evidence that heredity plays an important role in human intelligence. For example, the intelligence scores of identical twins raised either together or apart correlate almost +0.90 (Bouchard et al., 1990). One study of 543 pairs of identical twins and 134 pairs of nonidentical twins in Japan reported a substantial heritability of 0.58 for IQ (Lynn & Hattori, 1990). About two dozen studies conducted using magnetic resonance imaging (MRI) to measure the volume of the human brain have found an overall correlation with IQ (Vernon et al., 2000). Twenty-five percent of cases of mental retardation are caused by known biological defects (Grossman, 1983). Moreover, the intelligence scores of adopted children strongly correlate with the scores of their biological parents, whereas there is only a weak correlation between scores of adoptive parents and adopted children (Munsinger, 1978). The correlation between the IQ scores of two biologically unrelated individuals, who were raised together, is also relatively low: +0.20 (Bouchard & McGue, 1981). It is also known that vocabulary size, or the number of words a person remembers and uses in his or her communications, may depend on genetic predispositions. However, even though various data suggest high correlations between parents and children and brothers and sisters in terms of their intellectual skills, these data tell little about what would happen to people's IQ scores if they lived in a different social context than the one in which they actually grew up. Moreover, genetic links for individual differences and similarities do not imply that group differences—on the national level, for example—are also based on genetic factors (Sternberg, 2004). The fact that the heritability of IQ is high does not mean that individual differences in intellectual functioning are permanent. It shows that some individuals are probably genetically predisposed to be more teachable, more trainable, and more capable of learning skills than others, under current conditions and within specific cultural contexts (Lynn & Hattori, 1990).

Besides genetic factors, cross-cultural psychologists examine how particular environmental conditions affect human physiology and whether such biological changes influence cognitive skills. It was found, for instance, that the presence or absence of a particular chemical in a specific geographic region might have affected the overall cognitive performance of the population living in that territory. To illustrate, iodine-deficient areas are found in some regions of Indonesia as well as in Spain. Clinicians report that substantial iodine deficiency in the human body can cause severe mental and neurological abnormalities (see Bleichrodt et al., 1980). In accordance with predictions, cognitive test scores obtained from children living in iodine-deficient areas of Spain and Indonesia were much lower than the scores obtained from children residing in neighboring areas where the water contained sufficient amounts of iodine.

We now turn to a discussion of recent studies related to cognitive processes in order to illustrate how and to what extent they are shaped by cultural and social factors.

INCOMPATIBILITY OF TESTS: CULTURAL BIASES

In Chapter 2, we learned about equivalency, one of the important requirements of any comparative research. If a test were designed for a particular ethnic group, the test questions or tasks may not have similar meaning for other cultural groups. Many specialists (Berry, 1988; Mishra, 1988; Poortinga & Van der Flier, 1988) emphasize the importance of such issues as "culture fairness" and "test transfer."

Theoretically, cognitive processes are believed to be similar in virtually all healthy individuals of different groups. However, these processes are applied to various, person-specific environmental, social, psychological, and cultural circumstances (Cole et al., 1971). People develop dissimilar cognitive skills because they are shaped by different contexts. A girl who goes to a private school in Paris, stays with her 45-year-old single mother, and has her own bedroom and personal computer lives in an environment that is quite different from that of a North Korean boy who shares his room with two siblings, attends public school, does not have a personal computer, and has very young parents who work in a shoe factory. A test may adequately measure some elementary cognitive skills in these two children, but at the same time it can be of a little use in terms of measuring other, culture-specific cognitive skills.

Most intelligence tests benefit specific ethnic groups because of the test vocabulary—words and items used in the test questions. For instance, tests may contain internal bias because they use words that are familiar only to some groups. As a result, members of these groups receive higher scores than those who do not belong to these groups. For example, try to solve the following problem.

Find the odd man out: Rose   Tulip   Forget-me-not   Basil

The correct answer is "basil," because all the other words stand for flowers, and basil is not a flower. The critics of this type of question argue that unless the subject knows something about different flowers and plants, it will be very difficult for him or her to find the right answer. Those of us having access to flowers will benefit in this situation. Moreover, one may assume that there are more girls who are familiar with the names of flowers than there are boys. Therefore, girls will probably give more correct answers than boys.

Cultural experience may affect test scores, and some test designs demonstrate this. For example, in one study, British children were found to solve test problems more creatively than Asian students from Hong Kong, Indonesia, and Malaysia. One explanation for this finding is that the subjects were required to give numeric verbal responses to the test items, something that is not a typical problem-solving task for Asian cultures (Wright et al., 1978). Another example illustrates how a test can benefit members of a particular group. A culturally oriented vocabulary test unique to the African American community was given to kids of different ethnic groups.

Black kids scored around a mean of 87 out of a possible 100; however, white children's mean score was only 51 (Williams & Mitchell, 1991). In general, black youths perform better than white young people on free-word recall tasks when the categories (words) are related to African American daily experience (Hayles, 1991).

He who does not know one thing knows another.

KENYAN PROVERB

A WORD ABOUT "CULTURAL LITERACY"

Most verbal intelligence tests contain sections on general knowledge. Obviously, our "general knowledge" is based on events that took place in a particular cultural environment. Most U.S. kindergartners possess knowledge about George Washington. Later comes information about Benjamin Franklin, the Great Depression, Titanic, *Gone with the Wind*, Liberty Bell, Watergate, Ronald Reagan, Barack Obama, Lady Gaga, and LeBron James. In Italy, cultural knowledge is based on other facts, events, and developments that are different from those one can experience in the United States. For example, words and names such as Mussolini, Andreotti, Fiat, Brigate Rosse, Juventus, and Adriano Celentano would be identified in Italy with almost no difficulty. Could you identify all these names? The answer is "no," unless you have lived in Italy or possess great knowledge of Italian history, politics, soccer, and music.

Our literacy is culture based. There is no doubt that 2 + 2 = 4 in all countries. An antonym for "death" is "life" in virtually every literate community regardless of its cultural heritage or nationality. However, beyond these universal categories—at least they sound universal for most of us—there is always culture-specific knowledge. Could you come up with your own examples of culture-specific knowledge in the United States or any other country?

Those who disagree with the existence of bias argue that IQ scores can more or less accurately predict future success at school—high test scores are positively correlated with high scores on intelligence tests. The specialists who believe that IQ tests contain very little bias suggest that these tests predict the academic performance of any ethnic group in the same way that they predict performance of white children and adults: High IQs predict academic success and low IQs predict low school grades (Pennock-Roman, 1992). This means that any student of any ethnic group who scores high on an IQ test is likely to have fine grades in college.

ENVIRONMENT AND INTELLIGENCE

Compare yourself with any person in the classroom. You may find someone of the same age, height, weight, nationality, income, and even lifestyle as you are. However, we do not live in identical environments. Our diversity is determined by natural factors, such as individual, professional, educational, social, and cultural circumstances. This is a popular view in psychology—accepted by cross-cultural psychologists—that human intellectual skills can be influenced by external environmental factors (Carroll, 1983; Sternberg, 1985). In general, these factors include the overall availability of and access to resources, variety of perceptual experiences, predominant type of family climate, educational opportunities, access to books and travel, presence or absence of cultural magical beliefs, general attitudes, and cultural practices. These and other conditions have been found to influence performance on intelligence tests (Vernon, 1969). Settings such as educational incentives, quality of teaching, and teacher–student communications may also influence test scores (Irvine, 1983; Mackie, 1983). Special training programs (Keats, 1985) and additional instructional efforts (Mishra, 1997) can determine how well a person scores on an intelligence test as well. For example, Ogbu (1994) suggested that negative attitudes about testing in general, feelings of hopelessness, and exposure to stereotypes may lower the intelligence scores of African Americans and other minority groups in the United States. Research data suggest that at least some black students do not perform well on cognitive tests because they are inhibited by a concern of being evaluated according to a negative "you are not smart" stereotype and the fear of performing poorly that would inadvertently confirm that stereotype (Steele, 1999).

There is strong evidence that training can increase test scores on IQ tests (Skuy et al., 2002). Raven (2000) showed that students who were encouraged to engage in complex cognitive tasks improved substantially in self-direction, understanding, and competence.

Studies show that the acquisition of many mental functions depends on interaction with the environment (Macdonald & Rogan, 1990). Take, for instance, West African traders, who spend most of their adult life traveling and negotiating. One well-known study found that the merchants are better on cognitive tasks—including problem solving—than West African tailors, who spend most of their life in one place and do not have such diverse contacts as the merchants (Petitto & Ginsburg, 1982). In another example, Brazilian and Colombian street children who earn money by selling fruit and vegetables on the street—often at age 10 and 11—are able to conduct financial operations in their "minds" without making mistakes. Similar math operations, done in paper and pencil at the request of investigators, were not successful. The children did not receive formal schooling, and, as a result, they did not learn the algorithms of adding and subtracting on paper (Aptekar, 1989). In another study, after viewing a series of pictures, European children tended to describe the pictures as a sequence of events—as if they were a comic strip that appears in children's magazines. African children who were not exposed to comics tended to report that the pictures portrayed a single instant in time, not a sequence of events (Deregowski & Munro, 1974).

Aboriginal children obtain lower verbal scores than urban Australian children do, and one cause may be a lack of interaction. If Aboriginal children have a chance to live side by side with white children, their test scores on verbal classification tests are relatively similar (Lacey, 1971). In general, serious deprivation of stimulation may result in the disorganization of a number of cognitive processes (Sinha & Shukla, 1974).

Certain types of environmental influences determine the individual's experience with these influences. However, people's experiences determine their adaptive reactions. As a result, cognitive skills that play a crucial role in an individual's survival may develop earlier than other skills (Ferguson, 1956). For example, children in hunting and gathering societies develop spatial reasoning skills earlier than their peers in agricultural communities. However, children in agricultural cultures achieve understanding of concepts such as conservation of quantity, weight, and volume—knowledge necessary in agricultural activities—more rapidly than children from nomadic (traveling) groups (Dasen, 1975).

Environmental factors may affect higher mental operations, such as planning abilities. One such factor is stability of the environment. In a stable environment most changes are predictable. People are certain about their lives and feel that they are in control of their future. When conditions are unpredictable, people may lack planning strategies because of the assumption that it is impossible to control the outcome of whatever you plan. All in all, in societies and communities that are stable, people perhaps have better chances of developing their planning skills than people from unstable environments (Strohschneider & Guss, 1998).

Lack of systematic schooling may also contribute to the slow development of planning strategies. Certainly, the complexity of everyday life can provide conditions for the development of planning skills even if a person has little formal education. However, if there is no access to education and if environmental conditions require simple responses, the individual would tend not to develop complex planning strategies.

SOCIOECONOMIC FACTORS

Intelligence scores are, in general, positively correlated with the socioeconomic status of the individual (Neiser et al., 1996). The link between socioeconomic conditions and test performance may be revealed at an early age. It was found that a child's IQ and the socioeconomic status of the child's parents are positively correlated. The higher the child's IQ, the higher her parents' socioeconomic rank, and vice versa (White, 1982). Children who grow up in a privileged environment tend to show higher scores than their peers from a deprived environment (Masters, 1997). For example, Yoruba children, living in upper-class, educated families, demonstrated superior mental age scores when compared to Yoruba children from nonliterate families (Lloyd & Easton, 1977). A similar trend was found among four-year-old Maori and Pakeha Aboriginal children living in New Zealand (Brooks, 1976). Accordingly, no substantial differences were found in the cognitive abilities of disadvantaged children from both Australian Aboriginal and European decent (Taylor & deLacey, 1974).

According to the U.S. Census Bureau (2010), 18 percent of U.S. children under age 18 lived in families below the official poverty level. Poverty could contribute to these children's lower scores on tests of intelligence and lower levels of school achievement (McLoyd, 1998). Studies in the past showed links between breast-feeding, nutrition, and cognitive performance of the child. Breast-feeding reduces the infants' exposure to metal pollutants, while providing infants the long chains of proteins necessary for brain development. Mothers from low socioeconomic groups typically do not breast-feed their infants. Black mothers in the United States, for instance, in the past, were only one-third as likely to breast-feed their infants as white mothers (Jensen, 1998). A 40-year study showed that students from lower-income families making $37,000 or less are less likely to be proficient in both math and reading (Strauss, 2008). The individual's socioeconomic status may have both direct and indirect impact on test performance. For instance, social environments with limited amounts of resources may stimulate the development of particular cognitive traits that are useful only for those environments. If we compare large clusters of countries—for example, Western developed and traditional societies—we will find that people in Western countries generally outscore members of traditional societies on intelligence tests (including tests that do not include culture-specific tasks, questions, and problems).

Socioeconomic factors have a more pronounced effect on intelligence test scores in developing countries than in industrialized ones. One explanation of this phenomenon is that in developed countries the gap between the rich and the poor is not as profound as it is in developing countries. The official poverty level in the United States, which is slightly more than $22,000 per family of four per year, exceeds the average annual income of most other countries.

Some researchers suggest that high IQ scores may predict people's high social status and income (Herrnstein & Murray, 1994). The middle-class population generally has higher IQ scores than the lower-class population. Does this mean that individual socioeconomic success is possible only when an individual has high intellectual skills? This is not necessarily true. Yes, higher IQ scores may determine the success of the individual, in particular his social status and income. Nevertheless, availability and access to resources—or the lack thereof—may also affect the person's intellectual potential, which results in higher or lower IQ scores. One should not forget that the individual's social status determines her position in the society and access to resources and power. Both middle-class and well-to-do parents establish connections and develop personal and professional relationships with people from the same social stratum, thus paving the way for their own children to reach high levels on the social ladder. In other words, psychometric intelligence alone cannot decide social outcome; there are many other variables in this equation. For example, individuals who have the same IQ scores may be quite different from one another in their income and social and professional status.

Those who believe in the crucial role of socioeconomic factors in our intellectual functioning consider them the most salient influences contributing to the difference between intelligence test scores of blacks and whites in the United States. Generally, blacks have lower incomes, occupy less prestigious positions, and receive less adequate care than other minority groups. Poverty is also linked to inconsistent parenting and persistent exposure to stress that can and does affect cognitive functioning.

THE FAMILY FACTOR

An affluent and educated family is likely to provide a better material environment for a child and also has more resources to develop a child's intellectual potential than a poorer family. Middle-class parents typically have enough resources to stimulate the child's learning experience at home (Gottrfried, 1984). Such parents are likely to be educated and subsequently have general understanding of the importance of education. They are able to buy developmental toys, including video games and computer software. Most of them do not have problems that would prevent them from talking to their children about various topics, exposing them to interesting events, and stimulating their imagination. On the contrary, poor families have fewer resources and fewer opportunities to stimulate a child's intellectual development (Shiraev, 1988). If the parents' prime activity is to secure food and safety for the family members, then collective survival—not necessarily the intellectual development of the child—is the prime goal of the parents' activities.

In 2003, for instance, children of parents of Indian origin, living in England and Scotland, outperformed all other students at school. Similar data were received regarding students of Chinese and mixed backgrounds. One of the factors proposed by researchers is that, in most cases, immigrant parents start their lives with low-paid jobs and see in their children's education the key to their sons' and daughters' success in life. As a result, these parents pay special attention to their children's school performance (Sonwalkar, 2004). A similar conclusion was drawn in a study involving 6,000 U.S. middle-school students. Across ethnic groups, students whose parents were concerned about their children's academic performance and who were able to boost the educational aspirations of their children showed significantly higher academic scores than other students (Hong & Ho, 2005).

Studies show that parents from Southeast Asian immigrant groups—such as Chinese, Koreans, and Vietnamese—are often successful at promoting academic success in their children. It is also shown that parents from many Hispanic ethnic backgrounds are less successful in this regard. Does this mean that Hispanic parents are less invested in their children's future than are Asian parents? These differences are likely based on the social backgrounds of the immigrant families and the specific reasons why the families migrated: Some of them moved to escape violence, others to improve their economic conditions, yet others to provide a "better life" for their children (Schwartz et al., 2011). These reasons may be interconnected, and new studies are needed.

It has been found that intelligence scores decline as a function of birth order. According to one theory, this trend has little to do with biological factors (Munroe & Munroe, 1983). Every immature member of a family develops intelligence linked to the intellectual level of the older family members. The firstborn in the family has the initial advantage of an immediate environment consisting of only himself and the adult parents, who have a particular set of cognitive skills. When a second child is born, she enters an environment consisting of herself, the parents, and an individual with an immature intellectual level, that is, the older sibling. Thus, in general, the intellectual environment encountered by the firstborn is "superior" to that of the second born, and so on.

These data, although controversial, found additional support in some other studies. For example, a continuous increase in IQ scores in the African American population is correlated with the increasingly smaller family size since the 1970s. Children from smaller families tend to achieve higher IQ scores than their counterparts from larger families (Vincent, 1991). However, extra caution is needed in such interpretations. First, the relationship here may be reverse: higher scores on IQ tests stand for higher cognitive abilities, which, in turn, affect individual attitudes about pregnancy and unprotected sex. Another explanation for the change in IQ scores is a more significant increase in the educational level of parents in black families in the 1980s and 1990s.

Parental influence can be one of the factors contributing to the difference in IQ scores between white and some other ethnic groups—predominantly minorities—that represent the middle class. Minority parents—especially those who arrived in the United States before the 1960s—are likely to be less educated than the white population. As it was mentioned earlier, parents' cognitive skills contribute to the development of the child's cognitive skills. Moreover, some minority parents may pay less attention to educational opportunities for their children than white families do. Overall pessimism and a lack of opportunity and success can cause such attitudes. On the contrary, Chinese and Japanese Americans tend to emphasize the importance of education for their children and see it as the only opportunity for future advancement. Partly because of family values and partly because of their academic success, Asian Americans tend to seek and get appointments in professional, managerial, or technical occupations to a greater extent than any other ethnic group (Flynn, 1991; Schwartz et al., 2011).

"NATURAL SELECTION" AND IQ SCORES

According to the bell curve principle, a normal distribution of IQ scores in any given population can be roughly divided into three large categories: people with low, average, and high IQ scores. This same principle can also be used in the distribution of peoples' heights. However, although a bell curve of IQ scores and a bell curve of peoples' heights may paint a similar picture, the meanings people assign to these pictures may be quite different. For instance, we find people of all different heights in various social circles, with various occupations, and of varying intelligence. An individual's location on the bell curve of height may place him next to numerous types of people that he may never interact with in everyday life.

The bell curve of IQ scores is another story. In the United States, for example, people with high IQ scores are disproportionally represented among doctors, scientists, lawyers, and business executives. Individuals with low intelligence scores are disproportionately represented among people on welfare, prison inmates, single mothers, drug abusers, and high-school dropouts (see, e.g., Rushton & Jensen, 2005).

Perhaps there is nothing unusual about people with similar interests and occupations tending to communicate with one another significantly more often than with people of other occupations and interests. For example, a high IQ score indicates that you will be likely to (1) attend college, (2) gain employment in a setting conducive to meeting and making friends with people of similar educational levels and, perhaps intelligence, and (3) marry someone with an educational background similar to yours. Likewise, people with lower scores will likely seek love and friendship among people of the same cognitive level. Therefore, according to Herrnstein and Murray (1994), two polls of people have been "constructed" over the years: one with relatively high and the other with relatively low intelligence scores. The former is placed in an advantageous social niche with prestigious jobs, good income, and fine living conditions. The latter group finds itself in the disadvantaged stratum of low-paying jobs, unstable social environment, and low-quality living conditions.

Unfortunately, for a variety of reasons, many representatives of ethnic minorities remain in the disadvantaged group. Low IQ scores, as was mentioned earlier, predict low academic grades and fewer opportunities for individuals to get high-income jobs. Lack of resources would contribute greatly to keeping these individuals in low-income communities. Low salaries and low cost of property produce significantly less taxes than in affluent districts. Therefore, local schools—most of which depend on local property taxes—are not able to provide high-quality education comparable to the quality of education in affluent communities. Poor schooling conditions, lack of qualified teachers, and the absence of modern educational equipment affect the developing child's cognitive skills. In addition, as we saw earlier, poverty is responsible for a variety of indirect impacts on the intellectual development of children and adults.

He who knows others is learned; he who knows himself is wise.

LAO-TSE (604–531 B.C.E.)—**Chinese Philosopher**

CULTURAL VALUES OF COGNITION

Judging from an ethnocentric perspective, one might suggest that the most "valuable" features for any problem-solving process are analytical, rational skills, and quick reasoning. However, such a view—though prevailing in most contemporary societies—is not universal in all cultures. Some societies may have diverse sets of cognitive values different from the ones highly regarded, for example, in Western societies (Berry, 1988). In some societies holistic—emphasizing the importance of the whole—rather than analytic decision making is valued (Dasen, 1984; Serpell, 1993). In such cases, careful reflection rather than promptness is considered the most appropriate course of action. In these primarily agricultural societies, collective discussion rather than individual consideration is generally the preferred cognitive style. Therefore, in such cultures, individuals tested with a standard Western psychological instrument will likely display a low level of cognitive development according to criteria that measure only independence and speed of judgment.

Nisbett (2003) demonstrated the differences in cognitive styles between Western and East Asian students. Using experimental data, he showed that students from China, Korea, and Japan tend to be more holistic in their perceptions than do students of Western descent, as we saw in Chapter 4. In other words, East Asian students tend to see and remember objects as being interconnected, while Western students pay attention to details and issues that clearly stand out (Masuda & Nisbett, 2006). Studies also show that Western infants learn nouns faster than verbs, while East Asian infants tend to learn verbs (indicating connections between objects) more rapidly. Differences in reasoning styles between Chinese and European Americans were observed during a comparative study that revealed Chinese students, both bilingual and not speaking English, organized objects in pictures in a more relational and less categorical way than European Americans (Ji et al., 2004).

Desire to have things done quickly prevents their being done thoroughly.

CONFUCIUS (551–479 B.C.E.)—**Chinese Philosopher**

According to another approach to the interpretation of test scores on general intelligence, the problem is in the way people across cultures value and construe intelligence. For instance, as already mentioned, the conceptualization of intelligence as quick and analytic is not shared in all cultures. If one group's concept includes being detailed and precise in responding, and the other group does not mention these features (and mentions improvisation as an element of intelligence), then precision cannot be used as a criterion according to which the two groups are compared (Berry, 1969).

In the United States, different ethnic groups may use different frames of reference regarding intelligence (Heath, 1983; Okagaki & Sternberg, 1993). For instance, in most cases, European Americans emphasize the importance of cognitive skills such as memorization, classification, and problem solving, whereas other groups tend to emphasize characteristics such as motivation, social, and practical skills. In light of this, Sternberg (1997) found that the emphasis on formal mental abilities does not give a fair chance to many individuals with high creative and practical mental abilities. For example, on measures of creativity, flexibility, and originality, black children and other minority groups typically do as well, and frequently better, compared to white children (Hayles, 1991).

CRITICAL THINKING
A "Chinese Way" in Thinking? Comparing Socrates and Confucius

Do you believe that there is a special, unique, Chinese way of thinking and processing information? Do you think there is a special European style? According to one view, there ought to be a special "cultural" way rooted in customs and early European and Chinese philosophical systems. Supporters of this argument use an example of the teachings of two prominent philosophers of China and Greece—Confucius and Socrates—and their impact on the general learning principles cultivated in Chinese and Western (European) cultures. It is argued that Socrates, a major contributor to the Western scholarly thought, valued critical thinking and skepticism by encouraging the questioning of common knowledge. He taught his students and, subsequently, millions of followers of other generations, to be independent thinkers and generate their own ideas. Confucius, to the contrary, is viewed as valuing the effortful, respectful, and pragmatic acquisition of essential knowledge based on respect toward educators and the constant search for patterns of

useful behavior to follow (Tweed & Lehman, 2002; Yang & Sternberg, 1997). While Confucius urged his followers to respect elders, Socrates urged his followers to challenge them.

If you accept these arguments, you are likely to agree with the idea that there are culture-based patterns of learning and thinking. Thus, Socrates impacted the cultural characteristics of the "typical" European student who is primarily a critical thinker, while Confucius impacted the characteristics of the "typical" Chinese student who is an efficient follower and problem solver.

If you disagree, you are likely to suggest that respect of authority, acceptance of teachers, and search for practical applications of knowledge are, in fact, universal features of any educational system, whether it is Greek, or Chinese, or Mexican. Therefore, to attribute them exclusively to a particular culture or any other philosophy is simply inaccurate (Li, 2003).

Which side of the argument do you find easier to support and why?

We understand now that intellectual skills are judged according to a group's standards. For example, if a culture places an emphasis on hunting, a person's good vision and ability to make quick visual judgments will be considered extremely adaptive. In other cultures, the quickness of one's response will not be as essential as a critical evaluation of a task or problem at hand. In other words, the people, as representatives of a particular culture, define intelligence. If we argue for this, we inevitably move in the fields of cultural relativism (see Chapter 1). Why? Because we would challenge the existence of universal criteria for human mental activities. However, cultural relativism can also be challenged. For example, do you think that in an era of globalization of economy and informational revolution, people can, may, and probably should develop similar perceptions of what specific mental abilities are considered to be adaptive and valuable in the global community unified by the global economy?

There have been many attempts to explain the differences between Western and African cultural values and views on healthy cognitive functioning and intelligence. Boykin (1994), for example, suggested that blacks do not accept materialistic beliefs and do accept the influence of nonmaterial forces to a greater extent than other groups. They appreciate high levels of stimulation and energy and emphasize the importance of emotions and expressiveness. Furthermore, African American culture is rooted in spirituality, harmony, and affect, as well as verbal elements of communication. These features may not fit well into the Western values of rationality, calculation, discipline, individualism, and achievement, which are embodied in IQ tests. The author even suggests that the whole idea of intelligence assessment may be foreign to the African American mentality.

Most non-African theories of behavior, according to Baldwin and colleagues (1991), emphasize the critical role of the gratification of desires. The emphasis of black psychology is that the essential goal of human behavior is survival. Moreover, African theology assumes that the most direct experience of the self is one that goes through affect. Therefore, IQ measures, according to Baldwin, cannot measure the psychology of individuals who grew up in African or African American cultures. Intelligence, from the perspective of African psychology, is a collective moral responsibility.

Shade (1992) suggested that African Americans value a unique **cognitive style**—a way in which individuals organize and comprehend the world. In the study of 178 ninth-grade students, sampled African Americans tended to be spontaneous, flexible, open-minded, and less structured in the perception of people, events, and ideas. European Americans in the sample appeared to be self-regulated, judgmental, and less openminded than their counterparts. In another study, African American children generally learned in ways characterized by emotional emphasis, harmony, holistic perspectives, expressive creativity, and nonverbal communication (Wills, 1992). Some explain the below-average standardized test scores of African American children by referring to the tests' emphasis: the abstract, analytic thinking valued by Europeans—the features that are somewhat de-emphasized by blacks (Whethrick & Deregowski, 1982).

It was also implied that students of non-European origin use different cognitive styles of information processing: They are more field dependent than their European counterparts in the classroom (Kush, 1996). For example, **field-dependent** learners are more attentive to external references, contexts, and instructions in their learning tasks. **Field-independent** learners tend to be autonomous in learning, solving problems, and making decisions. It was found that in U.S. academic settings, field-independent students are more successful than field-dependent students. Although an individual's cognitive style is determined by many factors, studies also show that people in predominantly individualist cultures, such as Germany and the United States, tend to be more field independent than people in collectivist cultures, such as Russia and Malaysia, as is shown in cross-cultural studies (Kuhnen et al., 2001).

Certain ideological conditions may affect what people of a certain country value most in cognitive skills. Consider this example. If authorities, whoever they are—central government or local boss—make most decisions in your life, then apparently the number of choices you have may be restricted. Given a limited amount of choices, the number of activities available to you will also be limited, which is likely to affect your creativity and problem-solving ability. For example, creative thinking and self-expression are highly regarded in Western democratic societies. The paradox is that creative thinking is not a necessary asset in authoritarian societies. Why? Because this type of thinking may put the individual "above the crowd," which is neither appreciated nor tolerated by authorities. The same logic may be applied to those societies that promote dogmatic thinking and punish individuals for free exchange of ideas (Shiraev & Sobel, 2006).

Exercise 5.1

Please analyze the following theory differentiating dichotomous variables and continuous variables. Jackson (1991) introduces the following assumptions about the cognitive skills of African Americans:

- Blacks in the United States tend to perceive events as the whole visual picture, whereas whites perceive reality as broken down into parts.
- African Americans tend to prefer reasoning based on contextual and interpersonal factors, whereas European Americans prefer inductive and deductive reasoning.
- African Americans prefer to approximate space, numbers, and time. European Americans tend to prefer precision based on the concert of one-dimensional time and "objective" space between individuals.
- African Americans prefer to focus on people and their activities as opposed to Europeans, who show a propensity toward things based on a Eurocentric orientation and norms.
- African Americans prefer cooperation, preservation of life, affiliation, and collective responsibility; European Americans prefer competition, conflict, control of life, ownership, and individual rights.
- African Americans are more altruistic and concerned about the "next person," while European Americans value individualism and independence.
- African Americans prefer novelty, freedom, and personal distinction to a greater degree than European Americans.

GENERAL COGNITION: WHAT IS "UNDERNEATH" INTELLIGENCE?

Numerous facts about cultural diversity as well as empirical evidence about universal principles of cognition (see the definition of cognition in the section "Defining Intelligence") have contributed to the foundations of many theories exploring the links between culture and intelligence. There are several cognitive processes—recognition, categorization, thinking, and memory—the analysis of which will perhaps shed some light on differences and similarities in intellectual functioning among various ethnic groups.

Classification

Are there any differences in how people classify their environment? Humans tend to see things in highly similar fashions. One of the most universal classifications is the cognitive distinction made between plants and animals (Berlin, 1992). However, those plants and animals that are essential for the survival of individuals become most carefully distinguished and named. In general, the importance of objects and animals as well as a person's familiarity with them are the most significant factors that influence categorization. Groups that are relatively distant from each other should have some differences in classifications (Schwanenflugel & Rey, 1986). This may become a source of a potential bias in the testing of cognitive skills.

Sorting

If you ask a seven-year-old child of any nationality to sort 100 colored cards into color categories, the child should be expected to perform this operation without difficulty. Now ask an elderly resident of a small Ethiopian village to sort 100 compact discs according to the musical genres they represent—rock, classical, and hip-hop—and this person will likely experience serious difficulties (unless he is familiar with musical genres).

We can sort various objects even though no instructions are given on how to do it. Generally, we choose a dimension of categorization, that is, concept or characteristic. Linguists suggest that many categories used in sorting are universal. We use synonyms, such as "quick" and "fast"; antonyms, such as "clean" versus "dirty"; subcategories, such as "skunk" and "animal"; and parts, such as "heart" and "body" (Raybeck & Herrmann, 1990).

Research suggests that cultural groups tend to categorize objects in terms of their specific cultural experiences associated with these objects (Okonji, 1971; Wassmann, 1993; Wassmann & Dasen, 1994). In other words, according to experience people know what the objects are used for and then base their categorization on this knowledge (Mishra, 1997). It has also been shown that the degree of familiarity with the environment influences classificatory behavior. For example, according to a well-known study, rural Liberians performed at a lower level, compared with students from New Mexico, in a card-sorting task. However, the Liberians were superior at sorting bowls of rice (Irwin et al., 1974). In several studies, Middle Eastern immigrants to North America were found to have better integrative thinking than other immigrants who performed similar object-sorting tasks in laboratory experiments. These differences were likely to reflect differences in national educational systems (Zebian & Denny, 2001). It was also found that many African Americans may have superior skills of categorizing people, but not objects (Shade, 1992).

Memory

Many comparative tests on memory contain tasks that require the subject to remember storylike information and then recall it. Are there any cultural differences in memory? Mandler and colleagues (1980) found relatively few differences in the recollection of stories between U.S. and Liberian children and adults. Similarly, common patterns in immediate recall of information were found among such distant cultural groups as English, Polish, and Shona in Zimbabwe (Whethrick & Deregowski, 1982).

Common patterns in how people recall stories do not mean there are common patterns in what people recall or how fast they process this information. Cultural, social, and educational experiences affect what we remember. Two groups of students, Australians and Asians (including Chinese, Japanese, and Korean), were asked to provide information about so-called self-defining memories. These memories were to be autobiographical recollections of events they believed shaped them as individuals. Australians provided more elaborate self-focused memories' and Asians produced more elaborate memories involving other people and relationships (Jobson & O'Kearney, 2008). Children of higher socioeconomic status receive better scores on various memorization tests compared with other students (Ciborski & Choi, 1974). Steffensen and Calker (1982) tested U.S. and Australian Aboriginal women by asking them to recall two stories about a child getting sick. The child was treated by Western medicine in one story (a situation familiar to U.S. women) and by native medicine in the other (a situation familiar to Australian women). The stories were recalled better when they were consistent with the subjects' knowledge. Similar results have been reported by other psychologists working with different cultural populations (Harris et al., 1992). Deregowski (1974) showed that urban children in Zambia recalled more test information than did rural residents. Perhaps better educational opportunities of urban boys and girls and emphasis on memorization in school activities influence children's test performance.

Formal and Mathematical Reasoning

Formal reasoning is a basic cognitive operation that is based on abstract analysis of given premises and deriving a conclusion from them. It is particularly sensitive to systematic schooling (Scribner & Cole, 1981). Formal reasoning is different from **empirical reasoning**, which is drawn from everyday experience. A person may develop skills of empirical reasoning but do poorly on a test that measures formal reasoning skills. Russian psychologist Luria (1976) demonstrated in one of his studies that illiterate peasants in Uzbekistan, a republic of the former Soviet Union, were able to understand empirical reasoning—when objects involved in reasoning were observable—but often failed to comprehend abstract formal reasoning that required assumptions and imagination.

Many cross-cultural studies have specifically focused on mathematical problems. This was the case not only because these studies provided a good test of reasoning ability but also because math symbols appear to be culturally neutral. One of the important findings was that Eastern cultures—such as China and Japan—are often thought to be advanced in the development of numerical abilities in their members. Indeed, Chinese participants performed significantly better on several mathematical measures than did U.S. students (Geary et al., 1992; Stevenson et al., 1990). Davis and Ginsburg (1993) compared Beninese (African), North American, and Korean children and found little difference in performance on informal life-related mathematical problems. However, on formal problems, the Korean children performed best. Why does this trend exist? The most common explanation is based on the assumption that there is a particular set of social norms developed in East Asian countries. In particular, parents and teachers spend more time and effort on the development of formal mathematical skills in children than their overseas counterparts typically do. The differences in educational norms and attitudes most likely cause the differences in test performance between American and East Asian children (van de Vijver & Willemsen, 1993). It was shown that European American and Asian American students as groups tend to be different in terms of using speech while solving reasoning problems. Talking is apparently more helpful to Europeans than it is to Asians because, as researchers suggested, Asians tend to use internal speech less than do European Americans (Kim, 2002).

Creativity

If you write a verse in English and rhyme "forever" and "together," this cannot be called creative poetry. Why? Because **creativity** typically means originality or the ability to produce valued outcomes in a novel way. The rhyme "forever–together" has already been used in hundreds of verses and songs.

Creativity is typically defined as the process of bringing into being something that is both novel and useful. Specifically, the creative cognition approach identifies two kinds of cognitive processes implicated in creative thinking—generative processes and exploratory processes. First, people actively retrieve or seek out relevant information that might have creative potential. Next, they examine these ideas to determine which ones should receive further processing, such as modification, elaboration, and transformation (Leung et al., 2008). In cross-cultural psychology, studies examining the role of culture in creativity focus mainly on social factors and socialization practices (Harrington, 1990; Stein, 1991). For example, persistent parental support and positive stimulation appear as good predictors of creativity (Simonton, 1987). In a comparative Mexican American study, children from economically advantaged families showed higher creativity scores than did disadvantaged children (Langgulung & Torrance, 1972). It was also found that Arab subjects tended to score higher on verbal creativity than on spatial creativity, which is probably due to the emphasis Islamic cultures place on achieving verbal proficiency and the religious restrictions placed on pictorial reflections of reality (Abou-Hatab, 1997; Mari & Karayanni, 1982). The same study showed that in Arab cultures males score higher than females on creativity tests. However, those subjects who were equally exposed to television, Western education, and travel showed little evidence of sex differences in their scores of creativity.

Cultural experiences may either help or hinder creativity. Our learned routines often help us to coordinate our social behaviors (Chiu & Hong, 2006). On the other hand, when an individual is immersed in and exposed to only one culture, the learned routines and conventional knowledge of that culture may limit his or her creative responses and growth. Studies show that multicultural experience is positively related to a preference for sampling ideas from unfamiliar cultures. However, foreign living, but not necessarily short-term foreign traveling, affects creative thinking. When living abroad, we encounter many opportunities for cognitive and behavioral adaptation and change. In addition, multicultural experience does not improve an individual's performance in a creativity task unless the individual is predisposed to being open to experience (Leung et al., 2008).

In the worlds of education and employment, decision makers have become overly dependent on tests of cognitive abilities, knowledge, or skills for making high-stakes decisions affecting the life opportunities of many individuals (Helms, 2007).

A CASE IN POINT

Multicultural experience may foster the creative expansion of ideas. What do you think about expatriate artists and writers whose brilliant insights emerged when they left their home-land and settled in a foreign country? Explore the biographies of some writers, composers, and artists. Where did they create their major masterpieces? Gabriel G. Marquez (born in Colombia), Vladimir Nabokov and Sergei Rachmaninoff (both born in Russia), Paul Gauguin (born in France), Nâzım Hikmet (born in Turkey), and Rabindranath Tagore (born in India). Could you suggest other names of people who created their masterpieces mainly abroad? Does this mean that a different culture inspires imagination or stimulates creative work? We should understand, however, that there are many other artists and writers who did not travel much and yet no one has doubts about their creativity and talent. Take, for example, Nezami, a great Persian poet. He stayed in one place for his entire life.

COGNITIVE SKILLS, SCHOOL GRADES, AND EDUCATIONAL SYSTEMS

It has been shown in numerous studies that IQ scores correlate with school grades. In other words, if Ali has a higher IQ than John, one can anticipate that Ali's grades in math, science, literature, and social studies will be better than that of John. Can one then make a suggestion that higher intelligence scores determine higher school grades? Yes, such an assumption is correct, but it may contain a logical error. Why? Because the high grades one receives at school may also be determined by one's effort, motivation, interest in learning, and individual discipline. These characteristics, in turn, may be largely influenced by one's family. Add peers' influence, teachers' effort and commitment, and the availability of educational resources at school and home—all may determine a particular individual's grades and test scores.

We should not forget that around the globe, national school systems are organized differently. In the United States, public education is primarily based on the guidelines determined by local communities. The federal government cannot dictate to the states or counties what students have to study in kindergarten, middle school, or high school. In many other countries, however, schools use standard curricula and students nationwide have similar textbooks on every subject. To illustrate, children in Japan are generally more advanced than their U.S. counterparts in math. This is not happening because of a difference in IQ—the average scores are similar—but rather because the Japanese school curriculum places a heavy emphasis on mathematics.

Studies also show a high correlation between total years of education and IQ scores. To put it simply, people with a higher IQ are likely to continue their education at college; people with a college degree are likely to have a higher IQ than individuals with a high school diploma (Neiser et al., 1996). A higher IQ may predict higher grades; that, in turn, may increase a person's motivation to stay in school.

CRITICAL THINKING

Are U.S. children behind the rest of the world in math and other academic disciplines? The notion that "we are losing" in education is now a new phenomenon in mass media. A 1957 cover story in a March issue of *Life* magazine read as follows: "Crisis in Education." The article suggested that hard-working and disciplined students in the communist Soviet Union were surpassing languid and carefree Americans in educational achievement. Back in the 1980s, numerous reports about the achievements of Japanese students compared to their American counterparts implied an inevitable and rapid economic decline vis-à-vis the growing might of the Japanese economy rising on the shoulders of highly educated Japanese workers.

Today, when compared with students in the world's most industrialized countries, U.S. students are on the same level with the others in every subject. Moreover, Americans commonly outperform everyone in disciplines such as civics (studies dealing with public affairs and the rights and duties of citizens). Of course, being on the same level with others does not mean that everything is great in U.S. educational system. Educational challenges of the United States are related to institutional and cultural factors. First, with a few exceptions, U.S. public schools are locally funded and are not run by the federal government unlike in most countries in the world including Russia, China, and India. Second, college education is widely available to a majority of U.S. students (through a huge network of state universities and two-year colleges), which does not require the high school student to have perfect grades and highest scores. Third, the U.S. educational system has historically placed a special emphasis on individual development, freedom of choice, creativity, and unconventional problem solving. This focus subsequently diffuses attention away from test-taking preparations (Farhi, 2007).

The first mark of intelligence, to be sure, is not to start things; the second mark of intelligence is to pursue to the end what you have started.

PANCHATANTRA—**The Anonymous Collection of Sanskrit Animal Fables**

CULTURE, TESTS, AND MOTIVATION

IQ test scores may be determined not only by one's intellectual skills but also by the individual's motivation, anxiety, and attitudes toward testing. For example, why is there a gap in intelligence test scores between whites and African and Mexican Americans, whereas no such gap exists for other immigrant groups, such as Arabs, Chinese, or Iranians? Explaining the difference, scholars sometimes refer to the so-called **low-effort syndrome** (Ogbu, 1991). The low-effort syndrome is an example of a coping strategy: "No matter how hard I try, I will be held back."

Members of minority groups may view positive feedback from a dominant group member more negatively than do members of dominant cultural group. In one experiment, a white evaluator praised or did not praise either black or white students for a good academic performance. Praised black students rated the evaluator as less polite than did nonpraised black students, whereas praise did not affect the white students' evaluations of the evaluator's courtesy. Black students tended to attribute praise to the evaluator's low expectations, whereas the white students tended to attribute praise to high expectations (Lawrence et al., 2011)

Why does this syndrome exist? In the United States, and perhaps in some other countries, there are at least two kinds of minorities. The first is immigrant minorities, most of whom come voluntarily in search of better conditions and opportunities. These minorities make use of high academic achievement as a condition of success. Caste minorities, on the contrary, were brought to the United States through slavery or forceful colonization. They developed a different attitude that was based on an assumption that academic success does not lead to advancements because society does not want them to advance educationally.

It is hard to disagree with the idea that people ought to see successful results for their hard work. Otherwise, pessimism may discourage many of us from studying, learning, and striving for a better future (Raspberry, 2000). Those who argue that some ethnic minorities express less motivation on intelligence tests typically suggest that such individuals do not try to excel on these tests because they believe that they will not go to college anyway, the tests are biased against them, and test results are unimportant. Perceiving themselves as minority groups and understanding that power and resources do not belong to them, some individuals believe that there is no reason for them to try to succeed because success is not achievable and their effort will not be rewarded by society just because of their minority status. Moreover, tests may be seen by some as another instrument by which the government tries to advance the discrimination of minorities (Williams & Mitchell, 1991).

Such negative attitudes may be passed on to younger generations and become part of value systems, which encourage people to seek alternative ways to survive that do not include education. Moreover, some blacks stereotypically define academic achievement as "white" behavior that is inappropriate for nonwhite individuals, especially African Americans (Ogbu, 1986).

Some scholars argue that the motivational levels of blacks and whites—those who take intelligence tests—are not substantially different (Herrnstein & Murray, 1994). The authors give as an example the "digit span test." During this test, the subject is instructed to repeat a sequence of numbers in the order read to her, for example, 11, 17, 20, 16, 9, 49. After a certain number of forward sequences or a certain number of mistakes, the tester asks the subject to repeat a sequence of numbers backward. These two parts of the test are conducted immediately, one after the other, and have identical content: The person has to repeat the same numbers presented to her.

The black–white differences on this test are about twice as great on backward digits as on forward digits. The authors argue that it is impossible to suggest that lack of motivation in black subjects is responsible for such differences: How come the differences are minimal on the "forward" sequence and substantial on the "backward" sequence?

However, if you think critically, you may find that the two halves of the test are not equal in their meaning to the participant. The first half of the test requires a relatively simple operation of memorizing and repeating. The second half of the test—when the subject is asked to repeat numbers backward—requires a substantial mental effort. This may activate psychological resistance in subjects who consider such a difficult task impossible to overcome and therefore not worth the sustained effort.

Yet tests results are not necessarily and always produce negative reaction among disadvantaged groups. Tests also can help individuals make decisions related to their performance that lead to success outcomes (Griffore, 2007). While preparing for a test or analyzing its results, a student may start looking for the ways to improve his or her memory, comprehension, and critical-thinking skills.

A man of humanity is one who, in seeking to establish himself, finds a foothold for others and who, desiring attainment for himself, helps others to attain.

Confucius (551–479 b.c.e.)—**Chinese Philosopher**

IQ, CULTURE, AND SOCIAL JUSTICE

Is the power of the few based on their intellectual skills? Exceptions notwithstanding, in most contemporary societies the amount of education received by people should predict, in general, their social status. Indeed, the higher your educational degree, the more prestigious and well paid the profession you can apply for and eventually receive. Moreover, as indicated earlier, individuals with a higher educational degree should ultimately earn more than those with fewer years of completed education. For example, in most societies, occupations such as doctors, lawyers, dentists, college professors, and some other professions require up to 20 years of formal schooling. In other words, a high IQ score indicates higher grades in school and may eventually lead toward a higher social status—the value of which is measured by income generated and occupational prestige.

Now use your critical thinking. Can you hypothesize that there can be societies in which certain prestigious professions do not require the person to pass a series of tests or have a high academic degree? In such cases, the relationship between IQ and earning potential will not be so evident and, therefore, IQ would probably lose its discriminatory power over people's lives. Does this mean that in contemporary societies, people are divided into "upper" and "lower" social categories according to their test scores?

Some easily argue that in the contemporary democratic societies people are born to be equal and laws protect their equal rights. Therefore, it is fundamentally wrong to continue to divide people socially based on their test scores. Why does the contemporary system have to be accepted as fair if it discriminates against certain groups? For instance, some ethnic minorities, primarily blacks, Hispanics, and Native Americans, have less opportunity to go to college and fewer chances of getting better jobs than those individuals who show higher IQ scores. Looking at this situation from a slightly different perspective, one could ask a question: "How could we call this a democratic society if we have only one system, which links societal success to test scores and indicates what jobs people should pursue and eventually how much money they can make?"

Others may reply as follows: "So what is the problem? We are all different. Some people are tall and some other people are short. We have different skills. We want to achieve different goals. We are not entitled to perform in the same way. We have to accept diversity. Diversity assumes some sort of inequality." As it was mentioned, intelligence test scores predict what profession an individual is likely to obtain. In the United States and many other countries, certain occupations require an applicant to earn a particular college degree and pass special qualification tests. No doubt, these professions require individuals to use their intellectual skills. For example, imagine yourself as a physician. What do you have to do daily? Most likely, you have to examine different patients with different symptoms and problems; you have to develop your research skills and observation proficiency to come up with the correct diagnosis; you have to communicate with insurance companies and your supervisors; you have to understand how to write prescriptions; you have to know how to talk to patients and their relatives; and you must read scientific and other professional journals. Should we continue? This job requires a high academic degree. People with lower degrees or without formal schooling should be expected to perform less complex activities.

Perhaps people will compete with and discriminate against one another in certain walks of life. Maybe there is no way to achieve equal performance and, therefore, equal scores on school tests. However, wherever it is possible, people living in a democratic society can reduce the impact of discrimination, whether intentional or not. For the sake of argument, suppose that two children are born in the year 2005. Should we expect that they are both entitled to have an equal opportunity to compete for a better future? Perhaps. However, in reality, from the beginning of their lives they may join the race for happiness at different "speeds." One child will have better conditions for intellectual growth, whereas the other will not live in such a favorable environment.

Will these two children have equal chances to develop equal cognitive skills, given their unequal environments, even though they had equal potential at birth? The answer is likely to be "no." However, what can one do about this situation? Should the government force everyone to give up property and resources and be equal economically and ideologically? Such attempts were made in the twentieth century by many Communist and totalitarian governments. The attempts eventually failed.

Very few of us will demand that people be totally equal and receive the same benefits regardless of their effort, skills, and moral behavior. However, we believe that a wealthy democratic society is capable of creating better conditions for its citizens by helping the disadvantaged to compete for and pursue happiness. This debate, however, brings about not only psychological but also many moral and political questions that are beyond the scope of the present analysis.

The situation with IQ testing and scores may be changing, however. Flynn (1987, 2007) has shown an interesting tendency of a continuous and steady worldwide rise in intelligence test performance. Detected primarily in developed countries, this effect stands for a three-point increase in IQ scores every 10 years. From a broader perspective, one can suggest that every new generation is expected to be scoring higher than their parents and others and the difference will be from 6 to 9 points. Such a difference may be caused by an increase in the technological advancement of the population. As an example, in the 1980s most video games were simple and one-dimensional with two or three slow-moving objects. Today's video games—mostly three-dimensional and multicolored—require significant preparation and training before one can successfully play any of them. Increased access to television and the Internet also adds to the complexity of the surrounding world and perhaps stimulates the development of individual psychological skills. Technology and other resources make a difference in people's lives. For example, in recent years the gap in IQ scores between U.S. rural and urban populations has significantly decreased (Neiser et al., 1996), which may be explained by a changing environment. In rural areas, children have greater access to various sources of information, such as television and the Internet, compared to the situation 20 or 40 years ago.

High test scores and overall academic success involve knowledge and skill acquisition, as well as motivation for learning. As many specialists imply, although academic learning is a primary goal of education, ideas about how best to achieve this goal need to be broadened to include children's participation in learning, their self-confidence as students, and their capacity to work effectively with other children and with adults (Bemak et al., 2005).

An honest heart being the first blessing, a knowing head is the second.

Thomas Jefferson (1743–1826)—Third U.S. President

AND IN THE END, MORAL VALUES

All in all, the contemporary view supported by many psychologists is that the most essential elements of intelligence are so-called higher-level abilities, namely, reasoning, problem solving, and decision making. Intelligence is not just a reaction to changes in environmental conditions. It is also one's global capacity to learn about this environment. Persons with higher intelligence are more capable of noticing, understanding, and explaining surrounding phenomena—in various situations and forms of activities—than are persons with lower-level intelligence. One belief is that people who have higher IQs have a better chance of changing our environment (Sternberg, 2004).

However, a person with a high IQ score and a better potential for changing the environment may also possess little or no moral values and lack compassion, sympathy, or goodwill.

Back in the 1970s Chomsky (1976), one of the most renowned specialists in human development, criticized a very popular approach to intelligence. This approach was based on an assumption that the individual's success is based on the amount of money that person makes. In fact, income and prestige are not and should not be the only measure of social success. In many countries, social accomplishment is largely determined, not necessarily by the person's ability to score high on IQ tests but also, and most important, by her survival skills. This may include the ability to (1) carry on with a limited supply of food and resources, (2) adapt to the environment, and (3) change the environment despite the overwhelming pressure of lawlessness, violence, pollution, and disease. Moreover, many people do not base their individual happiness, reason for working, and success only on extrinsic rewards and material factors. There are also moral satisfaction, love, friendship, and many other elements of human experience that may not be related to scores on an IQ test.

Exercise 5.2

Memory and Experience

Our familiarity with a subject or topic can affect how precisely we memorize and retrieve information. Different cultural experiences, therefore, could affect the quality of our memory in particular circumstances. Consider the following sentence: *The quarterback threw an incomplete pass and his mistake forced the team to punt the ball right before the two-minute warning.* Select five people who are familiar with U.S. football and five people who know very little or nothing about this game. Read the sentence to people in both groups. Then ask them to write down what they remembered. What kinds of results will you expect to receive? Indeed, even though it is difficult to recall all 22 words of this sentence, people from the first group (those who know football) would correctly remember most of the words. On the contrary, those who are not familiar with football will, perhaps, make several mistakes trying to convey the meaning of the sentence. Could you test these hypotheses?

Exercise 5.3

Searching for a Possible Bias in Written Tests

Three-quarters of the nation's schoolchildren (sample of 60,000 in the fourth, eighth, and twelfth grades) were unable to compose a well-organized, coherent essay, according to results of a federally sponsored writing test. Most students were able to compose short essays they were asked to write. However, their writing had neither the sophistication nor proficiency expected by a national board of educators, state officials, and business leaders (Cooper, 1999). There was also a gap in the performance of different racial and ethnic groups. White and Asian students were writing better than African Americans, Hispanics, and Native Americans were. That gap was narrower in schools located on military bases, where minority students scored higher than their counterparts elsewhere. Perhaps minority students benefited from an equitable distribution of resources at the Defense Department schools and the attitudes, education, and financial security of the schools located on military bases.

A CASE IN POINT

Rational Calculations and Moral Values

What would you do in the following situation? Imagine you are captain of a spaceship that landed with a crew of 10 people on a remote planet to conduct scientific research. You learn, however, that due to some catastrophic problems, the ship cannot be launched from the planet with all the crewmembers aboard: It is 170 pounds over the carrying capacity. Now the oxygen tank is almost drained. What would you do? In a famous classical series of "Star Trek,"

Mr. Spock, a character with superior intellectual skills—far exceeding those of other crew members—offered a very "logical" solution: To leave the least valuable crew member on the planet (where this person would die and, by this sacrifice, save the lives of the other crew members). Apparently "less intelligent" characters opposed this heartless reasoning and offered an alternative solution. Moral values in this case overcame logical calculations.

However, did anyone examine the possibility of a cultural bias of the tests? Apparently no. Below are the sample questions used by the National Assessment Governing Board to test the writing skills of students in various grades. Could you examine them and write your suggestions about whether the assignments are biased against certain ethnic groups? Explain your arguments and try to achieve both sophistication and proficiency in your analysis.

FOURTH GRADERS   We all have favorite objects that we care about and would not want to give up. Think of one object that is important or valuable to you. For example, it could be a book, a piece of clothing, a game, or any object you care about. Write about your favorite object. Be sure to describe the object and explain why it is valuable or important to you.

EIGHTH GRADERS   Imagine this situation! A noise outside awakens you one night. You look out the window and see a spaceship. The door of the spaceship opens and out walks a space creature. What does the creature look like? What does the creature do? What do you do? Write a story about what happens next.

TWELFTH GRADERS   Your school is sponsoring a voter registration drive for 18-year-old high school students. You and three of your friends are talking about the project. Your friends say the following:

> **Friend 1:** "I'm working on the young voters' registration drive. Are you going to come to it and register? You're all 18, so you can do it. We're trying to help increase the number of young people who vote and it shouldn't be too hard—I read that the percentage of 18- to-20-year-olds who vote increased in recent years. We want that percentage to keep going up."

> **Friend 2:** "I'll be there. People should vote as soon as they turn 18. It's one of the responsibilities of living in a democracy."

> **Friend 3:** "I don't know if people should even bother to register. One vote in an election isn't going to change anything."

Do you agree with friend 2 or 3? Write a response to your friends in which you explain whether you will or will not register to vote. Be sure to explain why and support your position with examples from your reading or experience. Try to convince the friend with whom you disagree that your position is the right one.

Chapter Summary

- Most definitions of intelligence include phrases such as knowing and understanding the reality around us. Intelligence is also defined as a set of mental skills that helps individuals reach a goal. Intelligence is also seen as the ability to use knowledge and skills to overcome obstacles. And finally, intelligence is defined as helping one to adapt to a changing environment.
- Intelligence is inseparable from cognition, diversified processes by which the individual acquires and applies knowledge. It usually includes processes such as recognition, categorization, thinking, and memory. Altogether, cognitive development is neither totally culturally relative nor completely uniform everywhere.
- In psychology, most attention has been given to the so-called psychometric approach to intelligence. This view is based on the assumption that our intelligence can "receive" a numerical value.
- Today various tests show differences in intelligence scores among large cultural groups.

For example, in the United States, Asian Americans (of East Asian origins) score the highest, followed by European Americans, Hispanics, and, lastly, African Americans. Thus, on the average, African American schoolchildren score 10–15 percent lower on a standardized intelligence test than white schoolchildren.

- In an attempt to explain some group differences on intelligence test scores, Sternberg suggested distinguishing between intelligence and intelligent behavior. Intelligence, from his standpoint, is a mental process that may or may not result in particular behavioral patterns. These patterns of intelligent behavior may vary from culture to culture. Something considered to be intelligent among members of one culture may not be viewed as such in other cultures.

- According to the nativist approach to intelligence, human cognitive phenomena are inborn. They unravel as a result of biological "programming," and environmental perception requires little active construction by the organism. There is evidence that heredity plays an important role in human intelligence. However, genetic links for individual differences and similarities do not imply that group differences—on the national level, for example—are also based on genetic factors.

- Some specialists imply that most intelligence tests benefit specific ethnic groups because of the test vocabulary—words and items used in the test questions. Tests may contain internal bias because they use words that are familiar to only some groups. As a result, members of these groups receive higher scores than those who do not belong to these groups.

- Many environmental conditions have been found to influence performance on intelligence tests. Among them are availability of and access to resources, variety of perceptual experiences, predominant type of family climate, educational opportunities, access to books and travel, presence or absence of cultural magical beliefs, general attitudes, and cultural practices.

- Intelligence scores are, in general, positively correlated with the socioeconomic status of the individual and the link between socioeconomic conditions and test performance shows at an early age. A child's IQ and the socioeconomic status of the child's parents are also positively correlated. An affluent and educated family is likely to provide a better material environment for a child and also has more resources to develop the child's intellectual potential than a poorer family. Poverty is responsible for a variety of indirect impacts on the intellectual development of children and adults.

- In the United States, people with high IQ scores are disproportionally represented among doctors, scientists, lawyers, and business executives. Individuals with low intelligence scores are disproportionally represented among people on welfare, prison inmates, single mothers, drug abusers, and high school dropouts.

- There is a difference in the way people across cultures value and construe intelligence. For instance, the conceptualization of intelligence as quick and analytic is not shared in all cultures. If one group's concept includes being detailed and precise in responding, but the other group does not mention these features (and mentions improvisation as an element of intelligence), then precision cannot be used as a criterion according to which the two groups are compared.

- According to a theory, there are differences in cognitive styles revealed by Western and East Asian students: Students from China, Korea, and Japan tend to be more holistic in their perceptions than do students of Western descent.

- Cognitive processes have cross-cultural similarity but may also develop in different ways according to specific cultural norms and societal demands. People develop cognitive characteristics best adapted to the needs of their lifestyle. Cross-cultural findings suggest that differences in categorization, memorization, labeling, creativity, and formal reasoning may be rooted in cultural factors. Various cultural groups categorize stimuli differently in terms of their specific cultural experiences associated with these objects. Many cognitive processes can develop either in similar or in different ways according to specific cultural norms and societal demands.

- U.S. children, generally, are allowed more freedom in choosing school activities than their overseas counterparts. The emphasis is typically placed on individual development, enjoyable activities, and respect for the child's personality. In Asian countries, on the contrary, the active promotion of the mathematical development of children is crucial. From the beginning the child learns rules of discipline, perseverance, and sacrifice for the sake of educational goals.

- Some ethnic minorities may display the so-called low-effort syndrome, or low level of motivation on intelligence tests. This typically suggests that such individuals do not try to excel on these tests because they believe that they will not go to college anyway, the tests are biased against them, and test results are unimportant.

- Overall, in developed Western societies, high IQ scores are correlated with social success. The situation with IQ testing and scores may be changing, however. There is an interesting tendency of a continuous and steady world-wide rise in intelligence test performance. Detected primarily in developed countries, this effect stands for a three-point increase in IQ scores every 10 years and may be attributed to educational efforts and technological developments.

Key Terms

Cognition A general term that stands for a series of processes by which the individual acquires and applies knowledge.

Cognitive Style An individual way in which individuals organize and comprehend the world.

Creativity Originality or the ability to produce valued outcomes in a novel way.

Empirical Reasoning Experience and cognitive operations drawn from everyday activities.

Field-Dependent Style A general cognitive ability of an individual to rely more on external visual cues and to be primarily socially oriented.

Field-Independent Style A general cognitive ability of an individual to rely primarily on bodily cues within themselves and to be less oriented toward social engagement with others.

Formal Reasoning Basic cognitive operations based on abstract analysis of given premises and deriving a conclusion from them.

Intelligence Global capacity to think rationally, act purposefully, overcome obstacles, and adapt to a changing environment.

Low-Effort Syndrome Low level of motivation on intelligence tests based on the belief that the tests are biased and test results are unimportant for success in life.

Nativist View The view that all cognitive phenomena are inborn, that they unravel as a result of biological "programming," and that environmental perception requires little active construction by the organism.

Psychometric Approach to Intelligence A view based on an assumption that our intelligence can "receive" a numerical value.

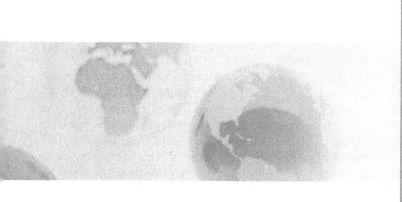

Emotion

Usually when people are sad, they don't do anything.
They just cry over their condition. But when they get angry,
they bring about a change.

MALCOLM X (1925–1965)—
U.S. Civil Rights Activist

Did you know that public kissing is not acceptable in Japan? No, this country doesn't have an antipecking law. It is simply an old and informal rule of conduct. Of course, if you travel to Japan, you may recall an episode or two when young couples are kissing goodbye at a train station or airport. However, these are rare exceptions to the main rule: affection and tenderness should not be publicly displayed. Groping, kissing, hugging, and puckering are extremely rare on Japanese streets. Do not think that this cultural ban on public displays of affection is linked to the prohibition of sex. It is very much alive and prominently displayed in the Japanese media. Just watch Japanese television, especially in the late hour. Or get a racy magazine—usually sealed in plastic—from a store's top shelf. So what is so unacceptable about public kissing? Ask any person who grew up in Japan, and he will tell you that people in this country, from the beginning of their lives, learn how to restrain their emotions in public. It is considered a sign of weakness if an individual cannot control anxiety, fear, joy, or sadness—any form of affection—and allows others to see it. If the expression of feelings is so tightly controlled by the rules, does this mean that the emotions are suppressed in Japan to the extent that they are not felt?

Right now, at this very moment, someone in Montreal is jumping for joy because he got a job promotion. At the other end of the planet, in Jerusalem, a girl is anxiously anticipating her first Bat Mitzvah. Stuck in traffic, an angry Moscow cab driver vents his frustration at other motorists. An army conscript in Korea is anxious before his first parachute jump. **Emotion**, or affect, is an evaluative response that typically includes some combination of physiological arousal, subjective experience (positive, negative, or ambivalent), and behavioral expression. Joy and disappointment, sadness and surprise, envy and pride, and dozens of other emotions accompany our daily lives regardless of where we live or what language we speak. We display emotions from the day we are born. We learn about them from the people around us, the books we read, and the movies we watch. Masterfully described in word, image, and sound, human emotions always draw significant interest from artists and poets. For centuries they illustrate, reflect, paint, and portray love, grief, guilt, and the excitement of human existence.

A brief educational tour through scholarly books reveals that human emotions always occupied philosophical minds. Sophisticated and fascinating observations about emotions can be found in the works of the Chinese educator and philosopher Confucius (fifth century B.C.E.), Epicureanians and Sophists in Greece (third to fifth centuries B.C.E.), the Persian physician and thinker Avicenna (eleventh century), Europeans Descartes and Spinoza (seventeenth century), and many others. However, the scientific study of emotion began only recently—just over a century ago.

One of the pioneers in this field, William James (1884), offered the theory that emotion is embedded into bodily experience. The physical experience leads the person to feel aroused, and the arousal stimulates the subjective experience of anxiety, joy, and so forth. According to James, people do not jump and clap their hands because they are happy; rather they become happy because they jump and clap their hands. James even gave advice about how to feel particular emotions: "The voluntary path to cheerfulness, if our spontaneous cheerfulness be lost, is to sit up cheerfully, and act and speak as if cheerfulness were already there. To feel brave, act as if we were brave, use all our will to that end, and courage will very likely replace fear" (compare Wallis, 1965, p. 156). At around the same time that James was putting forth his ideas in the United States, a Danish physiologist, Carl Lange (1885), proposed similar views on emotions. This view is now called the James–Lange theory.

Forty years later, Cannon and Bard published an alternative outlook, known as the Cannon–Bard theory of emotion. According to this approach, various life situations—such as a hairy spider crawling on your shoulder—can simultaneously elicit both an emotional experience, such as disgust or fear, and bodily responses, such as increased blood pressure or sweaty palms (Cannon, 1927). In the 1960s, another theory of emotion gained popularity among psychologists. According to the theory's authors (Schachter & Singer, 1962), there are two crucial elements of emotional experience: physiological arousal and the cognitive interpretation of this arousal. In every emotion, we first experience a state of physiological arousal. Then we try to explain to ourselves what the arousal means. If the situation suggests that we should experience pleasure, we call it joy. If somebody threatens us, we call this experience fear.

These theories were created in Western psychology. However, do they apply cross-culturally? To answer, we have at least two basic alternatives. According to one, all human emotions are universal. They have a similar underlying physiological mechanism and the specific cultural environment only applies some "make-up" on human affect. For example, in the United States, a group of happy friends will "high-five" each other when their favorite team scores a goal, whereas in Europe friends are more likely to shake hands in a similar circumstance.

However, the joy will be felt by both groups of friends in the same way regardless of the differences in its expression. In short, sadness is sadness and elation is elation no matter where you live, in Mexico, Bosnia, Nigeria, or Vietnam.

The other alternative emphasizes both cultural origin and cultural specificity of emotion. According to this view, all human emotions develop in specific cultural conditions and therefore can be best understood primarily within a particular cultural context. For example, an observer may identify a sarcastic smile on the face of a Polish worker if the observer understands both the nature of sarcasm—a form of expression in which meanings are conveyed obliquely—and the surrounding circumstances in which the sarcastic reaction was displayed.

Which one of these views received stronger empirical support? Consider evidence from both sides of the argument.

WHEN WE LAUGH WE ARE HAPPY: SIMILARITIES OF EMOTIONAL EXPERIENCE

People can tell other people's emotions. Even though we do not speak someone's language, we can often understand whether this person is happy or sad. If you understand what other people feel by judging their emotional expressions, and if they can judge your emotions correctly, that means human feelings are universal. This is exactly what Darwin (1872) suggested in his famous work, *Expression of the Emotions in Man and Animals.* He collected interviews from around the world and concluded that basic human emotional expressions are similar because they serve an adaptive purpose. Both animals and humans signal their readiness or willingness to help, fight, or run through gestures, postures, and facial expressions. Imagine, for example, you see your friend's eyes wide open, you hear his scream, and you observe him throwing away a cup of soda. This combination of reactions might alert you to the fact that it is likely your friend is scared or disgusted by something he found in the cup. Almost immediately, you will check to see if anything—a bug?—is in your cup too. Emotions regulate social behavior and may protect people from danger. Fear and anger, for example, produce greater acceleration of heart rate than does joy. This makes sense if one thinks in evolutionary terms. Anger and fear are related to fight-or-flight responses that require the heart to pump more blood to the muscles: All in all, you have to either defend yourself or run away from a threat. In people of all cultures, fear causes a particular defensive reaction in dangerous situations. Likewise, disgust prevents us from trying potentially toxic substances such as rotten food or spoiled water (Izard, 1977).

Empirical studies demonstrate many similarities in the ways people display their feelings. A comparison of emotional facial expressions of people from Western industrialized

CRITICAL THINKING

There is at least one serious methodological problem associated with survey-based studies of emotional expressions. Such expressions should be explained in survey questions and verbalized by the subjects. This issue presents a problem because many people cannot remember exactly how they express emotions and cannot describe with precision specific reactions other people display. Second, people have a tendency to give socially desirable answers assuming that some emotional expressions are not necessarily "good" or "moral" (such as laughing aloud or expressing anger openly). Therefore, many people may answer not in terms of how they react but in terms of how they should react (Oishi et al., 2004; Wang et al., 2006).

countries and non-Western settings showed significant resemblance (Ekman, 1980). Researchers found universal patterns in the vocal expression of emotion (Van Bezooijen et al., 1983) and cross-cultural invariance in the behavioral expression of complex emotions such as jealousy and envy (Hupka et al., 1985).

A 2004 comparative study involving 37 countries revealed that people in both Western and non-Western countries displayed the same general pattern as it pertains to the expression of emotions. Men, as compared to women, tended to express more anger, while women, in comparison to men, tended to express more sadness and fear (Fischer et al., 2004). Remember that these data reflected only general tendencies describing men and women as large groups.

Another interesting argument about similarities in human emotion derives from numerous studies about the process of identification, description, and explanation of an emotional expression, for short, **emotion recognition** (Ekman, 1980; Izard, 1971). For instance, in one such study, subjects in five countries—the United States, Brazil, Chile, Argentina, and Japan—were shown photographs of people, each of whom displayed one of six emotions: happiness, sadness, anger, fear, surprise, or disgust. Most subjects correctly identified these emotions (Ekman & Friesen, 1969). People show remarkable accuracy in the interpretation of eyebrow positioning and smiling (Keating et al., 1981). For instance, smiling is universally understood as a sign of happiness and lowered eyebrows as a sign of anger or domination. In another study, which included subjects from Estonia, Germany, Greece, Hong Kong, Italy, Japan, Scotland, Sumatra, Turkey, and the United States, Ekman and colleagues (1987) demonstrated that mixed emotional expressions, such as shame and frustration, are also easily recognizable across countries.

Research on cross-cultural recognition of emotional intonation in the voice has yielded similar results: People typically identify the speaking person's emotion in cases in which the speaker uses a foreign tongue and the voice is recorded on tape (Albas et al., 1976; Van Bezooijen et al., 1983). In a study, subjects from Western and non-Western cultures were asked to make the face they would show when they were happy to see somebody, angry with someone, sad about bad news, and so on. These facial expressions were recorded and later analyzed. The findings suggested the existence of the same facial muscular patterns in both subject groups (Ekman & Friesen, 1978). In other words, people across cultures not only can easily recognize basic emotions but also use the same muscle groups to express their feelings. Most people across the world are able to infer emotion from vocal cues. A study was conducted in nine countries in Europe, the United States, and Asia on vocal emotion portrayals of anger, sadness, fear, joy, and neutral voice as produced by professional German actors. Data show an overall accuracy of more than 60 percent across all emotions and countries (Scherer et al., 2001).

There is amazing similarity in the way people name emotions across different cultures and languages (Russell, 1991). In other languages, there are equivalent words for virtually every English term for emotions (Scherer & Wallbott, 1994; Scherer et al., 1988). All languages make distinctions between positive affect and negative affect, and this distinction is explained to young children, who begin to use words and phrases such as "nice," "mean," "good," "bad," "I like," and "I don't like" at a very early age. There are also similarities in the way in which different languages define so-called basic emotions. Although theorists may generate slightly different lists, most classifications include from five to nine emotions. Anger, fear, happiness, sadness, and disgust are present in almost every national classification. Surprise, contempt, interest, shame, joy, trust, anticipation, and guilt are present in others (Lynch, 1990; Russell, 1991; Vekker, 1978).

There is evidence that people living in distant parts of the world developed relatively similar linguistic labels for certain complex emotions, which probably indicates some common, universal roots of human emotional experiences. For example, in the Japanese and Middle English dialects,

CROSS-CULTURAL SENSITIVITY

A study of samples in 32 countries (including India, China, Turkey, Israel, Russia, Zimbabwe, the United States, Germany, and Mexico) showed that individualism was positively correlated with higher expressivity of emotions, especially happiness and surprise. Individualism was negatively correlated with expression of sadness. These findings suggest that cultural individualism, in general, is associated with endorsement of positive emotions (Matsumoto et al., 2008). Contempt, disgust, and fear were the least endorsed emotions in all samples. Most probably, negative emotions, particularly contempt and disgust, are perceived as disruptive to

social relationships, and this tendency is stronger in collectivist cultures (Butler et al., 2009). Sadness also signals distress (Izard, 2004), and this can also be interpreted as a clear sign of a person's weakness. However, these findings do not indicate that individuals from predominantly collectivist cultures are always reserved in their emotional expressions and people from mainly individualist cultures are not. When judging other people's emotional expressions, think about these people's unique personality features, the circumstances of the situation, and your role in this situation. Don't make a mistake of self-fulfilling prophecy (see Chapter 3).

there are two words—*amae* and *mardiness*—both apparently indicating an individual's need for affection (Lewis & Ozaki, 2009).

All in all, supporters of the idea of the universality of human emotion argue that similar emotions exist in all cultures. We react to external events and bodily signals with similar facial expressions, physiological changes, and subjective experiences of pleasure or displeasure. Cross-culturally, individuals are emotionally sensitive to the loss of relatives and friends, the birth of their children, the victories of their favorite sports team, and criticism from others. Across cultures, sadness can cause crying, anger can provoke aggression, and joy often helps people to forgive.

YOU CANNOT EXPLAIN PAIN IF YOU HAVE NEVER BEEN HURT: DIFFERENCES IN EMOTIONAL EXPERIENCE

Despite similarities in emotional experiences across cultures, there is no one single universal description of basic emotions. In the Buddhist tradition (accepted in Chinese language, for example), the basic seven emotions are described as happiness, anger, sorrow, joy, love, hate, and desire. There is no disgust in this lineup. Also, Russell and Yik (1996) reviewed studies of ancient Chinese texts reflecting dominant philosophies including Confucianism, Daoism, and Buddhism and found various sets of noted emotions, ranging from five to seven. Their English translations of all the emotion labels, totaling 12 names, did not include disgust. Recent studies of emotion recognition showed that subjects in China, compared to other groups, had more problems with recognition of disgust on photographed faces. However, other studies involving physiological measurements indicate that Chinese subjects tend to identify six basic emotions in the same way that people of other nationalities do (Wang et al., 2006). Differences in the expression of emotional experience, linguistic variety in the labeling of emotions, and distinct socialization practices all suggest culture-specific origins of human emotions. According to this view, people's emotions vary because they are based on different experiences that are related to the culture in which they originate.

Cultures may be at variance in the frequency and significance of common emotional reactions (Matsumoto et al., 1988). For example, some studies have pointed to cultural differences in the degree to which some groups experience positive emotions, such as joy (Markus & Kitayama, 1994b), and negative emotions, such as anger (Solomon, 1978). Shigehiro Oishi, a Japanese American psychologist, and several of his colleagues surveyed more than 350 college students in Japan, Korea, and the United States. They found that on average, European Americans report to be happier than Asian Americans, Koreans, or Japanese. However, European Americans become emotionally distracted by negative events (getting a parking ticket or receiving a bad grade) and recover from these setbacks slower than their counterparts of Asian ancestry. Alternatively, Koreans, Japanese, and, to a lesser extent, Asian Americans report that they are less happy in general but "recover" to their normal emotional state faster than European Americans. The researchers found that European Americans needed nearly two positive events to return to their normal level of happiness (e.g., getting an encouraging call or receiving an A). The Koreans, Japanese, and Asian Americans, on average, needed only one positive event to recover emotionally (Oishi et al., 2004). Cultures also vary in linguistic descriptions of emotion. The Tahitian language, for example, has 46 different words for anger but no word for sadness. In some African languages, the same word can represent both sadness and anger. In some local Russian dialects, the phrase "I pity you" can either stand for "I love you" or indicate one's condolence.

Despite obvious similarities in the facial recognition of emotions, subjects from various cultures also vary in the degree of agreement. In one study, for example, happiness was correctly identified by 68 percent of African participants and by 97 percent of their European counterparts (Izard, 1969). In another study, U.S. and European groups correctly identified from 75 to 83 percent of emotions in the facial photographs, whereas the Japanese group scored 65 percent and the African group only 50 percent. The recognition rate of facial expressions on photographs was lower when subjects had little previous contact with other cultures (Izard, 1971). Schimmack (1996), after conducting a meta-analysis of the existing studies of emotion, showed that white participants were better than nonwhite participants in recognizing happiness, fear, anger, and disgust, but not surprise and sadness. Other research has demonstrated that there are cultural differences in accuracy and speed with which emotions of other people can be judged (Elfenbein & Ambady, 2003).

Disgust, as an emotion, is associated with cultural requirements to reject certain foods or avoid particular situations related to eating. Once accepted, these requirements are supported by a powerful emotion and thus become less subject to temptation or modification. The classic cross-cultural study of disgust emphasized that people develop expectations about how children should react to particular foods and food consumption (Rozin & Fallon, 1987). For example, most of us are not continuously concerned about the regular food we chew; however, most of us would feel disgust and refuse to eat the food that we had spit out a second ago. Most of us wouldn't mind sucking our own blood from a cut finger, but a majority would be repulsed by the idea of ingesting our own blood after it had been accumulated onto a spoon. There is a worldwide aversion to eating animals that are physically similar to humans or have close interactive relations with humans, such as pets, including cats and dogs, in most countries. Such practices are learned usually early in our lives. We tend to avoid the situations in which disgust is induced. It happens without a significant conscious effort, almost automatically.

Disgust is associated with the perception of food contamination. If a person believes, for instance, that a glass of juice is contaminated, this individual is not likely to drink out of the glass unless something is done to "clean" the contaminated juice. People vary in their perceptions of which food products or drinks are contaminated. Some cultural differences exist as well. A study of 125 Hindu Indian and 106 U.S. children between the ages of four and eight

A CASE IN POINT
A United Nations Dinner Party

Imagine you are invited to attend a New Year reception at the UN headquarters in New York. There you have to try many kinds of ethnic dishes prepared by the ambassadors' chefs. Among the displayed foods you find steamed beef tongue, broiled dog meat, roasted lamb brains, and a bowl of fermented horse milk. You have to try them all! Will you be disgusted by these foreign foods? Perhaps yes, if your taste for food has been developed at McDonalds or Pizza Hut. However, is it fair to suggest that your disgust, as an emotion, can be experienced only by you and not by the people who cooked these foods? The answer, of course, is: Other people can experience disgust too, but feel it in different situations. Does this mean that we all have similar emotions "within" us but that they are "activated" only in particular situations? Does this mean that our knowledge about human emotions is relative to the situation in which emotions occur?

showed that most rejected food contaminated by contact with a cockroach, a human hair, or if the juice was tried by a stranger. Indian children, however, were more sensitive than U.S. children to contaminants. The Indian children responded significantly more strongly to stranger or cockroach contamination and did not accept "purifications" (such as boiling or a mother's touch). Specialists suggest that interpersonal disgust and contagion are a more substantial aspect of Hindu Indian culture than of most Western cultures. Any contact with the mouth, either direct (through biting or sipping) or indirect (through the hand or saliva), can make the food unacceptable. In particular, in this study, for Indian children no purification was accepted in removing stranger contamination; boiling of the juice was effective for most Americans (Hejmadi et al., 2004).

It was also found in several studies that Japanese participants relatively less often used descriptions such as "afraid" and more often used "surprised," compared with participants from Indian and North American groups. Americans relatively more often, in comparison to other groups, endorsed expressions as "afraid" and less often as "surprised" or "disgusted" (Elfenbein et al., 2002).

Differences in emotion recognition between representatives of two cultures may exist because some emotional expressions are cultivated in children during the socialization process and some are not. In an earlier example about the Japanese and English idioms standing for the need for affection, the English mardiness is considered childish in most cases and thus less acceptable than the Japanese amae, which is treated kindly and supportively (Lewis & Ozaki, 2009). On the other hand, the public display of emotions may be seen as disruptive and thus inappropriate. This may affect the Japanese perception of people from other cultures who do display their emotions freely. For instance, a Japanese observer may see such individuals as being hyper and disorderly. Differences in the perception of emotions were found in many other countries. When Greek and British individuals observe other people in embarrassing situations, the Greeks usually overestimate the intensity of the observed emotion of embarrassment, whereas the British observers usually underestimate the intensity (Edelman et al., 1989). Such a difference may be caused by more developed norms of collectivism in Greece compared with Great Britain. Therefore, people in Greece feel more interconnected and group oriented and that makes their embarrassment more intense than it is for the British.

Several studies found that both men and women identified angry expressions most quickly. But they also found that anger was more quickly identified on a male face than on a female face (Williams et al., 2007). Probably, the reason for this difference is that being able to spot an angry individual quickly has a survival advantage—and, since anger is more likely to turn into lethal violence in men than in women, the ability to spot angry males quickly is particularly valuable.

Now that we have learned about two distinct approaches to understanding the relationships between culture and emotion, how do we know which is correct? The first approach advocates cross-cultural universality, whereas the second suggests cultural origin and specificity of human emotion (Ekman, 1994; Mead, 1975; Russell, 1994). Before we suggest an answer, consider the following case.

EMOTIONS: DIFFERENT OR UNIVERSAL?

Is severe pain after a stumble likely to cause a negative emotion in any two individuals? Perhaps. What if one is born and raised in Puerto Rico and the other came from Iran? There is no difference: A stumble causes physical pain, and pain causes a negative emotion. Should detachment from a person you love make you sad? Possibly. If you are thirsty and get a glass of water, will you experience joy? Most likely, yes. But will you necessarily feel and show your emotions exactly in the same way as others do? Not really. How we feel and how we express our feelings is based on our personality, experiences, immediate circumstances, presence or absence of people, and many other factors. For example, you may hide frustration after a clumsy fall in a public place but scream and curse if such a fall happens in your home where no one can see you. Emotions can be seen as similar or different because we often perceive, analyze, and think about them from different points of view.

Cultural differences in emotions tend to grow larger as the level of description becomes more concrete. We can generally consider jealousy as sadness. Alternatively, by applying a "magnifying glass" for a more detailed analysis, jealousy may be interpreted as a blend of anger, fear, sadness, and frustration. High levels of abstraction cause us to see people from different cultures or social groups as similar in their emotions. Here we can all recall public stereotypes about "emotionless" Finns and Japanese, "hot-blooded" Italians and Brazilians, and "sensuous" Arabs and French.

For a more comprehensive cross-cultural analysis of emotions, we should look "inside" the emotion. First, looking again at the definition, we should try to understand emotion as a multicomponential process (Frijda, 1986; Scherer, 1984). First, an emotion is initiated, there is an underlying physiological process for the emotion, the emotion is experienced, then it is displayed or remains hidden, it somehow affects our decisions, the emotion may cause other emotions, and it eventually fades away. Are there any cross-cultural findings that shed some light on what role culture may play in these stages? In the beginning of the chapter we indicated that emotion includes physiological arousal. Let us describe it in some detail.

PHYSIOLOGICAL AROUSAL

There are significant cross-cultural similarities in the underlying physiological mechanisms of emotions. Universally, we detect stimuli from our surroundings and our body. The signal then goes to the brain. The amygdala serves as the brain's "emotional computer": It assesses the affective significance of the stimulus. Therefore, irrelevant stimuli may cause no emotion.

Then, the hypothalamus, as a part of the limbic system, activates sympathetic and endocrine responses related to emotion. The brain's cortex also plays several roles with respect to emotion, particularly in the appraisal of stimuli. Moreover, the right hemisphere is believed to be responsible for the facial displays of emotion (Borod, 1992). Current research also suggests that pleasant emotions are associated with the activation of the left frontal cortex, whereas unpleasant emotions are mostly associated with the activation of the right frontal lobe (Davidson, 1992).

Experimental studies show that when people of various national groups express their emotions, their blood pressure changes as well. Cross-culturally, embarrassment has common physiological responses, and one of them is increased body temperature (Edelman et al., 1989). In a classic study, researchers gave participants specific directions to contract their facial muscles in particular ways characteristic of anger, sadness, happiness, surprise, or disgust (Ekman et al., 1983). Subjects held these expressions for 10 seconds, during which particular physiological reactions were measured. The researchers found a connection between the simple act of changing facial expressions and patterns of physiological response. Different emotions produce differences in variables such as acceleration of heart rate, finger temperature, and a measure of sweat on the palms related to arousal or anxiety, also known as galvanic skin response. A comparison between the physiological changes reported by subjects from Southern and Northern European regions also yielded interesting results. The "hot-blooded" southerners reported significantly more blood pressure changes while experiencing joy, sadness, and anger, compared to the "cold" northerners (Rime & Giovannini, 1986). However, in other study, Asian Americans compared to European Americans expressed significantly larger increases in blood pressure when they were expressing negative emotions (Butler et al., 2009).

But what may cause such diverse physiological reactions?

Take away the cause, and the effect ceases; what the eye never sees, the heart never rues.

MIGUEL DE CERVANTES **(1547–1616)—Spanish Novelist and Poet**

THE MEANING OF PRECEDING EVENTS

There is always something that causes or initiates an emotion. A pain in your body, a lost soccer game, a meeting with a person you adore, a windy and rainy day, or an annoying flow of music streaming from a neighbor's window—many **preceding events** in our everyday lives bear particular emotional significance for us. However, do people across cultures agree that certain situations should elicit similar emotions? Do all people concede that the loss of a friend is a sad event, and that the birth of a child is a happy one? There is more than ample research data to confirm that this is the case: Cross-culturally, basic emotions are generally marked by similar types of events. Let us illustrate this statement with the results of several cross-cultural studies.

Subjects from the United States, South Korea, and Samoa were asked to write stories about an event causing one of six emotions: anger, disgust, fear, happiness, sadness, or surprise (Brandt & Boucher, 1985). Then, these stories were presented to other subjects for evaluation. Substantial similarities were found in the assignment of emotions related to stories among the examined cultures as well as within cultures. A year later, Wallbott and Scherer (1986) published a study that examined situations in which people experienced joy, fear, anger, sadness, disgust, shame, and guilt. Data collected in 27 countries suggested that although there were some differences among the samples, these differences were much lower than the ones within the countries. Evidence for similarity in preceding events is also shown in a study conducted by Scherer and his colleagues (1988), in which subjects were asked to describe a situation that had caused them to feel happy, sad, angry, or scared. After the task was complete, these situations were grouped into several categories. In all cultures, the most important event categories were birth and death, good and bad news about relatives, and friends, acceptance or rejection in relationships, meetings with friends, dates, temporary and permanent separation, listening to music, sexual experiences, interaction with strangers, and success or failure. In another study, both U.S. and Malay subjects were equally accurate in their identification of emotions caused by 96 different types of events (Boucher & Brandt, 1981). Matsumoto and colleagues (1988) found a large degree of cultural agreement in how people in Japan and the United States evaluate situations that evoke particular emotions. Cross-cultural similarities were found in the perception of events that cause people to experience jealousy and envy (Hupka et al., 1985).

CRITICAL THINKING

Example 1

If we limit our analysis of human emotion only to the question of whether an emotion is expected to occur, we will find many cross-cultural similarities among human feelings. Indeed, any starving person presumably will be happy to have a piece of bread. However, if we focus on how emotion is experienced and displayed in human activities, we are more likely to see cultural differences. Consider, for example, Japanese sumo wrestlers. If you have a chance to watch a sumo tournament (they are often broadcast on U.S. television), you will discover that the wrestlers never show their emotions. Even if a wrestler experiences a tough loss, spectacular victory, excruciating pain, or the spectators' loud ovation, he remains emotionless. Not a single muscle moves on his face. After seeing these pictures, one may conclude that sumo wrestlers do not experience emotions. However, it is more plausible to assume that emotions are indeed felt by the wrestlers, but they are not displayed. It takes many years of practice and education to become a professional sumo wrestler. During this time the candidates patiently learn how to hide their joy, frustration, and other feelings during the competition. In contrast to the sumo wrestlers' training, South American and European soccer players are not trained to hide their emotions on the field. Instead, they may find it beneficial to exaggerate their expression of pain after a collision with an opponent because referees—observing the

player's display of pain—might feel obliged to penalize the opposing team.

Other Examples

We have to pay special attention to a particular level of abstraction on which emotions are described. The very same emotion of joy, for example, may be culturally similar or cross-culturally different, depending on the level of generalization chosen for description. Perhaps many similarities in emotions are likely to be found when they are described at a high level of generality or abstraction. An emphasis in one's observations on specific emotional characteristics would perhaps highlight cultural differences. Many authors, for example, write about a "specific" fear that existed and still exists in people of totalitarian political cultures: These individuals are afraid of political persecution for speaking up (Gozman & Edkind, 1992; Smith, 1976). However, a more abstract analysis may yield an interpretation of a different kind: These individuals experience a typical fear based on an absolutely adequate evaluation of a threat. As soon as the threat of persecution is eliminated, the fear may disappear as well (Shiraev & Bastrykin, 1988). Likewise, millions of undocumented aliens may experience fear of deportation from the United States. This fear is unfamiliar to U.S. citizens if we see it as a special type of fear. Described in a more general way, this emotion loses its specificity, and fear of deportation becomes nothing more than a state of reluctant anticipation of an unpleasant event.

Grief diminishes when it has nothing to grow on.

PUBLILIUS SYRUS (FIRST CENTURY B.C.E.)—Roman Writer

Nevertheless, the same situations can be interpreted differently across cultures and, therefore, lead to different emotions. There is also scientific and anecdotal evidence for cultural differences in emotion-eliciting events. Most Europeans, as well as North and South Americans, for instance, consider the number 13 as unlucky, and some are even afraid to live in an apartment numbered 13 or on the thirteenth floor. People of many other ethnic groups, on the contrary, would pay little attention to this number. People in Russia, for example, are afraid to keep an even number of flowers in a vase: An even number of flowers is typically brought to a funeral. A Canadian student, however, is likely to be unaware of this foreign superstition and would be thrilled to receive six flowers from her fiancé.

Consistent with other studies, Chinese students were found to experience higher levels of anxiety in mathematics compared to students from Germany. They were also found to experience more enjoyment, pride, and shame, and less anger than German students (Frenzel et al., 2007). Liem (1997) analyzed the experience of shame and guilt in first- and second-generation Asian Americans and European Americans. The participants were asked to describe situations in which they felt guilty or were embarrassed. Some differences were found between the first-generation immigrants. According to this study, Europeans experienced guilt as an anticipated moral transgression: Guilt indicates that a person violated an internal standard of ethical behavior even though there is no public notice of such violation. In the stories reported by first-generation Asian Americans, the typical guilt-related situation is based on the feeling of failed or unfulfilled duty. For European Americans, shame centers on the presence of other people: It is shameful that other people discover your inappropriate actions. For first-generation Asian Americans, shame also involves the presence of outsiders. However, another element is present that is not typical in the picture of shame among European Americans. This is a group to which the person belongs, usually his or her family. Therefore, shame is also felt as regret for letting some important people down. It is interesting that the differences in experiencing shame and guilt are insignificant between the second generation of Japanese Americans and European Americans.

As you saw, a large number of preceding events can produce similar emotional responses in most human beings, regardless of their cultural origin or current identity. These studies suggest a high degree of similarity in human emotional sensitivity to particular life events or conditions. There is also evidence that particular emotions can be elicited by culture-specific events. People who are not familiar with various cultural norms and traditions may not recognize such emotions and may make mistakes in communications. What kinds of mistakes? Imagine, for example, a host who offers a beef sandwich to a Hindu guest at a party.

EMOTION AS AN EVALUATION

We are usually aware of our emotions, and we feel good or bad, scared, surprised, frustrated, or relieved at different times. Despite tremendous individual variations, there are some cultural norms and rules that regulate our **evaluations of emotions**. There is evidence that people may

CRITICAL THINKING
Being Alone

Have you ever had some time on your own when nobody was near you? How did you feel? Did you enjoy the time of being alone or did you long for someone to come and break the silence surrounding you? People perhaps would give different answers to these questions. "The way one feels about being alone depends on the circumstances," most of us would say. Researchers give more specific answers. In Western cultures, for example, being alone is likely to be regarded as an occasion of privacy that causes feelings of gratification or happiness (Mesquita et al., 1997, p. 271). On the contrary, for some Eskimo groups, the state of being alone is interpreted as a cause of sadness. Tahitians perceive loneliness as causing weird feelings and fear. For some Aboriginals of

Australia, "sitting alone" prevents one from experiencing happiness (see Briggs, 1970; Levy, 1973; Myers, 1979). Do you think that such a distinction between Western and non-Western experiences of being alone is too simplistic? Do you think that all human beings would consider any long isolation as an unpleasant event? Indeed, there are works that suggest that cross-culturally, loneliness is seen as a disturbing emotional event (Bowbly, 1982). Try to find some facts that would either confirm or disprove a hypothesis about cross-cultural similarity of emotions elicited from the condition of being alone. Most important, try to distinguish between conditions such as "to be alone" as a temporary situation and "loneliness" as a permanent state in one's life.

carry cultural beliefs about which emotions are most significant or suitable to particular social roles or social settings (Ellsworth, 1994; Markus & Kitayama, 1994a; White, 1994). Shame of fear for own "face loss" is launched when other people are present (Lin & Yamaguchi, 2011). For example, some emotions could be considered inappropriate and therefore suppressed, such as feeling envious of your brother's or sister's success. Other emotions may be absolutely legitimate and even desirable, such as feeling joy after recovering from an illness. These evaluations are attached to the situation in which an emotional response is anticipated. Pay attention, for example, to how many people react to so-called ethnic jokes. They may laugh at a joke that ridicules members of a particular ethnic group, if the joke-teller is a representative of the ethnic group about which the joke is being told. If there is no ethnic "match" between the teller and the joke, or the teller is not your good friend, you may feel disappointed or angry.

People of different cultures evaluate words that indicate particular emotions in similar ways (Frijda et al., 1995; Roseman, 1991). To illustrate, words that stand for anger are appraised similarly by Japanese, Indonesian, and Dutch subjects as indicating the experience of something unpleasant, as preventing one from reaching one's goals, or as standing for something that is unfair and for which there is something responsible.

Stipek (1998) examined how people would evaluate some hypothetical situations in a comparative Chinese–U.S. study that involved 200 students from Zhejiang Province in China and the University of California at Los Angeles. The participants were given six written stories. Half the situations involved the participants themselves: as a person who is caught cheating, who is expecting admittance to a prestigious university, and who participates in a sports game. The other half of the cases suggested the involvement of significant others. The study showed that, in general, U.S. students tended to attribute pride to the cases of personal accomplishments. On the contrary, Chinese were more likely to experience pride for outcomes that benefited others. Moreover, compared with Americans, Chinese respondents reported stronger positive emotional reactions to other people's achievements. For example, Chinese participants claimed that they would feel more pride if their child was accepted into a prestigious university than if they themselves were accepted into that same university. U.S. respondents claimed that they would feel equally proud in both circumstances.

The author of this study believes these differences might best be explained by the emphasis on the collective nature of emotional experiences in China. (The Chinese social orientation is based on the Confucian ideal that individuals should be mainly concerned about their place in the network of human relations.) This is not a new hypothesis. As many scholars point out, Chinese tend to identify themselves in the context of significant others (Triandis, 1990). As the authors mentioned, the findings of the study examined earlier are consistent with the demands of prevailing communist ideology of the People's Republic of China. This ideology—as all other types of Communist ideologies—demands the primacy of the group over individual interests.

The results of this study can be critically evaluated, in part, from another point of view. The Chinese system of higher education is quite different from the U.S. system because college admission is based on highly competitive written and oral examinations (some other countries have the same system of college entrance exams). Every year, a substantial number of students are not accepted, and many have to wait another year to try again. In the United States, a person who is not accepted to one school can apply to another school that accepts students with lower SAT scores and grade point averages. Therefore, it is expected that Chinese participants will rate these "acceptance to college" situations as more stressful than they are rated by the U.S. participants. As to sporting events, the differences in emotional experience can also be traced to public attitudes about sports in general. Because the government sponsors sports activities, a loss or victory becomes a public issue. If you win, you make a contribution to your group, school, province, or your entire country.

WE ARE EXPECTED TO FEEL IN A PARTICULAR WAY

Emotional experiences can certainly be influenced by social norms or popular expectations. **Feeling rules** refer to particular cultural rules about how to feel in particular situations. We often consider whether our laughter (an expression of joy) or head shaking (an expression of disappointment) might evoke either positive or negative reactions from others. Emotional experiences that contradict some basic social norms could be quite different from those emotions that are in line with the existing customs. Moreover, an emotion can be felt differently considering the context in which it is displayed or observed. A Chinese father may be deeply saddened by the fact that his son is leaving home for college. However, the father's emotion may also be suppressed by his unwillingness to show his weakness in front of other family members. Joy may be experienced in a totally different way when it is accompanied by the loss of something or somebody significant.

There is evidence suggesting that individuals feel more certain about the meaning of events and give more certain emotional responses when there are clear norms about how to interpret these events and how to respond to them (Frijda & Mesquita, 1994; Mesquita & Frijda, 1992). For example, a relationship exists between cultural and religious beliefs and anxiety related to the individual's sexual practices (Paige, 1973).

Emotional complexity or the co-occurrence of pleasant and unpleasant emotions simultaneously is more prevalent in East Asian than Western cultures (Spencer-Rodgers et al., 2010). In the West, on the level of folk beliefs, pleasant and unpleasant emotions are typically conceptualized as discrete, short-lived, and oppositional phenomena that seldom co-occur. In East Asia, constructs such as happy-sad are viewed as mutually dependent in a state of balance.

Sometimes, however, our anticipation of what people should or should not feel leads to errors in judgment. In one study, Tsai and Levenson (1997) compared 22 Chinese American and

20 European American dating couples, all of whom were college aged. The participants were asked about the emotion they experienced when they tried to resolve interpersonal conflicts. The study also included physiological measurements of the participating couples. A common expectation would be that Chinese Americans would place a greater emphasis on emotional moderation (see Chapter 1) than European Americans. However, the results of the study drew a different picture. There was neither disparity in feelings nor differences in most measures of physiological responses found in the results. Perhaps the college campus environment created particular norms that reinforced certain types of feelings similar in the two ethnic groups.

One important application of the study of feeling rules is a growing understanding that people can manage their emotional states. There is cross-cultural evidence, for example, that people can influence their level of happiness by learning how to feel positive. Cultural values and individual experiences are helpful. Studies show support for Buddhist view that many people are unhappy because they choose the wrong goals in life: What people think will make them happy, such as material possessions, does not lead to lasting well-being (Wallace & Shapiro, 2006). American psychologists demonstrate evidence in support of ancient philosophies that happiness is often based on our own ability to stay positive. For example, Davidson and colleagues (2003) found that some meditation practices were associated with significantly greater activity in the left prefrontal cortex of the brain associated with positive emotion. Happiness is also a factor of longevity and health. Angela Bryan showed experimentally that optimism is an important factor contributing to healthy habits (Bryan et al., 2004). People who really believe that they will get healthier tend to achieve more positive results compared to bitter pessimists. David Myers finds supportive evidence about the positive impact of our spiritual beliefs on good health (Myers, 2008). Professor Sonja Lyubomirsky (2007) showed that besides biological factors and luck affecting our well-being, people have the capacity to manage their happiness themselves. In short, both Western psychology and Buddhism claim that the happiness may be achieved through psychological training and not necessarily through stimulus-driven pleasures (Wallace & Shapiro, 2006).

HOW PEOPLE ASSESS EMOTIONAL EXPERIENCE

When people try to evaluate their emotional experience, they make assessments not only about the experience of the emotion along the dimensions of pleasure or displeasure but also along several other dimensions. For example, people try to determine whether their emotions (1) are caused by a familiar or unfamiliar event, (2) suggest the existence of an obstacle, (3) create a sense of being in charge or being out of control, (4) increase or decrease self-esteem, and (5) cause praise, reproach, or mockery by one's group (Ellsworth, 1994; Frijda, 1986; Matsumoto et al., 1988; Wallbott & Scherer, 1986). Expectedly, the frequency with which these dimensions are used in emotional assessment can vary. For example, those events that may have an impact on the individual's family or social group have greater importance in collectivist than in individualistic cultures. On the contrary, the events that may affect one's self-esteem, material success, and professional achievement become the primary emotional concerns of most people in individualistic cultures (Markus & Kitayama, 1994b). Research also suggests that some of our emotions are evoked by cultural beliefs (Abu-Lughod, 1986; Rosaldo, 1980). For instance, a simple phrase such as "an independent Palestinian state" may have little significance for a welder in Michigan. The same phrase, however, will bear emotional meaning for millions of people living in the Middle East. For some it will indicate pride and honor, and for others it will evoke frustration.

Appraisal of emotions may be linked to more complex psychological assessments such as guessing a person's cultural identity. For example, have you ever guessed a stranger's nationality by looking at his or her photograph? An individual's smiling face, apparently, contains some information that helps other individuals to make judgments about this person's ethnic group or nationality. Comparing pictures of Japanese subjects to Japanese Americans and Australian faces to American faces, people tend to guess nationality from photographs showing emotional rather than neutral facial expressions. In other words, if a person is smiling, people have a better chance to guess his or her nationality (Marsh et al., 2007). Socialization practices may also affect the process of appraisal (Williams et al., 2002). Markham and Wang (1996) compared samples of Chinese children in Beijing and Australian children in Sydney. The children were compared in terms of their ability to evaluate faces—both Chinese and white—and in their ability to express their opinions about the emotions they judged. An initial hypothesis was that the wide range of resources available to Australian children plus a diversity of social experiences that a child has in contemporary Australian society—including television and the Internet—would improve the child's ability to evaluate emotional expressions. However, the authors did not find any substantial differences in responses between the studied groups. Moreover, some Chinese children received better scores than their Australian counterparts. Why was this difference found? The authors explain this phenomenon by referring to the family norms in both societies. Typically, Chinese parents demand a higher degree of discipline from children than Australian parents. The more consistent Chinese socialization might reduce the range of evaluations applicable to emotional interpretations compared with the range of such interpretations in Australia. The authors also indicate that children from smaller families have been found to be superior in recognizing emotions. As you know, China's official demographic policy is "one family, one child," and this policy indicated the participation of smaller nuclear families in the Chinese sample.

Another study yielded comparable results. Jolley and colleagues (1998) studied how children in China and Great Britain described the mood of some picture characters. The study revealed that Chinese children were able to interpret emotions in pictures at an earlier age than the British children. The authors explain such a difference as a result of the two countries having different traditions of education. According to the Chinese art program for elementary schools—which is regulated by the central government—children are supposed to learn techniques of drawing and teachers should concentrate on how to interpret exact messages conveyed by picture characters. In Great Britain, as in most Western countries, art education curriculum may be different from school to school.

Worry often gives a small thing a big shadow.

SWEDISH PROVERB

Worries go down better with soup than without.

YIDDISH PROVERB

WHEN EMOTIONS SIGNAL A CHALLENGE: CROSS-CULTURAL RESEARCH ON STRESS AND ANXIETY

The realization of a challenge to a person's capacity to adapt to inner and outer demands is called **stress**. This definition points to two important aspects of stress: (1) It is a psychobiological process and (2) it entails a transaction between people and their environments (Lazarus, 1993).

If the challenge does not decrease, the organism remains constantly aroused and the body continues to divert its resources to respond to the demands (Cannon, 1932). One of the most stressful events any individual can experience is the death of a family member or close friend. Daily hassles—from the absence of food to a lack of free time—can also be sources of stress. Catastrophes and disasters such as earthquakes, floods, violence, and other traumatic events affect millions of people around the world. Cross-culturally, many survivors of such traumatic events continue to experience recurrent nightmares and difficulties in relationships and are prone to anxiety and depression (Allodi, 1991; Herman, 1992; Koopman, 1997; Nadler & Ben-Shushan, 1989).

The actual amount of stress and anxiety is difficult to measure because people have different coping strategies and evaluate stress using dissimilar criteria. The ways people evaluate stress, as well as the situations they consider stressful, are culturally determined, but they also may depend on individual traits (Lin & Peterson, 1990). Poor living conditions, political instability, violence, and many other factors can also contribute to people's evaluations. Even educational systems may have an impact on how students experience stress. For example, test anxiety has repeatedly shown as lower in the United States than in other countries, such as Brazil, South Africa, and Egypt (El Zahhar & Hocevar, 1991; Guida & Ludlow, 1989).

Studying stress in African Americans, Jenkins (1995) suggested that blacks may have developed a special emotional style of behavioral response that reflects the cultural value placed on the individual's ability to manage stressful life events. In African American culture, from the author's view, emphasis is placed on the active managing of difficult situations without displaying nervous tension. Thus, a difference between European Americans and African Americans may be found in their emotional assessments of reality. In blacks, their emotionality is displayed more often than it is in whites. This type of African American emotional response may be passed on from generation to generation as a cultural norm.

Self-critical, pessimistic evaluation of one's own life may be viewed as a cultural norm in other ethnic groups. For instance, higher levels—in comparison to other groups—of negative emotions, including anxiety and sadness, were measured in elderly Russian immigrants living in the United States (Consedine & Magai, 2002). Although most immigrant groups experience stress and a variety of negative emotions caused by the difficult process of adjustment to a new culture, Russian immigrants as a group typically report more anxiety and pessimism. This difference may be explained by a variety of reasons, including the fact that the majority of Russian immigrants are highly educated and most of them have to lower their aspirations and hopes for a quick and effortless success in the United States (Kliger, 2002).

Researchers also found that Asians consistently score higher than European Americans on measures of emotional distress including anxiety, sadness, and fear of negative evaluation (Norasakkunkit & Kalick, 2002). The difference may be explained by cultural norms as well. From the Western perspective, the absence of anxiety in most social situations is seen as a desirable characteristic associated with positive mental health and healthy interpersonal functioning. However, from an Asian perspective, a certain level of anxiety about social situations may be normative and even desirable (Okazaki et al., 2002). While following this social norm, many individuals develop a particular sensitivity to their own behavior and to other people's negative appraisals.

A human being should be aware how he laughs, for then he shows all his faults.

RALPH WALDO EMERSON (1803–1882)—U.S. Poet and Philosopher

EXPRESSION OF EMOTION

Eight-year-old Tom is looking at the scene of a car wreck with his eyes opened wide in a fixed stare. He is not hiding his fear. Anybody can read it on Tom's face. Tom's parents, who came from Taiwan, did not teach him how to express fear by turning his lips down. His U.S. school-teachers did not train him to lower his eyebrows in case of a threat. He expresses his fear in the same way billions of people on earth might display it through their facial expression, posture, and gestures.

The rules of emotional expression—called **display rules**—are acquired primarily during socialization (Birdwhistell, 1970). Every culture has particular sanctions that support display rules or patterns of emotional expression considered appropriate within that culture (Ekman & Friesen, 1975; Ekman et al., 1983). Throughout the history of human civilization, one way of managing an emotion has been to learn how to control its manifestation. It is interesting that such display rules are primarily concerned with the restraining of emotional expressions (Ekman, 1982). Beginning presumably with the Chinese thinker Confucius (fifth century B.C.E.) and the Greek philosopher Plato (fourth century B.C.E.), emotion has been viewed as a disruptive force in human affairs. Plato asserted that reason must restrain the passions, which otherwise distort rational thinking. Aristotle and Democritus (fourth century B.C.E.) had a similar view, suggesting that emotions are located in the "lower," more primitive level of the soul, whereas thinking is located on the "higher," more advanced layers. Stoicism, an ancient Greek and Roman school of philosophy, held that human beings should be free from the power of passion in order to accept both the fortunes and misfortunes of life. Most major world religions, for example, Islam, Judaism, Buddhism, and Christianity, introduced the rules by which human beings could become independent of "destructive" emotional forces, such as envy, pride, vanity, and jealousy (Smith, 1991).

There are at least two criteria for assessment of emotional expressions: frequency and intensity. For example, in the United States, many parents commonly say "I love you" to their children and vice versa. Contrarily, in the Ukraine, Russia, and Belarus, such a verbal expression of affection is considered to be too "strong" and intrusive and may be expressed only in a few critical life situations.

If emotions are cultural and social products, the cultural norms and environmental factors should regulate the ways people express their emotions (Kitayama & Markus, 1995). Perhaps then it shouldn't be a surprise that surveys reveal a very low admission level of personal happiness and lower overall expression of one's satisfaction with life in countries going through economic and social crises. Russia and Ukraine, for instance, scored the lowest on individual expression of happiness among other European countries studied (Glad & Shiraev, 1999). Likewise, an ongoing social conflict may elicit and reinforce particular emotional responses. To illustrate, in several experimental situations, Israeli subjects responded more aggressively than their U.S. counterparts (Margalit & Mauger, 1985). When a social situation requires an individual to be "tough," one's display of anger may become an adaptive response to stressful situations of ethnic conflict.

There are some cultural variations in the display of sadness. Tahitians report feeling tired in response to losses (Levy, 1973). Crying among the Bedouins in the Egyptian desert (Abu-Lughod, 1986) is considered a sign of weakness, whereas in other Islamic cultures, such as the Turkish, it is considered an acceptable social response in particular circumstances. Display rules differ not only by culture but also by gender. Some evidence suggests that women probably express emotions more intensely and openly than men do. This is true for all emotions except anger. Women are generally more comfortable in displaying emotions such as love, happiness, shame, guilt, and sympathy, which foster affiliation and caretaking. Men, however, avoid these "soft" emotions that display, according to their opinion, male vulnerabilities (Brody & Hall, 1993). For men raised in traditional cultures, a complex emotion of honor consists of being in control of their own family and of outperforming or impressing other men. Women's honor in these cultures consists of conforming to the rules of modesty and faithfulness. Likewise, shameful events have been reported to elicit different reactions in men and women: Men try to restore their honor by showing off through aggression, or by retaliation; women will react to shameful events with submissive behavior and avoidance (Abu-Lughod, 1986; Blok, 1981). During the process of anticipatory socialization (see Chapter 8), boys and girls receive different sets of instructions about the display rules for various emotions. Indeed, children as young as three years old recognize that females are more likely to express fear, sadness, and happiness, and males are more likely to display anger (Birnbaum, 1983).

The presence or absence of other people may also have various impacts on emotional expressions. Ekman and Friesen (1975) asked Japanese and U.S. students to watch stressful films in isolation and in the presence of an experimenter. Without the subjects' awareness the emotional expressions on their faces were recorded in both conditions. For the two samples, similar expressions were found in reaction to the same movie episodes when the subjects were alone. However, in the presence of the experimenter, the Japanese subjects showed far fewer negative expressions than did the Americans. Does this experiment partially explain why others often see the Japanese as unemotional?

In another study, researchers asked U.S. and Japanese students living in the United States to report on the frequency with which they experienced certain emotions in daily life (Markus & Kitayama, 1994b). The Americans reported an overwhelmingly greater frequency of experiencing positive than negative self-relevant feelings, but there was virtually no such effect among the Japanese. One can suggest that such differences could be caused by the Japanese subjects' unwillingness to reveal their emotions to strangers. There are also data suggesting that in Japan, for instance, the happiest people are those who experience primarily the "socially engaged emotions" of interdependence (such as friendly feelings). In the United States, on the contrary, the happiest people are generally those who experience the socially "disengaged" emotions of independence, such as pride (Matsumoto, 1994).

Researchers suggest that in the West, high levels of expressiveness are seen as signs of competence and likeability in contrast to Asian cultures. Educators report that Asian American college students are less expressive than European Americans, which is probably based on Asian cultural traditions valuing emotional self-restraint and attentiveness to others (Butler et al., 2009; Kim & Markus, 2002).

However, these trends in expressive behavior were not confirmed in another study. The participants from both countries were asked to rate their anticipated degree of comfort in the expression of independent and interdependent emotions (Stephan et al., 1998). The results did not reveal substantial differences between the samples. In another study, Aune and Aune (1994) studied three groups of subjects, Japanese Americans, Filipino Americans, and European Americans; each group completed self-report questionnaires in which they evaluated both positive and negative emotions experienced and expressed in romantic relationships. The participating students were asked to think about the relationship they have with their partner and the emotions they felt and expressed. The participants were also asked to rank their emotions using a special scale. The researchers did not find substantial cultural differences in how negative emotions are experienced and expressed in romantic relationships. Low scores on anger expression among the U.S. participants were perhaps due to substantial societal pressure to suppress the expression of negative emotions in daily settings.

How can we interpret the results of these studies? Can we say then that collectivism and individualism have little impact on how people feel and communicate their emotions? We shouldn't rush to such a categorical judgment. Do not forget that the subjects in these studies were people of "mixed" cultural backgrounds: They were born in the Philippines and Japan and were studying in the United States. Perhaps in the contemporary world people learn from other cultures and begin to understand many issues and behaviors that have not been available to them prior to the new era of satellite television and the Internet. Japanese and American society are more interconnected today than they were 10 years ago. For instance, if a Japanese woman from a traditional family is shown a photograph of a nude beach, this could cause a reaction of extreme shame. However, this woman can travel abroad, to Europe or Brazil, for example, and learn more about other cultures and their practices related to nakedness. Her experience may not change her negative opinion about public nudity; however, her emotional response will perhaps change.

Exercise 6.1

Embarrassment is regarded as a form of social anxiety, an unpleasant emotion excited by the realization of impropriety in one's behavior. A study of five European cultures (Greece, Great Britain, Italy, Spain, and Germany) showed that blushing and increased temperature plus smiling and grinning were reported consistently across cultures (Edelman et al., 1989). There are some other observations of embarrassment, such as sticking out one's tongue, as people in the Indian Orissa culture do (Menon & Shweder, 1994). Ask at least 10 people, preferably from various cultural backgrounds, to imagine that they encounter a very embarrassing situation. How would they react in terms of facial expression and body language? Ask them to play the role of an embarrassed person. Immediately write down what you see. Will they touch their face? Will they scratch their head? Will they stick out their tongue? Will they smile and turn away? Bring your observations to class to find out whether there are some consistencies and differences in the way people describe their embarrassment.

The best answer to anger is silence.

GERMAN PROVERB

WHEN EMOTION HURTS: CROSS-CULTURAL STUDIES OF ANGER

Cross-culturally, **anger**—an emotion aroused by one's perception of being interfered with or threatened and/or overt or covert activities of attack or offense—is seen as an interpersonal emotion because its experience usually involves some norm violation committed by other people. There are several universal anger-evoking events. They include problems in relationships, injustice, interaction with strangers, inconvenience, achievement, bad news, death, and several separation-related issues (Averill, 1982; Mauro et al., 1992; Wallbott & Scherer, 1986).

However, when a person speaking in a foreign language says, "I am angry," one should be careful not to rush to judgment because most human languages have several labels for anger (Klineberg, 1938; Tanaka-Matsumi, 1995). As an example, it is interesting to compare *anger*, as an English word, and, for instance, *song* in the Ifaluk (Pacific region) language. Both of these words refer to emotions involving appraisal of harm from another person. However, they can differ in the kind of action they bring about. *Anger* often leads to the tendency to return the other person's harm. *Song*, however, produces action that aims to alter the behavior of the offending person. Such action may include, of course, aggressive behaviors, but it may also consist of avoidant behavioral reactions, such as refusing to eat and attempted suicide (Lutz, 1988).

People get angry and interpret this emotion according to the norms of the culture in which they live. For instance, Japanese cultural traditions strongly inhibit public display of private emotions, particularly negative ones. This culture emphasizes homogeneity and conformity as necessary conditions for the maintenance of the society's interdependent network (Johnson, 1993). In collectivist cultures, anger is seen as an emotion of disengagement from the society, a threat to its integrity (Markus & Kitayama, 1994b) and, therefore, is generally discouraged. In individualist societies, such as the United States, the display of anger could be judged differently because people generally recognize other people's right to independence and self-expression.

Just as courage imperils life, fear protects it.

LEONARDO DA VINCI (1452–1519)—**Italian Artist and Thinker**

EMOTION AND INCLINATION TO ACT

Cross-culturally, the influence of emotions can cause us to avoid and reject some people, help and accept others, dominate or submit to some, and respect or despise others (Frijda, 1986; Frijda et al., 1995).

Some cross-cultural studies show similarities regarding action readiness evoked by certain emotions. In the extensive cross-national study cited earlier (Scherer & Wallbott, 1994), subjects were asked whether their emotional experience had led them to move toward, move away from, or move against the object of emotion. Significant cross-cultural similarities were found. Joy caused more approach behaviors, anger elicited more aggressive behaviors, and withdrawal was the most common reaction to sadness, disgust, shame, and guilt.

There are some cultural differences in how emotions affect behavioral readiness. In a comparative study of Japanese, Dutch, and Indonesian subjects, an impulse toward a hostile behavior, as a response to anger, was more common for the Dutch group. A more "internal" impulse was common in the Indonesian and Japanese groups. The Japanese group more often reported feelings of helplessness and urges to protect themselves. They also expressed a wish to depend on someone else and a feeling of apathy at a higher level than participating Dutch and Indonesian subjects (Frijda et al., 1995). These results partly support findings obtained in other studies that suggest that personal dependence on intimate others as well as acceptance by others are significant components of emotional experience in Japan (Lebra, 1983; Markus & Kitayama, 1994b).

An emphasis on the mastery of one's environment is more typical of highly technologically developed societies. Other cultures emphasize harmony and natural order. Therefore, active coping styles can be preferable in some cultures but not in others (Kluckhohn & Strodtbeck, 1961). One of the lessons we can learn is that coping with stress is relative to its cultural context. More important, some stress-coping therapeutic strategies that have been proven successful in one culture may not work well in other cultures.

The tongue of a wise man lays behind his heart.

ALI IBN-ABI-TALIB (600–661)—**Fourth Caliph of Muslims**

EMOTION AND JUDGMENT

In the famous classical American TV series *Star Trek*, one of the main characters, Mr. Spock, is a half-human, half-alien being who is naturally free from any emotions. His behavior is directed by pure logic. He is, of course, a fictional character, a product of creative imagination that often has little to do with real-life experiences. In reality, emotions and thought are closely linked. Emotions can influence the way people make judgments and predictions (Mayer et al., 1992). Vice versa, people's thoughts and beliefs influence their emotions. There is ample evidence that emotional states may shape cognitive processing in different ways. People who are depressed, for example, tend to underestimate the probability of their own success and overestimate the probability of bad events occurring in the future (Beck, 1991). People who experience positive affect differ from those who experience negative affect. The former have better memory and use different strategies for problem solving and categorization (Clore et al., 1994). Anger has been found to lead to more personal accusations, whereas sadness leads to a tendency to understand negative circumstances as more due to fate, chance, or unluckiness (Keltner et al., 1993).

Emotions lead to belief changes: Certain emotional appraisals can cause perceptual generalizations and stereotypes. For example, an individual's negative experience with, and emotional feeling toward, a representative of a particular ethnic group can cause prejudice toward all members of that group. There was a significant difference found between Japanese and U.S. subjects in their attribution of anger. Apparently, the Japanese subjects were comparatively more reluctant to identify anger as being caused by other people than the Americans (Matsumoto et al., 1988; Scherer et al., 1988). Japan is a collectivist culture, and perhaps societal interdependency is a factor that makes the inclusion of anger in cognitive attributions, which can be a potentially destructive force, difficult. Physical violence may be interpreted in accordance with individual beliefs. Researchers have found that prisoner activists with particularly strong political or religious convictions show the most emotional resilience to torture compared to those who do not hold such beliefs (Basoglu et al., 1994).

Exercise 6.2

Tietelbaum and Geiselman (1997) examined cross-race recognition for white and black faces with participants from four racial and ethnic groups: whites, blacks, Latinos, and Asians. The researchers found that same-race identifications tend to be more accurate than cross-race assessments. In other words, people from the same ethnic or racial groups have a tendency to evaluate pictorial emotions and moods more accurately than people from other social groups. The differences in accuracy were statistically significant in the range of 10–15 percent. It was also shown that being in the state of a pleasant mood increased accuracy of facial recognition within same ethnic groups. Another finding was that Latino and Asian participants had less difficulty recognizing emotions on white faces than on black faces.

Question:

The authors believe that these results can have implications for everyday life situations. What do you think these implications are?

Chapter Summary

- Classic theories of emotion provide little empirical evidence of cultural influences on emotional experiences. Trying to clarify the impact of the cultural factor in human emotions, cross-cultural psychologists have pursued at least two theoretical models. According to one, human emotions are universal and culture has a limited impact on them. The other view represents an assumption about the cultural origin and cultural specificity of emotion. Supporters of the universality of human emotion argue that similar emotions exist in all cultures and all emotions have similar underlying physiological mechanism.

- Compelling arguments about similarities in human emotion arrive from numerous studies on consistent cross-cultural similarities in emotion recognition and in the way people name emotions across different cultures and languages. Supporters of cultural specificity of emotion suggest that concrete emotional realities vary significantly from culture to culture. Differences in the expression of emotional behavior, linguistic variety in the labeling of emotions, and distinct socialization practices are all taken as evidence for the culture-specific origin of human emotions. According to this view, people learn how to feel and interpret other people's affects. This learning of emotional experience is related to the culture from which it originates.

- Emotions can be seen as similar or different because we often perceive, analyze, and think about them from different points of view. If we limit our analysis of human emotion to the question of whether an emotion is expected to occur, we will find many cross-cultural similarities among human feelings. We have to pay special attention to the particular level of abstraction on which emotions are described. Moreover, any emotion may be culturally similar or cross-culturally different, depending on the level of generalization chosen for description.

- Perhaps many similarities in emotions are likely to be found when they are described at a high level of generality or abstraction. An emphasis in one's observations on specific emotional characteristics would perhaps highlight cultural differences.

- It is useful to understand emotion as a multi-componential process. It generally includes the following components: preceding event, physiological response, assessment, expressive behavior, and change in some element of cognitive functioning. Cross-culturally, specific types of elicitors mark basic emotions. Despite tremendous individual variations, there are some cultural norms and conditions that regulate emotional experience. Some cultural differences may still be found in the different degrees to which certain emotional responses are tolerated or valued. Human emotional expression is generally acquired in the process of socialization. Cultural differences may result in differences in emotion-related cognitive processes. The prevalence of one particular emotion or of certain ways of experiencing an emotion can affect people's specific attitudes, beliefs, and even views on life. For example, disgust is associated with cultural requirements to reject certain foods or avoid particular situations related to eating. Once accepted, these requirements are supported by a powerful emotion and thus become less subject to temptation or modification.

- Human beings have the potential to experience the same basic emotions. However, our cultural differences and subsequent socialization practices encourage us to experience particular emotions and suppress others and be emotionally involved in particular issues to which other people remain indifferent. Therefore, psychologists should gain knowledge about cultural norms, display rules, and specific and universal antecedents of various emotions and examine them within particular cultural contexts.

Key Terms

Anger Emotion of displeasure aroused by a threat, overt (explicit) or covert (hidden), wrongdoing, attack, or offense.

Display Rules Patterns of emotional expression considered appropriate within a particular culture, age, or social group.

Emotion An evaluative response (a positive or negative feeling) that typically includes some combination of physiological arousal, subjective experience, and behavioral or emotional expression.

Emotion Recognition The process of identification, description, and explanation of an emotional expression.

Evaluations of Emotions An individual assessment of emotions according to certain criteria or principles.

Feeling Rules Particular cultural rules about how to feel in particular situations.

Preceding Events The environmental circumstances and individual reactions that have a strong impact on particular emotional experiences.

Stress Perception of a continuous challenge to a person's capacity to adapt to inner and outer demands.

7

Motivation and Behavior

Take away the motive and you take away the sin.

MIGUEL DE CERVANTES (1547–1616)—
Spanish Novelist and Poet

*Looking at small advantages prevents great
affairs from being accomplished.*

CONFUCIUS (551–479 B.C.E.)—
Chinese Philosopher

D aniel Crocker was a 38-year-old professional who lived peacefully in suburban Virginia with his wife and two children. One day he quit his job, consulted his minister and family, and boarded a plane to Kansas, where he willingly confessed to strangling a woman 19 years ago.

Continuous harassment, abuse, insults, and, finally, a 27-year imprisonment did not break Nelson (Rolihlahla) Mandela. Over the years, his beliefs grew stronger, and his motivation and faith became an extraordinary symbol of black resistance against racism in South Africa. He became South Africa's first black president.

Christopher Nolan from Ireland had cerebral palsy since birth. He couldn't walk. Neither could he talk, write, or even touch his face. Unable to move, he studied math, science, and literature like every child. He began to write poetry and prose. He did it with a rubber-tipped stick attached to his forehead and typed letters on a typewriter. His novel, *The Banyan Tree*, took about 10 years to finish. He began to publish his work at age 15. Recognition, raving reviews, and literary awards followed. He could master the words that he could never say. Christopher died when he was 43. People say his life was a miracle.

Where do people find resources to pursue their goals? Is it their family? Religion? Rational calculations? Individual desires or collective goals? To survive we all need to breathe, eat, and avoid unnecessary pain and discomfort. But how do we learn about compassion, greed, aggression, and success? Does culture have any influence on our motivation?

Motivation is a condition—usually an internal one—that initiates, activates, or maintains the individual's goal-directed behavior. The nature of human motivation is a subject of discussions and continuous attempts to find a universal theory that would explain it. Evolutionary psychologists, for example, generally believe that biological factors best explain social behavior. Some sociological theories claim the nature of human motivation is social or economic. Classical psychologists have also contributed to the theory of motivation by determining major psychological mechanisms that underlie basic human needs. A critical examination of these approaches provides cross-cultural psychologists with valuable ideas that can be used to analyze specific kinds of human motivation.

A GLANCE INTO EVOLUTION

The origin of human motivation is biological, according to the evolutionary view. Due to genetic variations, some organisms are more likely to survive than others. Those who survive pass on their "advantageous" genes to their offspring. Over many generations, genetic patterns that promote survival become dominant. For instance, hunters become successful seekers and killers of animals, and gatherers become excellent finders of berries, roots, and fruit. The struggle for survival within the human species motivates people to compete for scarce resources. Individuals who are skillful competitors, and who are fit for the struggle, will succeed and prosper. The unfit, or those who lack the motivation to compete, will fail. Life is unjust, but who says it should be so? (Summer, 1970). Survival needs can be individual and collective. Baldwin (1991), for example, suggested that the principle of collective survival is part of the psychology of African people. Continued existence of the group—and not necessarily individual survival—is closely linked to the collective responsibility and interdependence of Africans. Perhaps this explanatory principle is applicable not only to African culture but also to most social and ethnic groups that have been oppressed or continue to live under oppression.

The evolutionary approach to human motivation generally fails to explain the diversity of human motivation and overlooks the influence of individual choice and reason.

In contrast to evolutionary theories, the sociological approach emphasizes the crucial role of social factors in determining individual motivation. We illustrate the sociological approach by describing two theories.

SOCIAL SCIENCE: SEE THE SOCIETY FIRST

Consider, for example, the views of Max Weber (1922). As we mentioned earlier in the book, he drew a line between two types of societies: preindustrial (traditional) and industrial (nontraditional). People in preindustrial societies are inseparable from traditions and customs. In these societies, people's desires and actions are viewed as appropriate and inappropriate on the basis of their links—or lack thereof—to the existing customs and rules. For example, married couples in traditional societies are not likely to pursue divorce. It is inappropriate behavior because it destroys the traditional family. Capitalist societies, on the contrary, endorse rationality as a pillar of human motivation. People deliberately assess the most efficient ways of accomplishing a particular goal. If two spouses decide that they cannot live together any longer, they could break up their marriage. Why? Because this act serves their best interest. In such cases, reason overcomes emotion, calculation replaces intuition, and scientific analysis eliminates superstition. The scarcity and value of their time often motivate people in modern societies, whereas in traditional cultures time is not viewed as a commodity (see Chapter 10).

Conflict theories pay attention to socioeconomic and political conditions and their impact on motivation. They pay attention to social inequality or view consumerism as the main driving force behind human behavior in the West (Marcuse, 1964). Conflict theories generally cannot explain many other noneconomic and nonpolitical aspects of human motivation. For example, social equality, unfortunately, does not stop aggression and violence. Similarly, economic inequality does not necessarily cause conflict among people: They may give up their freedoms in exchange for stability and economic benefits. People often find the ways to cope with societal challenges. A study of women in power in China and the United States showed that although they both faced significant obstacles in the workplace, they integrated their work and family roles in ways that enabled them to harmonize both (Cheung & Halpern, 2010).

The next step is an overview of basic psychological theories of motivation: drive and arousal theories, as well as psychodynamic, humanistic, and learning approaches.

Drive and Arousal: Two Universal Mechanisms of Motivation

An internal aroused condition that directs an organism to satisfy some physiological need is called a **drive**. One of the central concepts of motivational theories is **need**, a motivated state caused by physiological or psychological deprivation (such as lack of food or water). According to drive theories, people across countries come to value what they do not have just as those who are hungry are especially likely to value food (Peng et al., 1997). The goal of behavior is to attain a state of stability or balance within the individual. Stimuli, such as hunger and pain, energize and initiate our behavior. Traditionally, needs are divided into two categories: *biological* and *social*. Biological needs are universal and direct human behavior toward self-preservation. Indeed, we all have to eat to survive. Social needs direct people toward establishing and maintaining relationships. The organism motivated by a need is said to be in a *drive state*. Being in a drive state, humans exhibit goal-directed behavior. The environment may press an individual to fight against an enemy, pray, and/or develop particular skills (Murray, 1938). The pressure of poverty may generate a need for financial security, causing a person to work harder and get an education (Van de Vliert, 2007). Influenced by different circumstances, another individual chooses a violent confrontation with the society that, in this person's view, caused his or her poverty.

Arousal theories of motivation suggest that people seek to maintain optimal levels of arousal by actively changing their exposure to arousing stimuli (Yerkes, 1911). Unlike hunger and thirst, the lack of sensory or other experience does not result in a physiological imbalance. Both human beings and animals always seek sensory stimulation. Ukrainian men might play chess on the park bench, an Uzbek man might stop by a teahouse for a chat, and a Boston student might pay $40 to see a Red Sox game. Each culture offers its own repertoire of activities, which people are motivated to seek out to maintain optimal levels of arousal.

Studies give partial support to arousal theories. More than a thousand men and women from six nations (Spain, Peru, Venezuela, the United Kingdom, Australia, and the United States) completed questionnaires about their procrastination. Results indicated no significant sex or nationality differences within or between nations. Overall, almost 30 percent of the respondents reported about their tendency to procrastinate. Half of them procrastinate for arousal reasons: They believe that they achieve better results when working under pressure. The other half are avoidant procrastinators: They do not perform well under the pressure of deadlines. These findings suggest that there are universal psychological mechanisms of procrastination (Ferrari et al., 2007).

One of the major weaknesses of drive and arousal theories is their treatment of culture as an "external factor" relatively independent of human activity. These theories discount the fact that people are not only responding bodies and minds but also active "architects and designers" of their own culture.

THE POWER OF THE UNCONSCIOUS: PSYCHOANALYSIS

The central concept of psychoanalysis, originally developed by Sigmund Freud (1938), is the unconscious. The unconscious is the level of consciousness that contains the thoughts, feelings, and memories that influence us without our awareness and that we cannot become aware of at will. All humans are born with two basic drives: the life instinct and the death wish. All the tendencies that strive toward the integration of a living substance, such as loving, liking, helping, caring, building, and creating, are driven by the life instinct. The death wish represents all the tendencies toward aggression and death. To survive, the individual tends to destroy alien objects and people.

The individual's personality comprises three major components. The most primitive part of the personality is the id, the component of the personality that contains inborn drives (the death wish and life instinct) and that seeks immediate gratification of its impulses according to the pleasure principle. A newborn child's behavior is guided by this principle: Infants in all cultures are unaware of social rules. Gradually, a growing child faces an increasing number of regulators of his behavior that systematically appear in the form of restrictions. The especially strict restrictions are usually applied to his developing sexual interests and aggressive impulses. This indicates the beginning development of the superego—the level of the personality that acts as a moral guide restraining the original impulses. The superego represents the values and the cultural standards of society, transmitted to the child through parents and other adults. Surrounded by the id and the superego is the ego, a level of the personality that adapts to external reality by making compromises between the id, the superego, and the environment. Freud was among the first to critically describe the psychological roots of human culture and the impact of culture on psychology. Psychologists made many attempts to apply this theory in cultural and cross-cultural studies. There were psychoanalytic studies on African witchcraft, research on social customs within Australian Aboriginal natives, the impact of white society on African Americans, and the power of self-restraint in Buddhist cultural communities of Burma, Cambodia, Laos, or Thailand (Tori & Bilmes, 2002). Yet, psychoanalysis was developed primarily within the cultural environment of the Western culture oriented toward individualism, rational thinking, and free choice. Non-Western cultures are, in general, different. Back in 1929, Girindrasekhar Bose, the founder and first president of the Indian Psychoanalytical Society, wrote to Freud to emphasize some differences related to gender identity in India and Europe. He believed that Indian culture, in general, was not prone to completely separate feminine and masculine features within the individual (Kakar, 1989). On the other hand, psychoanalysis failed to accept high-power distance in traditional cultures and did not understand well the structure of family ties and gender relations in Muslim cultures (Roland, 2006).

Carl Jung (1857–1961), one of the most prominent followers of the psychoanalytic tradition, was among the first psychologists to criticize the ethnocentric worldview of Western psychology. He confronted a widespread opinion of the time that the European type of thinking and behavior was far superior to Asian or African types of action and experience. Europe can be viewed as only a peninsula on the Asian continent, he liked to point out. Europeans, in fact, were merely catching up with other ethnic groups whose psychological world has been richer and more complex than Europeans had thought. The Western world, according to Jung, was based almost exclusively on rationality and needed to be in touch with a deeper view of self and other cultures. Contemporary psychology today has generally accepted Jung's encouragements to develop an inclusive, cross-cultural approach to psychological knowledge (Shiraev, 2011).

HUMANISTIC THEORIES

These theories focus on human dignity, individual choice, and self-worth. Abraham Maslow (1970), a pioneer of humanistic psychology, proposed that humans have a number of innate needs that are arranged in a hierarchy in terms of their potency (Table 7.1).

Maslow grouped these needs into five categorical levels: physiological, safety, love, esteem, and self-actualization. Once an individual has satisfied the cluster of needs at a particular level, he or she is able to progress to the next hierarchical level. Thus, for example, people typically are not prompted to seek acceptance and esteem until they have met their needs for food, water, and shelter.

Maslow noted that as one ascends the hierarchy of needs, one becomes less animal-like and more humanistic. If the person has been able to satisfy adequately the needs in the first four levels, he or she is in a position to fulfill the highest-order needs, namely, to actualize his or her unique potential. According to Maslow, once people enter the realm of **self-actualization**, they become qualitatively different from those who are still attempting to meet their more basic needs. The self-actualizing person's life is governed by the search for "being-values" (B-values), such as truth, goodness, beauty, wholeness, justice, and meaningfulness.

In contrast to most personality theorists preceding him, Maslow created his theory by studying healthy and successful people, rather than clinical cases of psychopathology. His interest in self-actualizing people began with his great admiration for Max Wertheimer, one of the founders of Gestalt psychology, and Ruth Benedict, the renowned cultural anthropologist. After discovering that these two individuals had many characteristics in common, Maslow began to search for others with the same qualities. The group that he finally isolated for more detailed study included Abraham Lincoln, Thomas Jefferson, Albert Einstein, Eleanor Roosevelt, Albert Schweitzer, Benedict Spinoza, Adlai Stevenson, and Martin Buber—all Europeans or European Americans.

Based on his informal research, Maslow developed a composite, impressionistic profile of an optimally functioning, mature, and healthy human being. Maslow concluded that

---

TABLE 7.1 Abraham Maslow's Hierarchy of Needs

Level 5: *Self-Actualization Needs*
Level 4: *Esteem Needs*
Level 3: *Belonging and Love Needs*
Level 2: *Safety Needs*
Level 1: *Physiological Needs*

Source: Based on Maslow, A. (1970). Motivation and personality (2nd ed.). New York: Harper & Row.

CRITICAL THINKING
One Need—Different Behaviors?

Would you agree that social needs are transposable? Do you think that an inability to satisfy one's needs in a particular area could motivate one to search for a way to satisfy those needs in other areas? For example, it is suggested that not all politicians become involved in public affairs because of their need to join politics. Political careers in different cultures may have diverse origins. But in general, the political career could have provided satisfaction for the leaders' individual needs and an opportunity for further expression of their creative skills or frustration. As Betty Glad wrote, U.S. President Jimmy Carter's career was propelled by his desire for recognition "in some field," rather than a strong, overwhelming interest in a political career (Glad, 1980). U.S. President Richard Nixon, at the beginning of his career, failed to obtain a job in a major New York law firm. Joseph Stalin, the Soviet dictator, was an ill-famed terrorist in his youth. Lech Walesa, the leader of an anticommunist movement in Poland, was a frustrated electrician. Adolf Hitler, the most notorious dictator of the twentieth century, tried first to become an artist. Václav Havel, the first president of the Czech Republic, was a dissident writer for many years. Nelson Mandela began his career as a lawyer. Could you give other examples? Do you think that human needs are basically universal and what differs is the set of circumstances that surrounds people? In other words, different life events motivate us to pursue different goals because of dissimilar environmental circumstances that we encounter. Do you agree?

self-actualizing persons exhibit a number of similar characteristics, including (1) an accurate perception of reality, (2) a continued freshness of appreciation and openness to experience, (3) spontaneity and simplicity, (4) a strong ethical awareness, (5) a philosophical (rather than hostile) sense of humor, (6) a need for privacy, (7) periodic mystical ("peak") experiences, (8) democratic leadership traits (see Chapter 11), (9) deep interpersonal relations, (10) autonomy and independence, (11) creativeness, (12) a problem-centered (rather than self-centered) orientation, (13) a resistance to enculturation, and (14) an acceptance of self, others, and nature.

Do you think that Maslow's theory is a valid depiction of a fully functioning person, or, instead, is a reflection of Maslow's own subjective value system? Did Maslow mix ethical and moral considerations with his logic? Consider, for example, his portrayal of self-actualizing people as open, realistic, spontaneous, possessing democratic leadership traits, resistant to enculturation, and accepting of self, others, and nature. Is this an objective description of human fulfillment? Or is it a *pre*scription—masked as a *de*scription—of Maslow's own subjective ideals? As noted by M. B. Smith (1978), perhaps Maslow simply selected his personal heroes and offered his impressions of them.

Although the structure of needs presented by Maslow may be appropriate for individuals of all cultures, the relative strengths of the needs are culture specific. Self-preoccupation could be seen as a Western characteristic not so dominant in some other cultures. The Chinese hierarchy of values, for instance, includes the promotion of interconnectedness, in contrast to the emphasis on self-development in Maslow's version. In one study, Nevis (1983) revised Maslow's hierarchy of needs and argued that one of the most basic needs of people in communist China is the need to belong, rather than physiological needs. Moreover, self-actualization could manifest as a devoted service to community. If a person self-actualizes by means of contributing to the group, this individual is realizing the value of collectivist self-actualization.

Maslow acknowledged that his theorizing and research on self-actualization lacked the rigor of strict empirical science. He fervently believed, however, that it was imperative to begin the process of rounding out the field of psychology by attending to "the highest capacities of the healthy and strong man as well as with the defensive maneuvers of crippled spirits" (Maslow, 1970, p. 33). Further, Maslow maintained that it would be misleading to believe that science is value free, since its methods and procedures are developed and utilized for human purposes.

A similar theory of motivation was formulated and empirically tested within a different cultural environment by the Soviet psychologist Arthur Petrovsky (1978), who claimed the existence of a collectivist orientation in most Soviet people. An individual is able to fulfill maximum potential when she accepts and internalizes the goals and values of the society. In both Chinese and Russian examples, environmental demands, socialist ideology, and traditions (like the Confucian work ethic in China or a communist moral code of behavior in the Soviet Union) advocated harmony and cooperation, but not individualist determination, which is usually promoted in the West.

LEARNING AND MOTIVATION

Learning theories associated primarily with the behaviorist tradition in psychology maintain that people are aware of their thought patterns and therefore can control their motivation and behavior because they control conditions within which this behavior occurs. People learn what they want and how to achieve rewards, mastery, and affiliation. There are two types of motivation: intrinsic and extrinsic. **Intrinsic motivation** engages people in various activities for no apparent reward except the pleasure and satisfaction of the activity itself. Deci (1972) suggested that people engage in such behaviors for two reasons: to obtain cognitive stimulation and to gain a sense of accomplishment, competency, and mastery over the environment. In contrast, **extrinsic motivation** comes from the external environment. Examples of extrinsic rewards include praise, a high grade, or money given for a particular behavior. Such rewards can strengthen existing behaviors, provide people with information about their performance, and increase feelings of self-worth.

Psychologists working within this tradition hoped to establish some universal scientific principles to explain behavior. Environment, educational conditions, cultural norms—all were the factors that condition people's responses to stimuli, help them to adjust to the environment, and direct their actions. Behaviorism appeared as a set of universal principles applicable in any cultural settings.

Let us now examine several specific types of human motivation. We will analyze hunger first, then move on to achievement motivation, and, finally, examine sexual and aggressive motivation.

A hungry stomach has no ears.

La Fontaine (1621–1695)—French Fabulist

An empty stomach will not listen to anything.

Spanish Proverb

A CARROT AND A BEEF TONGUE: HUNGER AND FOOD PREFERENCE

This is obvious: To live, people have to eat. There are no cultural exceptions: Hunger indeed is a biological need. The body transforms food into energy for further growth and functioning. Our eagerness to eat is pushed by a physiological state (i.e., bodily chemistry and hypothalamic activity in the brain) and pulled by our learned responses to external stimuli. The biological nature of hunger explains many cross-cultural similarities in eating preferences. People in all cultures learn to salivate in anticipation of appealing foods. Our preferences for sweet and salty tastes are probably genetic and universal. For most children, candy is a very desirable food product. However, individual experience creates particular taste preferences. For instance, when people are continuously given highly salted foods, they develop a liking for excessive salt (Beauchamp, 1987). Thus, a person who grew up in New Orleans or Syria will be likely to consider many types of Scandinavian food somewhat tasteless.

Typically, cultural norms and traditions regulate our eating habits, determine what we consider tasty and tasteless, and establish social taboos on particular foods and food products. Arab Bedouins could eat the eye of a camel, which most Europeans would find disgusting. In some European and Asian countries, beef tongue is a deli product, whereas for most North Americans it is unacceptable. Similarly, most North Americans will refuse to eat dog meat. This type of food is acceptable in Vietnam. Muslims eat beef, but Hindus wouldn't dare touch it. Muslims—as well as many Jews—stay away from pork. People from other ethnic and religious groups could eat pork without hesitation. In general, people typically are cautious about trying novel meat-based products and foods (Pliner & Pelchat, 1991). However, with repeated exposure, our appreciation for the new taste typically increases. In addition, exposure to a novel food product increases our willingness to try another (Pliner, 1982; Pliner et al., 1993).

WHEN HUNGER CAUSES DISTRESS: EATING DISORDERS

Is it true that eating disorders are more common in the West than they are in non-Western countries? That is correct. Eating disorders are more common in young females in industrial societies (countries such as Canada, the United States, European countries, Japan, and Australia) than they are in the young females of other countries (Castillo, 1997). Two types of eating disorders, *anorexia nervosa* and *bulimia*, are life-threatening illnesses. Being preoccupied with their body weight, people who suffer from an eating disorder—about 90 percent of them are women—go on starvation diets and fasting or engage in persistent food expulsion (i.e., vomiting, punishing exercises) to maintain a desirable but very low body weight.

Cultural norms have a significant impact on whether an individual develops a preoccupation with thin-body ideals and acquires an intense fear of gaining weight (*DSM-IV*, 1994). In most cultures, certain aspects of the female anatomy became signals of how feminine and sexual a woman is (Habermas, 1991). Today, in Western cultures, thinness is a major aspect of the definition of attractiveness, which increases perceived femininity. Along with some psychological factors that may predispose an individual to develop an eating disorder, social factors such as cultural models of beauty, fashion trends, and peer pressure could contribute to the formation of a self-image of being obese, fat, and unattractive (Thompson, 2003). In many nontraditional cultural settings, attractiveness is associated with a smaller, thinner body shape. A larger, rounded form is associated with the "wife and mother" stereotype that many younger women desperately try to avoid (see Chapter 10).

Anorexia is not a "new" disorder, and it does not occur only in Western countries. Although the term "anorexia" was introduced in 1874, several medical sources reveal the presence of its symptoms in people of the eighteenth century and much earlier. Using historical documents, Bell (1985) described a so-called *holy anorexia* involving food refusal accompanied by the person's belief that abstinence from food is connected to divine power. While researchers found evidence that both anorexia and bulimia have become more common during the twentieth century, the symptoms of anorexia have been observed in every non-Western region of the world.

With the exceptions of Japan and Iran, prevalence estimates of bulimia in non-Western nations were below the range reported for Western nations, and the attempts to find evidence of bulimia in earlier historical periods were fruitless (Keel & Klump, 2003).

VICTORY AND HARMONY: ACHIEVEMENT MOTIVATION

People constantly strive for achievement and excellence. Take a look at masterpieces of human creativity, the pyramids in Egypt and the Eiffel tower in Paris. Turn to a sports channel on television and see how athletes of different national, religious, and ethnic backgrounds compete for excellence. Read the poetry of Nizami, the great son of Persia, and any novel written by literary genius Gabriel García Marquez of Colombia. People try to achieve what others could not. **Need for achievement** is a social need that directs people to constantly strive for excellence and success, influence, and accomplishment. Activities not oriented toward these goals are not motivating and are usually performed without commitment.

Are we born with such motivation to achieve? One of the leaders in early studies of achievement motivation, David McClelland (1958), gave a categorical "no" to this question. He demonstrated that achievement motivation is learned during childhood. It is acquired from parents who stress excellence and display affection and emotional rewards to their children for high levels of achievement. During the individual's life, a wide range of social and psychological factors could further influence achievement motivation. If there is no such example set for the child, he or she will not develop the need for achievement.

Particular social norms may be linked to this motivation. For example, industrial managers in Czechoslovakia (when it was a unified communist country) were found to be significantly lower on achievement motivation than their counterparts in the United States (Krus & Rysberg, 1976). It was found that 11- to 12-year-old children in the United States already displayed more competitive and individualistic motivation than Chinese children of the same age (Domino, 1992). In another study, U.S. mothers repeatedly chose significantly more difficult achievement goals for their children than Mexican mothers (Madsen & Kagan, 1973). In a classic research study on motivation, McClelland (1987) analyzed children's stories in 22 cultures with respect to the degree to which the stories showed themes of achievement motivation. He then related these levels of motivation to measures of economic development in the studied countries. Achievement motivation scores were highly correlated with economic growth of the children's countries. In other words, the greater the emphasis placed on achievement in the stories told to children in various nations, the more rapid the economic development in these nations as the children grew up.

In a cross-national project that involved more than 12,000 participants, Furnham and colleagues (1994) showed a strong relationship between individual achievement motivation and economic growth. In particular, economic growth correlated with attitudes toward competitiveness. The stronger these attitudes, the higher the achievement motivation. The higher the achievement motivation, the greater the rate of economic growth. If the correlation does exist, what is the causal direction of the association? Quite a few scientists believe that economic development changes cultural syndromes. For example, nations with developing and strong economies subsequently increased their support for individualism and decreased their endorsement of power distance and authoritarianism (Hofstede, 1980). Others emphasized that cultural syndromes foster economic development: Values of hard work and gradual savings should boost economic developments, as it was predicted in earlier studies (McClelland, 1961; Weber, 1905). However, most recent studies show that the correlations here are likely bidirectional, and economic development and cultural change seem to move in consistent patterns (Allen et al., 2007). For example, Japan and Hong Kong, two very economically successful countries, were the strongest long-time backers of the so-called **Confucian work dynamism**: a cultural syndrome manifested in persistence at achieving economic goals, social stability, encouragement of prudence and savings, and promoting loyalty and trust by emphasizing shame (Hofstede & Bond, 1988). China most probably enforced similar values about 20 years ago. On the other hand, strong empirical data suggest that individuals who grew up during a time of economic prosperity show an increasingly greater endorsement of values such as egalitarianism, harmony, and autonomy (Allen et al., 2007). Feelings of financial insecurity tend to lead people to seek strong leaders, absolute rules, and social order, while feelings of financial security drive people toward self-expression and individual gratification (Inglehart, 1997).

One of the characteristics of high-achievement motivation is entrepreneurship. This trait gives rise to new ideas and initiative (Miller, 1983). Punishment generally does not promote the generation of new ideas. In addition, in families with authoritarian parents, children develop a relatively low level of achievement motivation (Segall et al., 1990). As a nine-country study revealed, entrepreneurship is typically associated with high-power distance—or tolerance for relative inequality in the workplace—high individualism, low uncertainty avoidance, and high masculinity (McGrath et al., 1992). Data obtained on a U.S. sample (Zheng & Stimpson, 1990) proved a difference between entrepreneurs and nonentrepreneurs in four psychological characteristics of entrepreneurship, such as innovation, achievement orientation, self-esteem, and personal control.

Where ambition ends happiness begins.

HUNGARIAN PROVERB

Falling hurts least for those who fly low.

CHINESE PROVERB

It shouldn't take much imagination to realize that any two individuals may develop two different types of achievement motivation: low and high. One strives for excellence and success, the other is happy doing what is required and does not need recognition from others. What definitely is intriguing is the idea of cultural differences in motivation. Do the results of the studies—mentioned previously—suggest that there are high- and low-achievement-oriented nations and cultures?

The key to the answer is that achievement or success can be understood in several ways. So-called **individualist-success motivation**—the type of motivation measured in most studies cited so far—affects one's attitudes and actions and is directed to the attainment of personal goals. On the contrary, **collectivist-success motivation** directs a person to connect with other people; the individual's contribution is seen as beneficial to the members of a particular group or society in general (Parsons & Goff, 1978).

Each society sets standards for excellence and determines what type of goals—individual or collective—a person is expected to achieve. The individualist type prevails among people in Western cultures, such as the United States, France, and Germany. The collectivist type was more common in Eastern cultures, such as India, Korea, and Japan (Maehr & Nicholls, 1983). In Korea, Thailand, and China, there is a special kind of work ethic, according to which future-oriented and harmonious interpersonal networks are essential for business success (Cho & Kim,

CRITICAL THINKING
Achievement Motivation and Wealth

Think again about the results suggesting that achievement motivation is higher in economically advanced countries (Inkeles & Smith, 1974; McClelland, 1961; Steers & Sanchez-Runde, 2002). As we already know, we have to be cautious when we interpret any correlational data. Correlation does not necessarily prove that high-achievement motivation *causes* economic growth. It is quite possible that a country's economic prosperity stimulates the development of achievement motivation in many successful citizens. Why? Here is the reasoning: "If I know that my effort will be rewarded, I will strive for achievement and excellence. However, if I know that because of poor economic conditions and inefficient governance, my individual effort will not be rewarded, it will be difficult to convince myself to desire achievement." Still, some psychologists suggest that studying achievement motivation could provide us with insights into why certain countries rise to economic prominence at particular times in their history (Allen et al., 2007). What do you think about the motivation–wealth connection?

1993). It was also found that Australian Aboriginal students placed greater emphasis on collectivist intentions, compared with non-Aboriginal students (Fogarty & White, 1994). Bass (1997) showed that bragging about success may be viewed as appropriate in some countries but not in others. For example, in Indonesia boasting about one's competence may be inspirational and builds confidence in subordinates, but in Japan this behavior is considered to be in most cases inappropriate.

Discussion about collectivist and individualist achievement motivation can be found in many cross-cultural studies. Consider, for instance, education. Task orientation is a form of achievement motivation that involves the goal of developing one's ability to learn and grow, whereas ego orientation implies illustrating one's superiority over others (Nicholls, 1989). In a comparative study of Chinese and U.S. elementary school students, it was found that these two types of achievement orientation were present about equally in the samples studied. This result came as a surprise to researchers. China—as was suggested previously—is typically portrayed as a country with a great emphasis on the importance of interpersonal harmony, modesty, and cooperation. The sampled Chinese students, therefore, were expected to have lower ego orientation than U.S. students. One explanation might be the Chinese educational system, which is different from the U.S. system in that it is highly selective and competitive. To succeed, one has to be better than others, especially in terms of grades. Therefore, success in competition with other students for better grades can be the primary source of motivation for the Chinese student (Xiang et al., 1997).

Interesting results were obtained in a bicultural study of Chinese and European New Zealanders. Chinese students were found to have stronger motivation toward academic and professional achievement than their European counterparts. However, Chinese students also showed a greater sense of obligation toward fulfilling their parents' expectations, and they were more fearful of parental response to failure than Europeans students. According to Chinese cultural norms, parents demand and expect high achievement from their children at school. Students must fulfill parental obligations and must appreciate parental sacrifice for the sake of their children (Sue & Okazaki, 1990). Maybe this would explain the fact that by the late 1990s, Chinese immigrants in New Zealand achieved great success in educational and occupational areas, getting higher-status positions in proportions larger than any other ethnic groups, including Europeans (Chung et al., 1997; Liu et al., 2005).

CROSS-CULTURAL SENSITIVITY

People often do not realize the extent to which they distort information when they stereotype. When Britain's Prince Phillip was visiting a high-tech company near Edinburgh, Scotland, a few years ago, he spotted a poorly wired fuse box and consequently made a remark to the company manager: "It looks as though it was put in by an Indian." The royal spokesperson apologized for the remark, but you can imagine how offensive it was to millions of hardworking and high-achieving Indians and their descendants living around the world.

Several years ago, former Mexican President Vicente Fox commented that Mexican immigrants to the United States take jobs "that not even blacks want to do." The Mexican president's office immediately issued a statement saying the president had misspoken and people should not interpret his words in a wrong way. Of course, the president did not want to offend blacks; he should have chosen his words more carefully.

There is further evidence of culture-related complexity in achievement motivation. An interview with more than 500 Anglo-Australians and Sri Lankans was conducted to compare achievement motivation in members of both groups. The individualist orientation was more prevalent in Australians than in Sri Lankans, who were predominantly family- and group-oriented (Niles, 1998). However, both groups were similar regarding the preferred means of achievement of their goals: They both strongly endorsed individual responsibility and the work ethic. The results did not show that one group was more motivated than the other. Most important, the study suggested that people are motivated to achieve different goals through different means or different goals through the same means. It is also argued that achievement can have different meaning in different cultural settings. In short, achievement-oriented behavior is not necessarily individualistic.

Achievement may be perceived differently based on cultural perceptions of specific behaviors. Take indecision, as an example. In some cultures, indecision is denigrated and even the word *indecisive* has negative connotations. In U.S. political and business environment, for instance, being perceived as indecisive is a liability. In other societies, such as in Japan, the very same indecisive behaviors might be evaluated positively (Yates et al., 2010). Cultural norms may encourage different types of achievement motivation. Research shows that Buddhist and Western societies may encourage two somewhat different types of motivation: "maximizing" and "satisfying." *Maximizers* are always in search of the best (which leave them frequently unhappy), whereas *satisficers* are satisfied with what they have achieved (Iyengar et al., 2006).

All cruelty springs from weakness.

SENECA (55 B.C.E.–39 C.E.)—**Roman Rhetorician**

AGGRESSIVE MOTIVATION AND VIOLENCE

"After each game we just wanted to beat somebody up. The best thing was to find [a person] who would challenge us. If no one dared, we would go and kick somebody's butt anyway." This was said to us by M.M., a 30-year-old father of two children, an Englishman who used to be a "soccer hooligan," as he called himself, in one of the London suburbs.

The desire to harm or injure others is called **aggressive motivation**. Physical abuse, verbal assault, angry retaliation, open hostility, and many other forms of aggressive behavior are part of our everyday life, no matter where we live. Aggressive motivation has multiple roots and

CRITICAL THINKING
Collectivism and Individualism

In the late 1990s, Japan and other industrialized nations in Southeast Asia were going through a painful period of economic difficulties. Some popular U.S. talk radio hosts repeatedly suggested that the economic crisis in Asian markets was caused by a cultural factor and, in particular, a collectivist approach to the management of economies. Asian governments pursuing collectivistic principles were very protective of their countries' economies and underestimated the main principle of free enterprise: Economic and financial success comes only as a result of free competition. The rapid pursuit of individualism in achievement motivation of the other hand can have negative social and psychological consequences. For example, it happened in Latin America, where the "capitalization" of the society—historically built on socialist egalitarian principles—could guarantee neither economic growth nor people's satisfaction with the reforms.

Questions:

Do you agree that capitalism in a society requires the acceptance of individualistic values? Or maybe you think that there *is* room for collectivist values in a capitalist society? Would you share an opinion that there are countries and cultures that have difficulties accommodating individualistic principles of free competition?

causes and cannot be explained by one theory, no matter how attractive it appears. Cross-cultural psychologists compare and combine the existing data into a comprehensive view that takes into account a wide range of psychological, political, biological, socioeconomic, and cultural factors that are linked to aggressive motivation and behavior.

Biologists found, for example, that the absence of a specific chemical in the brain—nitric oxide—can transform normal mice into violent and sexually aggressive miscreants. The same mechanism might be found in humans too (Brown, 1995). Even being psychologically predisposed to violent responses, most individuals are still capable of adjusting to existing social restraints and cultural requirements. In cultures in which violent conduct is rare, people become very sensitive to any form of violence and aggression and resist it. On the contrary, in communities in which violence is a common problem-solving technique, such as in a zone in which there is ethnic conflict, people may acquire this particular behavioral pattern of violent behavior as a norm (Buckley, 2000). Several cross-cultural studies bring additional support to the argument that the roots of violence may be found in society (Frey & Hoppe-Graff, 1994).

Aggression is positively reinforced when aggressive acts have utilitarian value and bolster the violent performance. The individual in such cases can gain power and control, obtain material resources, or resist provocation (Rohier, 1975). It was found, for example, that children of the same country who were raised in different social settings may display different patterns of aggressive behavior. A study of children from two Mexican regions found that those who lived in the town with a higher level of violence performed twice as many aggressive acts as those from the other town in which the violence level was lower (Fry, 1988). According to the report, parents who lived in high-violence areas tended to encourage their children to be aggressive and respond to violence with retaliatory actions. Moreover, aggressive behavior was higher in those families in which parents were neglecting, rejecting, lacking in affection, indifferent to the child's aggression, and abusive. This study provides an example of a bidirectional causation. On one hand, the dangerous social conditions induce parental encouragement of violence in "self-defense." On the other hand, the encouragement of aggressive behavior creates a particular social climate that permits new aggressive acts. This study, nevertheless, suggests little about why there are children and adults who do not respond to aggression with new aggression and maintain nonviolent behavior throughout their lives.

Staub (1996) investigated multiple factors of aggressive behavior in various cultural groups. Among these factors are a history of discrimination, exposure to violence, attitudes to authority, fulfillment of basic needs, lack of education, harsh treatment, abusive families, and joblessness. Violence increases in both black and white neighborhoods with a predominantly poor population. Why does it happen? Does it mean that the poor are more aggressive than other social groups? The author argues that in a society that develops materialistic values in its members, personal success is primarily determined by how much money one makes and whether one has access to power and resources. With all possibilities for economic and social success visible, but without the capacity to make use of them, the person may experience a sense of powerlessness. This mental set, in turn, may cause frustration and aggression. In addition, if a person adopts masculine values (see Chapter 1), his frustration can be easily channeled through various violent behaviors. Unfulfilled needs may bring a person closer to a group of people—a gang, for instance—that promotes a positive identity, promises power, and offers a connection to peers. Analyzing why there are many Hispanic gangs in U.S. cities, the author suggests that because of a rapid social change in the lives of the youth, the traditional attachment to the family is being rapidly destroyed. As a result, many young people are looking for affiliation and attachment elsewhere, and some of them end up being gang members.

One of the contemporary views on aggression is influenced by the frustration–aggression hypothesis (Berkowitz, 1962; Dollard et al., 1939). This theory describes aggression as the dominant response to frustration. Using this assumption, many social scientists attempted to explain the roots of aggressive behavior in a wide range of frustrating circumstances such as poverty, broken families, migration, urbanization, unemployment, and discrimination. There are numerous examples of studies relating aggression to unfavorable circumstances and absence of aggression to favorable conditions (Bernard, 1990). Thus, it was found that in India and the United States, positive parental affection was negatively correlated with children's aggression (Pinto et al., 1991). Parents' reaction to children's aggressive behavior is an important factor that controls and facilitates aggression. Studies show that punishment is not an effective means of aggression control (Weiss, 1992). Moreover, high levels of restriction (low permissiveness) could cause physical aggression (Schlegel & Barry, 1991).

Among psychological factors linked to aggression, specialists often mention self-esteem. Assumptions that a low level of self-esteem is related to a high frequency of delinquent behavior were taken into consideration by some researchers (Crain & Weissman, 1972; Jenkins, 1995). However, cross-cultural comparisons do not always prove this to be true. For example, three ethnic groups were examined to determine whether individual self-esteem is linked to delinquent conduct. The hypothesis was valid only for European Americans, but not for the black and Hispanic subjects (Leung & Drasgow, 1986). Aggressiveness can also be related to the child's poor social competence with peers. Without having such competency the child does not know how to negotiate conflicts, resolve difficult social situations, control emotions, or interpret the emotions of others (Asher et al., 1982).

Considerable experimental work yields evidence that aggression does not always have to be caused by underlying frustration (Kadiangandu et al., 2001). Albert Borowitz (2005) described a special kind of violence caused by a craving for notoriety or self-glorification. Borowitz coined the term "Herostratos syndrome" to refer to a person who believes that life has cheated him and the only way to compensate for the sense of injustice is to inflict pain on somebody else.

(The term refers back to the destruction of the Temple of Ephesus in 356 B.C.E. by a man who wanted to leave his name in history.) Violent impulses can develop as learned response patterns. Very often aggressive behavior is readily acquired through observation of aggressive models (Bandura, 1969).

Aggression can become manifest early in life in various forms of children's activities, including play. In a study of 120 children from the United States, Sweden, Germany, and Indonesia, the four-year-old children were asked to tell two stories using two toys with aggressive and neutral characteristics. The stories created by U.S. children contained more aggressive concepts, aggressive words, and hostile characters than the narratives of other studied groups (Farver et al., 1997). Perhaps early family experiences or children's exposure to aggression on television could have influenced the children's responses.

Are particular nations and cultures more aggressive than others? To address this question one should understand that there are no violence-free societies. Presidents and prime ministers have been assassinated in the United States and Israel, Pakistan, India and Sweden, Armenia and Chile. Terrorist groups attack innocent victims in Russia and in Argentina, Egypt and Peru, Tanzania and Spain. Violent acts are committed in the subways and streets of London, Tokyo, Oslo, and Moscow. There are countries in which the crime rate is declining and ones in which it is growing; there are regions with low rates of violence and areas with high rates of violence. The rates, however, vary among different groups. In the United States, boys are four times more likely to be arrested than girls are. Adolescents of lower socioeconomic status are almost twice as likely to be arrested as middle-class adolescents, and African American and Latino youths are close to twice as likely to be arrested as whites. European Americans themselves are more than twice as likely to be arrested as Asian Americans. Homicide, for instance, is the leading cause of death among young African American men, whereas among whites automobile accidents are the number one cause of premature death. In the 1990s, a 10-year-old black boy had a 1 in 21 chance of being murdered before reaching maturity (D'Souza, 1995). However, Adelbert Jenkins (1995), a prominent black psychologist from New York University, suggests that the very question about whether one ethnic group is more violent than the other cannot be addressed without looking at it from an historic perspective. For example, speaking of American Africans, he argues that one should take into consideration a few hundred years of direct and indirect discrimination and aggression against blacks committed primarily by white Europeans.

Societies have different thresholds of tolerance toward various acts of violence and aggression. As an illustration, in many nonindustrial societies, killing infants was not considered a crime (Minturin & Shashak, 1982). In other ethnic groups, killing is appropriate and even praised if it is committed in the name of God or retaliation. So-called honor killings of women still take place in many traditional cultures, including countries such as Pakistan, Saudi Arabia, Turkey, and Egypt. Many such cases are never brought to trial for a number of reasons. Many victims, especially uneducated women confined to their husbands' homes, are too intimidated to press charges. It is not a secret that police are easily bribed or persuaded by the men's families to dismiss the complaints. Moreover, under another Islamic legal concept called *qisas* and *diyat*, a blood relative of a victim can formally forgive a crime in exchange for payment (Constable, 2000). In most industrialized nations, killing in the context of war is considered to be legitimate because those who are targeted for killing belong to "outlawed" groups. Furthermore, in these societies, execution may be accepted not just because of what the convicted criminal did or because justice is administered by constituted authority but also because criminals put themselves outside the law and confront society.

A CASE IN POINT
Incarceration Rates

According to international studies, the highest rates of incarceration per 100,000 population were in Russia (606 people), the United States (701), Ukraine (415), South Africa (402), and Belarus (554). On the other end of the spectrum were countries such as Nepal (29 people per 100,000), India (29), and Indonesia (29). Low imprisonment rates should be interpreted with caution, however. These rates may reflect a low crime rate, such as in Japan (Struck, 2000), or poor police work or legal system, which allows many criminals to slip away. High imprisonment rates can reflect the abusive legal system of a repressive police state, a high rate of crime, relatively longer prison sentences, or the use of mandatory sentences. In the United States, for example, the high rate is significantly affected by the large number of prisoners convicted of drug-related crimes (Walmsley, 2006).

Numerous cross-cultural sources report that boys are more aggressive than girls (Segall et al., 1997). In virtually all cultures, most men and women are socialized differently: boys as fighters and problem solvers and girls as moderators and peacekeepers. It is generally assumed that boys receive more inculcation of and encouragement for aggression. However, empirical research does not provide compelling evidence that encouragement is the only factor that stimulates aggression. Some psychologists argue that men are more aggressive than women because of higher testosterone levels in males. However, factors such as poverty, abuse, violence, lack of male role models, the glorification of war and lawlessness, and drug abuse all seem to promote deviant destructive behavior in males to a greater extent than they do in females (Eagly, 1995). Comparing patterns of aggressive behavior in men raised in the historic South and North of the United States, researchers found that Southern males are more likely than their Northern counterparts to misinterpret and overestimate aggressive intentions of the opponent. Men in the South tend to believe that violent norms are supported by their peers to a greater extent than it actually is (Vandello et al., 2008).

In general, members of collectivist cultures can tolerate aggression when it comes from an in-group authority more often than when it comes from a lower-level in-group member or an outsider. In an experiment, two samples of Hong Kong Chinese and U.S. citizens were

CRITICAL THINKING
Aggression and Testosterone

A research study found that men with testosterone levels in the top 10 percent were more likely to belong to lower socioeconomic classes (Dabbis & Morris, 1990). Does this mean that people with higher testosterone levels are more likely to become or stay poor? That is quite possible. Why? If an individual is aggressive and violent, the person will not be able to succeed in a society that requires cooperation and demands compliance from its members. However, the other explanation is plausible too. We could suggest that unfavorable social conditions, abuse, and discrimination against a person may cause continuous frustration and stress that is responsible for the release of surplus amounts of testosterone in the body.

A CASE IN POINT
Sexual Jealousy and Aggression

Do males and females differ in aggression caused by sexual jealousy? Indeed, the incidence of husbands assaulting wives is much higher than the reverse (Daly & Wilson, 1988). The evidence that men are more likely to assault women than vice versa does not necessarily mean that males experience stronger sexual jealousy. Perhaps females experience jealousy that is just as strong and have equally powerful motives to punish their mates, but they simply lack the strength or expertise to do so: Males are generally stronger than females and have often had more experience with aggressive acts.

Despite high incidents of jealousy-based violence, sexual jealousy and subsequent aggression could decline in the future, as some researchers forecast. Why? As Archer (1996) argues, for females, jealousy may focus primarily on the potential loss of resources (males) needed

for child rearing. In this context, an unfaithful mate could threaten to leave and take resources with him. Therefore, females react very strongly to male sexual infidelity. For males, though, sexual jealousy may rest primarily on different concerns. If their mate has sexual relations with other men, the husband could end up raising other men's children. However, such a sociobiological view on the nature of jealousy is criticized. In Western societies today, women have become more independent from men than they were 30 or 70 years ago. The access to resources, power, and effective contraceptives has made a difference in the lives of many women. Therefore, the significance of both biological and economic factors of jealousy is substantially reduced. What is the conclusion? Today both men and women express almost equivalent levels of jealousy and—as a result—aggression.

compared. The Chinese were less critical of an attacker and of his or her actions as long as the attacker had a higher status than the in-group target of aggression. U.S. citizens made no consistent distinction as a function of the attacker's status or group membership. It is believed that the Chinese are high on collectivism and power distance and that Americans are low on collectivism and relatively low on power distance (see Chapter 1). In other words, people in the United States tend to respond and to fight back no matter who the attacker is (Bond, 1985).

Sexuality is the lyricism of the masses.

CHARLES BAUDELAIRE **(1821–1867)—French Poet**

CULTURE AND SEXUALITY

Hormones and other chemicals in our body could determine the dynamics of sexual arousal and the related psychological experiences (Byrne, 1982). Thus, **sexual motivation**, or motivation to engage in sexual activity, is certainly regulated, at least in part, by human physiology. However, genes, hormones, and other biological factors only change the probability of the occurrence of certain types of sexual behavior. Societal factors including laws, customs, and norms, in fact, determine what types of sexual behavior are acceptable, under what circumstances, and with what frequency. Every culture has its own set of requirements, beliefs, symbols, and norms regarding sexuality and its expression. This set of characteristics is called **sex culture**. Sex cultures vary greatly across the world and are influenced by current religious, ideological, political, and moral values developed by society.

What we consider sexual is determined by a combination of biological, psychological, and cultural factors. Evolutionary psychologists emphasize the importance of the adaptive role of human sexuality. For example, cross-cultural surveys suggest that men generally prefer to marry younger, physically attractive women who are perceived to be high in reproductive potential. Women, on the other hand, prefer to marry older and wealthier men, who generally excel in providing material resources and social status for the family. Other universal features of mating behavior can also be explained in adaptive terms. For example, marital stability around the world is associated with fertility: the more children, the less chance of divorce. In addition, divorce in almost every culture is predicted by infertility and infidelity, both of which may hinder individual fitness (Lucas et al., 2008). Many cultures consider sexual pleasure as normal, desirable, and natural, whereas others view it as primitive, sinful, and even abnormal. For instance, in many cultures, there is a popular belief that masturbation is a sin that could cause retardation and other serious psychological problems (Kon, 2001).

Cultural beliefs about sex may affect the quality of cross-cultural research on sex. For example, the so-called refusal rate (proportion of people who do not want to participate in a study as subjects) may affect the validity of surveys on sexuality. Why? People in one country may be open to talking about sex—because of the existing cultural norms of permissiveness—and agree to give interviews and answers to survey questions. People who grew up in more sexually restrictive environments are often very reluctant to give any kind of information about sex. For the aforementioned reason, it is difficult to compare cultures on criteria such as premarital and teenage sex, extramarital sex, frequency and number of sexual relationships, and sexual abuse. As we mentioned earlier, many women do not report sexual abuse against them because it is considered dishonorable for them to even mention the abuse. The shame of self-disclosure in such cases is overwhelming (Shiraev & Sobel, 2006).

Sexual values that regulate sexual motivation can be quite different across cultures. For example, chastity (no experience with sexual intercourse) is not regarded as a particularly important value in countries such as Sweden, Denmark, Germany, or Holland. On the contrary, in countries such as China, Iran, India, and many others, chastity is essential for a woman's position in the society (Halonen & Santrock, 1995). There are marked differences in the speed of labor and indicated extreme variations in the psychological environment during labor and delivery. Faster, easier labors appear to be related to acceptance of birth as a normal phenomenon uncomplicated by shame (Newton, 1970).

Traditional sex cultures endorse restrictive rules regarding the expression of sexuality among their members. These cultures also tend to suppress the expression of sexuality. For example, in some parts of Africa and the Middle East, many people practice female circumcision. It is believed that it helps keep a girl chaste, clean, and free from "sinful" sexual desires. In some cultures, this procedure is even considered to be religious. In the United States too, before the 1900s, female circumcision was practiced, but only by a few individuals.

In contrast, nontraditional sex cultures are generally permissive to different forms of sexual behavior. In nations such as Holland, Sweden, Russia, Australia, Denmark, and some others that represent the so-called nontraditional sex cultures, sex does not carry for a majority of people the same mystery, shame, and conflict it does in traditional cultures (see Table 7.2).

Even the style of clothing represents a particular sex culture. In traditional Islamic societies, women are typically veiled and cloaked from head to foot; contemporary European and U.S. fashion trends allow women to expose most parts of their bodies. Those who visit European countries know that on most public beaches many women appear topless.

TABLE 7.2 Type of Sex Culture and General Attitudes Toward Sex

Issues/Type of Culture	Traditional Sex Culture	Nontraditional Sex Culture
Expression of sexuality	Heavily regulated	Somewhat regulated
Premarital sex	Prohibited and rejected	Somewhat tolerated
Extramarital sex	Prohibited and rejected	Somewhat tolerated
Homosexuality	Prohibited and rejected	Somewhat tolerated
Chastity	High value	Low value

If you cannot be chaste, be cautious.

SPANISH PROVERB

Labels of "traditionalism" and "nontraditionalism" could be misleading, however. Many people who live in traditional sex cultures could express attitudes and behaviors that are more common to nontraditional sex cultures and vice versa. Family socialization, attitudes, adulthood experiences, and many other environmental factors affect an individual's sexuality—including his or her thoughts about sex, frequency of sexual acts, and type of sexual activities. For example, despite expectations, almost 70 percent of Chinese respondents (traditional sex culture) do not denounce extramarital affairs. This is a larger approval rate than is found in the United States. In China, among respondents aged 45 and above, about 25 percent of men and 10 percent of women said they had engaged in premarital sex, most of them with their future spouses. In the younger group, those who turned 20 around 1995, 40 percent of males and 25 percent of females had had premarital sex, the women typically with their future husbands, while young men also reported sex with other girlfriends or occasional partners (Braverman, 2002). Moreover, according to researchers at the Chinese Academy of Social Sciences, 60–70 percent of Chinese have had sex before marriage, up from 15 percent in 1989 (Associated Press, 2008). In the "nontraditional" sex culture of the United States, many prominent individuals, including politicians, movie stars, and opinion leaders, raise their voice in support of traditional values including chastity and abstinence (Edsall, 1998).

Different cultures may promote specific attitudes toward particular types of sexual lifestyles. Almost in all cases, gays and lesbians try to adapt to traditional norms and expectations. According to researcher Li Yinhe, most gay men in China eventually choose to marry a woman. In China, men are under serious social pressure to get married and have a family so that they commonly hide their sexual orientation in order to "fit" into traditional cultural norms (Associated Press, 2008). These norms are not just abstract principles. For example, a traditional Chinese marriage requires that the man perform his familial duties, including the birth of a male heir for the continuation of his family line, the acquisition of a daughter-in-law who should provide support for her husband's parents, and the begetting of sons who will provide for the family well-being. Traditional Chinese marriages also represent the formation of an alliance between two extended families (Lucas et al., 2008).

The finest people marry the two sexes in their own person.

RALPH WALDO EMERSON **(1803–1882)—American Poet and Philosopher**

There are two basic understandings of causes of homosexuality. According to the biological approach, a person's sexual orientation has strong genetic roots; culture has only some impact on homosexuality. According to the environmental approach, social and cultural factors cause homosexuality more than anything else. Some authors suggest that homosexuality in ancient Greece, for example, occurred under certain political and socioeconomic conditions. Among them were significant strong social stratification, a large poverty class, a decentralized political system, and an absence of formal education (Dickerman, 1993).

Several social and psychological conditions that may be linked to homosexuality were identified in a comprehensive ethnographic study of 70 preindustrial cultures (Barber, 1998). Despite initial predictions, homosexuality was not found to be higher in cultures with repressive attitudes toward premarital sex. Societies that practiced polygamy (multiple wives for one husband) were also low on homosexuality. Moreover, the frequency of homosexuality is very low in societies in which hunting and gathering are predominant activities. It increases in agricultural societies and goes up together with the growing complexity of modern cultures. A high density of population was also linked to homosexuality.

Male–female roles in homosexual relations are influenced by general cultural expectations of a given society. In Mexico, for example, with its strict gender-role divisions, homosexuals adhere more strictly to either male or female roles. In the United States and Canada, where gender roles are more flexible, many gay males frequently shift roles (Carrier, 1980). Homosexuality among males appears to be common in countries that value female virginity highly and separate men and women (Davenport, 1976). According to some researchers, the general public's attitudes toward homosexuality have social and cultural roots: Those countries that desire the expansion of the nation's population are less tolerant toward homosexuality (Ember & Ember, 1990). By way of illustration, in the 1930s, homosexuality was a serious crime in Nazi Germany. Before the 1990s, it was a crime in the Soviet Union. In fact, in both countries, the rapid growth of population was considered an important ideological and political goal. Homosexuals in those countries were considered criminals and mentally ill and were severely punished. For many years, even in the United States, homosexuality was considered a mental disorder. Only recently, in the early 1970s, based on the predominant opinion of U.S. mental health specialists, was male and female homosexuality removed from diagnostic manuals (*DSM-IV*, 1994). In the United States, individuals with college and postgraduate educational degrees, liberal ideological orientation, or who tend to vote for Democrats are inclined to express tolerance toward homosexuality. In contrast, people with no college degree, ideologically conservative, and Republican supporters tend to be less tolerant. These tendencies do not, of course, take into account individual variations in attitudes. In addition, younger people tend to me more tolerant than the older ones. Women have been somewhat more tolerant toward homosexuality than men (Shiraev & Sobel, 2006), but the opinion gap has narrowed significantly. Surveys taken after 2011 show that Americans' support for the moral acceptability of gay and lesbian relations is around 50 percent.

SEX AND SEXUALITY: SOME CROSS-CULTURAL SIMILARITIES

Psychologists suggest, for instance, that both men and women can respond erotically to mild pain. Betzig (1989) found that, cross-culturally, adultery and sterility (inability to conceive a child) were the most common reasons for divorce. Some aspects of interpersonal male–female attractiveness are also consistent across cultures. For example, characteristics such as kindness, understanding, intelligence, good health, emotional stability, dependability, and a pleasing disposition are considered to be cross-culturally attractive in women. Men everywhere react more negatively than women do when their partners share sexual fantasies about having sex with others. Women everywhere are more distressed than men are when their partner kisses someone else (Rathus et al., 1993). Many aspects of nonverbal communication appear to be universal too. For instance, courting and flirtation patterns are similar across many cultures and performed for the specific purpose of mate selection and reproduction (Aune & Aune, 1994).

There are many exceptions to the general rules, however. Kissing, for example, is a cross-cultural phenomenon. However, kissing is unknown to some cultures in Africa and South America. Touching may be viewed as a normal act of communication between two strangers in Mediterranean countries, but it could be totally inappropriate in the United States. Marital fidelity appears to be virtually a cross-cultural requirement as well. However, among some Arctic peoples, it is considered normal and hospitable to offer a host's wife to a guest. Around the world, males prefer females younger than themselves and vice versa. A study conducted across 33 countries showed similarities in preference for mate characteristics between men and women who ranked "kind and understanding" first, "intelligent" second, "exciting personality" third, "healthy" fourth, and "religious" last. Despite the overall cross-cultural gender similarity, there were some differences in preference. According to the survey, men almost universally prefer "good looks" in women, whereas women choose "good earning capacity" as the most important characteristic of the partner of the opposite sex (Buss, 1994).

Compared to Hispanic and white young males, ages 14–21, black youth are more sexually active. More than 35 percent of blacks report six or more sexual partners over their life. The rates for Hispanic and white youth are 12 points lower. Young African American women begin sexual life earlier than white women. However, if social class differences are taken into consideration, there were no differences between the two groups. Both groups were similarly affected by sexual abuse (Watt, 1990).

Data gathered across a large number of countries in Africa, Asia, South America, and Europe (Neto et al., 2000) showed that most people go through similar stages in romantic relationships. According to the Global Study of Sexual Attitudes and Behaviors, men and women around the world experience similar sexual problems related to aging. The study, based on in-person and telephone interviews with 27,500 men and women in 30 countries worldwide, found that among men, the most common problem is erectile dysfunction, which increases with age. Among women, the most common problems were lack of interest in sex and inability to experience orgasm (Laumann, 2002).

Cultural norms and receptions change with time. Not long ago, masturbation was widely considered a form of pathological behavior or even a serious chronic affliction that required therapeutic intervention or, sometimes, physical punishment. In publications and public speeches just several decades ago, doctors, psychologists, and psychiatrists routinely labeled masturbation and homosexuality as forms of degeneration and pathology. Overall, global changes in education, social norms, informational technology, and travel have changed many traditional views of human sexuality and sexual practices.

Exercise 7.1

Often humor helps us to understand ourselves better. Below is an assignment that could show that sexuality is a cultural phenomenon. The way we see ourselves and other people is often based on a starting point from which we make our judgments.

Teak is 18. Teal is 18. Both are foreign college exchange students, both are juniors, and both of them will study at the City University of New York. The tuition is paid, the books are bought, and the keys to the rooms are in the young men's pockets. The new life has begun.

Teak grew up on a small Atlantic island. People on this island know nothing about kissing. Nudity is strongly prohibited. People have DVDs; however, movies rated "R" are not available on the island. Premarital sex is punishable. Men and women believe that sexual experiences reduce their energy and are bad for their health. People do not even talk about sex. After a couple marries, the husband and wife are allowed to have sex once a week, at night, and as quickly as possible. Both partners should be dressed in nightclothes and cannot look at each other. Female orgasms are rare and considered to be abnormal. Sex education is prohibited by law.

Teal grew up on a small Pacific island. Children on this island, both boys and girls, are taught about sex as early as at the age of 7. Nudity is totally acceptable on the island. At the age of 13, the boys undergo a special ritual that initiates them into adult sexual life. Girls do the same at the age of 15. Every young man and woman at this age has an adult sexual partner of the opposite sex, who teaches them proficiency in sex. After a year of training, the students are allowed to have sex without supervision. Adults have sex practically every day, often in public places.

After spending a month in the United States, Teak and Teal decided to write letters to some close friends in their home countries about their experiences with sex culture in the United States. Please compose two brief letters on behalf of both young men. Compare the "letters." How could we help these young men to adjust better in the U.S. culture? Offer specific suggestions and discuss them in class.

Chapter Summary

- Motivation is any condition—usually an internal one—that initiates, activates, or maintains the individual's goal-directed behavior. Many interesting and valuable ideas about the nature of human motivation appear in classical works of prominent social scientists. Theories of sociobiology claim that general biological laws of evolution are perfectly suitable as a fundamental explanation of human motivation. Theories of *social instincts* emphasize the crucial and universal role of basic instincts, similar in both humans and animals, as motivations of behavior. The sociological approach emphasizes the crucial role of social factors, for example, values and economic inequality, in determining the individual's behavior.

- There are several psychological theories of motivation. Drive theories pay attention to needs, motivated states caused by physiological or psychological deprivation. Arousal theories of motivation suggest that people seek to maintain optimal levels of arousal by actively changing their exposure to arousing stimuli. Psychoanalysis emphasizes

the importance of unconscious processes. Humanistic theories focus on human dignity, individual choice, and self-worth. Cognitive psychologists maintain that we are aware of our thought patterns and therefore can control our motivation and overt behavior.

- In general, most of the theories emphasize the universal nature of human motivation that is influenced by various environmental factors. These factors, in turn, are products of historic, religious, political, cultural, and socioeconomic developments.

- Typically, cultural norms and traditions regulate hunger. Cultures establish culture-linked eating habits, determine what is considered tasty and tasteless, and establish social taboos on particular foods and food products. Eating disorders are more common in young white females in industrial societies compared to their peers in non-Western countries.

- Achievement motivation is acquired by the individual and influenced by his or her culture. On the national level, there is a strong relationship between individual achievement motivation and economic growth. However, there are "individually" oriented and "socially" oriented achievement motives. The first type is common in Western cultures. The latter is more common in Southwest Asian countries, Korea, Japan, and perhaps in other collectivist cultures.

- There are no aggression-free countries or cultures. Aggressive motivation has many underlying factors, from chemical and physiological, to socioeconomic, psychological, and political. Cultures have different thresholds of tolerance toward various acts of violence and aggression.

Poverty, lack of opportunities, socialization experiences, history of violence, and other factors contribute to violence.

- Sexual motivation is certainly regulated, at least in part, by human physiology, but culture determines various forms of its experience and behavioral manifestation. There are traditional and nontraditional sex cultures that practice either restrictive or permissive norms of sexuality. Sexual orientation, like homosexuality, for instance, as well as various forms of sexual disorders are linked to particular social practices and values.

Key Terms

Aggressive Motivation The desire to harm or injure others.

Arousal Theories Motivational theories based on an assumption that people seek to maintain optimal levels of arousal by actively changing their exposure to arousing stimuli.

Collectivist-Success Motivation A type of achievement motivation that directs a person to connect with others; the individual's contribution is seen as beneficial to the members of a particular group or society in general.

Confucian Work Dynamism A cultural syndrome manifested in persistence at achieving economic goals, social stability, encouragement of prudence and savings, and promoting loyalty and trust by emphasizing shame.

Drive An internal aroused condition that directs an organism to satisfy some physiological need.

Extrinsic Motivation A type of motivation that engages people in various activities for a particular reward.

Individualist-Success Motivation A type of achievement motivation that affects one's

attitudes and actions and is directed toward the attainment of personal goals.

Intrinsic Motivation A type of motivation that engages people in various activities for no apparent reward except the pleasure and satisfaction of the activity itself.

Motivation The psychological process that arouses, directs, and maintains behavior.

Need A motivated state caused by physiological deprivation (such as lack of food or water).

Need for Achievement A social need that directs people to strive constantly for excellence and success.

Self-Actualization A final level of psychological development in which individuals strive to realize their uniquely human potential to achieve everything they are capable of achieving.

Sex Culture A set of requirement, beliefs, symbols, and norms regarding sexuality and its expression.

Sexual Motivation A type of motivation that engages a person in sexual activity.

CHAPTER 8

Human Development and Socialization

Man is born a barbarian, and only rises himself
above the beast by culture.

BALTASAR GRACIAN (1601–1658)—
Spanish Writer and Jesuit Priest

He who opens a school closes a prison.

VICTOR HUGO (1802–1885)—
French Poet and Novelist

As Lynn headed out to go shopping, she already knew her four-year-old son was in a bad mood. All that day he had been doing all that he could to frustrate her. First, he chose not to eat breakfast and then he spilled apple juice all over the carpet. He categorically refused to put on his red jacket and continuously tried to unbuckle his seatbelt in the car. Since they had arrived at the shopping mall, he had been whining continuously for 20 minutes and demanding they go to the toy store immediately. The mother's patience finally ran out when her son ran away and started picking up coins from the fountain. Lynn pulled him out of the fountain and spanked him three or four times. The son reacted first with a brief and silent pause of embarrassment and then filled the shopping mall with a high-pitched scream. A couple of crystal tears rolled down his cheeks. "This is horrible. You cannot treat your child like this," a woman passerby said loudly as she pointed at Lynn. "You shouldn't do that, ma'am," uttered another woman. "At least not in a public place." Lynn could not understand why these strangers reacted in this way. She had arrived two years ago, as a Cambodian refugee, and thus far had had nothing critical said to her.

190

What had she done to upset these people? Traditional Cambodian child-rearing practices allow spanking. Moreover, this type of physical punishment is a major component of the child's learning process in her home country, where parental authority in the family is seldom challenged. Most parental behavior is supported by the extended family, the local community, and the Buddhist religion. A study found that more than 50 percent of Southeast Asian parents reported having used physical punishment of their children at some point (Tajima & Harachi, 2010). However, the same study found that among immigrant families, education and experience of living in the United States decrease spanking of children. Globally, affluence and education change parental attitudes toward the use of physical force against their family members. Hopefully, an open competition of ideas will deem spanking the least effective method of upbringing. However, this is only a wish. The competition of ideas continues. So does spanking of children.

DEVELOPMENT AND SOCIALIZATION

Psychologists distinguish between human development and socialization. **Human development** is viewed as the changes in physical, psychological, and social behavior that are experienced by individuals across the life span—from conception to death. **Socialization** is the process by which an individual becomes a member of a particular culture and takes on its values and behaviors. Neither human development nor socialization stops at age 18 or even 25. It is a lifelong process with accelerations and delays, changes in direction, sudden transitions, and long-term conversions. Human development is not only growth but also decline and modification.

Psychology as a scientific discipline began to study human development and socialization more than 100 years ago. Some psychologists, as you can see later in the chapter, believed in universal mechanisms of an individual's developments and saw cultural influences as some "external" elements affecting behavior and experience. Others were more skeptical and believed in cultural relativism (Edwards & Bloch, 2010). An early fundamental comparative study called *The Six Cultures Study of Socialization* began in 1954 and involved investigators from three universities (Harvard, Yale, and Cornell). The selected countries were the United States, Mexico, Japan, India, the Philippines, and Uganda (LeVine, 2010; Whiting, 1963). This was just an initiation of a long cross-cultural study into human development, which continues today.

We begin with an overview of the impact of culture on development and socialization and then—before describing specific life span stages—turn attention to several specific psychological theories of development.

QUALITY OF LIFE AND THE CHILD'S DEVELOPMENT

The overall quality of life—availability of food and other products, type of living conditions, quality of education and health care, presence or absence of violence in the family or neighborhood, and a number of other factors—significantly affects the individual's development. Countries vary in overall density of population and number of immediate family members. A unit of two adults living with their own children is common in Western societies, such as Canada, Sweden, or the United States, whereas the large extended family in which parents, children, grandparents, cousins, and even some distant relatives live in one household is common in non-Western countries, such as Pakistan, Rwanda, or Indonesia. Technological advancements and socioeconomic improvements affect the composition of the family (Berry, 1997). Immigration is also an important factor that changes substantially many century-old family traditions. In cross-cultural studies, it is extremely important to distinguish between several generations of immigrants because, among other things, they are likely to be different from the socioeconomic point of view (Schwartz et al., 2010).

A study of 799 students in Greece, Cyprus, the Netherlands, Great Britain, and Germany examined the relationship of family bonds to family structure but did not find substantial differences among families in the sampled countries in terms of emotional closeness, geographic proximity to relatives, and frequency of telephone contacts (Georgas et al., 1997). However, when the extended families were analyzed, differences were found between generally wealthy individualist countries in the sample (the Netherlands, Great Britain, and Germany) and predominantly collectivist countries (Greece and Cyprus). The extended families in the latter sample were emotionally and geographically closer to each other than the families from the individualist sample.

Access to resources and educational opportunities are likely to provide an advantageous environment for the developing child. Vygotsky (1932) established that guided interaction with a more knowledgeable partner should advance the intellectual development of the child. Middle-class parents answer children's questions with more elaborate explanations than do parents of a lower social class, who are generally less educated than middle-class families (see Chapter 5). One study showed that Mexican mothers from low-socioeconomic-status groups—contrary to mothers from other families—used tactile interaction, such as a touch and push, with their children more frequently than they used verbal means (Zepeda, 1985). In many working class communities in the United States, as well as in preindustrial communities in Africa and the Pacific, parents have low willingness to instruct their children themselves and tend to assume that children can learn things on their own (Rogoff, 1990).

Poverty may directly affect relationships within the family. In preindustrial and economically underdeveloped societies, partly because of limited access to resources, close cooperation within families becomes an economic necessity (see Chapter 1).

NORMS, CUSTOMS, AND CHILD CARE

The child's development and socialization depend on the people with whom the child interacts, the places where they spend time together, and the roles children play (Whiting & Whiting, 1975). Adults assign children to some roles and disallow others. For example, cross-cultural differences in the behavior of boys and girls may be partially due to different roles assigned to them by adults. Girls are more apt to stay close to home and are more involved in child-care activities compared to boys (Whiting & Edwards, 1988). Rough-and-tumble play is a common child's activity across cultures. However, in traditional Muslim countries, girls are seldom encouraged by their parents to engage in such games (Ahmed, 2002).

There are similarities in patterns of social support from children, spouses, relatives, and friends. However, comparative studies identify a number of national and cultural differences. For example, rocking or thumb sucking in children would be considered wrong by white South African mothers. For native African mothers, such behavior is absolutely normal. U.S. mothers respond more favorably to their babies' requests when the infants are playing with physical objects. Japanese mothers, on the other hand, are more responsive when their babies are engaged in play with them. Japanese parents, unlike U.S. parents, rarely leave their children with babysitters. These children learn how to interact with other adults, and this may explain why Japanese children display a higher rate of anxiety than U.S. boys and girls do when the parents are not present (Bornstein & Tamis-LeMonda, 1989). Studies on parent–child communication showed that French and Italian parents and children were more interactive than German pairs (Best, 1994).

An exaggeration in one's gratitude is considered normal and is even expected in Arab cultures (Triandis, 1994). "Thank you" letters are commonly sent by U.S. boys and girls to their birthday guests. This tradition is unknown in Russia, Ukraine, Armenia, and many other countries.

Cultural traditions of collectivism are positively correlated with the authoritarian style of parenting, which is based on strict demands, behavioral control, and sanctions (Rudy & Grusec, 2001). In other words, in predominantly collectivist cultures, more parents practice authoritarian methods than they do in individualist cultures. Of course, we should understand that besides collectivism, many societal factors contribute to authoritarian methods, including political authoritarianism, lack of education, social instability, and educational traditions. For instance, Russian adolescents perceived parents and teachers as more controlling than did U.S. students (Chirkov & Ryan, 2001). Observers see Russian elementary and secondary education and parenting styles as more authoritarian than the styles practiced in the United States.

Studies show that Indian mothers, compared to American and German mothers, tend to emphasize responsibility and interrelatedness in their children (Keller et al., 2010; Raghavan et al., 2010). Findings from a comparative study of white, Mexican American, and Mexican parents revealed that white parents reported less authoritarian parenting than Mexican Americans. However, no differences were found in authoritarian parenting style between white and Mexican parents (Varela et al., 2004). Adoptive parents of children with different ethnic backgrounds are likely to use similar strategies of adoption disclosure, caring above all about whether the truth about adoption causes a psychological trauma in the child and whether it is done at the appropriate time and under favorable circumstances (Alexander et al., 2004).

CROSS-CULTURAL SENSITIVITY

Are there any words that a teacher is not supposed to use in a multicultural classroom? Of course, profanities should be out. What about other words? Let us discuss a story in which good intentions are not always supported by the appropriate knowledge.

For example, if you were a teacher in a New York public school and all students in your class are black or Hispanic, would you choose to read them multicultural books? When Ruth Sherman, a 27-year-old teacher, read a story to her class about Brenda, a little black girl from Haiti, the students liked the reading very much. They really enjoyed the teacher's funny voice and good acting. They enjoyed it so much that some students asked Ms. Sherman to make a few copies of the story so that they could read it at home. This is where the controversy begins. No, it is not about the copyright law. The photocopy of the story caught some parents' eye and sparked their angry reactions (Clementson, 1998). The problem was in the title of the story: *Nappy Hair*. *Nappy* is a colloquialism for curly African hair. What is wrong with it?

Unfortunately, this word is sometimes used as a put-down or disrespectful expression. Some parents, therefore, believed that this title should not have been used in class because it ridicules people with a certain type of hair. Others suggested that the words were not the problem. The problem was the teacher—because she was white, she had no business to use such words with black children.

When we asked our colleagues to comment on this story, some of them—and they all were college professors and researchers of different backgrounds—emphasized to us that it always creates an unpleasant feeling when someone mentions anything about your body height, shape of your eyes, size of your nose, skin color, and texture of your hair in connection with your ethnicity or origin. As mentioned earlier, to be sensitive, one should develop empathy—the ability to understand and appreciate other people's feelings. The teacher in this story did nothing illegal. However, as a teacher, she touched a very sensitive string of people's identity and emotions attached to it.

Once a norm is established, it may be passed on from one generation to the next. In most traditional African cultures, obedience is a highly desired pattern of behavior for children, a pattern that is crucial for the child's survival in harsh living conditions (Klingelhofer, 1971). Most Western concepts of childrearing judge obedience critically and condemn most forms of adult–child coercion.

The parents' age must be remembered for both joy and anxiety.

CONFUCIUS (551–479 B.C.E.)—**Chinese Philosopher**

PARENTAL VALUES AND EXPECTATIONS

Before becoming a parent, many individuals have expectations about when and how many children they would love to have. More than 3,300 adolescents from 12 countries (the United States, Russia, Germany, France, China, India, Indonesia, Poland, South Africa, Turkey, Israel, and Japan) responded to the question about how many children they would love to have in the future. With the exception of Israel and China, adolescents preferred to have between two and three children. American and French adolescents reported a higher number of desired children than did adolescents from the other European countries. A noteworthy gender difference was established only in the United States, with female adolescents wanting to have more children than males (Mayer & Trommsdorff, 2010).

Parents typically have their own developmental timetables: They expect their children to acquire particular characteristics (such as walking, talking, or reasoning) at certain ages. Research shows that despite large individual variations, there are some cultural patterns in such expectations (Super & Harkness, 1997). In one study, for example, Israeli mothers of European background expected their children to develop certain cognitive skills earlier than did mothers of non-European origin (Ninio, 1979). U.S. mothers had earlier expectations of their children's assertiveness compared to Japanese mothers, and Japanese mothers had earlier expectations about their children's ability to control their emotions and express courtesy (Hess et al., 1980). According to Levy (1996), in societies that are small, egalitarian, and with little occupational specialization, children are expected to learn "on their own," whereas in industrialized democratic societies there are explicit expectations about what, with whom, when, and how children should learn.

Parents' particular beliefs are translated into behavior that, in reverse, influences other beliefs. Japanese mothers generally view autonomy of the child as her ability to interact with other children. For many Israeli mothers, the child's independence is the ability to perform certain instrumental tasks, such as answering the phone and setting the table (Osterweil & Nagano, 1991).

Parents from different cultural groups may hold different views on the formal education of their children and their role as parents in this process. Chao (1996) asked a sample of 48 immigrants of Chinese origin (Taiwan) and 50 European American mothers of preschool-age children to indicate their views on the role of parenting in the child's school success. The Chinese mothers expressed a greater interest in education and suggested that they were willing to sacrifice for the sake of the children to a greater extent than their U.S. counterparts. On the contrary, European American mothers stressed the importance of building their children's self-esteem and expressed less motivation regarding their children's education. Why did these differences occur? Most of the Taiwanese immigrants to the United States who were studied came from a middle-class stratum, and most of them emigrated from Taiwan for economic reasons. This might suggest a high level of achievement motivation in this group.

Parents who are afraid to put their foot down usually have children who step on their toes.

CHINESE PROVERB

· Two samples of Japanese and American mothers described the behavioral characteristics they found most desirable and undesirable in children and chose one characteristic in each list that they considered most highly positive or negative. In describing desirable characteristics, mothers in both cultures tended to emphasize social cooperativeness and interpersonal sensitivity. Comparisons of negative behaviors revealed cultural contrasts. U.S. mothers were far more likely than Japanese mothers to designate aggressive and disruptive behaviors as negative, whereas Japanese mothers tended to highlight social insensitivity and uncooperativeness (Olson et al., 2001).

In another study, 175 mothers from India, Japan, and England indicated the age at which they expect their child to achieve confidence in 45 different activities, including education, compliance, interaction with other children, emotional control, and environmental awareness (Joshi & MacLean, 1997). It was found that competence was expected at an earlier age in Japan than it was in England. Indian mothers expected competence at a later stage than mothers in both England and Japan. However, the expectations of Indian mothers were considerably different from the expectations of the other two groups on all items except environmental competence, in which they were "later" than Japanese but "earlier" than English mothers. Why did such differences occur? The subjects from Japan and England were taken from urban areas. Children in those regions live primarily in small families and the mother—who is likely to have a job—is expected to encourage her child's independence at an early age. In contrast, the Indian mothers may not be under such pressure to encourage their child's independence early. Indian children from the sample lived mainly in large extended families, with many relatives representing two or three generations in one household. Even though one might expect that Japanese and Indian societies share similar cultural characteristics such as collectivism and the priority of family values, such similarities may be overshadowed by particular socioeconomic factors such as quality of life, availability of diversified information, and access to computers and advanced technologies.

CRITICAL THINKING
Look at the Samples

The authors of the study of mothers conducted in India, Japan, and England mentioned in this chapter suggested that the differences among the samples could not be attributed to socioeconomic factors because all the samples were taken from suburban areas and the income was approximately the same in terms of its purchasing power. However, such direct comparisons can be misleading. Even though a family in country A can purchase the same amount of food as a family in country B, the quality of purchased food could be dramatically different. If two families in two countries have access to medical care, the quality of care in country B could be significantly higher than the quality in country A. In the case studied previously, the scope and depth of the problems that India faces—overpopulation, infectious diseases, corruption, environmental problems, to name a few—can only remotely resemble the daily problems of average U.S. and Japanese citizens.

ERIKSON'S STAGES OF PSYCHOSOCIAL DEVELOPMENT

German-born American psychologist Erik Erikson (1950) is known globally for his developmental and personality theories. Based on his early research of childhood and parenting among the Native American Lakota and the Yurok tribes, rooted in careful observations of hundreds of his patients, Erikson theorized that every person during his or her lifespan passes through eight developmental stages. Each stage is characterized by a developmental conflict, problem, or crisis. If the crisis has a positive resolution, the person's ego is strengthened by gaining a virtue that results in greater adaptation and a healthier personality. But if the crisis has a negative resolution, the ego loses strength, resulting in inhibited adaptation and an unhealthier personality. For instance, if a young girl's conflict between a desire to go and play on the street (an independent decision, initiative) and fear of retribution from parents (guilt) has a positive resolution, she will emerge with the virtue of purpose; a negative outcome, however, would result in a sense of unworthiness (see Table 8.1).

Erikson thus defined the healthy or mature personality as one that possesses the eight virtues (namely, hope, will, purpose, competence, fidelity, love, care, and wisdom) that emerge from a positive resolution at each stage of development. It was Erikson's belief that the outcome of every crisis resolution is reversible. The goal in his approach to psychotherapy, therefore, was to encourage the growth of whatever virtues the person was missing to achieve happiness (Erikson, 1968).

According to a comprehensive analysis (Gardiner et al., 1998), this theory could be applicable in a wide variety of cultural settings. However, as was the case with Maslow's theory (see Chapter 7), Erikson has been criticized by psychologists for mixing objective description with subjective prescription. Specifically, the virtues he uses to define the healthy individual are clearly in accordance with Western, Judeo–Christian ethics, values, and social institutions. In other words, Erikson, like many social theorists, may have been describing what he believes should be, rather than what is. We wish to emphasize that it is not our intention to impugn the value judgments implicit in the theory of Erikson; in fact, we find ourselves closely aligned with many of his beliefs. However, values and veracity are not synonymous. Further, we must remember that our perceptions of the world are inescapably colored by our own personal beliefs and that the distinction between description and prescription frequently is a jumbled one, indeed.

In Erikson's theory, the stages indicate a very general sequence that cannot always be paralleled in other countries. For most adults in economically developed societies, healthy and financially independent retirement is one of the prime areas of concern. Monetary savings

TABLE 8.1 Developmental Stages According to Erikson

Stage	Ego Crisis	Age	Positive Outcome
1	Basic trust versus mistrust	0–1 years	Hope
2	Autonomy versus shame and doubt	2–3 years	Will
3	Initiative versus guilt	3–5 years	Purpose
4	Industry versus inferiority	5–12 years	Competence
5	Ego identity versus role confusion	Adolescence	Fidelity
6	Intimacy versus isolation	Young adult	Love
7	Generativity versus stagnation	Adulthood	Care
8	Ego integrity versus despair	Maturity	Wisdom

Source: Based on Erikson, E. H. (1950). Childhood and society. New York: Norton.

and investments became a source of either elation or frustration for millions of individuals in the United States, Germany, Japan, and other countries. At the same time, billions of human beings have absolutely no money to save in the bank. Hunger, civil and ethnic wars, violence and oppression imposed by authorities, chronic ecological problems, and other cataclysms are the permanent focus of these people's daily concerns. Various unpredictable disturbances present a wide range of unpredictable problems, and the sequence of these problems is not as linear as it appears in Erikson's classification. Therefore, in many cases, more immediate strategies of survival may dominate people's lives. Studies of immigrants to the United States show that identity concerns can occupy people's minds during adulthood, long after the period Erikson had proposed in his classification (Birman & Trickett, 2001).

In industrialized, wealthy democracies, people can exercise a relative freedom of choice. They have available to them the choice of different foods, places to live, schools to attend, job opportunities, ideologies, lifestyles, and even religions. However, and this is a paradox, the process of individual development may be stressful in countries in which people are confronted with a wide variety of choices. Conversely, in many other cultures many people's identities and lifestyles are prescribed at birth. They accept a particular religion, political ideology, occupation, and place to live. People have fewer choices, and therefore their transition from one stage to another may be "smoother" than for people in the Western cultures, which have more choices. In other words, Erikson's theory could be more applicable to societies with so-called *broad socialization* practices that emphasize independence and free self-expression, than in countries with *narrow socialization* that prescribes an ideology that strictly identifies both right and wrong behaviors.

It is important to note that in some cultures, social maturation is not associated with increased independence, as Erikson believed, but rather with increased interdependence. In Buddhism, for example, isolation may be rewarding and should not necessarily be avoided. Intimacy may occur at earlier life stages in some ethnic groups. Moreover, role confusion may not be typical for individuals from traditional cultures but becomes significant for immigrants from these countries. Studies also show that in the West, parents tend to expect an increasing conflict between them and their children when they grow older. They also expect decreasing closeness between family members. This is not the case in other cultures. Among adolescents and parents in countries including India, Brazil, and Indonesia, the measures of conflict and closeness do not change. Adolescents reported they tend to enjoy being with their parents and feel even closer to them than to their friends (Larson et al., 2003). You can also reason, however, that adolescents in these countries might have given the socially "appropriate" answers and didn't reveal the real situation in their families—a tendency of responding somewhat common in collectivist cultures.

In general, when applying Erikson's theory to specific cultural conditions, try to analyze how each culture views each life crisis—assuming, of course, that the crisis takes place—and what is generally expected of an individual to perform, believe in, or reject to solve the crisis.

PIAGET'S STAGES OF COGNITIVE DEVELOPMENT

Swiss psychologist Jean Piaget (1963) was primarily interested in how children develop the process of thinking about themselves and the world around them. According to Piaget, the child's cognitive growth is a stage-by-stage process, consisting of four stages. In the first stage, the *sensorimotor* stage, infants learn about their interaction with their immediate environment. During the second stage, the *preoperational* stage, children develop the foundation for language acquisition. Here, children do not comprehend that other people may see things differently (*egocentrism*). At the third stage of *concrete operations*, children learn logic and realize that volume, amount, and weight may stay the same despite changes in the object's physical appearance (the process is called *conservation*). The final stage, *formal operations*, is when adolescents develop the ability to think abstractly.

Do children from all over the world move through these stages? Summarizing results from a handful of studies, Dasen (1994) suggested that the stage sequence—preoperational–operational–abstract thinking—appears to be universal across cultures. Children move from one stage to another as Piaget has predicted. Nevertheless, other psychologists were more cautious in their cross-cultural assessments of Piaget's findings (Gardiner et al., 1998). Most of the critical comments are related to the methodology and procedures used by Piaget and his colleagues. For instance, researchers who conducted earlier cross-cultural studies of language development using Piaget's theory had only limited knowledge of the language studied. Maybe because of this, researchers often used standardized tests that did not require the child to have language proficiency. Moreover, accurate birth dates of many children were not commonly available so that the actual age of the child studied was not always known.

Piaget's theory does a good job of explaining how children deal with conservation of volume, weight, and amount. Our everyday thinking, however, and ability to make practical decisions in a maze of daily circumstances are not explained well by this theory (Goodnow, 1990). Critics also pointed out that Piaget provoked a temptation to interpret some developmental stages as more "valuable" than others. This, in turn, leads to further categorizations. In reality, though, social success, satisfaction, or adaptation strategies, as well as certain activities and professions, do not require that the individual function on the level of formal operations. It is also questionable whether the formal operational stage is achieved by all adolescents in all societies. In both Western and non-Western settings, there are many healthy, happy, and successful individuals who basically fail on formal operational tasks (Byrnes, 1988).

A man may not transgress the bounds of major morals, but may make errors in minor morals.

Confucius **(551–479 b.c.e.)—Chinese Philosopher**

STAGES OF MORAL DEVELOPMENT ACCORDING TO KOHLBERG

American psychologist Lawrence Kohlberg (1981) described six stages of moral development in which children and adults are able to make several types of moral judgments. In brief, people go from lower stages of reasoning, where they prefer to avoid punishment for wrongdoing, to the higher stages, where they choose social contract and then universal principles to guide moral actions (see Table 8.2).

Snarey (1985) examined 45 empirical studies of moral judgment development conducted in 27 countries and suggested that the first four stages appear to be universal in the subjects of all cultures studied. However, some critics express skepticism about cross-cultural validity of this theory. Why?

The methodology used in cross-cultural studies on moral development was based on hypothetical stories about moral choices that were related well only to U.S. subjects (Shweder et al., 1990). For example, in one such story a woman is suffering from an illness. She is prescribed an expensive drug that may save her life; however, the pharmacist in the story charges an excessive amount of money for the prescription. The woman's husband does not have the money. The moral predicament in this vignette is whether it is moral to steal the drug.

TABLE 8.2 Kohlberg's Stages of Moral Development

Stage 1. Preconventional level: Judgments about what is right and what is wrong are based on fear of punishment.

Stage 2. Preconventional level: Moral conduct produces pleasure, whereas immoral conduct results in unwanted consequences.

Stage 3. Conventional level: Any behavior is good if it is approved by significant others.

Stage 4. Conventional level: The existing laws determine what is moral and immoral.

Stage 5. Postconventional level: Moral behavior is based on individual rights and underlying social circumstances.

Stage 6. Postconventional level: Moral conduct is regulated by universal ethical principles that may rise above government and laws.

It looks like a story that makes sense and the situation described is not unusual. However, in many countries, medicine is under government control, and pharmacists cannot charge patients market prices. Some items are in short supply, and briberies in these cases are common ways to get the prescription. Moreover, in some countries, physicians themselves—and not pharmacists—have access to medication and distribute it to their patients.

Another point of criticism is that the developmental stages are closely linked to values of Western liberalism and individualism based on moral choice. Liberal individualism, however, cannot always represent moral principles that are applicable to all cultures and peoples. In many cultures, moral judgment is based mostly on existing traditions, and not necessarily on free will and choice. For certain religious groups, certain types of moral behavior are strictly prescribed in the Bible, Torah, or other religious scriptures. Other studies point out that the individual's moral judgments are caused by circumstance and not necessarily based on a certain level of the person's moral development (Matsumoto, 1994; Vassiliou & Vassiliou, 1973).

An interesting cross-cultural examination of Kohlberg's theory was conducted by Ma and Cheung (1996), who compared moral judgments of more than 1,000 Hong Kong Chinese, English, and U.S. college and high school students. The test consisted of four stories, and each story contained a description of a moral problem. The subjects were asked to make judgments about the possible solutions to the problem. It was found that Chinese tended to emphasize the importance of the stage 3 judgments and considered stage 4 judgments as more similar to stage 5 and 6 judgments. The English and U.S. subjects tended to regard stage 4 judgments as more similar to stage 2 or 3 judgments.

The authors argue that moral judgments of the Chinese are reinforced by traditional norms and regulated by conformity to primary groups. Chinese see issues, such as concerns for social order, consensus, and abiding by the law, from a collectivist perspective. A strong orientation to perform altruistic acts for the sake of close relatives and friends is part of Chinese culture. According to the authors, Chinese are also influenced by the Confucian concept of the five cardinal relationships, which emphasizes the harmonious connection between sovereign and subject, father and son, husband and wife, sibling and sibling, and friend and friend. Social order, consensus, and law-abiding behavior are attached to the Chinese collective mentality. On the contrary, Western people are concerned primarily with individual rights and their interests being protected by the law. In the West, as the authors claim, people easily sue each other because the law mediates interpersonal relationship. Chinese tend not to resolve their conflicts in legal institutions. They prefer instead to resolve their conflicts by using interpersonal contacts.

This practice, however, can become a double-edged sword. On one hand, it may appear that interpersonal orientation is more humane and appealing than the law-based system. (Indeed, it seems healthier to settle a conflict than seek legal help.) On the other hand, an emphasis on an interpersonal system of communications may stimulate nepotism and corruption—two serious problems that Hong Kong officials themselves recognize very well.

DEVELOPMENTAL STAGES

According to most scientific and folk theories, human development takes place in stages. Typically, birth and physical death—as the initial and final points of physical existence—are present in developmental classifications. Beliefs in reincarnation and immortality promote the understanding of the life span as a cycle. Views on the beginning of a child's life (i.e., when does it start, at conception or at a certain later stage?) vary cross-culturally and are based on people's educational background, religion, and other ideological values.

Birthdays, initiation rituals, weddings, graduations, job promotions, the birth of children and grandchildren, retirement, and other significant life events mark the most important points of human transition. Several biological, behavioral, and physiological changes are also recognized cross-culturally as indicators of particular life stages. Among these natural events are emergence of permanent teeth, first words, first menstruation and menopause in women, and intensive growth of facial hair in young men. Gray hair is commonly viewed as a sign of maturity despite tremendous individual variations of hair pigmentation. There are also age categorizations based on folk beliefs or particular life events. Such events may symbolically identify either the beginning or ending of a life stage. One's first sexual intercourse could be seen as a confirmation of one's "manhood" or "womanhood." Reaching the drinking age—which is 21 in the United States and 18 in the Ukraine, for example—could also be interpreted as a sign of legal maturity.

Books on human development distinguish several common stages within the life span: prenatal period, infancy, childhood (divided into early and middle childhood), adolescence, and adulthood, which is, in turn, subdivided into three stages: early adulthood, middle adulthood, and late adulthood (see Table 8.3).

There can be slightly different categorizations of the life span, however. For example, according to Hindu tradition, infancy, early childhood, and middle childhood are not separate stages (Valsiner & Lawrence, 1997). In the Judeo-Christian tradition, life is represented linearly and its end is death. In Hinduism, life is represented circularly: People live and die many times (Fernandez et al., 2010). In more than half of the societies studied by Schlegel and Barry (1991), there was no special term for adolescence.

TABLE 8.3 The Periods of Human Development

Prenatal period	Infancy	Childhood	Adolescence	Adulthood
From conception to birth: It takes approximately 266 days in every ethnic, racial, or social group.	From birth to 2 years: The child acquires initial motor, cognitive, and social skills.	From 2 to 11–12 years: The child acquires language and learns about the most important social skills.	From 11–12 to 19–20 years: The child has reached sexual maturity but has not yet taken on rights and responsibilities of the adult status.	From 20 years onward: The individual has achieved adult status as prescribed by the norms and laws of a particular society.

LIFE BEFORE BIRTH: PRENATAL PERIOD

In London and Beijing, as well as in any other part of the planet, the **prenatal period**—typical time between conception and birth—is 38 weeks. From the beginning, the developing embryo in a mother's womb can be exposed to either favorable or unfavorable conditions. For instance, the natural environment around the mother could be stable or unstable, safe or dangerous. Across the world, environmental problems and perilous conditions, such as hunger, violence, excessive radiation, exposure to chemicals, and air and water pollution, to name a few, can cause various complications in pregnancy and serious birth defects. The availability or lack of professional prenatal care is also a crucial factor affecting the unborn child's development. There are many common cognitive and behavioral trends related to pregnancy. Studies show, for instance, that in most countries, when a family expects a child, boys are desired more than girls (Hortacsu et al., 2001), and, cross-nationally, teen pregnancies are more common in rural than in urban populations (Barber, 2001).

The fetus's life can be interrupted by a mother's decision to terminate her pregnancy. Nearly 50 million abortions are performed in the world each year. Almost 60 percent of them take place in developing countries, where close to 90 percent of the over 20 million illegal and unsafe abortions are performed each year. This is despite the fact that in many cases abortion in developing countries is restricted by law and condemned by religion. The risk of death from an unsafe, or illegal, abortion in a developing country is many times higher than the risk in developed countries. An estimated 21.6 million unsafe abortions took place worldwide in 2008, almost all in developing countries. Numbers of unsafe abortions remain relatively stable in the past decade: there are about 14 unsafe abortions per 1,000 women aged 15–44 years (WHO, 2011). Countries vary in terms of frequency of abortions performed.

Attitudes toward pregnancy also differ. In traditional collectivist countries, such as Malaysia, Singapore, Indonesia, Philippines, and Thailand, pregnancy is more family centered with active participation and guidance from family (Gardiner et al., 1998). In individualist societies, childbirth tends to be a rather private affair. However, one should be careful and try not to make stereotypical judgments. Many foreign exchange students, for example, mentioned to us how open many Americans are about their pregnancies: People make official statements, inform relatives and friends, and throw parties to spread the word about their condition. However, in many countries, such as Russia, pregnancy is commonly kept secret until the changes in the woman's body become obvious. Husbands are not only absent when their wives give birth but are also prohibited from entering birth clinics and may be escorted out by the police if they dare to enter the facility. Tradition and law often go hand in hand (see Table 8.4).

TABLE 8.4 A List of Selected Customs Followed by Some Immigrant Women in Families in the Maternity Ward in the United States

Region of the World	Custom Followed by Some Immigrants from that Region
Russia	A child is not supposed to be seen by strangers for at least one month so that he or she is protected from the "evil eye."
Vietnam	A new mother should not be exposed to cold because it disrupts the equilibrium that is believed crucial to good health.
Muslim countries	Examination or delivery must be done by female health workers only.
Some African countries	The tradition is to take the placenta home and bury it.
Latin American countries	Women do not breast-feed the child in the first couple of days after delivery.

Source: Based on Aizenman, N. (2002, May 12). A rebirth of traditions: Maternity wards adapt to immigrants' needs. Washington Post, p. A01.

Infancy conforms to nobody; all conform to it.

RALPH WALDO EMERSON (1803–1882)—U.S. Poet and Philosopher

FIRST STEPS: INFANCY

Infancy is period from birth to two years when the child acquires initial motor, cognitive, and social skills. A newborn child needs total care. It is obvious that environmental and social conditions in which the new life begins have a crucial impact on the child's life, health, and perhaps his or her personality traits. Infant mortality, for example, varies greatly from country to country and depends on the socioeconomic and political conditions of each particular nation. For example, infant mortality in Sierra Leone was 160 in 2001 (this many deaths per 1,000 live births) and it was the highest in the world. The lowest rate was 2.9 in Iceland. In the United States, the rate was 6.3, and in China it was 23.0 (United Nations Population Division, 2011).

The child's **temperament**, or personality traits present in infancy, presumably has a genetic basis (Buss & Plomin, 1985). Temperament may also be influenced by environmental factors. Parents respond differently when their child is crying. There are adults who easily neglect their children when they cry, and there are those who respond immediately. An immediate or delayed response to the child's crying may stimulate or inhibit certain emotions and other behavioral reactions in the infant. There are individual and cultural variations in such responses. For example, in one of the projects on cross-cultural similarities and differences in mother–infant communications, rural Kenyan and middle-class Bostonian mothers were compared. There were many similarities between the samples studied. Mothers in both locations would eagerly touch, hold, or talk to a child if he or she was crying. However, the U.S. mothers communicated more with words and less with physical contact than did Kenyan mothers (Berger, 1995).

Ask a mother who has raised a healthy infant, and she will probably tell you that her son or daughter was able to recognize human faces very early. Indeed, most infants feel calm when they see familiar faces and show signs of worry when they see a stranger's face near them. A study conducted in several countries showed that most infants develop a form of attachment around their seventh month of life (Kagan et al., 1978). Such attachment patterns in a strange situation are universal and can be divided into three categories (Gardiner et al., 1998):

- anxious and avoidant [children do not pay much attention to their parent(s)];
- anxious and resistant [children tend to stay very close to their parent(s) and worry about his/her/their whereabouts];
- securely attached [children are not threatened by a stranger in the presence of the parent(s)].

Some researchers found that the prevalence of the anxious-and-avoidant type is relatively higher in West European countries, whereas the anxious-and-resistant type is more prevalent in non-Western countries, such as Israel and Japan (Van Ijzendoorn & Kroonenberg, 1988). Consistent with attachment theories, findings of a comparative U.S.–Japanese study indicated that a clear majority of mothers in both countries perceive children with desirable characteristics as secure and children with undesirable characteristics as insecure (Rothbaum et al., 2007).

Right-handedness appears prevalent in all cultures, and, as studies show, this function is most likely genetic (Coren, 1992). However, different cultural practices and beliefs were found

A CASE IN POINT
Customs in Parental Behavior

It is an East European custom—well maintained in the twenty-first century—not to show a newborn child to anyone except close relatives during the first month of the baby's life. Reasons? This isolation is considered by some Russians a necessary precaution against an "evil eye." In other words, the child remains relatively deprived of other people and new experiences for some 30 days of his life.

Question:

Do you think that this practice—which is exercised, perhaps, by millions of parents and leads to a relative isolation of the child during the first 30 days of her life—may somehow affect the child's psychological development?

to affect the behavior of millions of children around the world. In many countries, for example, left-handedness was resisted, and both teachers and parents attempted to change this "anomaly," as they would call it, by forcing children to unlearn many of their skills that required the use of the left hand. Environmental factors also influence the ways children develop their motor activities. As an example, motor skills of African infants develop several months before they develop in white children: Parents use different training strategies when they teach their children to walk (Gardiner et al., 1998).

Societal changes shape patterns of parental behavior. For example, frequency of breast-feeding and the level of a nation's industrial development are negatively correlated. In other words, the more the nation becomes industrialized, the more breast-feeding declines, and that causes further societal changes. The availability of baby formula and other foods, changes in women's occupation and social status, a general change in public attitudes, and other factors all promote freedom of choice for women to decide whether to breast-feed.

Infants are constantly surrounded by a complex system of sounds that represents a particular language. Children make important sound distinctions at a very early age, and this may explain some linguistic differences that people experience when they learn a foreign language. For example, our mutual colleague from Japan has difficulties pronouncing the *L* when he speaks English (likewise, many Americans cannot pronounce the typically hard German *R*, the *KH* in Hebrew, or *GH* in the Ukrainian language). Japanese infants typically do not notice the difference between *L* and *R* because there is no *L* sound in the Japanese language and their parents do not use such sounds in their conversations. English-speaking infants are able to detect this difference, even if they cannot talk themselves. Perhaps our pronunciation difficulties have deep roots in our infancy, when we began to recognize and memorize sounds. For example, many Russians cannot distinguish the difference between sounds *i* (in *bit*) and *ee* (in *beat*). In the Russian language, there is no distinction between these two sounds. Some linguists suggest that the Danish language is especially difficult to speak because it contains so many unfamiliar sounds that non-Danish people were not exposed to as infants.

Life's aspirations come in the guise of children.

RABINDRANATH TAGORE (1861–1941)—**Bengali Poet and Novelist**

CRITICAL THINKING
On Labeling of Dependency

It is frequently emphasized that people in Japan are more interdependent and emotionally attached to each other than people in Western societies. There are many explanations and interpretations of this assumption. Some of them refer to early socialization experiences. According to one view, people in Japan develop a pattern called *amae* that makes them interdependent (Doi, 1989). *Amae* is described as the tendency of the self to merge with the self of another person. This tendency becomes part of everyday life in Japan and is especially encouraged in the early mother–child relationship (Lewis & Ozaki, 2009; Yamaguchi, 2004). In the United States, security is seen as leading primarily to autonomy, self-esteem, and self-expression. In Puerto Rico, security is seen as leading primarily to respect, obedience, and calmness. Finally, there are differences in perceived antecedents of attachment, with white American mothers placing greater emphasis on autonomy fostering and Puerto Rican mothers placing greater emphasis on controlling behavior (Carlson & Harwood, 2003). How different is the Japanese *amae* from dependency, a concept known in Western psychological schools? (Dependency is a need for comfort, approval, or attention and may be described at the behavioral level as a child crying, clinging, following the mother, and other behaviors that encourage attention from caregivers.) To compare the meanings of both concepts, Vereijken and colleagues (1997) evaluated descriptions given by Japanese experts to *amae* and by Western experts to dependency. The experts used a Q-sort method for the evaluation. First, they were given 90 cards that each contained a written description of a particular behavior that characterizes the mother-and-child relationship. Then, the experts were asked to arrange the cards in a certain order so that those chosen at the beginning would present the most salient behaviors, typical for *amae* (Japanese experts) and dependency (Western experts). The researchers found, despite predictions, a striking similarity between the behavioral definition of *amae*, given by Japanese experts, and the behavioral definition of dependency as provided by experts in the United States ($r = 0.77$). It is quite possible that in different cultures, certain universal behavioral patterns are labeled differently. In reality, different labels may describe similar behaviors.

DISCOVERING THE WORLD: CHILDHOOD

Mencius, an ancient Chinese philosopher, wrote that a great person is one who does not lose his childhood heart. Children are great because they are sincere and emotional. **Childhood** is a period of continuous growth, learning, and development. During early childhood, children's thinking is wishful and fantastic. Young children are often uncertain about the difference between reality and fantasy, and they often mix them together. They constantly check their thinking against the reality but still believe in the magical power of their ideas. During middle childhood, which lasts from approximately age 6–12 years, children continue to develop thinking and social skills. Abstract thinking begins to play a greater role in their daily events. Still, the child's thinking is primarily based on observations and direct experiences. If something is tangible or observable, it is easily comprehended and interpreted. As an example, several studies involving English, Japanese, and Norwegian children suggest that they develop elaborate conceptions of war earlier than they do of peace. The conceptions of war focus primarily on aspects such as killing, fighting, and the use of weapons. Conflicts are pervasive and have concrete aspects that can be observed. Peace, however, is a less tangible and notable phenomenon. It may not register in interpersonal experience early in life to the extent that violence and aggression do (Rosenau, 1975).

Childhood as a developmental stage is mediated by an array of practices that could be similar in different across cultures. It is a custom in many families the United States to praise their children and show positive emotions toward them for their accomplishments. Qualitative research in New Zealand with Samoan men shows that the overt expression of emotion or feelings toward children was generally regarded as improper because, as fathers tend to believe, their children have to learn the value of humility first (Anae et al., 2000).

Look at pictures that children draw. Some complex and colorful, some schematic and simple, they reflect what children see or wish for. Children see the reality around them and reflect it in their thoughts and fantasies. For example, Domino and Hannah analyzed 700 stories generated by 160 Chinese and U.S. elementary school students. Chinese stories showed greater concern with authority, greater concern with moral rectitude, fewer instances of physical aggression, and greater salience of the role of natural forces and chance than the U.S. sample did (Domino & Hannah, 1987). If children's drawings reflect reality, could adults make any suggestions about a child's life by discovering that themes of victimization constantly appear in drawings of Palestinian children living in Israel (Kostelny & Garbarino, 1994)? Could we explain why in U.S. children's drawings, boys were pictured as more powerful than girls (Rubenstein, 1987)?

In practically all cultures—with the exception of regions that suffer severe food shortages—mothers try to coax their children into eating. They use various methods for good eating: from punishment to reward and from persuasion to feeding games (Dettwyler, 1989). Eating habits and food preferences of an adult person are generally linked to early-age feeding practices (Schulze et al., 2001). Eating preferences show great variability among countries and families. Bread and many types of fruit and vegetables are common in most cultures; however, there are products that children begin to eat during childhood and that are considered inappropriate for other children living in other cultures. Muslim children do not eat pork, Hindu boys and girls may never try beef, and Europeans stay away from dog's meat (see Chapter 7).

If attempts to feed children appear to be similar across different countries, cosleeping, or the practice of allowing the child to sleep in one bed with the parents, usually varies from country to country. Typically, cosleeping is resisted by U.S. parents or at times allowed in some limited way. U.S. and Western mothers commonly put their children in separate bedrooms. This practice is largely uncommon among Indian Mexicans (Morelli et al., 1992). One should note, however, that cosleeping is practiced in some countries, in part, because of living conditions: Parents simply cannot afford a separate bedroom for each child in the family.

Many elements of social identity are formed during childhood. Children between the second and fourth grade are able to clearly identify themselves with their ethnic group, nationality, and social class (Dawson et al., 1977). At this stage, both Arab and Jewish schoolchildren in Israel were significantly different in their flag preference, clearly divided along the Arab–Jewish origins (Lawson, 1975).

Anyone can say without conducting research that children around the world love to play. There are some functions of play that are universal across cultures, such as teaching children about interaction patterns, cooperation, sharing, and competition (Farver et al., 2000). Despite these similarities, different cultural practices may develop different behavioral traits. In a study conducted in the early 1970s, playing children in North America appeared to be more competitive than children in many other societies studied (Madsen, 1971). These results, however, should be verified in contemporary conditions. Why? In the United States today, for example, a mother who signs her son or daughter up for a little league soccer team will perhaps get a note from the league explaining, very politely and cautiously, that the main purpose of the game is participation, not necessarily winning. In many contemporary children's sports leagues in the United States (i.e., baseball, football, basketball, soccer, ice hockey, and others), there are serious attempts made to emphasize a more nonachievement focus.

Is there evidence that societal norms restricting children's behavior in many ways may cause children to become aggressive and rebel? According to the suppression–facilitation hypothesis, behaviors that are discouraged in a culture will be seen infrequently in mental health facilities. For example, if parents punish children for being violent, there should not be many violent mental patients in this country's mental facilities. The suppression–facilitation model also assumes that behaviors that are rewarded will be seen excessively. From the standpoint of another hypothesis, the adult distress threshold hypothesis, the behaviors that were discouraged in childhood will be seen in clinics more often than "acceptable" behaviors. Weisz and his colleagues (1987) tested this model in a cross-cultural study that involved Thai and U.S. children. Buddhist traditions of Thailand are different from the U.S. cultural norms. The former emphasizes nonaggression, politeness, modesty, and respect for others. Parents are very intolerant toward impulsive, aggressive, and "undercontrolled" behavior in their children. As the first hypothesis predicted, "overcontrolled" problems (aloofness, withdrawal) were reported more frequently for Thai children than they were for U.S. children. Problems such as violence and disorderly behavior were reported more frequently for U.S. children. Thus, the suppression–facilitation hypothesis received some empirical support.

A boy becomes an adult three years earlier than his parents think he does, and about two years after he thinks he does.

Lewis Hershey (1893–1977)—U.S. General

MAJOR REHEARSAL: ADOLESCENCE

John and Jorge are two 16-year-old neighbors and friends of different ethnic backgrounds. At the same time, they are so much alike. They both wear adult-size clothes, both have a shadow of a mustache on their upper lip, both play computer games for many hours a day, both contemplate getting a summer job, and both think of attending a local college in two years. As adolescents, they both have reached sexual maturity but have not yet taken on the rights and responsibilities of the adult status.

Adolescence is viewed not only as a developmental stage but also as a cultural phenomenon. For instance, extended schooling in many developed countries stretches the period from childhood to adulthood. On the contrary, many nonindustrialized cultures encourage their members to take on adult roles as early as possible. Thus, the adolescent stage becomes almost indistinguishable. In some countries, such as Sudan and Brazil, many children begin to work full time and take care of other family members as early as age 12 and sometimes even earlier. In other societies, such as India, a girl can marry in her early teens and move to her husband's home to accept the roles of wife and mother. Cultural conditions can determine the recognition of an entire developmental stage.

The rapid changes in weight and height are important characteristics of adolescence. Cross-culturally, girls mature as much as two years earlier than boys. Since the beginning of observations in the 1800s in Europe and North America, girls have been maturing earlier than previously studied age groups of girls, approximately several months per every 10 years. For example, from 1850 to the 1950s, the average age of first menstruation in girls has decreased five years and became close to 12 years. This trend significantly slowed in the second half of the twentieth century and was apparently not observed in less-developed non-Western countries (Frisch & Revelle, 1970). One possible explanation for this earlier maturation is the improved health care, nutrition, and living conditions of most citizens of the developed regions of the world.

Formal thinking at this developmental stage replaces concrete thinking, and moral judgments are often made on the basis of the individual's values (Piaget, 1963). At the same time, adolescent thinking could be full of contradictions, unpredictable assumptions, and sudden turns. Despite their ability to make ethical judgments and tremendous cognitive reserves, adolescents do not have the vision or wisdom often found at a more mature age. Altruism and selfishness, enthusiasm and withdrawal, tolerance and impatience may easily exist together in the same individual at the same time. If the child's perception of the world is generally naive and trustful, adolescence is often associated with the development of cynicism (Sigel, 1989). Cynicism—which is the belief that people generally and repeatedly violate prescriptive moral standards for their behavior—can become salient in adolescence because of the young person's tendencies to grow increasingly independent and critical, or because of an increasing amount of discouraging information about society that one receives in late adolescence, especially in the countries where political scandals became a common practice (Schwartz, 1975). However, we should anticipate a lack of publicly expressed cynicism in countries in which the government strictly reinforces ideological and political homogeneity. In such cases, an adolescent may develop cynical views without exposing them to pollsters or social scientists (Gozman & Edkind, 1992). For more than a century, many Western psychological sources have been discussing the issue of teenage rebelliousness and defiance as an anticipated period of every young person's life (Glad & Shiraev, 1999; Hall, 1916; Kon, 1979). Psychologists and sociologists try to understand whether or not various antisocial fads associated with "youth culture" have deep psychological roots in the young person's desire for independence (Petersen, 1988). "Gangs" in North and Central America, "hooliganism" in Russia, or "ladette culture" of British girls (a behavioral pattern of "acting like boys"; involving in smoking, swearing, fighting, and drinking; and being disruptive in school) are just a few examples of such antisocial trends among the adolescents. Prevalence of young people among violent groups in non-Western cultures has been documented as well. Yet, it is quite doubtful that psychological reasons alone could explain why the young join various rebellious groups. Obviously, there are specific socioeconomic and political factors that must be taken into consideration. For example, there are scores of documented cases in Africa involving young adolescents and children being forced to join rebellious militant groups against their will (Beah, 2008).

Social and political conditions play a significant role in individual socialization. In a study conducted in Israel, children of North American and Soviet immigrants showed significantly different patterns of behavior in the classroom. Students from North America were peer-group oriented. Students from the Soviet Union were teacher oriented (Horowits & Kraus, 1984). The Soviet system of education, compared with the U.S. system, had a very strong emphasis on student discipline and obedience. Moving into a new cultural environment, Soviet adolescent immigrants did not change their obedience-oriented behavioral pattern. In another study conducted in Israel, Soviet-educated adolescents were significantly more realistically oriented in their moral judgments than the Israelis who grew up in Israel (Ziv et al., 1975). Perhaps, many years of personal humiliation and the struggle against the communist government for an opportunity to emigrate from the Soviet Union have contributed to the development of realistic and pragmatic attitudes (Kliger, 2002). Social and political factors affect adolescent's cultural identity. A study of Palestinian Arab Christian adolescents in Israel showed that most of them tend to maintain their ethnic and religious distinct identity. However, when compared to Muslim Arabs, they expressed more willingness to adopt elements of the Jewish society. They also feel stronger assimilation pressures coming from Israeli Jews. Christian Arabs are commonly viewed as a "double minority" because they are Arabs, and the majority of Arabs are Muslims and, in addition, they live in a predominantly Jewish country. The stronger willingness of Palestinian Christian Arabs to engage in social and cultural contact with Israeli Jews may reflect a desire to gain more access to important resources such as education and work. In addition, Palestinian Christian Arabs tend to distinguish themselves historically as a more Westernized cultural group (Horenczyk & Munayer, 2007).

Overall, social and political conditions in a particular country may affect attitudes and motivation of the young (Bronfenbrenner, 1970). For example, in the 1980s, young people in Poland—a socialist country at that time—reported more aggression in their attitudes than those in Finland (Fraczek, 1985). For several years, Poles lived under a state of emergency and violence initiated by the government, and this could have triggered more violence on an interpersonal level.

In another study, 1,500 high school students from Finland and Estonia were asked to imagine themselves in three hypothetical situations (Keltikangas-Jaervinen & Terav, 1996). For example, if one of your classmates is repeatedly teased by some of your other classmates, what would you do? If one of your classmates continues to be the target of a blackmailing, what would you do? If you see someone stealing money from one of your classmates, what would you do? The students then were offered several alternative solutions to these situations: aggressive, prosocial, social responsible, and avoiding. As a result, several tendencies were revealed. Estonian adolescents were more aggressive and less socially responsible in their answers than their Finnish counterparts. Moreover, avoidance was shown to be the most typical way of solving problems for Estonian students. How can one interpret the differences? The countries studied are very close geographically and share many elements of culture and history. The authors explain the results by referring to social and political factors. For more than 40 years, Estonia was a part of the Soviet Union, whereas Finland remained an independent country. Western values of individualism were persistently emphasized in child socialization in Finland. On the contrary, in Soviet Estonia, public education and socialization promoted the mantra of collectivism, obedience to authority, loyalty to the homeland, and a sense of social responsibility. Here comes some confusion in the interpretation: As far as we know, the system promotes loyalty, responsibility, and collectivism in socialist countries. Why did the actual attitudes of the young people in this study reveal the presence of aggression, avoidance, and lack of responsibility? The authors of the study suggest that despite the communist government's efforts, most young people in Estonia simply rejected the main values promoted by the authorities. However, other factors could also have contributed to the socialization of Estonian youth of the 1990s. The unprecedented political and ideological struggle in the country after it gained independence, rapid growth of crime and corruption, increasing social inequality, a virtual loss of guaranteed social security—these factors could have triggered a sense of disappointment and frustration in the population. Perhaps these negative developments of the most recent times, and not only the experiences of the early 1980s, affected the attitudes of Estonian youth revealed in this study.

Collectivist and individualist norms influence individual behavior and perceptions. Elbedour and colleagues (1997) compared perceptions of intimacy in the relationships among Israeli Jewish and Israeli Bedouin adolescents. More than 600 students, from grades 7 to 11, completed questionnaires in which students were asked to rate statements describing same-sex adolescent friendship on a four-point scale ranging from low (1) to high (4). Statements such as, "To what extent does the following statement characterize the relationship with a close friend?" were asked. Characteristics such as emotional closeness, control, conformity, and respect for the friend were studied. Each of these characteristics was measured with the help of eight questions. The results showed that Jewish adolescents (more individualist than collectivist), as opposed to

Bedouin adolescents (more collectivist than individualist), expressed less of a need to control or to conform to their friends. The Bedouin adolescents tended to emphasize both control of and conformity to friends.

Men are more like the time they live in than they are like their fathers.

ALI IBN-ABI-TALIB (600–661)—**Fourth Caliph of Muslims**

ADULTHOOD

In all cultures, **adulthood** represents maturity, responsibility, and accountability. This period is typically divided into three stages: early adulthood, middle adulthood, and late adulthood (Levinson, 1978). The early adulthood stage is usually linked to formative processes, whereas the middle and late adulthood stages are associated with accomplishments of various kinds. However, the line separating these periods is unclear. Many adults have been and are able to accomplish great things at a very young age. For example, George Washington became an ambassador to France at 21. He won his first battle as a colonel at 22. Luther was 29 when he started his religious reformation of Christianity. Newton was 24 when he began his work on universal gravitation, calculus, and the theory of colors. Einstein published his famous theory of relativity at 26. Overall, younger scientists primarily made the great scientific discoveries. Studies show, for example, that the average age for conducting the prize-winning research for all disciplines was around 38 years, with physicists doing their research the earliest, at 35 years (Stroebe, 2010).

Although some psychological functions decline with age, the individual's socialization during adulthood continues. Two models—the **persistence** and the **openness**—attempt to explain this process (Renshon, 1989). According to the first model, persistence, adults acquire attitudes and learn behaviors early in life and tend not to change them later. For example, if a child grows up in a religious family in Morocco, he or she will likely be religious no matter where he or she lives as an adult. The other model, openness, states the opposite: People do change their attitudes and behavior because they have to adjust to changing situations and the transformations can be substantial. In other words, early childhood and adolescent experiences do not necessarily determine who the person is today. Despite the fact that some students of socialization are intrigued by the persistence approach, most analysts agree that socialization does not stop at the age of 18 or 20. It was confirmed that socialization continues in the adulthood stage and many transitions in the individual's opinions and behavior take place during this developmental stage (Sigel, 1989).

Adulthood experiences vary across cultures and depend on age, gender, socioeconomic status, occupation, family structure, and a variety of life events. Violence, economic hardship, and hunger may affect the lives of an entire generation. As an example, social and political developments in Afghanistan during the last 25 years of the twentieth century were marked by a series of devastating developments. Among them were the revolution and dismissal of the king, the Soviet invasion in 1979, the war against the occupation, and the seemingly endless civil war that took tens of thousands of lives. An adult who was born in 1950, for example, during practically all stages of his adult life, was exposed to continuous stress, poverty, traumatic events, and fear for his life. At the same time, a person born in 1950 in a small Norwegian town could have lived a life absolutely free of cataclysms, significant events, and unexpected turns.

In adulthood, most people develop their sense of **identity**, the view about themselves as individuals and members of society. Identity formation cannot be understood outside of its cultural context. In traditional societies, for example, people accept their identity in the systematic and coherent environment. The society is supposed to provide a sense of certainty for its individuals. The individual constantly refers to others for evaluation (Kagitcibasi, 1985). Individuality is especially restricted on the level of ideology or religion. People learn about their roles and acquire them while gradually moving from one life period to another. In Western industrialized societies, the performance of social roles is more open to individuals because the roles are often not strongly formalized. Individuals take membership in a wide variety of diverse subgroups (Camilleri & Malewska-Peyre, 1997). Western societies, compared with non-Western ones, offer individuals a wide range of options. Individuals are not only given options but also encouraged to choose.

In the contemporary world, the amount of education required for young people to prepare for many jobs is expanding. As these people pursue education for longer periods, they also postpone transitions into adult roles. Moreover, when the power of traditional authority weakens and young people increasingly gain control over their own lives, they generally choose to wait longer to start families. The median ages for these adult transitions are in the late 20s in every industrialized society and rising rapidly in developing countries (Arnett, 2002). The fact that transitions into adult roles have become somewhat delayed in many societies has led to the spread of a new period of life, called *emerging adulthood*, that extends from the late teens to the mid-twenties and is characterized by self-focused exploration of possibilities in love, work, and worldviews. Young people in industrialized societies now go through this period, and it is growing in prevalence among young people in developing countries as well (Arnett, 2000).

I not only use all the brains I have but all I can borrow.

Woodrow Wilson (1856–1924)—Twenty-Eighth U.S. President

In people's minds, adulthood is linked to wisdom. The more mature a person is, the wiser he or she is expected to be. Societal expectations affect our perception of adult intelligence. For instance, quickness of thinking is linked to *fluid intelligence*, the ability to form concepts, think abstractly, and apply knowledge to new situations (see Chapter 5). *Crystallized intelligence* is the individual's accumulated knowledge and experience. In Western societies, speed of thinking is highly valued and fluid intelligence is interpreted as an indicator of success.

A CASE IN POINT

American Counselor Yola Ghammashi (personal interview, October, 2011) is developing a concept of a *frozen culture* to describe the lives and experiences of many adult immigrants within their new homelands. Some immigrant adults after they settle in a new country continue to maintain most of the customs, speech patterns, beliefs, and emotional attachments similar to what they had before immigration. They deliberately speak their old language, maintain most cultural habits, and resist learning or adapting to different cultural norms. Their home country, meanwhile, transforms over time. Customs, fashion, and speech patterns might change. Yet these immigrants continue to live in a self-created culture of the past. They think they do not belong to their new culture. Yet their "old" culture no longer exists in the form they remember. Do you know of such individuals? What can you tell about the elements of their "frozen cultures"? Is it necessary to particular individuals to maintain some elements of "frozen culture"?

In many non-Western societies, speed of operations is valued less, because experience, or crystallized intelligence, is perceived as more important than quickness (Gardiner et al., 1998). Many mediating individual circumstances and social factors affect crystallized intelligence. For example, a 60-year-old Iranian father can be a perfect mentor for his son who starts a business in a small town near the Caspian Sea. The same father could be less efficient and knowledgeable after his family immigrates to another country.

In some cultures of the nonindustrialized world, the concept of middle age is indistinct. For instance, a person may be described as "young woman" or "old man," but not "a middle-aged person." Similarly, some view midlife crisis as a stage for those who have the time and money to afford it.

The wine of life keeps oozing drop by drop, the leaves of life keep falling one by one.

OMAR KHAYYAM (TWELFTH CENTURY)—**Persian Poet and Astronomer**

LATE ADULTHOOD

When do people get old? Is aging a physical wearing and decline that takes place without a substantial change of attitudes? When do people slow down? Aging is a biological process. Although biologists haven't found conclusive explanations about universal characteristics of aging (Cox, 1988), most people of old age suffer from similar diseases (such as cancer, dementia, and arthritis), their skin becomes less elastic, and their hair loses its pigmentation. The muscles begin to atrophy, the bones become more brittle, and the cardiovascular system becomes less efficient. Most psychological functions decline too. Hearing and visual impairments are common. However, human beings defy the "rules" of nature. Since the classic work of the nineteenth century, the predominant view in scientific psychology was that memory declines over time. However, clinical and laboratory studies suggest that memory can also increase. Actually, memory simultaneously increases and decreases over time (Erdelyi, 2010). Goethe, a great German poet, completed his *Faust* when he was 80. Lamark completed his great zoological book, *The Natural History of Invertebrates*, when he was 78. Ronald Reagan became president when he was 70. Mahatma Gandhi reached the peak of his popularity when he was 75. Mother Teresa did not slow down her charitable work before she died at 87.

In many countries, the **late adulthood** period begins with retirement, when a person formally quits her job. If a person does not work outside the home, this period begins perhaps when the individual gives up his major family responsibilities. There are common national "deadlines" for formal retirement, which vary greatly. In Russia, a woman can retire at age 55 and men can do so five years later. In the United States, the common retirement age is 65. Norwegians push their retirement age up to 70. It is expected that so long as life expectancy goes up, the retirement age will go higher.

Countries vary greatly regarding their population's life expectancy. Japan and Switzerland have a life expectancy close to 80. Poverty, natural disasters, and chronic political and economic problems keep the life expectancy of some countries (Nigeria, Bangladesh, and Chad, for example) at the age of 60, 50, and even lower. This is at least 10 years or more below the average life expectancy in the developed countries (*The World Factbook*, 2011).

In collectivist cultures, the elderly usually occupy a high social status. In individualist societies, young people enjoy the greatest status, whereas the elderly can often be isolated and even rejected. Indeed, studies show that respect for the elderly is higher in Japan and China than it is in the United States (Yu, 1993). As in other Western countries, the parent–child relationship in the United States is more voluntary than it is, for example, in Asian countries, especially when the child reaches adulthood (Hsu, 1985; Tolbert, 2000). In most African and Asian societies, intergenerational families are the norm, and the younger family members customarily take care of older relatives (Gardiner & Kosmitzki, 2008). Asian and Latin American families in the United States come from cultural traditions that place great importance on the role of children to support, assist, and respect the family (Chilman, 1993; Uba, 1994). Changes in a sense of obligation to assist, support, and respect the family were examined among an ethnically diverse group of 745 U.S. individuals as they began to move from secondary school into young adulthood. A sense of family obligation increased for all young adults, with slight variations depending on ethnic and financial backgrounds. Young adults from Filipino and Latin American families reported the strongest sense of familial duty during young adulthood, as compared to people of other ethnic backgrounds (Fuligni & Pedersen, 2002). Some studies have observed greater familial support among teenagers from families experiencing economic crises (Elder & Conger, 2000). Gender can also shape family obligations, with traditional gender roles often urging girls, more so than boys, to provide more assistance to the family.

French author and historian Andre Maurois (1967) wrote that growing old is no more than a bad habit that a busy man has no time to form. Age and aging are strongly related to an individual's time perspective. In turn, this time perspective may affect an individual's attitudes (Cutler, 1975). In early childhood, the dominant perception is that time is virtually limitless. Early adulthood brings the realization that time is a scarce resource. Middle age and later stages lead to the perception that time becomes seriously limited. Gergen and Black (1965) pointed out that among public policy attitudes, orientations toward solutions to international problems are linked to one's perception of personal future time: Senior people have a sense of urgency and tend to settle conflicts, whereas the young may display stubbornness. Renshon (1989) argued that in the arts, the phenomenon of late-age creativity and boldness occurs often in different cultures. The last works of Shakespeare, Rembrandt, Verdi, Beethoven, and Tolstoy might suggest that the final stages of the life cycle can bring release from conventional concerns and free the artist to make major creative statements that represent a culmination of the person's vision.

A CASE IN POINT
Culture and Perception of Aging

There is a trend in many Western cultures to hide the signs of aging. In contemporary U.S. society, people often refrain from saying "old" and prefer to use a more neutral "senior" label. People surgically eliminate wrinkles on their faces and bodies, buy expensive cremes to keep their skin elastic, wear toupees and chignons, and try different "magic" colors to eliminate the natural gray of their aging hair. Do adults really dislike how they look when they get older? Do they believe that they become less attractive and therefore want to change their appearance to boost self-esteem? There is no evidence that this is actually true. Moreover, some studies suggest that self-esteem and perceived "attractiveness" are not correlated (Kenealy et al., 1991).

Question:

Do you think that the cosmetic industry and plastic surgeons—to boost their sales and get more clients—are interested in creating the "younger image" hype?

Exercise 8.1

Develop Critical Thinking Skills Working with Original Sources

Kim (2002) generalized comparative data on verbal communications between children and adults in several Asian countries and the United States. Japanese middle-class mothers speak much less frequently to their young children than do their U.S. counterparts. Moreover, Chinese preschool teachers see quietness as a means of control, rather than passivity, and appreciate silence more than U.S. teachers. Consequently, East Asian children tend to be not as verbal as their European American counterparts. Japanese children produce significantly fewer utterances per turn than North American children, and they use verbal expression to communicate emotions less frequently than do U.S. children.

Find this article:

Kim, H. (2002). We talk, therefore we think? A cultural analysis of the effect of talking on thinking. *Journal of Personality and Social Psychology, 83(4)*, 828–842.

Answer these questions:

What were the research data selected in this study? What were the samples selected for this study? In your view, were these samples representative (did they resemble the population of children in the studied countries)? What was the main method used in this study? How substantial were the differences found in this study? What conclusions does the author make? What explanations does the author offer? Could you give your own explanations?

Chapter Summary

- Since ancient times, many of the world's thinkers considered human development a result of the interaction between environment and natural individual predispositions. Contemporary theories of human development emphasize the meaning of both individual and cultural factors of socialization. However, many classical developmental theories were ethnocentric and failed to take into account the richness of human diversity.

- In the interdependent families commonly found in rural traditional societies, the family structure is characterized by interdependency on both dimensions: between parents and their children and among children themselves. In independent families—the typical middle-class nuclear family in most European and North American countries—the family structure is characterized by independence on both dimensions.

- The developing child is seen as an individual with inborn dispositions and skill potential. The child's environment is a part of a larger cultural system. Both the environment and the individual are seen as open and interchanging systems. The power of the culturally regulated environment comes from the coordinated action of the three elements of the niche. They relate to each other, to outside forces, and to the developing individual.

- According to Erikson, a developing individual moves through a series of psychological crises. Each crisis, or conflict, grows primarily out of a need to adapt to the social environment and develop a sense of competence. Once a crisis is resolved, the individual moves further. This theory, with some amendments, is applicable in a wide variety of cultural settings. However, Erikson has been criticized for mixing objective description with subjective prescription. Specifically, the virtues he uses to define the healthy individual are clearly in accordance with Western, Judeo–Christian ethics, values, and social institutions.

- Studies suggest that the stage sequence (preoperational, operational, abstract thinking) and reasoning styles described by Piaget appear to be, with some limitations, universal across cultures. The limitations refer to the methodology and some procedures used by Piaget and his colleagues that are viewed as ethnocentric. Moreover, the Piaget theory explains how children deal with conservation of volume, weight, and amount. However, everyday thinking and the ability to make practical decisions in particular cultural settings are not well explained by this theory.

- According to Kohlberg, there are six stages of moral development in which children and adults are able to make several types of moral judgments. In brief, people go from lower stages of reasoning, where they prefer to avoid punishment for wrongdoing, to the higher stages, where they choose social contract and then universal principles to guide moral actions. This theory may be applied to different cultural settings. Yet, the methodology used in the cross-cultural studies on moral development was based on hypothetical stories about moral choices that were related mainly to U.S. subjects. Another point of criticism is that the developmental stages are closely linked to values of Western liberalism and individualism based on moral choice, values which are not shared universally around the world.

- Cross-culturally, human development is understood as taking place in stages. Specialists refer to particular cultural norms and biological, behavioral, and physiological changes, which are identified cross-culturally with a particular life stage. Most books on human development distinguish several common stages within the life span: prenatal period, infancy, childhood (divided into early and middle childhood), adolescence, and adulthood, which is also divided into three stages: early adulthood, middle adulthood, and late adulthood.

- During the prenatal period, the developing embryo in the mother's womb can be exposed to either favorable or unfavorable conditions. One's access to resources and professional prenatal care along with a stressful social and psychological environment are crucial factors affecting the unborn child's development. Attitudes about pregnancy, abortion, and childbirth vary from culture to culture and are linked to local traditions and laws.

- Each culture provides a particular set of norms regarding parent–child relationships. Cross-culturally, the child's thinking is wishful. Each child's developmental niche includes social practices, values, and demands conveyed to him or her from parents and caregivers.

- Adolescence is viewed not only as a developmental stage but also as a cultural phenomenon rooted in social and economic conditions. Many nonindustrialized cultures encourage their members to assume adult roles as quickly as possible, almost skipping the adolescence stage. Adolescence marks the beginning of sexual maturation. Despite their ability to make ethical judgments and their tremendous cognitive reserves, adolescents do not have the vision or wisdom often found at a more mature age.

- In all cultures, adulthood represents maturity, responsibility, and accountability. This period is divided into stages of early, middle, and late adulthood. Early adulthood is usually linked to formative processes and middle adulthood is associated with accomplishments. In adulthood, individuals generally form their sense of identity, which is the view of themselves as individuals and members of society. The fact that transitions into adult roles have become somewhat delayed in many societies has led to the recognition of a new period of life, called *emerging adulthood*, that extends from the late teens to the mid-twenties and is characterized by self-focused exploration of possibilities in love, work, and worldviews.

- In many countries, the late adulthood period begins with retirement, when a person formally quits his or her job or gives up his or her major responsibilities. Late adulthood is linked to the physiological process of aging. Life expectancy, general socioeconomic conditions, individual psychological and physiological characteristics, and societal attitudes toward the elderly comprise the individual's final developmental niche.

Key Terms

Adolescence The period from 11–12 to 19–20 years. The child has reached sexual maturity but has not yet taken on the rights and responsibilities of the adult status.

Adulthood The period from 20 years onward. The individual has achieved the adult status prescribed by norms and laws of a particular society.

Childhood The time from 2 to 11–12 years. The child acquires language and learns about the most important social skills.

Human Development The changes in physical, psychological, and social behavior as experienced by individuals across the life span from conception to death.

Identity The view of oneself as an individual and a member of society.

Infancy The period from birth to two years when the child acquires initial motor, cognitive, and social skills.

Late Adulthood The period of physical wearing and decline.

Openness Model The theoretical view that suggests that adults change their attitudes and behavior to adjust to changing situations.

Persistence Model The theoretical view that suggests that adults acquire attitudes and behaviors early in life and tend not to change them later.

Prenatal Period The time between conception and birth, which lasts approximately 38 weeks.

Socialization The process by which the individual becomes a member of a particular culture and takes on its values, beliefs, and behaviors.

Temperament Personality traits (presumably of a genetic basis) present in infancy.

Psychological Disorders

The madman thinks the rest of the world is crazy.

PUBLILIUS SYRUS (FIRST CENTURY B.C.E.)—
Roman Writer

Several years ago, a 29-year-old Saudi man began to display unusual symptoms including occasional convulsions and body twists. His behavior rapidly deteriorated and became erratic. Soon he lost the ability to walk. His speech became disorganized. His relatives began to notice that "the voice of a woman" could be heard coming from the young man. The family didn't call the doctor. Instead, they brought the man to religious scholars who concluded that he was possessed by a jinn—an evil, supernatural creature or spirit. In Islamic tradition, these evil spirits are believed to be invisible but have the power to accept human or animal form. They have bad intentions because jealousy guides them to seek revenge. The scholars suggested that the family should isolate the man, chain him, and read prayers. The family agreed. The man's father even stated that when he was a little boy himself, a jinn invaded his body too but praying has eventually saved him and he is symptom-free now.

Was the young man in this case misdiagnosed? If this case was taking place in the United States, would you accept the diagnoses involving "evil spirits" and would you prescribe praying as a treatment? Or would you rather think of diagnostic symptoms associated with catatonia, disorganized speech, and delusions and prescribe hospitalization and medical treatment? Moreover, is the father delusional too because he insisted he had been invaded by a jinn? But hold on a second! Do we have the right to challenge some people's religious beliefs and reject their interpretation of the patient's behavior? The diagnostic manual used by clinicians in the United States (to which we will refer in this chapter several times) explicitly states that certain forms of behavior should not to be labeled delusional and abnormal if shared by members of a religion, culture, or subculture. If the members of a community or larger society interpret the symptoms in their own way, can we impose on them our secular views of how to diagnose and treat psychological disorders? Are the specialists able, in principle, to clearly separate a psychopathological syndrome from a cultural norm without confusing the two? We will try to answer these and many other questions related to culture and psychological disorders.

AMERICAN BACKGROUND: *DSM-IV*

According to the American Psychiatric Association's *Diagnostic and Statistical Manual of Mental Disorders*, fourth edition, text revision, or *DSM-IV-TR*, a **mental disorder** is "a clinically significant behavioral and psychological syndrome or pattern that occurs in an individual and that is associated with present distress (a painful syndrome) or disability (impairment in one or more important areas of functioning) or with a significantly increased risk of suffering death, pain, disability, or an important loss of freedom" (*DSM-IV*, p. xxi). U.S. clinicians usually assess the information that they have available to them about an individual from the standpoint of five axes, each of which helps professionals to examine the situation from five different viewpoints or domains of information (see Table 9.1). Today, the *DSM-IV* has become the main system of classification of psychological disorders in the United States. It is used by the vast majority of mental health professionals, including psychiatrists, psychologists, social workers, and counselors working in both private and government agencies (Mirin, 2002).

The *International Statistical Classification of Diseases and Related Health Problems* (*ICD*) is a detailed description of known diseases and injuries and is published by the World Health Organization, a branch of the United Nations. It is revised periodically and is currently in its tenth edition, known as the *ICD-10*. It also contains descriptions of mental disorders. Because of the help and cooperation from U.S. clinicians, the mental disorders section of *ICD-10-CM* is very close to the *DSM-IV* and its latest version in terms of terminology and structure.

TABLE 9.1 Multiaxial Diagnostic System

Axis I indicates clinical syndromes and other important conditions that could be a focus of clinical attention. Axis II is for reporting personality disorders or mental retardation. Axis III is for reporting the individual's current medical conditions that are potentially relevant to the understanding or management of the individual's mental disorder. Axis IV is for reporting psychosocial and environmental problems that may affect the diagnosis, treatment, and prognosis of mental disorders. Among these problems are ones related to social environment and primary support group, educational and occupational problems, housing and economic problems, problems related to access to healthcare services, and legal and other social problems. Axis V is for reporting the clinician's judgment of the individual's overall level of functioning. Those professionals who prefer not to use the multiaxial system list the appropriate diagnoses for the individual.

What is madness? To have erroneous perceptions and to reason correctly from them.

VOLTAIRE (1694–1778)—French Philosopher

TWO VIEWS ON CULTURE AND PSYCHOPATHOLOGY

Culture can affect psychological disorders in at least five areas. The first area is the individual's culture-based *subjective experience,* including knowledge about psychological problems. The second area is culture-based *idioms of distress,* that is, the ways individuals explain and express their symptoms according to culture-based display rules. The third area is culture-based *diagnoses* for various forms of psychological disorders, including professional and nonprofessional judgments. The fourth area is culture-based *treatment,* the way people, including professionals, attempt to overcome psychopathological symptoms. The fifth area is culture-based *outcome,* or principles, according to which the results of treatment are evaluated (Castillo, 1997).

Subjective experience, idioms of distress, and outcomes of treatment necessary for diagnosis of psychopathological symptoms can be assessed by judgments about at least three types of symptoms: physical, behavioral, and psychological. People tend to experience and explain their symptoms, largely, according to accepted cultural standards and their individual knowledge. The professional who evaluates the reported symptoms also places her judgment on the platform of a particular experience. Having these discourses in mind, we could propose two alternative hypotheses.

First: Human beings develop ideas, establish behavioral norms, and learn emotional responses according to a set of cultural prescriptions. Therefore, people from different cultural settings should understand psychological disorders differently, and the differences should be significant. This view is called the **relativist perspective** on psychopathology because it puts psychological phenomena in a relative perspective.

Second: Despite cultural differences, people share a great number of similar features, including attitudes, values, and behavioral responses. Therefore, the overall understanding of mental disorders ought to be universal. This view is called the **universalist perspective** on psychopathology because it suggests the existence of absolute, invariable symptoms of psychopathology across cultures.

From the relativist perspective, psychopathology is unique for each culture and cannot be understood beyond the context in which it develops. According to this view, psychopathology is culture specific and should have different meanings in different societies. Religious, social, and political norms of each country should therefore determine the way various psychological symptoms are displayed, understood, and treated. If we accept this view, we may no longer apply views on psychopathology formed in one cultural environment to other cultures' circumstances. Thus, it may be futile to study major depressive disorder in Japan using North American diagnostic methods because people in this Asian country may interpret and describe feelings and bodily reactions differently, compared to most Americans, Germans, or Canadians.

According to the relativist view, what is considered psychopathological in one culture could be regarded as normal in another cultural setting and vice versa. Spirit possession syndromes are common and considered natural for some indigenous cultures in Africa and South America. When one claims that the alien spirits possess his body, this symptom, often marked by overwhelming anxiety, is likely to be diagnosed as schizophrenia in any Western country. Similar to most U.S. citizens worrying about the possibility of contracting a contagious disease, people in some African societies experience fear of bewitchment.

A CASE IN POINT
Idioms of Distress

Have you heard expressions such as "I have a gut feeling" or "I am sick to the stomach"? The English language is rich in its range of terms for psychological distress, which are described differently in other languages. Thus, an African's complaint of "pain in the heart" or a Russian idiom "my soul hurts" may have to cover a range of symptoms for which we would use different names. Culture-based idioms of distress—the expressions in which the individual describes his or her symptoms—are very important channels through which the culture affects the subjective experience, clinical picture, and public expression of a disorder. This could include emotional expressions, cognitive emphasis on certain symptoms while ignoring others, as well as mannerisms; physical actions, including seeking out clinical care; and the culture-based explanations of mental disorders. For example, it is very common in many parts of the world to use both scientific and spiritual explanations for mental illness (Hinton & Kleinman, 1993). In Eastern Europe, in particular the Ukraine, Belarus, and Russia, an "average" patient may have a belief that his headaches are a direct consequence of fluctuations of atmospheric pressure; in this case, the patient will be looking for medicine that would make him invulnerable to that atmospheric disturbance (even newspapers publish medical recommendations for those people who suffer from such headaches). For the "average" U.S. resident, these atmosphere–headache connections do not fit into the repertoire of idioms of distress. Cultural relativists are highly skeptical about applicability of Western diagnostic criteria in other cultures. They believe that indigenous views, concepts, and expressions of distress are considered fundamental to understanding the cultural context of illness (Tanaka-Matsumi, 1995).

Dissociative fugue, a disorder marked by sudden travel away from home or work, is known only in few countries (*DSM-IV*, pp. 482, 485). Its prevalence could be caused by such conditions as a natural disaster or violence that targets particular ethnic or religious groups. In the United States, up until the 1960s, and in the former Soviet Union, until the late 1980s, homosexual behavior was considered criminal and pathological. An admission of homosexuality could carry a serious punishment, such as a prison term or mandatory psychiatric detention. Moreover, not long ago a sizable portion of Russians believed that homosexuals are ill and should be physically exterminated (Shiraev, 2010). In the 2000s, homosexuality is still considered pathological or even criminal in many countries such as Iran, Angola, Myanmar, Guyana, Cameroon and most Arabic and Islamic countries.

Defenders of the relativist view particularly target and criticize ethnocentrism, or judgment of one cultural reality from the position of the other. The most salient type of ethnocentrism, in the eyes of critics, is one promoted by cultural majorities. Values and norms accepted by any cultural majority—such as ethnic, religious, or racial—have great power because of the sheer size of the majority and because of the fact that its members hold most of the positions of power (Lewis-Fernández & Kleinman, 1994).

From the universalist view, the culture impact is important, but it should not be overstated (Beardsley & Pedersen, 1997). According to this position, psychopathological phenomena across countries and cultures tend to be universal in terms of their origin and expression. There are many examples that suggest such cross-cultural similarities. For instance, many disorders are characterized by almost identical symptoms. Among these symptoms are those of the Alzheimer's dementia, Parkinson's disease, schizophrenia, mental retardation, and autism. There are no reports of different incidences of bipolar disorder based on race or ethnicity (*DSM-IV*, p. 352). In a study of Japanese and U.S. women, both samples, despite many cultural dissimilarities between them, did not report and display significant differences in their symptoms of postpartum depression, a mood disorder occurring in some women after birth of a child (Shimizi & Kaplan, 1987). Across the world, people's experiences of caring for a family member with serious mental illness are very similar and involve negative stereotyping (stigma), guilt, shame, and hopelessness (Penny et al., 2009). Overall, the symptoms and related experiences have a similar origin, yet may manifest and felt somewhat differently in different cultural settings.

Central and Peripheral Symptoms: An Outcome of the Debate Between Universalists and Relativists

Which view, absolutist or relativist, describes psychological reality with a greater accuracy? While understanding both the relative cultural uniqueness and the universal nature of psychopathology, it is useful to implement an inclusive approach to psychopathology that combines the two previously described viewpoints. That is, major features of psychopathology—abnormality, maladaptiveness, and distress—should be considered universal. However, these features manifest by individuals in specific environmental, social, and cultural contexts. Each disorder, therefore, can manifest as follows:

- A set of **central symptoms** that can be observed in practically all world populations and
- A set of **peripheral symptoms** that are culture specific.

For example, central symptoms for a case of a major depressive episode, such as dysphoria, loss of energy, tension, and ideas of insufficiency, could be seen cross-culturally as

1. caused by biochemical factors;
2. a bodily syndrome manifested in the form of fatigue, lack of concentration, and various pains; and
3. psychological complaints such the inability to take pleasure in previously enjoyable activities.

A CASE IN POINT

Neurasthenia Across the Globe

Neurasthenia can be a diagnostic category. At the same time, it is a social construct with a variety of cultural connotations. Historically, the use of that diagnosis stemmed from the difficulty experienced by clinicians to explain the etiology of several symptoms including various forms of anxiety and depression. Clinicians attributed these symptoms to the weakness of the nervous system, assuming—mostly implicitly—that in the future the science will further progress and specific neurological causes of that disorder will be discovered. In addition, until the recent past, neurasthenia has been a popular diagnosis because it was very general and vague enough to be used with numerous patients who otherwise would be diagnosed with a more severe disorder. Neurasthenia was one of the most widely used diagnoses worldwide because, as a diagnosis, it almost never caused serious social limitations in the patient's life. Still, there is no cross-national consensus on what the "core" characteristics of neurasthenia are; however, this did not prevent clinicians all over the world from using this diagnostic label (Shiraev, 2011; Starcevic, 1999).

Peripheral (culture-specific) signs of this illness vary. Thus, many Canadian patients may display guilty feelings. Some of them would report preoccupations with suicidal thoughts. Most patients from Taiwan will be unlikely to report guilty feelings. Guilt, shame, bodily pain, or behavioral disturbance may be the dominant presentation, depending on one's learned expectation of what is relevant to his or her particular illness (Turner, 1997). In the section on schizophrenia, we will learn that hallucinations and delusions can be considered central symptoms of this disorder. However, the images and thoughts conveyed through these symptoms are profoundly affected by historic and cultural circumstances in which the patient lives.

CULTURE-BOUND SYNDROMES

Culture-bound syndromes comprise a set of psychological phenomena of particular interest to psychologists. The eclectic nature of the category makes it hard to define precisely. It has even invited much dispute over the best definition for it. *DSM-IV* defines a culture-bound syndrome as recurrent, locality-specific patterns of aberrant behavior, and troubling experience that may or may not be linked to a particular *DSM-IV* diagnostic category. Many of these patterns are indigenously viewed as "illnesses," or at least afflictions, and most have local names.

Culture-bound syndromes do not have a one-to-one correspondence with a disorder recognized by "mainstream" systems. Most of these syndromes were initially reported as confined to a particular culture or set of related or geographically proximal cultures. At least seven broad categories can be differentiated among phenomena often described as culture-bound syndromes:

1. An apparent set of psychopathological symptoms, not attributable to an identifiable organic cause, which is recognized as an illness in a particular cultural group, but does not fall into the illness category in the West. *Amok*, a sudden explosion of rage, recognizable in Malaysia, is an example. In London or New York, a person with these symptoms is likely to be described as "having anger-control problem."

2. An apparent set of psychopathological symptoms, not attributable to an identifiable organic cause, which is locally recognized as an illness and which resembles a Western disease category, but which (1) has locally salient features different from the Western disease and (2) lacks some symptoms recognizable in the West. One example is *shenjingshaijo* or neurasthenia in China, which resembles major depressive disorder but has more salient somatic features and often lacks the depressed mood that defines depression in the West.

3. A discrete disease entity not yet recognized by Western professionals. A fine example of this is *kuru*, a progressive psychosis and dementia indigenous to cannibalistic tribes in New Guinea. *Kuru* is now believed to result from an aberrant protein or "prion" that is capable of replicating itself by deforming other proteins in the brain. (A 1997 Nobel Prize was awarded for the elucidation of prions.) *Kuru* has also been compared to a form of Creuzfeldt–Jakob disease and may be equivalent or related to *scrapie*, a disease of sheep, and a form of *encephalopathy* labeled "mad cow disease."

4. An illness, the symptoms of which occur in many cultural settings; however, it is only elaborated as an illness in one or a few cultural settings. An example is *koro*, the fear of retracting genitalia, which may sometimes have a physiological–anatomical reality and appears to occur as a delusion or phobia in several cultural groups.

5. Culturally accepted explanatory mechanisms or idioms of illness, which do not match Western idioms of distress and, in a Western setting, might indicate culturally inappropriate thinking

and perhaps delusions or hallucinations. Examples of this include witchcraft, *rootwork* (in Caribbean), or the *evil eye* (common in Mediterranean and Latin American traditions).

6. A state or set of behaviors, often including trance or possession states: hearing, seeing, and/or communicating with the dead or spirits or feeling that one has "lost one's soul" from grief or fright. These may or may not be seen as pathological within their native cultural framework but, if not recognized as culturally appropriate could indicate psychosis, delusions, or hallucinations in a Western setting.

7. A syndrome allegedly occurring in a given cultural setting, which does not in fact exist but may be reported to the professional. A possible example is *windigo* (in Algonkian Indians), a syndrome of cannibal obsessions, the existence of which is questionable (Marano, 1985); this allegation, however, may be used to justify the expulsion or execution of a tribal outcast in a manner similar to the use of witchcraft allegations (see Table 9.2).

TABLE 9.2 Specific Culture-Bound Syndromes

These are recurrent, locally specific patterns of atypical behavior and troubling experiences that may or may not be linked to a particular *DSM-IV* diagnostic category (*DSM-IV*, p. 844). Culture-bound syndromes are generally limited to specific societies or areas and indicate repetitive and troubling sets of experiences and observations. Consider examples of some culture-bound disorders. Try to find both central and peripheral symptoms in each syndrome.

Amok. Known in Malaysia; similar patterns may occur elsewhere. Amok is a sudden rage in which an otherwise normal person goes berserk, sometimes hurting those in his path. Brooding is followed by a violent outburst; it is often precipitated by a slight or insult. The symptoms seem to be prevalent among men. It was well known to the British colonial rulers of Malaysia and has therefore passed into the English language: "running amok." To this day, cases of amok are reported in Malaysian newspapers (Osborne, 2001).

Ataque de nervios. Also known as "attack of nerves." Common in Latin America and Mediterranean groups. Symptoms include uncontrollable shouting, attacks of crying, trembling, heat in the chest rising to the head, and verbal or physical aggression. Ataque de nervios frequently occurs as a result of not only a stressful family event, especially the death of a relative, but also a divorce or fight with a family member. Studies of *ataque de nervios* revealed that 26 percent of people who suffer from this condition had a strong risk factor for other psychiatric disorders. More than 80 percent of these people have symptoms associated with anxiety, mood, suicidal, psychotic, or substance use dysfunctions (Tolin et al., 2007).

Bilis, colera, or muina. Part of a general Latin American idiom of distress and explanation of physical or mental illness as a result of extreme emotion that upsets the humors (described in terms of hot and cold). Other symptoms include tension, headache, trembling, screaming, and so on. Bilis and colera specifically implicate anger in the cause of illness. In Korea, similar symptoms are labeled *Hwa-byung* or *wool-hwa-bung*, or the "anger syndrome." Symptoms are attributed to suppression of anger and include insomnia, fatigue, panic, fear of impending death, indigestion, anorexia, palpitations, generalized aches and pains, and a feeling of a mass in the epigastrium.

Brain fag. Known in West Africa. Sometimes labeled "brain tiredness," this is a mental and physical reaction to the challenges of schooling, a condition experienced primarily by male high school or university students. Symptoms include difficulties in concentrating, remembering, and thinking. Students often state that their brains are "fatigued." Additional symptoms center around the head and neck and include pain, pressure, tightness, blurring of vision, heat, or burning. "Brain tiredness" or fatigue from "too much thinking" is an idiom of distress in many cultures. The symptoms resemble anxiety, depressive, or somatoform disorders in *DSM-IV*.

(Continued)

TABLE 9.2 Continued

Dhat. Occurs in India; similar conditions are described in Sri Lanka and China too. This syndrome is characterized by excessive concern about loss of semen through excessive sexual activity or in the urine. Dhat syndrome presents with weakness, depression, and sexual problems and symptoms, such as palpitations, in a rather nonspecific form; similar to *jiryan* (also in India), *sukrapremeha* (in Sri Lanka), and *shenkui* (in China). Symptoms are attributed to excessive semen loss from frequent intercourse, masturbation, nocturnal emission, or urine. Excessive semen loss is feared because it represents the loss of one's vital essence and can thereby be life threatening.

Falling out. Recognized in Southern United States, and "blacking out," as known in the Caribbean. Symptoms: sudden collapse; loss of sight even though eyes remain open. The person usually hears and understands what is occurring around him but feels powerless to move. These symptoms are labeled *obmorok* in Russian culture. May correspond to conversion disorder or dissociative disorder (*DSM-IV*).

Frigophobia. There is a condition that the Chinese call *weihanzheng*, or "fear of being cold." Patients bundle up in the steamy heat, wearing wool hats and gloves. Frigophobia seems to stem from Chinese cultural beliefs about the spiritual qualities of heat and cold; these symptoms are described primarily in the Chinese population of Singapore.

Ghost sickness. Reported in people from Native American Indian. Symptoms include preoccupations with death and the dead, bad dreams, fainting, appetite loss, fear, witchcraft, hallucinations, a sense of suffocation, confusion, and so on.

Koro. Is known to people of Chinese ethnicity in Malaysia; related conditions are described in some other parts of East Asia. Main symptom: People experience sudden and intense anxiety that sexual organs will recede into body and cause death.

Latah. Occurs in Malaysia, Indonesia, Thailand, and Japan. Symptoms include hypersensitivity to sudden fright, often with nonsense mimicking of others, and trancelike behavior. Over time, the person with these symptoms becomes so sensitive that trances can be triggered by a falling coconut. *Latahs* (people who display the symptoms of latah) tend to blurt out offensive phrases, much like sufferers of Tourette's syndrome. (Indeed, Georges Gilles de la Tourette, the French discoverer of the syndrome in the 1880s, explicitly compared it to latah.) *Latahs* also often mimic the actions of people around them or obey commands, including requests to take off their clothes. Afterward, people often claim to have no memory of what they said or did.

Locura. Incidents are known in the United States and Latin America. Symptoms include incoherence, agitation, auditory and visual hallucinations, inability to follow rules of social interaction, unpredictability, and possible violence.

Mal de ojo ("evil eye"). Known in people from the Mediterranean and elsewhere. Sufferers, mostly children, are believed to be under the influence of an "evil eye," causing fitful sleep, crying, sickness, and fever.

Pibloktoq. Known in people from the Arctic and sub-Arctic Inuit communities, such as Greenland Eskimos. The syndrome is found throughout the Arctic with local names. Symptoms include extreme excitement, physical violence, verbal abuse, convulsions, and short coma. During the attack, the individual may tear off his clothing, break furniture, shout obscenities, eat feces, flee from protective shelters, or perform other irrational or dangerous acts. The individual may be withdrawn or mildly irritable for a period of hours or days before the attack and will typically report complete amnesia of the attack.

Qi-gong. Known in China. A short episode of symptoms, such as auditory and visual hallucinations, occurs after engaging in Chinese folk practice of qi-gong, or "exercise of vital energy," which resembles meditation (Lim & Lin, 1996). In the United States, reports about persistent hallucinations are likely to suggest schizophrenia or schizophreniform disorder.

(Continued)

TABLE 9.2 Continued

Rootwork. Symptoms are known in the Southern United States and the Caribbean. They include anxiety, such as fear of poisoning or death, ascribed to those individuals who put "roots," "spells," or "hexes" on others.

Sin-byung. Known in Korea. This is the syndrome of anxiety and bodily complaints followed by dissociation and possession by ancestral spirits. The syndrome is characterized by general weakness, dizziness, fear, loss of appetite, insomnia, and gastrointestinal problems.

The sore neck syndrome. This is a syndrome observed in Khmer refugees. The main feature involves a fear that blood and wind pressures will cause vessels in the neck area to burst. Additional symptoms include palpitations, shortness of breath, panicking, headache, blurry vision, a buzzing in the ear, dizziness, and trembling.

Spell. Symptoms are described by some individuals in the Southern United States and elsewhere in the world. This is a trance in which individuals communicate with deceased relatives or spirits. At times this trance is associated with brief periods of personality change. This is not considered psychopathological in the folk tradition; however, this phenomenon is often labeled "psychotic episodes" in Western clinical settings.

Susto. Found in Latin American groups in the United States and labeled "fright" or "soul loss" among some people from the Caribbean. Symptoms are tied to a frightening event that makes the soul leave the body, causing unhappiness and sickness.

Taijinkyofusho. In Japan, it is an intense fear that one's body, body parts, or bodily functions are displeasing, embarrassing, or offensive to other people in appearance, odor, facial expressions, or movements. This malady is included in the official Japanese classification of mental disorders. The symptoms are perhaps similar, in some respect, to social phobia (*DSM-IV*).

Zar. Known in Ethiopia, Somalia, Egypt, Sudan, Iran, and elsewhere in North Africa and the Middle East. This is the belief in possession by a spirit, causing shouting, laughing, head banging, singing, or weeping. Individuals may show apathy and withdrawal, refusing to eat or carry out daily tasks, or may develop a long-term relationship with the possessing spirit. Such behavior is not necessarily considered pathological in local settings.

Debates over culture-bound syndromes often revolve around confusions or conflations among these different categories. Many so-called culture-bound syndromes actually occur in many unrelated cultures, or they appear to be merely locally flavored varieties of illnesses found elsewhere. This fact is especially interesting because it shows that culture-bound syndromes could be viewed as an accentuation of the universal trends. Specific cultures construe certain behaviors as syndromes of psychopathology, name them disorders, and treat them as illnesses. Some are not so much actual illnesses as explanatory mechanisms, such as beliefs in witchcraft or humoral imbalances (a shift in the balance of some "bodily liquids"). So-called "male pregnancy symptoms"—vomiting, fatigue, toothache, and food cravings during a partner's pregnancy were studied in On Wogeo, an island off the coast of New Guinea, the Garifuna (or Black Carib) of Central America, the Bimin-Kuskusmin of Papua New Guinea (Munroe, 2010). Are these special culture-bound syndromes or just local variations of sympathy pain, which many of us can experience? The concept of culture-bound syndromes is therefore useful insofar as it brings culture (religion and ethnic identity in particular) to the attention of psychiatrists and psychologists trained in a different cultural tradition (Simons & Hughes, 1985).

Our health is our sound relation with external objects.

RALPH WALDO EMERSON (1803–1882)—U.S. Poet and Philosopher

Now we will explore some specific mental disorders identified in the United States from a broader cross-cultural context.

ANXIETY DISORDERS

The definition of an **anxiety disorder** is subject to interpretations that are rooted in value judgments that may vary across cultures (Satcher, 2000). However, no matter where the person lives, each anxiety disorder can manifest itself as a set of central symptoms that can be observed in practically every culture as well as a set of peripheral symptoms that are culture specific. For example, symptoms of an anxiety disorder can be universally reported as a persistent worry, fear, or a constant state of apprehensive anticipation—the conditions are maladaptive and cause significant distress in the individual. Although one person may experience overwhelming fear of scorpions, and another person may develop a devastating fear of college examinations, they both report the existence of an emotion labeled "fear" that disrupts their daily functioning. For example, central symptoms for a case of generalized anxiety disorder could be seen cross-culturally as (1) a bodily syndrome manifested in the form of fatigue, lack of concentration, and muscle tension and (2) a psychological syndrome manifested as the individual's persistent worry about particular social performance or activity. Peripheral (culture-specific) signs of this specific anxiety disorder can vary. In most Western and some industrialized countries, individual anxiety is often related to the way people view their success.

Each national, religious, or ethnic group may develop conditions for the development of particular peripheral symptoms of various anxiety disorders. In Japan and Korea, for example, individuals with social phobia may express persistent fear of being offensive to others. Some cultural conditions may cause the development of "normal" concerns, which may be viewed differently from the standpoint of other cultures. Some Middle Eastern countries, for instance, restrict the participation of women in public life, and strict rules are applied to women's clothes and behavior in public places. Therefore, a woman's reluctance to appear in public should not be automatically considered by a U.S. professional as agoraphobia (*DSM-IV*, pp. 399, 413). The environment in which the individual lives often determines the type of fear he experiences. Fear of magic spirits, perhaps, should not be diagnosed as a phobia in a culture where this type of fear is culturally appropriate. However, if this fear becomes excessive, so that it disrupts the individual's everyday activities and causes extraordinary suffering, this condition can be labeled a phobia (*DSM-IV*, p. 407).

Take, for example, obsessive-compulsive disorder (OCD), which is manifested as recurrent and persistent thoughts and impulses. Should every type of compulsive behavior or obsessive thought be diagnosed as OCD? Not necessarily. Specific repetitive behavior—praying, for example—should be judged in accordance with the norms of the individual's culture and should clearly interfere with social role functioning to be diagnosed as OCD (*DSM-IV*, p. 420).

Despite the variety of culture-specific, peripheral symptoms of anxiety disorders, there are also significant similarities. For instance, various traumatic events have direct and indirect impact on the development of anxiety problems across countries. Cheryl Koopman (1997) found that traumatic events such as the Holocaust, terrorism, captivity, torture, and rape could produce similar behavioral responses in individuals of different national, cultural, and religious backgrounds. These reactions could be described as posttraumatic stress disorder, acute stress disorder, or acute stress reaction (*ICD-10*). Individuals who were exposed to such traumatic events—for example, political refugees, asylum seekers, and victims of ethnic "cleansing"—typically have highly elevated rates of posttraumatic stress disorder compared to the general population.

Similarities in symptoms do not necessarily suggest that the severity of the condition is the same across various cultural groups. In case of agoraphobia, for instance, it was established that this disorder is more prevalent among African Americans than among whites. Moreover, African Americans were less likely than other groups to seek treatment for agoraphobia (Chambless & Williams, 1995; Eaton et al., 1991).

DEPRESSIVE DISORDERS

In the past, **melancholy** (often **melancholia**) was the most common label for symptoms known today as **depressive disorders**. The word *melancholy* originates from the Greek *melas* (black) and *khole* (bile, the liver-generated bitter liquid stored in the gallbladder). Used throughout centuries, this term was replaced by the term *affective disorder*, with *depressive disorders* being a subtype. Various written accounts and detailed descriptions of mood-related maladies, depression in particular, are found in the texts of ancient civilizations including China, Babylon, Egypt, India, and Greece. According to the Old Testament, Saul, the ruler of Israel, was deprived of his favors with God and doomed to suffer from long-term distress and sorrow. He finally committed suicide. In *Ramayana*, the classical Indian epic, King Dasaratha goes through three episodes of deep sorrow caused by tragic family events. Depression figures prominently in another sacred Indian epic, *Mahabharata*. In this tale, a young man named Arjuna becomes afflicted with the symptoms of a serious depressive illness. These symptoms are later relieved by Lord Krishna. It is believed that Prince Gautama Siddhartha, the future Buddha, displayed symptoms of depression early in his life. To cheer him up, his worried father and foster mother built three palaces, one for cold weather, one for hot weather, and one for the rainy season. Various descriptions of manic and depressive states are found in the Homeric epics, the earliest known works of Greek literature.

The first scientific accounts of depressive disorders are associated with the works of Greek scholars, physicians, and philosophers who shared several common views on human emotions (Simon, 1978; Tellenbach, 1980). These views were largely supported by Roman and Middle Eastern scholars and physicians. The most remarkable observations and assumptions included the following:

- There are physical or somatic causes of depressive symptoms.
- The balance of bodily functions (either surplus or deficiency) is associated with certain problems manifested through emotions.
- Life events and experiences of the individual can predispose him to develop particular mood maladies.

The first English text entirely devoted to affective illness was Robert Burton's *Anatomy of Melancholy*, published in 1621 (later editions of the book are available today). Burton suggested that mood disorders have a wide variety of indicators, including many of those that are today considered symptoms of dissociative and anxiety disorders. He included environmental factors such as diet, alcohol, biological rhythms, and intense love as contributing forces to melancholy. During the period when Burton lived, melancholia was commonly considered a condition to which noblemen, artists, thinkers, and other intellectuals were predisposed because of their exceptional compassion. It was frequently labeled as "love sickness" (Gilman, 1988). In addition to this type, Burton also describes "religious" melancholia. Overall, the author not only discussed causes and symptoms of melancholy, but also introduced principles of their treatment.

Several cross-cultural studies of mood disorders showed that people tend to report a broad range of common symptoms. An earlier World Health Organization study (1983) found that more than three-quarters of individuals diagnosed with depression reported similar symptoms, such as sadness, tension, lack of energy, loss of interest, ideas of insufficiency, and an inability to concentrate

In a comprehensive cross-cultural analysis of depressive symptoms, Tanaka-Matsumi and Draguns suggested that *universal core symptoms* of depression include dysphoria, anxiety, tension, lack of energy, and ideas of insufficiency. Beyond these core symptoms, cultural variations in the expressions of depression are also found. *DSM-IV* refers to several peripheral symptoms of depression. The headaches reported by the patients in Latino and Mediterranean countries, weakness, imbalance, and tiredness in Chinese and Asian countries, and problems of the "heart" reported in Middle Eastern countries could all be interpreted as depressive. The combination of Asian cultures' belief in the unity of the mind and body with the Asian tendency not to express feelings openly may lead to the presentation of somatic complaints and the underreporting of psychological symptoms (Goldston et al., 2008).

At least three factors—(1) diagnostic practices, (2) understanding of the symptoms by the individual, and (3) disclosure of the symptoms—together influence the content of the clinical picture of mood disorders around the world.

Research in this field yielded results suggestive of particular cultural differences in diagnostic practices and reporting of affective symptoms. One of significant factors is the stigma of mental illness: People tend to hide or deny their abnormal psychological symptoms because of the fear of disapproval and rejection by other people. Ian Neary from University of Essex undertook a three-year-long study of diagnostic practices in Japan. He suggested that some medical professionals avoid giving the "depression" diagnosis, especially to young women, because such a verdict in the eyes of relatives and friends would automatically place the woman's condition in the category of "incurable" mental illness. As a result, the woman (or the man) could face serious problems finding a husband (or a wife) and starting a family: Many men (and women too) avoid any engagement with mentally ill individuals. Being aware of stigmatization of depression, clinicians try to avoid it by giving their patients different diagnoses, such as neurasthenia or any other dysfunction, which is seen as a bodily problem treatable by conventional means (Neary, 2000).

Health professionals in some countries—due to historic tendencies in their medical systems—are often trained not to recognize illness, in particular psychological symptoms. As an illustration, healthcare providers in African countries, chiefly in rural areas, tend to view mental illness predominantly as marked behavior with strong psychotic features, such as hallucinations and delusions. Affective disturbances are not overlooked, though. Instead, they are commonly explained by situational factors. A physician who spent two years working in Zimbabwe reported a case in which healthcare providers were given a case summary for evaluation. In this description, a 40-year-old woman expressed sadness, decreased motivation, lack of energy, loss of interest, and persistent ideas of personal ineptness. She reportedly said that life was not worth living and even said she once attempted suicide. What was the most common diagnosis? The most common interpretations of the woman's problem referred to her excessive thinking, preoccupation with her husband's infidelity, her neighbors' jealousy, and possible witchcraft conducted "against" her. A mood disorder was not mentioned in the evaluations (Patel, 1996). Besides identifiable cultural factors, diagnostic practice in any given country depends on the guidelines specified by the official national classification system.

Symptoms, if they are not directly observable by the clinician during an interview, are typically recorded according to the patient's own accounts. Could it be that some individuals have particular symptoms suggestive of an affective disorder, but do not report them? There is evidence in support of this assumption. It was found in one study that many Chinese patients do not acknowledge several of their own psychological symptoms, such as lack of joy, hopelessness, and loss of self-esteem. With further questioning, these symptoms were eventually revealed (Kleinman, 1986). Similarly, Yap (1965) initially noted that Chinese depressed patients had a low incidence of guilty feelings. However, additional observations and questions revealed the presence of affective experiences related to guilt. These examples suggest that affective and cognitive dimensions of depression were not necessarily "absent" in some Chinese patients. These symptoms were underreported, compared to other, primarily bodily, symptoms (Yen et al., 2000). One of the most interesting cross-cultural findings is a difference in displaying somatic versus psychological symptoms of affective illness. Some groups tend to "psychologize," whereas others tend to "somaticize" their distressful experiences (Keyes & Ryff, 2003; Marsella, 1980). A study of word associations to the word "depression" in Japan and the United States found that the Japanese subjects preferred to use more external referent terms, such as "rain" and "cloud," and somatic-referent terms, such as "headache" and "fatigue." In contrast, both Japanese Americans and European Americans associated predominantly mood-state terms, such as "sad" and "lonely" (Tanaka-Matsumi & Marsella, 1976). Studies conducted with Chinese and Chinese American populations in the United States supported other reporting of an emphasis on the expression of somatic symptoms among Chinese groups (Yen et al., 2000). Similar observations about cultural differences were established in a study by Ulusahin and colleagues (1994): Among British patients (representing a Western country) with depressive symptoms, there were high scores on psychological complaints such as sadness, guilt, and pessimism; the participating Turkish patients (representing a non-Western country) showed higher scores on somatic complaints such as sleep disturbances, pains, and aches. A more recent study found that the Turkish immigrants in Belgium report more somatic complaints than "native" residents in Turkey and Belgium (Smith, 2011).

In summary, there is evidence that people in non-Western cultures tend to "somatize" their distress, whereas Western cultures have the tendency to "psychologize" (Keyes & Ryff, 2003). Why do such differences in the reporting of bodily and psychological symptoms occur? Most authors refer to cultural rules of emotional display; others analyze the differences between Chinese on one hand and other ethnic groups on the other. Chinese interpersonal connectedness tends to dominate their attitudes and consequent behavior. In this context, duty, obligation, conformity, reciprocity, and avoidance of conflict, disapproval, and shame are highly valued. For the individual raised in Chinese culture, for instance, affective expression of depression is often perceived as self-centered, asocial, distancing, and threatening to interpersonal relationships. However, the expression of physical sufferings and bodily pain, which are amenable to treatment and do not threaten social ties, are more acceptable in the Chinese culture (Ying et al., 2000). Other experts theorize about a greater separation of psychological and bodily phenomena in Western countries compared to Chinese society. In Chinese culture and medicine, according to these observers, the mind and body are integrated with each other, as well as with the social context (Wu, 1982). Furthermore, aspects such as stigmatization of mental illness and inadequate mental health care resources, both of which exist in Communist China, may serve as mediating variables. In contrast, the reporting of somatic symptoms would facilitate the patient receiving support from family and friends. As a result, neurasthenia as a "medical" verdict became a preferred diagnosis over the psychological diagnosis of major depression in Chinese society (Cheung, 1995).

Even though cultural differences can have a significant impact on depressive symptoms, try not to rush to judgment when you analyze reported symptoms. Somatic complaints are not a unique set of characteristics typically found only in non-Western patients. Somatic symptoms can be frequently identified among "mainstream" Western patients. When carefully made by a practicing specialist, the diagnosis usually reads: "masked depression." There is also evidence that across countries, many symptoms of anxiety and depression overlap (Mak et al., 2011).

To be conscious is an illness—a real thorough-going illness.

FYODOR DOSTOYEVSKY (1821–1881)—**Russian Novelist**

SCHIZOPHRENIA

Schizophrenia is a disorder characterized by the presence of delusions, hallucinations, disorganized speech, and disorganized or catatonic behavior. If we used North American diagnostic practices, the opening case in this chapter was likely to have presented such symptoms. Historically, many symptoms of schizophrenia recognized today were labeled madness (also called insanity or lunacy) on 100 and 50 years ago. These symptoms included either gross excessiveness or overwhelming deficiency of certain features in an individual's behavior and experiences. This term described aggressive, violent behavior and dramatic emotional outbursts. It also concerned an individual's profound lack of will, desire, or emotion. Individuals developed these disturbing symptoms as young adults and almost never improved (Shiraev, 2011).

Approximately 1 percent of the world's population today is affected by schizophrenia, the symptoms of which appear to be universal. Despite general similar occurrence rates, there are some cultural variations. For example, there is a relatively high admission rate with this diagnosis in the Republic of Ireland. In the United States, blacks have relatively higher rates of schizophrenia than whites (Levinson & Simmons, 1992). Acute and catatonic cases of schizophrenia were more prevalent in developing countries compared with developed nations (Sartorius, 1992). Delusional ideas in one culture may be nondelusional in others. Visual and auditory hallucinations could have different interpretations in various places, and speech could be mistakenly diagnosed as disorganized due to different forms of verbal presentation.

Despite the assumed biological causes, social conditions can and do affect the course of schizophrenia. Higher educational statuses of patients, for instance, were predictive of whether the illness would remain chronic, but this trend was confirmed for only non-Western countries. People may internalize their environmental influences differently, such as peer pressure, requirements, and expectations from others. Warner (1994) explained this fact by suggesting that in the Third World countries, the better educated experience higher work-related stress. However, national differences in schizophrenia rates could also be explained by differences in access to hospitals. As far as this assumption goes, if access to medical services and facilities is limited, a more severe case is more likely to get attention than less severe cases of illness.

Schizophrenia is more common in men than in women in most parts of the world. However, a 2004 study conducted by Phillips and colleagues (2004) in China showed that this trend was reversed in China. Their results suggested that for every three Chinese men diagnosed with schizophrenia five cases of schizophrenia are established in females. The researchers used census data and information from the Ministry of Health and other sources to estimate that 4.25 million people in China have symptoms of schizophrenia. This research challenges the assumption that schizophrenia has a uniform prevalence worldwide with only minor variations. As researchers of this study suggested, cultural, social, and economic characteristics of communities may influence the onset and course of schizophrenia. The study raises further questions about diagnostic procedures, stigma associated with schizophrenia, and government control of the health statistics reported. Because of the substantial gender gap related to behaviors considered appropriate for men and women, doctors may be more reluctant to diagnose men with schizophrenia. However, this reluctance is not as likely to affect the diagnosis of women. In addition, the Communist authorities in China (as they did in the former Soviet Union) may for political reasons lower the number of cases reported. The researchers of this study also detected a link between schizophrenia and suicide. Their data suggested that nearly 10 percent of the 285,000 deaths from suicide in China each year are committed by people suffering from schizophrenia. Additionally, those who commit suicide are also more likely to be women than men.

In developed countries today, schizophrenia is treated primarily by neuroleptic drugs, which aims at reducing the most profound symptoms of this illness. Later, a variety of psychological methods can be used to reduce relapses. Therefore, the role of the caring family and community becomes extremely important in the life of the patient.

CULTURE AND SUICIDE

Approximately every 15 minutes somebody in the United States takes his or her life. In countries such as Germany, Taiwan, and the United States, suicide rates are much higher than in less economically advanced countries: the ratio, for instance, between the United States and India is approximately 2:1. Japan has even higher rates of suicide than the United States, especially among the elderly. In developed countries including Japan, Finland, France, and Russia, suicide rates vary from 12 to 20 suicides per 100,000 people per year. They are relatively lower (5–7 suicides per 100,000) in Italy, Great Britain, and Spain.

Countries such as Syria, Egypt, Jordan, and Kuwait have low suicide rates. Many nations in Central and South America have low rates also, with the exception of Guyana (23 per 100,000), Surinam (14), and Uruguay (13). Scandinavian countries, as well as Central and East European states, have higher suicide rates compared with other European nations. Some Asian countries, such as Japan, Singapore, and Sri Lanka, have relatively high rates. Elsewhere in the world, higher suicide rates are reported for males. The world's highest suicide rates are reported in Lithuania and South Korea (31 per 100,000). Most of the top 20 countries with the highest suicide rates are economically affluent. Suicide rates tend to be higher in those nations that rank high on subjective well-being (Inglehart, 1997). In other words, nations in which people tend to be happier than people in other nations have higher suicide rates. Perhaps being deeply unhappy in a society where everybody is expected to be happy is even more difficult than it would be in a society where most people believe that their lives are tough and full of misery.

Overall, suicide levels are lower in less developed countries, particularly African, Asian, and Latin American countries and Islamic nations. However, there are few reliable studies of suicide in the Muslim world (Leenaars et al., 2010). Suicide rates in Muslim countries can also be underreported due to shame and guilt associated with it (Eskin, 2004).

Suicide rates have always been high in Japan, where there are about the same number each year as in the United States (34,598 deaths in 2007), which has more than double the population.

Few religious prohibitions exist in Japan against suicide, and it has long been seen as a way to escape failure or to save loved ones from embarrassment. Moreover, in Japan, where honor is an ultimate virtue, many people have long regarded suicide as an "honorable" death, rather than an act of shame and cowardice. Suicide remains almost a taboo subject in Japan. The public awareness about the problem remains low, and individuals experiencing suicidal ideation are unlikely to seek help from psychology professionals.

Although the overall suicide rate among African Americans ages 10–19 years declined from 4.5 to 3.0 per 100,000 in the United States, suicide remains the third leading cause of death among African Americans aged 15–19 years old (CDC, 2007). Depressive illness remains the most serious contributor to suicide. Unfortunately, African American youths are underrepresented in outpatient mental health services and many, as a result, do not receive preventive care. Lack of preventive care is one of the risk factors of suicide. According to the National Institute of Mental Health (2011), American Indians, Alaskan Natives, and whites have the highest rates of suicide. The rates of blacks, Latinos, and Asian youths are almost two times lower. However, studies show that newly immigrated Latinos lack familiarity with the service system and are often apprehensive of it because of fear of being reported as being undocumented.

Suicide rates are generally lower in cultures in which religion strongly opposes "self-murder." There are relatively low levels of suicide in predominantly Catholic and Muslim countries compared with many Western and Protestant nations, where suicide is considered

A CASE IN POINT
Suicide in Finland: From a Conversation with a Finnish Doctor

Do you know that Finnish men are killing themselves at nearly the highest rate among Western nations? The suicide rates in this prosperous Scandinavian country are about 30 suicides per 100,000 population (the rate for the United States is about 19 per 100,000). The numbers for Finnish men are more than three times higher than they are for women. Remarkably, ethnic Swedes who live in Finland have lower suicide rates and ethnic Finns who live abroad still have higher suicide rates than those of native groups. How can we explain such high rates of suicide? Some would choose explanations that are easily accessible: "It's climate! It is too cold in Finland!" However, we know that people in Iceland live in a colder climate, and the suicide rates are much lower there. One may guess: "Is it alcoholism?" Indeed, Finland has high alcohol consumption rates and specialists suggest that suicides occur more frequently among the inebriated. However, there are countries with high alcohol consumption rates, such as Korea, but with lower suicide rates. "Is it societal violence? Could suicide be self-directed aggression?" The murder rates in Finland are among the highest in Europe. There are other countries that have higher rates of violence (the United States, for example) but lower rates of suicide, compared to Finland. "It is social and economic problems!" In fact, suicide rates jumped about 25 percent ten years ago during the years of economic prosperity for Finland. However, rapid economic development is not linked to higher suicide rates in other countries. Finally, the most knowledgeable could suggest: "Is it the linguistic factor? Finns, Hungarians, and Estonians all have high suicide rates and their languages belong to the Finno-Ugric linguistic family."

Questions:

How could the language be a cause of high suicide rates? What other social and cultural factors in your view could contribute to suicide?

by some as a legitimate way of escaping physical pain, personal loss, and other misfortunes of life. However, along with religious prescriptions, there are other cultural factors that might affect people's attitudes toward suicide. As an example, suicide rates in Puerto Rico are higher than those in Mexico, both of which are Catholic countries. The difference may be explained by the coexistence among Puerto Ricans of both Catholic doctrines and Indian folk beliefs (i.e., assumptions of communications between the dead and those who are alive). However, there are also suicides inspired by religious and ideological beliefs including the acts of terrorism. Several factors contribute to suicide. One is a major depressive disorder. Another risk factor is substance abuse. Severe or progressed alcohol and substance use is strongly associated with increased risk of suicidal behavior in most ethnic groups. In the United States, serious problems related to drinking affect suicidal rates among Native American and Mexican American youths (Goldston et al., 2008).

Another factor contributing to suicide is group pressure. In some groups, particularly Americans of Asian origin (primarily Chinese and Japanese), one of the most serious psychological problems is associated with shame or "loss of face" due to an individual's inappropriate behavior. Loss of face can serve as a precipitant for suicidal behavior if shame is perceived as intolerable or if the group views suicide as an honorable way of dealing with difficulties. On the other hand, if the group views suicide as a detestable act, the adolescent may be less likely to attempt suicide, even in the presence of loss of face (Goldston et al., 2008).

Studies also show that suicidal youths were more likely than nonsuicidal youths to have been born outside of the United States. English language proficiency, a present rather than past time orientation, and social support from families and ethnic communities protect against depression among Southeast Asians (Hsu et al., 2004).

Some classic theories of suicide suggest a relationship between societal complexity and frequency of suicide (Durkheim, 1897). A cross-cultural sample of 58 societies was selected to test this hypothesis formulated more than 100 years ago. Each selected society was rated on a scale of social development, and the number of cases of suicide in the literature for each society was recorded. There emerged a significant relationship between societal complexity (e.g., urbanization, organizational ramification, and craft specialization) and rate of suicide (Krauss, 1970).

Two main explanations for suicide statistics across the globe can be put forward. First, some religious beliefs may prevent people from considering self-killing during depression or a personal crisis. Second, some cultural norms increase the social supportiveness among people (Eskin, 2004).

PERSONALITY DISORDERS

Personality disorders are viewed as enduring patterns of behavior and inner experience that deviate markedly from the expectations of the individual's culture. It is not just a single act. It is a persistent behavioral pattern that leads to the individual's distress and impairment in one or several important areas of functioning (Akhtar, 2002). Professionals in many nations recognize personality disorders as a special diagnostic category. There is growing consistency in the way these disorders are diagnosed today. However, it is also important to consider which symptoms of personality disorders are relatively consistent across cultures and which symptoms are culturally bound.

The *DSM-IV* suggests that judgments about appropriate and inappropriate traits vary across cultures. Psychologists are expected to make a determination of whether the diagnosis is applicable to the individual, given the cultural context in which the patient lives. Someone's flashy, unusual clothes may get attention from people on the street; in the same way, personality traits may be seen as unusual and ambiguous when compared to a social standard. **Tolerance threshold** is a term that stands for a measure of tolerance or intolerance toward specific personality traits in a cultural environment. Low thresholds stand for relative societal intolerance against specific behaviors and underlying personality traits, while high thresholds stand for relative tolerance. If a society accepts the diversity of behaviors, then tolerance thresholds should be relatively high. In Table 9.3, you will find a description of the impact of specific cultural constructs on manifestation and evaluation of personality disorders. Overall, personality disorders represent a deviation from what is considered "standard" personality in a specific social and cultural environment.

TABLE 9.3 Assumptions about the Links Between Cultural Variables and Manifestation and Evaluation of Symptoms

Cultural Variables	Manifestations and Evaluations of Symptoms
Collectivism	Collectivist norms allow very limited deviance from what is considered appropriate behavior. Therefore, there should be less tolerance to and more social sanctions against any exhibition of histrionic or antisocial traits. Personality traits that disengage individuals from the group are also among the least tolerated; these include narcissistic, borderline, and schizoid features. Dependent and avoidant personality traits should be tolerated, in general. Obsessive-compulsive traits can be useful in cases that they help an individual to follow strict requirements and rules. Paranoid tendencies may not be seen as pronounced if most people share similar fears and concerns.
Individualism	Tolerance thresholds are relatively high. Individualist norms cultivate tolerance to independent behavior and a range of deviations from the norm. Many symptoms of personality disorders in their mild form could be accepted as signs of a person's unique individuality or the person's right to choose his own behavioral scripts. However, due to expectations that individualism is based on self-regulation and self-discipline, antisocial and borderline features may stand out and be rejected.
High-power distance	Tolerance thresholds are relatively high toward behavior that is in accordance with the power hierarchy. Narcissistic personality tendencies are tolerated in individuals of higher status. Antisocial traits are particularly resisted because they challenge the established order in relationships between older and younger family members, authority figures and lay people. Obsessive-compulsive traits can contribute to coping in interpersonal relationships because the person maintains the rules of subordination. Dependent personality traits are tolerated. Avoidant personality traits are likely to be tolerated. Schizoid personality traits are required for some social roles.
Low-power distance	Personality characteristics that are viewed antiegalitarian are not likely to be tolerated. Among these characteristics are narcissistic and dependent features for their association with the idea of personal subordination.
Traditionalism	Personality traits that are viewed as challenging the established order and tradition will likely be rejected. Therefore, there are very low tolerance thresholds toward histrionic and antisocial features. Other personality traits are evaluated based on the criterion of whether these traits help to maintain the existing traditional establishment.
Modernity	Traits that are not in line with the customs of openness, exchange of ideas, flexibility of customs, and individual freedom are likely to be resisted.

(Continued)

TABLE 9.3 Continued	
Cultural Variables	**Manifestations and Evaluations of Symptoms**
Specific social and cultural circumstances	Obsessive-compulsive and dependent personality traits are likely to be more appropriate in the context of social stability and less appropriate if a society is in transition. Antisocial personality traits can be useful as a means of self-preservation in especially difficult social conditions, such as rampant violence and lawlessness. Borderline personality traits can develop in extreme social circumstances. Narcissistic personality traits can develop within conditions of extreme social mobility, where individuals are able to achieve enormous success and wealth. Histrionic personality traits may be common in younger individuals from nontraditional settings. Paranoid personality traits are useful in dangerous situations, such as instances of social turmoil.

In a unique comparative study sponsored by the World Health Organization, Loranger and associates (1994) employed the help of 58 psychiatrists who interviewed 716 patients in 11 countries in North America, Europe, Africa, and Asia. A specially designed semistructured clinical interview was used (called International Personality Disorder Examination), which was compatible with evaluations used in the United States and in the *ICD-10*. The main result of the study was that personality disorders have relatively similar features that can be assessed with a reasonably high degree of reliability across different nations, languages, and cultures. Additional studies reveal similar outcomes, suggesting that certain symptoms can be diagnosed with a degree of consistency across different racial and national groups (Fountoulakis et al., 2002). Unfortunately, reliable comparative empirical evidence has been accumulated only for antisocial personality disorder (Murphy, 1976). Symptoms of this *personality* disorder can be recognized in all social and cultural groups (Robins et al., 1991). In particular, in the United States, individuals with symptoms of antisocial personality disorder are charged with a greater number and variety of criminal offenses than people without these symptoms, regardless of race (Cooke & Michie, 1999; Hare, 1991). However, at least at this stage of psychological research, there are many reasons to believe that personality disorders represent categories and symptoms that vary in a range of cultures.

Psychologists focus largely on two basic sets of assumptions related to the manifestation and diagnoses of these disorders. The first set includes hypothesis about specific culture-bound personality traits that are prevalent in some cultural groups and less prevalent in others. According to this view, similarities in coping strategies cause the development of similar traits in many individuals belonging to the same cultural group. As an example, conscientiousness and deeply seated habits of self-discipline, as some may argue, have been cultivated in the German culture for many years. Therefore, there should be many individuals raised in Germany who developed personality traits consistent with self-discipline and conscientiousness. Additionally, if a person is born outside Germany but raised there, this individual is likely to develop such traits. If this hypothesis is correct, there should be a higher statistical probability of the occurrence of the symptoms of obsessive-compulsive personality disorder. In other words, these symptoms should be found with a greater frequency in Germans than in people of other nations whose cultural conditions cultivate a set of different personality traits.

The second set embraces assumptions about the existence of specific social and cultural circumstances that determine our views serving as "filters" for evaluations of personality traits and personality disorders. Some traits can be seen as common and "standard" from a particular national or cultural standpoint, while they can be seen as excessive and even abnormal (if they fit specific criteria) from another cultural point of view. For instance, if a woman from a traditional culture does not go in public places often, prefers solitary activities at home, does not have close relationships with anyone outside her family, and appears "cold" or unemotional in conversations with a researcher, these characteristics should not be considered indicative of schizoid personality disorder. Her behavior should be judged from a broader cultural context, which contains specific gender scripts, or rules of behavior for men and women. Therefore, some symptoms of *DSM-IV* personality disorders could be valued as nonexcessive, nonpathological, and even normal in certain cultural settings. Thus, cultural sensitivity is essential when attempting to apply DSM-based diagnoses to individuals from different cultural environments.

The idea about the existence of culture-bound or specific "national" or "ethnic" personality traits was explored by many intellectuals of the past and present. From the times of the Greek philosopher Aristotle (fifth century B.C.E.) who claimed that the Greeks had a particular inclination to philosophy, while people of other nations develop skills, there were numerous written statements or even scientific theories about personality traits developed on entire peoples and cultural groups (Cooper, 2003). Little empirical evidence, of course, was produced to back up the theories espousing the existence of a distinct "Greek," "Babylonian," or any other collective personality. Even in more recent times, at the dawn of scientific psychology, there has been no shortage of such stereotypical theories about prevalence of specific personality traits in national or cultural groups. Most popular assumptions were established about the differences between European and Asian cultures. Karl Jung, for instance, believed in substantial differences between the Eastern and the Western types of individuals. The Western type is rooted in reason but little in intuition and emotion, which is more common in the Eastern type. The Western type is an extravert. To the contrary, the Eastern type is an introvert (Kleinman & Kleinman, 1991). While evaluating Chinese and European personality types, other authors focused their attention on the peasant roots of the Chinese civilization associated with pragmatism and down-to-earth considerations on one hand, and mercantilism of Europeans with their love of numbers and abstract theories on the other (Fung, 1948). Generalizations about personality traits appear in contemporary publications. Authors continue to make sweeping assumptions about fundamental cultural differences shaping different types of behavior in individuals who are brought up in different countries (Li, 2003; Mahbubani, 1999). Most of these assumptions—although intriguing—are not accompanied by strong empirical evidence or support. (See box "Critical Thinking.") It is very difficult to validate theories about the existence of "national" personality types and personality disorders for a host of reasons. The most substantial is that there is a tremendous diversity of personality traits within an ethnic or national group. Furthermore, studies show with consistency that the variation of characteristics within national samples is typically greater than the differences between any two national samples (Barrett & Eysenck, 1984; Zuckerman, 1990).

Certain personality traits may "flourish" in particular circumstances and be "suppressed" in others. Certain personality types can contribute to successful coping in a set of cultural conditions, while other personality types may interfere with an individual's successful coping. Take, for example, avoidant traits. In China, interpersonal relationships are largely based on a deep cultural tradition of exchange of favors, or, in Western terms, reciprocal relationships guided by moral norms. If a person believes that, under specific circumstances, she is not capable of exchanging favor with others, this could be an embarrassing blow to her reputation. Therefore, to save face, it is generally appropriate for such individuals to develop avoidant tendencies, because avoidance is perceived as less embarrassing than the inability to exercise appropriate social acts. Individuals from outside this social context may be inclined to perceive these behaviors as symptoms of avoidant personality disorder. Similarly, it is not uncommon for

CRITICAL THINKING
Stereotype-Based Anticipations Related to Personality Disorders

Even educated individuals are not free from making stereotypical assumptions about the psychological symptoms of other individuals (Funtowitz & Widiger, 1999). In one study, psychology students were asked to sort diagnostic characteristics of personality disorders by racial groups, according to the most common classification in the United States: white, black, Hispanic, and Native American. The results were quite surprising because psychology students were not expected to make judgments based on popular stereotypes. However, many students did in fact demonstrate such stereotypical judgments. Specifically, criteria for antisocial and paranoid personality disorders were assigned mostly to African Americans, criteria for schizoid personality disorders were mostly applied to Asian Americans, and criteria for schizotypal personality disorders were mostly applied to Native Americans. The study also revealed that five of the *DSM-IV* personality disorders were attributed mostly to whites and

practically none to Hispanics. You can see a sort of two-stepstereotyping: Some personality features are assigned to the racial groups and thus corresponding personality disorders are associated with the same racial groups (in the absence of empirical evidence to prove these assessments). The authors of this study used the term *pathologization*, which stands for assigning pathological characteristics to ordinary, nonpathological psychological phenomena (Iwamasa et al., 2000).

Could you find out about other personality traits ("labels") that are stereotypically assigned in folk theories (popular knowledge) to certain national or ethnic groups? To begin, think about your own cultural (either national, or ethnic, or religious) group. What kind of stereotypical judgments do you know exist about this group? Could you search for evidence about these judgments on the Web? Why do you think these stereotypical judgments exist? How do you think it will be possible to change them?

young adults from Greece to seek support (both emotional and financial) from their parents until the age of 30. However, a foreign observer may construe this as a form of dependent personality disorder (Fountoulakis et al., 2002).

Assumptions of the similar kind exist about obsessive-compulsive personality traits in Japan. As one Japanese expert in education put it, in Japanese society, many people are brought up to model themselves faithfully on "role models" or general behavioral standards. This environment creates conditions that stimulate people's preoccupation with discipline, formal rules, and procedures (Esaki, 2001). If these behavioral traits are taken out of cultural context, there could be a temptation to view them as symptoms of obsessive-compulsive personality disorder. However, within the Japanese context, to a certain degree, these personality traits are considered normal and mainstream.

IS SUBSTANCE ABUSE CULTURALLY BOUND?

There are cultural and national standards for substance use and abuse. There are also wide cultural variations in attitudes toward substance consumption, patterns of substance use, accessibility of substances, and prevalence of disorders related to substance (*DSM-IV*, p. 188) (Table 9.4). Marijuana is outlawed in most states of the United States, but is legal under certain conditions in Holland. The legal drinking age in the United States is 21. In contemporary Russia, however, it is 18, and the laws against selling alcohol to minors are not strictly enforced. You can buy wine in a student cafeteria in France, but this is impossible to do at UCLA or George Mason University. Smoking opium was legal in some Asian American communities at the turn of the century. Today, opium is an illegal substance.

TABLE 9.4 *DSM-IV* on Cultural Variations of Substance Abuse

Caffeine consumption varies across cultures with males drinking coffee more often than females. In European and other developed countries, the rates are 400 mg/day or more, whereas in the developing world the rate is approximately 50 mg/day. The cost of coffee may also be a factor contributing to consumption rates (p. 214). *Cannabis* (usually marijuana) is among the first drug of experimentation for all cultural groups in the United States (p. 219). Cocaine use affects all races, ethnic groups, and both sexes in the United States but is most commonly found in 18–30-year-olds (p. 228). Hallucinogens may be used as part of established religious practices. Inhalants are more commonly abused by the young from economically depressed areas (p. 241). The prevalence of smoking is decreasing among industrial nations, but increasing among developing countries. Prevalence of smoking is decreasing more rapidly among males than females (p. 246). Opioid dependence historically is more common in members of minority groups living in economically deprived areas in the United States. However, at the beginning of the twentieth century, opioid dependence has been seen more often among middle-class individuals (p. 254). Prescription drug abuse is more common in women, but the prevalence has many cultural variations, partly caused by different prescription practices around the world (p. 268).

Source: American Psychiatric Association (1994). Diagnostic and statistical manual of mental disorders(DSM-IV) (4th ed.). Washington, DC: APA.

Worldwide consumption of alcohol during the last decade was approximately 6 liters (1.6 gallons) of pure alcohol per person aged 15 years or older. Almost 30 percent of this consumption was homemade, illegally produced or sold (WHO, 2011b). There is no universal criterion that would distinguish normal from abnormal drinking. There is also heavy episodic drinking in 12 percent of drinkers. The highest consumption levels are not only in rich countries of the Northern Hemisphere but also in Argentina, Australia, and New Zealand. Medium consumption levels are in southern Africa and in the Americas. Low consumption levels are in the countries of North Africa and sub-Saharan Africa, the Eastern Mediterranean region, and southern Asia and the Indian Ocean (WHO, 2011b). Muslims, Hindus, and Mormons prohibit any alcohol consumption. In contrast, other religious groups accept occasional and moderate drinking. Europeans, although only 15 percent of the world population, consume about 50 percent of the alcohol on earth. The top consumers are Portugal and France. Their residents consume seven times as much as the lowest consumer, Israel (countries in which alcohol is outlawed, such as Saudi Arabia, were not included in the analysis). The United States is in the middle of the list. In most Asian countries (except Korea), the overall prevalence of alcohol-related disorders is relatively low, and the male–female ratio is very high. Various East Asian populations have a sort of "protective mechanism" against alcohol abuse. It was found that approximately 50 percent of Korean, Japanese, and Chinese individuals lack a particular chemical in their blood, *aldehyde dehydrogenase*, that eliminates the first breakdown product of alcohol. When such individuals consume alcohol, they experience a flushed face and palpitations. Therefore, they are not as likely to consume large amounts of the substance. Cultural norms and peer pressure could change behavioral patterns, though. When Asian youth immigrate to the United States, they tend to drink more than their peers who live in their home countries (Halonen & Santrock, 1995).

Some researchers refer to biological factors that cause differences in addictive behavior in certain cultural groups. For example, the *Journal of the American Medical Association* reported that cells of blacks who smoke absorb more nicotine than do cells of white or Hispanic smokers. This difference, as experts suggest, could explain why blacks tend to suffer more from tobacco-related diseases—lung cancer, for example—and have more trouble quitting the habit (Schwartz, 1998).

A CASE IN POINT

Hikikomori is a complex form of withdrawal behavior, observed in Japan, that resembles the symptoms of schizoid personality disorder. This behavioral pattern has become the subject of worldwide attention and the topic of numerous television documentaries and newspaper and magazine articles (Rees, 2002). According to a government survey, approximately 1 million people in Japan choose to live for a long time in relative isolation (Tolbert, 2002). These individuals, typically male, shut themselves in the homes of their parents, seldom go out, and have very limited face-to-face contact with other people. They spend their days browsing the Web or chatting online and only occasionally see their parents, who continue to support their adult children financially. Economic and social conditions of contemporary Japan may contribute to this form of self-isolation. Young individuals lose the incentive for hard work and abandon ambitions, partly because the society in which they live guarantees a certain level of well-being. In addition, electronic communication and computer games give these shut-ins a chance to interact with others without face-to-face contact. Studies suggest that this phenomenon is growing in other countries, too (Sax, 2007). But do these people display symptoms of schizoid personality disorder? Again, you analyze the symptoms within the cultural context in which they appear. For a professional, who tends to base his or her evaluations on the existing culture-bound model of a "normal" personality (someone who is outgoing, balanced, and ambitious), many cases of the shut-ins would likely be linked to schizoid personality traits. However, if the standard for normality were to change, a different type of evaluation ought to follow. One important observation: The Japanese survey mentioned earlier did not find any evidence that the shut-ins displayed a higher prevalence of any psychological disorders compared to the general population.

Alcohol-related disorders are associated with lower educational levels, lower socioeconomic status, and higher rates of unemployment. However, it is difficult to say what is cause and what is effect. For example, people who drop out from either high school or college have particularly high rates of alcohol-related disorders (*DSM-IV*, p. 201). Does the individual develop a substance-related problem because he dropped out of school or did this person drop out from school because of the substance-related problem?

PSYCHODIAGNOSTIC BIASES

The cultural background of the professional can influence his perception of different behaviors. Psychologists are likely to have their own perceptions and attributions about the links among culture, ethnicity, and mental illness (Lopez, 1989). It is also known that doctors can misdiagnose particular diseases due to cross-cultural differences in the perception and expression of signs of illness. Psychological findings in North America may not be automatically generalized to the rest of the world (Arnett, 2008). Individuals often hold multiple interacting national, ethnic, and religious memberships, not just one (Hays, 2001). Not all people from a predominantly collectivist culture such as China or India share its norms. Likewise, not all Americans are supposed to embrace individualism and low power distance (Kitayama et al., 2010).

As another illustration of the diagnostic bias in the clinical setting, consider how therapist's beliefs and expectations may predispose them to "see" psychopathology wherever they look.

A CASE IN POINT
Some Smoking Patterns

Worldwide, approximately 1.4 billion people (1 billion of them men) currently smoke cigarettes or other tobacco products. Tobacco use continues to be the leading global cause of preventable death killing approximately 6 million people each year (WHO, 2001a). Globally, the prevalence of tobacco use is substantially higher in men (47 percent) than in women (12 percent), but significantly increasing smoking rates among women in the past 10 years were noted in Cambodia, Malaysia, and Bangladesh. Female smoking prevalence is actually higher than male smoking prevalence in the Cook Islands, Nauru, Norway, Papua New Guinea, and Sweden, thanks largely to aggressive tobacco industry marketing of cigarettes to women. In the 2000s, more smokers lived in low- and middle-income countries (933 million) than in high-income countries (209 million). About 35 percent of men in developed countries smoke, compared to almost 50 percent of men in developing nations and almost two-thirds of men in China. Currently, more than 600,000 annual smoking-attributable deaths occur in China alone. If current smoking patterns continue, deaths from smoking in Asia—home to one-third of the world's population—are expected to increase to 4.9 million per year by 2020 despite the tougher antismoking policies (Shafey et al., 2003).

Suppose you were to ask a therapist to explain the meaning of behaviors that clients might exhibit on arriving for their scheduled therapy session. Let us imagine further that this therapist happens to view the world through a densely filtered cultural schema of psychopathology. The therapist thus calmly and confidently offers you the following interpretations:

If the patient arrives early for his appointment, then he's anxious. If he arrives late, then he's hostile. And if he's on time, then he's compulsive.

This witticism about psychoanalysis dates back to the 1930s. Although originally intended as a joke, it was far more prophetic than most people at that time could have anticipated. It is not just a humorous illustration of "noncritical" thinking; it is also a revealing and sobering parable that alerts us to the dangers inherent in maintaining schemas that allow—and even encourage—virtually any human behavior to be subsumed under one or another of pathological categories (Levy, 2010).

As we suggested earlier, some specialists are skeptical about the applicability of Western diagnostic criteria in other cultures and vice versa. They insist that distress is experienced and manifested in many culture-specific ways. Different cultures may either encourage or discourage the reporting of psychological or physiological components of the stress response (Draguns, 1996). In some traditional cultures, persistent nightmares are often viewed as a spiritual and supernatural phenomenon, whereas others observe nightmares as indicators of mental or physical disturbance (*DSM-IV*, p. 581).

Some existing culture-specific disorders are difficult to interpret in terms of other national classifications. A neurological weakness, typically diagnosed in China, includes symptoms of weakness, fatigue, tiredness, headaches, and gastrointestinal complaints (Tung, 1994). The Western diagnostic assessments of patients with this disorder varied with different diagnostic procedures employed. It could be anxiety disorder, depressive disorder, or bipolar disorder (Kleinman, 1986).

Some symptoms, however, can be consistent across different national samples. A study in Russia conducted by V. Ruchkin, D. Sukhodolsky, and colleagues (2007) showed that prevalence rates of attention deficit/hyperactivity disorder were similar to those of many other countries. Recent studies on culture-specific disorders suggest that different cultures have specific labels for behavioral disorders. Culture-bound syndromes challenge any universal categorization because of the culturally specific content of the disorders (Tanaka-Matsumi & Draguns, 1997). But no matter how you describe a problem, it would manifest as a maladaptive and distressful symptom, as inability to cope with stressful situations. The key to success in diagnostic practices is to identify distress and maladaptive symptoms correctly and in their cultural context.

> Much unhappiness has come into the world because of bewilderment and things left unsaid. The greatest happiness is to know the source of unhappiness.
>
> *FYODOR DOSTOYEVSKY* **(1821–1881)—Russian Novelist**

PSYCHOTHERAPY

If different cultural settings can affect diagnostic practices, one can assume that culture may also play a significant role in **psychotherapy**, which is the treatment of psychological disorders through psychological means, generally involving verbal interaction with a professional therapist. Research cases show, for example, that many drug rehabilitation and prevention programs designed for one particular ethnic and social category (white middle-class subjects) are applicable to other ethnic and social categories. In tolerant and supportive cultures (as well as in supportive communities and families), individuals with mental disorders may function better than those in less-tolerant surroundings. In Japan, depressed patients could rely on other people to make decisions for them. In U.S. culture, depressed patients rely more on individual decision making and therefore are more avoidant and show lower self-esteem than Japanese patients (Radford et al., 1991). It was also shown in a World Health Organization study (1979) that patients from collectivist cultures had a better prognosis for schizophrenia, whereas patients from individualist cultures showed fewer signs of improvement (Tanaka-Matsumi & Draguns, 1997).

A CASE IN POINT
Openness and Psychotherapy

The twenty-first century brought rapid changes to many countries' attitudes toward mental illness and psychotherapy. In China, for example, rising wealth and growing complexity of life have produced a stressful environment of competition and uncertainty, to which many people have difficulty adjusting. People in China will inevitably face more stressful problems than those faced two or three decades ago. The society is becoming more open, and stigma attached with mental illness and psychotherapy is gradually disappearing. More people see psychological problems as conditions that they should not be ashamed of. Scores of young psychologists graduate from Chinese universities. They travel globally and earn their advanced degrees in the North America and Europe. Psychoanalysis, behavioral, and cognitive therapies attract significant attention. Over this decade, Chinese psychologists will be answering studying a very important question: Do western therapies work in China?

Studies show that Mexican Americans are significantly less likely to use outpatient mental help than other ethnic groups. Asian Americans also seek disproportionately fewer treatment services and are more likely to be severely ill at point of receiving help (Hwang, 2006).

African Americans and Native Americans appear to use outpatient mental health services at higher rates than whites. Some studies have found that ethnic minority patients have a tendency to drop out of treatment before it can be effective more frequently than whites. Many factors can contribute to the above tendency, for example, whether those providing mental health services are themselves members of an ethnic minority group, fluent in the language of their patients, or aware of culturally specific therapeutic procedures. However, the differences in the dropout rates among various ethnic groups do not appear to be statistically significant.

Many psychologists today argue that professionals could use religion as a factor facilitating psychotherapy. A person turning to God for strength and hope is, in fact, looking for inner resources that help at times of adversity and pain. Therapeutic interventions involving spiritual healing are gaining popularity. Studies show, for example, that for African Americans, the sense of spiritual connectedness and wholeness helps to improve quality of life by influencing the way that individuals cope with adversity. Individuals higher in spirituality have greater inner resources that facilitate adaptive coping and positive health outcomes. Overall, the current findings are consistent with the extensive literature indicating that spirituality has historically been an important mechanism by which African Americans manage adverse life circumstances (Utsey et al., 2007). Native Americans, compared to other groups, have stronger beliefs in the healing nature of traditional practices (frequently based on folk beliefs) even when they seek professional health services. For example, one study has found that about 40 percent of American Indian adolescents and adults with a lifetime history of depressive or anxiety disorders sought services from a mental health professional, but almost 50 percent also sought help from a traditional healer (Beals et al., 2005). More studies are necessary to verify the effectiveness of spiritual treatment as well as the use of traditional healing techniques. We don't know yet if, for example, the principles of therapeutic relaxation used in Western countries could be effectively combined with Chinese folk traditions and meditative practices of breathing, exercising, relaxing, and so on and used with clients of Asian origin. Would, for example, Japanese immigrants in North America who are experiencing headaches and bodily pains benefit from receiving a shiatsu massage and Zen meditation (Hwang, 2006)? There should be empirical studies verifying the effectiveness of traditional Buddhist methods of anxiety reduction through mental training and introspection (Ricard, 2006; Wallace and Shapiro, 2006). Treatment practices combining traditional Islamic and modern psychological methods also need careful studies in many countries (Penny et al., 2009). Some studies show the importance of the immigrant community in prevention of psychological problems; but more studies are necessary (Lim et al., 2011).

The stigma of mental illness continues to be a major obstacle preventing many individuals from seeking professional help. Shame of mental illness may facilitate the development of so-called repressive adaptive style rooted in an individual's desire to hide the symptoms (e.g., elevated anxiety and depressive symptoms that are actually present) and prove that he or she is fine and healthy. Several studies (Steele et al., 2003) reported a higher prevalence of repressors among children with a serious illness than among healthy children. Psychologists also report that people in collectivist cultures are more likely to display repressive adaptive style than people from other groups. This was shown, for example, in an interesting study of European American, Mexican American, and Mexican children (Varela et al., 2007). Probably, because collectivism rewards behavior that brings positive outcomes to a group or community, individuals learn to hide some of their distressful symptoms so that they will not attract unnecessary attention to

A CASE IN POINT

Cross-cultural Sensitivity

Clinicians point out that many Asian and Asian American patients undergoing psychotherapy tend to observe the social etiquette of formal hierarchical expectations of age and gender in which they are supposed to show deference, respect, and agreement with the superior and keep most disagreements and negative feelings to themselves (Roland, 2006). Immigrant Asian clients, for example, may often see the therapist as an expert authority figure who can help them solve their problems (Hwang, 2006). These observations are interesting but lack empirical support. How many clients do express this attitude toward therapists? What are the specific circumstances under which such observations were made? Without reliable empirical facts, even the most prolific observations about a client's behavior may feed ethnic stereotypes and misconceptions (Whaley & Davis, 2007). Imagine, your next client is an Asian American woman. Would you undoubtedly expect that she sees you as an "authority figure" and uncritically accepts every word of wisdom that you convey to her?

themselves. In fact, this assumption is probably consistent with the fact that Latin American children tend to manifest many of their emotional problems through somatic symptoms such as pains, aches, and other forms of physical discomfort (Canino, 2004). Complaining about abdominal pain looks more appropriate than acknowledging one's own panic attacks. However, these assumptions need further studies. It is also probable that cultural traditionalism is a serious factor preventing millions of people around the world from acknowledging their abnormal psychological symptoms without fear of being considered "sick" or "crazy."

CULTURE MATCH?

Many factors can affect therapists' diagnostic judgments. Among these factors is the cultural background of both the therapist and the client. We should always keep in mind that every therapist is not destined to make erroneous decisions about her client of a different cultural background. However, the mistakes are made, and there are at least two reasons for possible misjudgments. First, some clinicians may not understand the cultural backgrounds of their clients and therefore may misinterpret their responses. Moreover, some clients express their thoughts and emotions according to the common rules in their culture. Second, knowledge of certain cultural trends may be lacking critical thinking emphasis and thus distort diagnosis. Stereotypes and schemas create expectations about the "typical" symptoms of particular ethnic groups.

Scores of research studies have concluded that schemas greatly influence what we perceive and the manner in which we perceive it (see, e.g., Bruner & Potter, 1964; Kelley, 1950; Reason & Mycielska, 1982; Vokey & Read, 1985). For instance, Li-Repac (1980) investigated the effect of sociocultural differences between therapists and clients on clinical impressions, perceptions, and judgments. In her study, a sample consisting of white therapists and Chinese American therapists assessed a series of videotaped clinical interviews. The therapists were told that they would be evaluating both white and Chinese clients. They were not, however, informed of the experiment's true purpose, namely, to compare therapists' clinical perceptions as a function of their own ethnicity.

CRITICAL THINKING

Imagine a psychotherapist tells you that "Most every ethnic minority patient I've treated has dropped out of therapy prematurely." What are some possible explanations for this correlation? Can you propose that ethnicity is the factor affecting the patients' commitment? Remember that correlation does not necessarily prove causation. Could you suggest some other factors?

1. _____
2. _____
3. _____

Suppose you read an article reporting an inverse correlation between religiosity and depression (i.e., the less religious, the more depressed). What factors could account for this relationship?

1. _____
2. _____
3. _____

Results showed that although both groups of therapists agreed in their general conceptions of psychological "normality," they differed significantly in their actual assessments of the same clients. Specifically, in comparison to the Chinese American therapists, the white therapists viewed the Chinese clients as more depressed and inhibited and as possessing less social poise and interpersonal capacity. Conversely, Chinese American therapists judged the white clients to be more severely disturbed than did the white therapists. These findings may demonstrate that "cultural stereotyping is a two-way street" (Li-Repac, 1980, p. 339).

As evidenced in this experiment, the impact of culture on diagnosis of mental disorders can be profound. In essence, each group of therapists had filtered (i.e., assimilated) the clients' behavior through their respective sociocultural schemas, and, as a consequence, arrived at strikingly different judgments. The underlying principle here again becomes manifest: More than believing what we see, we tend to see what we believe.

Ethnic match, that is, a situation where the psychotherapist and his client belong to the same ethnic group, may determine several developments. For instance, if the therapist and the client are "matched," it is a meaningful predictor of the duration of psychotherapy (Sue et al., 1991). African Americans with depressive symptoms tend to be misdiagnosed with schizophrenia if they are evaluated by nonblack professionals. In general, matched therapists judge clients to have higher psychological functioning than do mismatched therapists. This means that ethnically matched therapists see less pathology in their clients than therapists from a different culture. Overall, although there is a common view that "matching" counselors or psychotherapists are more culturally competent in working with ethnic groups than their white American counterparts, recent studies suggest that such a view does not have strong empirical support (Karlsson, 2005). More studies will be necessary.

These results can be interpreted in several ways. It appears that an ethnic match between a patient and a therapist reduces diagnostic mistakes. So far, so good, but should we then always match patients and therapists? Not until we first consider the finding that ethnically matched professionals may not see some significant symptoms in their clients, thus underdiagnosing them (Russell et al., 1996).

Another potential factor that may affect therapy is the counselor's accent. If she speaks English (or French, German, Spanish, etc.) with an accent, it is not clear yet if it is helpful or not in terms of the therapy's effectiveness (Fuertes et al., 2002). Some clients may develop a

A CASE IN POINT

Arab Americans and Treatment of Psychological Disorders

Some Arab Americans resist seeking psychological treatment, in part because of a general skepticism about therapists and in part because they hold negative attitudes about mental illness in general. Clients may have strong fears about being branded *majnun*, or crazy. Another factor contributing to Arab Americans' reluctance to seek mental health services is a lack of experience with or exposure to contemporary counseling approaches. When an Arab person develops a psychological problem, he seeks out the help of a family member of the same gender. Talking about family or personal problems with a professional may be seen as a threat to group honor or as being disloyal to the family. Many patients (and especially immigrants of the Arab descent) with significant needs for psychotherapeutic services often resist referrals to mental health counselors or therapists. Encouragement about a client's mental stability and the confidential nature of the counseling relationship should help clients feel more comfortable in making the most of mental health services.

Sources: Abudabbeh (1996); Erickson and Al-Timimi (2001); Jackson (1997); Nassar-McMillan, S. and Hakim-Larson, J. (2003).

---

sense of "solidarity" with the therapist because he will be seen as a member of the same group (particular ethnic or general immigrant group), whereas others may devaluate this therapist's status and competence.

Components of cognitive and behavioral therapies frequently require some linguistic adaptations so that instructions and explanations provided by therapists become more relevant to people's experiences. For example, Muñoz and Mendelson (2005) gave the culturally relevant example from Latino culture of using the saying *la gota de agua labra la piedra*(which means, a drop of water carves a rock) to illustrate how an individual's thoughts can gradually influence one's view of life and contribute to depression.

Different countries have different laws and rules regarding the hospitalization of mental patients. In most totalitarian societies (such as Nazi Germany in the 1930s and the Soviet Union prior to 1991), it was the state's prerogative to decide whether a person should be hospitalized. In the history of the twentieth century, psychiatry has been used countless times for political and ideological purposes. In U.S. society today, only those who show signs of imminent danger to themselves or others may be held in mental facilities against their will. In many other countries, the rules required for hospitalization are not as strict as in the United States. But in general, studies indicate that mental health specialists show substantial agreement among themselves as to which patients should be considered dangerous, suicidal, or unable to testify or take care of themselves (Swenson, 1993).

All in all, the context of therapy should be consistent with the client's culture (Bemak & Chung, 2004; Tanaka-Matsumi, 1989). For example, Kleinman (1978) offered a framework for successful patient–therapist interactions. At the beginning, the therapist asks clients to give their interpretation of the existing problem. Then the therapist offers her explanation of the problem. Then both types of explanations are compared. Finally, both therapist and clients come up with a joint explanatory concept, so that they communicate in the same language and can discuss therapy and its potential outcome.

Snacken (1991) described three desirable types of therapy between the specialist and the patient who represent different cultures. *Intercultural* therapy includes a professional who knows the language and culture of the client (he could belong to this cultural group). *Bicultural* therapy includes two types of healers: both the Western and the native who work together. *Polycultural* therapy involves the patient's meetings with several therapists who represent different cultures.

Exercise 9.1

Here is a list of some culture-bound psychological problems. Using *DSM-IV*, please find analogies in the U.S. classification of mental disorders to each of the syndromes below. Write down and critically examine your findings.

- Possession (in some African countries) is a belief that one's body has been taken over by a spirit, which leads to profound behavioral manifestations and experiences.
- *Koro* (in China) is a severe anxiety based on the assumption that the penis is retracting; this fear leads to another belief of inevitable death.
- *Latah* is a syndrome known in some Asian and African countries that is marked by altered states of consciousness, including exaggerated obedience and impulsivity.
- *Malgri* is a severe abdominal pain that is believed to be caused by entering forbidden territory without purification rituals.
- Nuptial psychosis occurs among very young women in India whose lives are disrupted by arranged marriages. Sexual trauma, separation from the family, and stress contribute to symptoms of confusion, hysteria, and suicidal intentions.
- Kayak angst is an extreme anxiety, known among the Eskimos of Western Greenland. This anxiety strikes after hours of solitary hunting in unfavorable environments.

Chapter Summary

- Two perspectives on psychological disorders and culture—relativist and universalist—have been developed in cross-cultural psychology. The relativist perspective on psychopathology puts psychological phenomena in a relative perspective and pays attention to unique cultural context of psychological disorders. According to the universalist perspective on psychopathology, there are absolute, invariable symptoms of psychopathology across cultures.
- Attempting to diagnose and treat an individual, the professional should know the client's reference groups and the ways in which cultural context is relevant to clinical care, including psychotherapy. In particular, the specialist should pay attention to the following: (1) the cultural identity of the individual, that is, his or her ethnic, religious, and other cultural reference groups; (2) the cultural explanations of the individual's illness; (3) the cultural interpretations of social stressors and social supports, such as religion, level of functioning, and disability; and (4) the cultural elements of the relationship between the individual and the clinician.
- American clinicians use a special diagnostic manual (*DSM-IV*) to diagnose mental disorders. Clinicians usually assess information available to them about the individual from the standpoint of five axes, each of which helps professionals to examine the situation from five different viewpoints or domains of information. There are disorders that may or may not be linked to a particular

DSM-IV diagnostic category. These are recurrent, locally specific patterns of aberrant behavior and troubling experiences that are called culture-bound syndromes. They are generally limited to specific societies or areas and indicate repetitive and troubling sets of experiences and observations.

- Cultural norms, availability of resources, national standards on health, access to technology, social inequality, and many other environmental factors could affect the individual's health and general well-being.

- Despite general similar occurrence rates, there are some cultural variations in how schizophrenia is viewed, diagnosed, and treated. There are some substantial ethnic variations in the expression of depression, which are also based on various individual differences, socialization experiences, cultural definitions of disorders, and stress. There is empirical evidence concerning the links between suicide and religiosity, age, sex, nationality, substance use, and various cultural traditions. There are substantial cultural variations in the expression of anxiety that range from somatic to cognitive to behavioral symptoms. Differences in diagnostic practices account in some way for cross-cultural differences in reported symptoms and could explain great cross-cultural variability for anxiety disorders. It is suggested that personality disorders should be viewed, diagnosed, and treated in the context of each culture's norms and thresholds of tolerance for a particular behavior. There are cultural and national standards for substance use and substance abuse. There are also wide cultural variations in attitudes toward substance consumption, patterns of substance use, accessibility of substances, and prevalence of disorders related to substance use.

- The cultural background of the professional can influence his or her perception of different behaviors. Psychologists are likely to have their own perceptions and attributions about the links of culture, ethnicity, and mental illness. It is also known that doctors can misdiagnose particular diseases due to cross-cultural differences in the perception, attribution, and expression of signs of disease. Psychotherapy across countries has different historical and cultural roots and varied cultural expressions. Different countries have different laws and rules regarding the hospitalization of mental patients. General psychological and cultural factors may affect the cross-cultural relationship between the professional and his or her client. Different ethnic groups could have various attitude patterns about mental health services. In general, the context of therapy should be consistent with the client's culture to achieve the goal of cultural accommodation.

Key Terms

Anxiety Disorders A category of mental disorders characterized by persistent anxiety or fears.

Central Symptoms Symptoms of mental disorders observable in practically all cultures.

Culture-Bound Syndromes Recurrent, locally specific patterns of aberrant behavior and troubling experience that may or may not be linked to a particular *DSM-IV* diagnostic category. Culture-bound syndromes are generally limited to specific societies or areas and indicate repetitive and troubling sets of experiences and observations.

Depressive Disorder A category of psychological disorders characterized by a profound and persistent feeling of sadness or despair, guilt, loss of interest in things that were once pleasurable, and disturbance in sleep and appetite.

Melancholy The most common label used in many countries in the past for symptoms known today as depression (often spelled *melancholia*).

Mental Disorder A clinically significant behavioral and psychological syndrome or pattern that occurs in an individual and that is associated with present distress (a painful syndrome) or disability (impairment in one or more important areas of functioning) or with a significantly increased risk of suffering death, pain, disability, or an important loss of freedom.

Peripheral Symptoms Symptoms of mental disorders that are culture specific.

Personality Disorders Enduring patterns of behavior and inner experience that deviate markedly from the expectations of the individual's culture.

Psychotherapy The treatment of psychological disorders through psychological means, generally involving verbal interaction with a professional therapist.

Relativist Perspective A view of psychological disorders, according to which human beings develop ideas, establish behavioral norms, and learn emotional responses according to a set of cultural prescriptions. Therefore, people from different cultural settings should understand psychological disorders differently, and the differences should be significant.

Schizophrenia A disorder characterized by the presence of delusions, hallucinations, disorganized speech, and disorganized or catatonic behavior.

Tolerance Threshold A measure of tolerance or intolerance toward specific personality traits in a specific cultural environment.

Universalist Perspective A view of psychological disorders, according to which people, despite cultural differences, share a great number of similar features, including attitudes, values, and behavioral responses. Therefore, the overall understanding of psychological disorders ought to be universal.

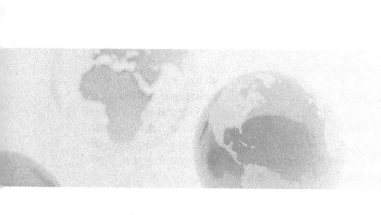

Social Perception
and Social Cognition

Freedom and slavery are mental states.

MOHANDAS GANDHI (1869–1948)—
Indian Spiritual Leader

Don't find fault in what you don't understand.

FRENCH PROVERB

D o people pay too much attention to symbols? At a soccer match in Great Britain, fans of the Scottish soccer club the Rangers (who are largely Protestant) jeered during a moment of silence meant to commemorate the death of Pope John Paul II. As a result, the tribute was cut short. The Celtics, the Ranger's rivals, have predominantly Catholic fans who expressed their disappointment and anger over the incident. Why? Because symbols have meanings and they are different for different people who associate themselves with different groups. Indeed, a burning flag for some people is an act of disgrace; for others it is just a piece of cloth on fire. It is appropriate to call somebody "white" in America but "whitee" would be offensive to some. An extended middle finger is an obscene gesture barred from U.S. public television. Meanwhile, a villager in Siberia would not understand this gesture. We interpret and explain people and events using our own emotions and values filtered through our individual and cultural experiences. People create meanings of reality in their perception and then change reality using the power of their perceptions. If you disagree, this means you see things differently than do the authors of this textbook. "There is no good and bad; our thinking makes it so," wrote Shakespeare. Was he right?

The process through which we try to understand other people and ourselves is called **social perception**. It is an established view in psychology that people acquire judgments, attitudes, and beliefs through socialization experiences from their cultural milieu. If perception is influenced by experience, then there should be commonalities and differences in social perception. People who grow up in similar environments may learn to interpret many elements of this environment in a similar way. People who were exposed to different stimuli are likely to see the world from divergent perspectives. Despite differences in educational systems, studies show that people tend to see some global events similarly: The world wars, especially World War II, and Hitler continued to be considered across cultures as the most important events and figure, respectively, in world history (Liu et al., 2009).

In short, the way we see things changes according to our experience with them (Matsumoto, 1994). The experiences of two individuals are not alike. For instance, eyewitnesses to criminal events are typically inaccurate in what they report. But when the witness belongs to a different ethnic group than the suspect, inaccuracies tend to increase (Platz & Hosch, 1988).

The process of social perception contributes to the means of thinking about the world. **Social cognition** is the process through which we interpret, remember, and then use information about the world and ourselves. In general, social cognition tends to be conservative (Aronson, 1995). We retain our past experiences and use them to make today's judgments. For instance, until recently, despite great medical advancements, organ transplantation was unacceptable to many patients in Japan because of particular ancient religious interpretations about the unity of the body and soul (see Chapter 12). Ethnic groups engaged in a conflict against one another see the cause of their hostility differently, each from the biased lenses of centuries-old negative stereotypes of the other.

We begin a cross-cultural analysis of social perception and cognition with an examination of attitudes and values. Then we explore how people balance their attitudes and whether consistency in attitudes is a universal trend. Next, the chapter analyzes how people explain the behavior of others and how they view justice, success, and failure. Finally, moral values, self-perception, and popular stereotypes are contemplated.

Three Spaniards, four opinions.

Spanish Proverb

VALUES

Attitudes also tend to change. For example, Rehza disliked baseball when he arrived in the United States from Iran. Above all other sports, he liked soccer, the game he played growing up in Tabriz. Things change. A few years later, Rehza became a fan of baseball and even began to attend the Dodgers games in Los Angeles. Does Rehza's opinion of baseball help us judge what type of a person he is? The likely answer is "no." An emotional attachment to the game is not typically considered a strong indicator of anything significant in a person's character. However, there are other attitudes that represent Rehza's most important views on life. Such views are called values.

Values are attitudes that reflect a principle, standard, or quality considered by the individual as the most desirable or appropriate. Values are stable and enduring views that a specific behavior (often called instrumental value) or goal (called terminal value) is preferred to another behavior or goal. Evolutionary psychologists suggest that values allow human groups to adjust better to their environments. They become embedded in cultures and passed on to new genera-tions (Confer et al., 2010).

Terminal values usually refer to social and personal concerns, whereas instrumental values designate morality and competency issues. Values generally hold a more central position than attitudes and therefore lead individuals to form particular views on a variety of issues (Rokeach, 1973). It is likely, for example, that an Indian woman in the United States would not eat a beef sandwich served to her at a friend's party because abstinence from beef (a Hindu value) is stronger than "being polite" to the host (an attitude). Likewise, an Italian autoworker strongly attached to the value of equality is likely to support (an attitude) government actions aimed at helping people from neighboring Yugoslavia (Shiraev, 2000). A study in Hong Kong showed that values of cultural solidarity are reflected in people's positive perceptions of their country's historical figures and that perception was positive and strong (Ho-Ying Fu & Chi-Yue, 2007).

Are there noticeable national or cultural differences in values? Do people around the world share the same values? If they do, what are these values? Or if there are cultural differences, do we know what values are most important? Hofstede (1980, 1991) conducted a remarkable international study of 117,000 people employed by IBM in 50 nations. To simplify the analysis, he divided the countries studied into eleven clusters: Nordic, Anglo (including the United States), Germanic, Near Eastern, developing Asian, developing Latin, developed Latin, and Japan as a separate developed Asian country. He described the following cultural dimensions that reflect four major ways people cope with their most important problems: (1) individualism and collectivism, (2) power distance, (3) masculinity and femininity, and (4) uncertainty avoidance (see Chapter 1 for a description of most of these features).

The investigator described each of the national clusters studied. The Nordic and Anglo samples demonstrated values low on power distance, high on individualism, and low on uncertainty avoidance. The Anglo group was high on masculinity (power and risk-taking), but the German group was low on masculinity. The less developed Asian countries and the Near Eastern bloc were both high in power distance and low in individualism. But the most remarkable comparison was made between the Anglo and Nordic cultures on the one hand and Near Eastern and less-developed Asian countries on the other. The Anglo and Nordic groups were low on power distance and high on individualism. This pattern was called *individualist.* The opposite pattern—high-power distance and low individualism—common for non-Western countries, was labeled *collectivist.*

In another study, Schwartz (Smith & Schwartz, 1997) argued about cultural differences in individual values. He suggested individual values as being connected to the way various groups cope with basic societal problems. Three basic issues make various social groups different from one another: (1) the extent to which people are independent of or dependent on groups; (2) their views on prosperity and profit; and (3) their views on whether it is appropriate to exploit, fit in, or submit to the outside world. An analysis of people's responses revealed their basic views dis-tributed between two opposite ends of the spectrum of human values (Lee et al., 2011; Schwartz et al., 2001).

Type 1. Conservatism vs. Autonomy. The conservative views are shared by individu-als who believe in the status quo, advocate self-discipline, and care about family, social order, and tradition. Those who share values of autonomy emphasize the right of individu-als to pursue their own ideals and to enjoy the variety of life for the sake of pleasure and excitement.

Type 2. Hierarchy vs. Egalitarianism. If a person supports the hierarchy values, he jus-tifies the legitimacy of an unequal distribution of power, resources, and social roles. If a person has egalitarian values, she sees individuals as equals, who share basic interests and should be treated equally as human beings.

Type 3. Mastery vs. Harmony. Mastery values encourage individuals to exercise control over society and exploit its natural resources. Ambition and high self-esteem are important individual traits that accompany mastery values. Harmony values are based on assumptions that the world should be kept as is: preserved and cherished rather than violated and exploited.

Schwartz's study included 40 countries, which were divided into several groups: West European, Anglo (including the United States), East European, Islamic, East Asian, Japan (as a single country), and Latin American. East Asian nations were especially high on hierarchy and conservatism and low on egalitarianism and autonomy. West European participants showed the opposite trend. The Anglo profile fell somewhere in between the West European and East Asian samples. One interesting finding was the established correlation between the size of the household and the values of conservatism and hierarchy. Values such as order, discipline, and compliance were promoted more often in large families living under one roof than in smaller family units. Cultures high on hierarchy (and low on egalitarianism) tend to emphasize power and status differences among people. Cultures low on hierarchy (and high on egalitarianism) tend to minimize such differences and attempt to distribute resources more equally. Power distance is positively correlated with hierarchy and negatively correlated with egalitarianism on the national level (Schwartz, 2004, 2007). Studies also showed that the more a nation prioritized egalitarianism versus hierarchy values and harmony versus mastery values, (a) the higher was children's well-being, (b) the more generous was maternal leave, (c) the less advertising was directed at children, and (d) the less CO_2 the nation emitted (Kasser, 2011).

Predominant cultural values that have been developed in a community or country, of course, can determine people's views on a wide range of social, political, and personal issues. Take, for example, a psychological construct such as honor, which in the English language typically stands for high respect, good name, or reputation. The results collected by Mosquera and colleagues (2002) indicated that people in Spain and the Netherlands tended to understand honor in different ways. Notions of honor in Spain were closely related to the values associated with family and social interdependence. In the Netherlands, to the contrary, honor was typically associated with values of self-achievement and autonomy.

Cultural values tend to change slowly under the influence of economic, political, demographic, and even climatic conditions of societies (Schwartz, 2011).

WESTERN AND NON-WESTERN VALUES

For many years now, journalists, political scientists, sociologists, and psychologists have discussed the differences between two major cultural clusters of attitudes called Western and non-Western values. According to a philosophical tradition developed by Weber, the most fundamental values of Western civilization are work, achievement, striving for efficiency, and consumption of material goods. It is then argued that in non-Western civilizations, these values are somewhat important but not considered critical. The essence of non-Western values is respect for tradition, reverence to authority, and overall stability.

There are also other areas of contraposition between Western and non-Western values. Two of the most frequently mentioned are Western individualism and non-Western collectivism.

The value of individualism was not as salient in the non-Western developing nations as it was in more economically developed Western countries (Hofstede, 1980). For example, individualistic values were found to be stronger in Western countries, such as the United States, Germany, and Sweden, than they were in Taiwan, Japan, and India (Segall et al., 1990). The value of competition was reportedly higher in urban, industrial areas than in rural regions (Munroe & Munroe, 1997). However, the differences may diminish due to the ongoing global social and economic changes.

It is commonly stated in the media that Western values are linked to economic prosperity and democratic attitudes. Therefore, these values are important to all countries. An opposite view that challenges the universal importance of Western values appeared and gained strength (see discussion in Chapter 7 on motivation). It was argued that the pursuit of Western values does not produce a climate of social satisfaction. The most fundamental Western values are no longer adaptive because they have outlived their historical usefulness (Clark, 1995). In particular, assumptions such as:

- the nature of human beings is selfish (Freud and Marx),
- scarcity is a primary condition of nature (Darwin), and
- progress means growth, complexity, competition, and freedom (Weber)

should be changed to "softer," non-Western concepts based on the values of harmony, inner accord, and cooperation.

Huntington (1993) predicted a deepening of the gap between Western and non-Western values. He suggested that billions of people on earth would vigorously discuss and challenge the leadership role of the West and its materialistic Judeo–Christian values. This would further attenuate the differences between Western and non-Western values and representing them countries. Empirical studies give only little support to these predictions.

How do people acquire attitudes and values? How do they use them to make judgments about other people and themselves? There are theories of attitudes that have been tested cross-culturally. Let us examine some of them.

A CASE IN POINT

We want you to think about the opinion that Western values, including civil freedoms and individual rights, were forced on other countries by the Western world as a direct instruction of what is good and what is not. The whole idea of individual rights can be criticized because the pursuit of these rights may encourage individuals to perform completely independent actions and disregard the views of other people. Such actions may distance the person from his or her family, culture, and religion. Criticizing Western values, some political activists argue that human rights—understood from a different perspective—do not consist only of individual political and civil liberties. They suggest that rights for economic security, social protection, and preservation of tradition are just as important as individual liberties.

Questions:

Do you think that there are values more attuned to Western culture than to non-Western cultures? Do you think Western countries impose those values on other countries? Which values do you think are shared by most people regarding their cultural affiliations?

STRIVING FOR CONSISTENCY: THE COGNITIVE BALANCE THEORY

Heider's theory of attitude balance (Heider, 1959) states that people seek consistency among their attitudes. In general, a balance is achieved if you and a person you like agree on something or when you and a person you dislike disagree about something. It is expected that we should overestimate positive traits in persons and groups we enjoy, and that we underestimate positive traits in those persons or groups we do not favor, even if the facts suggest that our adversaries are not as bad as we had previously thought (Pratkanis, 1988). The theory of attitude balance examines consistency pressures within a simple, three-element, cognitive evaluation process. The first element (A) is a person who develops evaluations. The other two elements (B, C) are objects, issues, or other people who are being evaluated. For example, a young woman (A) adores the music of Puerto Rican singer Ricky Martin (B) who made a critical remark about the president of the United States (C). The woman (A) is likely to agree with the singer (B) about the president of the United States (C). If, however, she dislikes the criticism of the president, her attitude about Ricky Martin would probably change from very positive to somewhat positive or even negative.

Experimental research shows that the principles of cognitive balance are universal in virtually all countries studied (Triandis, 1994). It was found, however, that cognitive consistency also varies across cultures. For instance, in the United States people are more concerned about the consistency of their attitudes than individuals in Japan, where the ability to handle inconsistency is considered a sign of maturity. In the former communist countries of the Soviet bloc, moral consistency required personal modesty, honesty, sacrifice on behalf of society, and public criticism of others who did not follow these standards (Gozman & Edkind, 1992; Shiraev & Bastrykin, 1988). In Islamic societies, being consistent in one's religious attitudes requires a more complex behavioral reaction than the religious behavior of many people in other societies. For instance, such consistency requires regularity of prayers, abstention from alcohol, paying of Islamic taxes, and following the proclamations of religious leaders (Moghaddam, 1998).

AVOIDING INCONSISTENCY: COGNITIVE DISSONANCE

People experience psychological tensions when they perceive mismatch (dissonance) between (1) attitudes and behavior, (2) two or more decisions, or (3) two or more attitudes. These tensions are known as **cognitive dissonance** (Festinger, 1957). Whenever we must decide between two or more alternatives, the final choice will be inconsistent—to some extent—with some of our beliefs or previous decisions. This inconsistency generates dissonance, an unpleasant state of emotions. As a result, we feel compelled to reduce the dissonance and avoid unnecessary discomfort. There are three techniques for reducing dissonance: (1) improving our evaluation of the chosen alternative ("This is the best dress I have ever bought"), (2) lowering our evaluation of the alternative not chosen ("The dress I didn't buy was overpriced"), and (3) not thinking or talking about the decision we made ("I bought the dress, the topic is closed").

Why do people across cultures attempt to reduce dissonance (Camilleri & Malewska-Peyre, 1997)? One reason may be the attractive value of a harmonious, consistent, and meaningful view of the world. To avoid frustration or discomfort, we may cut off a relationship with somebody we dislike or disagree with and begin to ignore evidence inconsistent with our beliefs. Yet studies show that inconsistency of views maybe more acceptable in some cultures, such as East Asian, but not in others, such as the United States (Boucher et al., 2009).

Men of principle are sure to be bold, but those who are bold may not always be men of principle.

CONFUCIUS (551–479 B.C.E.)—Chinese Philosopher

PSYCHOLOGICAL DOGMATISM

Not long ago, the absolute monarch of the African country Swaziland claimed that women who wore slacks and jeans caused the world's problems. He also condemned human rights as a disgrace before God. He referred to the *Bible* when promising punishment for those women who wore pants. When speaking of human rights, he suggested that God created people unequal and, therefore, humans should not attempt to change what is a divine creation.

Generally, people dislike being called "dogmatic." **Dogmatism** is a tendency to be extremely selective, rigid, and inflexible in opinions and subsequent behavior. This is a powerful alliance of attitudes and beliefs, usually organized around one central idea. This idea has absolute authority over the individual and usually causes intolerance toward other people or issues (Rokeach, 1973). The dogmatic individual has a very limited way of thinking and acting, is rigid about other people's opinions, and uncritically accepts people who represent the central dogmatic idea. The dogmatic individual typically rejects those who disagree with him or her and has difficulty assimilating new information. Dogmatism and democratic values are negatively correlated (Schwartz, 2000).

What causes some groups of people to be more dogmatic than others? Ofer Feldman (1996), an Israeli-born researcher who lives and works in Japan, offered an interesting explanation. He compared dogmatism in politicians from the United States, Italy, and Japan. Japanese public officials were found to be less dogmatic than Italian politicians but more dogmatic than their U.S. counterparts. The findings were explained in the context of differences in political systems in the countries studied. In Italy, at the time the survey was conducted, there were eight major national political parties, and each of them was advancing a different political doctrine and philosophy of life. In-group ideological pressures within each political party were high. In the United States, two major political parties were weakly organized and highly decentralized. In-group ideological pressure was not expected to be high. The author argued that the Japanese political system contained characteristics of both Italian and U.S. political systems: high ideological solidarity and relative independence from the central party. One fact should be noted, however. The data for the U.S. sample were gathered on the local level: Only state legislators participated in the study. Local politics is traditionally different from politics at the national level and is expected to be "pragmatic."

SOCIAL ATTRIBUTION

A student came to the professor after class and asked a question about the topic discussed 10 minutes ago. Then, he asked a couple of other questions and, finally, made a personal remark: "Sorry, I see you are divorced. Am I right?" The professor replied, "No, I am married. What made you think that I am divorced?" "Well, I saw your golden ring on your right hand—not on the left—and assumed that you are divorced," replied the student. The professor smiled, "In the country where I was born, we wear the wedding ring on the right hand. This is a tradition." Moral? The student made an assumption about the professor just by looking at his wedding ring. This episode—that really happened to one of the authors—is a demonstration of **social attribution**, the process through which we seek to explain and identify the causes of the behavior of others as well as our own actions.

Are there any common cross-cultural trends of social attribution? Across countries, we tend to evaluate more positively the persons and objects we like, and we view negatively those who are considered to be our adversaries, even if the facts suggest that they are not as bad as we think (Pratkanis, 1988). Groups to which we belong are commonly perceived as more heterogeneous (i.e., made up of dissimilar elements) than groups to which we do not belong (Gudykunst & Bond, 1997). Across cultures, people tend to rate faces that have even a minor scar as less sociable, less attractive, and more dishonest than the same faces without the scar (Bull & David, 1986). Both Korean and U.S. subjects see "baby-faced" adults and interpret their behavior in a similar way (McArthur & Berry, 1987).

Research in the fields of communications, psycholinguistics, and social psychology suggests that most people tend to make quick assessment of other people based on whether they speak with an accent (Giles, 1970; Kim, 1986). Moreover, speech accents have been shown to affect listeners' evaluations of other people's competence, social status, social attractiveness, and personality characteristics such as openness, honesty, and assertiveness (Ryan & Sebastian, 1980). Studies in the United States also show that standard-accented speakers (people who speak with so-called TV network accent, a derivative of an accent used by newscast anchors) receive higher ratings of intelligence, wealth, education, and success when they are compared to other people (Lippi-Green, 1997). These assessments of speech then could direct the listeners' behaviors toward the speaker: Speech accents have been shown to stimulate positive or negative stereotypes, cause certain responses, and even instigate discriminatory behavior (Abrams & Hogg, 1987).

Research on social attribution provides some evidence that people across countries, despite many similarities, express different attributions. Consider, for instance, a study in which U.S. and Japanese subjects were asked to look at smiling or nonsmiling white and Japanese faces and rate them on how attractive, intelligent, and sociable they were. The Americans normally rated the smiling faces higher on all three dimensions. The Japanese, in general, rated the smiling faces only as more sociable and the neutral faces as more intelligent (Matsumoto, 1994).

ATTRIBUTION AS LOCUS OF CONTROL

One of our most powerful psychological drives is our need to explain things around us. Without a sense of understanding, the world would seem unsafe, threatening, and dangerous. An important way of gaining this understanding is by seeking explanations for the causes of events in and around our lives. If we explain causations, the world may become more predictable and, therefore, controllable (Kelley, 1967). Rotter (1966) showed that, theoretically, people could be placed into two large groups. One group, the "internals" (those who have an internal locus of control), prefer to explain events as influenced by controllable internal factors. The other group, the "externals" (those who have an external locus of control), prefer to explain events as influenced by uncontrollable external factors. It has been shown in numerous studies that people with an external **locus of control** are more easily engaged in risky enterprises—such as gambling—than are internals. The latter are also likely to become political activists. People with an internal locus of control may tend to be "difficult" patients because they may be less likely than externals to follow the doctor's recommendations. The "internals" are not easily persuaded and they tend to have stronger achievement motivation than externals.

Early publications about locus of control inspired interest in testing its cross-cultural characteristics (Semin & Zwier, 1997). Do people in a particular region or culture display a particular locus of control? Could we say, for instance, that French men are more "externally controlled" than Chinese men? Or are collectivist cultures more likely to develop an external locus of control in its members? Are we motivated to prefer one type of causal attribution to another? It would appear so. Think, for example, about Western countries. Most individuals born in Western countries are socialized to believe that people can control their destiny and are the masters of their fate. As such, society generally condones dispositional attributions and discourages situational attributions. One consequence, however, is that we frequently fool ourselves into overestimating the degree of control that we actually do have, while underestimating the impact of external factors that lie beyond our control. Put another way, we simply do not have as much control over people and events as we would like to believe that we do. Nevertheless, making dispositional attributions provides us with a comfortable illusion of control.

Despite some exceptions, individuals from Western countries are more likely to display a stronger internal locus of control than non-Western people because "Westerners" are generally suspicious of powerful governments (external forces) and possess material resources that make them less dependent on external factors. If we follow this logic, are we justified in expecting every male who is a city dweller, is of a religious or ethnic majority, and has a high socioeconomic status to have an internal locus of control? Are we also making accurate predictions when we imply that every woman who is a minority from a rural area, with a low socioeconomic status will have an external locus of control? These expectations were not confirmed in comparative studies (Hui, 1982; Tobacyk, 1992). Overall, the general pattern for locus of control across the groups, countries, and cultures studied was inconsistent. A few studies, however, have yielded some differences between social groups, such as one revealing that ethnic minorities in the United States participate in lotteries more often than nonminorities (Chinoy & Babington, 1998). Persistent gambling may be a behavioral pattern typical for "externals." However, one behavioral pattern cannot stand for the individual's locus of control.

Why has cross-cultural research found little or no difference in locus of control among cultures? There could have been a methodological problem: The participants in these cross-cultural studies were getting standard, preselected questions that could have had different meanings in different countries (Munro, 1986). There is also an opinion that the locus of control scores yielded in the studies could have reflected the actual, "individualized" degree of control that people exert in the real world, not only one determined by their social status and cultural identity (Collins, 1974; Dyal, 1984). For instance, a person is expected to have an external locus of control because he is poor and lives in a rural area controlled by an authoritarian government. However, this person is a father, a husband, an older brother, and a breadwinner for his family—the roles that would actually indicate an internal locus of control.

Both external and internal factors may be viewed as contributors to an individual's sense of personal happiness. More than 200 participants from Canada (both of French and English descent), El Salvador, and the United States, all undergraduate students, were asked open-ended questions: "What makes you happy?" "What does a person need to be happy?" "What is a happy person?" It was found that factors contributing to happiness were perceived similarly across the cultures studied (Chiasson et al., 1996). For example, the most important factors of happiness were family relationships, the ability to reach one's goals, and positive self-esteem. However, there were some differences. The participants from El Salvador referred to religious values as well as political conditions in the country as factors affecting their happiness. North Americans mentioned personal success and enjoyable life episodes.

There is no idea, no fact, which would not be vulgarized and presented in a ludicrous light.

Fyodor Dostoyevsky (1821–1900)—Russian Novelist

Morality is simply the attitude we adopt toward people whom we personally dislike.

Oscar Wilde (1854–1900)—Irish-Born English Poet

ATTRIBUTION OF SUCCESS AND FAILURE

The prevalence of external or internal explanations of people's behavior is measured in studies of how people explain their success or failure. It was found that cross-culturally, when people explain why individuals succeed or fail, at least three explanations are commonly used (Fletcher & Ward, 1988):

- individual ability ("I have skills" or "I do not have skills")
- effort ("I tried hard" or "I didn't try")
- task difficulty ("It was not so difficult" or "It was very difficult")

If a person tends to take credit for personal success and avoid responsibility for failure, this person displays the **self-centered bias**. Imagine you take a French class but decide to drop it. If you say that your failure to learn French is caused by a lack of time (task difficulty), you are expressing a self-centered bias. Several attempts were made to examine how people in different countries use this bias in their comments about themselves. For example, a self-centered bias was found in samples studied from the United States, Yugoslavia, India, and South Africa. However, in Japanese samples, such bias was not found. Instead, researchers identified an **unassuming bias**: a tendency to explain personal success as a result of external factors, such as luck or help from others, and failure as a result of one's personal mistakes or weaknesses (Chandler et al., 1981).

Different studies suggested the existence of the unassuming bias in Asian and East Asian cultures. For example, Japanese subjects attribute failure to themselves more frequently, and success to themselves less frequently, than do their U.S. counterparts. In addition, Japanese subjects display a group-serving bias, a tendency to explain the success of other people by internal factors and failure by external ones (Kashima & Triandis, 1986; Yamaguchi, 1988). Group-serving bias is particularly strong when individuals express their opinions in front of their group members (Bond, 1985). It was also shown that an individual's minority status typically affects his or her attribution of success. If you see yourself as a representative of a minority group that has a tense or rival relationship with the majority, you should not be expected to express a majority group-serving bias (Hunter et al., 1993).

A major change of immediate social environment—emigration from a home country as an example—can affect the way people explain their success and failure. By way of illustration, Indian women are expected to display the unassuming bias in their social perception. However, this bias did not appear in the responses of Indian female immigrants to Canada: Both success and failure were attributed to internal causes (Moghaddam et al., 1990). Perhaps the influence of the norms of an individualist society influenced the women's social perception.

Different trends in interpretation of success can be found in the media. Authors of a study comparing U.S. and Hong Kong newspapers were looking for similarities and differences in the portrayal of winners and losers in various sporting events. It was found that U.S. journalists were praising victorious athletes more often than Hong Kong reporters were. Moreover, those in the United States were making primarily internal attributions for their success. In Hong Kong, the reporters made mostly external attributions for losers (Hallahan et al., 1997).

Man is so made that if he is told often enough that he is a fool he believes it.

BLAISE PASCAL **(1623–1662)—French Scientist and Philosopher**

CRITICAL THINKING
Assumptions About Individualism and Collectivism

As we already saw in Chapter 3, people's appeals to commonsense logic may lead to incorrect assumptions. Knowing about the individualistic and materialistic nature of U.S. society, some might assume that romantic relationships are not a great psychological value in the United States. Research provides evidence that challenges this assumption. In a survey conducted among U.S., Japanese, and German students, romantic love was valued higher in the United States and Germany than it was in Japan. Overall, romantic love is valued higher in nontraditional cultures than in traditional ones, and in nontraditional cultures, it plays a more central role in people's decisions to marry. In collectivist cultures, family obligations often play a crucial role in marriage arrangements (Simmons et al., 1986).

Consider another example. Common sense would perhaps lead some people to the assumption that in collectivist cultures people lose their individuality and are unable to act independently because they must comply with formal rules of conduct. Following this logic, one might consider that intimacy, for instance, is not common among members of collectivist cultures. Research, however, indicates an opposite trend: Intimacy is greater in collectivist societies than it is in individualist ones (Triandis, 1994).

Now think about the daily greetings exchanged between your colleagues and friends. People habitually exchange the universal: "Hello, how are you doing?—I am fine, thank you" on nearly all occasions. Rarely when we ask, "How are you?" are we genuinely interested in knowing how the person is actually doing. Similarly, by answering, "I am all right," we are revealing virtually nothing. On most occasions, people exchange these phrases because this is a formal way of greeting. The privacy barrier is not broken. Collectivists, however, are likely to feel strong obligations to know about you and take care of you if you belong to or identify yourself with their group.

SELF-PERCEPTION

People can make distinctions between the world within them and the world outside. Both individual traits and environmental circumstances shape our self-perception in a variety of ways and can reflect the most prominent characteristics of an underlying culture. Research shows that many tendencies in self-perception are similar across countries: It is a common tendency, for instance, for men to overestimate their own IQ and give themselves an average three points higher score than do females (Furnham & Baguma, 1999; Furnham et al., 1999). On online dating sites, people routinely portray themselves as taller and more athletic than they actually are (Levitt & Dubner, 2009). There are, of course, cultural differences. For centuries, as an example, the predominant form of social organization in India was the caste system that reinforced inequality and hierarchy among all people. Expectedly, 30 years ago, Indians viewed themselves and their interpersonal relationships as more hierarchically structured than U.S. citizens do (Sinha & Verma, 1983).

A study conducted by Biswas and Pandey (1996) compared the self-perceptions of male members of three social groups in India. The respondents were asked to evaluate their quality of life, and then each respondent's answer was matched with his socioeconomic status. The researchers found that socioeconomic upward mobility—measured as an increase in income and occupational status—did not substantially affect the respondents' self-image or perception of their social status. A respondent may earn more money than he did several years ago, have a better job, have a higher academic degree, and still perceive himself as a person of a lower status. What conclusion can be drawn from these findings? Socioeconomic changes alone do not necessarily bring about changes in the way people see themselves. Because many societies are still deeply divided along the old class, gender, ethnic, and caste lines, the "old" identities may be more salient than "new" ones despite significant changes taking place in many people's lives.

It is also shown that self-critical elements of self-perception are more typical in Japanese individuals than in U.S. citizens (Heine et al., 1999). In fact, lower self-esteem scores in East Asian countries compared to North America and Europe have been revealed in many studies conducted over years (Boucher et al., 2009; Brown & Cai, 2010). The findings do not suggest that Chinese, Japanese, or Korean individuals feel worse about themselves than their counterparts in the United States or the Netherlands. Probably, these lower scores are a form of expressed self-criticism, which derives from a large and complex cultural tradition of self-restraint. For example, as one study suggests, the linguistic and behavioral emphasis in Japan on *kenson* (modesty) and *enryo* (reserve or restraint) does not have an analogy in Western social life. This emphasis does not allow to speak or write something that might be perceived as arrogant, presumptions, or impudent. In contrast, in the West people tend to be conditioned to avoid statements that would portray them as weak and insecure (Tafarodi et al., 2011).

There are findings pointing to a correlation between individualism and collectivism on the one hand and self-esteem on the other. Tafarodi and Swann (1996) examined the self-esteem of more than 600 U.S. (a predominantly individualist culture) and Chinese (a generally collectivist culture) college students. The study revealed that the Chinese participants were lower in perceived self-competence but higher in self-liking than were the U.S. students. The authors argued that in collectivist cultures—which require sensitivity to the needs of others and subordination of personal goals to collective needs—it is expected that individuals develop self-liking. However, because of a relative loss of individual control often found in collectivist societies, these cultures promote restraints on feelings of self-competence. In individualist cultures, on the contrary, independence and the priority of the self are emphasized. Perhaps competence is related to material status, and in the United States, people feel more secure in terms of achievement than do people in China. However, it is unclear why positive feelings of self-competence in U.S. students appear to have caused a decrease in positive feelings of self-liking. Perhaps one should be looking here for a reverse causation: A relatively low level of self-liking generates compensatory thoughts and behaviors that push individuals to achieve, produce, and accomplish.

One of the popular hypotheses derived from cross-cultural research on self-perception is an idea about the existence of a "private" and "public" self (Benedict, 1946; Shiraev & Fillipov, 1990; Triandis, 1994). Private self indicates feeling and thoughts about oneself and for oneself. Public self is a concept of self in relation to others and for others. Do you think people from collectivist cultures produce more group-centric and fewer self-centric descriptions of self than people from individualist cultures? Indeed, in collectivist, and therefore interdependent, cultures (such as China, Japan, and Korea), people tend to identify their self not as an independent entity but rather as part of particular social groups (Triandis, 1994, 1989). Moreover, U.S. subjects, when they describe themselves, tend to identify a great number of abstract traits—relatively unrelated to particular social groups. Asian subjects identify fewer of the same abstract traits (Bond & Tak-Sing, 1983). Surveys show that most Japanese subjects, for example, accept differences between their public and private self. Those who cannot accept these differences may experience social alienation and insecurity (Naito & Gielen, 1992). U.S. respondents, on the contrary, try to eliminate the inconsistency between public and private self (Iwato & Triandis, 1993).

A young woman called Fatima explains in an interview that she doesn't identify herself as being Dutch or Moroccan. Rather, she feels as though she is something in between. She recalls that while traveling in Morocco she was referred to as the girl from Holland. However, while in Holland she does not feel a "hundred percent" Dutch. When asked to describe her identity, she replies "I'm only Fatima" (Richburg, 2003).

There is a popular opinion that in response to economic and cultural globalization, most people would likely adapt to the changes. Many people would develop and are already developing new self-perceptions based on old and "local" customs, ideas, and symbols, and new, cross-cultural ones (including new fashions, foods, leisure activities, and educational principles). However, for some people the process of change is more difficult than it is for others. The new values, norms, and behaviors may seem frightening and challenging when compared to old and "convenient" cultural images and norms. Some people may experience themselves as excluded from both their local culture and the global culture, truly belonging to neither (Arnett, 2002).

DO SOCIAL NORMS AFFECT THE WAY WE SEE OUR OWN BODY?

Research has shown that bodily symmetry, which is considered a cross-culturally accepted feature of a beautiful body or face, is one of the strongest predictors of healthy attributes such as a strong immune system. Evolutionary psychologists suggest that many of our visual preferences may have evolutionary roots (Thornhill & Gangestad, 2008). Sobal and Stunkard (1989) reviewed several anthropological studies that measured correlation between the individual's body weight and socioeconomic status. They established a remarkable tendency. In rich countries the correlation is negative: People who are thinner than others tend to be richer than others are as well. Or, if one takes a slightly different view, people who are richer tended to be thinner. In undeveloped countries the correlation is positive: Thinner people, in general, are usually poorer than others who weigh more.

Cogan and colleagues (1996) examined attitudes toward obesity and fitness in university students in the United States and Ghana, in Western Africa. The participants answered questions about their weight, restrictions on eating and dieting, the degree to which their weight interferes with some social activities, perception of ideal bodies, and stereotypes of thin and heavy people. Students in Ghana rated heavier bodies more favorably than U.S. students did. U.S. students were more likely to be dieting than were their African counterparts, and U.S. females were the most likely to diet among the students interviewed. Moreover, U.S. females scored significantly higher on eating restriction problems and interference of their body weight with social behavior.

In the United States, most people hold negative attitudes toward body fat. According to surveys, people attribute increased body weight to being poor or having poor health. The obese are blamed for their weight, which is assumed to be under their voluntary control. Obese women, more than men, are rated negatively by peers. These stereotypical views about one's weight do not exist in many other cultures around the world. In developing countries, for example, in which major causes of death are due to malnutrition and infection, thinness is not really desired. In countries such as India, China, the Philippines, and some Latin American countries, an increased standard of living was correlated with increasing body weight (Rothblum, 1992). A more recent study in Indonesia and Great Britain, showed that participants in Indonesia rated a wider range of female figures as attractive compared with Britons (Swami et al., 2011).

Despite different cultural views of body weight, comparative studies show some evidence that men across continents always prefer women with slim waists. A comparative study of British literature of the sixteenth to eighteenth centuries, analyses of the Indian epics *Mahabharata* and *Ramayana*, and an examination of Chinese sixth dynastic Palace poetry, compared with statistics of top U.S. fashion models showed a positive bias toward a small waist (Singh et al., 2007).

There are cross-cultural similarities in the way people perceive the leg-to-body ratio. A study of 3,103 participants from 27 nations rated the physical attractiveness of seven male and seven female silhouettes. Male and female silhouettes with the average ratio were perceived as more attractive than more extreme ones. The silhouettes with short and excessively long legs were perceived as less attractive across all nations (Sorokowski et al., 2011).

To know what is right and not to do it is the worst cowardice.

Confucius (551–479 B.C.E.)—**Chinese Philosopher**

DUTY AND FAIRNESS IN INDIVIDUALIST AND COLLECTIVIST CULTURES

People say, "Do not kill, do not steal, and do not lie." Even though general moral principles of behavior may be universal, the interpretations of these principles are influenced by culture. There are two basic views on morality. The first view, a justice-based view, emphasizes the autonomy of the individual and her personal rights. It argues that autonomy and personal rights should be impartial and applicable to every human being. This view is supported primarily in individualist cultures. The second view, a duty-based view, is based on the belief that obligation to others is the basis of morality. This view is common in collectivist cultures. For example, in experimental situations when participants are asked to assess the behavior of other people, U.S. subjects preferred to endorse an individual's personal choice, whereas Indian subjects tended to appeal to regulations and required norms (Miller, 1994). A study of Arab teachers' attitudes found that the feeling of personal obligations to the group was the dominant factor in the teachers' work ethic (Abu-Saad, 1998).

Are there any cultural trends in people's views on the fair distribution of resources? People tend to like success stories involving individuals who initially had nothing but later became better off because of their effort. Myths and fairy tales from all continents show a consistent pattern: "Good" characters are those who obtained their success due to their effort, and "bad" individuals are those who enrich themselves by harming others or doing nothing. Empirical studies support these assumptions. People in the United States and Australia perceived stories about initially poor and subsequently rich individuals as more competent and likeable than initially rich and subsequently poor individuals (Mandisodza et al., 2006). Political psychologists suggest that there are at least two major views on fairness. The first stems from the merit standpoint, arguing that people have to have access to resources according to their skills and accomplishment. A person who contributes to society can get a bigger share of the benefits from society than those who contribute less—for whatever reason. The second originates from the need standpoint, asserting that people have to receive equal shares of the benefits regardless of their "worth" to society (Sears, 1996). Children, the elderly, and the ill all may contribute little to society; however, they deserve to be treated as anybody else.

As you might anticipate, there are national differences in the way people perceive fair distribution of resources. For example, college students in the United States were more merit oriented than students in Germany, who were more need oriented (Bernman & Murphy-Bernman, 1996). Results of national surveys show that, compared to U.S. students, twice as many young Germans endorse statements such as (1) "the government should guarantee everyone a minimum standard of living," (2) "the government should place an upper limit on the amount of money anyone can make," and (3) "people should help the needy even if this means getting money from those who have money." The prevailing attitudes among U.S. students were that individuals themselves are responsible for their material success (Cockerham et al., 1988). Even in countries that can be considered similar in terms of democratic principles of government, education, and social tradition, there could be substantial differences in how people view justice and what they consider a "fair" distribution of resources.

The differences between the United States and Germany are, in part, based on different social traditions in these countries. True, social welfare policies exist in both nations. In Germany, however, the government is involved in social welfare programs to a larger degree than is the government in the United States. The situational context of the surveys could also have affected the results. The studies mentioned here were conducted in the late 1980s and early 1990s when prevailing attitudes among Germans were influenced by the necessity to provide for German unification. However, a few years later, according to opinion surveys, many Germans became skeptical of social welfare and the amount of help given to the needy (Shapiro et al., 2000).

STEREOTYPES AND THE POWER OF GENERALIZATIONS

We often do not have the necessary time or psychological resources to analyze every fact as new and unique. We categorize almost everything we see, hear, and deal with. **Stereotypes** are categorical assumptions that all members of a given group have a particular trait. Stereotypes could be positive or negative, simple or differentiated, and held with or without confidence (Smith & Bond, 1993). These qualities could also vary in their degree. For example, it was found in a study that Anglo-Australians held very positive stereotypes of themselves and very negative stereotypes about Aboriginal Australians. The latter held somewhat favorable stereotypes about Anglo-Australians and only moderately positive stereotypes about themselves (Marjoribanks & Jordan, 1986).

The process of social perception often makes us simplify the incoming information and categorize it by groups. For instance, Israeli Arabs saw Jews as more intellectually advanced; however, the Arabs saw themselves as far superior socially—thus referring to their friendships, love, family traditions, and overall collectivism (Bizman & Amir, 1982). Stereotypical beliefs such as "most illegal immigrants are criminals," or "interracial marriages are less stable than same-race marriages," or "all Jews are wealthy" may be expressed in our daily judgments despite the fact that many times these stereotypes are incorrect. There are some undocumented aliens who commit crimes, but they represent a small proportion of all undocumented aliens in the United States. Interracial marriages are as stable as same-race matrimony. There are both rich and poor Jews.

Exercise 10.1

The following is a description of interpersonal communications of "typical" U.S., Japanese, and Arab individuals adopted from a best-selling book (Fast, 1970).

There are distinct differences in the way an American, Japanese, and an Arab handle their personal "territory." In Japan, crowding together is a sign of warm and pleasant intimacy. Like the Japanese, the Arabs tend to cling to one another. But while in public they are crowded together, in the privacy of their houses the Arabs have almost too much space: their houses are generally large and empty, with the people clustered together in one small area. Arabs do not like to be alone, so partitions between rooms are usually avoided. The Arab likes to touch his companion and feel him. The Japanese avoid touching and prefer to keep physical boundaries. Americans too tend to have boundaries in public places. You do not push or intrude into the space of another person. Arabs have no concept of privacy in a public place. Americans very seldom shove, push, or pinch other people in public. When two Arabs talk to each other, they look each other in the eyes with great intensity. The same intensity is rarely exhibited in the American culture.

Questions:

Do you think all these statements are erroneous? What exactly is inaccurate in them? Or maybe you suggest that these judgments are somewhat accurate? Where should we draw the line between being fairly accurate and being stereotypical?

Members of an ethnic group may hold stereotypes about themselves similar to what others think about this group. For example, Walkey and Chung (1996) examined attitudes toward Chinese immigrants in New Zealand. More than 300 schoolchildren of both Chinese and European backgrounds showed that the stereotypes held by these two groups were similar. Both groups mentioned the work ethics of Chinese, especially their effort. Both interviewed groups saw Europeans as relatively less positive on work ethics and more individually, rather than socially, controlled than Chinese immigrants.

In the course of evaluating similarities and differences between phenomena, we are subject to committing errors of at least two kinds: First, we allow genuine differences to be obscured by similarities, and second, we allow genuine similarities to be obscured by differences. Stereotyping is, in fact, permitting similarities between phenomena to eclipse their differences. Those who stereotype other people are prone to habitually, systematically, and automatically overestimate within-group similarities, while minimizing (or even ignoring) within-group variability (Fiske & Taylor, 1984). In other words, the individual perceives group members to be more alike than they really are and, at the same time, does not recognize many of the ways in which they are different from one another.

Moreover, groups we like and groups we do not like are seen as more different than they really are (Keen, 1986). As you can readily discern, in its most extreme form, this process is a fundamental component underlying prejudice, bigotry, chauvinism, racism, sexism, ageism, and so forth, wherein all members of the particular "out-group" are seen as essentially the same, while their individuality goes virtually unnoticed.

Consider, for example, cross-cultural counseling. Some therapists may fail to respect or even recognize the uniqueness indigenous to each individual client. Unfortunately, these therapists may perceive a client from one sociocultural group as basically the same as every other client from that group. In this way, clients are viewed *not* as distinct and varied individuals, each possessing a separate and unique constellation of life experiences, memories, feelings,

CROSS-CULTURAL SENSITIVITY

For a psychologist, it is crucial to understand that negative stereotyping may emerge in subtle forms that are often difficult to recognize (Sue et al,. 2007). For example, it may appear in the form of so-called micro-aggressions conveyed in daily conversations, remarks, jokes, and gestures. One may say jokingly to a Vietnamese-American student, "So, did you get a summer job? Probably at your parents' nail salon?" People who produce such stereotypical jokes tend to dismiss their words and actions as innocent and meaningless (Franklin, 2004) and not offensive (Solórzano et al., 2000). Unfortunately, they may appear offensive to others. To illustrate, a person may compliment a student from an African country, "You are speaking English well" ignoring the fact that English could be this student's first language. It appears that the initial expectation was that the African student is not supposed to be proficient in English!

perceptions, values, beliefs, hopes, fears, and dreams. Instead, they are spontaneously filtered through the therapist's own sociocultural stereotypes, from which they emerge as Koreans, blacks, Jews, Latinos, Vietnamese, and so on. In this less-than-therapeutic environment, irrespective of individual clients' unique situations, problems, or needs, they would offer essentially the same "cookie-cutter" approach to diagnosis and treatment.

Stereotyping is making erroneous judgments. However, beware and do not reject the possibility that two or many people can have something similar in their behavior, emotion, and attitudes. How many times have you heard someone make the following pronouncement (or any derivation thereof): "You cannot compare these two people because they are totally and completely different from each other!" Here we have a vivid illustration of a person who is making the converse mistake of allowing similarities between people to be overshadowed by their differences. Thus, the individual who staunchly and adamantly maintains that "One should *never* stereotype" is effectively blinding himself or herself to authentic commonalities that actually do exist within specific groups. However, by obstinately clinging to this position, such individuals practically ensure that they will remain oblivious to true similarities within (as well as between) groups of people.

Similarly, psychotherapists who tenaciously cling to their belief that "Every client should be viewed and treated as totally unique and without regard for his or her cultural background" runs the risk of allowing true—and potentially helpful—similarities between persons to be overlooked, neglected, or omitted. Unfortunately, the therapists' overemphasis on individual differences typically is realized at the expense of minimizing interpersonal commonalities. As a consequence, for instance, deeply powerful and universal life experiences that appear to be intrinsic to the human condition—such as needs for love, acceptance, empathy, esteem, or meaning—are prone to be minimized, disregarded, or even outright rejected.

Is it possible to eliminate stereotypes? Some researchers are skeptical (Devine, 1989). But it is possible to reduce the influence of stereotypes on our daily judgments. Human diversity can be greater than human sameness. There are rich and poor, educated and illiterate, happy and angry Americans, Japanese, and Arabs, who live in big cities and small towns, who either work or do not, travel or stay in one place. Above all, people have unique personal characteristics hardly placed within the narrow confines of popularly held stereotypes. What we might anticipate from an individual based on our expectations does not often match who that person really is. Please be prepared for such inconsistencies.

A CASE IN POINT

In Search of Commonalities

The principle is to "look for both similarities and differences" that can be constructively applied in the cross-cultural counseling setting. Despite apparent differences, two individuals can share something in common. Members of the same cultural group may be different in virtually every personality trait. Consider the following brief vignette as an example of a search for commonalities in two people.

Client: "There's no way that you can understand how I feel. After all, you're white, and I'm black. And you've never been discriminated against because of your race."

Therapist: "You are right. I can never know exactly what that feels like. We are truly different in that respect. But at the same time, I know what it's like to be discriminated against because of my religion. And I have had the experience of being persecuted out of ignorance and hatred. To that extent, we do share a common experience. We are indeed both similar and different."

ON "NATIONAL CHARACTER"

Studies show that compared with Asians, the British and the Germans tend to be less holistic in attention, more oriented toward personal happiness, and more egocentric in their relationships. Compared with Western Europeans, European Americans are more "personal" in happiness, and much more egocentric in social relations (Kitayama et al., 2009). Does this mean that all Americans have consistent personal traits that make them different from people in China or Germany? Not necessarily. Yet people's perceptions tend to emphasize such differences.

National character can be described as perceived predominant behavioral and psychological features and traits common in most people of a nation. Quite frequently, people of one's own nation are seen as "good" and "decent," while the neighbors are considered "bad" or "mean." Some of these assumptions are fleeting and relate to specific events. Others have a long history. Some of them are offensive. Others are perceived as humorous. For three generations, for example, Europeans have been teasing about their "characters" by telling this joke: "What is Heaven and Hell? Heaven is when the restaurant chef is French, the cop is British, the auto mechanic German, the planner is Swiss, and the lover is Italian. In Hell, everything is out of order: The chef is British, the policeman is German, the mechanic is French, the planner Italian, and the lover is Swiss." In folk beliefs, Russians these days may frequently appear as drunkards spending oil money frivolously in famous resorts. Chinese may be portrayed as hardworking, math obsessed, and having no fun in life. Indians may be frequently depicted as computer-savvy nerds. And the French may appear as coffee-drinking, fashion-driven critics of everything. We understand, however, that these are inaccurate labels. Some notable facts, sensationalistic coverage in the media, or individual experiences create and maintain specific stereotypes associated with "national characters." International surveys, for example, show that Americans, for the most part, are described as assertive and open minded, but antagonistic. The Pew Research Center (2005) found in an international poll that more than 50 percent of people around the world rated Americans as hardworking and inventive but also greedy and violent. Americans are seen as high in competence and low in warmth. However, do these stereotypical perceptions have basis in reality? Are most people in Switzerland excellent planners? Are most people in China exceptionally polite? Are most people in Britain terrible in the kitchen? If you are an American, would you personally agree that Americans are hardworking and cold?

Views of national character are enshrined in literature, embedded in various interpretations of history, disseminated through jokes, and perpetuated by travelers' tales. For centuries, there is a relatively widespread popular belief that national character is related to climate: Some nations have "hot" blood while others are "cold." Wars between two countries, lasting colonialist policies, exclusive facts, long-standing folk beliefs, and sensationalistic coverage by the media—all can create and maintain specific stereotypes associated with "national characters" (see Table 10.1). People in some nations may have a tendency to distinguish themselves from their neighbors and show that they are different. Lithuanians, for example, have a long tradition to distinguish and dissociate themselves from Russians (Yushka & Gaidys, 2008). Canadians see themselves as having the "opposite" image of Americans, perhaps in an effort to differentiate themselves and establish an independent national identity (Cuddy et al., 2005).

Uncritical thinking plays a powerful role in shaping and maintaining these stereotypical beliefs. On the other hand, many people make a distinction between a country's foreign policy from this country's ordinary people. The Iraq war had a slight negative effect on perceptions of the typical American, but people around the world seem to draw a clear distinction between U.S. foreign policy and the character of the American people (Terracciano & McCrae, 2007).

TABLE 10.1 Some Sources of Stereotypes About "National Character"

Factors Affecting Stereotypical Perceptions Related to "National Character"

Specific events. Wars between two countries or serious international incidents commonly generate the "aggressor" image attached to people of a particular nation many years after the end of open hostilities. Many years after World War II, Germans and Japanese had to deal with negative stereotypes attached to their countries. Similarly, British, French, Russian, and American people as well as people of several other nations have also had to deal with negative perceptions attributed to their countries after past wars or international incidents.

A history of oppression. Lasting colonialist policies and other examples of one country's domination or exploitation of another country frequently produce mutual antagonistic perceptions. People in the oppressed country are generally seen by the opposite side as "troublemakers" and "violent," while people of the dominant country are seen as "arrogant" and "immoral." Take a look at the history of world empires, read about the relations between Israel and its Arab neighbors or the Soviet Union and its former ethnic states. These histories clearly illustrate how one country's domination over other countries produced negative perceptions on both sides.

Wealth and poverty. People of wealthy countries are commonly perceived by people in poor countries (especially in neighboring countries) as "egotistical" and "mean," while people in poorer nations are stereotypically dismissed by some as "lazy" and "messy." In folklore, popular tales, and daily conversations, these negative mutual stereotypes are enforced and maintained. Many people tend to believe in such stereotypes because they don't have access to experience or information that would challenge such stereotypes.

How people view their own "national characters" is also based on a large number of factors. Americans, for example, in one international study perceived themselves as both assertive and disagreeable. Indonesians reported that they were agreeable but not conscientious. Yet, Argentines reported a rather undesirable profile, describing themselves as impulsive, arrogant, and careless (Terracciano et al., 2005). One survey revealed that people in South American and European countries tend to receive high scores on the openness dimension (Chile was ranked first). On the other hand, the bottom of the openness rankings belonged to mostly East Asian cultures, such as Hong Kong, Japan, South Korea, and Taiwan. Measurements produced by personality tests also showed that people from African cultures tend to be low on anxiety scores (Smith et al., 2007).

Nonetheless, all these and other data do not produce distinct evidence that people of particular nations have strong personality features different from people of other nations (McCrae, 2002). One of the most comprehensive international studies across 49 countries comparing various personality traits showed that national character stereotypes have only little basis in reality (Terracciano & McCrae, 2007). As a matter of principle, psychologists should remind everyone that such stereotypes are a poor guide to understanding the people in any country or culture.

Exercise 10.2

Imagine that you are on a cruise where you meet the following people: (1) a man from Japan, (2) a woman from Brazil, (3) a man from France, (4) a woman from Jordan, (5) a man from Germany, and (6) a woman from Italy. You spend a great week in their company. Back home, you finally realize that your initial stereotypes about these people were confirmed. Could you match the following behaviors with the nationalities displayed above? (Complete the statements below, please.) Four hundred students in Virginia and Washington DC have also given their assessments of popular stereotypes. You can then compare your answers with the most frequently displayed stereotypes (see the book's website). Discuss why these stereotypes are inaccurate.

Question:

Who was this person (Japanese, Italian, French, German, Jordanian, Brazilian)?

1. This person was never late for breakfast, lunch, or dinner.
2. This person talked too much.
3. This person had three video cameras with him/her.
4. This person was the best samba dancer in the group.
5. This person was drinking beer continuously.
6. This person was trying to date several people in the group.
7. This person was the quietest in the group.
8. This person kept smiling continuously and kept saying "yes."
9. This person said he (she) had never played poker and won't be playing.
10. This person was drinking wine continuously.
11. Military marches have been this person's favorite music.
12. This person said that after marriage he (she) would love to stay home with his/her kids.
13. This person knew a lot about cheese.

Exercise 10.3

Both Hofstede (1980) and Smith and Schwartz (1997) found that the value of individualism and economic development of a country are strongly and positively correlated. In other words if a country is wealthy, it is more likely that its citizens will express more individualistic attitudes than citizens of a poor country will. The most convenient explanation of the link could be as follows:

> • *Wealthy economies provide people with a variety of opportunities and therefore allow freedom of choice to and relative independence of individuals.*

However, a different explanation is also possible:

> • *Individualistic values shared by people motivate them to work hard and develop productivity.*

Using these two types of explanations, please justify strong negative correlations between the economic wealth of a nation (evaluated on the basis of income per capita) and power distance and uncertainty avoidance. Refer to Chapter 3 if you need to refresh your memory about positive and negative statistical correlation.

Chapter Summary

- It is an established view in psychology that social perception is culturally rooted. We acquire judgments, attitudes, and beliefs from our cultural milieu.

- One of the most fundamental elements of the process of social perception and social cognition is attitude. Cross-culturally, attitudes help us understand and make sense of the world. They serve an ego-defensive function assisting us to feel better about ourselves. Finally, attitudes serve a function that allows us to express our values.

- Cultures develop, maintain, and justify particular sets of values along the following dimensions: conservatism versus autonomy, hierarchy versus egalitarianism, and mastery versus harmony. There could be collectivist and individualist patterns in human values. There are also debates about the existence of so-called Western and non-Western values.

- Cognitive balance and cognitive dissonance theories suggest that people seek consistency among their attitudes. Notwithstanding limitations, this trend was established among individuals in different countries. One of the forms of consistency seeking is psychological dogmatism, which has a wide range of cultural manifestations.

- Research on social attributions provides some evidence that people across countries, despite many similarities, could express different attribution styles, and these differences are deeply rooted in people's social and cultural background.

- Despite expectations about culture-bound manifestations of locus of control, its general pattern across many countries studied was highly inconsistent.

- Culture can have an impact on various individual manifestations of the fundamental attribution error and other patterns of social attribution.

- Even though general moral principles of behavior may be universal, the interpretations of these principles can be strongly influenced by each particular culture. There are two basic views on morality. The first view, a justice-based view of morality, is associated with beliefs that emphasize the autonomy of the individual and his or her individual rights. The second view, a duty-based view, is based on the belief that obligation to others is the basis of morality.

- Individuals make distinctions between the world within them and the world outside them. Both individual traits and environmental circumstances shape people's self-perception in a variety of ways.

- The process of social perception often makes people simplify the incoming information and categorize it by groups. Stereotypes can lead people to think that all members of a given group have a particular trait. Research suggests that stereotypes could have a number of universal characteristics common in different cultural settings

Key Terms

Cognitive Dissonance Psychological tensions caused by the perceived mismatch (dissonance) between (1) attitudes and behavior, (2) two or more decisions, or (3) two or more attitudes.

Dogmatism The tendency to be closed minded, rigid, and inflexible in one's opinions and subsequent behavior.

Locus of Control The generalized beliefs that the control of one's reinforcements rests either on controllable internal factors (internal locus of control) or on uncontrollable external factors (external locus of control).

National Character The perceived predominant behavioral and psychological features and traits common in most people of a nation.

Self-Centered Bias The tendency to take credit for successes and avoid responsibility for failures.

Social Attribution The process through which we seek to explain and identify the causes of the behavior of others as well as our own actions.

Social Cognition The process through which we interpret, remember, and then use information about the social world.

Social Perception The process through which we seek to know and understand other people and ourselves.

Stereotypes Traits or characteristics generally attributed to all members of specific groups.

Unassuming Bias The tendency to explain one's own success as a result of external factors, and one's failure as a result of personal mistakes or weaknesses.

Value A complex belief that reflects a principle, standard, or quality considered by the individual as the most desirable or appropriate.

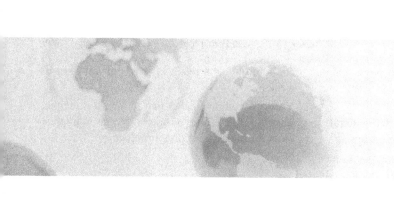

Social Interaction

What you do not want done to yourself, do not do to others.

CONFUCIUS (551–479 B.C.E.)—
Chinese Philosopher

Thirty years ago, the authors of this book, two teenagers living on opposite sides of the planet, were told an anecdote. It was not particularly funny—just an amusing story about bargaining. Born in two different cultures, living under two different governments, separated by mountains of stereotypes and mistrust, we both nevertheless understood what bargaining was.

Two old friends meet in a bar in New York City. "You know," says one, "My son was a loser until I decided to give him a jump start in life." "What kind of a jump start?" the second asked. "Well, my son married a Saudi princess last week and got a job as vice president of Chase Manhattan Bank." "Married to a Saudi princess and vice president of a bank? How did you arrange this? You are a cab driver!" "Oh, I used the shuttle diplomacy method." "The shuttle diplomacy method? What is that?" "It is simple. A month ago I called the Saudi embassy and asked them if there was a princess available to marry my son. They said 'No.' I then told them that I forgot to mention that my son is vice president of Chase Manhattan Bank. They immediately said, 'That makes a difference. We would be glad to find a princess for your son.'" "But wait a minute. Your son is a drummer at a night club, not a banker!" "Well, I fixed that too. I called Chase Manhattan Bank and asked them if my son could apply for the position of vice president. They said 'No.' Then I told them that I forgot to mention that my son is married *to a Saudi princess. They immediately told me, 'That makes a difference. Your son can begin work tomorrow.' So, this is what I call the shuttle diplomacy."*

This anecdote is popular in many countries. The expression "shuttle diplomacy" comes from the decision-making strategies of Henry Kissinger, secretary of state in the Nixon adminis- tration. But the political context of the anecdote is perhaps not so important. The most fascinat- ing aspect of this story is that despite our cultural, political, and socioeconomic differences, we easily understood some basic rules of human interaction. But are there any empirical facts to suggest that people across countries and cultures recognize and make use of the same rules of interaction? If no such facts exist, then in what areas are we different?

UNIVERSAL INTERACTION

Human beings cannot survive living in total isolation from other people. During our lives, we join various groups, voluntarily or forcibly, deliberately or by chance. People tend to form groups in all known human societies (Coon, 1946). A **group** consists of two or more figures forming a complete unit in a composition. Groups to which we belong are called in-groups, and groups to which we do not belong are called out-groups. Geographic proximity is not a necessary or suf- ficient condition for belonging to the same in-group. For instance, a Catholic and a Protestant may live side by side in a town in Northern Ireland, but they will probably not belong to similar in-groups. Almost every group to which one of them belongs—a school, a church, or a circle of close friends—will be an out-group for the other. Alternatively, a Hindu boy from New York and a Muslim child from California may never see each other in person, but they can belong to the same fantasy baseball league on the Internet.

When we join a group, we attain a **status**: a relative social position within a group that can be either formal or informal. Cultures differ in the way societal norms facilitate or inhibit social mobility. For instance, status can be earned (achieved) or given at birth (ascribed). One might expect, for example, that in democratic societies individual merit serves as a foundation for social status. The old Indian system of castes, however, determined one's social position with little or no opportunity for social mobility. If one belonged to the lower caste, one's chances of becoming powerful and wealthy were slim.

By becoming a member of different groups, people may accept more than one social sta- tus. For example, one can be an immigrant, a mother, a daughter, a nurse, a soccer coach, and a patient—all at the same time. Having a multitude of social positions inevitably affects the way people reflect their identities, including their cultural identity.

Norms are established by a group and indicate how members of that group should and should not behave, including manners, simple responses, and complex behaviors. Physical prox- imity, common values, and language influence cultural norms, making them culturally unique (Pika et al., 2009). New online networks, however, may affect the existing cultural norms and form new ones. It was common in the United States, for example, to send written invitations to join a celebration or a party. This type of formal communication was unusual in most collectivist cultures. Until now. The Internet is eliminating many cultural differences by inviting people to join social networks sharing similar global norms of communication and interaction. Social **roles** are sets of behaviors that individuals occupying specific positions within a group are expected to perform. As soon as we become part of a group, we encounter that group's norms, and as soon as we obtain a status, we begin performing social roles. For instance, in some families, children always ask for their parents' blessing when making an important decision. In many Asian and African countries, parents do not allow their children to date before marriage. These are cultural norms. Mayan children living in Guatemala learned not to give advice to an elder—a local norm of showing respect for adults (Berger, 1995), which is probably changing today. Religious norms can be very restrictive against certain foods or products.

A group can establish **sanctions**—certain actions reward those who follow the norms (positive sanctions) and reprove those who are deviant (negative sanctions). In most cases, norms cannot exist without sanctions attached to them. These vary from physical punishment to friendly criticism, from material rewards to verbal appreciation. As we saw in Chapter 1, many collectivist cultures (e.g., Russia, Pakistan, and Mexico) have stronger system sanctions and rewards than most of the individualist cultures (e.g., Switzerland, the United States, and Germany). There are, of course, also cultural similarities. Both U.S. and Japanese managers use direct and indirect forms of praise (positive sanctions) for their employees (Barnlund & Araki, 1985).

Population density can have an impact on interaction because it determines how many people will have direct contacts over a certain period. There are countries and regions in which people live in crowded social environments, and there are regions in which large gatherings of people are rare. Just to compare, Monaco in Europe has maybe the highest population density (23,000 people per square kilometer). At the same time, Cambodia has a very low population density (78 people per square kilometer).

You are a king by your own fireside, as much as any monarch on his throne.

MIGUEL DE CERVANTES (1547–1616)—Spanish Novelist and Poet

As a universal cross-cultural trend, people tend to identify and protect territory on which they live. Territorial behavior includes actions that stake out or identify territory, ownership, or belongings. A fence around one's house or a bag placed on a classroom desk indicates our territorial behavior. Anthropologists suggest that territorial behavior is natural for both individuals and social groups (Schubert & Masters, 1991). Territorial behavior can be instinctual. For example, some fish will defend their territory even without the presence of their natural competitors (Lorenz, 1966). Although rejecting the idea about human instincts, psychologists show that groups that are inclusive will tend to tolerate "trespassers," whereas exclusive groups will be particularly territorial.

Cultures can be different in terms of their so-called **embeddedness** or the degree to which individuals and groups are enmeshed together. Cultures high on embeddedness focus on their own internal group solidarity, shared goals, way of life, and resist actions disrupting their in-group solidarity. People in embedded cultures are not particularly concerned for the well-being of those outside their groups. In practical terms, the more embedded the culture in a country, the less people should help strangers. According to studies, several countries scored high on embeddedness: Singapore, Malaysia, Bulgaria, Thailand. Countries in "the middle" are the United States, China, and Brazil. Low-embedded countries are Austria, Spain, Denmark, Sweden, and the Netherlands (Knafo et al., 2009).

Collectivism and individualism, as fundamental cultural attributes, may significantly influence social interaction in a wide variety of situations. We learned in Chapters 1, 7, and 8 that in individualistic cultures, people usually care primarily for themselves and their individual family, whereas in collectivist cultures, people are expected to first look after their in-groups and then themselves. In individualist cultures, the importance of achievement and the individual's initiative are stressed during socialization. In collectivist societies, the emphasis is placed on belonging to groups (Chiu & Hong, 2006). Therefore, it is likely that people in collectivist cultures will interact more frequently and more intensely with in-group members than will members of individualist cultures. In most societies with collectivist norms, people tend to belong to fewer groups, but such groups tend to be more stable and enduring than the groups in individualist societies. People in individualist cultures are more inclined to belong to a large variety of groups, but for shorter periods of time (Moghaddam, 1998). It is also expected that in-group favoritism and mutual influence will be stronger in collectivist cultures than in individualist ones (Gudykunst & Bond, 1997).

Is it accurate to say that Westerners tend to view a person as independent and separate from other people, while Asians tend to view a person as fundamentally connected with others? Are Asians and Asian Americans more or less likely to seek social support for dealing with stress than European Americans? The answer is not that simple. On the one hand, the collectivist orientation of Asian countries might promote the sharing of stressful problems; on the other hand, efforts to maintain group harmony might discourage such efforts: You are not supposed to display your selfish concerns. In two empirical studies, Koreans (study 1) and Asians and Asian Americans in the United States (study 2) reported using social support less for coping with stress than did European Americans. Why? East Asian cultural norms appear to discourage the active engagement of one's social support network for help in solving problems or for coping with stress. Thus, people from an interdependent culture may feel they have less to gain personally and could lose socially by calling on others for help. That is, people may prefer not to burden their social network and attempt to solve their problems individually instead. Thus, cultural differences exist in the way a person copes with stressful events (Taylor et al., 2004).

Nations and communities may develop similar or area-specific norms related to helping behavior. Independent experiments in 23 large cities around the world measured three types of helping: alerting a pedestrian who dropped a pen, offering help to a pedestrian with a hurt leg trying to reach a pile of dropped magazines, and assisting a blind person to cross the street (Levine et al., 2001). The results showed that the "helping" rate in every city was relatively stable across the three measures. This means if most people noticed a dropped pen, then most people in this city would also help the blind or disabled pedestrian. However, cross-cultural variations in helping occurred. As an example, in Brazil (Rio de Janeiro), the rate was 93 percent. In Kuala Lumpur (Malaysia), the rate was 40 percent. Overall, helping across cultures was related to a country's economic productivity: The higher the productivity, the lesser the helping behavior. Other studies showed that helping strangers was more frequent in poorer countries. It was also more frequent in Latin American cultures compared to others (Levine et al., 2001).

One would not be alone even in Paradise.

Italian Proverb

No matter what our cultural background is, the presence or absence of others may significantly alter our behavior: Bystanders, spectators, or even passersby can either enhance or inhibit our performance (Zajonc, 1965). This phenomenon is called **social facilitation**. The influence of others on individual performance was studied as early as the 1900s, when the first pathbreaking experiments in social psychology demonstrated that social facilitation could be viewed as a cross-cultural phenomenon (Yaroshevski, 1996).

Another important cultural dimension that is related to individual interaction, which was discussed in Chapter 1, is *uncertainty avoidance*. Compared to individuals from cultures with low-uncertainty avoidance rules, individuals who live in cultures with high-uncertainty avoidance tend to be less tolerant of uncertainty and ambiguity. They tend to express culturally "approved" emotions more frequently, have a stronger desire for group consensus, are less tolerant of those who are different, and have a greater need to follow formal rules of behavior (Hofstede, 1980). Tolerance of behaviors that deviate from the expected normative patterns is a characteristic behavior in nontraditional societies. Bear in mind that tolerance and intolerance are issue specific and are better understood when studied from a comparative perspective: One should examine a specific group, under specific circumstances, and the extent to which that group experiences intolerance or tolerance for a particular issue. For example, many people are intolerant of homosexuality; however, the scope and scale of such intolerance are different in democratic and authoritarian societies, in traditional and nontraditional cultures (see Chapter 7).

DIRECT CONTACTS AND BODY LANGUAGE

Can an individual's cultural origin be guessed by watching his or her counting? Germans, for example, gesture numbers usually starting with the thumb, whereas English Canadians gesture numbers usually starting with the index finger (Pika et al., 2009). However, in the modern age of travel and communication, these national differences tend to diminish. Whether in Argentina, Sweden, Australia, the Congo, or India, people have common understandings of many signs of body language: They identify belligerent gestures, recognize friendly smiles, and may panic in similar ways when feeling frightened. For example, without saying a word, almost any person can show he does not know the answer to a question by using the universal body language of shrugging the shoulders. It has also been found that typically the higher the social status of an individual, the greater the vocal volume, that is, the louder she speaks. This is especially true in competitive interactions. People tune their vocal intensity by increasing it when interacting with those closer to them in rank and decreasing it when interacting with those further above and below in status (Schubert, 1991a).

The rules of greeting and introducing oneself to other people appear to be comparable across cultures. When two or more people meet for the first time, they tend to tell something about themselves, or as psychologists say, disclose themselves to each other. They say a greeting, tell their names, and usually smile. Studies show significant consistency in the rules of address across different cultures (Frager & Wood, 1992). There are also differences, of course. In some countries, as in the United States, people give each other a handshake when they meet for the first time and typically do not shake hands when they then see each other daily. In many Arab countries and in Russia, on the contrary, people shake hands with their friends and colleagues daily. Remember the effects of the naturalistic fallacy in our evaluation of observable facts? Some people in the United States may consider such attempts at daily handshaking as annoying and intrusive behavior. In the same way, a U.S. professional traveling abroad may be perceived as "cold and detached" because he will not shake hands with his foreign colleagues every morning. Why? Because people tend to consider things that are familiar or "typical" as normal and more acceptable than "atypical" behaviors.

Cultural traditions also regulate our initial contacts, for example, situations of so-called high- or low-cultural contexts (Berry et al., 1992). Within high-context situations, much of the most important information is present in the context. If one person says to another, "Let us have lunch sometime," this does not always mean that the first individual is actually going to have lunch with the other. Based on the situational context, the other person should make an evalua-tion and decide if it was an invitation for lunch or just a polite way to end the relationship. Within low-context situations, almost all the information is in the conveyed message. Most Western countries, including the United States and Canada, are considered to be low-context cultures, whereas countries such as Japan, Korea, and Vietnam are considered to be high-context cultures. It is likely, for example, that personal self-disclosure may be more difficult for Japanese when they communicate with people in the United States than vice versa. Japanese inner life is often communicated more by hints and overtones than by direct interaction. Therefore, when Japanese communicate with U.S. citizens, they may look less relaxed and less flexible than their counter-parts from California or Texas (Hedstrom, 1992). However, do not let your expectations create reality (please remember an element of critical thinking): When a Japanese person communi-cates with a U.S. counterpart, in most cases they will speak English. In this context, who should feel more relaxed: a person who speaks English since birth or one whose foreign-language pro-ficiency is somewhat limited?

There are various social, religious, and cultural factors that regulate our direct contact with others. Eye contact plays a central role in interpersonal relations (Grumet, 1983). In most cultures, people are taught not to stare at strangers. Eye contact during a conversation is a sign of sincerity and interest in most cultures. However, it is generally not the case in Korea: You have to know another person well before you start looking in this person's eyes. In one study, the authors measured the eye gaze displays of Canadian, Trinidadian, and Japanese participants as they answered various questions. When the participants already knew the answers, Trinidadians maintained the most eye contact, while Japanese maintained the least. When the participants had to think about the answers, Canadians and Trinidadians looked up, whereas Japanese looked down (McCarthy et al., 2006).

When people talk to each other, they almost always produce so-called back-channel feedback, which is based on several verbal signals or gestures. For example, in the United States, people use short utterances such as *okay, hmm,* or *I see.* People who speak Arabic as their first language tend to use different back-channel feedback in a conversation: It is a steep pitch downslope (as a native Arabic speaker to demonstrate this). As a study showed, Americans tend to misinterpret this feedback as an expressed negative emotion or a sign of disapproval (Ward & Al Bayyari, 2010). However, such misperception disappears after a short training exercise.

Pointing your finger toward a person is extremely disrespectful among Navajos and native Russians. Touching is more common in cultures around the Mediterranean Sea and in some Slavic nations than it is in European countries such as Holland, Germany, and Finland. In Japan, people follow rules that restrain them from touching friends of the opposite sex below the waist. This restriction is not considered to be important for many individuals from European and American countries (Barnlund, 1975). Latinos interact using smaller physical distances than Japanese and other East Asians. In cultures within the Mediterranean basin, it is accept-able to speak loudly. This type of communication would be considered impolite in Scandinavia. Overall, people's understanding of cultural, ethnic, and national customs can be very useful in cross-cultural communications.

Great players are willing to give up their own personal achievement for the achievement of the group. It enhances everybody.

KAREEM ABDUL-JABBAR (1947–) Professional Basketball Player (www.brainyquote.com)

CONFORMITY

How often do we do things simply because other people do them? **Conformity** is a form of social influence in which individuals change their attitudes and/or behavior to adhere to a group or social norm. Experimental social psychology provides many interesting examples and explanations of human conformity. In a series of classic studies conducted by Asch in the early 1950s, subjects were put into situations in which there were no particular rewards for conformity and no explicit punishment for deviance (Asch, 1956). When faced with an absolute majority of their fellow students agreeing on the same incorrect judgments (in the series of 12 attempts), almost 75 percent of the subjects conformed at least once by responding incorrectly as the group did. In total, 35 percent of the overall responses conformed to the deliberately incorrect judgments expressed by the "actors." It was mentioned that each group applies a variety of sanctions to members who do not accept the group norms. Does this mean that we always conform to avoid negative social sanctions against us? The answer is "no." We conform not only to escape sanctions but for a variety of other reasons.

One reason that we might conform, other than to escape sanctions, is to live up to the expectations of others and therefore remain in their good graces. This is especially true when the "others" represent a majority. For example, many European women cover their heads with a scarf when they arrive in a Muslim country even though this is not required of foreigners. Decision making, especially in an unfamiliar situation, might increase conformity, whereas prior commitments might reduce conformity (Deutsch & Gerard, 1955). Reduced conformity may be due to a prior commitment: A person who does not drink alcohol because of her religious responsibility has fewer chances of starting to drink with her friends than those who do not have such strong commitments.

Either do as your neighbors do, or move away.

MOROCCAN PROVERB

Conformity could be directly motivated by a desire to gain reward or avoid punishment. This form of behavior, often called **compliance**, may also bring people hope. If people are poor, desperate, and depressed, then the promise of a convincing solution might force them to comply with those who make such promises. Compliance, however, is not only a sign of

CROSS-CULTURAL SENSITIVITY

Professional ice hockey players are tough. They shoot the puck and throw body checks. Sometimes, some of them drop their gloves and fight with their bare fists. They are not joking around. The fights are for real. So are the injuries they may inflict on each other. What is the maximum penalty for fighting? Five minutes on a penalty bench. And then the player is back in the game. If you are hit, you hit back. Do not complain. Physical fighting is a part of ice hockey.

However, some words that you say on the ice rink are more painful than cuts and bruises. We are not talking about sexual profanities—if you watch any U.S. professional game from the stands, you know that these obscenities are thrown in every game and basically are left unnoticed by sports officials and the public. We are talking about ethnic and racial slurs—disparaging and extremely offensive remarks about or related to one's ethnicity, religion, or race (origin). The National Hockey League has established "zero tolerance" for racial and ethnic slurs on the ice. Moreover, the league severely punishes some players for using such slurs during the game. Apparently, words can hurt more than fists.

personal weakness and desperation. Take, for example, the 1977 Jonestown suicide and the 1997 Heaven's Gate suicide (you can easily "google" these tragic incidents): The members of these two cult groups were persuaded by group leaders into believing that death was the only acceptable resolution for suffering and the only way to obtain spiritual salvation. Thinking critically about these and other cases of group suicide and various forms of compliance, consider that some powerful leaders who make people follow their orders may themselves display serious abnormal symptoms such as delusions of grandeur and persecution, serious personality dysfunctions, obsession with suicide, and sadistic tendencies (Osherow, 1993; Zimbardo, 1997).

IS CONFORMITY UNIVERSAL ACROSS CULTURES?

Social conformity varies across cultures. For example, there is a positive correlation between individualism and economic wealth. In countries low on individualism, conformity is popular and autonomy is rated as less important (Berry et al., 1992). Therefore, economically wealthy countries, when compared with poorer countries, will conceivably show fewer examples of conformity. Conformity is typically lower in upper–middle-class groups and higher in lower socioeconomic groups. It is higher in stratified and authoritarian societies as well, where parents are concerned about making their children conform to existing social norms (Kohn, 1969; Shiraev & Bastrykin, 1988). All in all, collectivist norms are likely to facilitate conformity, and individualistic norms should not (Matsuda, 1985). In multicultural and diverse societies, such as the United States and Canada, the dominance of a single mainstream culture will be present to a lesser extent than the influence of a single uniform culture in less diverse societies, such as Norway or Korea. Even in an ethnically diverse country such as the Soviet Union, the influence of mainstream Russian culture and single Marxist ideology was enforced by the totalitarian government, which facilitated conformity among its citizens (Gozman & Edkind, 1992).

Anticipation of negative sanctions may limit the expression of views that contradict the majority's opinion and can result in the individual's silent agreement with others. As formulated by Noelle-Neumann (1986), what individuals fear most with respect to their private opinions is social isolation. To avoid isolation, people try to determine what opinions other people hold. If an individual subscribes to the dominant opinion, this judgment is likely to be freely discussed and expressed. Moreover, the absence of resistance or criticism from others will strengthen the individual's opinion. If, however, an individual subscribes to a perceived minority opinion, that individual will fear social isolation and will not express that opinion as freely in public. This situation results in an opinion-voicing spiral into silence, as minority opinions, being less publicly shared, appear less and less widely held. The moral? Social norms of the rejection of and intolerance to different ideas may affect not only the frequency of expression of certain ideas but also their salience among people's thoughts and attitudes. Moreover, lack of expression of such ideas leaves the existing social norms unchallenged.

Social and environmental conditions also influence individual conformity. For example, Berry (1967) showed that conformity is higher in societies with high-food-accumulation practices (e.g., the Temme of Sierra Leone) and lower in societies with low-food-accumulation practices (such as the Canadian Eskimo). In this case, low levels of conformity are perhaps conditioned by socialization practices: A young Eskimo learns very early in life how to be independent as a hunter. Studies conducted in many Asian countries indicate that people there engage in conforming behavior to a greater degree than Europeans. Specifically, Chinese were shown in the past to be more conforming than Americans (Huang & Harris, 1973). Moreover, conformity is valued among Asians (such as Indonesians and Japanese) to a greater degree than among

A CASE IN POINT
Sexual Harassment

"I do what others do." Is conformity a social norm? In the tradition articulated by Lewin (1951), human behavior is a function of two factors: situational and personal. Within the frame of reference of this tradition, many interesting observations can be made. For example, consider sexual harassment. Certain individuals, as a result of their life experience and personality traits, may possess proclivities toward sexual harassment. At the same time, the social norms in a given society or within specific organizational settings may be tolerant of sexual harassment. To illustrate, in the Russian language, there is no exact equivalent for the phrase "sexual harassment." There are virtually no official rules or regulations that aim at preventing or even discouraging sexual harassment. There is a predominant belief among many Russians that women should take the majority of the responsibility for what happens in their sexual relationships. If a woman is acting "provocatively," then it is only she who can be blamed for any harassment or violence against her (Glad & Shiraev, 1999). If there are no words to label sexual harassment, then is it easy to discount or completely deny its very existence. As a result of this cultural norm,

when individuals with a proclivity for sexual harassment are placed in social situations that permit or accept this sort of behavior, tolerance of harassment is more likely to occur (Pryor et al., 1995). In short, those Russians who routinely engage in sexual harassment behavior routinely get away with it because of societal tolerance: There are so many other people who practice the same behavior. However, if these individuals were to move to the United States, it is likely there would be a substantial change in their behavior on learning how sexual harassment is viewed in the United States.

A study of the effects of sexual harassment on a sample of 1,500 women of various ethnic groups showed that more than two-thirds of avoidant negotiators were members of collectivist, patriarchal cultures. Compared to European Americans, Hispanic and Turkish women reported more avoidance, denial, and attempts to cope themselves, without asking for help from others. Such behaviors are likely to reflect collectivist concerns about doing "what others do" by protecting the ongoing relationship and allowing harassers to avoid consequences for their actions (Cortina & Wasti, 2005).

Europeans (Matsumoto, 1994). For example, among participants of a Rokeach Value survey, Asian subjects endorse values such as conformity and obedience, whereas West European subjects emphasize independence and personal freedom (Punetha et al., 1987). Other studies show differences in conforming behavior among representatives of countries that are "similar" to one another, such as Italy and Australia (both predominantly Christian and democratic societies). Italians were found to be more conforming than British Australians (Cashmore & Goodnow, 1986). Contemporary studies, however, tend to challenge the results obtained 15 to 20 years ago. Studies show that conformity is likely to be attached to specific situations and is not, contrary to popular assumptions, typical in some ethnic or national groups. One of the recent studies of Japanese college students demonstrated that Japanese conformed in experimental situations no more than Americans did (Takano & Sogon, 2008).

Remember that conformity should be considered a continuous variable. One can describe both high and low levels of conformity only when contrasting two or more samples. Moreover, within a single culture, different social sanctions are applied to different groups in regard to their conforming behavior.

When comparing conformity cross-culturally, one should take into consideration the social context in which the behavior occurs. With a certain degree of generalization, we can suggest that all human behavior may be viewed as acts of conformity because most healthy individuals tend to adjust their behavior to particular sets of norms. Some forms of conformity can be facilitated. For instance, we conform easily and eagerly when the conforming behavior falls into the category of socially acceptable and when there is no serious moral dilemma present. That is probably why people conform readily when they see other people engaged in socially "good" and "desirable" behavior (Aronson & O'Leary, 1982–1983; Cialdini et al., 1990).

> To go beyond is as wrong as to fall short.
>
> *CONFUCIUS* **(551–479 b.c.e.)—Chinese Philosopher**

If the United States is such a diverse and heterogeneous country, should we expect that most of its citizens are less conformist than other people living in, for instance, Turkey, Brazil, or India? Experimental research does not provide us with impressive evidence in support of this belief. Further, some studies confirm that people in the United States are not less conformist than people from other cultures tested in similar experimental situations. The results of one study conducted in Japan were rather surprising. The data showed the lowest rates of conformity on the Asch experiment in Japan, lower than in the same experiment in the United States (Frager, 1970). Hypothetically, Japanese subjects, who represent a collectivist culture, were expected to conform more frequently than subjects from individualistic cultures, such as the United States. What was the cause of such unexpected results? Was it an error in experimental procedure? Apparently, in collectivist cultures, people conform toward their in-groups and behave less cooperatively toward out-groups. In the Asch experimental procedure, the participants knew each other very little or not at all. This situation could not be termed as "in-group pressure." Studying research on conformity in Japan, Matsuda (1985) explained this phenomenon by hypothetically dividing Japanese groups into three categories. The first category—groups selected by the experimenter—does not show conformity; the second category—mutually selected friends—shows some conformity; and the third category—cohesive groups—shows maximum conformity. Moghaddam (1998) also interprets the findings about low rates of conformity in some Japanese subjects as a demonstration of how different social norms may affect experimental procedures. Most of the experiments on conformity were conducted in colleges and universities and most participants were students. For some of them, situations such as experimental interaction with "strangers" were not as significant as interaction with their families and other important groups, where conformity is apparently high. It is also interesting how uncertainty avoidance may be used to explain conformity. For example, Frager (1970) and later Gudykunst and his colleagues (1992) explained that in the United States, where uncertainty avoidance is low, people tend to have less similar "standard" rules in many social situations. In Japan, however, where uncertainty avoidance is high, people tend to have clear rules of behavior in different social contexts. Therefore, behavior with strangers could be quite different from behavior with in-group members.

Still, when we ask our students to express their opinions on how people in the United States compare with other national groups in regards to conformity, most say that Americans are much less conforming than people of other nationalities. Why does it appear this way? Those who travel can easily see that people who live in North America, Europe, and industrialized countries of the Far East have more choices in life. The choices are not only related to products and services, but also to political diversity, ideological choices, lifestyle, and religious orientations. When John has more choices in life than Mary, he can choose more possible ways to act

CRITICAL THINKING
"We All Conform"

Russian social psychologist Arthur Petrovsky (1978) believed that most of the research on conformity collected by Western psychologists contained a logical error. His main argument was that the error takes place when psychologists describe a person's act of conformity—in the face of group pressure—as a dichotomous variable: The person has only two choices, to conform and not to conform. Moreover, in individualist cultures those who conform are often considered negatively in the public eye as "the led," "the followers," "people without guts," and so on. Conversely, those who do not conform are often labeled as "the leaders," "the daring," and "the independent."

Petrovsky proposed that we could avoid the availability bias (when observers pay attention to what is visible or salient) and examine conformity from a broader perspective. People, especially when they make important decisions, often take into consideration not only the factors that are influencing them in the present situation, but also their values and broader social norms. In some situations, people appear to be exercising

nonconforming behavior, whereas, in fact, they are conforming, but to different norms. For example, a group of students decides to stop by a steak house for dinner; one of the students does not follow the group because, due to his religious views, he does not eat beef. Or a young woman, contrary to what her friends are doing, refuses to get into a car with a drunken driver behind the wheel because she believes this drink-and-drive behavior is dangerous. Should these examples, behaviors in which individuals did not side with the majority, be considered nonconforming behavior? The answer is no, but why? Recall how conformity is defined: This is a form of social influence in which individuals change their attitudes or behavior to adhere to group or social norms. In other words, when it appears to others that somebody does not yield to group pressure, this person still exercises an act of conformity. However, the person conforms to a different set of norms. In the examples given above, the man conformed to the norms of his religion and the woman conformed to the norms of "responsible" behavior, that is, a "do not drink-and-drive" imperative.

than Mary can. In this situation, when we examine John's and Mary's behaviors, we would find that John's behavior is more "complex and diverse." However, this fact could not lead us to the conclusion that John is less conforming than Mary. Mary has fewer choices and opportunities in life, therefore her behavior is confined into a frame of the required behavioral models, but this does not necessarily mean she is more conforming than John.

When you don't command obedience, don't issue orders.

ARABIC PROVERB

FOLLOWING ORDERS

At the very moment that you are reading this, somewhere on the planet someone is giving an order to someone else. For example, someone is commanding others to rise, to move, to work, to rescue, to build, or to kill. People obey other people—parents, teachers, police officers, military commanders, husbands, wives—in every culture. **Obedience** is a form of conformity when a person simply follows orders given by others. Obedience to authority is defined as following orders given by an authority figure. This type of behavior is usually based on a belief that those with authority have the right to issue requests and give such orders.

Research on obedience in the United States and around the world is most notably associated with the name Stanley Milgram, a prominent scientist from Yale University (see Milgram, 1963).

As some psychologists point out, Milgram's publications are among the most famous and widely recognized in psychology's history (Hock, 1995).

Milgram showed in his experiments that some people easily obey others and by doing that, they also readily violate their own moral standards of behavior. Moreover, he found that the circumstances under which people become obedient do not have to be extraordinary. We sometimes obey even in insignificant social situations. The Milgram experiment and many of those that have followed show that obedience to authority is not only typical of the extremely weak, frustrated, or pathological, but also of many "normal" individuals when under psychological pressure. It has also been found that we tend to obey with less hesitation when somebody assumes responsibility for our actions. In these situations, we may do something that we otherwise consider unthinkable.

The Milgram experiment on obedience was reproduced in many countries, apparently with similar results: People tend to obey other people who have power. Despite variations, it is more likely that in countries with high-power distance, rates of obedience will be higher than in countries with low-power distance. (Power distance, discussed earlier in the book, is the extent to which there is inequality between supervisors and subordinates in an organization.) The power distance index is high when the members of a society accept that power in institutions is distributed unequally. Similarly, the power distance index is low when the members of a society tend to accept equality within the institutions (Hofstede, 1980).

Another factor that may affect obedience is the predominant leadership style in a studied society. An authoritarian style of leadership, for example, presumes direct communications from the leader to the led. The leader or any authority figure gives the orders, and the led must obey. Discussions and exchanges of information are significantly limited. In postwar Germany, for example, 40 percent of students who were age 12 between 1946 and 1953 reported actual participation in school discussions and debates, whereas only 6 percent of the students who were age 12 between 1941 and 1945, during the last period of the Nazi dictatorship, reported participation in discussions (Almond & Verba, 1965). It was also found that obedience was one of the most important values cultivated by the system of German socialization during at least the past 200 years (Miller, 1983).

CRITICAL THINKING
Cultural Norms and Obedience

Acts of obedience committed by other people are described and evaluated by us, the observers. When we evaluate, we often use our own standards to either disapprove of or support an individual who obeys. How can person B interpret the obedience of person A if they belong to different cultures? To think critically about an issue also means to ask additional questions about it. In the case of obedience, such a question might be why did *this* particular person follow *this* particular order? Consider, for example, an arranged marriage in India where a young woman follows her parents' suggestion to marry a man she has never seen. Might this appear to a U.S. observer as an act of obedience (Saroop, 1999)? Perhaps it would from the standpoint that the woman simply followed a direct order coming from other people. But from the woman's point of view, her parents' decision may not be an order, but instead a suggestion based on her parents' wisdom, love, and sincere intentions. Moreover, by agreeing with her parents' choice, the young woman honors a centuries-old cultural tradition of arranged marriages. In any situation, we should not forget about the impact of external factors—such as traditions, customs, and mores—on individual behavior and obedience in particular. Please refer to the discussion of the fundamental attribution error in Chapter 3.

According to other studies, parents from low socioeconomic status groups valued obedience more than middle-class families do (Kohn, 1969). Similar results were received in a large-scale study conducted in nine countries, in which parents were asked to say what characteristics in their children were considered to be most desirable. The answers from parents who lived in the United States and other industrialized countries, such as Korea, stressed the importance of personal independence and self-reliant behavior. Parents from less industrialized nations, such as Turkey and Indonesia, indicated the importance of obedience in their children and did not endorse independence (Kagitcibasi, 1996). Among the world's different cultural areas, African societies are rated the highest in the socialization of compliance and obedience (Munroe & Munroe, 1972). Political ideologies also seem to influence the frequency of obedient reactions. In totalitarian countries, obedient reactions were reported to be more frequent than in democratic societies (Triandis, 1994).

A thousand curses never tore a shirt.

ARABIC PROVERB

SOCIAL INFLUENCE

Social Influence in the context of psychology stands for efforts on the part of one person to alter the behavior or attitudes of one or more people. The capacity or ability of an individual to exercise control and/or authority is called **power**. Power can be formal or informal. Formal power is exercised mostly within activities that are defined by official regulations, laws, and institutional rules. Informal power is exercised by individuals in situations without official regulations. In most traditional cultures, parents do not have formal power over their family members. But informally, most parents possess and exercise parental authority over their adult children (Shiraev & Bastrykin, 1988).

Experiments show that the simple presence of a cultural symbol representing a different country or ethnic group may influence people to think spontaneously in terms of the values of that country or cultural group. For example, seeing a red lantern (a cue of Chinese culture) may spontaneously make you think of the value of fulfilling interpersonal duties (a Chinese cultural value) (Ho-Ying et al., 2007).

Research has shown that the way people perceive power of other individuals may affect many aspects of group behavior. Even a simple joke may be interpreted differently by people who have power and those who do not (McGhee & Duffey, 1983).

Compared with people high in power, individuals low in power are more likely to be pessimistic about their own life; the status of their country; and the past, present, and future of the world (Larsen, 1972). Members of low-power groups are expected to have more empathy for members of high-power groups than vice versa. For example, it was found that Arab Lebanese students in the United States were more successful in identifying typical "American" responses than Americans were in identifying typical "Arab" responses (Lindgren & Tebcherani, 1971).

There is an expression in sociology called "soft power." It refers to the influence of ideas transmitted through culture, movies, literature, fashion, and human exchanges. Some nations, like the United States, have enormous economic and financial potential to promote their own culture. Japan, for example, is spreading its "soft power" by introducing its pop culture, including music,

A CASE IN POINT
Challenging the Boss

The copilot and flight engineer of Korean Air jet Boeing 747 knew that the situation was not right: All indicators suggested a serious problem. But neither of them said anything to the captain, who failed to detect any danger. A few seconds later, the airplane slammed into the top of a hill, killing 228 passengers. Investigators confirmed that the crew—even though they knew about the problem—failed to challenge the captain. This tragedy was interpreted as an emblematic cultural issue: The pilots showed a traditional Korean deference to authority (Phillips, 1998). Would a U.S. or Mexican pilot challenge a captain in a similar situation?

It is very difficult to predict specific behavior in hypothetical situations. Studies, however, show that general cultural norms can regulate pilots' behavior in the cockpit. Survey data collected from 9,400 male commercial airline pilots in 19 countries (Merritt, 2000) show that norms of collectivism and individualism, respect to authority, and power distance may determine specific actions of the pilot.

clothing design, toys, food, and martial arts, to the rest of the world. According to Japanese sources, more than 3 million people around the world have been studying the Japanese language as of late, compared with only 127,000 in 1997 (Faiola, 2003).

FEELING GOOD ABOUT SOME VIEWS

Across the world, individuals in social groups show tendencies to adhere to their shared views so strongly that they ignore information inconsistent with those views (see discussion of "belief perseverance" in Chapter 3). There are some cultural differences in the way people express their agreement with the views of others. Studies show, for example, that Koreans tend to show more acquiescence or agreeableness in written answers than Americans do. However, the differences were relatively small (Locke & Baik, 2009). This occurrence of agreement with others in a group decision-making process is called **groupthink**. Irving Janis, who described this amusing phenomenon, believed that groupthink is associated with concurrence seeking, and that it may often override any realistic appraisals of alternative decisions or courses of action (Brandstatter et al., 1984). In April 1961, President Kennedy agreed to support an invasion of Cuba with the help of U.S.-trained Cuban exiles to dismiss the communist regime there. This operation ended in a disaster and serves as a perfect example of groupthink. The cabinet members apparently knew that the invasion would not succeed, but nobody brought those issues to light because they apparently wanted to maintain **cohesiveness** within the inner circle of presidential advisers. Psychologist Aronson proposed that the tragic failure of the space shuttle Challenger in 1986 was also the result of groupthink. The NASA engineers, in their pursuit of a common goal, ignored several warning signs of a potential disaster (Aronson, 1995). Discussions continue today on whether groupthink was a factor influencing the U.S. decision on war in Iraq in 2003.

Groupthink is a very compelling group mechanism among members of fundamentalist religious, radical political, and militant ethnic groups. When you join a group, you may be hesitant to express doubts regarding group decisions and group activities because your hesitation might be considered a sign of weakness and disloyalty.

Another group phenomenon, known as **group polarization,** is almost in direct contrast to groupthink. Group polarization is the tendency of group members to shift, as a result of group discussion, toward more extreme positions than they initially held. In the case of group polarization, group cohesiveness may not be as important for the group members. In some cases, the risky shift phenomenon occurs, which means that group decisions are often riskier than individual views held by the members before discussion or decision making (Moscovici & Zavalloni, 1969). Found in various experimental situations in the United States, in many European, and some African countries, the risky shift phenomenon is also explained as being based on particular cultural norms (Brown, 1965). In other words, if a culture values risky behavior in its individuals, the risky shift is likely to occur. The risky shift phenomenon was confirmed to be present in many countries, including France, England, Canada, Israel, and New Zealand (see, e.g., Rim, 1963; Vidmar, 1970). The data on risk taking across cultures are somewhat inconsistent (Foxall & Payne, 1989), but several studies place U.S. managers in a higher risk-taking category compared with other national samples.

IS SOCIAL LOAFING UNIVERSAL?

Imagine you are working alone on a project. You have been asked to compare divorce rates around the world and collect statistical data through the Internet. You hope to finish the project in a few days. Unexpectedly, your professor tells you that two people have been assigned to help you finish the project. After hearing this news, will you feel relief? Will you slow down your efforts, anticipating that your helpers will contribute to the work load? Indeed, many people slow down under similar circumstances, thus demonstrating **social loafing,** the tendency of group members to exert less effort on a task than they would if they were working alone or when the size of the group is expanded. Is social loafing common in every social group?

The results of several cross-cultural studies show that social loafing is not a universal phenomenon. For example, research conducted in China and Japan suggests that social loafing does not occur in the group behavior studied in these countries. In some cases, the opposite phenomenon appeared. It is called "social striving," when a group enhances the individual performance of its members (Earley, 1989). It was found in some studies that people in the United States ("individualists") manifested social loafing, whereas people in China ("collectivists") tended to show the opposite pattern (social striving), performing better in pairs than alone (Gabrenya et al., 1985). Perhaps in many cultures in which social loafing does not occur, the existing collectivist norms stimulate interpersonal interdependence. In other words, hypothetically, in collectivist cultures social loafing is not typical. However, this does not mean that in individualistic cultures social loafing will always be part of group relationships. Also, we should not discount the fact that the more cohesive a group becomes, the lower the occurrence of loafing (Petrovsky, 1978). Loafing is based on social circumstances and may also be increased or decreased according to psychological phenomena such as members' individual **identification** with, and loyalty and responsibility toward, the group.

COOPERATION AND COMPETITION

Some of us are either more or less competitive compared with others. Circumstances may change and we may also adjust our competitive patterns, becoming more cooperative or more competitive. There are circumstances that stimulate **competition**, and there are conditions that facilitate **cooperation** among group members. What are those conditions?

- In competitive reward conditions, a person gains when other members lose. The worse they are, the better you are. Almost all sport competitions are based on the competitive reward principle. The same situation occurs when several companies are competing for a contract and only one can win it. Competitive elections for any public office in the United States are also based on the win–lose principle. One may win not only by improving one's record but also by "going negative," that is, downgrading the accomplishments of the competitors.
- In cooperative reward conditions, people's rewards are positively linked. If one does poorly, the whole group may go down. The better each member does, the more chance the whole group has to win. A group of surgeons and nurses working in an operating room, a football team on the field, or automobiles on the freeway during rush hour all represent cooperative reward structures.
- In individualistic reward conditions, the outcomes of individuals are independent of each other. If a professor gives an "A" to everyone who gains more than 100 points in the class, this system of grading is based on an individualistic reward structure. Shoppers in a food store, casino gamblers sitting side by side in front of slot machines, and patrons in a restaurant are all relatively independent of one another.

There are some cultural influences on the group reward conditions. For example, in Japanese organizations, plans are typically drafted at the lower levels of an organization. Then, employees are encouraged to develop their own ideas into a draft. Finally, the plan gradually moves up, from lower offices to higher offices for approval (Berry et al., 1992). This type of plan drafting is not as common in the United States.

Cross-cultural studies show that U.S. citizens are among the most competitive people on earth. In business, according to the law, most government contracts to private firms must be awarded on a competitive basis. Experiments also show that in general children from Western technological societies are less cooperative than children from Latin American, African, and Middle Eastern countries. Additionally, there is a cross-cultural tendency for children from urban areas to be more competitive than children from rural regions, and for middle-class children to compete more often than children from lower-class environments (Madsen, 1986). In cultures with strong collectivist features, such as Ukraine, helping behavior is stronger associated with societal orientation than in more individualist cultures where cooperation is based on personal responsibility (Mullen & Skitka, 2009).

A comparative French–Congolese study showed that, in the predominately collectivistic Congolese culture, forgiveness toward criminals was associated with the restoration of cooperation, sympathy, affection, and trust toward them—all leading to behavioral reconciliation. Within the predominately individualistic culture of France, on the other hand, forgiveness and reconciliation were not commonly associated. You may forgive someone but will not start cooperating or restore your relationship with that person (Kadiangandu et al., 2007).

There are cultural similarities too. For example, a comparative Sudanese–British study showed that in both countries people are less willing to cooperate with others when they are in the city, when the situation is not urgent, and when helping entailed high personal cost (Hedge & Yousif, 1992). In ethnic conflicts, as research shows, one of key problems is that the competing sides consider compromise as a sign of weakness. Both Israeli and Palestinians, in the Middle East, for example, struggle to accept a new set of perceptions according to which sharing territory and power is not actually losing (Kelman & Chin, 2010).

One man with courage makes a majority.

ANDREW JACKSON (1767–1845)—Seventh U.S. President

LEADERSHIP

Leadership can be compared to the ability or capacity to lead: to guide, manage, and direct the actions and opinions of individuals. For the most part of the twentieth century, understanding of leadership has been largely based on the results of studies carried in the United States and a few other countries (Ayman & Korabik, 2010). Gradually, researchers embraced cross-cultural studies in this field. **Leadership** is the process through which some individuals (leaders) influence other group members toward attainment of specific group goals. The leader's behavior is frequently described along two dimensions. The first dimension represents performance, that is, task-related actions, such as explaining goals, distributing roles, explaining requirements, and so on. The other dimension (maintenance) is a set of psychological supports provided by the leader to subordinates. This description of leadership has found support in several countries, such as Japan, India, Iran, and Russia (Hui & Luk, 1997; Schmidt & Yeh, 1992; Sventsitsky, 1988), and these characteristics seem to be universal in every culture. Psychological research shows that two types of leadership roles for problem-solving behavior—labeled "adaptors" and "innovators"—appear in many national environments (Kirton, 1976, 1994). For example, cross-nationally, at least for a sample of European countries, those with a more adaptive style (the "adaptors") would be attracted to occupations and professions that require close attention to detail and more organized and methodical styles of work. By contrast, those with a more innovative style ("the innovators") would prefer occupations where systems and procedures of operation are more loosely defined and emphasis is placed more on "the bigger picture" than on the detail (Tullett, 1997).

There is less agreement about what makes an effective leader. The contingency theory suggests that a leader's success should be determined by the person's traits and by various features of the situation. The normative theory implies that a leader's success be based on whether support and participation are accepted from followers and subordinates. *Participative* leadership that allows subordinates' participation could be very effective in some conditions, especially when individuals are educated and responsible for their actions. However, it could backfire when employees are not ready to act independently, whether due to lack of education or skill, or because of their unwillingness to accept responsibilities.

Special attention in cross-cultural psychology is paid to transformational leadership, often known as charismatic leadership. There is little agreement on how to define this phenomenon. However, specialists concede that charismatic leaders become personally attractive to their followers and are able to unify people to perform difficult tasks with enthusiasm and devotion. The history of human civilization gives many examples of charismatic leadership: Dr. Martin Luther King, Jr. in the United States, Napoleon in France, Simon Bolivar in South America, Indira Gandhi in India, Ayatollah Khomeini in Iran, Mikhail Gorbachev in Russia, and many others. Cultural conditions and traditions determine what traits are necessary for a successful charismatic leader (Glad & Shiraev, 1999). Across cultures, stereotypes exist about the differences between men and women as leaders. Eagly and Carli (2007) showed a gender bias in the way people perceive leadership roles. The male style of leadership has been accepted as "command and control," while the female style is commonly viewed as "facilitative and collaborative." In simple terms, women are often expected to lead within a narrow band described as the small range between not too "wimpy" and not too "bitchy" (Bronznick & Goldenhar, 2008). There were studies showing that men were more effective in masculine leadership roles, while women were more effective in more feminine leadership roles (Eagly et al., 1995), which may suggest that people judge about a leader's effectiveness by how well she or he fits into the roles "prescribed" to them.

Sexist attitudes could prevent a woman—even though she has outstanding leadership skills—from becoming a national leader (Starovoitova, 1998). In short, across countries, gender can affect access to leadership positions (Ayman & Korabik, 2010). Specialists also point out that in certain periods in history, the leader's role of a benevolent father was especially attractive in Iran (Ayman & Chemers, 1983), Germany (Koenigsberg, 1992), and Russia (Gozman & Edkind, 1992). A moral person is the best charismatic model in China, and a "nurturant" manager is more suitable for Indian conditions (Hui & Luk, 1997) than for North American circumstances.

Traditionally, psychologists recognize three major leadership styles that are described in practically all social psychology textbooks around the world. In the *authoritarian* style, the leader makes all decisions. This person is very controlling, directive, and demanding and gives few explanations regarding group activities. In these cases, members are not allowed to choose their own strategies or courses of action. Roles are precisely assigned to the group members, and any deviation from group norms is punishable. Negative sanctions usually outweigh positive sanctions. In the *democratic* style, the leader makes decisions after consulting with the group members. The leader often allows group members to choose their own implementation strategies after decisions are made. The democratic leader tries to share as much information (related to the group activities) as possible with the group members. Positive and negative sanctions are equally applicable. These two styles were first described by Kurt Lewin, a prominent psychologist who immigrated to the United States as a refugee from Nazi Germany (Lewin et al., 1939). The third style is called *laissez-faire*. The leader does not try to exercise control over the group. This person gives the group members general instructions and advice. The group members are then expected to act on their own, choosing their own methods and strategies for actions.

Which of these styles is the most effective? Initially, Lewin and his colleagues believed the democratic style to be the best and most effective one. Even the label "democratic" was most likely chosen for ideological reasons in order to emphasize the advantages of the democratic society (please refer to discussion of the "Evaluative Bias of Language" in Chapter 3). However, despite some obvious advantages, this style cannot be ranked as the most effective. For example, in emergency situations, the authoritarian style may be more effective than the other styles. Moreover, in paternalistic and post-totalitarian societies, the group members might not accept the democratic style. Why? Because in many difficult life situations, people need guidance with decision making because they do not have enough experience to make important life decisions for themselves. Totalitarian cultures in a process of transition are apt to present especially difficult problems along these lines. Because the authorities in such regimes make so many life choices for members and use the threat of force to prevent independent action, psychological dependency is likely to be characteristic of many members of the group. Dependency is promoted and people come to need the all-powerful leaders who feed the people's needs (Koenigsberg, 1992; Marlin, 1990).

Thinkers prepare the revolution; bandits carry it out.

MARIANO AZUELA **(1873–1952)—Mexican Novelist**

Over the years, social psychologists have created at least two types of explanations for the causes of leadership behavior. The first view is called "the trait approach." According to this standpoint, to become a leader one should have a set of specific predispositions or traits. These traits are universal and typical in leaders in every culture. In other words, one should expect that U.S. and French presidents as well as Japanese and Turkish prime ministers have a somewhat similar ensemble of personality traits related to leadership. Among the most frequently mentioned traits are abilities to accomplish group goals, intellectual skills, strong motivation, and abilities to sustain pressure.

However, not every person who has these traits has the chance to become a leader. According to the other common view, leadership is mostly situational. Leaders surface when the situation requires their presence. According to this approach, dictators may emerge only in the case of a national crisis. In a simple way, great leaders emerge only when the society is going through great difficulties. If everything is all right in a group or in a society, great leaders will not emerge. Why? Because they are not needed. Of course in reality, leadership is probably a function of both "trait" and situational factors (see discussion of "multiple causation" in Chapter 3).

To conclude, cross-cultural research of leadership brings new questions. We don't know very well how could race, ethnicity, and nationality influence the leader's behavior. Think about this: Will a woman president remain less forceful during times of crisis? Will a leader with a mixed ethnicity be more sensitive to global problems? Would a leader from a collectivist culture such as India be different from a leader who grew up in an individualist culture such as Denmark or the United States? (Chin, 2010). Research in this field continues.

Exercise 11.1

Brainstorming is a group discussion technique that allows participants to generate as many different suggestions or solutions to the problem as they can in a limited period of time. The rules of brainstorming are relatively simple (Osborn, 1957). First, the group needs your ideas. The more ideas you generate, the better, because the quantity of ideas will influence the quality of the final decision. Second, you are free to generate any ideas you want. Perk up, do not tame down! You should not worry about being "crazy," "naive," or "stupid." There are no crazy, naive, or stupid suggestions in this situation. Third, criticism of other members' ideas and proposals is taboo. Be positive and generous. You will have time later to veto those ideas that you do not like. Fourth, you will help improve on the ideas and suggestions of other group members. Be constructive by showing how those ideas you support can be implemented.

Question:

Do you think that brainstorming as a method of group decision making may have different effects in collectivist and individualist cultures? Which culture's norms would be most beneficial for successful brainstorming? Consider two hypotheses:

First, in individualist cultures, people are freer to express their individual opinions than in collectivist cultures. Therefore, brainstorming is naturally "fit" into any individualist culture: People do not care about criticism and express their ideas freely.

Second, in collectivist cultures, individuals are more interconnected and interdependent. Therefore, any group discussion that requires mutual support and understanding is naturally in agreement with the norms of a collectivist culture. Which of the two hypotheses would you consider to be more plausible? Explain your answer.

Chapter Summary

- Anthropologists confirm that people tend to form groups in all known human societies. By joining a group, we attain a status, a relative social, formal, or informal position, or rank within the group. As soon as we obtain a status, we begin to perform our social roles, the sets of behaviors individuals occupying specific positions within a group are expected to perform. Each group has a set of norms, or rules within a group indicating how its members should or should not behave. Most of us identify our own in-groups, that is, groups to which we belong, and out-groups, that is, groups to which we do not belong. There are groups to which we may not belong but with which we identify ourselves: reference groups. Anthropologists suggest that territorial behavior is natural for both individuals and social groups. Groups that are inclusive will tend to tolerate "trespassers," whereas exclusive groups will be particularly territorial.

- Studies show significant consistency in the rules of address across different cultures. Despite many similarities across countries, there are various social, religious, and cultural factors that regulate our specific contacts.
- Conformity is a form of social influence in which individuals change their attitudes and/or behavior to adhere to existing group or broader group or social norms. Conformity is a universal phenomenon, which has some variations across cultures. There is a positive correlation between individualism and economic wealth. In addition, in countries low on individualism, conformity is popular, and autonomy is rated as less important. In countries with high individualism, variety is valued. In particular, studies conducted in many Asian countries indicate that people of these cultures engage in conforming behavior to a greater degree than do people in the United States. Conformity is high in agricultural societies and low in hunting and gathering societies. It is typically lower in upper–middle-class groups and higher in lower socioeconomic groups. It is also higher in stratified societies.
- Obedience is a form of conformity when a person simply follows orders. People tend to obey other people who have power. Despite variations, it is more likely that in

countries with high power distance, rates of obedience will be higher than in countries with low power distance.

- Groupthink is the tendency of members of groups to adhere to the shared views so strongly that they ignore information inconsistent with those views. There is evidence suggesting that groupthink is common in every culture. Group polarization is the tendency for group members to shift, as a result of group discussion, toward more extreme positions than those they initially held. In the case of group polarization, group cohesiveness may not be as important for the group members. In some cases, the risky shift phenomenon occurs, which means that group decisions are often riskier than individual views held by the members before discussion or decision making. If a culture values risky behavior in its individuals, the risky shift is likely to occur.
- Social loafing is the tendency of group members to exert less effort on a task than they would if working alone or when the size of the group is expanding. In many cultures in which social loafing does not occur, the existing collectivist norms stimulate interpersonal interdependence. In competitive reward structure, a person gains when other members lose. In a cooperative reward structure, people's rewards are positively linked. In an individualistic reward structure, the outcomes of individuals are independent of each other.
- Leadership is the process through which some individuals (leaders) influence other group members toward attainment of specific group goals. Goal-oriented leaders organize their activities around the group's prime goals. The group-oriented leader is concerned first with in-group relationships. The self-oriented leaders' concerns have to do with their own power. Traditionally, there are three major leadership styles recognized. In the authoritarian leadership style, the leader makes important decisions. In the democratic style, the leader makes

decisions after consulting with the group members. The third is called *laissez-faire*, and in this style, the leader does not try to exercise control over the group, but gives the group members general instructions and advice. The usefulness of these styles is based on particular situational or cultural conditions.

Key Terms

Cohesiveness All forces acting on group members to cause them to remain part of a group, including mutual attraction, interdependence, and shared goals.

Competition A form of social interaction in which individuals or groups attempt to maximize their own outcomes, often at the expense of others.

Compliance Doing or saying what others say or do.

Conformity A form of social influence in which individuals change their attitudes or/and behavior to adhere to existing social norms.

Cooperation A form of social interaction in which individuals or groups coordinate their behavior to reach a shared goal.

Embeddedness The degree to which individuals and groups are enmeshed together.

Group Two or more individuals forming a complete unit in a composition.

Group Polarization The tendency of group members to shift, as a result of group discussion, toward more extreme positions than those they initially held.

Groupthink The tendency of members of groups to adhere to the shared views so strongly that they ignore information inconsistent with those views.

Identification The process wherein the individual so strongly feels that he or she is a member of a group that he or she adopts its opinions, attitudes, and values.

Leadership The process through which some individuals (leaders) influence other group members toward the attainment of a specific group goal or activity.

Norms Rules within a group indicating how its members should (or should not) behave.

Obedience A form of social influence in which one person simply orders one or more people to perform some action(s).

Power The capacity or ability of an individual to exercise control and/or authority.

Roles The sets of behaviors that individuals occupying specific positions within a group are expected to perform.

Sanctions Actions that reward those who follow the norms (positive sanctions) and reprove those who are deviant (negative sanctions).

Social Facilitation Effects on performance resulting from the presence of others.

Social Influence Efforts on the part of one person to alter the behavior or attitudes of one or more people.

Social Loafing The tendency of some group members to exert less effort on a task than they would if working alone.

Status Relative social (formal or informal) position or rank within a group.

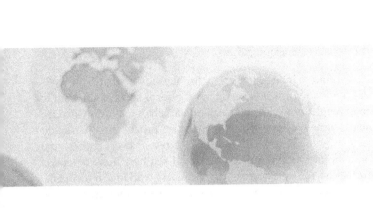

Applied Cross-Cultural Psychology: Some Highlights

None will improve your lot if you yourself do not.

BERTOLT BRECHT—
Twentieth-Century German Playwright

Symbols of pride in one country often mean something else in others. Not long ago, Chinese officials privately asked the U.K. prime minister and his delegation before they arrived in China to remove the poppy symbol that many Britons wear every November. Red poppies are Britain's symbol of remembrance. The tradition stems from the times of World War I, when these flowers grew on battlefields. Charitable organizations regularly sell paper poppies to raise funds for veterans. However, this flower means something else in China. Back in the nineteenth century, China fought and lost two wars with Britain. Called Opium Wars, they resulted in Britain gaining the territory of Hong Kong and forced China to open their borders to trade, including in the drug ingredients derived from the poppy. In this case of international diplomacy, the British delegation politely refused to remove the poppy symbol. But if you were to advise the prime minister, would you recommend him to remove the flower out of respect to the hosts? Or, if you were to advice the Chinese government, would you advise them not to ask about the flower, out of respect to the guests?

Psychology remains a theoretical discipline so long as it answers the questions "what?" "when?" and "why?" It becomes a practical field when it starts searching for some specific answers to the question, "How to apply?" For example, how can one teach effectively in culturally diverse classrooms, use western therapies in non-Western settings, advertise products to particular ethnic groups, or reduce prejudice? Psychologists try to find some concrete answers to these and many other questions related to human interaction in diverse cultural settings. It is an applied field that can provide helpful information for thousands of professionals working in medicine, psychotherapy, education, community services, business, sports, and many other areas of life (Chung, Bemak, & Talleyrand, 2007).

Psychologists are not magicians. Psychologists most of the time are not policy makers either. However, they can influence policy by creating a particular "policy climate" around almost every social issue, problem, or development. Via books, conferences, articles, public lectures, the media, online social networks, and face-to-face contacts, psychologists can disseminate their ideas, influence people's opinions, change stereotypes, and manage people's actions.

Cross-cultural psychology can provide valuable data and suggestions to psychotherapy. Psychological knowledge can be useful in international diplomacy and negotiation, advertising, and marketing. Specialists in cross-cultural psychology can help thousands of migrants adjust in a new cultural environment. We believe that as intercultural contacts increase in all parts of the world, interest in this area of cross-cultural training will almost certainly grow.

Let us examine just a few practical problems that cross-cultural psychologists may face and what kinds of solutions they may offer.

Cultivate health instead of treating disease.

JOHN RUSKIN (1819–1900)—English Writer

HEALTH

When most people in a wealthy side of the world care mostly about improving the quality of their lives, for almost a billion of people, their chief daily concern is survival. Every year, the World Health Organization publishes data about major causes of illness and premature death. It will not be a surprise that environmental problems, poverty, and poverty-related issues are mentioned among prime causes of health problems around the world. For example, more than 50 million people live in countries in which the life expectancy is close to 45 years, and these countries are the poorest in the world. Despite tremendous changes in the prevention and treatment of childhood illnesses, by 2025 there will still be 5 million deaths a year among children under five years of age. It is expected that 97 percent of these deaths will take place in the developing world, and most of them will be due to infectious diseases and malnutrition, which alone account for 50 percent of deaths among young children. On a positive side, stomach cancer will generally become less common, mainly because of improved food conservation and healthy dietary changes. Time and again we see how availability and access to resources affect the overall health of the population in any country. We still don't know much how genetic factors affect health problems in various ethnic groups. In the United States, African Americans have the highest mortality on most causes of death, along with Native Americans. Asian Americans generally have the lowest rates of disease. Hispanics have higher incidences of diabetes, but relatively lower rates of cardiovascular problems. Non-Hispanic Whites are second after African Americans in rates for many diseases and in mortality (Adler, 2009).

Overall, poverty and ecological problems significantly affect people's health-related activities. However, are there any cultural factors, such as norms and values that could have some effect on people's attitudes and actions related to their health. Cultural myths, inaccurate folk beliefs, and fear of sanctions affect many people's reluctance to admit the existence of AIDS. In Africa, for example, many doctors are often unwilling to record AIDS as the cause of death. Instead, other diseases such as tuberculosis are often recorded on certificates. Studies show that a key source in the transmission of AIDS in Africa is men who migrate to urban areas in search of work, where they have unprotected sex with HIV-infected prostitutes before returning to their rural areas and unintentionally infecting their wives (Kalipeni et al., 2008). Knowledge of this cultural pattern would be very useful in developing HIV prevention programs in Africa.

See Table 12.1 for a few examples of how particular cultural beliefs and practices contradict international health initiatives and scientific evidence. The United Nations endorses a policy to encourage lower birth rates in the world's poor regions. One of the main arguments to support this policy is that lower birth rates are likely to reduce poverty, improve health, and increase educational opportunities for women and children. Serious socioeconomic and psychological factors, however, prevent people from having fewer children. Availability of contraceptive methods is seriously limited in most rural areas. Erroneous folk beliefs about contraceptives negatively affect their use. Religious and cultural restrictions also keep people away from using birth control methods. In the traditional family, communication about sex is virtually nonexistent, and women often leave the decision about contraceptive use to their husband (Leenen et al., 2008).

TABLE 12.1 Health Policies, Research, and Common Health-Related Beliefs

Health Policies and Research Findings	Popular Beliefs and Common Practices
Certain practices especially involving abuses of women and children such as child labor or systematic spousal cruelty should be condemned. Governments and communities should curb such practices.	There are cultural practices that do not follow Western standards of abuse. People from other countries should not tell local communities what they should and should not do regarding traditions.
In poor countries, low fertility rates and smaller families improve people's economic opportunities, educational possibilities, and general health. High fertility rates should be reduced.	Fertility rates are beyond people's control. Contraceptives and other birth-control methods should not be used. Women should not discuss with men issues related to birth control.
It is imperative to provide detailed information about how many people are affected by AIDS and related problems. People should be educated about AIDS.	AIDS is not caused by an infection. It is embarrassing to reveal that the family member has an AIDS-related problem. The number of cases should be underreported to avoid accusations of sinful behavior or poor health policies.
Certain psychological problems such as depression or schizophrenia should be recognized and diagnosed. Treatment for such problems should be provided, including medication and counseling.	There is no such thing as mental disorder. All psychological dysfunctions are a form of punishment for sinful or inappropriate behavior in the past. The remedy for such dysfunctions is beyond the abilities of contemporary medicine or psychology.

Recompense injury with justice, and recompense kindness with kindness.

Confucius (551–479 b.c.e.)—**Chinese Philosopher**

Cultural factors affect medical decisions related to life and death. In 2001, the Dutch parliament allowed doctors to inject a sedative and a lethal dose of muscle relaxant into an adult terminal patient suffering great pain in instances where conscious consent is given. Christian, Jewish, and Islamic scholars are generally in favor of life-support machines. However, opinions differ about when life support should be discontinued. Legal rules are relatively strict. In the United States, France, and scores of other countries, the death of the brain, that is, the secession of electrophysiological activities, is the evidence of death. Many religious experts tend to agree that once the brain is dead, the person is no longer alive. Yet some argue that the person lives so long as the heart is beating. Consider "A Case in Point".

One of the key activities that psychologists can help with is the creation of educational, culture-sensitive programs that can help people to take immediate steps and improve their health, deal with abuse, or cope with consequences of natural and human-made disasters (Bemak et al., 2003). Most of these programs have already been created in the United States and Western Europe. Yet, we do not know if these programs and "psychological interventions" are effective in different cultural environments. Therefore, successful, culture-specific educational or counseling programs attract much attention these days. Among these projects, for example, is the highly acclaimed work of Fred Bemak and Rita Chung (2008) on cross-cultural counseling for survivors of natural disasters. Another example is the innovative project by Iwin Leenen and colleagues on the effectiveness of a Mexican health education program in poor rural areas in Guatemala (Leenen et al., 2008). This program aimed at imparting knowledge as well as enabling changes in behavior with respect to everyday life issues like nutrition, hygiene, sanitation, and sexual and reproductive health.

The primary target of this program is changing behavior of specific individuals in existing circumstances. The program was implemented with some 400 indigenous women in rural

A CASE IN POINT
Life and Death

What criteria constitute the death of the human body? Absence of all movements including breathing? Absence of heartbeat? Permanent nonattendance to stimulation? Irreversible loss of consciousness? Even though there are ongoing and heated debates about when life begins—at conception or at some point during prenatal development—there are some national standards of what is considered death of the body. In the United States, in the beginning of the 1980s, a presidential commission and state courts reached a consensus that brain death signals the end of human life. In Japan, however, there is a prominent belief that it is not only the brain that makes us human. Even a brain-dead person is alive until the last beat of that person's heart. Therefore, organ transplants, until the end of the 1990s, were banned in Japan (except cornea, kidney, and bone marrow transplants because they do not require a brain-dead donor). But despite recent changes in the government's stand on organ transplant, donors are few because of the Japanese belief that bodies must remain intact for the trip to the afterlife. Besides, Japanese people tend to be very uncomfortable bringing part of someone else's body into their own. It is like you have part of their soul.

Guatemala living under dire poverty and was carried out through a closely supervised cascade process in which specially trained local women conducted workshops to their fellow country-women. The program can be broken down into four consecutive modules or stages.

Stage 1. The goal here is to explain the factors affecting the health of rural women. Discussions center on how a submissive role of women can prevent them from addressing their feelings and needs. Exercises deal with domestic violence, stress, and the use of tobacco and alcohol. Women also learn about human rights, women's rights, and self-knowledge. They learn how to negotiate and make health-related decisions in the family.

Stage 2. In this stage, women learn about the relation between health and nutrition and the right and necessity to have a sufficient and balanced diet. Special attention is given to women's nutritional needs related to menstruation, pregnancy, and breast-feeding. The women learn how to prepare healthy and low-cost meals and how to maintain a family vegetable garden.

Stage 3. Here, women discuss hygiene and sanitation and learn basic rules related to the prevention of infectious diseases. Emphasis is given to a clean home environment and preventive actions such as removing household garbage, protection against pests, and keeping toilets clean. Assuming responsibility for hygiene by all members of the family is emphasized.

Stage 4. In this stage, discussions focus on sexuality, cultural taboos, and reproductive health. The women gain knowledge about fertility, contraception, sexual rights and values, sexually transmitted diseases, and cervical cancer. They learn how to talk about these "embarrassing" topics and to negotiate sexual matters with their husbands.

Science without religion is lame; religion without science is blind.

ALBERT EINSTEIN **(1879–1955)—German-Swiss-American Physicist**

SPIRITUALITY, SCIENCE, AND HEALTH

Historically, many psychologists provide **counseling**, psychological direction or advice as to a decision or course of action. Such advice and directives are frequently made from a contemporary Western position of science that accepts biomedical treatment or behavioral modification as the main approach to psychological problems. During the past century, psychological science in most Western countries developed in the context where there was a distinct separation between psychology and religion. As a result, a researcher's appeals involving "spiritual" issues were rejected in the mainstream psychology of many countries, including the United States, England, Canada, Russia, and France. Most professional psychologists attending colleges and universities in developed Western countries have little knowledge about the use of spirituality in counseling and psychotherapy. Any mention of spirituality was rejected altogether as nonscientific and therefore undeserving of attention.

As a result, many contemporary psychologists are only at the beginning stages of understanding spirituality, a source of motivation and reasoning for many people living in traditional cultures and modern settings (Penny et al., 2009). **Spirituality** refers to a broad range of phenomena concerning "nonmaterial" matters related to faith, trust, and hope, in contrast to "material" matters related to ownership, accumulation of possessions, and competition. In a psychological context, spirituality emphasizes mind over matter, being over having, and mental effort over physical action. Individuals develop a strong belief in existence of a spiritual essence that fills everything in the universe, including human beings. This essence exists before, after, and beyond material existence.

Using a multidisciplinary approach, psychologists try to understand spirituality and its effects on treatment and health. Rejecting sheer speculations about the "power of the mind," psychologists currently try to apply scientifically sound methods of comparative analysis. In a typical methodology, two groups of subjects are selected. One group represents individuals who accept spirituality and regularly practice their beliefs. Such practices vary and depend on cultural conditions and characteristics of populations: Some people indicate their deep belief in God; some attend religious services (in a mosque, church, synagogue, etc.); some pray regularly; yet others may emphasize meditation, trance, and other activities indicating their belief in spiritual power. The control groups in such studies comprise people who show very little or no inclination to spirituality.

On the basis of such comparative studies, researchers have found evidence that meditation and prayer are associated with and cause lower blood pressure and pulse, lower endocrine activity, and overall lower body metabolism (Ray, 2004). Another set of studies is based on finding various physiological mechanisms of spirituality (Chopra, 2000, 2010).

Overall, the contemporary view of spirituality is that spiritual factors such as strong religious beliefs, prayer, meditation, and combinations of these affect at least four interacting physiological systems: the brain, the endocrine system, the peripheral nervous system, and the immune system.

There is also growing scientific evidence about the possible impact of spirituality on health (see Table 12.2).

We have to be cautious, however, because the results are mixed. In some areas, the impact was established; in others it was not. For example, contemporary science has no evidence that spirituality improves recovery from acute illness or that deeply religious people have higher life expectancy. Yet, there is some strong evidence that spirituality protects against cardiovascular diseases.

What is the evidence about the effectiveness of spirituality as a method of treatment? Multidisciplinary research suggests that spiritual meditation reduces stress and enhances confidence and optimism in people across various age groups. Spiritual-based coping can be a useful

TABLE 12.2 Evidence on the Impact of Spirituality on Health

Assumptions	Research Evidence
People attending religious services tend to live longer	Persuasive
Deeply religious people have higher life expectancy	No evidence
Spirituality protects against cardiovascular diseases	Some evidence
Spirituality protects against cancer mortality	Inadequate
Spirituality slows cancer progression	No evidence
Spirituality protects against disability	Inadequate evidence
Spirituality improves recovery from acute illness	No evidence
Being prayed for improves recovery from acute illness	Some evidence

Sources: Powell, L. et al. (January 2003). Religion and spirituality: Linkages to physical health. *American Psychologist*, 58(1), 36–52; Ray, O. (January 2004). How the mind hurts and heals the body. *American Psychologist*, 59(1), 29–40.

strategy to improve the quality of life for people with some crippling injuries. Because spirituality provides the courage and motivation to deal with difficulties and limitations of the moment, it gives psychological protection and helps people to develop habits to buffer emotional difficulties such as ineffectiveness, frustration, defeat, depression, and anger (Ray, 2004).

Working overseas, psychologists often find that many individuals attempting to explain psychological disorders embrace traditional beliefs and folk theories clearly based on what would be considered **pseudoscience** among many Western health practitioners. Beliefs in supernatural forces, spiritual healing, or occult phenomena are very common around the world. In particular, people in many traditional communities believe that various psychological problems originate as God's punishment for evil acts. A remedy for the punishment is typically sought in symbolic actions, including ritualistic prayer or meditation, which is led by local healers. Nevertheless, as observers acknowledge, people who receive such traditional treatment are often passive in their approach to the healing process, instead of being actively involved, as more frequently occurs in Western-style therapies. This evidence suggests that in some communities, people accept that forces beyond one's control could largely determine these people's health outcomes.

Spirituality includes a vast number of human activities and beliefs not limited only to faith in God or supernatural forces. To some people who are not religious, spirituality is their deep belief in positive outcomes, good luck, protection, and the power of circumstances that provides these people with the sense of competence and strength. Psychologists refer to this as possessing strong *external locus of control* (see Chapter 10). To other people, spirituality is mostly their adherence to rituals and customs, such as meditation and prayer, which also helps them to avoid confusion and guilt, helps reduce stress, and provides relaxation. Yet to other people, spirituality is a powerful source of motivation. It provides them with joy, a sense of power, meaning to their actions, and purpose.

What should a healthcare worker do in situations when people in local communities embrace "nonscientific" (from the Western standpoint) views of psychological problems and disorders? Does a university-trained professional have an obligation to raise doubts in the minds of the local population about the validity of supernatural beliefs explaining the nature and causes of psychological problems? A common opinion today is that it is reasonable to work within the client's belief system and culture-specific components of the client's illness, without necessarily endorsing the validity of such beliefs (Martínez-Taboas, 2005). In other words, psychologists are encouraged to respect their clients' beliefs, but do not have to accept them as valid.

BUSINESS DECISIONS

Contemporary cross-cultural psychology can make a strong contribution to **organization development**, which is a set of planned changes targeted at improving organizational and individual performance and well-being in a private business or government company. Applied to cross-cultural psychology, organization development involves the creation of an atmosphere that incorporates cultural and cross-cultural knowledge into the work process, the aim of which is to increase both the overall efficiency (i.e., profit) and psychological satisfaction in the workplace. Consider a few examples related to psychological aspects of business negotiations, language, and advertising in multicultural environments.

You have probably come across comments that in business deals, entrepreneurs from Japan or China tend to move slowly, carefully, and often appear indecisive? Their Western business partners—who tend to view themselves as fast and decisive—often attribute such tentativeness of their East Asian partners to bureaucratic restrictions. However, the differences in business negotiations may also be based on cultural dissimilarities. As studies show, in America's political and business discourse being perceived as indecisive tends to be liability: A person who appears indecisive is also regarded as a week idler. However, in Japan, similar behaviors tend to be evaluated positively because they are associated with care, thoughtfulness, and attention (Yates et al., 2010). Applied to business, these data suggest that a group on one side of the negotiation table (the Americans) may see their partners moving too slow, when the other side (the Japanese) may see their partners as too impatient.

Several negotiation strategies in different countries were studied by Graham and his associates (Graham, 1983; Graham et al., 1992). They investigated which of two strategies are used during negotiations: problem solving (consensus oriented) or competitive (winning oriented). In the United States, according to some studies, successful negotiators try to exchange information at the negotiation table and the strategies are primarily problem solving. In Japan and Korea, negotiators with a higher status have some sort of advantage, and if they adopt problem-solving strategies, the other side follows. Russian and Taiwan Chinese negotiators tend to use competitive bargaining strategies. Brazilian managers prefer to use different forms of influence and persuasion to demonstrate their competitive strategies. These observations, however, were made a few years ago in an experimental classroom environment and should be interpreted with caution (Hui & Luk, 1997).

Have you heard from some people that they can recognize faces of strangers belonging to their own ethnic group but all other people "look alike" to them? Elfenbein and Ambady (2003) showed, predictably, that facial recognition of emotions in different national groups is more accurate if a person has had significant contact with those groups. The study has shown the importance of training of police, customs, and immigration officers working with a large number of people of different ethnic backgrounds: The more often you see people of different backgrounds, the more accurately you recognize their faces during direct contacts, and on photographs and videos.

Negative stereotypes hurt communication and business. Studies show that African Americans are sometimes stereotyped as antagonistic and lacking competence. Hispanics are viewed as uneducated and unambitious, and Asian Americans as quiet and unassertive (Eagly & Chin, 2010). Therefore, psychologists should dismiss such stereotypes and pay attention to facts established through research. It would be wrong, however, to refer to some experimental facts as describing entire cultural groups. Ask a person who has some experience with international business, and that businessperson would tell you that perhaps in every country there are patient and impatient partners, those who understand humor and those who do not, those well prepared for negotiations, and those who are not ready to strike a deal.

Some cross-cultural studies refer to self-confidence, job satisfaction, work environment, and plans for retirement. Studies show that professionals are generally overconfident in their judgments or decisions and that overconfidence in general knowledge is typically stronger among Asian than among Western subject groups (Li et al., 2011). A comparative U.S.–Dutch study showed that American workers were more anxious and less trusting of their retirement plan managers, while the workers in the Netherlands were more confident in their future financial situation. Do American financial officers need more training or maybe this is a reflection of differences between American and West European social security systems: Many Europeans express long-standing reliance on central government, which might have reduced some people's desire to take initiative and be concerned and demanding regarding their retirement plans (Hershey et al., 2007).

In cross-cultural psychology, conflict resolution is one of the most vital fields for research applications. Specialists on conflict resolution have to understand group dynamics, group decision-making processes, and the major characteristics of social perception. Their knowledge in psychology should help them establish strategies that, if accepted by conflicting parties, could eventually lead to successful resolutions of existing conflicts. Peter Smith and Schwartz (1997), for example, conducted a 23-nation study that examined how power distance was linked to conflict resolution procedures. In countries with high-power distance, formal rules and procedures were used to handle disagreements with other groups. In countries with low-power distance, sides relied primarily on informal contacts and their own experience.

Psychologists recognize several universal types of resolutions to a conflict. An imposed solution is based on an assumption that there are no win–win situations. Every solution will benefit one party—for example, an ethnic group—and harm the other. Negotiations based on the imposed solutions may take forever. That is why the moderator should take decisive measures, if, of course, the moderator has enough power and authority to take control of the situation and implement a decision. A distributive solution involves mutual compromises or concessions. Distributive solutions offer proposals that are midway between the initial positions of both (or all) conflicting parties. Integrative solutions are often called win–win solutions because both sides can benefit simultaneously, without losing anything substantial (Pruitt & Rubin, 1986). See the following exercise.

Exercise 12.1

The Cooperation Dilemma

The class should be divided into several groups (teams). There should be at least three teams, with up to seven people in each. As a rule of the exercise, each team represents a "country." All participating countries should secretly decide what kind of foreign policy they will have toward each of the other participating countries. The participating teams have only two choices: "peace" or "war." Countries can negotiate with one another. However, they cannot know what decisions other teams are making. In other words, as in the real world, countries can negotiate and make agreements, but the actual decisions are made secretly by each team (country). As soon as all decisions are made, they must be written on a piece of paper and turned over to the professor. Here is the catch. If any two countries declare peace with each other, each gets a hypothetical reward of $1 million each. If any two countries declare war on each other, each loses $2 million. However, if team 1 declares peace with team 2, and team 2 declares war on team 1, the aggressor, team 2, gets $3 million, and the victim, team 1, loses $1 million. The winner is the team that collects more money than the other teams. One may ask: "Where is the problem that must be solved? Each team establishes peace with one another and each team receives $1 million for the peace with each of the participating teams!" However, in reality such a peaceful development of events does not often happen.

Note: From 1991 to 2012, one of the authors of this book conducted almost 50 such exercises in different schools around the United States, and peace was established among all the participating teams only twice. In all other cases, at least one team always declared war on one or more of its neighbors. The most common argument for declaring war was that "it is difficult to trust other teams." As one student said: "You may agree on peace, and yet, they [the other teams] can secretly declare war on you and you lose." How will you and your classmates handle such a situation? What are the strategies to prevent war and guarantee peace in this exercise?

In business, language is frequently a barrier hampering direct communication. Although the United Nations has official languages of communication (and both French and English are considered official languages of diplomacy), English remains the most prevalent language in international business and other international communications, including e-mail. Some governments attempt to protect their own cultural environment by limiting the use of foreign languages, especially English. For example, at the beginning of this century, the French government demanded that the English word "e-mail" be replaced with the French word *le courriel*, in the attempt to curtail the incursion of American English. Some original French words were accepted as a result. The French reportedly use *ordinateur* instead of "computer" and *moteur de recherche* instead of "search engine." However, not all English terms have been expunged. The term "mouse" is still more frequently used than the French word *souris*.

Some business decisions may appear as culture wars. For example, in Rome, the local government has set the rules that limit Chinese commerce in certain districts. Wholesale outlets, a popular type of commerce for the Chinese, are banned. If a previous owner had, for instance, a bakery or a coffee shop for some time, new owners must not change the nature of the business for two years. Also, police have begun to enforce an old regulation that required all signs on walls and doors in foreign languages to be smaller than those in Italian. Supporters of such measures argue that they are necessary to protect local business. However, if you look carefully, a growing number of new so-called ethnic stores are open by individuals, the second-generation immigrants, who are born in Europe. In other words, they are "local" too.

The body pays for a slip of the foot and gold pays for a slip of the tongue.

MALAY PROVERB

WORKING WITH IMMIGRANTS

Psychologists have to fight a common stereotype that all immigrants are alike. In fact, they come from different socioeconomic backgrounds and face different psychological challenges. Those who migrate as young children are more likely to acquire new norms and values easily than those who migrate at older ages. Adults and especially older adults may experience the most difficulty in adopting the practices, values, and identifications of their new country. Some immigrants grow up in ethnic enclaves—areas where a majority of residents are from the same ethnic group. Others live away from such areas. Yet others live in mixed communities. In large cities such as New York, Los Angeles, Boston, San Francisco, Toronto, Sydney, London, Paris, Moscow, and Amsterdam migrants comprise substantial shares of the populations (Schwartz et al., 2010).

Immigrants also differ because of the reasons why they left their countries and because of their activities now. These facts often determine other people's views of immigrants (Kitayama et al.,

2010). Those who are seen as contributing to the receiving country's economy or culture—such as voluntary immigrants who work as nurses, doctors, engineers, or other professionals—may be welcomed. However, immigrants from lower socioeconomic brackets and those who immigrate illegally may be viewed as a drain on the receiving country's resources (Steiner, 2009).

Psychologists working with various groups, in particular **refugees** (individuals who have left their country and are unwilling or unable to return to it because of persecution or fear of persecution), encounter a number of problems. One of the most significant is **acculturation**, which, in the context of immigration, is the process of an individual's adjustment to a new culture. One popular approach to acculturation research is based on the presumption that a person can appreciate, practice, or identify with two different cultures independently of each other. Regardless of the cultures in question, the topic, or the intent, four generic types of acculturation are now commonly labeled: (1) Assimilation refers to individuals' acceptance of the customs and values of their new culture and subsequent rejection or abandonment of the behaviors and values of their old culture. (2) The second type involves individuals favoring their "older" culture. (3) Integration results from the acceptance of the major features of both cultures. (4) Finally, marginalization involves the rejection of both cultures. Critics of this classification maintain that it should be expanded to include, for example, a greater focus on subcultures and the interactions between cultures (Berry, 1997; Rudmin, 2003). As we have argued, a migrant in the United States might be fluent in both English and one or several other languages, endorse individualistic values in some contexts (e.g., at work) and collectivistic values in other contexts (e.g., with the family or at school), and identify both with the United States and with her or his country of origin (Chen et al., 2008). A host of factors may affect an individual's acculturation. Some of them are intriguing. For example, in a study of Americans with both Japanese and European ancestors, those who looked distinctly Japanese tended to associate more with Japanese American identity. Yet those who looked distinctly European associated more with European American identity (Ahnallen, Suyemoto, & Carter, 2006).

Studies in other countries may help understand immigrant and ethnic groups in the United States better. For example, a study in Taiwan showed that political competition between several ethnic clusters there prompts different ethnic identification among these relatively similar groups who share biological and cultural heritage: Some identify more with China and others with Taiwan (Lee & Pratto, 2011). It is remains to be seen if immigrants in the United States or Great Britain tend to identify themselves more with their new countries than with the countries of their origin because this brings them significant economic and political benefits.

Specialists understand *acculturaltive stress* as a distressful psychological reaction to any unfamiliar cultural environment. "Culture shock" or acculturative stress is typically defined as a set of complex psychological experiences, usually unpleasant and disruptive (Tsytsarev & Krichmar, 2000). Almost 40 years ago, in early path breaking studies on this subject, it was empirically confirmed that people arriving in a new culture may rapidly develop negative psychological symptoms (Oberg, 1960). It was noticed, for example, that there were increased rates of psychiatric hospitalization among foreign immigrants and their newly arrived children compared with nonimmigrants (Fried, 1964). It wasn't clear, however, whether culture shock itself had been causing higher hospitalization rates or if there were other, undetected factors, such as the health of migrants prior to their arrival to their new home. But what became apparent for psychologists was that persons and groups undergoing any social and cultural change should experience a certain amount of psychological displeasure or distress, the extent of which is based on many circumstances, both psychological and social (Berry & Annis, 1974). In general, many early definitions focused on culture shock as a syndrome, a reactive state of specific pathology or deficit: The individual moves into an unfamiliar environment and then develops negative symptoms (Berry & Sam, 1997). Assuming this approach, researchers have focused on descriptions of culture shock, its duration, and relationships between culture shock and various psychological problems (Barankin et al., 1989). It was shown that many emotional disorders, such as depression and anxiety, experienced by newcomers have been directly related to culture shock. It became apparent that aliens may alternate between anger and depression, especially during the initial stages of their adjustment in a new culture (Mirsky et al., 1992). In-depth research of the problems that African exchange students experience in the United States showed that most of them had difficulties communicating their problems and sharing their concerns with their peers and counselors. This communication barrier affected their adjustment process (Constantine et al., 2004, 2005).

Many immigrants are afraid to speak up against inhumane practices and customs, such as domestic violence and psychological abuse, for fear of dishonoring their families or exposing their family members to arrest or deportation.

However, there is reasonable skepticism about the expected existence of psychopathology in all individuals adapting to new cultures. For example, Furnham and Bochner (1986) described culture shock as a learning experience that includes the acquisition and development of the skills, rules, and roles required in the new cultural setting. Harry Triandis, a renowned psychologist, views culture shock as a loss of control that people experience when they interact with members of a different culture (1994, p. 239). Loss of control is in most cases maladaptive but does not necessarily cause marked psychological disturbances. In one of the most recently developed theories, culture shock is seen as the process of initial adjustment to an unfamiliar environment. Culture shock is associated with individual development, education, and even personal growth (Pedersen, 1995, pp. 1–2).

CRITICAL THINKING
Is This Culture Shock?

Sabir, a 23-year-old man and son of a political emigrant from the Middle East, thinks that the United States is not a healthy environment in which to live. For the past five years he has been in America, and his life has been filled with disappointment, sleepless nights, frustration, and depressive thinking. For Sabir, the new culture is seen as "unacceptable, unfriendly, and too selfish." Sabir attempted to attend two colleges, but dropped out in both cases because of, as he explained, "tremendous pressure and lack of free time." He started as a business partner in his father's consulting company, but soon quit because of a serious disagreement with his dad over their views on life. However, one of Sabir's friends said that Sabir simply wasn't motivated to work hard. Within a year, Sabir started two companies on his own, but in both cases failed to earn enough money to even return the initial investments. During the past three years, he dated several women but broke up with all of them. In an interview, Sabir emphasized that his culture shock has persisted over these years because of the "coldness and unfriendliness of this culture."

Comment

It is always difficult to separate symptoms of culture shock from all other individual problems that might be unrelated to culture shock. In this particular case, one shouldn't deny that some elements of culture shock are present in Sabir. However, a person who speaks nearly flawless English, gets some reasonable financial support from his father, and has not experienced discrimination against him in this country perhaps is unhappy with the way his life is turning out. U.S. culture and its traditions are used as easy scapegoats for his business failures and personal problems. It is difficult to condemn yourself for your own mistakes and easier to instead place blame on something or someone else. Sabir didn't have symptoms of distress prior to his arrival in the United States; his emotional problems began with the start of his independent adult life. Therefore, it is always important to find out whether a culture change itself has become the major cause of distress.

TABLE 12.3 Some Symptoms of Acculturative Stress and Their Descriptions

Symptoms of Acculturative Stress	Description of Symptoms
Acculturative stress as nostalgia	The person may feel longing for relatives, friends, and familiar cues and experiences.
Acculturative stress as disorientation and loss of control	Familiar cues about how another person is supposed to behave are missing. Disorientation creates anxiety, depressive thinking, and a sense of desperation.
Acculturative stress as dissatisfaction over language barriers	Lack of or difficulties in communication may create frustration and feelings of isolation.
Acculturative stress as loss of habits and lifestyle	The individual is not able to exercise many previously enjoyed activities; this causes anxiety and feelings of loss.
Acculturative stress as perceived differences	Differences between the host and home cultures are typically exaggerated and seem difficult to accept.
Acculturative stress as perceived value differences	Differences in values are typically exaggerated; new values seem difficult to accept.

Source: Based on Shiraev, E., & Boyd, J. (2001). The accent of success. Englewood Cliffs, NJ: Prentice Hall.

See also Table 12.3. In a study of Asian American youths, it was found that family conflicts and the lack of acculturation were among the most significant risk factors contributing to stress, emotional problems, and suicide (Lau et al., 2002).

Today, researchers studying cultural adjustment usually focus on the description of stress factors related to adjustment, factors associated with successful adaptation (Mok et al., 2007), and psychological skills that people develop to overcome negative consequences of stress (Shupe, 2007).

CROSS-CULTURAL SENSITIVITY

Cultural adjustment is also the process of adaptation to various smells and odors. For example, J.K., an ESL college student in Virginia, says in an interview, "Koreans eat kimchi, a traditional food with garlic and pepper. It gives you nice garlic breath. I realized how people here [in America] disliked this. I stopped eating it after being here for two weeks and that was very difficult for me because traditional American food was tasteless for me at that time" (cf. Shiraev & Boyd, 2008). This example demonstrates at least two important points. First, there are cultural norms regarding what odors or smells are considered appropriate and inappropriate. For example, if almost everyone eats foods with garlic, these people can hardly notice that they, or others, have garlic breath.

However, if you had a dish with garlic in it for lunch, and no one else did, then people around you would certainly notice that you smell of garlic. Second, most of us are able to adapt to particular smells and dominant odors in a new country that we live in or travel to (remember, sensory adaptation is a universal psychological process). Most travelers, for instance, say that they quickly get used to the smell of soy sauce in Japan. If the situation requires, many can adjust to unpleasant street odors in some world cities not equipped with sewer systems. Nonsmoking travelers can adapt to the smell of cigarette smoke in most countries in eastern and southern Europe, where smoking regulations are relatively loose compared to strict antismoking rules in the United States.

EDUCATION

Minority children, as a group, often show lower scores on intelligence and other cognitive skills tests. Assuming that the test is not biased against particular cultural groups and the child has adequate proficiency in the language of testing, what can a teacher or parent do to improve the child's test performance?

Jenkins (1995), in his well-known work on the psychology of African Americans, suggests that there are several ways by which adults can improve intelligence test scores of minority children. He suggested that even though many minority children lack developmental experiences—due to poverty, overcrowded housing, and inadequate parenting—this deficit can be overcome. To achieve this, some children may need the teacher to pay special attention to their cognitive functioning. For others, it is important to give extra attention to the emotional context in which intellectual learning takes place. For example, it is beneficial to create a particular cooperative classroom environment and, in addition, include parents in the educational process. If formal intellectual problem-solving procedures involve interesting and pleasing challenges, the child is likely to appreciate such an academic situation and become engaged in such activities more frequently than previously. The problem is that many minority children begin to feel competence in nonacademic situations, basically in the street game contexts. In other words, the street often shapes these children's intellectual skills, not the educators.

Of course, one of the most difficult tasks for the psychologist is the engagement of parents in the educational process. Overall, on the larger world scale, success has not been great. However, many national cases demonstrate the possibilities of such interactions. For example, in Turkey, Kagitcibasi (1995) developed a special educational, community-based project with the local mothers. The interactive training included analyses of special cognitive tasks and biweekly group discussions about children, their problems, and parent–child communications.

The debate about the language of test administration for a bilingual child continues for some time (Griffore, 2007). On some concept acquisition and reasoning skills tests, bilingual children tend to perform at a slightly higher level if tested in their native language, that is, the language they speak at home (Keats et al., 1976; Takano & Noda, 1993). However, Stephen Wright and colleagues (1997) found that in those cases of ethnic student diversity, the language of instruction, and the teacher's ethnicity had no significant impact on student success in class. Perhaps language becomes a factor only at the early stages of the second-language acquisition. Moreover, a 2001 ruling of the U.S. Supreme Court clears the legal path for the use of the "English only" rule in public schools and during examinations conducted by the states, including testing for a driver's license (Lane, 2001). But from the psychological and social viewpoint, being bilingual has definite benefits, the discussion of which is beyond our tasks. One study though revealed that being bilingual is associated with higher creativity (Kharkhurin, 2010).

CULTURE, BEHAVIOR, AND THE LAW

In contemporary multicultural communities, customary rules of behavior shared by the people of one group may appear strange and even unacceptable to others. Many national judicial systems are often placed in a position where they have to rule in favor of a particular group, thus leaving others displeased. Although psychologists do not have the power of judges and legislators, they can express their opinion regarding a wide range of legal issues related to culture and behavior across ethnic and national lines. Consider a few examples.

After eating a sandwich, a Florida woman was fired from her job. Is it illegal to have a sandwich for lunch now in Orlando? Why was she fired? Her termination was apparently the result of the slices of bacon on her sandwich. This was a violation of the company policy that pork and pork products were not permissible on the company premises. A central Florida telecommunications company with strong Muslim ties gave this woman, who was Catholic, a warning about eating "unclean" products considered inappropriate in the Muslim faith. After she again violated the company's rule, she was fired. The critics of the company's decision maintained that this was a case of religious discrimination, because the company's food policy was based on clear theological principles and not on the law, which guarantees every employee equal opportunity. Some people may have cultural objections about certain products or habits, but these objections should not be imposed on everyone in the workplace. The other side argued that the policy was stated clearly and employees should respect cultural rules suggested in the employment agreement. Besides, the Koran forbids Muslims from eating pork and most of them would feel uncomfortable or be offended if someone was doing so nearby.

What do you think about this case? Both sides have strong points, but which side's arguments are more sound? How far could cultural limitations be implemented in businesses and public activities? Imagine you own a business and you have great intentions to respect your employees' cultural and religious beliefs. How would we deal with an employee who would openly eat dog meat for lunch?

Governments decide on the appropriateness of particular traditions. For instance, in Germany, a woman was refused a job as a teacher because she, as a Muslim, chose to wear a headscarf. When she sued in court and won, most German regions initiated legislation to ban headscarves from public schools. A similar law was passed in France in 2004. In Italy, a court ruled in favor of a Muslim parent who contended that in his child's small-town schoolteachers could not display a crucifix in class, a widespread practice in a predominately Catholic nation (Richburg, 2003).

A CASE IN POINT

How far could people go on challenging deep-seated customs and values of a traditional community? Which is more important in your life: to respect all traditions, even though you disagree with some them, or to challenge them, thus undermining a society's cultural foundations? Could a compromise be found?

A 25-year-old handyman and a 67-year-old widow have decided to marry. Such a decision would definitely raise eyebrows, as the age difference between the groom and the bride is quite abnormal. What makes this case even more remarkable is that the marriage was proposed in Kenya, a country of strong traditional customs. It is also important to consider that in this case the man is younger. This marriage provoked a heated debate in Kenya between those who support individual rights and especially the woman's right to choose, and those who insisted that marriage should be based on tribal tradition and values established many generations ago. While in the United States and Europe, people argue about gay marriage, in Kenya, the arguments were revolving around the appropriateness of a union between a young man and an older woman (Wax, 2003). The supporters of this marriage argued that in the country in which older men regularly marry teenage girls, and on the continent where the prominent leader, Nelson Mandela, married a woman 28 years younger than he was, this couple did nothing wrong. Opponents consider this marriage a violation of cultural traditions.

In Nebraska, a court dispute between two parents ended with a decision that the father would jeopardize his visitation rights if he continued to speak Spanish to his five-year-old daughter (Fears, 2003). The case was brought to court because the father, a Mexican American, would bring his daughter to visit relatives and friends. The problem arose when the daughter complained that her father usually spoke in Spanish, a language that she did not understand. The mother wanted her daughter to learn English first, while the father believed it was important for his daughter to learn Spanish as well. Which side would you support and why?

The real fault is to have faults and not to amend them.

Confucius (551–479 b.c.e.)—**Chinese Philosopher**

HUMAN RIGHTS

What if cultural norms of a particular country or ethnic group violate universal human rights determined by international law? Would psychologists recommend choosing between indigenous practices and international standards? International human rights law has been specifically designed to protect the full range of human rights required for people to "have a full, free, safe, secure and healthy life" (UN, 1948). It is stated that the right to live a dignified life can never be attained unless all basic necessities of life—work, food, housing, health care, education, and culture—are adequately and equitably available to everyone. Based squarely on this fundamental principle of the global human rights system, international human rights law has established individual and group rights relating to the civil, cultural, economic, political, and social spheres.

Consider a case of children's rights. According to the United Nations, children should be able to express their views freely, the state should respect children's freedom of thought and religion, and children also "have the right to privacy and adults cannot unlawfully interfere in the child's privacy" (UN, 1959). Meanwhile, in many countries, according to cultural customs and religious norms, children's rights are suppressed. There is opposition from many states, for example, to the right of children to choose their own religion. The rights of children that emphasize self-expression can be easily challenged in countries with authoritarian governments. Further, the United Nations requires that states ensure that children have access to a wide variety of resources, including a standard of living that is adequate for physical, mental, spiritual, moral, and social development. These requirements are impossible to fulfill in poor countries.

Earlier in the book, we learned that "real" socialization practices are quite different from those endorsed by the United Nations. For example, in theory, states should guarantee the right to an education. This requirement is very difficult to implement, especially in countries such as Brazil, India, and Indonesia in which millions of children begin to work at a very early age and may quit school altogether to provide food for their families.

In addition, the United Nations declares the priority of children's individual rights over their rights within a social group, such as family. Many argue that these provisions indicate the individualistic values of Western society that are very difficult to accept for individuals living in traditional communities in other countries—such as Pakistan, Botswana, and Thailand—with different cultural conditions, specifically of a collectivist tradition.

Countries and governments vary in beliefs about the property distribution of power in the family, the degree to which behavior should be regulated by individuals themselves versus external rules, the importance of individual rights versus group and family loyalties, and the scope of responsibility individuals should have for themselves and their families (Murphy-Bernman et al., 1996). These examples, perhaps, suggest that culture may have a significant impact on how individuals and governments define the best interest of the child.

The United Nations also recognizes fundamental rights of women. Any exclusion or restriction made on the basis of gender, which has the effect or purpose of discrimination against women in political, economic, social, cultural, civil, or any other fields, should be deemed unlawful and therefore condemned (UN, 1967). However, such demands directly contradict many cultural traditions and religious practices in some places. Forceful female circumcision, forceful marriage, and sexual exploitation of girls continue in many countries. One of the most troubling facts associated with these rights violations is that many men don't see the problem here arguing that men and women are different and require different treatment. Abuse against women may be subtle. In many poor countries, due to today's technologies and lower birth rates, some expecting parents after determining the sex of their fetus choose a selective abortion because they want to have a son, not a daughter (Guilmoto, 2009). Because in affluent, educated countries this practice is not widespread, one of the keys to address this problem in developing countries is education.

WORKING AND SERVING ABROAD

Working abroad as a diplomat, journalist, peacekeeper, entrepreneur, or counselor, you are likely to deal with the restrictive practice of reviewing and determining what is appropriate for publication or broadcasting for moral, ideological, or political considerations. Such practice is called **censorship**. Camouflaged under different labels, such as local "regulations" or domestic "restrictions," censorship is a powerful tool used by social and religious institutions to filter out and prohibit certain information. You have to understand the reasons used to justify the practice of censorship, and respect customs and laws, yet be critical if such practices violate people's fundamental rights.

Defenders of *political* censorship argue that restrictions on information are necessary to protect social order and stability. Therefore, you will not be allowed to disseminate information that undermines the political authority of the government. You may not criticize the government, its representatives, and political leaders. Caricatures portraying these countries' political leaders are prohibited. Such political restrictions often become customs that regulate what people

CRITICAL THINKING

Cross-cultural psychologists should have the courage to ask questions about something that many people often consider "obvious" and therefore "normal" (see Chapter 3). For example, is the American view on democracy ethnocentric? Do American and West European politicians make ethnocentric judgments when they demand democracy in countries such as Cuba, China, Serbia, or Rwanda, to name a few? Some specialists imply that holding of free and open elections, which is considered democratic and therefore "good" for the West, may bring chaos and instability to some other countries (Pei, 1998, p. 69). Without asking these questions and looking for answers, one can follow an easy path of dogmatic thinking (Chung & Bemak, 2002).

can write and say about the government. Traditional cultural attitudes related to high-power distance (see Chapter 1) may also justify political censorship suggesting that authorities must be respected, not criticized.

Under *ideological* censorship, various societal institutions, including organized religion and government, establish principles about the society's past, present, and future. Information that challenges these principles is prohibited from publication. In Communist countries, ideological censorship is compulsory. Articles, reports, or essays about the advantages of the free market, civil freedoms, and successful social programs in Western countries are outlawed. However, any information about disasters or lingering social problems in the West is welcomed. It is against the law in Germany today to publish or air any material that endorses Nazism. However, these materials and items could be produced in the United States or Russia, among other countries. Religious censorship is part of ideological censorship. There are many countries in which criticism of the country's dominant or official religion is strictly prohibited by law. In the most fundamentalist governments of the beginning of the twenty-first century, such as Iran or Saudi Arabia, a journalist who dares to publish critical materials about Islam—the official religion in these countries—could be prosecuted. A foreign journalist will be expelled from these countries. In various forms, ideological censorship is enforced in many regions today.

Moral censorship is people's cultural and psychological guard. Local communities develop particular informal standards of decency and morality. In addition, some laws prescribe the standards to be followed in communications among businesses, institutions, and the media. For example, it was long tabooed in Europe before the twentieth century to expose depictions of nude bodies on paintings unless these were the bodies of biblical characters. Today, in the United States, movie ratings warn parents about the use of profanities or depictions of nudity and violence on television and in films. Sexually explicit materials or violent documentary scenes are also excluded from major prime-time networks' programs in the United States and Canada. There are certain words that radio and television commentators may not say on the air. In many Islamic countries, sex scenes are cut from Western movies, and even kissing is not shown. Cultural reasons are often cited to justify particular restrictions. For example, in 2003, the Egyptian government banned the Hollywood blockbuster *Matrix Reloaded*. The justification for the ban was based on the reviews suggesting that the movie portrayed God in a human form, which is deemed inappropriate for Egyptian moviegoers (see Table 12.4).

TABLE 12.4 Censorship and Culture

Type of Censorship	Description
Political	Defenders of this form of censorship argue that restrictions on information are necessary to protect social order and stability.
Ideological	These are ideas or principles about society, past, present, and future. Any information that challenges these principles and measures is prohibited from dissemination.
Moral	Society develops a set of standards of decency and public morality. In addition, there are laws that prescribe the standards to be followed in communications among businesses, institutions, and the media.

Source: SHIRAEV, ERIC B.; SOBEL, RICHARD, PEOPLE AND THEIR OPINIONS, 1ST EDITION, 2005. Reprinted with permission of Pearson Education, Inc., Upper Saddle River, NJ

Specialists participating in peacekeeping or other community and missions should be aware of attempts by some local authorities to use the idea of culture to set particular political priorities in their countries. For example, any help or assistance coming from any Western country could be criticized on the grounds that this help threatens the local customs or way of living. Books, medication, computers, technologies, new forms of communications, or therapeutic procedures are criticized and even rejected. Although the preservation of valuable traditions is one of the top priorities of specialists working overseas, arguments about culture could be used for political purposes: Quite often local authorities interpret changes in their communities as a threat to the leaders' own power. Unfortunately, humanitarian help is often curtailed or criticized by uninformed or corrupt officials to continue the dependency of local populations.

RELIGION: A CAMPUS CONTEXT

We learn about tolerance and respect for the customs, rules, and religious views of others. One way of learning about tolerance is information exchange. If a college student wants to tell other students about his religion, will it benefit other students? Is there evidence that free expression of religious views fosters mutual understanding among students? According to a number of polls, almost 90 percent of people in the United States identify with a religion; in other words, they can tell which religion they belong to. The United States is home to many world religions. As you perhaps know, many Pilgrims—the first European settlers in America—came to this country with a particular religious vision. Moreover, back in Europe many of them were subject to discrimination, persecution, and quite often physical extermination. Today, like throughout all U.S. history, those individuals who are persecuted in their home countries for their religious beliefs and practices can receive asylum in the United States.

As a free individual, you have the right to choose to follow any religion or no religion. The U.S. Constitution permits private religious activity in colleges and universities. However, you have to understand some rules and regulations related to religious activity on campuses. These rules are generally the same for both public and private schools (some private institutions of higher education may have their own guidelines about religious behavior on their campuses). This is one of the cases in which all people, that is, students, teachers, counselors, and administrators, should follow formal rules.

All in all, in the United States, the government and religion are separated. Therefore, state-funded colleges and universities will not have courses in their curricula designed to promote any particular religion. However, you may find courses on the history of religion, comparative religion, and others that teach about the role of religion in the history of the United States and other countries.

Students have the right to pray individually or in groups and to discuss any religious views with their peers so long as these discussions are not disrupting the peace. Students can read any religious scripture, say grace before meals, and pray before tests. However, students must not forget that their school activities come first. For example, do not pray during the test for an hour and then ask the professor for extra time to finish the test.

Can students express religious beliefs in the form of projects and reports? Yes, they can, and no one should reject their work because of its religious content, such as quotes, symbols, and examples. However, remember that the work should be relevant to the assignment.

Anyone can talk about any religion during classroom discussion. It constitutes free speech. Similarly, people can criticize religion and promote atheistic views. Your professor may not silence you, for example, just because you make critical statements against religion.

However, do not forget that other students also have the right to speak and they may criticize your views too.

Please remember that any criticism against a particular religion should not become excessive and overwhelming. In this case, such criticism may be called religious harassment. Surprisingly, any intrusive attempts to promote one's religion by soliciting someone's participation are qualified as harassment too.

Religious messages on shirts, jackets, and hats may not be prohibited on campus and if you wear such printed messages, you should not be persecuted for this. Students may wear religious attire, such as crosses, yarmulkes, turbans, and headscarves. If your religious beliefs do not allow you to wear gym clothes because they are too revealing, you may not be forced to do so.

Exercise 12.2

Could Governments Impose Culture?

In some countries, governments make sure that state employees do not use foreign words, English words in particular. A few years ago, France launched a campaign to eliminate English terms from computer-related vocabulary. Similarly, in Venezuela, the government instructed a state-owned telephone company to forget about words such as "marketing" and "password" and switch to using Spanish terms. Sometimes such campaigns can be successful, but most of the time they fail. Officials forget about an important psychological phenomenon: If you want to promote a trend or a fashion style, ban it. Yet, attempts to "preserve culture" by legal means continue.

By the end of the 1990s, France placed strict limits on the number of non-French films that could be shown in its theaters. French leaders say this is important to support their film industry and to protect French culture from U.S. cultural imperialism. Other commentators say this rule unfairly excludes U.S. films from the market and promotes instead French ethnocentrism and nationalism.

Questions:

Do you think France—as well as any other country—should be able to put limits on the showing of non-French films? Do you consider such actions a culture war that severely limits free exchange of information and ideas? Do you think that every country's culture should be protected by limiting foreign cultural influences? Please explain your answers. (*Source:* Reprinted with permission of The Center on Policy Attitudes, University of Maryland, 2007–2008)

CONCLUSION

Psychologists cannot make everyone equal and happy. Despite economic progress, 20 percent of the world population lives in absolute poverty. At the beginning of the twenty-first century, there were more than 30 low-intensity wars in the world and more hidden ethnic conflicts. Civil hostilities and bloody coups continue to tear nations and regions apart. Cross-cultural psychology can respond to the emerging global challenges and opportunities and become a scientific and applied field that accumulates research data from many other disciplines. Psychologists are able to offer suggestions for dissolution of both local and global problems, especially those that include ethnic, religious, and other tensions. As a result, a more intense cultural dialogue may start that would signify the beginning of the exchange of values and ideas that different cultures can offer to each other. Among these values could be materialism and spiritualism, consumption and recycling, family planning, and greater respect for the elderly.

Cross-cultural psychology should accept diversity of ideas, values, and opinions. Indeed, centuries-old customs are rooted in economic, religious, political, and other cultural foundations. Many human traditions should be respected. However, specialists should denounce and reject promotion or justification of ethnic discrimination, racism, religious intolerance, physical and sexual abuse, and ideas of the inferiority of particular groups and the superiority of others.

Of course, cross-cultural psychology alone cannot offer solutions to every global and local problem. However, your knowledge in this field, the skills you develop studying cross-cultural psychology, and the ideas you share with others will definitely help you become better prepared to seek out solutions. A great Chinese thinker, Lao-tse, said that any journey of a thousand miles begins with one step. So let us take this step together and see what we can do to make this world a better place. Here, now, and everywhere.

Chapter Summary

- Psychology remains a theoretical discipline so long as it answers the questions "what?" "when?" and "why?" It becomes an applied field when it starts searching for some specific answers to the questions "How to use?" or "How to change?"

- Overall, poverty, social, and ecological problems affect people's health-related activities. There are also cultural practices that are considered unhealthy or wrong, including spousal abuse and child labor.

- Many contemporary psychologists are only at the beginning stages of understanding spirituality, a source of motivation and reasoning for many people living in traditional cultures. Spirituality refers to a broad range of phenomena concerning "nonmaterial" matters related to faith, trust, and hope.

- Contemporary cross-cultural psychology makes a contribution to organization development, which is a set of planned changes targeted at improving organizational and individual performance and well-being in a private business or government company.

- There are similarities and differences in negotiating styles and conflict-resolution strategies. Knowledge about the other side's cultural strategies is a key to successful negotiation.

- Assuming that cognitive tests are not biased against particular cultural groups and the child has adequate proficiency in the language of testing, the teacher or parent can improve the child's test performance.

- Working with immigrants, psychologists often help them to overcome an acculturative stress: an initial reaction of adjustment to a new culture. Specialists understand acculturative stress as a distressful psychological reaction to any unfamiliar cultural environment, a set of complex psychological experiences, usually unpleasant and disruptive.

- Although psychologists do not have the power of judges or legislators, they can express their opinion regarding a wide range of legal issues related to culture and behavior across ethnic and national lines.

- Working abroad in nondemocratic countries, specialists are likely to deal with the restrictive practice of censorship and resistance to change.

Key Terms

Acculturation Considered in the context of immigration, the process of an individual's adjustment to a new culture.

Censorship The restrictive practice of reviewing and determining what is appropriate for publication or broadcasting—according to moral, ideological, or political considerations.

Counseling The act of providing psychological direction or advice as to a decision or course of action.

Organization Development A set of planned changes targeting at improving organizational and individual performance and well-being in a private business or government company. Applied to cross-cultural psychology, organization development means the creation of an atmosphere that incorporates cultural and cross-cultural knowledge into the work process to increase both the overall efficiency and psychological satisfaction in the workplace.

Pseudoscience Knowledge and its applications that appear scientific but are not based on the scientific method.

Refugee One who has left one's native country and is unwilling or unable to return to it because of persecution or fear of persecution (because of race, religion, membership in a particular social group, or political opinion).

Spirituality A broad range of phenomena concerning "nonmaterial" matters related to faith, trust, and hope, in contrast to "material" matters related to ownership, accumulation of possessions, and competition. In psychological context, spirituality emphasizes mind over matter, being over having, and mental effort over physical action.

REFERENCES

Abou-Hatab, F. (1997). Psychology from Egyptian, Arab, and Islamic perspectives: Unfulfilled hopes and hopeful fulfillment. *European Psychologist, 2*(4), 356–365.

Abrams, D., & Hogg, M. A. (1987). Language attitudes, frames of reference, and social identity: A Scottish dimension. *Journal of Language and Social Psychology, 6*, 201–213.

Abudabbeh, N. (1996). Arab families. In M. McGoldrick, J. Giordano, & J. K. Pearce (Eds.), *Ethnicity and family therapy* (2nd ed., pp. 333–346). New York: Guilford Press.

Abu-Lughod, L. (1986). *Veiled sentiments.* Berkeley, CA: University of California Press.

Abu-Saad, I. (1998). Individualism and Islamic work beliefs. *Journal of Cross-Cultural Psychology, 29*(3), 377–383.

Adams, F., & Osgood, C. (1973). A cross-cultural study of the affective meaning of color. *Journal of Cross-Cultural Psychology, 4*(2), 135–156.

Adler, N. E. (2009). Health disparities through a psychological lens. *American Psychologist, 64*(8), 663–673.

Ahmed, A. A. (2002). *Intisar: A story of a Muslim girl.* Bloomington, IN: Authorhouse.

Ahnallen, J. M., Suyemoto, K. L., & Carter, A. S. (2006). Relationship between physical appearance, sense of belonging and exclusion, and racial/ethnic self-identification among multiracial Japanese European Americans. *Cultural Diversity and Ethnic Minority Psychology, 12*, 673–686.

Aizenman, N. (2002, May 12). A rebirth of traditions: Maternity wards adapt to immigrants' needs. *Washington Post*, p. A01.

Akbar, N. (1991). The evolution of human psychology for African Americans. In R. Jones (Ed.), *Black psychology* (3rd ed., pp. 99–123). Berkeley, CA: Cobb & Henry.

Akhtar, S. (2002). *Broken structures: Severe personality disorders and their treatment.* Northvale, NJ: Aronson.

Albas, D. C., McCluskey, K. W., & Albas, C. A. (1976). Perception of the emotional content of speech. *Journal of Cross-Cultural Psychology, 7*, 481–490.

Alexander, L., Hollingsworth, L., Dore, M., & Hoopes, J. (2004). A family of trust: African American parents' stories of adoption disclosure. *American Journal of Orthopsychiatry, 74*(4), 448–455.

Alexander, M. G., & Fisher, T. D. (2003). Truth and consequences: Using the bogus pipeline to examine sex differences in self-reported sexuality. *The Journal of Sex Research, 40*, 27–35.

Allen, M., Sik Hung Ng, Ken'Ichi Ikeda, Jawan, J. A., Sufi, A. H., Wilson, M., & Kuo-Shu Yang (2007). Two decades of change in cultural values and economic development in eight East Asian and Pacific Island nations. *Journal of Cross-Cultural Psychology, 38*(3), 247–269.

Allodi, F. A. (1991). Assessment and treatment of torture victims. *The Journal of Nervous and Mental Disorders, 179*, 4–11.

Almond, G., & Verba, S. (1965). *The civic culture.* Boston, MA: Little, Brown.

Amenomouri, M., Kono, A., Fournier, J., & Winer, G. (1997). A cross-cultural developmental study of directional asymmetries in circle drawing. *Journal of Cross-Cultural Psychology, 28*(6), 730–742.

American Psychiatric Association. (1994). *Diagnostic and statistical manual of mental disorders (DSM-IV)* (4th ed.). Washington, DC: APA.

Anae, M., Fuamatu, N., Lima, I., Mariner, K., Park, J., & Suaalii-Sauni, T. (2000). *Tiute ma matafaioi a nisi tane samoa i le faiga o aiga: The roles and responsibilities of some Samoan men in reproduction.* Auckland, New Zealand: Pacific Health Research Centre, University of Auckland.

Anderson, C. (1987). Temperature and aggression: Effects on quarterly, yearly, and city rates of violent and nonviolent crime. *Journal of Personality and Social Psychology, 52*, 1161–1173.

Andreason, N. J. C., & Canter, A. (1974). The creative writer: Psychiatric symptoms and family history. *Comprehensive Psychiatry, 15*(2), 123–131.

Andreason, N. J. C., & Powers, P. S. (1975). Creativity and psychosis: An examination of conceptual style. *Archives of General Psychiatry, 32*, 70–73.

Antrobus, J. (1991). Dreaming: Cognitive processes during cortical activation and high afferent thresholds. *Psychological Review, 98*, 96–121.

Aptekar, L. (1989). Colombian street children: Gamines and Chupagruesos. *Adolescence, 24*, 783–794.

Archer, J. (1996). Sex differences in social behavior: Are the social role and evolutionary explanations compatible? *American Psychologist, 51*(9), 909–917.

Arnett, J. J. (2000). Emerging adulthood: A theory of development from the late teens through the twenties. *American Psychologist, 55*, 469–480.

Arnett, J. J. (2002). The psychology of globalization. *American Psychologist, 57*(10), 774–783.

Arnett, J. J. (2008). The neglected 95%: Why American psychology needs to become less American. *American Psychologist, 63*, 602–614.

Aronson, E. (1995). *The social animal.* New York: W. H. Freeman.

Aronson, E., & O'Leary, M. (1982–1983). The relative effectiveness of models and prompts on energy conservation: A field experiment in a shower room. *Journal of Environmental Systems, 12*, 219–224.

Asch, S. (1956). Studies of independence and conformity: A minority of one against unanimous majority. *Psychological Monographs, 70*(9) (whole no. 416).

Asher, S., Renshaw, P., & Hymel, S. (1982). Peer relations and the development of social skills. In S. Moore (Ed.), *The young child: Reviews of research.* Washington, DC: NAEYC.

Aune, R., & Aune, K. (1994). The influence of culture, gender, and relational status on appearance management. *Journal of Cross-Cultural Psychology, 25*(2), 258–272.

Averill, J. (1982). *Anger and aggression: An essay on emotion.* New York: Springer-Verlag.

Ayman, R., & Chemers, M. M. (1983). Relationship of supervisory behavior ratings to work group effectiveness and subordinate satisfaction among Iranian managers. *Journal of Applied Psychology, 68*, 338–341.

Ayman, R., & Korabik, K. (2010). Leadership: Why gender and culture matter. *American Psychologist, 65*(3), 157–170.

Bahl, V., Prabhakaran, D., & Karthikeyan, G. (2001). *Coronary artery disease in Indians. The Internet Journal of Cardiology.* Retrieved from http://www.ispub.com/ostia/ index.php?xmlFilePath=journals/ijc/vol1n2/cadi.xml

Baldwin, J. (1991). African (Black) psychology: Issues and synthesis. In R. Jones (Ed.), *Black psychology* (3rd ed., pp. 125–135). Berkeley, CA: Cobb & Henry.

Baldwin, J., Brown, R., & Hopkins, R. (1991). The black self-hatred paradigm revised: An Africentric analysis. In R. Jones (Ed.), *Black psychology* (3rd ed., pp. 141–161). Berkeley, CA: Cobb & Henry.

Bandura, A. (1969). *Principles of behavioral modification.* New York: Holt, Rinehart & Winston.

Barankin, T., Konstantareas, M. M., & de Bosset, F. (1989). Adaptation of recent Soviet Jewish immigrants and their children to Toronto. *Canadian Journal of Psychiatry, 34*, 512–518.

Barber, N. (1998). Ecological and psychological correlates of male homosexuality: A cross-cultural investigation. *Journal of Cross-Cultural Psychology, 29*(3), 387–401.

Barber, N. (2001). On the relationship between marital opportunity and teen pregnancy: The sex ratio question. *Journal of Cross-Cultural Psychology, 32*(3), 259–267.

Barkow, J. H., Cosmides, L., & Tooby, J. (Eds.). (1992). *The adapted mind: Evolutionary psychology and the generation of culture.* New York: Oxford University Press.

Barnlund, D. (1975). *Public and private self in Japan and the United States.* Tokyo: Simul Press.

Barnlund, D., & Araki, S. (1985). Intercultural encounters: The management of compliments by Japanese and Americans. *Journal of Cross-Cultural Psychology, 16*(1), 9–26.

Barnlund, D. C. (1989). *Communicative styles of Japanese and Americans: Images and realities.* Belmont, CA: Wadsworth.

Baron, R., & Kalsher, M. (1996). The sweet smell of… safety? *Proceedings of the Human Factors and Ergonomics Society, 40*, 1282.

Barrett, P., & Eysenck, S. B. G. (1984). The assessment of personality factors across 25 countries. *Personality and Individual Differences, 5*, 615–632.

Basoglu, M., Paker, M., Paker, O., Ozmen, E., Marks, I., Sahin, D., et al. (1994). Psychological effect of torture: A comparison of tortured with nontortured political activists in Turkey. *American Journal of Psychiatry, 151,* 6–81.

Bass, B. M. (1997). Does the transactional–transformational leadership paradigm transcend organizational and national boundaries? *American Psychologist, 52,* 130–139.

Beah, I. (2008). *A long way gone: Memoirs of a boy soldier.* New York: Farrar, Straus and Giroux.

Beals, J., Novins, D., Whitesell, N., Spicer, P., Mitchell, C., & Manson, S. (2005). Prevalence of mental disorders and utilization of mental health services in two American Indian reservation populations: Mental health disparities in a national context. *American Journal of Psychiatry, 162,* 1723–1732.

Beardsley, L., & Pedersen, P. (1997). Health and culturecentered intervention. In J. Berry & C. Kagitcibasi (Eds.), *Handbook of cross-cultural psychology: Social behavior and applications* (Vol. 3, pp. 413–448). Boston, MA: Allyn & Bacon.

Beauchamp, G. (1987). The human preference for the excess salt. *American Scientist, 75,* 27–33.

Beck, A. (1991). Cognitive therapy: A 30-year retrospective. *American Psychologist, 46,* 368–375.

Bell, R. M. (1985). *Holy anorexia.* Chicago, IL: University of Chicago Press.

Bemak, F., & Chung, R. C.-Y. (2004). Culturally oriented psychotherapy with refugees. In U. Gielen, J. Fish, & J. Draguns (Eds.), *Culture, therapy and healing* (pp. 121–132). Mahwah, NJ: Lawerence Erlbaum Associates.

Bemak, F., & Chung, R. C.-Y. (2008). Counseling disaster survivors: Implications for cross-cultural counseling. In P. B. Pedersen, J. Draguns, W. Lonner, & J. Trimble (Eds.), *Counseling across cultures* (6th ed., pp. 325–340). Thousand Oaks, CA: Sage.

Benedict, R. (1934/2006). *Patterns of Culture.* Boston, MA: Mariner Books.

Benedict, R. (1946). *The chrysanthemum and the sword: Patterns of Japanese culture.* Boston, MA: Houghton Mifflin.

Berger, K. (1995). *The developing person through the life span.* New York: Worth Publishers.

Berkowitz, L. (1962). *Aggression: A social psychological analysis.* New York: McGraw-Hill.

Berlin, B. (1992). *Ethnobiological classification: Principles of categorization of plants and animals in traditional societies.* Princeton, NJ: Princeton University Press.

Berlyne, D. E. (1960). *Conflict, arousal, and curiosity.* New York: McGraw-Hill.

Berlyne, D. E. (1971). *Aesthetics and psychobiology.* New York: Appleton-Century-Crofts.

Berlyne, D. E. (1974). *Studies in the new experimental aesthetics.* New York: Wiley.

Berman, A. L., & Jobes, D. A. (1992). Suicidal behavior of adolescents. In B. Bongar (Ed.), *Suicide: Guidelines for assessment, management and treatment.* New York: Oxford University Press.

Bernard, T. (1990). Angry aggression among "truly disadvantaged." *Criminology, 28,* 73–96.

Bernman, A., Jobes, D., & Silverman, M. (2005). *Adolescent Suicide: Assessment and Intervention.* Washington, DC: American Psychological Association.

Bernman, J., & Murphy-Bernman, V. (1996). Cultural differences in perceptions of allocators of resources. *Journal of Cross-Cultural Psychology, 27*(4), 494–509.

Berry, J. W. (1967). Independence and conformity in subsistence level societies. *Journal of Personality and Social Psychology, 7,* 415–418.

Berry, J. W. (1969). On cross-cultural comparability. *International Journal of Psychology, 4,* 119–128.

Berry, J. W. (1971). Ecological and cultural factors in spatial perceptual development. *Canadian Journal of Behavioral Science, 3,* 324–336.

Berry, J. W. (1988). Cognitive values and cognitive competence among the bricoleurs. In J. W. Berry, S. H. Irvine, & E. B. Hunt (Eds.), *Indigenous cognition: Functioning in cultural context* (pp. 9–20). Dordrecht, The Netherlands: Nijhoff.

Berry, J. W. (1997). Immigration, acculturation and adaptation. *Applied Psychology: An International Review, 46,* 5–68.

Berry, J. W., & Annis, R. (1974). Acculturative stress. *Journal of Cross-Cultural Psychology, 5*(4), 382–397.

Berry, J. W., Poortinga, Y. H., Segall, M. H., & Dasen, P. R. (1992). *Cross-cultural psychology: Research and applications.* New York: Cambridge University Press.

Berry, J. W., & Sam, D. (1997). Acculturation and adaptation. In J. W. Berry, M. H. Segall, & C. Kagitcibasi (Eds.), *Handbook of cross-cultural psychology: Social behavior and applications* (Vol. 3, pp. 291–326). Boston, MA: Allyn & Bacon.

Berscheid, E. (1982). Attraction and emotions in interpersonal relationships. In M. S. Clark & S. T. Fiske (Eds.), *Affect and cognition: The 17th Annual Carnegie Symposium on Cognition.* Hillsdale, NJ: Erlbaum.

Best, D. (1994). Parent-child interactions in France, Germany, and Italy. *Journal of Cross-Cultural Psychology, 25*(2), 181–193.

Best, D., Naylor, C., & Williams, J. (1975). Extension of color bias research to young French and Italian children. *Journal of Cross-Cultural Psychology, 6*(4), 391–400.

Betzig, L. (1989). Causes of conjugal dissolution: A cross-cultural study. *Current Anthropology, 30*(5), 654–676.

Beveridge, W. M. (1940). Some differences in racial perception. *British Journal of Psychology, 30,* 57–64.

Birdwhistell, R. L. (1970). *Kinesics and context.* Philadelphia, PA: University of Philadelphia Press.

Birman, D., & Trickett, E. (2001). Cultural transitions in firstgeneration immigrants: Acculturation of Soviet Jewish refugee adolescents and parents. *Journal of Cross-Cultural Psychology, 32*(4), 456–477.

Birnbaum, D.W. (1983). Preschoolers' stereotypes about sex differences in emotionality: A reaffirmation. *Journal of Genetic Psychology, 143,* 139–140.

Biswas, U. N., & Pandey, J. (1996). Mobility and perception of socioeconomic status among tribal and caste group. *Journal of Cross-Cultural Psychology, 27*(2), 200–215.

Bizman, A., & Amir, Y. (1982). Mutual perceptions of Arabs and Jews in Israel. *Journal of Cross-Cultural Psychology, 13*(4), 461–469.

Blakemore, C., & Cooper, G. F. (1970). Development of the brain depends on the visual environment. *Nature, 228,* 477–478.

Bleichrodt, N., Drenth, P. J., & Querido, A. (1980). Effects of iodine deficiency on mental and psychomotor abilities. *American Journal of Physical Anthropology, 53,* 55–67.

Blok, A. (1981). Rams and Billy-goats: A key to Mediterranean code of honor. *Man, 16,* 427–440.

Boduroglu, A., Shah, P., & Nisbett, R. E. (2009). Cultural differences in allocation of attention in visual information processing. *Journal of Cross-Cultural Psychology, 40*(3), 349–360.

Bond, M. (1985). How are responses to verbal insult related to cultural collectivism and power distance? *Journal of Cross-Cultural Psychology, 16*(1), 111–127.

Bond, M., & Tak-Sing, C. (1983). College students' spontaneous self concept: The effects of culture among respondents in Hong-Kong, Japan, and the United States. *Journal of Cross-Cultural Psychology, 14,* 153–171.

Bornstein, M. H., & Tamis-LeMonda, C. (1989). Maternal responsiveness and cognitive development in children. In M. H. Bornstein (Ed.), *Maternal responsiveness: Characteristics and consequences* (pp. 49–61). San Francisco, CA: Jossey-Bass.

Borod, J. (1992). Interhemispheric and intrahemispheric control of emotion: A focus on unilateral brain damage. *Journal of Consulting and Clinical Psychology, 60,* 339–348.

Borowitz, A. (2005). *Terrorism for self-glorification: The herostratos syndrome.* Kent, OH: Kent State University Press.

Bouchard, T., Lykken, D., McGue, M., Segal, N. L., & Tellegen, A. (1990). Sources of human psychological differences: The Minnesota study of twins reared apart. *Science, 250,* 223–228.

Bouchard, T., & McGue, M. (1981). Familial studies of intelligence: A review. *Science, 212,* 1055–1059.

Boucher, H. C., Peng, K., Shi, J., & Wang, L. (2009). Culture and implicit self-esteem: Chinese are 'good' and 'bad' at the same time. *Journal of Cross-Cultural Psychology, 40*(1), 24–45.

Boucher, J., & Brandt, M. (1981). Judgment of emotion: American and Malay antecedents. *Journal of Cross- Cultural Psychology, 12*(3), 272–283.

Bourguignon, E. E. (1954). Dreams and dream interpretation. *American Anthropologist, 56*(2), 262–268.

Bourguignon, E. E. (1976). *Possession*. San Francisco, CA: Chandler & Sharp.

Bourguignon, E. E. (1994). Trance and meditation. In P. K. Bock (Ed.), *Psychological anthropology* (pp. 297–314). Westport, CT: Praeger.

Bowbly, J. (1982). *Attachment* (Vol. I). New York: Basic Books.

Boykin, A. (1994). Harvesting talent and culture: African- American children and educational reform. In R. Rossi (Ed.), *Schools and students at risk* (pp. 116–138). New York: Teachers College Press.

Boykin, A. W., Jagers, R. J., Ellison, C. M., & Albury, A. (1997). Communalism: Conceptualization and measurement of an Afrocultural social orientation. *Journal of Black Studies, 27,* 409–418.

Brace, C. (2005). *Race is a four letter word*. New York: Oxford University Press.

Brandstatter, H., Davis, J., & Stocker-Kreichgauer, G. (Eds.). (1984). *Group decision making*. New York: Academic Press.

Brandt, M. E., & Boucher, J. D. (1985). Judgment of emotions from antecedent situations in three cultures. In I. R. Lagunes & Y. H. Poortinga (Eds.), *From a different perspective: Studies of behavior across cultures* (pp. 348–362). Lisse, The Netherlands: Swets & Zeitlinger.

Braverman, A. (2002). Open-door sexuality. *University of Chicago Magazine, 95*(1), Retrieved October 2002, from Retrieved from http://magazine.uchicago.edu/0210/research.

Brenton, D. (March 2004). The anthropology of adolescent risk-taking behaviors. *Body & Society, 10,* 1–15.

Briggs, D. (2001). The effect of admissions test preparation: Evidence from NELS: 88. *Chance, 14*(1), 10–21.

Briggs, J. L. (1970). *Never in anger: Portrait of an Eskimo family*. Cambridge, MA: Harvard University Press.

Brislin, R. (1970). Back-translation for cross-cultural research. *Journal of Cross-Cultural Psychology, 1*(3), 185–216.

Brislin, R. (1993). *Understanding culture's influence on behavior*. Fort Worth, TX: Harcourt Brace Jovanovich.

Brislin, R. (2000). *Understanding culture's influence on behavior* (2nd ed.). Fort Worth, TX: Harcourt.

Brody, L., & Hall, J. A. (1993). Gender and emotion. In M. Lewis & J. Haviland (Eds.), *Handbook of emotions* (pp. 447–460). New York: Guilford Press.

Bronfenbrenner, U. (1970). *Two worlds of childhood: U.S. and U.S.S.R.* New York: Russell Sage Foundation.

Bronfenbrenner, U. (1979). *The ecology of human development: Experiments by nature and design*. Cambridge, MA: Harvard University Press.

Bronznick, S., & Goldenhar, D. (2008). *21st century women's leadership*. New York, NY: Research Center for Leadership in Action.

Brooks, I. (1976). Cognitive ability assessment with two New Zealand ethnic groups. *Journal of Cross-Cultural Psychology, 7*(3), 347–355.

Browder, L. (2000). *Slippery characters: Ethnic impersonators and American identities*. Durham: The UNC Press.

Brown, D. (1995, November 23). Aggression tied to chemical. *Washington Post*, p. A1.

Brown, J. D., & Cai, H. (2010). Self-esteem and trait importance moderate cultural differences in self-evaluations. *Journal of Cross-Cultural Psychology, 41*(1), 116–123.

Brown, P., & Wald, G. (1964). Visual pigments in single rods and cones in the human retina. *Science, 144,* 45–52.

Brown, R. (1965). *Social psychology*. New York: Free Press.

Bruner, J., & Goodman, C. (1947). Value and need as organizing factors in perception. *Journal of Abnormal and Social Psychology, 42,* 33–44.

Bruner, J. S., & Potter, M. C. (1964). Interference in visual recognition. *Science, 144,* 424–425.

Buckley, S. (June 17, 2000). Brazil's brutal economic gap. *Washington Post*, p. A13.

Buda, R., & Elsayed-Elkhouly, S. (1998). Cultural differences between Arabs and Americans: Individualism and collectivism revisited. *Journal of Cross-Cultural Psychology, 29,* 487–492.

Bull, R., & David, I. (1986). The stigmatizing effect of facial disfigurement. *Journal of Cross-Cultural Psychology, 17*(1), 99–108.

Buss, A. H., & Plomin, R. (1985). *Temperament: Early developing personality traits.* Hillsdale, NJ: Erlbaum.

Buss, D. (1994). Sex differences in human mate preferences. *Behavioral and Brain Sciences, 12*, 1–49.

Butcher, J., Jeeyoung, L., & Nezami, E. (1998). Objective study of abnormal personality in cross-cultural settings. *Journal of Cross-Cultural Psychology, 29*(1), 189–211.

Butler, E. A., Lee, T. L., & Gross, J. J. (2009). Does expressing your emotions raise or lower your blood pressure?: The answer depends on cultural context. *Journal of Cross-Cultural Psychology, 40*(3), 510–517.

Bynum, E. B. (1993). *Families and the interpretation of dreams: Awakening the intimate web.* New York: Harrington Park Press/Haworth Press.

Byrne, D. (1982). Predicting human sexual behavior. In A. G. Kraut (Ed.), *The Stanley Hall lecture series* (Vol. 2, pp. 363–368). Washington, DC: American Psychological Association.

Byrnes, J. P. (1988). Formal operations: A systematic reformulation. *Developmental Review, 8*, 66–87.

Camilleri, C., & Malewska-Peyre, H. (1997). Socialization and identity strategies. In J. W. Berry, P. R. Dasen, & T. S. Saraswathi (Eds.), *Handbook of cross-cultural psychology: Basic processes and human development* (Vol. 2, pp. 41–67). Boston, MA: Allyn & Bacon.

Campbell, D. (1967). Stereotypes and the perception of group differences. *American Psychologist, 22*, 817–829.

Canino, G. (2004). Are somatic symptoms and related distress more prevalent in Hispanic/Latino youth? Some methodological considerations. *Journal of Clinical Child and Adolescent Psychology, 33*, 272–275.

Cannon, W. B. (1927). The James-Lange theory of emotions: A critical examination and an alternative theory. *American Journal of Psychiatry, 39*, 106–124.

Cannon, W. B. (1932). *The wisdom of the body.* New York: W.W. Norton.

Cantor, N., & Mischel, W. (1979). Prototypes in person perception. In L. Berkowitz (Ed.), *Advances in experimental social psychology* (Vol. 12, pp. 3–52). New York: Academic Press.

Caprio, F. (1943). A psycho-social study of primitive conceptions of death. *Criminal Psychotherapy, 5*, 303–317.

Carlson, V. J., & Harwood, R. L. (2003). Attachment, culture, and the caregiving system: The cultural patterning of everyday experiences among Anglo and Puerto Rican mother–infant pairs. *Infant Mental Health Journal, 24*, 53–73.

Carrier, J. (1980). Homosexual behavior in cross-cultural perspective. In J. Marmor (Ed.), *Homosexual behavior: A modern reappraisal.* New York: Basic Books.

Carroll, J. B. (1983). Studying individual differences in cognitive abilities: Implications for cross-cultural studies. In S. H. Irvine & J.W. Berry (Eds.), *Human assessment and cultural factors* (pp. 213–235). New York: Plenum.

Cartwright, R. D. (1992). "Masochism" in dreaming and its relationship to depression. *Dreaming, 1*, 147–159.

Cashmore, J., & Goodnow, J. (1986). Influences on Australian parents' values: Ethnicity vs sociometric status. *Journal of Cross-Cultural Psychology, 17*, 441–454.

Castillo, R. J. (1997). *Culture and mental illness.* Pacific Grove, CA: ITP.

Chambless, D., & Williams, K. E. (1995). A preliminary study of African Americans with agoraphobia: Symptom severity and outcome of treatment with in vivo exposure. *Behavior Therapy, 26*, 501–515.

Chandler, T. A., Shama, D. D., Wolf, F. M., & Planchard, S. K. (1981). Multi-attributional causality: A five cross-national samples study. *Journal of Cross-Cultural Psychology, 12*, 207–221.

Chao, R. K. (1996). Chinese and European American mother's beliefs about the role of parenting in children's school success. *Journal of Cross-Cultural Psychology, 27*, 403–423.

Chen, S. X., Benet-Martínez, V., & Bond, M. H. (2008). Bicultural identity, bilingualism, and psychological adjustment in multicultural societies: Immigration-based and globalization-based acculturation. *Journal of Personality, 76*, 803–838.

Cheung, F. M. (1995). Facts and myths about somatization among the Chinese. In T. Y. Lin, W. S. Tseng, & E. K. Yeh (Eds.), *Chinese society and mental health* (pp. 156–166). Hong Kong: Oxford University Press.

Cheung, F. M., & Halpern, D. F. (2010). Women at the top: Powerful leaders define success as work + family in a culture of gender. *American Psychologist, 65*(3), 182–193.

Cheung, F. M., Leung, K., Fan, R. M., Song, W. Z., Zhang, J. X., & Chang, J. P. (1996). Development of the Chinese personality assessment inventory (CPAI). *Journal of Cross-Cultural Psychology, 27,* 181–199.

Chiasson, N., Dube, L., & Blondin, J.-P. (1996). Happiness: A look into the folk psychology of four cultural groups. *Journal of Cross-Cultural Psychology, 27*(6), 673–691.

Child, I. E. (1969). Esthetic. In G. Lindsey & E. Aronson (Eds.), *The handbook of social psychology* (Vol. 3, pp. 853–916). Reading, MA: Addison-Wesley.

Chilman, C. S. (1993). Hispanic families in the United States: Research perspectives. In H. P. McAdoo (Ed.), *Family ethnicity: Strength in diversity* (pp. 141–163). Newbury Park, CA: Sage.

Chin, J. L. (2010). Introduction to the special issue on diversity and leadership. *American Psychologist, 65*(3), 150–156.

Chinoy, I., & Babington, C. (1998, May 3). Low-income players feed lottery cash cow. *Washington Post,* p. A1.

Chirkov, V., & Ryan, R. (2001). Parent and teacher autonomy-support in Russian and U.S. adolescents: Common effects on well-being and academic motivation. *Journal of Cross-Cultural Psychology, 32*(5), 618–635.

Chiu, C.-Y., & Hong, Y. (2006). The social psychology of culture. New York: Psychology Press.

Cho, Y., & Kim, Y. (1993). The cultural roots of entrepreneurial bureaucracy: The case of Korea. *Public Administrative Quarterly, 16,* 509–524.

Chomsky, N. (1976). The fallacy of Richard Herrnstein's IQ. In N. J. Block & G. Dworkin (Eds.), *The IQ controversy* (pp. 285–298). New York: Pantheon Books.

Chopra, D. (2000). *How to know God.* New York: Harmony Books.

Chopra, D. (2010). *Reinventing the body, resurrecting the soul: How to create a new you.* New York: Three Rivers Press.

Chung, R. C.-Y., & Bemak, F. (2002). The relationship of culture and empathy in cross-cultural counseling. *Journal of Counseling and Development, 80,* 154–159.

Chung, R. C.-Y., Bemak, F., & Talleyrand, R. (2007). Mentoring within the field of counseling: A preliminary study of multicultural perspectives. *International Journal for the Advancement of Counseling, 29,* 21–32.

Chung, R. C.-Y., Walkey, F., & Bemak, F. (1997). A comparison of achievement and aspirations of New Zealand, Chinese, and European students. *Journal of Cross-Cultural Psychology, 28*(4), 481–489.

Cialdini, R., Reno, R., & Kallgren, C. (1990). A focus theory of normative conduct: Recycling the concept of norms to reduce littering in public places. *Journal of Personality and Social Psychology, 58,* 1015–1029.

Ciborski, T., & Choi, S. (1974). Nonstandard English and free recall: An exploratory study. *Journal of Cross-Cultural Psychology, 5*(3), 271–279.

Clark, H., & Clark, E. (1980). Pain response in Nepalese porters. *Science, 209,* 410–412.

Clark, M. (1995). Changes in Euro-American values needed for sustainability. *Journal of Social Issues, 51,* 63–82.

Clementson, L. (1998, December 14). Caught in the crossfire. *Newsweek,* pp. 38–39.

Clore, G. L., Schwarz, N., & Conway, M. (1994). Affective causes and consequences of social information processing. In R. S. Wyer & T. K. Strull (Eds.), *Handbook of social cognition* (Vol. 1, pp. 323–417). Hillsdale, NJ: Erlbaum.

Cockerham, W., Kunz, G., & Lueschen, G. (1988). Social stratification and health styles in two systems of health care delivery: A comparison of the United States and West Germany. *Journal of Health and Social Behavior, 29,* 113–126.

Cogan, J., Bhalla, S., Sefa-Dedeh, A., & Rothblum, E. (1996). A comparison study of United States and African students on perceptions of obesity and thinness. *Journal of Cross-Cultural Psychology, 27*(1), 98–113.

Cole, M., Gay, J., Glick, J. A., & Sharp, D. W. (Eds.). (1971). *The cultural context of learning and thinking.* New York: Basic Books.

Collings, G. (1989). Stress containment through meditation. *Prevention in Human Services, 6,* 141–150.

Collins, B. E. (1974). Four components of the Rotter internal-external scale: Belief in a difficult world, a just world, a predictable world, a politically responsive world. *Journal of Personality and Social Psychology, 29,* 381–391.

Comas-Díaz, L. (2001). Hispanics, Latinos, or Americanos: The evolution of identity. *Cultural Diversity and Ethnic Minority Psychology, 7*(2), 115–120.

Consedine, N., & Magai, C. (2002). The uncharted waters of emotion: Ethnicity, trait emotion and emotion expression in older adults. *Journal of Cross-Cultural Gerontology, 17*(1), 71–100.

Constable, P. (2000, February 23). Roiling sacred waters: Hindus halt the shooting of a film along the Ganges, calling it defamatory. *Washington Post,* p. A15.

Constantine, M., Anderson, G., Berkel, L., Caldwell, L., & Utsey, S. (2005). Examining the cultural adjustment experiences of African international college students: A qualitative analysis. *Journal of Counseling Psychology, 52*(1), 57–66.

Constantine, M. G., Myers, L. J., Kindaichi, M., & Moore, J. L. (2004). Exploring indigenous mental health practices: The roles of healers and helpers in promoting wellbeing in people of color. *Counseling and Values, 48,* 110–125.

Cooke, D., & Michie, C. (1999). Psychopathy across cultures: North America and Scotland compared. *Journal of Abnormal Psychology, 1*(108), 58–68.

Coon, C. (1946). The universality of natural groupings in human societies. *Journal of Educational Sociology, 20,* 162–168.

Cooper, D. (2003). *World philosophies.* Malden, MA: Blackwell.

Cooper, K. J. (1999, September 29). Students weak in essay skills. *Washington Post,* p. A3.

Coren, S. (1992). *The left-hander syndrome.* New York: Free Press.

Cortina, L., & Wasti, S. A. (2005). Profiles in coping: Responses to sexual harassment across persons, organizations, and cultures. *Journal of Applied Psychology, 90*(1), 182–192.

Costa, P. T., & McCrae, R. M. (1997, May). Personality trait structure as a human universal. *American Psychologist, 52*(5), 509–516.

Cox, H. G. (1988). *Later life: The realities of aging.* Englewood Cliffs, NJ: Prentice Hall.

Crain, R., & Weissman, C. (1972). *Discrimination, personality, and achievement: A survey of northern blacks.* New York: Seminar Press.

Crick, F., & Mitchison, G. (1983). The function of dream sleep, *Nature, 304*(5922), 111–114.

Cuddy, A. J. C., Norton, M. I., & Fiske, S. T. (2005). This old stereotype: The pervasiveness and persistence of the elderly stereotype. *Journal of Social Issues, 61,* 267–285.

Cutler, N. (1975). Toward a generational conception of political socialization. In D. Schwartz & S. Schwartz (Eds.), *New directions in political socialization* (pp. 363–409). New York: Free Press.

Cutler, W. B., Preti, G., Krieger, A., Huggins, G. R., Garcia, C. R., & Lawley, H. J. (1986). Human axillary secretions influence women's menstrual cycles: The role of donor extract from men. *Hormones and Behavior, 20,* 463–473.

Dabbis, J., & Morris, R. (1990). Testosterone, social class, and antisocial behavior in a sample of 4,462 men. *Psychological Science, 1,* 209–211.

Daly, M., & Wilson, M. (1988). Evolutionary social psychology and family homicide. *Science, 242,* 519–524.

Darwin, C. (1872/1979). *The expression of the emotions in man and animals.* London: John Muray/Julan Friedman; New York: Philosophical Library.

Dasen, P. R. (1975). Concrete operational development in three cultures. *Journal of Cross-Cultural Psychology, 6*(2), 156–163.

Dasen, P. R. (1984). The cross-cultural study of intelligence: Piaget and the Baoule. *International Journal of Psychology, 19,* 407–434.

Dasen, P. R. (1994). Culture and cognitive development from a Piagetian perspective. In W. J. Lonner & R. Malpass (Eds.), *Psychology and culture* (pp. 145–150). Boston, MA: Allyn & Bacon.

Dasen, P. R., Berry, J., & Witkin, H. (1979). The use of developmental theories cross-culturally. In L. Eckenberg, Y. Poortinga, & W. Lonner (Eds.),

Cross-cultural contributions to psychology. Amsterdam, The Netherlands: Swets & Zeitlinger.

Davenport, W. (1976). Sex in cross-cultural perspective. In F. A. Beach (Ed.), *Human sexuality in four perspectives* (pp. 115–163). Baltimore, MD: Johns Hopkins University Press.

Davidson, R. (1992). Emotion and affective style: Hemispheric substances. *Psychological Science, 3,* 39–43.

Davidson, R. J., Kabat-Zinn, J., Schumacher, J., Rosenkranz, M., Muller, D., Santorelli, S. F., et al. (2003). Alterations in brain and immune function produced by mindfulness meditation. *Psychosomatic Medicine, 65,* 564–570.

Davis, J., & Ginsburg, H. (1993). Similarities and differences in the formal and informal mathematical cognition of African, American and Asian children: The role of schooling and social class. In J. Altarriba (Ed.), *Cognition and culture: A cross-cultural approach to cognitive psychology* (pp. 343–360). Amsterdam, The Netherlands: Elsevier Science.

Dawes, R. M. (1994). *House of cards: Psychology and psychotherapy built on myth.* New York: Free Press.

Dawson, J. (1975). Socioeconomic differences in size judgments of discs and coins by Chinese primary VI children in Hong Kong. *Perceptual and Motor Skills, 41,* 107–110.

Dawson, R., Prewitt, K., & Dawson, K. (1977). *Political socialization.* Boston, MA: Little, Brown.

Dehaene, S. (2002). *The cognitive neuroscience of consciousness.* Cambridge, MA: The MIT Press.

Deregowski, J. B. (1974). Teaching African children pictorial depth perception: In search of a method. *Perception, 3,* 309–312.

Deregowski, J. B., Muldrow, E. S., & Muldrow, W. F. (1972). Perceptual recognition in a remote Ethiopian population. *Perception, 1,* 417–425.

Deregowski, J., & Munro, D. (1974). An analysis of "Polyphasic Pictorial Perception." *Journal of Cross-Cultural Psychology, 5*(3), 329–339.

Dettwyler, K. A. (1989). Style of infant feeding. Parental/caretaker control of food consumption in young children. *American Anthropologist, 91,* 696–703.

Deutsch, M., & Gerard, G. (1955). A study of normative and informational social influence upon individual judgment. *Journal of Abnormal and Social Psychology, 51,* 629–636.

Devine, P. G. (1989). Stereotypes and prejudice: Their automatic and controlled components. *Journal of Cross-Cultural Psychology, 9,* 259–284.

Dickerman, M. (1993). Reproductive strategies and gender construction: An evolutionary view of homosexuals. *Journal of Homosexuality, 24,* 55–71.

Dickson, D. H., & Kelly, I.W. (1985). The "Barnum Effect" in personality assessment: A review of the literature. *Psychological Reports, 57,* 367–382.

Diener, E., Gohm, C., Suh, E., & Oishi, S. (2000). Similarity of the relations between marital status and subjective well-being across cultures. *Journal of Cross-Cultural Psychology, 31*(4), 419–436.

Dole, A. (1995). Why not drop race as a term? *American Psychologist, 50*(1), 40.

Dollard, J., Doob, L., Miller, N., Mowrer, O., & Sears, R. (1939). *Frustration and aggression.* New Haven, CT: Yale University Press.

Domino, G. (1986). Sleep in advanced age: A comparison of Mexican American and Anglo American elderly. *Hispanic Journal of Behavioral Sciences, 8,* 259–273.

Domino, G. (1992). Cooperation and competition in Chinese and American children. *Journal of Cross-Cultural Psychology, 23*(4), 456–467.

Domino, G., & Hannah, M. T. (1987). A comparative analysis of social values of Chinese and American children. *Journal of Cross-Cultural Psychology, 18*(1), 58–77.

Draguns, J. G. (1996). Multicultural and cross-cultural assessment of psychological disorder: Dilemmas and decisions. In J. Impara & G. R. Sodowsky (Eds.), *Buros-Nebraska symposium on motivation and testing* (pp. 37–84). Lincoln, NE: Buros Institute of Mental Measurements.

D'Souza, D. (1995). *The end of racism.* New York: Free Press.

Durkheim, E. (1924/1974). *Sociology and philosophy.* New York: Free Press.

Durkheim, E. (1897/1964). *Suicide.* New York: Free Press.

Dyal, J. (1984). Cross-cultural research with the locus of control construct. In H. Lefcourt (Ed.), *Research with the locus of control construct* (Vol. 3, pp. 209–306). New York: Academic Press.

Dziurawiec, S., & Deregowski, J. (1992). "Twisted perspective" in young children's drawings. *British Journal of Developmental Psychology, 10*, 35–49.

Eagly, A. (1995). The science and politics of comparing women and men. *American Psychologist, 50*(3), 145–158.

Eagly, A. H., & Carli, L. L. (2007). *Through the labyrinth: The truth about how women become leaders.* Boston, MA: Harvard Business School Press.

Eagly, A. H., & Chin, J. L. (2010). Diversity and leadership in a changing world. *American Psychologist, 65*(3), 216–224.

Eagly, A. H., Karau, S. J., & Makhijani, M. G. (1995). Gender and the effectiveness of leaders: A meta-analysis. *Psychological Bulletin, 117*, 125–145.

Earley, P. (1989). Social loafing and collectivism: A comparison of the United States and the People's Republic of China. *Administrative Science Quarterly, 34*, 565–581.

Eaton, W., Dryman, A., & Weissman, M. (1991). Panic and phobia. In L. Robins & D. Reiger (Eds.), *Psychiatric disorders in America* (pp. 155–179). New York: Free Press.

Edelman, R., Asendroff, J., Contarello, A., Zammuner, V., Georgas, J., & Villanueva, C. (1989). Self-reported expression of embarrassment in five European cultures. *Journal of Cross-Cultural Psychology, 20*(4), 357–371.

Edsall, T. (1998, September 28). Candidates find virtue in chastity as an issue. *Washington Post*, p. A11.

Edwards, C. P., & Bloch, M. (2010). The whitings' concepts of culture and how they have fared in contemporary psychology and anthropology. *Journal of Cross-Cultural Psychology, 41*(4), 485–498.

Ekman, P. (1980). *The face of man.* New York: Garland Press.

Ekman, P. (1982). *Emotion in the human face.* New York: Cambridge University Press.

Ekman, P. (1994). Strong evidence of universals in facial expression: A reply to Russell's mistaken critique. *Psychological Bulletin, 115*, 268–278.

Ekman, P., & Friesen, W. V. (1969). The repertoire of nonverbal behavior: Categories, origins, usage and coding. *Semiotica, 1*, 49–98.

Ekman, P., & Friesen, W. V. (1975). *Unmasking the face.* Englewood Cliffs, NJ: Prentice Hall.

Ekman, P., & Friesen, W. V. (1978). *The facial action coding system.* Palo Alto, CA: Consulting Psychologists Press.

Ekman, P., Friesen, W. V., O'Sallivan, M., Diacoanni-Tarlatris, I., Krause, R., Pitcarin, T., et al. (1987). Universals and cultural differences in the judgments of facial expressions of emotion. *Journal of Personality and Social Psychology, 17*, 124–129.

Ekman, P., Levenson, R., & Friesen, W. (1983). Autonomic nervous system activity distinguishes between emotions. *Science, 221*, 1208–1210.

Elbedour, S., Shulman, S., & Kedem, P. (1997). Adolescent intimacy: A cross-cultural study. *Journal of Cross-Cultural Psychology, 28*(1), 5–22.

Elder, G., & Conger, R. (2000). *Children of the land: Adversity and success in rural America.* Chicago, IL: University of Chicago Press.

Elfenbein, H. A., & Ambady, N. (2003). When familiarity breeds accuracy: Cultural exposure and facial emotion recognition. *Journal of Personality and Social Psychology, 85*, 276–290.

Elfenbein, H., Mandal, M., Ambady, N., Harizuka, S., & Kumar, S. (2002). Cross-cultural patterns in emotion recognition: Highlighting design and analytical techniques. *Emotion, 2*(1), 75–84.

Ellsworth, P. (1994). Senses, culture, and sensibility. In S. Kitayama & H. Markus (Eds.), *Emotion and culture: Empirical studies of mutual influence* (pp. 23–50). Washington, DC: American Psychological Association.

El Zahhar, N., & Hocevar, D. (1991). Cultural and sexual differences in test anxiety, trait anxiety, and arousability: Egypt, Brazil, and the United States. *Journal of Cross-Cultural Psychology, 22*(2), 238–249.

Ember, C., & Ember, M. (1990). *Anthropology.* Englewood Cliffs, NJ: Prentice Hall.

Erdelyi, M. H. (2010). The ups and downs of memory. *American Psychologist, 65*(7), 623–633.

Erickson, C., & Al-Timimi, N. (2001). Providing mental health services to Arab Americans: Recommendations and considerations. *Cultural Diversity and Ethnic Minority Psychology, 7*(4), 308–327.

Erikson, E. H. (1968). *Identity: Youth and crisis.* New York: Norton.

Erikson, E. H. (1950). *Childhood and society.* New York: Norton.

Esaki, L. (2001, April 1). Connecting to the 21st century educational reform in Japan and reflections on global culture. *The Daily Yomiuri,* p. 6.

Eskin, M. (2004). The effects of religious versus secular education on suicide ideation and suicidal attitudes in adolescents in Turkey. *Social Psychiatry and Psychiatric Epidemiology, 39,* 536–542.

Estes, C. P. (2003).*Women who run with the wolves.* New York: Ballantine Books.

Faiola, A. (2003, December 27). Japan's empire of cool: Country's culture becomes its biggest export. *Washington Post,* p. A01.

Farhi, P. (2007, January 21). Five myths about U.S. kids outclassed by the rest of the world. *Washington Post,* p. B02.

Farver, J. A., Kim, Y. K., & Lee-Shin, Y. (2000). Within cultural differences examining individual differences in Korean American and European American preschoolers' social pretend play. *Journal of Cross-Cultural Psychology, 31*(5), 583–602.

Farver, J. A., Welles-Nystrom, B., Frosch, D., Wimbarti, S., & Hoppe-Graff, S. (1997). Toy stories: Aggression in children's narratives in the United States, Sweden, Germany, and Indonesia. *Journal of Cross-Cultural Psychology, 28*(4), 393–420.

Fast, J. (1970). *Body language.* New York: Pocket Books.

Fears, D. (2003, October 17). Judge orders Nebraska father to not speak "Hispanic." *Washington Post,* p. A3.

Feldman, O. (1996). The political personality in Japan: An inquiry into the belief system of Diet members. *Political Psychology, 17,* 657–682.

Ferguson, G. A. (1956). On transfer and abilities of man. *Canadian Journal of Psychology, 10,* 121–131.

Fernandez, S., Castano, E., & Singh, I. (2010). Managing death in the burning grounds of Varanasi, India: A terror management investigation. *Journal of Cross-Cultural Psychology, 41*(2), 182–194.

Ferrari, J., Díaz-Morales, J. F., O'Callaghan, J., Díaz, K., & Argumedo, D. (2007). Frequent behavioral delay tendencies by adults: International prevalence rates of chronic procrastination. *Journal of Cross-Cultural Psychology, 38,* 458–464.

Festinger, L. (1957). *A theory of cognitive dissonance.* Stanford, CA: Stanford University Press.

Fijeman, Y. A., Willemsen, M. E., & Poortinga, Y. H. (1996). Individualism-collectivism: An empirical study of a conceptual issue. *Journal of Cross-Cultural Psychology, 27,* 381–402.

Fischer, A., Rodriguez Mosquera, P. M., van Vianen, A. E. M., & Manstead, A. (2004). Gender and culture differences in emotion. *Emotion, 4*(1), 87–94.

Fischer, R., & Smith, P. (2003). Reward Allocation and Culture: A Meta-Analysis. *Journal of Cross-Cultural Psychology, 34*(3), 251–268.

Fiske, S. T., & Taylor, S. E. (1984). *Social cognition.* Reading, MA: Addison-Wesley.

Fiske, S. T., & Taylor, S. E. (1991). *Social cognition* (2nd ed.). New York: McGraw-Hill.

Fletcher, G. J. O., & Ward, C. (1988). *Attribution theory and process: A cross-cultural challenge to social psychology.* Beverly Hills, CA: Sage.

Flynn, J. (1987). Massive IQ gains in fourteen nations: What IQ tests really measure. *Psychological Bulletin, 101,* 171–191.

Flynn, J. (1991). *Asian-Americans: Achievement beyond IQ.* Hillsdale, NJ: Erlbaum.

Flynn, J. R. (2007). *What is Intelligence?: Beyond the Flynn effect.* New York: Cambridge University Press.

Fogarty, G., & White, C. (1994). Differences between values of Australian Aboriginal and non-Aboriginal students. *Journal of Cross-Cultural Psychology, 25*(3), 394–408.

Forer, B. R. (1949). The fallacy of personal validation: A classroom demonstration of gullibility. *Journal of Abnormal and Social Psychology, 44,* 118–123.

Foulkes, D. (1985). *Dreaming: A cognitive-psychological analysis.* Hillsdale, NJ: Erlbaum.

Fountoulakis, K. N., Iacovides, A., Ioannidou, C., Bascialla, F., Nimatoudis, I., Kaprinis, G., et al. (2002). Reliability and cultural applicability of the Greek version of the International Personality Disorders Examination. *BMC Psychiatry, 2*(1), 6.

Fowers, B. J., & Richardson, F. C. (1996). Why is multiculturalism good? *American Psychologist, 51,* 609–621.

Foxall, G. R., & Payne, A. F. (1989). Adaptors and innovators in organizations: A cross-cultural study of the cognitive styles of managerial functions and sub-functions. *Human Relations, 42,* 639–649.

Fraczek, A. (1985). Moral approval of aggressive acts. *Journal of Cross-Cultural Psychology, 16*(1), 41–54.

Frager, R. (1970). Conformity and anti-conformity in Japan. *Journal of Personality and Social Psychology, 15,* 203–210.

Frager, R., & Wood, L. (1992). Are the rules of address universal? *Journal of Cross-Cultural Psychology, 23*(2), 148–162.

Frake, C. (1980). The ethnographic study of cognitive systems. In C. Frake (Ed.), *Language and cultural descriptions* (pp. 1–17). Stanford, CA: Stanford University Press.

Franklin, A. J. (2004). *From brotherhood to manhood: How black men rescue their relationships and dreams from the invisibility syndrome.* Hoboken, NJ: Wiley.

Frenzel, A., Thrash, T., Pekrun, R., & Goetz, T. (2007). Achievement emotions in Germany and China: A cross-cultural validation of the academic emotions questionnaire—mathematics. *Journal of Cross-Cultural Psychology, 38*(3), 302–309.

Freud, S. (1938). *The basic writings of Sigmund Freud.* New York: Random House.

Frey, C., & Hoppe-Graff, S. (1994). Serious and playful aggression in Brazilian boys and girls. *Sex Roles, 30,* 249–268.

Fried, M. (1964). Effects of social change on mental health. *American Journal of Orthopsychiatry, 34,* 3–28.

Friedman, T. L. (2000). *The Lexus and the olive tree: Understanding globalization.* New York: Anchor.

Frijda, N. H. (1986). *The emotions.* Cambridge, MA: Cambridge University Press.

Frijda, N. H., Markam, S., Sato, K., & Wiers, R. (1995). Emotions and emotion words. In J. A. Russell, A. S. R. Manstead, J. C. Wellenkamp, & J. M. Fernandez-Dols (Eds.), *Everyday conceptions of emotion: An introduction to the psychology, anthropology and linguistics of emotion* (pp. 121–143). Dordrecht: Kluwer.

Frijda, N. H., & Mesquita, B. (1994). The social roles and functions of emotions. In S. Kitayama & H. Markus (Eds.), *Emotion and culture: Empirical studies of mutual influence* (pp. 51–88). Washington, DC: American Psychological Association.

Frisch, R. E., & Revelle, R. (1970). Height and weight at menarche and a hypothesis of critical body weights and adolescent events. *Science, 169,* 397–398.

Fry, D. (1988). Intercommunity differences in aggression among Zapotec children. *Child Development, 59,* 1008–1019.

Fuertes, J., Potere, J., & Ramirez, K. (2002). Effects of speech accents on interpersonal evaluations: Implications for counseling practice and research. *Cultural Diversity and Ethnic Minority Psychology, 8*(4), 346–356.

Fuligni, A., & Pedersen, S. (2002). Family obligation and the transition to young adulthood. *Developmental Psychology, 38*(5), 856–868.

Fung, Y.-L. (1948). *A short history of Chinese philosophy.* New York: Free Press.

Funtowitz, M., & Widiger, T. (1999). Sex bias in the diagnosis of personality disorders: An evaluation of the *DSM-IV* Criteria. *Journal of Abnormal Psychology, 108*(2), 195–201.

Furnham, A., & Baguma, P. (1999). A cross-cultural study from three countries of self-estimates of intelligence. *North American Journal of Psychology, 1,* 69–77.

Furnham, A., & Bochner, S. (1986). *Culture shock.* London: Methuen.

Furnham, A., Kirkcaldy, B., & Lynn, R. (1994). National attitudes to competitiveness, money, and work among young people: First, second, and third world differences. *Human Relations, 47*(1), 119–132.

Furnham, A., Rakow, T., Sarmany-Schuller, I., & Fruyt Filip (1999). European differences in self-perceived multiple intelligences. *European Psychologist, 4*(3), 131–138.

Futuyma, D. J. (1979). *Evolutionary biology.* Sunderland, MA: Sinauer.

Gabrenya, W., Wang, Y., & Lataner, B. (1985). Social loafing on an optimizing task. *Journal of Cross-Cultural Psychology, 16*(2), 223–242.

Gabriel, U., Beyeler, G., Daniker, N., Fey, W., Gutweniger, K., Lienhart, M., et al. (2001). Perceived sexual orientation and helping behavior: The wrong number technique, a Swiss replication. *Journal of Cross-Cultural Psychology, 32*(6), 743–749.

Galanti, G.-A. (2003). The Hispanic family and male–female relationships: An overview. *Journal of Transcultural Nursing, 14*, 180–185.

Gardiner, H. W., & Kosmitzki, C. (2008). *Lives across cultures: Cross-cultural human development.* Boston, MA: Allyn and Bacon.

Gardiner, H., Mutter, J., & Kosmitzki, C. (1998). *Lives across cultures: Cross-cultural human development.* Boston, MA: Allyn & Bacon.

Gardner, H. (2007). *Five minds for the future.* Cambridge, MA: Harvard Business School Press.

Geary, D., Fan, L., & Bow-Thomas, C. (1992). Numerical cognition: Loci of ability differences comparing children from China and the United States. *Psychological Science, 3*, 180–185.

Georgas, J., Poortinga, Y., Angleitner, A., Goodwin, R., & Charalambous, N. (1997). The relationship of family bonds to family structure and function across cultures. *Journal of Cross-Cultural Psychology, 28*(3), 303–320.

Gergen, K., & Black, K. (1965). Aging, time perspective, and preferred solutions to international conflicts. *Journal of Conflict Resolution, 9*, 177–186.

Giddens, A. (2000). *Runaway world: How globalization is reshaping our lives.* New York: Routledge.

Giles, H. (1970). Evaluative reactions to accents. *Educational Review, 22*, 211–227.

Gilman, S. L. (1988). *Disease and representation: Images of illness from madness to AIDS.* Ithaca, NY: Cornell University Press.

Glad, B. (1980). *Jimmy Carter: In search of the big White House.* New York: Norton.

Glad, B., & Shiraev, E. (Eds.). (1999). *The Russian transformation.* New York: St. Martin's.

Goldston, D., Molock, S., Whitbeck, L., Murakami, J., Zayas, L., & Hall, G. C. N. (2008). Cultural considerations in adolescent suicide prevention and psychosocial treatment. *American Psychologist, 63*(1), 14–31.

Goodnow, J. J. (1990). The socialization of cognition: What's involved? In J. W. Stigler, R. A. Shweder, & G. Herdt (Eds.), *Cultural psychology: Essays on comparative human behavior* (pp. 259–286). Cambridge, MA: Cambridge University Press.

Goodnow, J. J., & Levine, R. A. (1973). The grammar of action: Direction and sequence in children's copying. *Cognitive Psychology, 4*, 82–98.

Gosso, Y., Morais, M., & Otta, E. (2007). Pretend play of Brazilian children: A window into different cultural worlds. *Journal of Cross-Cultural Psychology, 38*(5), 539–558.

Gottrfried, A. W. (Ed.). (1984). *Home environment and early cognitive development: Longitudinal research.* New York: Academic Press.

Gould, S. J. (1994, November 15). The geometer of race. *Discover*, pp. 65–81.

Gould, S. J. (1997). This view of life: Unusual unity. *Natural History, 106*, 20–23, 69–71.

Gozman, L., & Edkind, A. (1992). *The psychology of post-totalitarianism in Russia.* London: Centre for Research into Communist Economies.

Graham, J. L. (1983). Brazilian, Japanese, and American business negotiations. *Journal of International Business Studies, 14*, 47–61.

Graham, J. L., Evenko, L. I., & Rajan, M. N. (1992). An empirical comparison of Soviet and American business negotiations. *Journal of International Business Studies, 23*, 387–418.

Granovetter, M. (1973). The strength of weak ties. *American Journal of Sociology, 78*(6), 1360–1380.

Greenwald, J. (1986, January 13). Is there cause for fear of flying? *Time*, pp. 39–40.

Gregory, R. (1978). *Eye and brain: The psychology of seeing.* New York: McGraw-Hill.

Griffith, R. C., Miyagi, O., & Tago, A. (1958). The universality of typical dreams: Japanese Americans. *American Anthropologist, 60*, 1173–1179.

Griffore, R. J. (2007). Speaking of fairness in testing. *American Psychologist, 62*(9), 1081–1082.

Grossman, H. J. (1983). *Classification in mental retardation.* Washington, DC: American Association on Mental Deficiency.

Grumet, G. (1983). Eye contact: The core of interpersonal relatedness. *Psychiatry, 46*, 172–182.

Gudykunst, W., & Bond, M. H. (1997). Intergroup relations across cultures. In J. W. Berry, M. H. Segall, & C. Kagitcibasi (Eds.), *Handbook of cross-cultural psychology: Social behavior and applications* (Vol. 3, pp. 119–161). Boston, MA: Allyn & Bacon.

Gudykunst, W. B., Nishida, T., & Morisaki, S. (1992). Cultural, relational, and personality influences on uncertainty reduction process. *Western Journal of Speech Communication, 53,* 13–29.

Guida, F., & Ludlow, L. (1989). A cross-cultural study of test anxiety. *Journal of Cross-Cultural Psychology, 20*(2), 178–190.

Guilmoto, C. Z. (2009). "The Sex Ratio Transition in Asia." *CEPED Working Paper, 5.* Retrieved from http://www.ceped.org/biblio/files/guilmoto/2009/95_Guilmoto2009.pdf

Gussler, J. (1973). Social change, ecology, and spirit possession among the South African Nguni. In E. Bourguignon (Ed.), *Religion, altered states of consciousness, and social change* (pp. 88–126). Columbus, OH: Ohio State University Press.

Habermas, T. (1991). The role of psychiatric and medical traditions in the discovery and description of anorexia nervosa in France, Germany, and Italy, 1873–1918. *Journal of Nervous and Mental Disease, 179,* 360–365.

Hall, E. T. (1959). *The silent language.* Greenwich, CT: Fawcett.

Hall, S. (1916). *Adolescence.* New York: Appleton-Century-Crofts.

Hallahan, M., Lee, F., & Herzog, T. (1997). It's not just whether you win or lose, it's also where you play the game: A naturalistic, cross-cultural examination of the positivity bias. *Journal of Cross-Cultural Psychology, 28,* 768–778.

Hallowell, A. (1955). *Culture and experience.* Philadelphia, PA: University of Pennsylvania Press.

Halonen, D., & Santrock, J. (1995). *Psychology: Contexts of behavior.* Madison, WI: Brown & Benchmark.

Halperin, D. (1996, January). Trance and possession: Are they the same. *Transcultural Psychiatry, 33,* 3–41.

Hamermesh, D. (2003). *Economics is everywhere.* New York: McGraw-Hill.

Hamilton, D. L. (1979). A cognitive-attributional analysis of stereotyping. In L. Berkowitz (Ed.), *Advances in experimental social psychology* (Vol. 12, pp. 53–81). New York: Academic Press.

Hamilton, D. L. (1981). *Cognitive processes in stereotyping and intergroup behavior.* Hillsdale, NJ: Erlbaum.

Hare, R. D. (1991). *The Hare psychopathy checklist—revised.* Toronto, ON: Multi-Health Systems.

Harkness, S. (1992). Human development in psychological anthropology. In T. Schwartz, G. M. White, & C. A. Lutz (Eds.), *New directions in psychological anthropology* (pp. 102–121). New York: Cambridge University Press.

Harrington, D. M. (1990). The ecology of human creativity: A psychological perspective. In M. A. Runco & R. S. Albert (Eds.), *Theories of creativity* (pp. 143–169). Newbury Park, CA: Sage.

Harris, R. J., Schoen, L. M., & Hensley, D. L. (1992). A cross-cultural study of story memory. *Journal of Cross-Cultural Psychology, 23,* 133–147.

Haslam, N. (2005, March). Dimensions of folk psychiatry. *Review of General Psychology, 9*(1), 35–47.

Hayles, R. V. (1991). African-American strength: A survey of empirical findings. In R. Jones (Ed.), *Black psychology* (3rd ed., pp. 379–400). Berkeley, CA: Cobb & Henry.

Hays, P. (2001). *Addressing cultural complexities in practice: A framework for clinicians and counselors.* Washington, DC: American Psychological Association.

Heath, S. B. (1983). *Ways with words.* New York: Cambridge University Press.

Hedayat-Diba, Z. (2000). Psychotherapy with Muslims. In P. S. Richards & A. E. Bergin (Eds.), *Handbook of psychotherapy and religious diversity* (pp. 289–314). Washington, DC: American Psychological Association.

Hedge, A., & Yousif, Y. (1992). Effects of urban size, urgency, and cost on helpfulness. *Journal of Cross-Cultural Psychology, 23*(1), 107–115.

Hedstrom, L. (1992). Interpersonal style: Contrasting emphases on individuality and group conformity in Japan and America. In U. Gielen et al. (Eds.), *Psychology in International Perspective.* Amsterdam: Swets & Zeitlinger.

Heider, F. (1959). *The psychology of interpersonal relations.* New York: Wiley.

Heiman, G. (1996). *Basic statistics for the behavioral sciences.* Boston, MA: Houghton Mifflin.

Heine, S., Lehman, D., Markus, H., & Kitayama, S. (1999). Is there a universal need for positive self-regard? *Psychological Review, 106*(4), 766–794.

Heine, S., Lehman, D., Peng, K., & Greenholtz, J. (2002). What's wrong with cross-cultural comparisons of subjective Likert scales? The reference-group effect. *Journal of Personality and Social Psychology, 82*(6), 903–918.

Hejmadi, A., Rozin, P., & Siegal, M. (2004). Once in contact, always in contact: Contagious essence and conceptions of purification in American and Hindu Indian children. *Developmental Psychology, 40*(4), 467–476.

Helms, J. (2006). Fairness is not validity or cultural bias in racial-group assessment: A quantitative perspective. *American Psychologist, 61*(8), 845–859.

Helms, J. (2007). Implementing fairness in racial-group assessment requires assessment of individuals. *American Psychologist, 62*(9), 1083–1085.

Herman, J. L. (1992). *Trauma and recovery: The aftermath of violence. From domestic violence to political terror.* New York: Basic Books.

Hermans, J. M., & Kempen, J. G. (1998). Moving cultures: The perilous problems of cultural dichotomies in a globalizing society. *American Psychologist, 53*(10), 1111–1120.

Herrnstein, R. J., & Murray, C. (1994). *The bell curve: Intelligence and class structure in American life.* New York: Free Press.

Hershey, D., Henkens, K., & Van Dalen, H. (2007). Mapping the minds of retirement planners: A cross-cultural perspective. *Journal of Cross-Cultural Psychology, 38*(3), 361–382.

Hess, R. D., Kashiwagi, K., Azuma, H., Price, G. G., & Dickinson, W. P. (1980).Maternal expectation for mastery of developmental tasks in Japan and the United States. *International Journal of Psychology, 15*, 259–271.

Hinton, L., & Kleinman, A. (1993). Cultural issues and international psychiatric disorders. *International Review of Psychiatry, 1*, 111–134.

Ho, D. (1998). Indigenous Psychologies: Asian Perspectives. *Journal of Cross-Cultural Psychology, 29*(1), 88–103.

Hobson, J. A. (2002). *Dreaming: An introduction to the science of sleep.* Oxford: Oxford University Press.

Hock, R. (1995). *Forty studies that changed psychology.* Englewood Cliffs, NJ: Prentice-Hall.

Hofstede, G. (1980). *Culture's consequences: International differences in work-related values.* Beverly Hills, CA: Sage.

Hofstede, G. (1991). *Cultures and organizations: Software in the mind.* London: McGraw-Hill.

Hofstede, G., & Bond, M. H. (1984). Hofstede's cultural dimensions: An independent validation using Rokeach's value survey. *Journal of Cross-Cultural Psychology, 15*, 417–433.

Hofstede, G., & Bond, M. H. (1988). The Confucius connection: From cultural roots to economic growth. *Organizational Dynamics, 16*, 4–21.

Hofstede, G., de Hilal, A. V. G., Malvezzi, S., Tanure, B., & Vinken, H. (2010). Comparing regional cultures within a country: Lessons from Brazil. *Journal of Cross-Cultural Psychology, 41*(3), 336–352.

Holcomb, H. R. (1996). Moving beyond just-so stories: Evolutionary psychology as protoscience. *Skeptic, 4*(1), 60–66.

Hong, S., & Ho, H. Z. (2005). Direct and indirect longitudinal effects of parental involvement on student achievement: Second-order latent growth modeling across ethnic groups. *Journal of Educational Psychology, 97*(1), 32–42.

Horenczyk, G., & Munayer, S. J. (2007). Acculturation orientations toward two majority groups: The case of Palestinian Arab Christian adolescents in Israel. *Journal of Cross-Cultural Psychology, 38*, 76–86.

Horowits, R., & Kraus, V. (1984). Patterns of cultural transition. *Journal of Cross-Cultural Psychology, 15*(4), 399–416.

Hortacsu, N., Bastug, S., & Muhammetberdiev, O. (2001). Desire for children in Turkmenistan and Azerbaijan: Son preference and perceived instrumentality for value satisfaction. *Journal of Cross-Cultural Psychology, 32*(3), 309–321.

Ho-Ying Fu, J., & Chi-Yue Chiu. (2007). Local culture's responses to globalization: Exemplary persons and their attendant values. *Journal of Cross-Cultural Psychology, 38*(5), 636–653.

Ho-Ying Fu, J., Chi-Yue Chiu, Michael W. Morris, & Maia J. Young. (2007). Spontaneous inferences from cultural cues: Varying responses of cultural insiders and outsiders. *Journal of Cross-Cultural Psychology, 38*, 58–75.

Hsu, E., Davies, C., & Hansen, D. (2004). Understanding mental health needs of Southeast Asian refugees: Historical, cultural, and contextual challenges. *Clinical Psychology Review, 24*, 193–213.

Hsu, F. L. K. (1985). The self in cross-cultural perspective. In A. J. Marsella, G. DeVos, & F. L. K. Hsu (Eds.), *Culture and self: Asian and western perspectives* (pp. 24–55). New York: Tavistock.

Huang, L., & Harris, M. (1973). Conformity in Chinese and Americans. *Journal of Cross-Cultural Psychology, 4*(4), 427–434.

Hudson, W. (1960). Pictorial depth perception in sub-cultural groups in Africa. *Journal of Social Psychology, 2*, 89–107.

Hui, C. H. (1982). Locus of control: A review of crossnational research. *International Journal of Intercultural Relations, 6*, 301–323.

Hui, H., & Luk, C. L. (1997). Industrial/organizational psychology. In J. W. Berry, M. H. Segall, & C. Kagitcibasi (Eds.), *Handbook of cross-cultural psychology: Social behavior and applications* (Vol. 3, pp. 371–411). Boston, MA: Allyn & Bacon.

Hunter, J. A., Stringer, M., & Coleman, J. T. (1993). Social explanations and self-esteem in Northern Ireland. *The Journal of Social Psychology, 133*, 643–650.

Huntington, S. (1993). Clash of civilizations. *Foreign Affairs, 72*, 22–49.

Hupka, R., Buunk, B., Falus, G., Fulgosi, A., Ortega, E., Swain, R., et al. (1985). Romantic jealousy and romantic envy: A seven-nation study. *Journal of Cross-Cultural Psychology, 16*(4), 423–446.

Hurlbert, A., & Ling, Y. (2007, August). Biological components of sex differences in color preference. *Current Biology, 17*, 623–625.

Hwang, W., Wood, J., Lin, K., & Cheung, F. (2006). Cognitive-behavioral therapy with Chinese Americans: Research, theory, and clinical practice. *Cognitive and Behavioral Practice, 13*, 293–303.

Inglehart, R. (1997). *Modernization and post modernization: Cultural, economic, and political change in 43 societies.* Princeton, NJ: Princeton University Press.

Inkeles, A., & Smith, D. (1974). *Becoming modern: Individual changes in six developing countries.* Cambridge, MA: Harvard University Press.

Irvine, S. H. (1983). Testing in Africa and America: The search for routes. In S. H. Irvine & J. W. Berry (Eds.), *Human assessment and cultural factors* (pp. 45–58). New York: Plenum.

Irwin, M., Schafer, G., & Feiden, C. (1974). Emic and unfamiliar category sorting of Mano farmers and U.S. undergraduates. *Journal of Cross-Cultural Psychology, 5*, 407–423.

Iusitini, L., Gao, W., Sundborn, G., & Paterson, J. (2011). Parenting practices among fathers of a cohort of Pacific infants in New Zealand. *Journal of Cross-Cultural Psychology, 42*(1), 39–55.

Iwamasa, G., Larrabee, A., & Merritt, R. (2000). Are personality disorder criteria ethnically biased? A card-sort analysis. *Cultural Diversity and Ethnic Minority Psychology, 6*(3), 284–296.

Iwato, S., & Triandis, H. (1993). Validity of auto- and heterostereotypes among Japanese and American students. *Journal of Cross-Cultural Psychology, 24*(4), 428–444.

Iyengar, S., Wells, R., & Schwartz, B. (2006). Doing better but feeling worse: Looking for the "best" job undermines satisfaction. *Psychological Science, 17*, 143–150.

Izard, C. E. (1969). The emotions and emotional constructs in personality and culture research. In R. B. Catell (Ed.), *Handbook of modern personality theory.* Chicago, IL: Aldine.

Izard, C. E. (1971). *The face of emotion.* New York: Appleton-Century-Crofts.

Izard, C. E. (1977). *Human emotions.* New York: Plenum.

Izard, C. E. (2004). *The psychology of emotions.* New York: Springer.

Jackson, G. (1991). The African genesis of the black perspective in helping. In R. Jones (Ed.), *Black psychology* (3rd ed., pp. 533–558). Berkeley, CA: Cobb & Henry.

Jackson, M. (1997). Counseling Arab Americans. In C. Lee (Ed.), *Multicultural issues in counseling: New approaches to diversity* (2nd ed., pp. 333–349). Alexandria, VA: American Counseling Association.

Jahoda, G., & Krewer, B. (1997). History of cross-cultural and cultural psychology. In J. W. Berry, Y. H. Poortinga, & J. Pandey (Eds.), *Handbook of cross-cultural psychology: Theory and method* (Vol. 1, pp. 1–42). Boston, MA: Allyn & Bacon.

James, W. (1884). What is emotion? *Mind, 19*, 188–205.

Jamison, K. R. (1993). *Touched with fire: Manic-depressive illness and the artistic temperament.* New York: Free Press.

Jane's Information Group. (2008). *A one-year investigation and analysis of 235 countries.* Retrieved from www.janes.com

Jenkins, A. (1995). *Psychology and African Americans* (2nd ed.). Boston, MA: Allyn & Bacon.

Jensen, A. R. (1973). *Educability and group differences.* London: Methuen.

Jensen, A. R. (1998). *The G factor.* Westport, CT: Praeger.

Ji, Li-Jun., Zhang, Z., & Nisbett, R. (2004, July). Is it culture or is it language? Examination of language effects in cross-cultural research on categorization. *Journal of Personality & Social Psychology, 87*(1), 57–65.

Jobson, L., & O'Kearney, R. (2008). Cultural differences in retrieval of self-defining memories. *Journal of Cross-Cultural Psychology, 39*(1), 75–80.

Johnson, F. (1993). *Dependency in Japanese socialization.* New York: New York University Press.

Jolley, R., Zhi, Z., & Thomas, G. (1998). The development of understanding moods methaphorically expressed in pictures. *Journal of Cross-Cultural Psychology, 29*(2), 358–376.

Joshi, M. S., & MacLean, M. (1997). Maternal expectations of child development in India, Japan, and England. *Journal of Cross-Cultural Psychology, 28*(2), 219–234.

Kadiangandu, J. K., Gauché, M., Vinsonneau, G., & Mullet, E. (2007). Conceptualizations of forgiveness: Collectivistcongolese versus individualist-French viewpoints. *Journal of Cross-Cultural Psychology, 38*, 432–437.

Kadiangandu, J. K., Mullet, E., & Vinsonneau, G. (2001). Forgiveness: A Congo-France comparison. *Journal of Cross-Cultural Psychology, 32*(4), 504–514.

Kagan, J., Kearsley, R. B., & Zealazo, P. (1978). *Infancy: Its place in human development.* Cambridge, MA: Harvard University Press.

Kagitcibasi, C. (1985). Culture of separateness—culture of relatedness. *Papers in Comparative Studies, 4*, 91–99.

Kagitcibasi, C. (1995). Is psychology relevant to global human development issues? Experience from Turkey. *American Psychologist, 50*, 293–300.

Kagitcibasi, C. (1996). *Family and human development across cultures: A view from the other side.* Mahwah, NJ: Erlbaum.

Kakar, S. (1989). The maternal-feminine in Indian psychoanalysis. *International Review of Psycho-Analysis, 16*, 355–362.

Kalipeni, E., Craddock, S., Ghosh, J., & Oppong, J. R. (2008). *HIV and AIDS in Africa: Beyond epidemiology.* New York: Wiley.

Kamin, L. (1976). Heredity, intelligence, politics, and psychology. In N. J. Block & G. Dworkin (Eds.), *The IQ controversy* (pp. 374–382). New York: Pantheon Books.

Kanazawa, S. (2010). Evolutionary psychology and intelligence research. *American Psychologist, 65*(4), 279–289.

Karlsson, R. (2005). Ethnic matching between therapist and patient in psychotherapy: An overview of findings, together with methodological and conceptual issues. *Cultural Diversity and Ethnic Minority Psychology, 11*(2), 113–129.

Kashima, Y., & Triandis, H. (1986). The self-serving bias in attributions as a coping strategy. *Journal of Cross-Cultural Psychology, 17*, 83–97.

Kasser, T. (2011). Cultural values and the well-being of future generations: A cross-national study. *Journal of Cross-Cultural Psychology, 42*(2), 206–215.

Kassinove, H., Sukhodolsky, D., Eckhardt, C., & Tsytsarev, S. (1997). Development of a Russian state-trait anger expression inventory. *Journal of Clinical Psychology, 53*(6), 543–557.

Kaufman, M. (2003, October 3). Breast implants linked to suicide. *Washington Post.* Retrieved from http://www.thewashingtonpost.com

Keating, C. F., Mazur, A., Segall, M., Cysneiros, P. G., Divale, W. T., Kilbride, J. E., et al. (1981). Culture and perception of social dominance from facial expressions. *Journal of Personality and Social Psychology, 40,* 615–626.

Keats, D. M. (1985). Strategies in formal operational thinking: Malaysia and Australia. In I. R. Lagunes & Y. H. Poortinga (Eds.), *From a different perspective: Studies of behavior across cultures* (pp. 306–318). Liss, The Netherlands: Swets & Zeitlinger.

Keats, D., Keats, J., & Rafael,W. (1976). Concept acquisition in Malaysian bilingual children. *Journal of Cross-Cultural Psychology, 7*(1), 87–99.

Keel, P., & Klump, K. (2003). Are eating disorders culturebound syndromes? Implications for conceptualizing their etiology. *Psychological Bulletin, 129*(5), 747–769.

Keen, S. (1986). *Faces of the enemy.* New York: Harper & Row.

Keller, H., Borke, J., Chaudhary, N., Lamm, B., & Kleis, A. (2010). Continuity in parenting strategies: A crosscultural comparison. *Journal of Cross-Cultural Psychology, 41*(3), 391–409.

Kelley, H. H. (1950). The warm-cold variable in first impressions of persons. *Journal of Personality, 18,* 431–439.

Kelley, H. H. (1967). Attribution theory in social psychology. In D. Levine (Ed.), *Nebraska Symposium of Motivation* (Vol. 15, pp. 192–240). Lincoln, NE: University of Nebraska Press.

Kelley, J. (1994, January 12). Frustrated Russians cool to the USA. *USA Today,* p. 1.

Kelman, H. C., & Chin, J. L. (2010). The Israeli-Palestinian peace process and its vicissitudes: Insights from attitude theory. Introduction to the special issue on diversity and leadership. *American Psychologist, 65*(3), 150–156.

Keltikangas-Jaervinen, L., & Terav, T. (1996). Social decision-making strategies in individualist and collectivist cultures: A comparison of Finnish and Estonian adolescents. *Journal of Cross-Cultural Psychology, 27*(6), 714–732.

Keltner, D., Ellsworth, P. C., & Edwards, K. (1993). Beyond simple pessimism: Effects of sadness and anger on social perception. *Journal of Personality and Social Psychology, 64,* 740–752.

Kenealy, P., Gleeson, K., Frude, N., & Shaw, W. (1991). The importance of the individual in the "causal" relationship between attractiveness and self-esteem. *Journal of Community and Applied Social Psychology, 1,* 45–56.

Kern, C., & Roll, S. (2001). Object representations in dreams of Chicanos and Anglos. *Dreaming: Journal of the Association for the Study of Dreams, 11*(3), 149–166.

Kern, M., & Just, M. (1995). The focus group method, political advertising, campaign news, and the construction of candidate images. *Political Communication, 12,* 127–145.

Keyes, C., & Ryff, C. D. (2003). Somatization and mental health: A comparative study of the idiom of distress hypothesis. *Social Science and Medicine, 57,* 1833–1845.

Kharkhurin, A. V. (2010). Sociocultural differences in the relationship between bilingualism and creative potential. *Journal of Cross-Cultural Psychology, 41*(5–6), 776–783

Kim, H. (2002). We talk, therefore we think? A cultural analysis of the effect of talking on thinking. *Journal of Personality and Social Psychology, 83*(4), 828–842.

Kim, H. S., & Markus, H. R. (2002). Freedom of speech and freedom of silence: An analysis of talking as a cultural practice. In R. Shweder, M. Minow, & H. R. Markus (Eds.), *Engaging cultural differences: The multicultural challenge in liberal democracies* (pp. 432–452). New York: Russell Sage.

Kim, U., & Berry, J. W. (1993). *Indigenous psychologies.* Thousand Oaks, CA: Sage.

Kim, Y. Y. (1986). *Interethnic communication.* Newbury Park, CA: Sage.

Kirton, M. (1976). Adaptors and innovators: A description and measure. *Journal of Applied Psychology, 61,* 622–629.

Kirton, M. (1994). A theory of cognitive style. In M. J. Kirton (Ed.), *Adaptors and innovators: Styles of creativity and problem solving* (2nd ed., pp. 1–33). London: Routledge.

Kitayama, S., Conway, L. G., III, Pietromonaco, P. R., Park, H., & Plaut, V. C. (2010). *American Psychologist, 65*(6), 559–574.

Kitayama, S., & Markus, H. R. (1995). Culture and self: Implications for internationalizing psychology. In N. R. Goldberg & J. B. Veroff (Eds.), *The culture and psychology reader* (pp. 366–383). New York: New York University Press.

Kitayama, S., Park, H., Sevincer, A. T., Karasawa, M., & Uskul, A. K. (2009). A cultural task analysis of implicit independence: Comparing North America, Western Europe, and East Asia. *Journal of Personality and Social Psychology, 97*, 236–255.

Kleinman, A. (1978). Clinical relevance of anthropological and cross-cultural research: Concepts and strategies. *American Journal of Psychiatry, 135*, 427–431.

Kleinman, A. (1986). *Social origins of distress and disease: Depression, neurasthenia, and pain in modern China.* New Haven, CT: Yale University Press.

Kleinman, A., & Kleinman, J. (1991). Suffering and its professional transformation: Toward an ethnography of interpersonal experience. *Culture, Medicine, and Psychiatry, 15*, 275–301.

Kliger, S. (2002). Russian immigrants in America: Fears and hopes. In V. Shlapentokh & E. Shiraev (Eds.), *Fears in post-communist societies* (pp. 111–120). New York: Palgrave.

Klineberg, O. (1938). Emotional expression in Chinese literature. *Journal of Abnormal and Social Psychology, 33*, 517–520.

Klingelhofer, E. (1971). What Tanzanian secondary school students plan to teach their children. *Journal of Cross-Cultural Psychology, 2*(2), 189–195.

Kluckhohn, F., & Strodtbeck, F. (1961). *Variations in value orientation.* Evanston, IL: Row & Peterson.

Knafo, A., Schwartz, S. H., & Levine, R. V. (2009). Helping strangers is lower in embedded cultures. *Journal of Cross-Cultural Psychology, 40*(5), 875–879.

Ko, S.-G., Lee, T.-H., Yoon, H.-Y., Kwon, J.-H., & Mather, M. (2011). How does context affect assessments of facial emotion? The role of culture and age. *Psychology and Aging, 26*(1), 48–59.

Koenigsberg, R. (1992). *Hitler's ideology.* New York: Library of Social Science.

Kohlberg, L. (1981). *The philosophy of moral development: Moral states and the idea of justice.* San Francisco, CA: Harper & Row.

Kohn, M. (1969). *Class and conformity.* Homewood, IL: Dorsey.

Kon, I. S. (1979). *Psychologya yunosheskogo vozrasta* [*Psychology of adolescence*]. Moscow: Prosveshenie.

Kon, I. S. (2001). *Adolescent sexuality on the eve of 21st century* (in Russian). Dubna: Fenix.

Koopman, C. (1997). Political psychology as a lens for viewing traumatic events. *Political Psychology, 18*(4), 831–847.

Kostelny, K., & Garbarino, J. (1994). Coping with consequences of living in danger: The case of Palestinian children and youth. *International Journal of Behavioral Development, 17*, 595–611.

Krauss, H. (1970). Social development and suicide. *Journal of Cross-Cultural Psychology, 1*(2), 159–167.

Krippner, S. (1996). The dream models of the Mapuches in Chile. *Dream Time, 13*(2), 14–15.

Krus, D., & Rysberg, J. (1976). Industrial managers and NACH. *Journal of Cross-Cultural Psychology, 7*(4), 491–499.

Kuhnen, U., Hannover, B., Roeder, U., Ali Shah, A., Schubert, B., Upmeyer, A., et al. (2001). Crosscultural variations in identifying embedded figures: Comparisons from the United States, Germany, Russia, and Malaysia. *Journal of Cross-Cultural Psychology, 32*(3), 365–374.

Kurman, J., & Sriram, N. (2002). Interrelationships among vertical and horizontal collectivism, modesty, and self-enhancement. *Journal of Cross-Cultural Psychology, 33*(1), 71–87.

Kush, J. (1996). Field-dependence, cognitive ability, and academic achievement in Anglo American and Mexican American students. *Journal of Cross-Cultural Psychology, 27*(5), 561–575.

Lacey, P. (1971). Classificatory ability and verbal intelligence among high-contact Aboriginal and low socioeconomic white Australian children. *Journal of Cross-Cultural Psychology, 2*(1), 39–49.

Laing, D. G., Preskott, J., Bell, G. A., & Gillmore, A. (1993). A cross-cultural study of taste discrimination with Australians and Japanese. *Chemical Senses, 18*, 161–168.

Lane, C. (2001, April 25). English only: A legal decision that may affect testing. *Washington Post*, p. A01.

Langaney, A. (1988). *Les hommes, passe, present, conditionnel* [*The men, past, present, conditional*]. Paris: Armand Colin.

Lange, C. G. (1885/1922). The emotions: A psychophysiological study. In C. G. Lange & W. James (Eds.), *Psychology classics* (Vol. 1). Baltimore, MD: Williams & Wilkins.

Langgulung, H., & Torrance, E. (1972). The development of causal thinking of children in Mexico and the United States. *Journal of Cross-Cultural Psychology, 3*, 315–320.

Larsen, K. (1972). Determinants of peace agreement, pessimism-optimism, and expectation of world conflict: A cross-national study. *Journal of Cross-Cultural Psychology, 3*(3), 283–292.

Larson, R., Verma, S., & Dworkin, J. (2003). Adolescence without disengagement: The daily family lives of Indian middle-class teenagers. In T. S. Saraswathi (Ed.), *Cross-cultural perspectives in human development: Theory, research and applications* (pp. 258–286). New Delhi, India: Sage.

Lau, A., Jernewall, N., Zaine, N., & Myers, H. (2002). Correlates of suicidal behaviors among Asian American outpatient youths. *Cultural Diversity & Ethnic Minority Psychology, 8*(3), 199–213.

Laughlin, C., McManus, J., & d'Aquili, E. (1992). *Brain, symbol, and experience.* New York: Columbia University Press.

Laumann, E. (2002). The impact of biological aging effects on the reporting of sexual dysfunctions in women aged 40–80: Results of an international survey. *The University of Chicago Chronicle, 22*(3), October 24. http://chronicle.uchicago.edu/021024/sex-study.shtml

Lawrence, J. S., Crocker, J., & Blanton, H. (2011). Stigmatized and dominant cultural groups differentially interpret positive feedback. *Journal of Cross-Cultural Psychology, 42*(1), 165–169.

Lawson, E. (1975). Flag preference as an indicator of patriotism in Israeli children. *Journal of Cross-Cultural Psychology, 6*, 490–499.

Lazarus, R. S. (1993). From psychological stress to the emotions: A history of changing outlooks. *Annual Review of Psychology, 44*, 1–21.

Leach, M. L. (1975). The effect of training in the pictorial depth perception of Shona children. *Journal of Cross-Cultural Psychology, 6*, 457–470.

Lebra, T. S. (1983). Shame and guilt: A psychocultural view of the Japanese self. *Ethos, 11*, 192–209.

Lee, I.-C., & Pratto, F. (2011). Changing boundaries of ethnic identity and feelings toward ingroup/outgroup: Examining Taiwan residents from a psychohistorical perspective. *Journal of Cross-Cultural Psychology, 42*(1), 3–24.

Lee, I.-C., Pratto, F., & Li, M.-C. (2007). Social relationships and sexism in the United States and Taiwan. *Journal of Cross-Cultural Psychology, 38*, 595–612.

Lee, J. A., Soutar, G. N., Daly, T. M., & Louviere, J. J. (2011). Schwartz values clusters in the United States and China. *Journal of Cross-Cultural Psychology, 42*(2), 234–252.

Lee, R., & Ackerman, S. (1980). The sociocultural dynamics of mass hysteria: A case study of social conflict in West Malaysia. *Journal of Cross-Cultural Psychiatry, 43*, 78–88.

Leenaars, A. A., Sayin, A., Candansayar, S., Leenaars, L., Akar, T., & Demirel, B. (2010). Suicide in different cultures: A thematic comparison of suicide notes from Turkey and the United States. *Journal of Cross-Cultural Psychology, 41*(2), 253–263.

Leenen, I., Givaudan, M., Pick, S., Venguer, T., Vera, J.,& Poortinga, Y. H. (2008). Effectiveness of a Mexican health education program in a poverty-stricken rural area of Guatemala. *Journal of Cross-Cultural Psychology, 39*(1), 198–214.

Lerner, M. J. (1970). The desire for justice and reactions to victims. In J. McCauley & L. Berkowitz (Eds.), *Altruism and helping behavior.* New York: Academic Press.

Leung, A. K., Maddux, W. W., & Galinsky, A. D. (2008). Multicultural experience enhances creativity: The when and how. *American Psychologist, 63*(3), 169–181.

Leung, K., & Drasgow, F. (1986). Relation between self-esteem and delinquent behavior. *Journal of Cross-Cultural Psychology, 17*(2), 151–167.

Levin, M. (1995). Does race matter? *American Psychologist, 50*(1), 45–46.

LeVine, R. (2010). The six cultures study: Prologue to a history of a landmark project. *Journal of Cross-Cultural Psychology, 41*(4), 513–521.

Levine, R., Norenzayan, A., & Philbrick, K. (2001). Cross-cultural differences in helping strangers. *Journal of Cross-Cultural Psychology, 32*(5), 543–560.

Levinson, D. (1978). *The seasons of a man's life.* New York: Knopf.

Levinson, D., & Simmons, G. (1992). Blacks, schizophrenia, and neuroleptic treatment. *Archives of General Psychiatry, 49,* 165.

Levitt, S., & Dubner, S. (2009). *Freakonomics: A Rogue Economist Explores the Hidden Side of Everything.* New York: Harper.

Levy, D. A. (1985). Optimism and pessimism: Relationships to circadian rhythms. *Psychological Reports, 57*(3), 1123–1126.

Levy, D. A. (1993). Psychometric infallibility realized: The one-size-fits-all psychological profile. *Journal of Polymorphous Perversity, 10*(1), 3–6.

Levy, D. A. (2010). *Tools of Critical Thinking: Metathoughts for Psychology* (2nd ed.). Long Grove, IL: Waveland Press.

Levy, D. A., Kaler, S. R., & Schall, M. (1988). An empirical investigation of role schemata: Occupations and personality characteristics. *Psychological Reports, 63,* 3–14.

Levy, R. (1996). Essential contrasts: Differences in parental ideas about learners and teaching in Tahiti and Nepal. In S. Harkness & C. M. Super (Eds.), *Parents' cultural belief systems: Their origins, expressions, and consequences* (pp. 123–142). New York: Guilford.

Levy, R. I. (1973). *Tahitians: Mind and experience in the Society Islands.* Chicago, IL: University of Chicago Press.

Lewin, K. (1951). *Field theory in social science: Selected theoretical papers* (D. Cartwright, Ed.). New York: Harper Torchbooks.

Lewin, K., Lippitt, R., & White, R. (1939). Patterns of aggressive behavior in experimentally created social climates. *Journal of Social Psychology, 10,* 271–299.

Lewis, J. R., & Ozaki, R. (2009). Amae and Mardy: A comparison of two emotion terms. *Journal of Cross-Cultural Psychology, 40*(6), 917–934.

Lewis-Fernández, R., & Kleinman, A. (1994). Culture, personality, and psychopathology. *Journal of Abnormal Psychology, 103*(1), 67–71.

Li, J. (2003). The core of Confucian learning. *American Psychologist, 58*(2), 146–147.

Li, S., Bi, Y.-L., & Rao, L.-L. (2011). Every science/nature potter praises his own pot—Can we believe what he says based on his mother tongue? *Journal of Cross-Cultural Psychology, 42*(1), 125–130.

Liddell, C. (1997). Every picture tells a story—or does not? Young South African children interpreting pictures. *Journal of Cross-Cultural Psychology, 28*(3), 266–283.

Liem, R. (1997). Shame and guilt among first-and-second generation Asian Americans and European Americans. *Journal of Cross-Cultural Psychology, 28*(4), 365–392.

Lim, M., Stormshak, E. A., & Falkenstein, C. A. (2011). Psychosocial adjustment and substance use of Cambodian and Vietnamese immigrant youth. *Journal of Cross-Cultural Psychology, 42*(1), 104–119.

Lim, R. F., & Lin Keh-Ming. (1996). Cultural formulation of psychiatric diagnosis: Case No. 03: Psychosis following qi-gong in a Chinese immigrant. *Culture, Medicine, and Psychiatry, 20,* 369–378.

Lin, C.-C., & Yamaguchi, S. (2011). Under what conditions do people feel face-loss? Effects of the presence of others and social roles on the perception of losing face in Japanese culture. *Journal of Cross-Cultural Psychology, 42*(1), 120–124.

Lin, E., & Peterson, C. (1990). Pessimistic explanatory style and response to illness. *Behavioral Therapy and Research, 28,* 243–248.

Lin, Y. (2002). Age, sex, education, religion, and perception of tattoos. *Psychological Reports, 90*(2), 654–658.

Lindgren, H., & Tebcherani, A. (1971). Arab and American auto- and heterostereotypes: A cross-cultural study of empathy. *Journal of Cross-Cultural Psychology, 2*(2), 173–180.

Lippi-Green, R. (1997). *English with an accent: Language, ideology, and discrimination in the United States.* New York: Routledge.

Li-Repac, D. (1980). Cultural influences on clinical perception: A comparison between Caucasian and

Chinese-American therapists. *Journal of Cross-Cultural Psychology, 11*(3), 327–342.

Liu, J. H., Goldstein-Hawes, R., Hilton, D. J., Huang, L. L., Gastardo-Conaco, C., Dresler-Hawke, E., et al. (2005). Social representations of events and people in world history across twelve cultures. *Journal of Cross-Cultural Psychology, 36*(2), 171–191.

Liu, J. H., McCreanor, T., McIntosh, T., & Teaiwa, T. (Eds.). (2005). *New Zealand identities: Departures and destinations.* Wellington, NZ: Victoria University Press.

Liu, J. H., Paez, D., Slawuta, P., Cabecinhas, R., Techio, E., Kokdemir, D., Sen, R., Vincze, O., Muluk, H., Wang, F., & Zlobina, A. (2009). Representing world history in the 21st century: The impact of 9/11, the Iraq war, and the nation-state on dynamics of collective remembering. *Journal of Cross-Cultural Psychology, 40*(4), 667–692.

Lloyd, B., & Easton, B. (1977). The intellectual development of Yoruba children. *Journal of Cross-Cultural Psychology, 8*(1), 3–11.

Locke, K. D., & Baik, K.-D. (2009). Does an acquiescent response style explain why Koreans are less consistent than Americans? *Journal of Cross-Cultural Psychology, 40*(2), 319–323.

Lonner, W. J. (1980). The search for psychological universals. In H. C. Triandis & W. W. Lambert (Eds.), *Handbook of cross-cultural psychology: Perspectives* (Vol. 1, pp. 143–204). Boston, MA: Allyn & Bacon.

Lopez, S. R. (1989). Patient variable biases in clinical judgment: Conceptual overview and methodological considerations. *Psychological Bulletin, 106*, 184–204.

Loranger, A. W., Sartorius, N., Andreoli, A., Berger, P., Buchheim, P., Channabasavanna, S. M., et al. (1994). The international personality disorder examination. *Archives of General Psychiatry, 51*(3), 215–224.

Lord, C. G., Ross, L., & Lepper, M. (1979). Biased assimilation and attitude polarization: The effects of prior theories on subsequently considered evidence. *Journal of Personality and Social Psychology, 37*, 2098–2109.

Lorenz, K. (1966). *On aggression.* New York: Harcourt, Brace & World.

Lucas, T., Parkhill, M. R., Wendorf, C. A., Imamoglu, E. O., Weisfeld, C. C., Weisfeld, G. E., et al. (2008). Cultural and evolutionary components of marital satisfaction: A multidimensional assessment of measurement invariance. *Journal of Cross-Cultural Psychology, 39*, 109–123.

Luria, A. R. (1976). *Cognitive development: Its cultural and social foundations.* Cambridge, MA: Harvard University Press.

Lutz, C. (1982). The domain of emotion words on Ifaluk. *American Ethologist, 9*, 113–128.

Lutz, C. (1988). *Unnatural emotions: Everyday sentiments on a Micronesian atoll and their challenge to western theory.* Chicago, IL: University of Chicago Press.

Lynch, O. M. (1990). The social construction of emotion in India. In O. M. Lynch (Ed.), *Divine passions: The social construct of emotion in India* (pp. 3–34). Berkeley, CA: University of California Press.

Lynn, R. (1996). Racial and ethnic differences in intelligence in the United States on the differential ability scale. *Personality and Individual Differences, 20*, 271–273.

Lynn, R., & Hattori, K. (1990). The heritability of intelligence in Japan. *Behavior Genetics, 20*, 545–546.

Lynn, R., & Vanhanen, T. (2002). *IQ and the wealth of nations.* Westport, CT: Praeger.

Lyubomirsky, S. (2007). *The How of Happiness: A Scientific Approach to Getting the Life You Want.* New York: Penguin Press.

Ma, H. K., & Cheung, C. K. (1996). A cross-cultural study of moral stage structure in Hong Kong Chinese, English, and Americans. *Journal of Cross-Cultural Psychology, 27*(6), 700–713.

Macdonald, M., & Rogan, J. (1990). Innovation in South African science education (Part II): Factors influencing the introduction of instructional change. *Science Education, 74*(1), 119–131.

Mackie, D. (1983). The effect of social instruction on conservation of spatial relations. *Journal of Cross-Cultural Psychology, 14*(2), 131–151.

Madsen, M. (1986). Developmental and cross-cultural differences in the cooperative and competitive behavior of young children. *Journal of Cross-Cultural Psychology, 2*, 365–371.

Madsen, M. C. (1971). Developmental and cross-cultural differences in the cooperative and competitive behavior of young children. *Journal of Cross-Cultural Psychology, 2*, 365–371.

Madsen, M., & Kagan, S. (1973). Mother-directed achievement of children in two cultures. *Journal of Cross-Cultural Psychology, 4*(2), 221–228.

Maehr, M., & Nicholls, J. (1983). Culture and achievement motivation: A second look. In N. Warren (Ed.), *Studies in cross-cultural psychology* (Vol. 2, pp. 221–226). London: Academic Press.

Mahbubani, K. (1999). *Can Asians think?* Singapore: Times Books International.

Maher, T. (1976). "Need for resolution" ratings for harmonic musical intervals. *Journal of Cross-Cultural Psychology, 7*, 259–276.

Mak, W. W. S., Law, R. W., & Teng, Y. (2011). Cultural model of vulnerability to distress: The role of self-construal and sociotropy on anxiety and depression among Asian Americans and European Americans. *Journal of Cross-Cultural Psychology, 42*(1), 75–88.

Mandisodza, A. N., Jost, J. T., & Unzueta, M. M. (2006). "Tall poppies" and "American dreams" reactions to rich and poor in Australia and the United States. *Journal of Cross-Cultural Psychology, 37*(6), 659–668.

Mandler, G. (1975). *Mind and emotion.* New York: Wiley.

Mandler, J. M., Scribner, S., Cole, M., & DeForest, M. (1980). Cross-cultural invariance in story recall. *Child Development, 51*, 19–26.

Marano, L. (1985). *Windigo* psychosis: The anatomy of an emic-etic confusion. *Current Anthropology, 23*(4), 385–421.

Marcuse, H. (1964). *One-dimensional man.* Boston, MA: Beacon Press.

Margalit, B., & Mauger, P. (1985). Aggressiveness and assertiveness. *Journal of Cross-Cultural Psychology, 16*(4), 497–511.

Mari, S., & Karayanni, M. (1982). Creativity in Arab culture: Two decades of research. *Journal of Creative Behaviour, 16*, 227–238.

Marjoribanks, K., & Jordan, D. (1986). Stereotyping among aboriginal and Anglo-Australians. *Journal of Cross-Cultural Psychology, 17*(1), 17–28.

Markham, R., & Wang, L. (1996). Recognition of emotion by Chinese and Australian children. *Journal of Cross-Cultural Psychology, 27*(5), 616–643.

Markus, H. R., & Kitayama, S. (1991). Culture and self: Implications for cognition, emotion, and motivation. *Psychological Review, 98*, 224–253.

Markus, H. R., & Kitayama, S. (1994a). The cultural shaping of emotion: A conceptual framework. In S. Kitayama & H. Markus (Eds.), *Emotion and culture: Empirical studies of mutual influence* (pp. 339–351). Washington, DC: American Psychological Association.

Markus, H. R., & Kitayama, S. (1994b). The cultural construction of self and emotion: Implications for social behavior. In S. Kitayama & H. Markus (Eds.), *Emotion and culture: Empirical studies of mutual influence* (pp. 89–130). Washington, DC: American Psychological Association.

Marlin, O. (1990). Group psychology in the totalitarian system: A psychoanalytic view. *Group, 141*, 44–58.

Marsella, A. J. (1980). Depressive experience and disorder across cultures. In H. Triandis & J. Draguns (Eds.), *Handbook of cross-cultural psychology* (Vol. 6, pp. 233–262). Boston, MA: Allyn & Bacon.

Marsella, T. (1998). Toward a "global-community psychology": Meeting the needs of a changing world. *American Psychologist, 53*(12), 1282–1291.

Marsh, A., Elfenbein, H., & Ambady, N. (2007). Separated by a common language: Nonverbal accents and cultural stereotypes about Americans and Australians. *Journal of Cross-Cultural Psychology, 38*(3), 284–301.

Marshall, R. (1997). Variances in values of individualism and collectivism across two cultures and three social classes. *Journal of Cross-Cultural Psychology, 28*(4), 490–495.

Masuda, T., & Nisbett, R. E. (2006). Culture and change blindness. *Cognitive Sciences, 30*, 381–399.

Martínez-Taboas, A. (2005). The plural world of culturesensitive psychotherapy: A response to Castro-Blanco's (2005) comments. *Psychotherapy: Theory, Research, Practice, Training, 42*(1), 17–19.

Maslow, A. (1970). *Motivation and personality* (2nd ed.). New York: Harper & Row.

Masters, R. (1997). Brain biochemistry and social status: The neurotoxity hypothesis. In E. White (Ed.), *Intelligence, political inequality, and public policy* (pp. 141–183). Westport, CT: Praeger.

Matsuda, N. (1985). Strong, quasi- and weak conformity among Japanese in the modified Asch procedure. *Journal of Cross-Cultural Psychology, 16*, 83–97.

Matsumoto, D. (1992). American-Japanese cultural differences in the recognition of universal expressions. *Journal of Cross-Cultural Psychology, 23*(1), 72–85.

Matsumoto, D. (1994). *People: Psychology from a cultural perspective.* Pacific Grove, CA: Brooks/Cole.

Matsumoto, D. (2007). Individual and cultural differences on status differentiation: The status differentiation scale. *Journal of Cross-Cultural Psychology, 38*(4), 413–431.

Matsumoto, D., Hee Yoo, S., & Fontaine, J. (2008). Mapping expressive differences around the world: The relationship between emotional display rules and individualism versus collectivism. *Journal of Cross-Cultural Psychology, 39*(1), 55–74.

Matsumoto, D., Kudoh, T., Scherer, K., & Wallbott, H. (1988). Antecedents of and reactions to emotions in the United States and Japan. *Journal of Cross-Cultural Psychology, 19*(3), 267–286.

Mauro, R., Sato, K., & Tucker, J. (1992). The role of appraisal in human emotions: A cross-cultural study. *Journal of Personality and Social Psychology, 62*, 301–317.

Maurois, A. (1967). *Collected stories.* Washington Business.

Mayer, B., & Trommsdorff, G. (2010). Adolescents' value of children and their intentions to have children: A cross-cultural and multilevel analysis. *Journal of Cross-Cultural Psychology, 41*(5–6), 671–689.

Mayer, J., Gasche, Y., Braverman, D., & Evans, T. (1992). Mood-congruent judgment is a general effect. *Journal of Personality and Social Psychology, 63*, 119–132.

McArthur, L., & Berry, D. (1987). Cross-cultural agreement in perceptions of baby-faced adults. *Journal of Cross-Cultural Psychology, 18*(2), 165–192.

McCarthy, A., Lee, K., Itakura, S., & Muir, D. W. (2006). Cultural display rules drive eye gaze during thinking. *Journal of Cross-Cultural Psychology, 37*(6), 717–722.

McClelland, D. C. (1958). The use of measures of human motivation in the study of society. In J. Atkinson (Ed.), *Motives in fantasy, action, and society* (pp. 518–554). Princeton, NJ: Van Nostrand.

McClelland, D. C. (1961). *The achieving society.* Princeton, NJ: Van Nostrand.

McClelland, D. C. (1987). *Human motivation.* New York: Cambridge University Press.

McCrae, R. R. (2002). NEO-PI-R data from 36 cultures: Further intercultural comparisons. In R. R. McCrae & J. Allik (Eds.), *The five-factor model of personality across cultures* (pp. 105–126). New York: Kluwer Academic/Plenum.

McGhee, P., & Duffey, N. (1983). Children's appreciation of humor victimizing different racial-ethnic groups. *Journal of Cross-Cultural Psychology, 14*(1), 29–40.

McGrath, R., Yang, E., & Tsai, W. (1992). Does culture endure, or is it malleable? Issues for entrepreneurial economic development. *Journal of Business Venturing, 7*, 441–458.

McLoyd, V. (1998). Socioeconomic disadvantage and child development. *American Psychologist, 53*(2), 185–204.

McLuhan, M. (1971). *The Gutenberg galaxy: The making of typographic man.* London: Routledge and Kegan Paul.

McManus, J., Laughlin, C. D., & Shearer, J. S. (1993). The function of dreaming in their cycles of cognition. A biogenic structural account. In A. Moffit, M. Kramer, & R. Hoffmann (Eds.), *The function of dreaming* (pp. 21–50). Albany, NY: SUNY Press.

McShane, D., & Berry, J. (1988). Native North Americans: Indian and Inuit abilities. In S. H. Irvine & J. W. Berry (Eds.), *Human abilities in cultural context* (pp. 385–426). New York: Cambridge University Press.

Mead, M. (1975). Review of Darwin and facial expression. *Journal of Communication, 25*, 209–213.

Meissner, C. A., & Brigham, J. C. (2001). Thirty years of investigating the own-race bias in face memory: A meta-analytic review. *Psychology, Public Policy, and Law, 7*, 3–35.

Meleis, A. I. (1982). Arab students in Western universities. *Journal of Higher Education, 53*, 439–447.

Menon, U., & Shweder, R. (1994). Kali's tongue: Cultural psychology and the power of shame in Orissa, India. In S. Kitayama & H. Markus (Eds.), *Emotion and culture* (pp. 241–284). Washington, DC: American Psychiatric Association.

Merritt, A. (2000). Culture in the cockpit: Do Hofstede's dimensions replicate? *Journal of Cross-Cultural Psychology, 31*(3), 283–302.

Mesquita, B., & Frijda, N. H. (1992). Cultural variations in emotion: A review. *Psychological Bulletin, 112*, 179–204.

Mesquita, B., Frijda, N., & Scherer, K. (1997). Culture and emotion. In J. W. Berry, P. R. Dasen, & T. S. Saraswathi (Eds.), *Handbook of cross-cultural psychology: Basic processes and human development* (Vol. 2, pp. 255–297). Boston, MA: Allyn & Bacon.

Milgram, S. (1963). Behavioral study of obedience. *Journal of Abnormal and Social Psychology, 67*, 371–378.

Miller, D. (1983). The correlates of entrepreneurship in three types of firms. *Management Science, 29*, 770–791.

Miller, G. (2000). *The mating mind: How sexual choice shaped the evolution of human nature.* London: Heineman.

Miller, J. (1983). *States of mind.* New York: Pantheon Books.

Miller, J. G. (1994). Cultural diversity in the morality of caring: Individually oriented versus duty based interpersonal moral codes. *Cross-Cultural Research, 28*, 3–39.

Mills, E., & Singh, S. (2007). Health, human rights, and the conduct of clinical research within oppressed populations. *Globalization and Health, 3*(10). Retrieved from http://www.globalizationandhealth.com/content/pdf/ 1744-8603-3-10.pdf

Miner, M., & Rawson, H. (1994). *The new international dictionary of quotations* (2nd ed.). New York: Signet.

Minturin, L., & Shashak, J. (1982). Infanticide as a terminal abortion procedure. *Behavioral Science Research, 17*, 70–90.

Mirin, S. (2002). Testimony of Steven M. Mirin, M.D. Medical Director for the American Psychiatric Association on the HIPAA code set issues/ICD-10-CM implementation before the National Committee on Vital and Health Statistics Standards and Security Subcommittee, May 29, 2002.

Mirsky, J., Barasch, M., & Goldberg, K. (1992). Adjustment problems among Soviet immigrants at risk. Part I: Reaching out to members of the 1000 "families" organization. *Israel Journal of Psychiatry Related Sciences, 29*, 135–149.

Mishra, R. C. (1988). Learning strategies among children in the modern and traditional schools. *Indian Psychologist, 5*, 17–24.

Mishra, R. C. (1997). Cognition and cognitive development. In J. W. Berry, P. R. Dasen, & T. S. Saraswathi (Eds.), *Handbook of cross-cultural psychology: Basic processes and human development* (Vol. 2, pp. 143–176). Boston, MA: Allyn & Bacon.

Moghaddam, F. (1998). *Social psychology.* New York: Freeman.

Moghaddam, F., Ditto, B., & Taylor, D. (1990). Attitudes and attributions related to psychological symptomatology in Indian immigrant women. *Journal of Cross-Cultural Psychology, 21*, 335–350.

Mok, A., Morris, M. W., Benet-Martínez, V., & Karakitapoglu-Aygün, Z. (2007). Embracing American culture: Structures of social identity and social networks among first-generation biculturals. *Journal of Cross-Cultural Psychology, 38*, 629–635.

Monroe, K., & Kreidie, L. (1997). The perspective of Islamic fundamentalists and the limits of Rational Choice Theory. *Political Psychology, 18*(1), 19–44.

Morelli, G. A., Rogoff, B., Oppenheim, D., & Goldsmith, D. (1992). Cultural variations in infants' sleeping arrangements: Questions of independence. *Developmental Psychology, 28*, 604–613.

Morse, J. M., & Park, C. (1988). Differences in cultural expectations of the perceived painfulness of childbirth. In K. Michaelson (Ed.), *Childbirth in America: Anthropological perspectives.* South Hadley, MA: Bergin & Garvey.

Moscovici, S., & Zavalloni, M. (1969). The group as a polarizer of attitudes. *Journal of Personality and Social Psychology, 12*, 125–135.

Mosquera, P. M. R., Manstead, A. S. R., & Fischer, A. (2002). Honor in the Mediterranean and Northern Europe. *Journal of Cross-Cultural Psychology, 33*(1), 16–37.

Moss, R. (1996). Dreaming with the Iroquois. *Dream Time, 13*(2), 6–7.

Mullen, E., & Skitka, L. J. (2009). Comparing Americans' and Ukrainians' allocations of public assistance: The role of affective reactions in helping behavior. *Journal of Cross-Cultural Psychology, 40*(2), 301–318.

Muñoz, R. F., & Mendelson, T. (2005). Toward evidence based interventions for diverse populations: The San Francisco General Hospital prevention and treatment manuals. *Journal of Consulting and Clinical Psychology, 73*, 790–799.

Munro, D. (1986). Work motivation and values: Problems and possibilities in and out of Africa. *Australian Journal of Psychology, 38*, 285–296.

Munroe, R. L. (2010). Following the whitings: The study of male pregnancy symptoms. *Journal of Cross-Cultural Psychology, 41*(4), 592–604.

Munroe, R. L., & Munroe, R. H. (1972). Obedience among children in an East African society. *Journal of Cross-Cultural Psychology, 3*(4), 395–399.

Munroe, R. L., & Munroe, R. H. (1983). Birth order and intellectual performance in East Africa. *Journal of Cross-Cultural Psychology, 14*(1), 3–16.

Munroe, R. L., & Munroe, R. H. (1997). A comparative anthropological perspective. In J. W. Berry, Y. H. Poortinga, & J. Pandey (Eds.), *Handbook of cross-cultural psychology* (Vol. 1, pp. 171–213). Boston, MA: Allyn & Bacon.

Munroe, R. L., Munroe, R. H., & Whiting, B. B. (Eds.). (1981). *Handbook of cross-cultural human development.* New York: Garland.

Munsinger, H. A. (1978). The adopted child's IQ: A critical review. *Psychological Bulletin, 82*, 623–659.

Murphy, J. M. (1976, March 12). Psychiatric labeling in cross-cultural perspective: Similar kinds of disturbed behavior appear to be labeled abnormal in diverse cultures. *Science, 191*, 1019–1028.

Murphy-Bernman, V., Levesque, H., & Bernman, J. (1996). U. N. convention on the rights of the child. *American Psychologist, 51*, 1257–1261.

Murray, H. (1938). *Explorations in personality.* New York: Oxford University Press.

Murray, W. (1999). The angel of dreams: Toward an ethnology of dream interpreting. *Journal of the American Academy of Psychoanalysis, 27*(3), 417–429.

Myers, D. (2008). *A friendly letter to skeptics and atheists: Musings on why god is good and faith isn't evil.* New York: Jossey-Bass/Wiley.

Myers, F. (1979). Emotions and the self. *Ethos, 7*, 343–370.

Nadler, A., & Ben-Shushan, D. (1989). Forty years later: Long-term consequences of massive traumatization as manifested by holocaust survivors from the city and the kibbutz. *Journal of Consulting and Clinical Psychology, 57*, 287–293.

Naito, T., & Gielen, U. (1992). Tatemae and Honne: A study of moral relativism in Japanese culture. In U. Gielen, L. Adler, & N. Milgram (Eds.), *Psychology in international perspective.* Amsterdam: Swets & Zeitlinger.

Nasar, J. L. (1984). Visual preferences in urban street scenes. *Journal of Cross-Cultural Psychology, 15*, 79–93.

Nassar-McMillan, S., & Hakim-Larson, J. (2003). Counseling considerations among Arab Americans. *Journal of Counseling & Development, 81*(2), 150–159.

Neary, I. (2000). Rights and psychiatric patients in East Asia. *Japan Forum, 12*(2), 157–168.

Neiser, U., Boodoo, G., Bouchard, T., Boykin, W., Brody, N., Ceci, S., et al. (1996). Intelligence: Knowns and unknowns. *American Psychologist, 51*(2), 77–101.

Neto, F., Mullet, E., Deschamps, J. C., Barros, J., Benvindo, R., Camino, L., et al. (2000). Cross-cultural variations in attitudes toward love. *Journal of Cross-Cultural Psychology, 31*(5), 626–635.

Nevis, E. C. (1983). Cultural assumptions and productivity: The United States and China. *Sloan Management Review, 24*, 17–29.

New, J., Cosmides, L., & John, T. (2007). Category-specific attention for animals reflects ancestral priorities, not expertise. *Proceeding of the National Academy of Sciences of the USA.* Retrieved October 1, 2007, from http://www.pnas.org/cgi/content/abstract/104/42/16598

Newton, N. (1970). The effect of psychological environment on childbirth: Combined cross-cultural and experimental approach. *Journal of Cross-Cultural Psychology, 1*(1), 85–90.

Ng, S. H., & Lai, J. C. L. (2011). Bicultural self, multiple social identities, and dual patriotisms among ethnic Chinese in Hong Kong. *Journal of Cross-Cultural Psychology, 42*(1), 89–103.

Ng, T. W. H., Sorensen, K. L., & Yim, F. H. K. Does the job satisfaction—job performance relationship vary across cultures? *Journal of Cross-Cultural Psychology, 40*(5), 761–796.

Nicholls, J. (1989). *The competitive ethos and demographic education.* Cambridge, MA: Harvard University Press.

Nicholson, J., Seddon, G., & Worsnop, J. (1977). Teaching understanding of pictorial special relationships to Nigerian secondary school students. *Journal of Cross-Cultural Psychology, 8,* 401–414.

Niles, S. (1998). Achievement goals and means: A cultural comparison. *Journal of Cross-Cultural Psychology, 29*(5), 656–667.

Ninio, A. (1979). The native theory of the infant and other material attitudes in two subgroups in Israel. *Child Development, 50,* 976–980.

Nisbett, R. (2003). *The geography of thought: How Asians and Westerners think differently and why.* London: Nicholas Brealey Publishing.

Nobles, W. (1991). African philosophy: Foundations for black psychology. In R. Jones (Ed.), *Black psychology* (3rd ed., pp. 47–63). Berkeley, CA: Cobb & Henry.

Noelle-Neumann, E. (1986). *The spiral of silence: Public opinion—our social skin.* Chicago, IL: University of Chicago Press.

Norasakkunkit, V., & Kalick, S. M. (2002). Culture, ethnicity, and emotional distress measures: The role of self-construal and self-enhancement. *Journal of Cross-Cultural Psychology, 33*(1), 56–71.

Oberg, K. (1960). Culture shock: Adjustment to new cultural environments. *Practical Anthropology, 7,* 177–182.

Offermann, L., & Hellmann, P. (1997). Culture's consequences for leadership behavior: National values in action. *Journal of Cross-Cultural Psychology, 28*(3), 342–351.

Ogbu, J. (1986). The consequences of the American caste system. In U. Neisser (Ed.), *The school achievement of minority children: New perspectives* (pp. 19–56). Hillsdale, NJ: Erlbaum.

Ogbu, J. (1991). Minority coping responses and school experience. *Journal of Psychohistory, 18,* 434–456.

Ogbu, J. (1994). From cultural differences to differences in cultural frames of reference. In P. M. Greenfield & R. R. Cocking (Eds.), *Cross-cultural roots of minority child development* (pp. 365–391). Hillside, NJ: Erlbaum.

Oishi, S., Diener, E., Scollon, C. N., & Biswas-Diener, R. (2004). Cross-situational consistency of affective experiences across cultures. *Journal of Personality and Social Psychology, 86,* 460–472.

Okagaki, L., & Sternberg, R. (1993). Parental beliefs and children's school performance. *Child Development, 64,* 36–56.

Okazaki, S., Liu, J., Longworth, S., & Minn, J. (2002). Asian American-White American differences in expressions of social anxiety: A replication and extension. *Cultural Diversity and Ethnic Minority Psychology, 8*(3), 234–247.

Okonji, O. M. (1971). A cross-cultural study of the effects of familiarity on classificatory behavior. *Journal of Cross-Cultural Psychology, 2*(1), 3–49.

Olson, S., Kashiwagi, K., & Crystal, D. (2001). Concepts of adaptive and maladaptive child behavior: A comparison of U.S. and Japanese mothers of preschool-age children. *Journal of Cross-Cultural Psychology, 32*(1), 43–57.

Ornstein, R. E. (1977). *The psychology of consciousness.* New York: Penguin Books.

Osborn, A. (1957). *Applied imagination.* New York: Scribners.

Osborne, L. (2001, May 6). Case study: Latah. *The New York Times.* Section 6, p. 98.

Osherow, N. (1993). Making sense of the nonsensical: An analysis of Jonestown. In E. Aronson (Ed.), *Readings about the social animal* (pp. 68–86). New York: W.H. Freeman.

Osterweil, Z., & Nagano, K. (1991). Maternal views on autonomy. *Journal of Cross-Cultural Psychology, 22*(3), 362–375.

Oyserman, D., Coon, H. M., & Kemmelmeier, M. (2002). Rethinking individualism and collectivism: Evaluation of theoretical assumptions and meta-analyses. *Psychological Bulletin, 128*(1), 3–72.

Paige, K. (1973, September 4). Women learn to sing the menstrual blues. *Psychology Today,* pp. 41–46.

Park, K. (1988). East Asians' responses to western health items. *Journal of Cross-Cultural Psychology, 19*(1), 51–64.

Park, J., Cho, Y.-S., Yi, K.-H., Rhee, K.-Y., Kim, Y., & Moon, Y.-H. (1999). Unexpected natural death among Korean workers. *Journal of Occupational Health, 41,* 238–243.

Park, Y. S., & Kim, B. S. K. (2008). Asian and European American cultural values and communication styles among Asian American and European American college students. *Cultural Diversity and Ethnic Minority Psychology, 14*(1), 47–56.

Parker, D., & Deregowski, J. (1990). *Perception and artistic style.* Amsterdam: North-Holland.

Parsons, T. (1951/1964). *The social system.* New York: Free Press.

Parsons, J., & Goff, S. (1978). Achievement motivation: A dual modality. *Educational Psychologist, 13*, 93–96.

Patel, V. (1996). Recognition of common mental disorders in primary care in African countries: Should "mental" be dropped? *Lancet, 347*(9003), 742–744.

Pearce, A. R., Chuikova, T., Ramsey, A., & Galyautdinova, S. (2010). A positive psychology perspective on mate preferences in the United States and Russia. *Journal of Cross-Cultural Psychology, 41*(5–6), 742–757.

Pedersen, P. (1995). *The five stages of culture shock: Critical incidents around the world.* Westport, CT: Greenwood Press.

Pei, M. (1998, January/February). Is China democratizing? *Foreign Affairs*, pp. 68–82.

Peng, K., Nisbett, R. E., & Wong, N. Y. C. (1997). Validity problems comparing values across cultures and possible solutions. *Psychological Methods, 2*, 329–344.

Pennock-Roman, M. (1992). Interpreting test performance in selective admissions for Hispanic students. In K. F. Geisinger (Ed.), *Psychological testing of Hispanics* (pp. 95–135). Washington, DC: American Psychological Association.

Penny, E., Newton, E., & Larkin, M. (2009). Whispering on the water: British Pakistani families' experiences of support from an early intervention service for first-episode psychosis. *Journal of Cross-Cultural Psychology, 40*(6), 969–987.

Persinger, M. (2003). The temporal lobe: The biological basis of the God experience. In R. Joseph (Ed.), *Neuro-Theology: Brain, science, spirituality, religious experience.* San Jose, CA: University Press.

Petersen, A. C. (1988). Adolescent development. *Annual Review of Psychology, 39*, 583–607.

Petitto, A., & Ginsburg, H. (1982). Mental arithmetic in Africa and America: Strategies, principles, and explanations. *International Journal of Psychology, 17*, 81–102.

Petrovsky, A. (1978). *The psychological theory of the collective.* Moscow: Academy of Sciences.

Pew Research Center. (2005). *U.S. image up slightly, but still negative.* Washington, DC: Author.

Phillips, D. (1998, March 18). Is a culture a factor in air crashes? *Washington Post*, p. A17.

Phillips, M., Yang, G., Li, S., & Li, Y. (2004, September 18). Suicide and the unique prevalence pattern of schizophrenia in mainland China: A retrospective observational study. *The Lancet, 364*(9439), 1062–1068.

Piaget, J. (1952). *The origins of intelligence in children.* New York: International Universities Press.

Piaget, J. (1954). *The construction of reality in the child.* New York: Basic Books.

Piaget, J. (1963). *The child's conception of the world.* Paterson, NJ: Littlefield, Adams.

Piaget, J. (1972). *The psychology of intelligence.* Totowa, NJ: Littlefield Adams.

Pika, S., Nicoladis, E., & Marentette, P. (2009). How to order a beer: Cultural differences in the use of conventional gestures for numbers. *Journal of Cross-Cultural Psychology, 40*(1), 70–80.

Pinto, A., Folkers, E., & Sines, J. (1991). Dimensions of behavior and home environment in school-age children: India and the United States. *Journal of Cross-Cultural Psychology, 22*, 491–508.

Platz, S. G., & Hosch, H. M. (1988). Cross-racial/ethnic eyewitness identification: A field study. *Journal of Applied Social Psychology, 13*, 972–984.

Pliner, P. (1982). The effects of mere exposure on liking for edible substances. *Appetite: Journal for Intake Research, 3*, 283–290.

Pliner, P., & Pelchat, M. (1991). Neophobia in humans and the special status of foods of animal origin. *Appetite: Journal for Intake Research, 16*, 205–218.

Pliner, P., Pelchat, M., & Grabski, M. (1993). Reduction of neophobia in humans by exposure to novel foods. *Appetite: Journal for Intake Research, 20*, 111–123.

Pollack, R. (1963). Contour detectability thresholds as a function of chronological age. *Perceptual and Motor Skills, 17*, 411–417.

Poortinga, Y. H., & Van der Flier, H. (1988). The meaning of item bias in ability tests. In S. H. Irvine & J. W. Berry (Eds.), *Human abilities in cultural context* (pp. 166–183). New York: Cambridge University Press.

Powel, L., Shahabi, L., & Thorensen, C. (2003). Religion and Spirituality: Linkages to Physical Health. *American Psychologist, 58*(1), 36–52.

Pratkanis, A. (1988). The attitude heuristic and selective fact identification. *British Journal of Social Psychology, 27*, 257–263.

Pratt, K. (2000). Dream as symptom, dream as myth: A cross-cultural perspective on dream narratives. *Sleep & Hypnosis, 2*(4), 152–159.

Pruitt, D., & Rubin, J. (1986). *Social conflict: Escalation, stalemate, and settlement.* New York: Random House.

Pryor, J., Giedd, J., & Williams, K. (1995). A social psychological model for predicting sexual harassment. *Journal of Social Issues, 51*(1), 69–84.

Punamaki, R. L., & Joustie, M. (1998). The role of culture, violence, and personal factors affecting dream content. *Journal of Cross-Cultural Psychology, 29*(2), 320–342.

Punetha, D., Giles, H., & Young, L. (1987). Ethnicity and immigrant values: Religion and language choice. *Journal of Language and Social Psychology, 6*, 229–241.

Radford, M., Nakane, Y., Ohta, Y., Mann, L., & Kalucu, R. (1991). Decision making in clinically depressed patients: A transcultural social psychological study. *Journal of Nervous and Mental Disease, 179*, 711–719.

Raghavan, C., Harkness, S., & Super, C. (2010). Parental ethnotheories in the context of immigration: Asian indian immigrant and euro-American mothers and daughters in an American town. *Journal of Cross-Cultural Psychology, 41*(4), 617–632.

Raspberry, W. (2000, June 2). Testing stereotype. *Washington Post*, p. A33.

Rathus, S., Nevid, J., & Fischer-Rathus, L. (1993). *Human sexuality in a world of diversity.* Boston, MA: Allyn & Bacon.

Raven, J. (2000). The Raven's progressive matrices: Change and stability over culture and time. *Cognitive Psychology, 41*, 1–48.

Ray, O. (2004). How the mind hurts and heals the body. *American Psychologist, 59*(1), 29–40.

Ray, V. F. (1952). Techniques and problems in the study of human color perception. *South Western Journal of Anthropology, 8*, 201–219.

Raybeck, D., & Herrmann, D. (1990). A cross-cultural examination of semantic relations. *Journal of Cross-Cultural Psychology, 21*(4), 452–473.

Reason, J., & Mycielska, K. (1982). *Absent-minded? The psychology of mental lapses and everyday errors.* Englewood Cliffs, NJ: Prentice-Hall.

Rees, P. (2002, October 20). Japan: The missing million. *BBC News, World Edition.* Retrieved from http://News.bbc.co.uk

Renshon, S. (1989). Psychological perspectives on theories of adult development and the political socialization of leaders. In R. Sigel (Ed.), *Political learning in adulthood: A sourcebook of theory and research.* Chicago, IL: University of Chicago Press.

Reuning, H., & Wortley, W. (1973). Psychological studies of the Bushmen. *Psychologia Africana, Monograph Supplement*, No. 7.

Ricard, M. (2006). *Happiness: A guide to developing life's most important skill.* New York: Little Brown.

Rich, J. (1999). *The culture of fear: Why Americans are afraid of the wrong things.* New York: Basic Books.

Richburg, K. (2003, November 27). Europe's Muslims treated as outsiders: Moroccan family seeks acceptance. *Washington Post*, p. A01.

Rim, Y. (1963). Risk-taking and need for achievement. *Acta Psychologica, 21*, 108–115.

Rime, B., & Giovannini, D. (1986). The psychological patterns of reported emotional states. In K. R. Scherer, H. G. Wallbott, & A. B. Summerfield (Eds.), *Experiencing emotion: A cross-cultural study* (pp. 84–97). Cambridge, MA: Cambridge University Press.

Rivers, W. H. R. (1901). Vision. In A. Haddon (Ed.), *Psychology and physiology: Reports of the Cambridge anthropological exhibition to Torres straits* (Vol. 2, Pt. 1). Cambridge: Cambridge University Press.

Robins, L. N., Tipp, J., & Przybeck, T. (1991). Psychiatric disorders in America. In L. N. Robins & D. A. Regier (Eds.), *Antisocial personality disorder* (pp. 258–290). New York: Free Press.

Roer-Strier, D., & Kurman, J. (2009). Combining qualitative and quantitative methods to study perceptions of immigrant youth. *Journal of Cross-Cultural Psychology, 40*(6), 988–995.

Rogers, P., & Soule, J. (2009). Cross-cultural differences in the acceptance of Barnum profiles supposedly derived from Western versus Chinese astrology. *Journal of Cross-Cultural Psychology, 40*(3), 381–399.

Rogoff, B. (1990). *Apprenticeship in thinking: Cognitive development in social context.* New York: Oxford University Press.

Rohier, I. (1975). A social-learning approach to political socialization. In D. Schwartz & S. Schwartz (Eds.), *New directions in political socialization.* New York: Free Press.

Rokeach, M. (1973). *The nature of human values.* New York: Free Press.

Roland, A. (2006). Across civilizations: Psychoanalytic therapy with Asians and Asian Americans. *Psychotherapy: Theory, Research, Practice, Training, 43*(4), 454–463.

Roll, S. (1987). Dreams. In T. M. Abel, R. Metraux, & S. Roll (Eds.), *Psychotherapy and culture* (pp. 176–195). Albuquerque, NM: University of New Mexico Press.

Roll, S., Rabold, K., & McArdle, L. (1976). Disclaimed activity in dreams of Chicanos and Anglos. *Journal of Cross-Cultural Psychology, 7*(3), 335–342.

Rosaldo, M. Z. (1980). *Knowledge and passion: Ilongot notions of self and social life.* Cambridge, MA: Cambridge University Press.

Roseman, I. J. (1991). Appraisal determinants of discrete emotions. *Cognition and Emotion, 5,* 161–200.

Rosen, G. (1968). *Madness in society.* London: Routledge and Kegan Paul.

Rosenau, N. (1975). The sources of children's political concepts: An application of Piaget's theory. In D. Schwartz & S. Schwartz (Eds.), *New directions in political socialization.* New York: Free Press.

Rosenthal, R., & Jacobson, L. (1968). *Pygmalion in the classroom: Teacher expectation and pupils' intellectual development.* New York: Holt, Rinehart, & Winston.

Ross, L. (1977). The intuitive psychologist and his shortcomings: Distortions in the attribution process. In L. Berkowitz (Ed.), *Advances in experimental social psychology* (Vol. 10). New York: Academic Press.

Ross, L. D., & Lepper, M. R. (1980). The perseverance of beliefs: Empirical and normative considerations. In R. A. Shweder (Ed.), *New directions for methodology of behavioral science: Fallible judgment in behavioral research.* San Francisco, CA: Jossey-Bass.

Ross, L., Lepper, M. R., & Hubbard, M. (1975). Perseverance in self-perception and social perception: Biased attribution processes in the debriefing paradigm. *Journal of Personality and Social Psychology, 32,* 880–892.

Rothbaum, F., Kakinuma, M., Nagaoka, R., & Azuma, H. (2007). Attachment and amae: Parent—child closeness in the United States and Japan. *Journal of Cross-Cultural Psychology, 38,* 465–486.

Rothbaum, F., & Tsang, B. Y.-P. (1998). Love songs in the United States and China. *Journal of Cross-Cultural Psychology, 29*(2), 306–319.

Rothblum, E. (1992). Women and weight: An international perspective. In U. Gielen, L. Adler, & N. Milgram (Eds.), *Psychology in international perspective.* Amsterdam: Swets & Zeitlinger.

Rotter, J. (1966). Generalized expectations for internal vs. external control of reinforcement. *Psychological Monographs, 80,* 1–28.

Rozin, P., & Fallon, A. (1987). A perspective on disgust. *Psychological Review, 94*(1), 23–41.

Rubenstein, J. (1987). A cross-cultural comparison of children's drawings of same- and mixed-sex peer interaction. *Journal of Cross-Cultural Psychology, 18*(2), 234–250.

Ruchkin, V., Lorberg, B., Koposov, R., Schwab-Stone, M., & Sukhodolsky, D. (2007, August). ADHD symptoms and associated psychopathology in a community sample of adolescents from the European North of Russia. *Journal of Attention Disorders.* Retrieved from http://jad.sagepub.com

Rudmin, F. (2003). Critical history of the acculturation psychology of assimilation, separation, integration, and marginalization. *Review of General Psychology, 7*(1), 3–37.

Rudy, D., & Grusec, J. (2001). Correlates of authoritarian parenting in individualist and collectivist cultures and implications for understanding the transmission of values. *Journal of Cross-Cultural Psychology, 32*(2), 202–212.

Rushton, J. P. (1994). Sex and race differences in cranial capacity from International Labour Office Data. *Intelligence, 19,* 281–294.

Rushton, J. P. (1995). *Race, evolution, and behavior.* New Brunswick, NJ: Transaction.

Rushton, J. P., & Jensen, A. R. (2005). Thirty years of research on race differences in cognitive ability. *Psychology, Public Policy, and Law, 11,* 235–294.

Russell, C. (1995, July, 10–12). Do you know what your kids are doing? *Washington Post Health,* p. 10.

Russell, G., Fujino, D., Sue, S., Cheung, M.-K., & Snowden, L. (1996). The effects of therapist-client ethnic match in the assessment of mental health functioning. *Journal of Cross-Cultural Psychology, 27*(5), 598–615.

Russell, J. (1994). Is there universal recognition of emotion from facial expression? A review of cross-cultural studies. *Psychological Bulletin, 115,* 102–141.

Russell, J. A. (1991). Culture and the categorization of emotions. *Psychological Bulletin, 110,* 426–450.

Russell, J. A., & Yik, M. S. M. (1996). Emotion among the Chinese. In M. H. Bond (Ed.), *The handbook of Chinese psychology* (pp. 166–188). Hong Kong: Oxford University Press.

Ryan, E. B., & Sebastian, R. J. (1980). The effects of speech style and social class background on social judgements of speakers. *British Journal of Social and Clinical Psychology, 19,* 229–233.

Sadie, S. (1980). *The new grove dictionary of music and musicians* (Vol. 9). London: Macmillan.

Sarfati, L. (2010). *Objects of worship: Material culture in the production of shamanic rituals in South Korea.* Dissertation Abstracts International Section A: Humanities and Social Sciences, p. 610.

Saroop, S. (1999). *Indian American attitudes regarding arranged marriages in the United States* (Unpublished manuscript).

Sartorius, N. (1992). Prognosis for schizophrenia in the Third World: A re-evaluation of cross-cultural research. A Commentary. *Culture, Medicine, and Psychiatry, 16,* 81–84.

Sarver, D., Brown, G., & Evans, D. (2007). Cosmetic breast augmentation and suicide. *American Journal of Psychiatry, 164,* 1006–1013.

Satcher, D. (2000). Executive Summary: A Report of the Surgeon General on Mental Health, Public Health Rep 2000; 115: 89–101. Assistant Secretary for Health and U.S. Surgeon General.

Sax, L. (2007). *Boys adrift: The five factors driving the growing epidemic of unmotivated boys and underachieving young men.* New York: Basic Books.

Schachter, S., & Singer, J. (1962). Cognitive, social, and psychological determinants of emotional state. *Psychological Review, 69,* 379–399.

Scherer, K., Banse, R., & Wallbott, H. (2001). Emotion interferences from vocal expression correlate across languages and cultures. *Journal of Cross-Cultural Psychology, 32*(1), 76–92.

Scherer, K. R. (1984). Toward a concept of "modal emotions." In P. Ekman & R. J. Davidson (Eds.), *The nature of emotion: Fundamental questions* (pp. 25–31). Oxford: Oxford University Press.

Scherer, K. R., & Wallbott, H. G. (1994). Evidence for universality and cultural variation of different emotional response patterning. *Journal of Personality and Social Psychology, 66,* 310–328.

Scherer, K. R., Wallbott, H. G., Matsumoto, D., & Kudoh, T. (1988). Emotional experience in cultural context: A comparison between Europe, Japan, and the United States. In K. R. Scherer (Ed.), *Faces of emotions* (pp. 5–30). Hillsdale, NJ: Erlbaum.

Schimmack, U. (1996). Cultural influences on the recognition of emotion by facial expressions: Individualistic or Caucasian cultures? *Journal of Cross-Cultural Psychology, 27*(2), 37–50.

Schlegel, A., & Barry, H. (1991). *Adolescence: An anthropological inquiry.* New York: Free Press.

Schlinger, H. D., Jr. (1996). How the human got its spots: A critical analysis of the just so stories of evolutionary psychology. *Skeptic, 4*(1), 68–76.

Schmidt, S., & Yeh, R.-S. (1992). The structure of leader influence. *Journal of Cross-Cultural Psychology, 23*(2), 251–264.

Schmitt, D., Allik, J., McCrae, R., & Benet-Martínez, V. (2007). The geographic distribution of big five personality traits: Patterns and profiles of human self-description across 56 nations. *Journal of Cross-Cultural Psychology, 38*(2), 173–212.

Schubert, G. (1991a). Human vocalizations in agonistic political encounters. In G. Shubert & R. Masters (Eds.), *Primate politics.* Carbondale: Southern Illinois University Press.

Schubert, G., & Masters R. (Eds.). (1991). *Primate politics.* Carbondale: Southern Illinois University Press.

Schulze, P., Harwood, R., & Schoelmerich, A. (2001). *Journal of Cross-Cultural Psychology, 32*(4), 397–406.

Schwanenflugel, P. J., & Rey, M. (1986). The relationship between category typicality and concept familiarity: Evidence from Spanish- and English-speaking monolinguals. *Memory & Cognition, 14,* 150–163.

Schwartz, B. (2004). *The paradox of choice: Why more is less.* New York: Ecco.

Schwartz, J. (1998, July 8). Blacks absorb more nicotine, suffer greater smoking toll, studies say. *Washington Post,* p. A3.

Schwartz, S. (1975). Patterns of cynicism: Differential political socialization among adolescence. In D. Schwartz & S. Schwartz (Eds.), *New directions in political socialization.* New York: Free Press.

Schwartz, S. (1994). Are there universal aspects in the structure and content of human values? *Journal of Social Issues, 50,* 19–45.

Schwartz, S. (2000).Value consensus and importance. *Journal of Cross-Cultural Psychology, 31*(4), 465–498.

Schwartz, S. H. (2004). Mapping and interpreting cultural differences around the world. In H. Vinken, J. Soeters, & P. Ester (Eds.), *Comparing cultures, dimensions of culture in a comparative perspective* (pp. 43–73). Leiden, The Netherlands: Brill.

Schwartz, S. H. (2007). Universalism values and the inclusiveness of our moral universe. *Journal of Cross-Cultural Psychology, 38*(6), 711–728.

Schwartz, S. H. (2011). Studying values: Personal adventure, future directions. *Journal of Cross-Cultural Psychology, 42*(2), 307–319.

Schwartz, S. J., Unger, J. B., Zamboanga, B. L., & Szapocznik, J. (2010). Rethinking the concept of acculturation: Implications for theory and research. *American Psychologist, 65*(4), 237–251.

Schwartz, S. J., Unger, J. B., Zamboanga, B. L., & Szapocznik, J. (2011). How selective is acculturation? Broadening our perspective. *American Psychologist, 66*(2), 155–157.

Schwartz, S., Melech, G., Lehmann, A., Burgess, S., Harris, M., & Owens, V. (2001). Extending the cross-cultural validity of the theory of basic human values with a different method of measurement. *Journal of Cross-Cultural Psychology, 32*(5), 519–542.

Scribner, S., & Cole, M. (1981). *The psychology of literacy.* Cambridge, MA: Harvard University Press.

Sears, D. (1996). Presidential address: Reflections on the politics of multiculturalism in American society. *Political Psychology, 17*(3), 409–420.

Sears, D., Huddy, L., & Jervis, R. (Eds.). (2003). *Oxford handbook of political psychology.* Oxford: Oxford University Press.

Segall, M. H., Campbell, D. T., & Herskovits, M. J. (1966). *The influence of culture on visual perception.* Indianapolis, IN: Bobbs-Merrill.

Segall, M. H., Dasen, P. R., Berry, J. W., & Poortinga, Y. H. (1990). *Human behavior in global perspective: An introduction to cross-cultural psychology.* New York: Pergamon.

Segall, M. H., Ember, C. R., & Ember, M. (1997). Aggression, crime, and warfare. In J. W. Berry, M. H. Segall, & C. Kagitcibasi (Eds.), *Handbook of cross-cultural psychology* (Vol. 3, 3rd ed., pp. 213–254). Boston, MA: Allyn & Bacon.

Segall, M., Dasen, P., Berry, J., & Poortinga, Y. (1999). *Human behavior in global perspective.* Boston, MA: Allyn & Bacon.

Semin, G., & Zwier, S. (1997). Social cognition. In J. Berry, M. Segall, & C. Kagitcibasi (Eds.),

Handbook of cross-cultural psychology (Vol. 3, pp. 51–76). Boston, MA: Allyn & Bacon.

Serpell, R. (1993). *The significance of schooling: Life journeys in an African society.* Cambridge, MA: Cambridge University Press.

Shade, B. (1991). African American patterns of cognition. In R. Jones (Ed.), *Black psychology* (3rd ed., pp. 47–63). Berkeley, CA: Cobb & Henry.

Shade, B. (1992). Is there Afro-American cognitive style? An exploratory study. In K. H. Burlew, W. C. Banks, H. P. McAdoo, & D. A. ya Azibo (Eds.), *African American psychology* (pp. 246–259). Newbury Park, CA: Sage.

Shafey, O., Dolwick, S., & Guindon, G. (Eds.). (2003). *Tobacco control country profiles 2003.* Atlanta, GA: American Cancer Society.

Shapiro, R., Nacos, B., & Isernia, P. (Eds.). (2000). *Decisionmaking in the glass house.* Boulder, CO: Rowman & Littlefield.

Shea, J. D. (1985). Studies of cognitive development in Papua New Guinea. *International Journal of Psychology, 20,* 33–61.

Shimizi, Y., & Kaplan, B. (1987). Postpartum depression in the United States. *Journal of Cross-Cultural Psychology, 18*(1), 15–30.

Shiraev, E. (1988). I semya v otvete [The family is responsible]. In A. Sventsitsky (Ed.), *The power of discipline.* Leningrad: Lenizdat.

Shiraev, E. (2000). People say, advisers advise, and officials decide. In R. Shapiro, B. Nacos, & P. Isernia (Eds.), *Decision-making in the glass house.* Boulder, CO: Rowman & Littlefield.

Shiraev, E. (2011). *A history of psychology: A global perspective.* Thousand Oaks, CA: Sage.

Shiraev, E., & Bastrykin, A. (1988). *Fashion, idols, and the self.* St. Petersburg: Lenizdat.

Shiraev, E., & Boyd, G. (2008). *The accent of success.* Ann Arbor, MI: University of Michigan Press.

Shiraev, E., & Boyd, J. (2001). *The accent of success.* Englewood Cliffs, NJ: Prentice Hall.

Shiraev, E., & Fillipov, A. (1990). Cross-cultural social perception. *St. Petersburg University Quarterly, 13,* 53–60.

Shiraev, E., & Sobel, R. (2006). *People and their opinions.* New York: Longman.

Shupe, E. I. (2007). Clashing cultures: A model of international student conflict. *Journal of Cross-Cultural Psychology, 38,* 750–771.

Shweder, R., Mahapatra, M., & Miller, J. (1990). Culture and moral development. In J. Stigler, R. Shweder, & G. Herdt (Eds.), *Cultural psychology* (pp. 130–204). New York: Cambridge University Press.

Sidanius, J., & Pratto, F. (2001). *Social dominance: An intergroup theory of social hierarchy and oppression.* Cambridge, MA: Cambridge University Press.

Sigel, R. (Ed.). (1989). Introduction: Persistence and change. In *Political learning in adulthood: A sourcebook of theory and research.* Chicago, IL: University of Chicago Press.

Simmons, C., vomKolke, A., & Shimizu, H. (1986). Attitudes toward romantic love among American, German, and Japanese students. *Journal of Social Psychology, 126,* 327–336.

Simon, B. (1978). *Mind and madness in ancient Greece: The classical roots of modern psychiatry.* Ithaca, NY: Cornell University Press.

Simons, R., & Hughes, C. (Eds.). (1985). *The culture-bound syndromes: Folk illnesses of psychiatric and anthropological interest.* Dordrecht, The Netherlands: D. Reidel Publishing Company.

Simonton, D. (1987). Developmental antecedents of achieved eminence. *Annals of Child Development, 5,* 131–169.

Singh, D., Renn, P., & Singh, A. D. (2007). Did the perils of abdominal obesity affect depiction of feminine beauty in the sixteenth to eighteenth century British literature? Exploring the health and beauty link. *Proceedings of the Royal Society of London. Biological Sciences, 274,* 891–894.

Sinha, D., & Shukla, P. (1974). Deprivation and development of skill for pictorial depth perception. *Journal of Cross-Cultural Psychology, 5*(4), 434–445.

Sinha, J., & Verma, J. (1983). Perceptual structuring of dyadic interactions. *Journal of Cross-Cultural Psychology, 14,* 187–199.

Skrypnek, B. J., & Snyder, M. (1982). On the selfperpetuating nature of stereotypes about women and men. *Journal of Experimental Social Psychology, 18,* 277–291.

Skuy, M., Gewer, A., Osrin, Y., Khunou, D., Fridjhon, P., & Rushton, J. P. (2002). Effects of mediated learning experience on Raven's matrices scores of African and non-African university students in South Africa. *Intelligence, 30,* 221–232.

Smith, H. (1976). *The Russians.* New York: Quadrangle.

Smith, H. (1991). *The world's religions.* San Francisco, CA: Harper.

Smith, M. B. (1978). Psychology and values. *Journal of Social Issues, 34,* 181–199.

Smith, K. D., Smith, S. T., & Chambers, J. (2007). What defines the good person? Cross-cultural comparisons of experts' models with lay prototypes. *Journal of Cross-Cultural Psychology, 38,* 333–360.

Smith, P. B. (2011). Communication styles as dimensions of national culture. *Journal of Cross-Cultural Psychology, 42*(2), 216–233.

Smith, P. B., & Bond, M. H. (1993). *Social psychology across cultures: Analysis and perspectives.* Hemel Hempstead, UK: Harvester/Wheatsheaf.

Smith, P. B., & Schwartz, S. (1997). Values. In J. Berry, M. Segall, & C. Kagitcibasi (Eds.), *Handbook of cross-cultural psychology* (Vol. 3, pp. 77–118). Boston, MA: Allyn & Bacon.

Snacken, J. (1991). Guide pour le pratique dans un contexte multiculturel et interdisciplinaire. In J. Leman & A. Gailly (Eds.), *Therapies interculturelles* (pp. 135–140). Bruxelles, Belgium: Editions Universitaires, De Boeck Universite.

Snarey, J. (1985). Cross-cultural universality of social-moral development: A critical review of Kohlbergian research. *Psychological Bulletin, 97,* 202–232.

Snyder, C. R., Shenkel, R. J., & Lowery, C. R. (1977). Acceptance of personality interpretations: The "Barnum Effect" and beyond. *Journal of Consulting and Clinical Psychology, 45*(1), 104–114.

Snyder, M. (1984). When belief becomes reality. In L. Berkowitz (Ed.), *Advances in experimental social psychology* (Vol. 18). New York: Academic Press.

Snyder, M., & Swann, W. B., Jr. (1978). Behavioral confirmation in social interaction: From social perception to social reality. *Journal of Experimental Social Psychology, 14,* 148–162.

Snyderman, M., & Rothman, S. (1988). *The IQ controversy: The media and public policy.* New Brunswick, NJ: Transaction Books.

Sobal, J., & Stunkard, A. J. (1989). Socioeconomic status and obesity: A review of the literature. *Psychological Bulletin, 105*(2), 260–275.

Solomon, R. S. (1978). Emotions and anthropology: The logic of emotional world views. *Inquiry, 21,* 181–199.

Solórzano, D., Ceja, M., & Yosso, T. (2000, Winter). Critical race theory, racial microaggressions, and campus racial climate: The experiences of African American college students. *Journal of Negro Education, 69,* 60–73.

Somer, E., & Saadon, M. (2000, December). Stambali: Dissociative possession and trance in a Tunisian healing dance. *Transcultural Psychiatry, 37,* 580–600.

Sonwalkar, P. (2004, April 2). Children of Indian origin outshine others in Scotland. *The Hindustan Times.* Retrieved from http:// www.hindustantimes.com

Sorokowski, P., Szmajke, A., Sorokowska, A., Cunen, M. B., Fabrykant, M., Zarafshani, K., Amiri, M., Bazzazian, S., Blazevska-Stoilkovska, B., Casellas, V., Cetinkaya, H., Coutino, B. L., Chavez, M., Cheng, C., Cristea, I., David, D., Dural, S., Dzięcioł, A., Fauzee, S., Frichand, A., Gulbetekin, E., Hromatko, I., Javahishvili, T., Jgenti, A., Kartasasmita, S., Moradi, K., Musil, B., Nongmaithem, S., Oladipo, E., Oluyinka, O., Patil, K., Schell, W., Serpekian, H., Slavchev, B., Stoyanova, S., Tadinac, M., Tripathi, N., & Fang, T. (2011). Attractiveness of leg length: Report from 27 nations. *Journal of Cross-Cultural Psychology, 42*(1), 131–139.

Sorrentino, R. M., Nezlek, J. B., Yasunaga, S., Kouhara, S., Otsubo, Y., & Shuper, P. (2008). Uncertainty orientation and affective experiences: Individual differences within and across cultures. *Journal of Cross-Cultural Psychology, 39*(2), 129–146.

Spearman, C. E. (1927). *The abilities of man.* London: Macmillan.

Spence, I., Wong, P., Rusan, M., & Rastegar, N. (2006). How color enhances visual memory for natural scenes. *Psychological Science, 17,* 1–6.

Spencer-Rodgers, J., Peng, K., & Wang, L. (2010). Dialecticism and the co-occurrence of positive and negative emotions across cultures. *Journal of Cross-Cultural Psychology, 41*(1), 109–115.

Spielberger, C. (1980). *Test anxiety inventory. Preliminary professional manual.* Palo Alto, CA: Consulting Psychologist Press.

Sporer, S. L., Trinkl, B., & Guberova, E. (2007). Matching faces: Differences in processing speed of out-group faces by different ethnic groups. *Journal of Cross-Cultural Psychology, 38*, 398–412.

Starcevic, V. (1999). Neurasthenia: Cross-cultural and conceptual issues in relation to chronic fatigue syndrome. *General Hospital Psychiatry, 21*(4), 249–255.

Starovoitova, G. (1998, March 5–11). An interview to *Obshchaya Gazeta*, p. 1.

Staub, E. (1996). Cultural-societal roots of violence: The examples of genocidal violence and of contemporary youth violence in the United States. *American Psychologist, 51*(2), 117–132.

Steele, C. M. (1999, August). Thin ice: "Stereotype threat" and black college students. *The Atlantic Monthly, 284*(2), pp. 44–47, 50–54.

Steele, R. G., Elliott, V., & Phipps, S. (2003). Race and health status as determinants of anger expression and adaptive style in children. *Journal of Social and Clinical Psychology, 22*, 40–58.

Steers, R., & Sanchez-Runde, C. (2002). Culture, motivation, and work behavior. In M. Martin & K. Newman (Eds.), *Handbook of cross-cultural management.* Malden, MA: Blackwell.

Steffensen, M., & Calker, L. (1982). Intercultural misunderstandings about health care: Recall of descriptions of illness and treatments. *Social Science and Medicine, 16*, 1949–1954.

Stein, M. (1991). On the socio-historical context of creativity programs. *Creativity Research Journal, 4*, 294–300.

Stephan, C. W., Stephan, W., Saito, I., & Barnett, S. (1998). Emotional expression in Japan and the United States: The nonmonolithic nature of individualism and collectivism. *Journal of Cross-Cultural Psychology, 29*(6), 728–748.

Sternberg, R. (1985). *Beyond IQ: A triarchic theory of human intelligence.* New York: Cambridge University Press.

Sternberg, R. (1997). The concept of intelligence and its role in lifelong learning and success. *American Psychologist, 52*(10), 1030–1037.

Sternberg, R. (2004, July–August). Culture and intelligence. *American Psychologist, 59*(5), 325–338.

Sternberg, R. (2007). *Wisdom, intelligence, and creativity synthesized.* Cambridge: Cambridge University Press.

Sternberg, R., & Grigorenko, E. (2001). Unified psychology. *American Psychologist, 56*(12), 1069–1070.

Stevenson, H., Lee, S. Y., Chen, C., Lummis, M., Stigler, J., Fan, L., et al. (1990). Mathematical achievement of children in China and the United States. *Child Development, 61*, 1053–1066.

Stipek, D. (1998). Differences between Americans and Chinese in the circumstances evoking pride, shame, and guilt. *Journal of Cross-Cultural Psychology, 29*(5), 616–629.

Strauss, V. (2008, May 20). No crisis for boys in schools, study says. *Washington Post*, p. A1.

Stroebe, W. (2010). The graying of academia: Will it reduce scientific productivity? *American Psychologist, 65*(7), 660–673.

Strohschneider, S., & Guss, D. (1998). Planning and problem solving: Differences between Brazilian and German students. *Journal of Cross-Cultural Psychology, 29*(6), 695–716.

Struck, D. (2000, August 11). Gun use intrudes on Japanese serenity. *Washington Post*, p. A17.

Sue, D. W., Capodilupo, C. M., Torino, G. C., Bucceri, J. M., Holder, A. M. B., Nadal, K. L.. & Esquilin, M. (2007). Racial microaggressions in everyday life: Implications for clinical practice. *American Psychologist, 62*(4), 271–286.

Sue, S., Fujino, D., Hu, L., Takeuchi, D., & Zane, N. (1991). Community mental health services for ethnic minority groups. *Journal of Counseling and Clinical Psychology, 59*, 533–540.

Sue, S., & Okazaki, S. (1990). Asian American educational achievements: A phenomenon in search of an explanation. *American Psychologist, 45*, 913–920.

Suh, E. M., Diener, E. D., & Updegraff, J. A. (2008). From culture to priming conditions: Self-construal influences on life satisfaction judgments. *Journal of Cross-Cultural Psychology, 39*(1), 3–15.

Sukhodolsky, D. G., Golub, A., & Cromwell, E. N. (2001). Development and validation of the anger rumination scale. *Personality and Individual Differences, 31*, 689–700.

Sullivan, H. S. (1954). *The psychiatric interview.* New York: Norton.

Summer, W. (1970). *What social classes owe to each other.* Caldwell, ID: Caxton.

Super, C., & Harkness, S. (1997). The cultural structuring of child development. In J. W. Berry, P. R. Dasen, & T. S. Saraswathi (Eds.), *Handbook of cross-cultural psychology: Basic processes and human development* (Vol. 2, pp. 1–41). Boston, MA: Allyn & Bacon.

Suzuki, L., & Valencia, R. (1997). Race-ethnicity and measured intelligence: Educational implications. *American Psychologist, 52*(10), 1103–1114.

Sventsitsky, A. (Ed.). (1988). *Avtoritet distsipliny [The power of discipline].* Leningrad: Lenizdat.

Swami, V., Henderson, G., Custance, D., & Tovée, M. J. (2011). A cross-cultural investigation of men's judgments of female body weight in Britain and Indonesia. *Journal of Cross-Cultural Psychology, 42*(1), 140–145.

Swenson, L. C. (1993). *Psychology and law.* Pacific Grove, CA: Brooks/Cole.

Symons, D. (1979). *The evolution of human sexuality.* New York: Oxford University Press.

Tafarodi, R. W., Shaughnessy, S. C., Lee, W. W. S., Leung, D. Y. P., Ozaki, Y., Morio, H., & Yamaguchi, S. (2009). Disregard for outsiders: A cultural comparison. *Journal of Cross-Cultural Psychology, 40*(4), 567–583.

Tafarodi, R. W., Shaughnessy, S. C., Yamaguchi, S., & Murakoshi, A. (2011). The reporting of self-esteem in Japan and Canada. *Journal of Cross-Cultural Psychology, 42*(1), 155–164.

Tafarodi, R. W., & Swann, W. (1996). Individualism-collectivism and global self-esteem: Evidence for a cultural trade-off. *Journal of Cross-Cultural Psychology, 27*, 651–672.

Tajima, E. A., & Harachi, T. W. (2010). Parenting beliefs and physical discipline practices among southeast Asian immigrants: Parenting in the context of cultural adaptation to the United States. *Journal of Cross-Cultural Psychology, 41*(2), 212–235.

Takano, Y., & Noda, A. (1993). A temporary decline of thinking ability during foreign language processing. *Journal of Cross-Cultural Psychology, 24*(4), 445–462.

Takano, Y., & Sogon, S. (2008). Are Japanese more collectivistic than Americans? Examining conformity in in-groups and the reference-group effect. *Journal of Cross-Cultural Psychology, 39*(3), 237–250.

Tanaka-Matsumi, J. (1989). The cultural difference model and applied behavior analysis in the design of early childhood intervention. In L. L. Adler (Ed.), *Cross-cultural research in human development: Lifespan perspectives* (pp. 37–46). New York: Praeger.

Tanaka-Matsumi, J. (1995). Cross-cultural perspectives on anger. In H. Kassinove (Ed.), *Anger disorders: Definition, diagnosis, and treatment.* Washington, DC: Taylor and Francis.

Tanaka-Matsumi, J., & Draguns, J. (1997). Culture and psychopathology. In J. W. Berry, M. H. Segall, & C. Kagitcibasi (Eds.), *Handbook of cross-cultural psychology* (Vol. 3, pp. 449–491). Boston, MA: Allyn & Bacon.

Tanaka-Matsumi, J., & Marsella, A. (1976). Cross-cultural variations in the phenomenological experience of depression. *Journal of Cross-Cultural Psychology, 7*(4), 379–390.

Taub, J. (1971). The sleep-wakefulness cycle in Mexican adults. *Journal of Cross-Cultural Psychology, 2*(4), 353–362.

Taves, A. (1999). *Fits, trances, and visions: Experimenting religion and explaining experience from Wesley to James.* Princeton, NJ: Princeton University Press.

Taylor, L., & deLacey, P. R. (1974). Three dimensions of intellectual functioning in Australian Aboriginal and disadvantaged European children. *Journal of Cross-Cultural Psychology, 5*(1), 49–55.

Taylor, S. E., & Fiske, S. T. (1975). Point of view and perceptions of causality. *Journal of Personality and Social Psychology, 32*, 439–445.

Taylor, S. E., Peplau, L. A., & Sears, D. O. (1994). *Social psychology* (8th ed.). Englewood Cliffs, NJ: Prentice-Hall.

Taylor, S. E., Sherman, D., Kim, H. S., Jarcho, J., Takagi, K., & Dunagan, M. (2004). Culture and social support: Who seeks it and why? *Journal of Personality & Social Psychology, 87*(3), 354–362.

Tedlock, B. (1987). Dreaming and dreamer research. In B. Tedlock (Ed.), *Dreaming: Anthropological and psychological interpretations*. Cambridge, MA: Cambridge University Press.

Tellenbach, H. (1980). *Melancholy*. Pittsburgh, PA: Duquesne University Press.

Terracciano, A., Abdel-Khalek, A. M., Ádám, N., Adamovová, L., Ahn, C. K., Ahn, H. N., et al. (2005). National character does not reflect mean personality trait levels in 49 cultures. *Science, 310*, 96–100.

Terracciano, A., & McCrae, R. (2007). Perceptions of Americans and the Iraq invasion: Implications for understanding national character stereotypes. *Journal of Cross-Cultural Psychology, 38*(6), 695–710.

Thompson, K. (2003). *Body image, eating disorders, and obesity*. Washington, DC: American Psychiatric Association.

Thornhill, R., & Gangestad, S. W. (2008). *The evolutionary biology of human female sexuality*. New York: Oxford University Press.

Thouless, R. H. (1932). A racial difference in perception. *Journal of Social Psychology, 4*, 330–339.

Thurstone, E. L. (1938). *Primary mental abilities*. Chicago, IL: University of Chicago Press.

Thwala, A., Pillay, A., & Sargent, C. (2000). The influence of urban/rural background, gender, age and education on the perception of and response to dreams among Zulu South Africans. *South African Journal of Psychology, 30*(4), 1–5.

Tietelbaum, S., & Geiselman, E. (1997). Observer mood and cross-racial recognition of faces. *Journal of Cross-Cultural Psychology, 28*(1), 93–106.

Tobacyk, J. J. (1992). Changes in locus of control beliefs in Polish university students before and after democratization. *Journal of Cross-Cultural Psychology, 13*(2), 217–222.

Tolbert, K. (2000, April 28). Japan's elderly: Once revered, now unemployed. *Washington Post*, p. A01.

Tolbert, K. (2002, May 29). Japan's voluntary shut-ins: Locked in their rooms, young men shun society. *Washington Post*, p. A01.

Tolin, D. F., Robison. J. T., Gaztambide, S., Horowitz, S., & Blank, K. (2007). *Ataques de Nervios* and psychiatric disorders in older Puerto Rican primary care patients. *Journal of Cross-Cultural Psychology, 38*(6), 659–669.

Tori, C. D., & Bilmes, M. (2002). Multiculturalism and psychoanalytic psychology: The validation of a defense mechanisms measure in an Asian population. *Psychoanalytic Psychology, 19*(4), 701–721.

Triandis, H. (1989). The self and social behavior in different social contexts. *Psychological Review, 96*, 506–520.

Triandis, H. (1990). Cross-cultural studies of individualismcollectivism. In J. Berman (Ed.), *Nebraska Symposium on Motivation 1989*. Lincoln, NE: Nebraska University Press.

Triandis, H. (1994). *Culture and social behavior*. New York: McGraw-Hill.

Triandis, H. C. (1996). The psychological measurement of cultural syndromes. *American Psychologist, 51*(4), 407–415.

Triandis, H. C., Lambert, W. W., Berry, J. W., Lonner, W. T., Heron, A., Brislin, R., et al. (Eds.). (1980). *Handbook of cross-cultural psychology* (Vols. 1–6). Boston, MA: Allyn & Bacon.

Tsai, J., & Levenson, R. (1997). Cultural influences on emotional responding: Chinese American and European American dating couples during interpersonal conflict. *Journal of Cross-Cultural Psychology, 28*(5), 600–625.

Tsytsarev, S. V., & Krichmar, L. (2000). Relationship of perceived culture shock, length of stay in the US, depression and self-esteem in elderly Russian speaking immigrants. *Journal of Social Distress and the Homeless, 9*(1), 35–49.

Tullett, A. (1997). Cognitive style, not culture's consequence. *European Psychologist, 2*(3), 258–267.

Tung, M. P. M. (1994). Symbolic meanings of the body in Chinese culture and "somatization." *Culture, Medicine and Psychiatry, 18*, 483–492.

Turner, J. F. (1920). *The frontier in American history*. New York, NY: Henry Holt.

Turner, T. (1997, October). Ethnicity and psychiatry. *The Practitioner, 241*, pp. 612–615.

Tutty, L., Rothery, M., & Grinnell, R. (1996). *Qualitative research for social work*. Boston, MA: Allyn & Bacon.

Tversky, A., & Kahneman, D. (1973). Availability: A heuristic for judging frequency and probability. *Cognitive Psychology, 5*, 207–232.

Tversky, A., & Kahneman, D. (1974). Judgment under uncertainty: Heuristics and biases. *Science, 185*, 1124–1131.

Tversky, A., & Kahneman, D. (1982). Judgments of and by representativeness. In D. Kahneman, P. Slovic, & A. Tversky (Eds.), *Judgment under uncertainty: Heuristics and biases.* New York: Cambridge University Press.

Tweed, R. G., & Lehman, D. R. (2002). Learning considered within a cultural context: Confucian and Socratic approaches. *American Psychologist, 57*, 89–99.

Uba, L. (1994). *Asian Americans: Personality patterns, identity, and mental health.* New York: Guilford Press.

Ullman, M., & Zimmerman, N. (1979). *Working with dreams.* New York: Delacorte Press/Eleanor Friede.

Ulusahin, A., Basoglu, M., & Paykel, E. S. (1994). A cross-cultural comparative study of depressive symptoms in British and Turkish clinical samples. *Social Psychiatry and Psychiatric Epidimeology, 29*, 31–39.

UN. (1948). Universal Declaration of Human Rights. Retrieved from http:// www.un.org

UN. (1959). Declaration of the Rights of the Child. Retrieved from http:// www.un.org

UN. (1967). Declaration on the Elimination of Discrimination against Women. Retrieved from www.un.org

United Nations Population Division. (2011). Retrieved from http://www.un.org/esa/population/

U.S. Bureau of the Census. (2000). United States Census 2000. Retrieved from http://www.census.gov/main/www/cen2000.html

U.S. Bureau of the Census. (2008). *Current population survey.* Washington, DC: U.S. Department of Commerce.

U.S. Bureau of the Census. (2010). Retrieved from http://www.census.gov/hhes/www/poverty/

Utsey, S., Bolden, M., Williams, O., Lee, A., Lanier, Y., & Newsome, C. (2007). Spiritual well-being as a mediator of the relation between culture-specific coping and quality of life in a community sample of African Americans. *Journal of Cross-Cultural Psychology, 38*, 123–136.

Valsiner, J., & Lawrence, J. (1997). Human development in culture across the life span. In J. W. Berry, P. R. Dasen, & T. S. Saraswathi (Eds.), *Handbook of cross-cultural psychology: Basic processes and human development* (Vol. 2, pp. 69–106). Boston, MA: Allyn & Bacon.

Van Bezooijen, C., Otto, S., & Heenan, T. (1983). Recognition of vocal expression of emotion: A three-nation study to identify universal characteristics. *Journal of Cross-Cultural Psychology, 14*(4), 387–406.

Vandello, J. A., Cohen, D., & Ransom, S. (2008). U.S. Southern and Northern differences in perceptions of norms about aggression: Mechanisms for the perpetuation of a culture of honor. *Journal of Cross-Cultural Psychology, 39*(2), 162–177.

van de Vijver, F. J. R., & Leung, K. (1997). *Methods and data analysis for cross-cultural research.* Thousand Oaks, CA: Sage.

van de Vijver, F., & Willemsen, M. E. (1993). Abstract thinking. In J. Altarriba (Ed.), *Cognition and culture: A cross-cultural approach to cognitive psychology* (pp. 317–342). Amsterdam: Elsevier Science.

Van de Vliert, E. (2006). Autocratic leadership around the globe: Do climate and wealth drive leadership culture? *Journal of Cross-Cultural Psychology, 37*, 42–59.

Van de Vliert, E. (2007). Climatoeconomic roots of survival versus self-expression cultures. *Journal of Cross-Cultural Psychology, 38*, 156–172.

Van Ijzendoorn, M. H., & Kroonenberg, P. M. (1988). Crosscultural patterns of attachment: A meta-analysis of the strange situation. *Child Development, 59*, 147–156.

Varela, R. E., Steele, R., & Benson, E. (2007). The contribution of ethnic minority status to adaptive style: A comparison of Mexican, Mexican American, and European American children. *Journal of Cross-Cultural Psychology, 38*, 26–33.

Varela, R. E., Vernberg, E., Sanchez-Sosa, J., Riveros, A., Mitchell, M., & Mashunkashey, J. (2004). Parenting style of Mexican, Mexican American, and Caucasian non-Hispanic families: Social context and cultural influences. *Journal of Family Psychology, 18*(4), 651–657.

Vassiliou, V., & Vassiliou, G. (1973). The implicative meaning of the Greek concept of philomoto. *Journal of Cross-Cultural Psychology, 4*(3), 326–341.

Veenhoven, R. (2008). Sociological theories of subjective well-being. In M. Eid & R. Larsen (Eds.), *The science of subjective well-being: A tribute to Ed Diener* (pp. 44–61). New York: Guilford Publications.

Vekker, L. (1978). *Psikhicheskie protsessy* [*Psychological processes*] (Vol. 2). Leningrad: Leningrad State University Press.

Vereijken, C., Riksen-Walraven, J. M., & Van Lieshout, C. (1997). Mother-infant relationships in Japan: Attachment, dependency, and amae. *Journal of Cross-Cultural Psychology, 28*(4), 442–462.

Vernon, P. (1969). *Intelligence and cultural environment.* London: Methuen.

Vernon, P. A., Wickett, J. A., Bazana, G., & Stelmack, R. M. (2000). The neuropsychology and psychophysiology of human intelligence. In R. J. Sternberg (Ed.), *Handbook of intelligence* (pp. 245–264). Cambridge, UK: Cambridge University Press.

Vesaluoma, M., Linda Müller, L., Gallar, J., Lambiase, A., Moilanen, J., Hack, T., et al. (2000). Effects of oleoresin capsicum pepper spray on human corneal morphology and sensitivity. *Investigative Ophthalmology and Visual Science, 41*, 2138–2147.

Vidmar, N. (1970). Group composition and the risky shift. *Journal of Experimental Social Psychology, 6*, 153–166.

Vincent, K. (1991). Black/white IQ differences: Does age make the difference? *Journal of Clinical Psychology, 47*, 266–270.

Vokey, J. R., & Read, J. D. (1985). Subliminal messages: Between the devil and the media. *American Psychologist, 40*, 1231–1239.

Vygotsky, L. (1932/1978). *Mind and society.* Cambridge, MA: Harvard University Press.

Walker, B. (1993). *The art of the Turkish tale.* Lubbock: Texas Tech University Press.

Walker, W., & Uysal, A. E. (1990). *Tales alive in Turkey.* Lubbock: Texas Tech University Press.

Walkey, F., & Chung, R. C.-Y. (1996). An examination of stereotypes of Chinese and Europeans held by some New Zealand secondary school pupils. *Journal of Cross-Cultural Psychology, 27*(3), 283–292.

Wallace, B. A., & Shapiro, S. L. (2006). Mental balance and well-being: Building bridges between Buddhism and Western psychology. *American Psychologist, 61*(7), 690–701.

Wallbott, H. G., & Scherer, K. R. (1986). How universal and specific is emotional experience? Evidence from 27 countries on five continents. *Social Science Information, 25*, 763–795.

Wallis, C. (1965). *The treasure chest.* New York: Harper and Row.

Walmsley, R. (2006). *World prison population list.* London: UK Home Office Research.

Wang, K., Hoosain, R., Lee, T. M. C., Meng,Y., Fu, J., & Yang, R. (2006). Perception of six basic emotional facial expressions by the Chinese. *Journal of Cross-Cultural Psychology, 37*, 623–629.

Ward, C. (1994). Culture and altered states of consciousness. In W. Lonner & R. Malpass (Eds.), *Psychology and culture* (pp. 59–64). Boston, MA: Allyn & Bacon.

Ward, N. G., & Al Bayyari,Y. (2010). American and Arab perceptions of an Arabic turn-taking cue. *Journal of Cross-Cultural Psychology, 41*(2), 270–275.

Warner, R. (1994). *Recovery from schizophrenia: Psychiatry and political economy* (2nd ed.). New York: Routledge.

Wassmann, J. (1993).When actions speak louder than words: The classification of food among the Yupno of Papua-New Guinea. *Newsletter of the Laboratory of Comparative Human Cognition, 15*, 30–40.

Wassmann, J., & Dasen, R. R. (1994). "Hot" and "Cold": Classification and sorting among the Yupno of Papua-New Guinea. *International Journal of Psychology, 29*, 19–38.

Watt, G. (1990). Reexamining factors predicting Afro-American and white American women's age at first coitus. *Archives of Sexual Behavior, 18*, 271–298.

Wax, E. (2003, July 25). Marriage stokes debate over gender roles. *Washington Post*, p. A18.

Wearden, J., Wearden, A., & Rabbitt, P. (1997). Age and IQ effects on stimulus and response timing. *Journal of Experimental Psychology: Human Perception and Performance, 23*(40), 962–979.

Weber, M. (1922/1968). *Economy and society: An outline of interpretive sociology.* New York: Bedminster Press.

Weber, M. (1905/1930). *The protestant ethic and the spirit of capitalism.* London: Allen and Unwin.

Wechsler, D. (1958). *The measurement and appraisal of adult intelligence.* Baltimore, MD: Williams & Wilkins.

Weiner, B. (1980). A cognitive (attribution)-emotion-action model of motivated behavior: An analysis of judgment of help-giving. *Journal of Personality and Social Psychology, 39*, 186–200.

Weinstein, L. B. (1989). Transcultural relocation: Adaptation of older Americans to Israel. *Activities, Adaptation & Aging, 13*, 33–42.

Weiss, B. (1992). Some consequences of early harsh discipline: Child aggression and a maladaptive social information processing style. *Child Development, 63*, 1321–1335.

Weisz, J. R., Rothbaum, F. M., & Blackburn, T. C. (1984). Standing out and standing in: The psychology of control in America and Japan. *American Psychologist, 39*, 955–969.

Weisz, J., Suwanlert, S., Chaiyasit, W., & Walter, B. (1987). Over and undercontrolled referral problems among children and adolescents from Thailand and the United States. *Journal of Counseling and Clinical Psychology, 55*, 719–726.

Whaley, A., & Davis, K. (2007). Cultural competence and evidence-based practice in mental health services: A complementary perspective. *American Psychologist, 62*(6), 563–574.

Whethrick, N. E., & Deregowski, J. B. (1982). Immediate recall: Its structure in three different language communities. *Journal of Cross-Cultural Psychology, 13*(2), 210–216.

White, G. M. (1994). Affecting culture: Emotion and morality in everyday life. In S. Kitayama & H. Markus (Eds.), *Emotion and culture: Empirical studies of mutual influence* (pp. 219–239). Washington, DC: American Psychological Association.

White, K. (1982). The relation between socioeconomic status and academic achievement. *Psychological Bulletin, 91*, 461–481.

Whiting, B. B. (Ed.). (1963). *Six cultures: Studies of child rearing.* New York: John Wiley.

Whiting, B. B., & Edwards, C. P. (1988). *Children of different worlds: The formation of social behavior.* Cambridge, MA: Harvard University Press.

Whiting, B. B., & Whiting, J. W. M. (1975). *The children of six cultures: A psycho-cultural analysis.* Cambridge, MA: Harvard University Press.

Whittaker, J., & Whittaker, S. (1972). A cross-cultural study of geocentrism. *Journal of Cross-Cultural Psychology, 3*(4), 417–421.

WHO. (2011). Unsafe abortion: Global and regional estimates of the incidence of unsafe abortion and associated mortality, 6th ed. http://www.who.int/reproductive health/publications/unsafe_abortion/9789241501118/en/.

Williams, J. E., & Best, D. (1990). *Sex and psyche: Gender and self viewed cross-culturally.* London: Sage.

Williams, M. A., Berberovic, N., & Mattingley, J. B. (2007). Abnormal fMRI adaptation to unfamiliar faces in a case of developmental prosopamnesia. *Current Biology, 17*, 1259–1264.

Williams, R., & Mitchell, H. (1991). The testing game. In R. Jones (Ed.), *Black psychology* (3rd ed., pp. 193–206). Berkeley, CA: Cobb & Henry.

Williams, Y., Kino, J., Goebert, D., Hishinuma, E., Miyamoto, R., Anzai, N., et al. (2002). A conceptual model of cultural predictors of anxiety among Japanese American and part-Japanese American adolescents. *Cultural Diversity & Ethnic Minority Psychology, 8*(4), 320–333.

Wills, M. G. (1992). Learning styles of African American children: A review of the literature and interventions. *African American Psychology* (pp. 260–278). Newbury Park, CA: Sage.

Winkelman, M. (2000). *Shamanism the neural ecology of consciousness and healing.* Westport, CT: Bergin and Carvey.

Wispe, L. G., & Drambarean, N. C. (1953). Physiological need, word frequency, and visual duration threshold. *Journal of Experimental Physiology, 46*, 25–31.

Word, C. H., Zanna, M. P., & Cooper, J. (1974). The nonverbal mediation of self-fulfilling prophecies in interracial interaction. *Journal of Experimental Social Psychology, 10*, 109–120.

World Health Organization. (1979). *Schizophrenia: An international follow-up study*. Geneva, Switzerland: WHO.

World Health Organization. (1983). *Depressive disorders in different cultures*. Geneva, Switzerland: WHO.

Wright, G., Phillips, L., Whalley, P., Choo, G., Tan, I., & Wishuda, A. (1978). Cultural differences in probabalistic thinking. *Journal of Cross-Cultural Psychology, 9*(3), 285–297.

Wright, R. (1994). *The moral animal: The new science of evolutionary psychology*. New York: Vintage.

Wright, S., Horn, S., & Sanders, W. (1997). Teacher and classroom context effects on student achievement: Implications for teacher evaluation. *Journal of Personnel Evaluation in Education, 11*, 57–67.

Wu, D. Y. H. (1982). Psychotherapy and emotion in traditional Chinese medicine. In A. J. Marsella & G. M. White (Eds.), *Cultural conceptions of mental health and therapy* (pp. 285–301). Dordrecht, The Netherlands: D. Reidel Publishing Company.

Wundt, W. (1913). *Elemente de Völkerpsychologie*. Leipzig, Germany: Alfred Kroner Verlag.

Xiang, P., Lee, A., & Solomon, M. (1997). Achievement goals and their correlates among American and Chinese students in physical education: A cross-cultural analysis. *Journal of Cross-Cultural Psychology, 28*(6), 645–660.

Yamaguchi, H. (1988). Effects of actor's and observer's roles on causal attribution by Japanese subjects for success and failure in competitive situations. *Psychological Reports, 63*, 619–626.

Yamaguchi, S. (2004). Further clarifications of the concept of amae in relation to dependence and attachment. *Human Development, 47*, 28–33.

Yang, S., & Sternberg, R. J. (1997). Conceptions of intelligence in ancient Chinese philosophy. *Journal of Theoretical and Philosophical Psychology, 17*, 101–119.

Yap, P. (1965). Phenomenology of affective disorder in Chinese and other cultures. In A. V. S. de Reuck & R. Porter (Eds.), *Transcultural psychiatry* (pp. 84–114). Boston, MA: Little, Brown.

Yaroshevski, V. (1996). *Istoriya psychologii [A history of psychology]*. Moscow: Prosveshenie.

Yates, J. F., Ji, L.-J., Oka, T., Lee, J.-W., Shinotsuka, H., & Sieck, W. R. (2010). Indecisiveness and culture: Incidence, values, and thoroughness. *Journal of Cross-Cultural Psychology, 41*(3), 428–444.

Yen, S., Robins, C. J., & Lin, N. (2000, December). A cross-cultural comparison of depressive symptom manifestation: China and the United States. *Journal of Consulting & Clinical Psychology, 68*(6), 993–999.

Yerkes, R. (1911). *Introduction to psychology*. New York: Holt.

Ying, Yu-Wen, Lee, Peter A., Tsai, Jeanne L., Yeh, Yei-Yu, & Huang, John S. (2000). The conception of depression in Chinese American college students. *Cultural Diversity & Ethnic Minority Psychology, 6*(2), 183–195.

Yu, L. C. (1993). Intergenerational transfer of resources within policy and cultural contexts. In S. H. Zarit, L. I. Pearlin, & K. W. Schaie (Eds.), *Caregiving systems*. Hillsdale, NJ: Erlbaum.

Yushka, A., & Gaidys, V. (2008). A case in point: Lay discourses on Soviet Lithuania during Brezhnev period (1964–1982). In V. Shlapentokh, E. Shiraev, & E. Carroll. *The Soviet Union: Internal and external perspectives on Soviet society*. New York: Palgrave.

Zajonc, R. B. (1965). Social facilitation. *Science, 149*, 269–274.

Zajonc, R. B. (1968). The attitudinal effect of mere exposure. *Journal of Personality and Social Psychology, Monograph Supplement, 9*, 1–27.

Zajonc, R. B. (1980). Feeling and thinking: Preferences need no inferences. *American Psychologist, 35*, 151–175.

Zaller, J. (1992). *The nature and origins of mass opinion*. Cambridge, MA: Cambridge University Press.

Zebian, S., & Denny, P. (2001). Integrative cognitive style in Middle Eastern and Western groups. *Journal of Cross-Cultural Psychology, 32*(1), 58–75.

Zendal, I., Pihl, R., & Seidman, B. (1987). The effects of learning sets on torque. *Journal of Clinical Psychology, 43*, 272–275.

Zepeda, M. (1985). Mother-infant behavior in Mexican and Mexican-American women: A study of the relationship of selected prenatal, perinatal and post-natal events. *Dissertation Abstracts International, 45*(9-A), 2756.

Zheng, R., & Stimpson, D. (1990). A cross-cultural study of entrepreneurial attitude orientation. *Information on Psychological Sciences, 6*, 23–25.

Zimbardo, P. (1997, May).What messages are behind today's cults? *APA Monitor*, p. 14.

Ziv, A., Shani, A., & Nebenhaus, S. (1975). Adolescents educated in Israel and in the Soviet Union. *Journal of Cross-Cultural Psychology, 6*(1), 108–121.

Zuckerman, M. (1990, December). Some dubious premises in research and theory on racial differences: Scientific, social, and ethical issues. *American Psychologist, 45*(12), 1297–1303.

AUTHOR INDEX

SUBJECT INDEX